WALKING by FAITH

Three / The Church

Parish Teaching Guide

Principal Program Consultants

Rev. Terry M. Odien, MA

Rev. Michael D. Place, STD

Dr. Addie Lorraine Walker, SSND

Nihil Obstat
Rev. James E. Hayes
Censor Deputatus

Imprimatur
✝ Most Rev. Jerome Hanus, OSB
Archbishop of Dubuque
November 4, 1997
Feast of Saint Charles Borromeo, Patron of Catechists

> The Ad Hoc Committee to Oversee the Use of the Catechism, National Conference of Catholic Bishops, has found this catechetical series to be in conformity with the *Catechism of the Catholic Church*.

The nihil obstat and imprimatur are official declarations that a book or pamphlet is free of doctrinal or moral error. No implication is contained herein that those who granted the nihil obstat and imprimatur agree with the contents, opinions, or statements expressed.

For permission to reprint copyrighted material, grateful acknowledgment is made to the following sources:

BROWN-ROA: Prayers from *Catholic Source Book*, revised edition edited by Rev. Peter D. Klein. Text copyright © 1990 by BROWN-ROA.

Confraternity of Christian Doctrine, Washington, D.C.: Scripture selections from *NEW AMERICAN BIBLE*. Text copyright © 1991, 1986, 1970 by the Confraternity of Christian Doctrine. Used by license of the copyright owner. All rights reserved. No part of *NEW AMERICAN BIBLE* may be reproduced, by any means, without permission in writing from the copyright holder.

English Language Liturgical Consultation (ELLC): English translation of the "Lord's Prayer." Text © 1988 by the English Language Liturgical Consultation.

International Committee on English in the Liturgy, Inc. (ICEL): From the English translation of *Rite of Baptism for Children*. Text © 1969 by ICEL. From the English translation of *The Roman Missal*. Text © 1973 by ICEL. From the English translation of *Rite of Penance*. Text © 1974 by ICEL. From the English translation of *Rite of Confirmation*, Second Edition. Text © 1975 by ICEL. From the English translations of *A Book of Prayers* and *Pastoral Care of the Sick: Rites of Anointing and Viaticum*. Text © 1982 by ICEL. All rights reserved.

Cover illustration by Lori Lohstoeter

Copyright © 1999 by BROWN-ROA, a division of Harcourt Brace & Company

All rights reserved. No part of this publication may be reproduced or transmitted in any form or by any means, electronic or mechanical, including photocopy, recording, or any information storage and retrieval system, without permission in writing from the publisher.

Requests for permission to make copies of any part of the work should be mailed to: Permissions Department, Harcourt Brace & Company, 6277 Sea Harbor Drive, Orlando, Florida 32887-6777.

Additional credits and acknowledgments appear on page 192A.

Printed in the United States of America

ISBN 0-15-950354-X

10 9 8 7 6 5 4 3 2

A Blessing for Beginnings

"So we are always courageous . . . for we walk by faith. . . ."
—2 Corinthians 5:6–7

Leader: Today we come together to continue our journey of faith. We are ready to learn from one another and from our Church community. And so we pray: God our Father, you called us into the Church through the saving waters of Baptism. Help us grow in love as a community of faith as we do your work in the world.

Reader: Listen to God's message to us: (Read Romans 12:4–10.) The word of the Lord.

All: Thanks be to God.

Leader: Let us ask God's blessing on our journey this year.

All: Holy Trinity, be with us on our journey. Help us live every day as members of Christ's Body, the Church. Give us the courage to use our gifts wisely for the sake of your kingdom. We pray in the words that Jesus taught us. (Pray the Lord's Prayer.)

Leader: May the Lord be with us, now and always.

All: Amen!

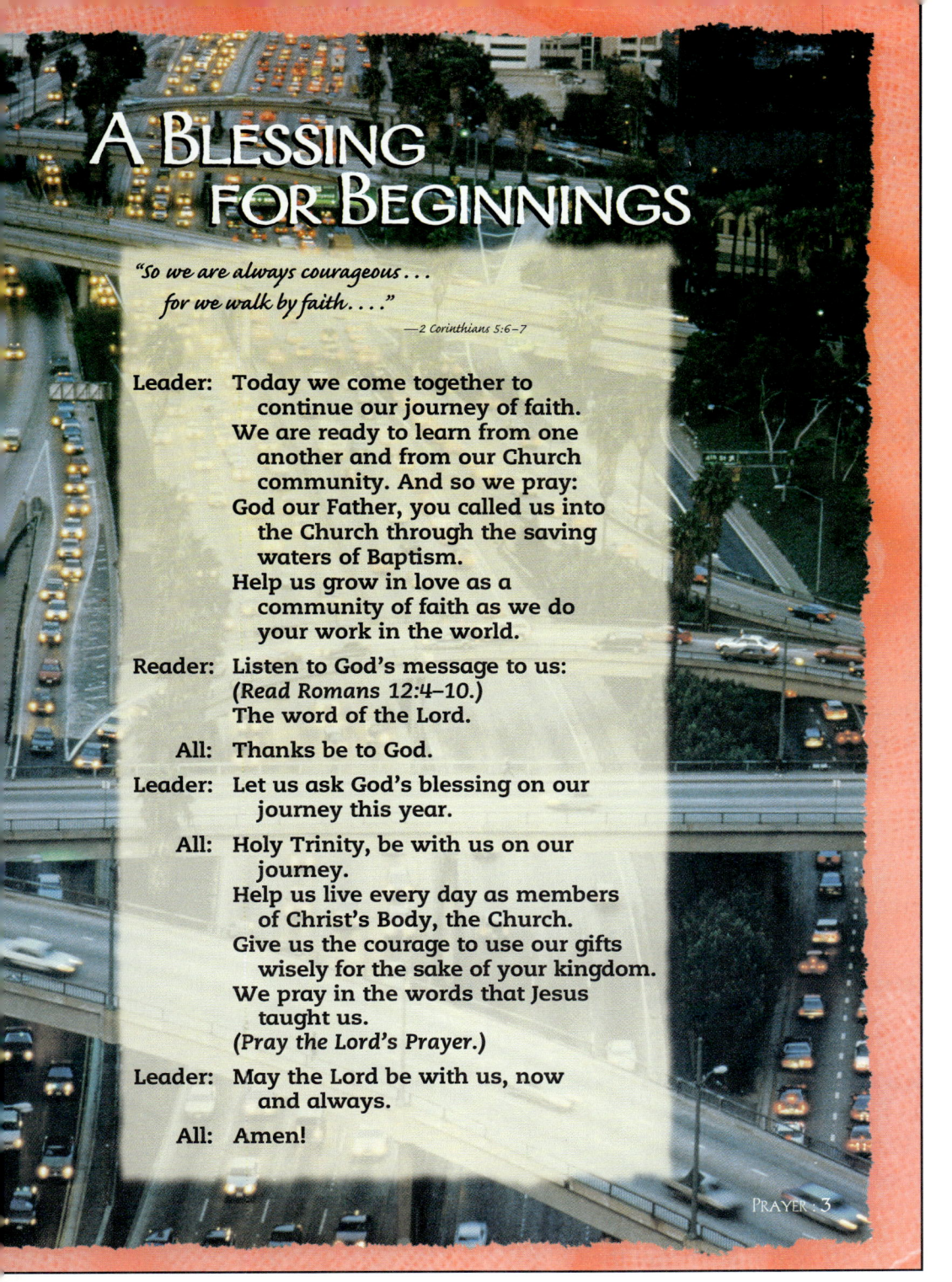

A Blessing for Beginnings

- Use this brief prayer service to begin your year together. Consider scheduling the prayer service as part of the first class session. It would be good to celebrate this service in the classroom as a way of dedicating the space. If possible, invite the students' families to join you for the celebration.

- To prepare for the prayer service, choose a reader (a student or family member) and provide him or her with a Bible opened to *Romans 12:4–10*. Point out the part of the prayer service in which the reading occurs.

- Gather the students and any other participants. Have them join you in the prayer corner or some other comfortable classroom setting. You may wish to play some instrumental music or sing one of the songs from the *Walking by Faith* Music and Liturgy Resources to set the tone.

- Take the part of *Leader*. Invite the students and others present to follow along and respond together at the parts marked *All*.

- You may wish to include a gesture of blessing (traditionally, laying hands on the top of a person's head or signing him or her with a cross) to accompany the final blessing. If family members attend the prayer service, they may join you in blessing their children.

- If possible, close the service by singing "Walking by Faith," the program theme song from the Music and Liturgy Resources. Tell the students they will be learning this song as the year goes on, and they should feel free to join in singing the chorus as soon as they feel comfortable doing so.

Resource Center

Working with the Cover Image

Use the *Walking by Faith* Three cover art to introduce the students to this year's theme—the Church as an active, evangelizing presence in the midst of the world. Have the students study the cover illustration, which continues around to the back cover, and describe what they see. Explain that the illustration shows a large Catholic church or cathedral in the middle of a busy urban area. The reflection of the church in the skyscraper next to it and the streams of people entering and leaving the church are meant to show that as Church we are not separate from the world. We are meant to be the active presence of the Holy Spirit in our own communities and neighborhoods, small or large, urban or rural. Ask a student to read aloud the quotation from Scripture on the back cover. Discuss how the cover illustration relates to the words of Jesus.

Artist Lori Lohstoeter received her first artistic award when she was in the second grade. A graduate of the University of Arkansas at Little Rock and the Art Center College of Design in Pasadena, California, Lohstoeter now lives and works in Connecticut. She has illustrated numerous popular children's books, some of which have been made into videos. Lohstoeter's colorful palette reflects the influence on her painting of Bellows, Van Gogh, and Gaugain. She feels blessed to have received so much joy from the work to which she gives her heart and soul.

WALKING by FAITH
Three / The Church

A Blessing for Beginnings **T3**

Introductory Material
Program Overview **T9**
Program Scope and Sequence **T15**
Principal Consultants' Messages **T18**
Grade Three Overview **T22**
Grade Three Scope and Sequence **T24**
Using the Teaching Guide **T27**
Preparing to Teach **T28**
Teaching a Chapter **T30**
Using the Faith Journal **T32**
Using Unit Reviews **T33**
Using Program Resources **T34**
Scheduling **T35**

Lesson Plan Pages
Introduction **T39**

Unit One — Created for Community
Chapter 1 Made for Each Other **5A**
Chapter 2 The Family of Creation **11A**
Chapter 3 Light of the World **17A**
Unit One Checkpoint **24**

Chapter 4 We Celebrate Mary: Mother of the Church **25A**

Unit Two — People of God
Chapter 5 We Believe in God **29A**
Chapter 6 We Worship God **35A**
Chapter 7 We Belong to God **41A**
Unit Two Checkpoint **48**

Chapter 8 We Celebrate All Saints: Honoring Their Memory **49A**

Unit Three — The Body of Christ
Chapter 9 Jesus Brings Good News **53A**
Chapter 10 New Life in Jesus **59A**
Chapter 11 Jesus Works Through Us **65A**
Unit Three Checkpoint **72**

Chapter 12 We Celebrate Advent: A Time to Remember **73A**

Unit Four — Guided by the Holy Spirit

- **Chapter 13** The Church Works Together **77A**
- **Chapter 14** One and Holy **83A**
- **Chapter 15** Catholic and Apostolic **89A**
- **Unit Four Checkpoint** **96**
- **Chapter 16** We Celebrate Christmas: The First Nativity Scene **97A**

Unit Five — Temple of the Holy Spirit

- **Chapter 17** Jesus' Law of Hope **101A**
- **Chapter 18** The Church Helps **107A**
- **Chapter 19** Faith, Hope, and Love **113A**
- **Unit Five Checkpoint** **120**
- **Chapter 20** We Celebrate Lent: Strength Through Practice **121A**

Unit Six — Belonging, Healing, Serving

- **Chapter 21** We Become Part of the Church **125A**
- **Chapter 22** The Church Celebrates Healing **131A**
- **Chapter 23** Sacraments of Service **137A**
- **Unit Six Checkpoint** **144**
- **Chapter 24** We Celebrate Holy Week: Hosanna! **145A**

Unit Seven — Yesterday, Today, and Tomorrow

- **Chapter 25** Connected to the Past **149A**
- **Chapter 26** The Church Today **155A**
- **Chapter 27** Hope for the Future **161A**
- **Unit Seven Checkpoint** **168**
- **Chapter 28** We Celebrate Easter: Signs of New Life **169A**

Catholic Prayers and Resources **174**
The Language of Faith **183**
Index **191**

Idea Files

This section contains information on ten topics of significance to religious educators. Each Idea File contains a number of practical hints and successful strategies to assist you in your ministry of religious education.

Introduction **T41**

1. Establishing Group Atmosphere **T42**
   Suggestions for gathering and classroom management

2. Building Faith Community **T44**
   Suggestions for helping the students see themselves as part of the Church

3. Meeting Individual Needs **T46**
   Suggestions for addressing multiple learning styles and for adapting lessons for students with special needs

4. Dealing with Popular Culture **T48**
   Suggestions for incorporating the best (and eliminating the worst) of the messages students receive from society and the media

5. Appreciating Diversity **T50**
   Suggestions for incorporating multicultural experiences

6. Connecting with Families **T52**
   Suggestions for strengthening the classroom-home link

7. Connecting with the Parish **T54**
   Suggestions for integrating your class into the life of the faith community

8. Overcoming Scheduling Limitations **T56**
   Suggestions for dealing with busy schedules, time limitations, and housekeeping chores

9. Fostering Catholic Morality **T58**
   Suggestions for introducing and reinforcing Catholic moral teaching

10. Assessing Progress **T60**
    Suggestions for evaluating your own and the students' growth in faith, using a multitude of means

Your Faith Journal

This section of the Teaching Guide offers you a way to nourish your own spiritual development as you walk by faith with the students.

Your Faith Journal features one page of reflections for each chapter in the student book. Each page includes the *Catholics Believe* statement and its relevant citation from the *Catechism of the Catholic Church*, as well as the following:
- **Reflect**—questions and prompts for your own reflection on the chapter topic
- **Continue the Journey**—suggested activities for deepening your spiritual growth and understanding
- **Affirm**—a personal resolution to inspire and guide you

Introduction	J1
Chapter 1 Reflections	J2
Chapter 2 Reflections	J3
Chapter 3 Reflections	J4
Chapter 4 Reflections	J5
Chapter 5 Reflections	J6
Chapter 6 Reflections	J7
Chapter 7 Reflections	J8
Chapter 8 Reflections	J9
Chapter 9 Reflections	J10
Chapter 10 Reflections	J11
Chapter 11 Reflections	J12
Chapter 12 Reflections	J13
Chapter 13 Reflections	J14
Chapter 14 Reflections	J15
Chapter 15 Reflections	J16
Chapter 16 Reflections	J17
Chapter 17 Reflections	J18
Chapter 18 Reflections	J19
Chapter 19 Reflections	J20
Chapter 20 Reflections	J21
Chapter 21 Reflections	J22
Chapter 22 Reflections	J23
Chapter 23 Reflections	J24
Chapter 24 Reflections	J25
Chapter 25 Reflections	J26
Chapter 26 Reflections	J27
Chapter 27 Reflections	J28
Chapter 28 Reflections	J29

Notes

Walking by Faith is three-dimensional religious education—active learning that translates into active faith.

What We Believe about Religious Education and Walking by Faith

We believe *that growth in faith is a lifelong journey, undertaken in community and guided by the Spirit.*

We believe *that the family is the primary community in which faith is shared and nurtured. The whole Church community, beginning at the parish level, puts itself at the service of the family to help form young Catholics. Formal religious education, in the parish school of religion or the Catholic school, is intended to support the family and the Church community in this mission.*

We believe *that the goal of any religious education program is active learning that translates into active faith.*

What **we believe** *about children and the ways in which they best experience the transmission of faith shapes this program in many ways.*

- **We believe** that children deserve to experience, integrate, and express the fullness of mature Christian faith—what we believe and how we celebrate, live, and pray—at every age level, according to their stage of development.
- **We believe** that children grow in faith best as members of a faith community that includes their families, their classmates and catechists, and the parish community, with extension into the wider world.
- **We believe** that children need education in faith that is three-dimensional: connected to a shared and meaningful past, directly applicable to the realities of the present, and preparatory to the challenges of the future.
- **We believe** that children learn best through engaging, interactive strategies that challenge their natural curiosity and creativity and that effectively balance formation and information.
- **We believe** that children benefit from explicit instruction in Catholic vocabulary and practices.
- **We believe** that children are capable of developing a lasting appreciation of sacred Scripture and familiarity with the Bible from a Catholic perspective.
- **We believe** that children need to be supported and affirmed in living their faith by being provided with the tools to make difficult moral choices, to act justly, and to witness to their beliefs in word and in deed.
- **We believe** that children come to a fuller understanding of the sacramental dimension of faith and life when they are encouraged—through immersion in and exploration of word and image, picture and symbol and ritual—to cultivate wonder and awe and to be open to the mystery of God's presence.
- **We believe** that children develop vitally important self-esteem and active concern for others when they see themselves as part of a richly diverse faith community, celebrating the gifts and contributions of people of all cultures and abilities.
- **We believe** that children can take responsibility for and be assisted in assessing and evaluating their own growth in faith, measured against the standards and expectations of the Christian community.

WALKING by FAITH

is **3**-dimensional Religious Education

Three-dimensional in content and organization, with an innovative scope and sequence that presents… *1* the complete Catholic catechesis at every grade level, *2* seen through the lens of grade-level themes, *3* experienced within the context of the Church community. **Three-dimensional** in participation, with a learning process that fully engages… *1* students in Catholic schools and parish religious education programs, *2* families at all levels of growth in faith, *3* teachers and catechists at all levels of experience. **Three-dimensional** in approach, with a lesson plan designed to help young people… *1* experience their Catholic identity, *2* integrate their Catholic values, *3* express their Catholic beliefs. **Three-dimensional** in outlook, with a commitment to… *1* sharing the richness of our past, *2* engaging the realities of our present, *3* developing skills to meet the challenges of our future.

Student Books One to Six

- One colorful and engaging student book for both School and Parish
- Three-dimensional scope and sequence
- 21 content chapters, 7 integrated seasonal chapters
- Chapter structure flows from the catechetical process:

  We Are Invited
  We Explore
  We Reflect
  We Celebrate

- Chapters incorporate stories, activities, Scripture, prayer, discussion, and reflection
- Checkpoint unit reviews
- *Catholic Prayers and Resources* reference section
- *The Language of Faith* glossary section

Student Book Features

- **Stepping Stones**
  Important Catholic practices and skills presented in a step-by-step format that encourages learning and practice

- **Catholics Believe**
  Doctrinal summary statements, with references to the *Catechism of the Catholic Church*

- **Scripture Signpost**
  Scripture verses keyed to chapter content, with discussion questions

- **Our Moral Guide**
  Summaries of chapter moral teaching, with references to the *Catechism of the Catholic Church* and discussion questions

- **Saints Walk with Us**
  Profiles of holy men and women whose lives give witness to the chapter teaching

- **Landmark**
  Captioned photographs of persons, places, and customs of special significance to our global Catholic history and culture

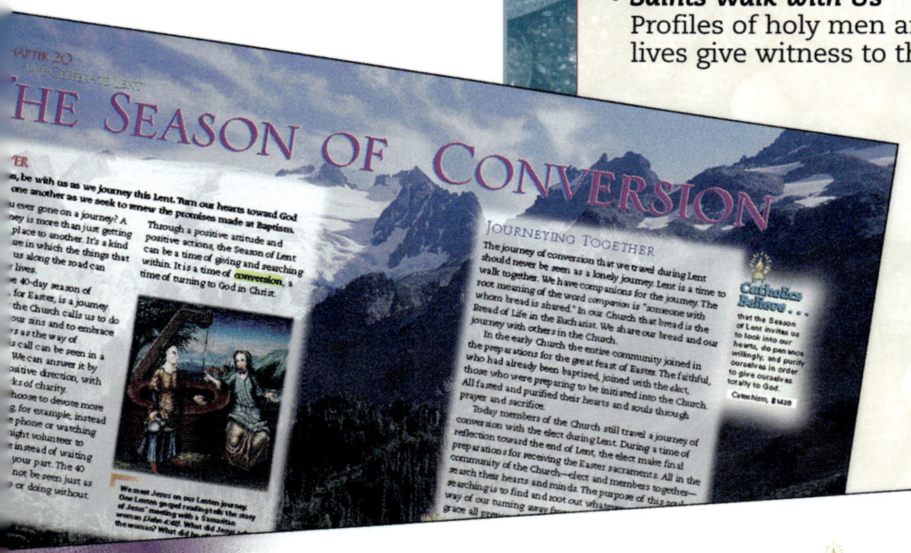

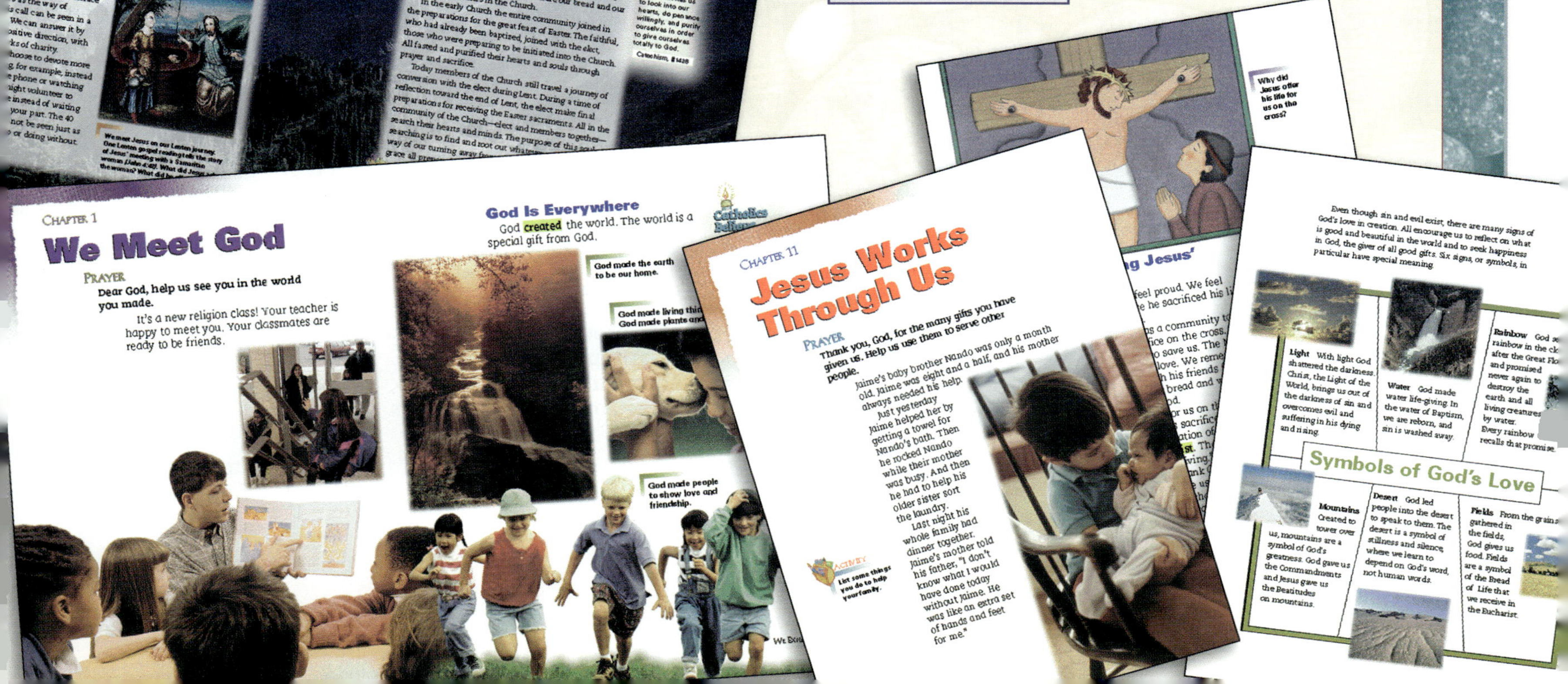

Faith Journals One to Six

The *Faith Journal* is a component unique to *Walking by Faith*. Moving beyond the traditional notions of pupil workbooks and activity sheets and family handbooks, the *Faith Journal* involves students and their families in the catechetical process in real and immediate ways.

Each *Faith Journal* contains 2 pages for each chapter of the student book.

- One page contains questions, prompts, and exercises for the student's own personal exploration of the chapter themes.
- The second page involves the whole family, with a chapter summary, an on-the-page activity, suggestions for continuing the family's growth in faith, and a family prayer.
- A resource section at the back of each *Faith Journal* contains traditional Catholic prayers in English and Spanish.

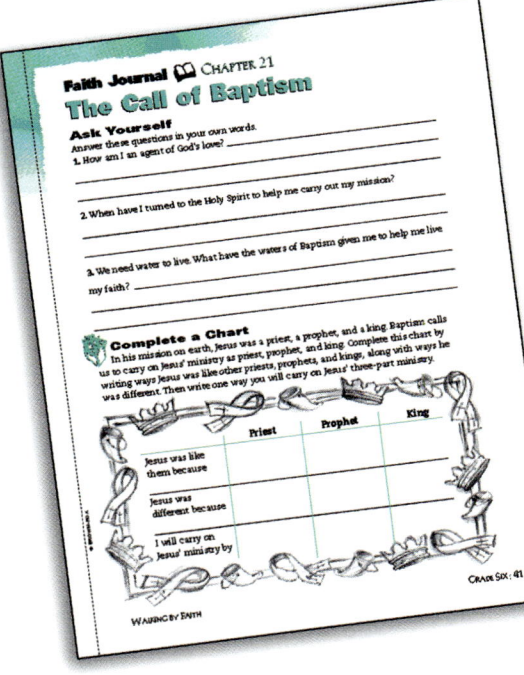

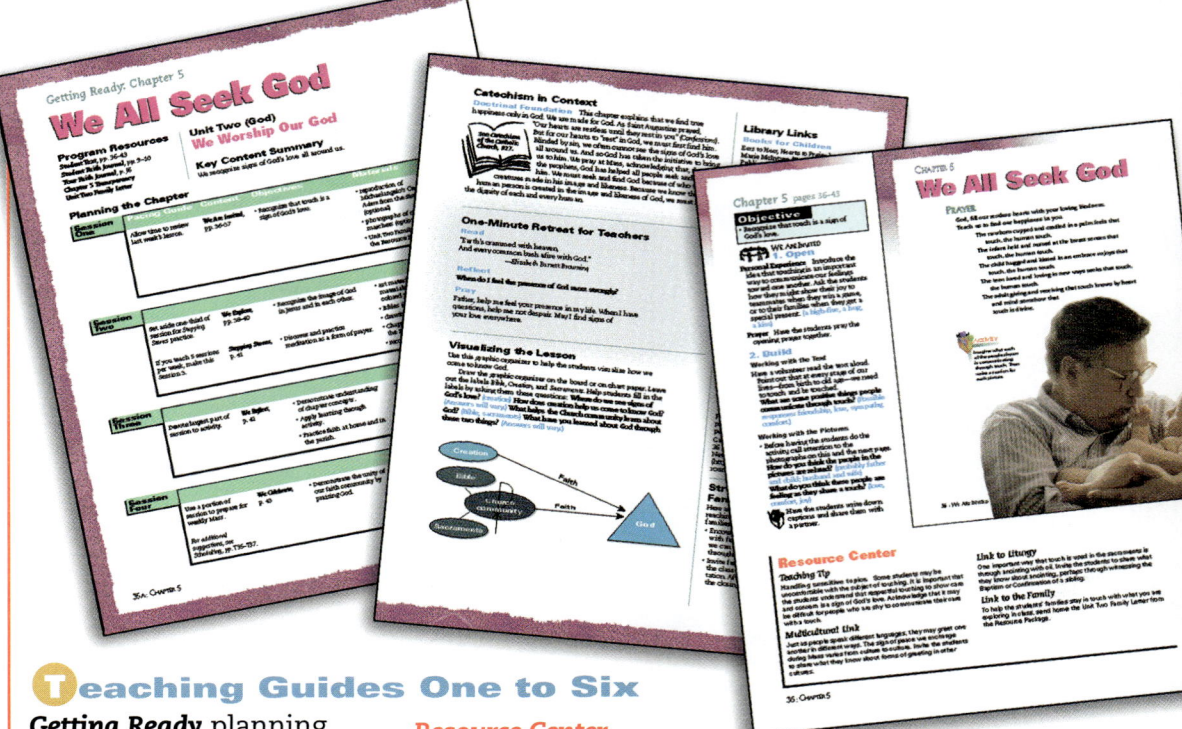

Teaching Guides One to Six

Getting Ready planning pages help organize each chapter's teaching with . . .

- *Planning Chart* (pacing, objectives, materials)
- *Catechism in Context* (doctrinal foundation)
- *One-Minute Retreat* (reflection and prayer)
- *Visualizing the Lesson* (graphic organizer)
- *Library Links* (books, multimedia, organizations for children, families, teachers)
- *Connecting with the Family* (hints for involving students' families)

Wraparound lesson plan pages contain full-color reduced Pupil Edition pages and reduced *Faith Journal* pages.

Core lesson column features . . .

- objectives
- simple, three-step lesson plan *(Open, Build, Close)*
- *Working with the Text* and *Working with the Pictures* teaching suggestions
- notes for incorporating all student book features
- answers to all student book and Teaching Guide questions

Resource Center features . . .

- **Background** (including Art, Scripture, Catechism) Key information at point of use
- **The Language of Faith** Expanded definitions of highlighted terms, rooted in the Catechism
- **Profiles** Background information on saints and other holy men and women
- **Multicultural Links** Information and activities exploring the Church's global diversity
- **Link to the Family, Link to the Faith Community, Link to Liturgy, Link to Justice** Suggestions for linking the class to the home, the parish, and the liturgical life and social concerns of the community
- **Meet Individual Needs** Strategies for adapting teaching situations to the various learning styles and pedagogical needs of students
- **Teaching Tips** Suggestions for classroom management, clarifying content, handling sensitive topics, and answering questions
- **Assessment Tips** Tips for assessing students' progress in class and growth in faith, using a variety of strategies including self-assessment

Additional features/School

- Links to other subject areas (including Language Arts, Social Studies, Music, Art, Health, Science, Mathematics, Other Languages)—strategies for incorporating religious teaching across the curriculum
- Continuing Project—a year-long project tying the grade-level theme to the seven content areas, stressing cooperative learning
- Portfolio suggestions—*Assessment Tips* designed to assist students in creating and filling portfolios of their work

Additional features/Parish

- *Notes* space for Opening, Building, and Closing the Chapter—handy write-in boxes for noting successful teaching strategies, classroom management reminders, and evaluations

T12 : PROGRAM OVERVIEW

Resource Packages One to Six

- **Transparencies**
  21 full-color graphics, one per content chapter, present the lesson content for overhead projection
- **Family Letters in English and Spanish**
  Reproducible copy masters for each unit, with room for personalizing the message and a tear-off response form
- **Assessment Resources**
  Reproducible copy masters include seven unit assessments and a two-part year-end assessment, with answer keys
- **Music and Liturgy Resources**
  Music, including "Walking by Faith," the program theme song, and original liturgical services keyed to the units and the liturgical seasons

Walking by Faith Kindergarten

For children and families
- Colorful, engaging, consumable child's book.
- Same three-dimensional scope and sequence as in Grades One through Six
- 21 content chapters, 7 integrated seasonal chapters
- All take-home pages
- Family notes for each chapter
- Take-home Scripture Story booklets with family activities
- *Catholic Prayers and Resources* reference section
- *The Language of Faith* illustrated ABC glossary

For teachers and catechists
- Single Teaching Guide provides lesson-planning for a wide variety of teaching situations
- Lesson plan consistent with Grades One through Six
- Idea Files offer helpful hints on 10 topics
- *Your Faith Journal* supports adult spiritual growth

Kindergarten Resource Package
- Reproducible family letters in English and Spanish
- Music and Liturgy Resources

PROGRAM OVERVIEW : T13

Notes

Walking by Faith is built on an innovative scope and sequence that presents the complete Catholic catechesis at every grade level, seen through the lens of grade-level themes, and experienced within the context of the Church community.

Walking by Faith
A Three-Dimensional Scope and Sequence
Kindergarten–Grade Six

The chart on the following pages presents the scope and sequence for all seven levels of the *Walking by Faith* series. Through color coding, the chart shows how the seven key content areas are taught at each grade level. Each of these seven areas also serves as a grade-level "lens" through which the total catechetical message is focused.

The *Walking by Faith* series was created using the *Catechism of the Catholic Church* as its foundation, source, and inspiration. The key Catechism reference for each chapter of each grade is indicated on the scope and sequence chart. The structure of the Catechism's "four pillars"—doctrine, liturgy and sacramentality, morality, and prayer—is echoed throughout *Walking by Faith*.

In finding the *Walking by Faith* series in conformity with the Catechism, the Ad Hoc Committee to Oversee the Use of the Catechism, National Conference of Catholic Bishops, took note of its comprehensive presentation of the catechetical message, balanced by a concentration on particular issues at each grade level.

Walking by Faith also conforms to the catechetical principles outlined in *Sharing the Light of Faith: National Catechetical Directory for Catholics of the United States* and to the catechetical guidelines of particular dioceses and archdioceses.

For a detailed grade-level scope and sequence, see pages T24–T25.

Grade Theme	Kindergarten Creation	Grade 1 God	Grade 2 Jesus Christ
Unit One Creation	*Creation*	*God's Creation*	*God's Gift to Our World*
Chapter 1	A Wonderful World Catechism, #32	We Meet God Catechism, #32	Beginnings Catechism, #423
Chapter 2	All God's Gifts Catechism, #2637	Gifts from God Catechism, #293	A World of Signs Catechism, #1147
Chapter 3	Caring for God's World Catechism, #307	We Care Catechism, #373	God's Promise Is Forever Catechism, #457
Chapter 4 We Celebrate Mary	Mary, Our Mother Catechism, #963	Mother of God Catechism, #968	Saying Yes to God Catechism, #494
Unit Two God	*God*	*The Holy Trinity*	*Jesus Teaches Us About God*
Chapter 5	We Love God Catechism, #214	A Loving Father Catechism, #239	The Father of Jesus Catechism, #240
Chapter 6	God Our Father Catechism, #239	The Son of God Catechism, #423	God Gives Us Life Catechism, #1997
Chapter 7	God Is with Us Catechism, #729	The Holy Spirit Catechism, #233	The Holy Spirit Is with Us Catechism, #259
Chapter 8 We Celebrate All Saints	All Saints' Day Catechism, #828	Friends of God Catechism, #956	Stars for God Catechism, #2030
Unit Three Jesus Christ	*Jesus Christ*	*Jesus, the Son of God*	*Jesus Shares Himself with Us*
Chapter 9	God Sent Jesus Catechism, #606	Jesus and His Family Catechism, #464	Jesus Shows Us How to Love Catechism, #1709
Chapter 10	The Holy Family Catechism, #531	Jesus Teaches Catechism, #516	Jesus Feeds Us Catechism, #549
Chapter 11	Follow Jesus Catechism, #520	New Life Catechism, #654	Jesus Forgives Us Catechism, #270
Chapter 12 We Celebrate Advent	Advent Catechism, #524	The Waiting Time Catechism, #524	Come, Lord Jesus! Catechism, #523
Unit Four The Church	*The Church*	*God's Church*	*Jesus Lives in the Church*
Chapter 13	Children of God Catechism, #759	Invited to the Kingdom Catechism, #831	The Church Is a Community Catechism, #752
Chapter 14	Our Church Family Catechism, #782	The Spirit and the Church Catechism, #737	Doing the Work of Jesus Catechism, #863
Chapter 15	Mother of Our Church Catechism, #986	A Church of Saints Catechism, #957	The Church Remembers Jesus Catechism, #1366
Chapter 16 We Celebrate Christmas	Christmas Catechism, #526	The Light of Christ Catechism, #525	Jesus Is Born Catechism, #525
Unit Five Christian Morality	*Christian Morality*	*Living God's Love*	*The Sacrament of Reconciliation*
Chapter 17	We Are Special Catechism, #357	Love and Serve Catechism, #1723	Jesus Invites Us to Love Catechism, #1970
Chapter 18	Our Choices Catechism, #1954	We Can Choose Catechism, #1732	We Make Choices Catechism, #1732
Chapter 19	Choose Love Catechism, #2093	God Forgives Us Catechism, #1847	We Celebrate Forgiveness Catechism, #1468–1469
Chapter 20 We Celebrate Lent	Lent Catechism, #1438	Following Jesus Catechism, #1438	A Time of Sacrifice Catechism, #1163
Unit Six The Sacraments	*The Sacraments*	*Signs of God's Love*	*Jesus Gives Us the Sacraments*
Chapter 21	Signs of God's Love Catechism, #1147	Sacraments Catechism, #1153	The Church Welcomes Us Catechism, #1212
Chapter 22	God Created Water Catechism, #1218	Baptism Catechism, #1267	Jesus Is with Us Catechism, #1374
Chapter 23	Family Meals Catechism, #1333	At Mass Catechism, #1359	Members of the Church Catechism, #2041
Chapter 24 We Celebrate Holy Week	Holy Week Catechism, #1344	Time to Remember Catechism, #610	Good Friday Catechism, #618
Unit Seven Salvation History	*Salvation History*	*God Saves Us*	*Jesus, Lord of All Creation*
Chapter 25	Heaven Is a Perfect World Catechism, #1024	God's Love Is Forever Catechism, #220	God Invites Us Catechism, #1419
Chapter 26	New Life Forever Catechism, #2683	Home with God Catechism, #1721	Jesus Will Come Again Catechism, #681
Chapter 27	God Makes Us Happy Catechism, #1721	The New Creation Catechism, #1042	We Care for the World Catechism, #2443
Chapter 28 We Celebrate Easter	Happy Easter Catechism, #638	Signs of Joy Catechism, #655	New Life in Jesus Catechism, #654

Grade 3: The Church	Grade 4: Christian Morality	Grade 5: The Sacraments	Grade 6: Salvation History
Created for Community	**Created to Love**	**Creation Celebrates God's Love**	**In the Beginning**
Made for Each Other — Catechism, #1879	God Created the World — Catechism, #299	God Our Creator — Catechism, #290	Our Story of Faith — Catechism, #104
The Family of Creation — Catechism, #344	Creation Has Order — Catechism, #1959	Signs of God's Love — Catechism, #385	Why Are We Here? — Catechism, #1721
Light of the World — Catechism, #1999	We Are Responsible — Catechism, #358	Caring for God's Creation — Catechism, #306	Good and Evil — Catechism, #401
Mother of the Church — Catechism, #969	The Immaculate Conception — Catechism, #493	Sign of the New Creation — Catechism, #966	Daughter of Zion — Catechism, #489
People of God	**Choosing to Love God**	**We Worship Our God**	**The Journey and the Promise**
We Believe in God — Catechism, #234	A Relationship with God — Catechism, #2062	We All Seek God — Catechism, #27	Called on a Journey of Faith — Catechism, #1080
We Worship God — Catechism, #752	Freedom and Grace — Catechism, #1730	In Prayer and Worship — Catechism, #1083	God Wants to Save Us — Catechism, #1164
We Belong to God — Catechism, #781	Gifts of the Spirit — Catechism, #260	God in Us — Catechism, #1102	Our Relationship with God — Catechism, #2056
Honoring Their Memory — Catechism, #957	They Chose God — Catechism, #2030	Called to Holiness — Catechism, #957	A Consecrated People — Catechism, #61, 828
The Body of Christ	**The Way of Jesus**	**Jesus Is a Sacrament**	**The One Who Is to Come**
Jesus Brings Good News — Catechism, #763	The Law of Love — Catechism, #1970	The Image of God — Catechism, #458	Leader of Leaders — Catechism, #2579
New Life in Jesus — Catechism, #609	Beatitudes — Catechism, #1719	Stories and Signs — Catechism #546–547	God's Wisdom — Catechism, #272
Jesus Works Through Us — Catechism, #794	Forgiveness and Peace — Catechism, #2844	The Way to New Life — Catechism, #1115	The Promised One — Catechism, #702
A Time to Remember — Catechism, #524	The Lord Is Coming — Catechism, #672	Waiting for the Light — Catechism, #524	O Come, O Come, Emmanuel! — Catechism, #524
Guided by the Holy Spirit	**The Christian Community**	**The Church Is a Sacrament**	**Founded on the Gospels**
The Church Works Together — Catechism, #872	Mother and Teacher — Catechism, #169	A Sign to the World — Catechism, #776	Sharing the Good News — Catechism, #125
One and Holy — Catechism, #813	The Work of Love — Catechism, #2046	Steps on Our Journey — Catechism, #1267	The Church Grows — Catechism, #767
Catholic and Apostolic — Catechism, #857	Communities of Love — Catechism, #916	Answering God's Call — Catechism, #1546	Together as One Body — Catechism, #669
The First Nativity Scene — Catechism, #525	The Prince of Peace — Catechism, #2305	Following a Star — Catechism, #528	The Promise Fulfilled — Catechism, #437
Temple of the Holy Spirit	**Faithful to the Covenant**	**The Life of Grace**	**True to the Promise**
Jesus' Law of Love — Catechism, #1970	Failure to Love — Catechism, #1849	Called to God's Kingdom — Catechism, #1717	The Way of Love — Catechism, #1823
The Church Helps — Catechism, #1785	Loving God — Catechism, #2083	Our Call to Do Good — Catechism, #1804	Living in Justice and Peace — Catechism, #2419
Faith, Hope, and Love — Catechism, #1813	Loving Our Neighbor — Catechism, #2196	Forgiveness and Healing — Catechism, #1421	The Holy Spirit in Action — Catechism, #1830
Strength Through Practice — Catechism, #1438	Spiritual Discipline — Catechism, #2043	The Season of Conversion — Catechism, #1428	Forty Days in the Desert — Catechism, #540
Belonging, Healing, Serving	**Celebrating the Sacraments**	**The Eucharist, Our Great Sacrament**	**Sacraments of Salvation**
We Become Part of the Church — Catechism, #1212	Life in the Spirit — Catechism, #1266	Gathered Around the Altar — Catechism, #1348	The Call of Baptism — Catechism, #1268
The Church Celebrates Healing — Catechism, #1421	Welcome Home — Catechism, #1469	God's Word Lives — Catechism, #1154	Called to Serve — Catechism, #1547
Sacraments of Service — Catechism, #1534	With Us Always — Catechism, #1392	We Celebrate the Eucharist — Catechism, #1355	Together in Love — Catechism, #1641
Hosanna! — Catechism, #559	Walking with Jesus — Catechism, #618	Christ's Passover — Catechism, #611, 613	Sacrifice and Salvation — Catechism, #608
Yesterday, Today, Tomorrow	**The Love that Never Ends**	**The Paschal Mystery**	**Journey to the Future**
Connected to the Past — Catechism, #759	Now and Forever — Catechism, #214	Celebrating Our Jewish Roots — Catechism, #1096	All the Faithful — Catechism, #957
The Church Today — Catechism, #2046	Judged by Love — Catechism, #1041	Death and Resurrection — Catechism, #1682	Christians as One — Catechism, #820
Hope for the Future — Catechism, #1042	Seeds of the Kingdom — Catechism, #865	The Life of the World to Come — Catechism, #672	Waiting for the New Creation — Catechism, #1048
Signs of New Life — Catechism, #638	Love Lives Again — Catechism, #654	The Great Vigil — Catechism, #1217	Our Story of Salvation — Catechism, #652

Principal Consultants' Messages

From the very beginning of its development, **Walking by Faith** *has benefited from the contributions of three Principal Program Consultants. The consultants have been actively involved at every step of the journey—from development of the scope and sequence through rigorous content review—bringing their combined theological, catechetical, and pastoral experience and expertise to the creation of materials for students, families, and catechists.*

Father Michael D. Place was appointed Research Theologian to the Curia of the Archdiocese of Chicago in 1986. In this capacity he is theological consultant to the Archbishop of Chicago and to the agencies and programs of the Archdiocese. In November 1990 Father Place was appointed by Cardinal Bernardin as Consul for Policy Development and a member of the Archbishop's cabinet. As Consul for Policy Development he coordinates the development of Archdiocesan policy, advises the Archbishop on matters of public policy, and chairs ad-hoc task forces.

Father Place serves as Chair of the Archdiocesan HealthCare Ethics Commission, as the Archbishop's representative to the Archdiocesan Pastoral Council, Presbyteral Council, and Archdiocesan Women's Commission, and as an advisor to the Catholic Conference of Illinois. Currently he serves as a member of the Theology and Ethics Resource Group of the Catholic Health Association and as a member of several other medical ethics committees; as a member of the Euthanasia Advisory Committee for the National Conference of Catholic Bishops; and as a member of and immediate past-chair of the Chicagoland Catholic/Jewish Scholars' Dialogue.

Ordained as a priest of the Archdiocese of Chicago from St. Mary of the Lake Seminary in 1970, Father Place holds Masters degrees in Divinity and Ecclesiastical History, and a Doctorate in Sacred Theology with highest honors from the Catholic University of America. He is a member of the adjunct faculty of the Institute of Pastoral Studies of Loyola University and Mundelein Seminary of St. Mary of the Lake.

Dr. Addie Lorraine Walker, SSND is currently a member of the formation faculty and the Director of Liturgy and Liturgical Formation at Assumption Seminary in San Antonio, Texas. She is also a member of the adjunct faculty at the Oblate School of Theology in San Antonio. Concurrently, she is the Associate Director for the Institute of Black Catholic Studies at Xavier University of Louisiana in New Orleans. As Associate Director for the Institute, she is involved in catechetics and the training of pastoral ministers. Sister Addie conducts various workshops and presentations at national and diocesan events throughout the United States.

Sister Addie is a member of the Association of Professors and Professional Religious Educators (APPRE) and of the National Black Sisters' Conference (NBSC). From 1986 to 1993 she served as Co-Director and Instructor for the IMANI Master Catechist Program at the Institute for Black Catholic Studies in New Orleans. She has designed and facilitated workshops on Ministry, Catechesis, and the RCIA in the Black Community and has authored numerous articles for catechetical publications. She was one of the organizers and designers of the Lafayette (Louisiana) Diocesan Black Youth Congress. She serves as a retreat director and program development consultant.

In 1996 Sister Addie received her Ph.D. in Religion and Education from the Institute of Religious Education and Pastoral Ministry of Boston College. She is a member of the Formation Committee of the School Sisters of Notre Dame in San Antonio.

Father Terry M. Odien currently serves as pastor of Holy Saviour Church in Westmont, New Jersey. Father Odien conducts workshops and gives presentations at national and diocesan congresses throughout the United States.

Father Odien is currently a member of the National Conference of Catechetical Leadership. He served as President of the NCCL from 1993 to 1994 and as a member of the NCCL Board of Directors from 1987 to 1995. He represented the conference at national gatherings such as the Future Search Conference of the National Catholic Young Adult Ministry Association and Catholic Campus Ministry Association, and the Planning Seminar for a National Hispanic Catholic Media Center sponsored by the Hispanic Telecommunications Network.

From 1979 to 1995 Father Odien served as the Diocesan Director of Religious Education for the Diocese of Camden in New Jersey. During this time Father Odien developed a Diocesan Catechist Formation Program, planned and executed an annual Diocesan Religious Education Institute, and gave numerous presentations to adult education groups.

Ordained in 1973 with a Masters in Religious Education from LaSalle University, Philadelphia, Pennsylvania. Father Odien has participated in the Catholic Jewish Symposium of the Institute for Christian-Jewish Studies in Baltimore, Maryland, and the Catholic Education Future Project of the University of Dayton, Ohio. He has been a member of the adjunct faculty at Holy Family College in Philadelphia.

On the following pages, the Principal Program Consultants share their insights into the program they helped to develop.

Walking by Faith and the Catechism of the Catholic Church

Rev. Michael D. Place, STD

The meaning of catechetical ministry is best understood in the context of the Church being an evangelizing community—a community that brings the good news to people in every time and place. In his apostolic exhortation Pope Paul VI reminded us that evangelization is not a "thing" but a complex process with many interrelated parts. And catechesis is one of the moments or elements of evangelization. The purpose of catechesis is to make it possible for those who are catechized to be in touch with and in communion with Jesus Christ and, through Christ, with the Triune God. It is Christ who is taught—who is the "content" of catechesis—and it is Christ who teaches.

We also know that catechesis is more than *kerygma* (proclamation). Catechesis is an education of the total person. The catechetical process is itself many-faceted, involving an experience of Christian living, personal as well as liturgical and sacramental prayer, and participation in the life of the community of faith through apostolic witness. Essential to this catechetical process is the handing on of Christian doctrine in a systematic manner.

The documents of the magisterium and of our own bishops have pointed out that this educational aspect of the catechetical process has some core elements. In addition to being systematic, it should deal with the essentials of our faith tradition, be sufficiently complete, and be integrated with other aspects of the catechetical process.

The Catechetical Context

It was with the core elements of catechesis in mind that *Walking by Faith* was developed. The series asks the students and their families to reflect through the eyes of faith on their experience of Christian living. It integrates personal and liturgical prayer into the catechetical series, and it invites the students to engage in apostolic activity appropriate to their age level.

What brings these elements together and provides for their integration is *Walking by Faith*'s handing on of Christian doctrine. For perhaps the first time in the United States, both the content and the presentation of doctrine in a series is based on the *Catechism of the Catholic Church*. This series is designed to provide at each grade level an integral presentation of the fundamental elements of Church teaching as presented in the Catechism. In addition, the series makes reference throughout both pupil and teacher materials to the Catechism by citing paragraph numbers and summarizing content. Specific lesson plans in *Walking by Faith* clearly reflect the Catechism's integration of the teaching of the Second Vatican Council with the wealth of earlier ecclesial teaching, as well as its attention to the rich heritage of the Eastern Catholic tradition.

The Pillars of Faith

Great care was taken to ensure that student, family, and catechist would come to appreciate and understand the distinctive manner in which each of the "pillars of faith" has been organized in the *Catechism of the Catholic Church*. The series reflects the strong attention to Trinitarian themes found in Part One. It grounds its discussion of the individual sacraments in an awareness of the sacramental economy that moves throughout Part Two. The series' emphasis on morality as a vocational call to conversion and holiness, made possible by God's grace and lived out by obeying the commandments, reflects the emphasis in Part Three of the Catechism. Finally, *Walking by Faith* expresses the dynamic nature of the personal relationship with God that is prayer, as outlined in Part Four.

Challenges for Today

The challenge has been to do all of this in a manner that is appropriate to the developmental level of the student and sensitive to the great diversity of student backgrounds that are found in school and parish religious education programs. As daunting as those challenges are, it has also been imperative that the series respond to those dimensions of our culture that might impede the students' gaining a full appreciation of the faith that is being handed on to them. What many today might consider to be "counter-cultural" values, such as community, stewardship, and truth, are woven into the entire series.

In the end, however, the success of this new catechetical series will be determined by how well families, catechists, and indeed the entire parish come to see themselves as participating in the Church's ministry of evangelization and make their own the truth that it is Christ who is taught and Christ who teaches.

Creating the Catechetical Environment

Dr. Addie Lorraine Walker, SSND

Walking by Faith, as the title implies, is a catechetical series that views religious education and formation as an ongoing or lifelong process of developing a faith that is alive and active in the world today. Community is at the heart of our catechetical process, and so the series challenges students and teachers to build community in all areas of their lives. Personal faith grows most naturally within community and in fact requires the involvement of the whole community.

But community is not automatically created. Only by careful and intentional preparation of the catechetical environment do we provide an atmosphere where community can happen—a place of warmth and acceptance, a place where each person is respected and cared for, a place where the challenges of life and students' questions of faith are taken seriously and attended to, a place where our diversity of cultures, customs, and devotional practices is shared and celebrated. This kind of atmosphere reminds students and teachers alike that we are not just individuals alone in relationship to God. We are called to be the people of God. Our Church, as a community of faith, must be an active sign of God's reign.

In creating the catechetical atmosphere, there are at least three dimensions to consider: the physical space, the social-relational environment, and the academic-intellectual space.

Physical Space

The physical space refers to just how the room is prepared for the session. What does the space look and feel like? Are religious symbols, especially a Bible, displayed with reverence? Do the pictures and other visual cues reflect that we are Catholics of many cultures? How are the chairs arranged? Is there a place in the room where work done by the students can be displayed?

In a catechetical atmosphere the visible elements should speak to our religious faith, reminding us subtly or explicitly that God is with us. The arrangement of chairs in circles rather than rows suggests that this is not a class in the academic sense (though this arrangement would be ideal for many academic settings as well) but is a faith group coming together to pray, to study, to learn new information, to ask new questions, to get support and encouragement from each other as we "walk by faith" together. A warm, inviting physical space predisposes students to the possibility of bonding as a community of faith.

Social-Relational Environment

The social-relational environment describes how the students and teacher relate to one another. How are students welcomed by the teacher? Is there an atmosphere of openness and freedom for sharing? Since faith formation, not just information sharing, is the goal of our coming together, creating a positive social-relational environment is crucial. An atmosphere of respect, trust, and care gives students a safe space in which to open themselves to the faith development process. This atmosphere for faith formation is not static but must be created and recreated at each gathering. A first step in establishing this atmosphere of safety, respect, trust, and care is what I call *gathering*. In liturgy we do this in the gathering and introductory rites before we listen to the word of God and partake of the Bread of Life. In our homes we do this in our greeting, welcoming, and making our guests feel comfortable before we share stories and break bread together. Attention to gathering is extremely important here in the catechetical setting where we come together to ponder the mysteries of life and faith. When we don't attend to the social-relational environment, we find it difficult to translate catechetical sessions into mature, living, and active faith.

Academic-Intellectual Space

The academic-intellectual space points to the content of study as well as the teaching-learning strategies used in instructional designs. Do students have the opportunity to be exposed to the fullness of Catholic doctrine at an age-appropriate level? Are students exposed to the richness of Catholic customs and devotional practices? What connections are made with other academic learning and with what is happening in the world? How is Christian action for justice supported? Are a variety of teaching and learning styles employed in order to reach every student? *Walking by Faith* has been developed to provide the best possible academic-intellectual support for the catechetical process in all these areas.

Careful attention to creating the catechetical environment each session will ready both teacher and students for the infinite possibilities of growing in faith. It will allow for a depth of sharing and for many wonderful surprises by the Holy Spirit. Careful attention to creating the catechetical environment will foster and support the values of Catholic Christian community for students and teachers, families, and local parish communities as we all continue "walking by faith."

Catechesis for the Twenty-First Century

Rev. Terry M. Odien, MA

Françoise Darcy-Berube, the renowned catechist, told a story that has had lasting impact on me and on my life as a catechist. While teaching at Fordham University, she surveyed adolescents from a Catholic high school to find out who God was for them, and what prayer meant to them after ten years of Catholic education. One student responded that he didn't pray. He went on to say that for ten years catechists and teachers had been talking to him about God, but that no one had ever introduced him to God.

Since hearing that story I have wondered whether the young people I have catechized over the past 30 years have been introduced to God by me—or have I only talked to them about God? Pope John Paul II reminds us that "at the heart of catechesis we find, in essence, a Person, the Person of Jesus of Nazareth" (*Catechesi Tradendae*, p. 6).

Where We Come From

We have come a long way catechetically in the past 30 years. We have moved away from a question-and-answer approach and toward a learning model that is interactive, experiential, and aimed at inviting the learner to interact with "the mystery of love that we call God" (Karl Rahner). We have come to realize that catechesis is not only concerned with providing information but must also be about the work of formation. The National Catechetical Directory, *Sharing the Light of Faith*, tells us that the goal of all religious education is to "help individuals and communities acquire and deepen Christian faith and identity through rites, instruction, and formation of conscience" (NCD, #5).

Challenges Ahead

As we move into the twenty-first century, we are challenged to identify the ways American children learn information and form values. We are living in a world that is changing at a rapid pace. It is almost impossible to keep up with the developments in technology. Even the youngest child is comfortable sitting at a computer and accessing information as desired. This may be effective for gathering information. However, if we are about the work of formation—forming the disciples of Jesus Christ—our efforts must include a willingness to share our faith with those we are catechizing. Pope Paul VI stated it well: "Modern man listens more willingly to witnesses than to teachers, and if he does listen to teachers, it is because they are witnesses" (*On Evangelization in the Modern World*, 1975).

If we are to catechize effectively, not only must we witness to our faith and be willing to share our faith story with those we are catechizing, but we must also employ the best pedagogical tools. I am reminded of the Chinese proverb:

> "I hear . . . and I forget.
> I see . . . and I remember.
> I do . . . and I understand."

Meeting the Challenge

Walking by Faith recognizes the catechetical realities we've mentioned. And so we bring to this series the best insights of religious educators and the additional strengths of pedagogical expertise from other disciplines. We supply a variety of lesson modalities. We promote interactivity at all levels and in all components. Integral to the series is the student and family *Faith Journal*, a unique tool for helping young people reflect on their own growth in faith, internalize the content and experiences of the religion class, and explore and practice their faith at home and in the larger world.

Along with utilizing the best teaching methods, we must recognize that children grow in faith best as members of a faith community. This faith community includes their families, their classmates, and the wider parish family. We have come to realize once again, as did the Church in its earliest centuries, that catechesis is the shared faith life of the entire parish community. We cannot expect that a child will grow into a person of mature faith if his or her religious formation is confined to a weekly catechetical session, or even to daily instruction in a Catholic school classroom.

Walking by Faith is a catechetical series whose language, pedagogy, and philosophy is communal rather than individualistic. Every aspect of the series is geared toward developing the community of faith.

In their pastoral letter to religious educators, the Catholic Bishops of New Jersey say that "it is no longer sufficient to catechize for an intellectual assent to beliefs, creeds, and doctrines. While these beliefs are integral to our tradition, we need to extend our understanding of what catechesis means. The goal of catechesis is the conversion of the whole person" (*Pastoral Letter to Religious Educators: Statement of the Catholic Bishops of New Jersey*, September, 1992).

Walking by Faith is a series that will more than adequately facilitate that conversion in the lives of our young people today, with results that will carry them into the future.

Walking by Faith Grade Three

The "lens" through which the Christian message is presented this year is **The Church**. Third graders are especially open to exploring their faith as members of a community. Here is how the seven key areas of catechesis will be presented through the lens of **The Church** this year:

Unit One / Creation

The students learn that God created people to be in community with him and with one another. They identify themselves as members of the Church. They are introduced to the Church's mission of announcing the gospel to the whole world.

Unit Two / God

The students see the Trinity as the model for Christian community. They see how members of the Church express their faith in God through prayer, worship, and the sacraments.

Unit Three / Jesus Christ

The students learn about Jesus' mission to invite all people into God's kingdom of justice, love, and peace. They see how Jesus commissioned his followers, the Church, to carry out his work in the world.

Unit Four / The Church

The students explore the Church as both community and institution. They see that all members of the Church have a share in the Church's ministry according to their state in life. The students see how the marks of the Church, signs of the Spirit's presence, are lived today.

Unit Five / Christian Morality

The students see that Jesus gave his followers the law of love. They learn to look to the Church for moral guidance as they grow in the virtues of faith, hope, and love.

Unit Six / The Sacraments

The students explore the sacramental nature of the Church. Each of the seven sacraments is presented in detail so that the students can grow in their understanding of and participation in the Church's sacramental life.

Unit Seven / Salvation History

The students come to understand the Church as a community with roots in the past, an active ministry in the present, and hope for the future coming of the kingdom of God in fullness.

Walking by Faith and Uncatechized Children

Because *Walking by Faith* presents the complete catechetical message at each grade level, you should have little difficulty integrating uncatechized students into the class. Students who have had no formal religious education or whose religious education has been interrupted for a period of time will still receive the full catechetical message at their appropriate age level. The *Catholic Prayers and Resources* section at the back of the student book is a valuable reference for students who may be unfamiliar with common prayers and practices.

Catechesis and the Third Grader

Jesus, the model for all catechesis, always approached his listeners on their own level, in the midst of their daily lives. Jesus used familiar language and images, along with provocative questions, to invite people to walk with him in faith.

As a catechist it is your task and your joy to follow Jesus' example with the students in your class. The best "lesson planning" you can do is to get to know the students and their world.

All children are individuals, with unique gifts and challenges. Yet the following list of general characteristics of eight- and nine-year-olds may be useful in coming to understand the world of the third grader.

- The third grader understands that he or she is not the only person in the world. Third graders can learn to see things from other perspectives than their own, and are developing qualities of empathy and compassion.
- Third graders identify themselves and others as members of groups. Children at this age are joiners, devoting energy to communal activities such as team sports, hobby clubs, and scouting. The family, the class, and the parish community remain strong influences in the child's world. Third graders need help in resisting the tendencies to stereotype others and to form cliques which are the negative sides of the communal instinct.
- At eight or nine years of age, children are capable of making moral choices. Given good example and clear moral guidelines, they can choose between right and wrong. They can begin to form their conscience. Psychologically and spiritually, a child of this age is not likely to be capable of serious sin, but third graders comprehend the nature of acts that violate the natural moral law. As the children mature, they benefit from a continued mystagogical catechesis of Reconciliation, a sacrament most of them celebrated for the first time while in second grade.
- The third grader generally maintains a sunny, optimistic disposition. While children of this age go through many different moods, prolonged sadness or anger in a third grader may be an indication of emotional problems, reaction to a difficult home situation, or frustration resulting from learning disabilities. Follow school or parish policies for offering help to troubled children.

Multiple Learning Styles

All students learn in several different ways. Educators and psychologists may refer to these learning styles as modalities or multiple intelligences, but the important thing for you to remember is the necessity to vary your presentation of information in order to stimulate all the students' capacities.

Here are some of the learning styles identified by educators and some suggestions for addressing them:

- *linguistic intelligence* (using words)—storytelling, poetry, spoken prayer
- *logical/mathematical intelligence* (using numbers, making logical connections)—listing, categorizing, ordering events in time, matching
- *spatial intelligence* (thinking visually)—drawing, painting, collage, learning from photographs and illustrations
- *musical intelligence* (sensitivity to sound and rhythm)—singing songs, making up rhymes, chanting, meditating to instrumental music, making music with simple instruments
- *bodily intelligence* (learning through touch, movement, three-dimensional objects)—dance, gesture prayer, dramatization, three-dimensional art
- *interpersonal intelligence* (learning from and responding to others)—group projects, cooperative games, discussion, group prayer
- *intrapersonal intelligence* (self-knowledge, goalsetting)—reflection questions, journaling, meditative prayer

The lesson plans and optional activities for *Walking by Faith* Three have been designed to touch all learning styles and to help the children make use of all their capabilities.

In the Resource Center section of the *Walking by Faith* Three lesson plan pages, you will find a feature entitled *Meeting Individual Needs*. This feature provides suggestions for tailoring the lesson content or activity to the needs of specific kinds of learners.

- **Auditory learners** learn best by listening. These suggestions may also be useful for children with visual impairments.
- **Visual learners** learn best through a graphic presentation of information. These suggestions may also be useful for children with hearing impairments.
- **Kinesthetic learners** learn best through touch and movement. These suggestions may also be useful for children with attention deficit disorders.
- **Learners acquiring English** need particular help with vocabulary and language arts exercises. These suggestions also apply to children with reading and writing difficulties.

For more on addressing multiple learning styles and adapting lessons for children, see Idea File #3, Meeting Individual Needs, pages T46–T47.

Scope and Sequence

Chapter	Key Content	Catholics Believe
Unit One (Creation) Created for Community		
1 Made for Each Other	God created humans to live in community; the Church; second creation story; Saint Paul; unity of Christians; litany	Catechism, #1879
2 The Family of Creation	Interrelatedness of God's creation; goodness of created world; chart of sacramentals; blessings; Saint Francis of Assisi; Canticle of the Sun	Catechism, #344
3 Light of the World	Church as sign of the kingdom; grace; original sin; sin; heaven; the fall; God's promise of redemption; "This Little Light of Mine"	Catechism, #1999
4 We Celebrate Mary: Mother of the Church	Mary's care for the Church; Our Lady of Guadalupe; Blessed Juan Diego; Mary as patron of Americas; "Las Mananitas"	Catechism, #969
Unit Two (God) People of God		
5 We Believe in God	Mystery of the Holy Trinity; creed; belief; witness; Saint Patrick; Glory to the Father (doxology)	Catechism, #234
6 We Worship God	Prayer and worship as response to God's love; Eucharist as central prayer of the Church; forms of prayer; psalms; *Praying; Glory to God*	Catechism, #752
7 We Belong to God	Covenant; Abraham and Sarah; Ten Commandments; faithfulness; chart on ways to keep the commandments; Mary's faithfulness; Magnificat	Catechism, #781
8 We Celebrate All Saints: Honoring Their Memory	Saints; witness of martyrs; early Church; Saint Polycarp; All Saints' Day; prayer from Mass of All Saints' Day	Catechism, #957
Unit Three (Jesus Christ) The Body of Christ		
9 Jesus Brings Good News	Kingdom of God; Jesus as Messiah; Jesus' mission; parables; gospel; doing God's will; *Hearing Good News*; the Lord's Prayer	Catechism, #763
10 New Life in Jesus	Sacrifice; resurrection; Passover; new covenant; Paschal mystery; chart comparing Passover and Eucharist; memorial acclamation	Catechism, #609
11 Jesus Works Through Us	The Church carries out Jesus' mission; the Body of Christ; service; the last judgment; gifts and talents; Saint Teresa of Avila; litany of service	Catechism, #794
12 We Celebrate Advent: A Time to Remember	Advent; Old Testament prophecies; second coming; prayer based on the Jesse tree	Catechism, #524
Unit Four (The Church) Guided by the Holy Spirit		
13 The Church Works Together	Church as organization; structure; hierarchy; roles and ministries; missionary efforts; Peter as head of the Church; Pope John XXIII; general intercessions	Catechism, #872
14 One and Holy	Marks of the Church; Church unity; Pentecost; presence of the Holy Spirit; holiness; prayer to the Holy Spirit	Catechism, #813
15 Catholic and Apostolic	Universality of the Church; apostles; apostolic succession; mission of the Church; sharing good news; creed; Apostles' Creed	Catechism, #857
16 We Celebrate Christmas: The First Nativity Scene	Christmas; Francis of Assisi and the crèche; Jesus' birth; blessing of nativity scene; carols	Catechism, #525

Chapter	Key Content	Catholics Believe
Unit Five (Christian Morality) Temple of the Holy Spirit		
17 Jesus' Law of Love	The law of love; the Great Commandment; the Beatitudes; good Samaritan; prayer of Saint Richard of Chichester	Catechism, #1970
18 The Church Helps	The role of the Church in teaching morality and forming conscience; God's word; conscience; the Holy Spirit's action; *Examining Your Conscience*; litany from Rite of Penance for Children	Catechism, #1785
19 Faith, Hope, and Love	Virtues; theological virtues in the life of the Church; Saint Thomas the Apostle; chart of precepts of the Church; Act of Faith, Hope, and Love	Catechism, #1813
20 We Celebrate Lent: Strength Through Practice	Lent; spiritual discipline; Lenten practices; fasting; abstinence; charity; Psalm 119	Catechism, #1438
Unit Six (The Sacraments) Belonging, Healing, Serving		
21 We Become Part of the Church	Sacraments of Initiation (Baptism, Confirmation, Eucharist); Christian identity; chart of Sacraments of Initiation; baptismal profession of faith	Catechism, #1212
22 The Church Celebrates Healing	Sacraments of Healing (Reconciliation and Anointing of the Sick); Jesus' ministry; chart of Sacraments of Healing; prayer from Rite of Anointing	Catechism, #1421
23 Sacraments of Service	Sacraments of Service (Matrimony and Holy Orders); vows; Saint Isidore the Farmer; chart of Sacraments of Service; prayers for priests, families	Catechism, #1534
24 We Celebrate Holy Week: Hosanna!	Jesus' entry into Jerusalem; Passion Sunday; Holy Week; Jesus' Passion; Palm Sunday celebrations; prayer based on Palm Sunday sequence	Catechism, #559
Unit Seven (Salvation History) Yesterday, Today, and Tomorrow		
25 Connected to the Past	Church history; roots in Judaism; early Church; persecutions; development around the world; Saint Bede; prayer of Saint Clement	Catechism, #759
26 The Church Today	Kingdom of God in fullness; witness; solidarity; justice, love, and peace; Jean Donovan; *Giving Witness*; Prayer to the Holy Spirit	Catechism, #2046
27 Hope for the Future	Looking to the challenges of the future; the Spirit's continued presence; last judgment; second coming; new Jerusalem; spontaneous litany of thanks	Catechism, #1042
28 We Celebrate Easter: Signs of New Life	Easter; resurrection; Church as community of risen Savior; prayer from Easter Mass	Catechism, #638

Note: Titles in italics indicate *Stepping Stones* features.

Notes

Walking by Faith offers a learning process that fully engages students in Catholic schools and parish religious education programs, families at all levels of growth in faith, and teachers and catechists at all levels of experience.

How to Use the Walking by Faith
Grade Three Teaching Guide

This Teaching Guide has been developed to assist you in your ministry of walking by faith with your students and their families. On the following pages, you will find information on using this guide to plan and teach your lessons. You will also find suggestions for incorporating other *Walking by Faith* program resources and guidance on scheduling your year.

Whatever your level of catechetical experience, you will find this Teaching Guide to be your greatest ally in carrying out your ministry. But no Teaching Guide or textbook, no matter how comprehensive, can take the place of the personal witness of the catechist. You—with your experience, your faith, your commitment—are the best gift you bring to the classroom.

Walking by Faith lessons are designed around a mutual journey of exploration, a common pilgrimage undertaken by students and catechist together, with the assistance of families and the full faith community. On that journey you are encouraged to adapt Teaching Guide strategies and suggestions to suit the needs of your particular classroom community.

As blessing and inspiration, keep in mind the words of the Letter to the Ephesians:

> *"Out of the riches of his glory,*
> *may God grant you the power through the Spirit*
> *for your innermost self to grow strong,*
> *so that Christ may dwell in your heart through faith,*
> *and so that—planted in love and built on love—*
> *you may have the strength to understand*
> *what all the holy ones know:*
> *the breadth, length, height, and depth*
> *of the love of Christ,*
> *that is beyond all knowing.*
> *May you be filled with the fullness of God.*
> *And to the One who, working in us,*
> *is able to do infinitely more*
> *than we can ever ask or imagine,*
> *let us give glory through Christ's Church*
> *forever and ever."*
>
> —based on Ephesians 3:16–21

USING THE TEACHING GUIDE : T27

Preparing to Teach

Preceding each chapter in this Teaching Guide are two preparatory pages called *Getting Ready*. These pages help you plan your lesson, organize materials, prepare yourself spiritually, and locate any additional resources you might need.

Before you teach each chapter:

- take time to review the *Getting Ready* pages
- read through the chapter lesson plan pages
- make notes on the steps you will follow and the optional activities you will carry out
- gather any necessary materials (including copies of program resources)
- preview additional resources

Here is what you will find on the *Getting Ready* pages for each chapter.

Planning Chart

The planning chart provides a simple, easy-to-follow outline of the chapter. Chapter content, which is designed to correlate to one class session, is broken into four parts—*Open, Build, Review,* and *Close*—corresponding to the *We Are Invited, We Explore, We Reflect,* and *We Celebrate* pages of the student book. A section of the chart entitled *Pacing Guide* provides suggested durations for each part and note space for your own pacing.

For other pacing suggestions, see Scheduling, *pages T35–T37, and Idea File #8,* Overcoming Scheduling Limitations, *pages T56–T57.*

The planning chart also lists key objectives for each part of the lesson and indicates any necessary materials or additional program resources.

Catechism in Context

This section of the *Getting Ready* pages provides a brief reflection on the doctrinal foundation of the chapter, keyed to the Catechism paragraph referenced in the *Catholics Believe* feature in the student book. You are encouraged to read the particular paragraph from the *Catechism of the Catholic Church* to add to your own understanding.

The *Catechism in Context* reflections were prepared by Rev. Douglas K. Clark, a member of the committee that prepared the English translation of the *Catechism of the Catholic Church*.

One-Minute Retreat

This feature gives you a way to prepare yourself spiritually to teach the chapter. A thought-provoking quotation focuses on the chapter theme. A reflection question helps you look at the chapter theme as it is lived out in your own experience. Finally, a brief prayer invites God to be present with you as you teach.

To continue your own spiritual growth, make use of Your Faith Journal *for each chapter, beginning on page J1 at the back of this Teaching Guide.*

Visualizing the Lesson

This section features a graphic organizer plus a suggested activity for you to use with the students. The graphic organizer provides a visual summary of key chapter content. Suggestions for when to use the graphic organizer are provided in the core lesson plan column of the lesson plan pages.

Library Links

This section of the *Getting Ready* pages offers annotated suggestions for additional resources tied to the chapter theme, including:

- **Books for Children**
  These may be read to the children or suggested for outside reading. They are available in libraries or through publishers' catalogs.

- **Books for Teachers and Families**
  These resources add to your understanding of the topic. They are available in libraries or through publishers' catalogs.

- **Multimedia**
  This section lists videos, audiotapes, music, and other media resources, available from catalogs or by rental from commercial video stores. Those labeled for children may be used in class. Others may be recommended for adult reference or for family sharing at home.

- **Organizations**
  This section lists organizations that may provide additional information. Mailing addresses, telephone numbers, and e-mail addresses or websites, where available, are provided. *(Note that contact information, while correct at time of publication, is subject to change.)*

For ideas on incorporating popular media into your class, see Idea File #4, Dealing with Popular Culture, *pages T48–T49.*

It is important to review all additional resources carefully before using them in class. Although care has been taken to choose resources with acceptable content appropriate to the users' developmental level, you know your class and your needs best. Preview multimedia to be sure that all projection and sound equipment, as well as the resource itself, is in good working order.

Strengthening the Family Link

This section of the *Getting Ready* pages offers simple strategies for involving the students' families, providing suggestions for at-home discussion or in-class participation.

For a description of the Family Letters, *see* Using Program Resources, *page T34. For other suggestions on strengthening the family link, see* Idea File #6, Connecting with Families, *pages T52–T53.*

Teaching a Chapter

The Importance of Gathering

The first thing you will see in each session's core lesson plan column is the *Gathering* icon. This is a reminder of the importance of bringing the students together in an effective and personal way to share their religion class. When you see the *Gathering* icon, you are reminded to use one of the suggestions listed here (or a strategy of your own) to help the students make a graceful and grace-filled transition into the catechetical experience. Vary these strategies as the occasion requires.

- **Sing a song.** Teach the students some of the simpler hymns and responses sung in your parish. Make use of the *Walking by Faith* Music and Liturgy Resources. Set Scripture verses or simple faith statements to familiar folk or popular tunes. Allow the students to suggest, lead, and teach songs.

- **Play instrumental music.** Experiment with different moods and types of music—a lively folk tune to start a rainy-day class, a quiet meditation to mark a transition from playground games. Incorporate music into guided meditations or use it with simple dance gestures. Be sure to explore music from many different ethnic and cultural traditions.

- **Form a circle.** Sometimes just gathering to hold hands makes a good transition into religion class. Form your circle by moving chairs or desks, or just take time to stand in a circle to pray.

- **Share joys and cares.** The students bring their everyday lives to religion class. A great way to gather is to allow the students to mention particular happy times or concerns they have. You may find that the events of the "outside world" have a profound impact on the course of the class. Especially when these events impact all the students—as, for example, when a storm or other natural disaster strikes the community—it's important to let life lead the lesson plan.

- **Touch base.** Spend a few moments following up on previous class discussions and activities to help the students gather themselves for this session's explorations. Allow the students to report on the progress of ongoing events in their lives.

- **Bring in those you love.** When you gather, mention students who are absent. Ask the students to name family members and friends for whom the class can pray.

- **Tell a story.** Capture attention and set the mood for the class with storytelling. A simple story from a book, a news clipping read aloud, or a piece of "human interest" from the Internet can become the focus for gathering.

- **Move in procession.** Activity helps students make the transition from one part of the school day to the next. You can gather the students by moving in procession out the door and back in again, around the room, to the church and back, or around the yard. Sing or chant as you go. Students can walk single file or with partners and can move solemnly or joyfully.

- **Acknowledge special days.** Keep a class calendar of birthdays or feast days of the students' patron saints. Mention special days, and allow the students to share good wishes.

- **Share silence.** Don't enforce quiet as a disciplinary measure or use prayer as a silencer. But do occasionally begin the class by gathering to share a moment of silence. Encourage the students to become comfortable with peaceful silence and to listen to God in their hearts.

Although the *Gathering* icon appears only once in each chapter (at step **1. Open**), you should use a gathering strategy every time you begin a new session.

For other gathering suggestions, see Idea File #1, Establishing Group Atmosphere, *pages T42–T43.*

Lesson Plan

The lesson plan pages of this Teaching Guide take you through the chapter in a simple, easy-to-follow process. Each lesson plan page consists of a full-color reduced version of the student book page, surrounded by a wraparound lesson plan. Next to the student page, in the vertical column, you will find the core lesson plan. These are the steps you will follow to communicate the chapter content.

Below the student page, across the bottom of the Teaching Guide page, you will find the Resource Center, which contains background information, links, tips, and optional activity suggestions.

The Core Lesson Plan

At the beginning of the chapter, the objectives for the whole chapter are provided for you. The core lesson itself is divided into three simple steps:

1. **Open**—strategies for introducing the chapter content, tied to the *We Are Invited* pages of the student book

2. **Build**—strategies for developing the chapter content, tied to the *We Explore* pages of the student book, and strategies for reviewing the content, tied to the *We Reflect* page

3. **Close**—strategies for ending the chapter with prayer and celebration, tied to the *We Celebrate* page of the student book

Here are some of the features of the core lesson plan column:

Personal Experience Suggestions for connecting the lesson content with the students' everyday lives. These suggestions may be combined with or used to extend the gathering idea with which you begin each session.

Prayer Suggestions for praying the opening and closing prayers for each session and for celebrating the closing prayer portion of the *We Celebrate* page.

Working with the Text Teaching directions for exploring the words on the page. These simple steps include ideas for addressing varied learning styles. You may expand on these steps by drawing from the Resource Center at the bottom of the Teaching Guide page. Among these steps you will find suggestions for answering in-text questions, exploring concepts in depth, and addressing the many features on the student page.

Working with the Pictures Teaching directions for exploring the photographs and illustrations on the page. Some of the important religious content of *Walking by Faith* is communicated visually, and these steps will help you guide the students' understanding of what they see. This part of the core lesson column includes suggestions for answering caption questions and working with in-text activities.

Alternative Suggestions for varying the core column directions. Alternatives often provide opportunities for maximizing use of class time.

Stepping Stones, Practice Accompanies a *Stepping Stones* feature in the student book. This special core lesson column helps you present, explore, and reinforce a particular Catholic practice or skill with the students.

Recall, Think and Share, Continue the Journey, We Live Our Faith These suggestions correspond to the parts of the *We Reflect* page in the student book. They include answers to review questions, directions for guiding discussion and carrying out the in-text activity aimed at applying the content of the lesson, and suggestions for assisting the students in extending the lesson into the home and the community. Prompts in the core column of the *We Reflect* page also remind you to have the students begin working on their *Faith Journal* activities and direct you to *Your Faith Journal*.

For more on how to use the core lesson plan column, see Lesson Plan Pages, page T39.

The Resource Center

This section contains background features and optional activities to extend and enrich the core lesson.

Here are the features you will find in the *Walking by Faith* Three Resource Center:

Background (including Art, Scripture, Catechism) Provides key information at point of use, to deepen your own and the students' understanding

The Language of Faith Introduces and develops the students' understanding of key religious terms, with definitions rooted in the Catechism

Multicultural Link Offers information and optional activities for exploring the Church's global diversity and helping the students appreciate their own cultural and religious heritage

For more suggestions on developing multicultural understanding, see Idea File #5, Appreciating Diversity, pages T50–T51.

Link to the Family, Link to the Faith Community, Link to Liturgy, Link to Justice Provides suggestions for linking the class to the home, the parish, and the liturgical life and social concerns of the community

Meeting Individual Needs Offers strategies for adapting teaching situations to the various learning styles and pedagogical needs of students

For more suggestions on tailoring lesson plans to your students, see Idea File #3, Meeting Individual Needs, pages T46–T47.

Teaching Tips Provides suggestions for classroom management, clarifying content, handling sensitive topics, and answering questions

Assessment Tips Offers tips for assessing the students' progress in class and growth in faith, using a variety of strategies including self-assessment

Enrichment Optional activities for in-class and at-home exploration of the chapter content

The Resource Center section of the Teaching Guide also provides handy note spaces for recording your planning and evaluation of each section of the lesson.

For more information on teaching Walking by Faith Three, see Lesson Plan Pages, page T39.

Using the Faith Journal

The *Faith Journal* is a component unique to the *Walking by Faith* series. Bound separately from the student book, it gives each student a way to keep track of his or her faith journey for the year.

This *Faith Journal* contains one two-sided page for each chapter of the *Walking by Faith* student book. On the front of the page, there are questions and activities designed to help the student think and pray about what he or she is learning in class. Some activities provide the students with ideas for living their Catholic faith every day.

The back of each page contains *Family Faith Journal* activities and prayers. By sharing these pages with their families every week, students invite family members to walk by faith with them. At the back of each *Faith Journal* is a collection of traditional Catholic prayers (in English and Spanish) and resources to use for family reference.

The *Faith Journal* is not a test. Students should not be graded on how they or their families complete the pages. Nor should students be compelled to share journal reflections with anyone, though they may be invited to do so if they choose. A direction on the *Checkpoint* pages at the end of each unit encourages students to choose favorite *Faith Journal* pages and share them.

In the core lesson column for each *We Reflect* page in this Teaching Guide, you will find a prompt to remind students to complete their *Faith Journal* pages. The *Faith Journal* pages for the chapter are reproduced in reduced form in the Resource Center section of this page. However, you may choose to remind students to use their Faith Journals at any point during the chapter. Students may begin completing the personal side of the page in class, completing it and the *Family Faith Journal* activities at home.

Here are some other ideas for using the *Faith Journal*:

- Encourage students to include godparents and other members of their parish family in the *Family Faith Journal* activities when possible.

- Devote part of a Family Night or open house to a practice session showing students and their families how to use the *Faith Journal*.

- Occasionally allow time for students to share the results of *Family Faith Journal* activities if they so choose.

- Remind students to look back through completed *Faith Journal* pages at regular intervals during the year. In this way they can begin to evaluate their own progress.

- If students will not be taking the *Faith Journals* home to use with their families, you may wish to do the *Family Faith Journal* activities in class, perhaps in small groups. It is important that these activities be viewed as group reflection and application, not as tests or graded exercises.

To facilitate your own growth in faith, be sure to make use of Your Faith Journal, *beginning on page J1 of this Teaching Guide.*

Using Unit Reviews

Following every three content chapters in the student book there is a two-page review spread called *Unit Checkpoint*. The lesson plan pages for the *Unit Checkpoints* provide you with the necessary materials to help the students review the units and measure their own progress. In the core lesson column you will find:

- **Chapter Summaries** Succinct statements summarize each chapter's key content, to aid in student review.

- **Tips for evaluating student review exercises** Answers for Matching, Fill in the Blanks, and other review exercises are provided in blue annotation type on the reduced student book pages. The core lesson column contains necessary directions for completing and evaluating these exercises.

- **Share Your Faith** This section of the *Unit Checkpoint* pages encourages students to put what they have learned into their own words. This question may be used as oral or written review. Suggestions for evaluation are found in the core lesson column.

- **Show How Far You've Come** This section of the *Unit Checkpoint* pages invites students to complete a graphic organizer with the key concepts of the unit. Use *Chapter Summaries* to evaluate student work.

- **What Else Would You Like to Know?** This section helps students clarify remaining questions. Resources for exploring student questions are listed in the Resource Center section of the page.

- **Continue the Journey** The core lesson column provides suggestions for carrying out these additional activities and projects.

The Resource Center of the *Unit Checkpoint* pages in this Teaching Guide provides suggestions for additional means of assessment, resources for answering student questions, and ideas for *Continuing Project*.

The Unit Checkpoint *pages are not designed to test material presented in the seasonal chapters. For more detailed unit assessments that test seasonal material as well as content chapters, see* Using Program Resources, *page T34.*

USING UNIT REVIEWS : T33

Using Program Resources

In addition to the *Walking by Faith* Three student book and Teaching Guide, a Resource Package is available. The Resource Package for *Walking by Faith* Three contains Family Letters, Transparencies, Assessments, and Music and Liturgy Resources.

Family Letters

Reproducible masters are provided for keeping in touch with the students' families. There is one Family Letter for each unit, designed to be sent home after the first session of Chapters 1, 5, 9, 13, 17, 21, and 25. Family Letters are available in both English and Spanish. They sum up the unit content and encourage family members to stay involved in their children's religious education. Letters may be reproduced on school or parish stationery and are designed with room for personalization. A tear-off-and-return response form allows family members to communicate with you during the year.

For other suggestions on strengthening the family link, see Idea File #6, Connecting with Families, *pages T52–T53.*

Transparencies

The Resource Package includes 21 full-color transparencies to enhance your presentation of the *Walking by Faith* Three content chapters. Transparencies are reproductions of key charts, graphics, lists, and other content summaries, including the *Stepping Stones* features, from the student book.

In addition to their use within the appropriate chapter lesson plans, transparencies may be used for unit review and content reinforcement throughout the year.

Assessments

The Resource Package includes reproducible masters for seven unit assessments and one year-end assessment. These assessments enable you to monitor students' progress in areas including key ideas, religious knowledge and beliefs, and religious practices. Material tested is correlated to the student book, and answer keys are provided.

The unit assessments include the seasonal chapters as well as the content chapters. These assessments are best given after all four chapters in a unit have been explored, even if the seasonal chapter falls out of numerical sequence.

For additional assessment suggestions, see Idea File #10, Assessing Progress, *pages T60–T61.*

Music and Liturgy Resources

Throughout the year you may wish to use the *Walking by Faith* Music and Liturgy Resources from the Resource Package to enhance your prayer and celebration. The Music and Liturgy Resources include music by noted Catholic pastoral musician David Haas, featuring the *Walking by Faith* theme song. (Additional components available from BROWN-ROA include the music CD or cassette, a student hymn book, and the full musical score.)

Also included in the Music and Liturgy Resources are liturgical celebrations especially created for *Walking by Faith* by liturgist Robert W. Piercy Jr. The book contains five school- or parish-wide celebrations (Beginning the Year, Advent, Lent, Reconciliation, and Ending the Year) and seven grade-specific celebrations geared to the unit themes. Directions are supplied for celebrating the liturgies as Masses or as prayer services.

When you see the music and liturgy icon in this Teaching Guide, it will serve as a reminder to make use of the Music and Liturgy Resources. Of course you may feel free to use or adapt the Music and Liturgy Resources at any time during the year.

For other suggestions on prayer, liturgy, and interaction with the parish community, see Idea File #2, Building Faith Community, *pages T44–T45, and* Idea File #7, Connecting with the Parish, *pages T54–T55.*

Scheduling

One of the greatest challenges facing catechists of all experience levels is scheduling sessions. Use the material on these pages to help determine how to allocate class time throughout the year.

Take Inventory of Your Situation

To give yourself the background you need to schedule *Walking by Faith* Three, ask yourself the following questions:

- How frequently will my class meet?
- How long does an average session last?
- How many sessions are scheduled for the year?
- How many students will I be teaching? Will I have classroom assistance?
- How will scheduled holidays and vacation periods affect the year's schedule?
- Do I anticipate any other times when I will be absent from class? How will my absence, scheduled or unscheduled, be handled?
- What impact will other parish or school activities (retreat days, liturgies, assemblies, sacramental preparation) have on my class schedule?

With this information in hand, you can begin to plan your year. The chart on page T37 will give you a model to follow.

Covering the Chapters

Walking by Faith Three contains 28 chapters. Each chapter is designed to correlate with approximately one weekly session of class time, based on a model duration of 90 minutes. If your class year contains fewer than 28 weeks (or 28 sessions), you should plan to combine chapters rather than eliminate any. If your year contains more than 28 weeks or sessions, you may choose to spread certain chapters over more than one week or session.

Seasonal Chapters

Walking by Faith Three contains seven chapters tied to specific feasts and seasons of the Church year. These chapters are interspersed throughout the student book, with one seasonal chapter following each content unit. The order of the seasonal chapters is approximately chronological. However, you will need to adjust your presentation of the seasonal chapters to suit the calendar. You do not need to have completed a content unit in order to schedule the seasonal chapter that follows it. For example, depending on the Church calendar, you may wish to teach Chapter 28 (Easter) ahead of Chapters 25–27 (Unit Seven). In planning your year, follow the Church calendar to see where these feasts and seasons will fall and where the seasonal chapters may best be taught.

You may wish to expand your teaching of the seasonal chapters to include a classroom or parish-wide liturgy incorporating the *Walking by Faith* Music and Liturgy Resources.

Scheduling

Adapting to Scheduling Limitations

The Planning Chart on the *Getting Ready* pages for each chapter of *Walking by Faith* Three gives you suggestions for spreading the chapter content across one 90-minute weekly session. These guidelines are very general and should be tailored to your own situation. Here are some additional suggestions for dealing with the limited class schedule many parish religious education programs face:

- Evaluate your class schedule. You may gain by dividing your one weekly session into two shorter sessions, perhaps alternating between the parish setting and neighborhood family clusters. Or lengthen your existing session to allow time for students to gather, explore the material, and celebrate.

- Assign chapters as pre-reading to be completed at home in advance of each session. This can be a good way to involve family members in the catechetical experience.

- In most cases it is impractical to attempt to combine the teaching of a basal religious education series like *Walking by Faith* and a lectionary-based catechetical program. The celebration of the children's Liturgy of the Word in the parish should not be turned into a religion class, nor should the exploration of the key religious content contained in *Walking by Faith* Three be crammed into a brief period during Sunday Mass. You may choose to develop a model in which religious education follows and flows from the Sunday liturgy, perhaps involving family members.

- For seasonal chapters (such as Advent or Easter) you may wish to shift the balance of your teaching time to the *We Celebrate* section, devoting any additional session time to preparing for and celebrating the liturgical feasts and seasons.

- Even if your time is very limited, be careful not to skip the *We Celebrate* page. Prayer and celebration are not "extras." They are integral parts of the *Walking by Faith* experience.

Integrating Non-basal Religious Education

One difficulty in scheduling your year may be the need to integrate non-basal elements into your already crowded catechetical sessions. The most common non-basal elements are sacramental preparation of some or all of the students and the presentation of Catholic family life and sexuality material. The best way to integrate these aspects into your religion class schedule is to use sacramental preparation and family life materials correlated with *Walking by Faith*. Here are some additional hints for balancing class time:

- *Walking by Faith* Three contains sufficient material to support catechetical preparation for the Sacraments of Initiation and Reconciliation. However, if you wish to use a supplementary sacramental preparation program, you may devote some designated portion of the session each week to supplementary sacramental catechesis.

- You may choose to schedule students' participation in a parish-wide sacramental preparation program that meets outside of the regular religion class. This separate arrangement has several advantages. It allows students in both Catholic school and parish religion programs to prepare together for the sacraments. It offers flexible scheduling that encourages family involvement in catechesis. And it allows the regular religion class schedule to unfold without interruption.

- Specific diocesan requirements may call for Catholic family life and sexuality education. As with sacramental preparation, you may choose to devote some portion of the weekly session to this material. Alternately, you may choose to treat Catholic family life education as a unit which may be added to, or substituted for one of, the seven units of *Walking by Faith* Three.

- Scheduling a separate, parish-wide family life education class may be the best choice, for the same reasons outlined above with regard to sacramental preparation. In family life education as in sacramental preparation, the involvement of family members is especially to be encouraged.

Scheduling Chart

Use or adapt this chart to plan your year. The chart is based on a 32-week year; add or subtract weeks as needed according to your schedule. Be sure to indicate seasonal celebrations, special activities, and holidays or vacation periods.

1 Week of _____ to _____ Chapter _____	**2** Week of _____ to _____ Chapter _____	**3** Week of _____ to _____ Chapter _____	**4** Week of _____ to _____ Chapter _____
5 Week of _____ to _____ Chapter _____	**6** Week of _____ to _____ Chapter _____	**7** Week of _____ to _____ Chapter _____	**8** Week of _____ to _____ Chapter _____
9 Week of _____ to _____ Chapter _____	**10** Week of _____ to _____ Chapter _____	**11** Week of _____ to _____ Chapter _____	**12** Week of _____ to _____ Chapter _____
13 Week of _____ to _____ Chapter _____	**14** Week of _____ to _____ Chapter _____	**15** Week of _____ to _____ Chapter _____	**16** Week of _____ to _____ Chapter _____
17 Week of _____ to _____ Chapter _____	**18** Week of _____ to _____ Chapter _____	**19** Week of _____ to _____ Chapter _____	**20** Week of _____ to _____ Chapter _____
21 Week of _____ to _____ Chapter _____	**22** Week of _____ to _____ Chapter _____	**23** Week of _____ to _____ Chapter _____	**24** Week of _____ to _____ Chapter _____
25 Week of _____ to _____ Chapter _____	**26** Week of _____ to _____ Chapter _____	**27** Week of _____ to _____ Chapter _____	**28** Week of _____ to _____ Chapter _____
29 Week of _____ to _____ Chapter _____	**30** Week of _____ to _____ Chapter _____	**31** Week of _____ to _____ Chapter _____	**32** Week of _____ to _____ Chapter _____

Notes

Walking by Faith provides lesson plans designed to help young people experience their Catholic identity, integrate their Catholic values, and express their Catholic beliefs.

Lesson Plan Pages

This section of the Teaching Guide contains the lesson plan pages. Each chapter's lesson plan is preceded by two *Getting Ready* pages. (See *Preparing to Teach*, pages T28–T29, for how to use these pages.)

Each lesson plan page contains a full-color, reduced student page surrounded by a wraparound lesson plan. The core lesson plan appears in the vertical column next to the reduced student page. The Resource Center at the bottom of the page contains background information and optional activities. (See *Teaching a Chapter*, pages T30–T31, for how to use the lesson plan pages.)

You will see several icons on the lesson plan pages. Here is the key to their significance:

This icon is your reminder to gather the students.

For gathering strategies see The Importance of Gathering, *page T30, and* Idea File #1, Establishing Group Atmosphere, *pages T42–T43.*

This icon points to suggestions for working with the *Catholics Believe* feature on the student page.

This icon points to suggestions for working with the *Scripture Signpost* feature on the student page.

This icon points to suggestions for working with the *Our Moral Guide* feature on the student page.

This icon points to suggestions for carrying out activities suggested on the student page.

This icon highlights an optional activity suggested by a Resource Center feature.

When you see this icon, you are reminded to use the Music and Liturgy Resources from the Resource Package.

Getting Ready: Chapter 1

Made for Each Other

Program Resources
Student Text, pp. 6–11
Student Faith Journal, pp. 1–2
Your Faith Journal, p. J2
Chapter 1 Transparency
Unit One Family Letter

Unit One (Creation)
Created for Community

Key Content Summary
The Church is a community gathered by God.

Planning the Chapter

	Pacing Guide Suggested time/Your time	Content	Objectives	Materials
Open	10–15 min./_____ min.	*We Are Invited*, pp. 6–7	• Recognize that God created us to be related, or connected, to others.	• chart paper
Build	20–25 min./_____ min.	*We Explore*, pp. 8–9	• Identify the variety of communities to which we belong. • Distinguish the Church community from all other communities.	• Chapter 1 Transparency from the Resource Package
Review	15–20 min./_____ min.	*We Reflect*, p. 10	• Demonstrate understanding of chapter concepts. • Apply learning through activity. • Practice faith at home and in the parish.	• *Student Faith Journal*, pp. 1–2 • *Your Faith Journal*, p. J2
Close	10–15 min./_____ min.	*We Celebrate*, p. 11	• Recognize that the Church began as a community and continues to be one.	• Unit One Family Letter from the Resource Package

For additional suggestions, see Scheduling, pp. T35–T37.

Catechism in Context

Doctrinal Foundation This chapter explains that God created humans to live in community and fellowship with one another: "It is not good for man to live alone." God made a helper suitable for Adam and formed a people from the union of Abraham and Sarah, brought them out of Egypt, made a formal covenant with them, led them into the promised land, and sent his prophets to warn them to stay together even when they began to separate. In the fullness of time, God sent his Son into our fragmented community to bring us into communion with him and with one another. The fullest expression of that communion on earth is the Church, which is the new People of God, the mystical Body of Christ in the world, and the Temple of the Holy Spirit here and now. We were made to live in this communion. We were not created to live in isolation from one another and from God.

See Catechism of the Catholic Church, #1879.

One-Minute Retreat for Catechists

Read
"A Christian is a keyhole through which other folk see God."
—*Robert E. Gibson*

Reflect
How can I give my students a better sense of what it means to be an active member of a Church community?

Pray
Lord, the Church is a binding force for all of us. Please help my students understand that being part of a Church community is an important responsibility.

Visualizing the Lesson

Use this graphic organizer to help the students visualize the relationship between the family community and the Church community.

Draw the graphic organizer on the board or on chart paper. **What do the family community and the Church community have in common?** (Possible answers: In both communities people share life and love; both are human gatherings; in both, being together teaches us more about God.)

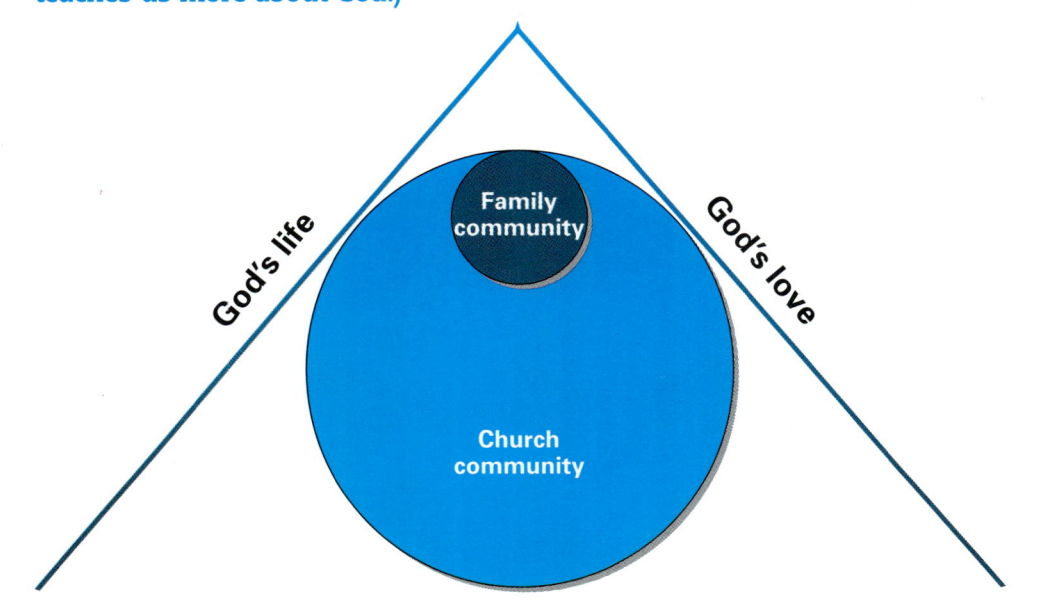

Library Links

Books for Children
Our Church by Graham English (The Liturgical Press, 1-800-858-5450).
Children of many cultures in a Catholic parish share their religious customs and traditions.

Books for Parents and Teachers
Catholic Customs and Traditions by Greg Dues (Twenty-Third Publications, 1-800-321-0411).
Vast traditions, customs, and ritual practices make up the Catholic experience.

Multimedia
For children:
Together in Faith produced by Salt River Production Group (video) (BROWN-ROA, 1-800-922-7696).
This video presents a brief overview of the community of the Catholic Church.

For parents and teachers:
Do I Really Need a Community? (video) (Paulist Press, 1-800-218-1903).
There is no spirituality without community.

Organizations
For helpful resources on teaching about our faith community, contact:
Catholic Audio Visual Education Association (CAVE)
P.O. Box 9257
Pittsburgh, PA 15224
(1-412-561-3583)

Strengthening the Family Link

Here are some suggestions for reaching out to your students' families:

- Encourage the students to talk with family members about community and the communities to which their families belongs.
- As a community-building exercise to begin the year, invite family members to join the class for a day. Have each student introduce his or her family members to the class. Explain that the class itself is a community. If possible, have each person decorate a card with his or her name on it, and hang the cards on a bulletin board titled *Our Class Community*.

Chapter 1 pages 6–11

Objectives
- Recognize that God created us to be related, or connected, to others.
- Identify the variety of communities to which we belong.
- Distinguish the Church community from all other communities.

Gathering WE ARE INVITED
1. Open

Personal Experience Brainstorm with the students a list of things they would like to learn about religion, the world, and their lives. Be sure to include a question about what it means to be part of the Church community. Write the list on chart paper and refer to it occasionally throughout the year.

Prayer As you begin the session, pray the opening prayer together.

Working with the Text
Read or summarize the text, focusing on the fun we can have with other people. **How did God make sure we would never be alone?** *(He created other people.)*

Working with the Pictures
- Point out that the girl in the picture seems to be all alone and looks sad. **How do you feel when you are all alone?** *(sad, lonely, worried)* **What could you do to help the girl feel better?** *(talk with her, invite her to play, offer to share a game)*
- Read the caption aloud and ask volunteers to respond to the question. *(Possible responses: family, friends, and neighbors.)* Work as a class to make the lists.

CHAPTER 1
Made for Each Other

PRAYER

God our Creator, bring us together in your love this year. Help us learn what it means to be part of the Church.

"Leave me *alone!*"

How many times have you shouted those words? Your mom reminds you to do your chores. A younger brother wants you to read him a story. Your friends tease you.

But what would happen if people took you seriously?

Being alone wouldn't be much fun after the first few minutes. Imagine a world with only you in it. No family, no friends. No third-grade class, no parish. No soccer team, no pets, no one to play games or laugh with.

It's a good thing being alone can't really happen. God made sure from the very beginning that we would never be left completely alone.

ACTIVITY
Whom would you miss if you were alone in the world? Make a list of all the groups to which you belong.

6 : WE ARE INVITED

Resource Center

Teaching Tip
Handling sensitive topics Be aware that some students feel alone at home or left out at school. Help these students feel included in class. Be sure all the students understand that God loves everyone and wants us to be a community of loving people.

Optional Enrichment
Ask the students why *Made for Each Other* is a good title for this chapter. Invite the students to think of people who are special to them. Ask the students to write brief notes or poems at home, telling the people why they are important to each other. Encourage the students to give the notes or poems to their special people.

Notes: Opening the Chapter

God **created**, or made from nothing, all things. The Bible tells a story to show that God does not want anyone to be alone. The story tells how God made a partner for the first human.

SCRIPTURE STORY
We're Partners

God made a man, the first human. God gave the man a beautiful garden to live in. But something was missing.

"It's not good for this person to be alone," God said. "He should have a partner." So God made all kinds of birds and fish and animals and brought each one to the man. The man liked all these living creatures, but none of them was the partner he was longing for.

Then God caused the man to fall asleep. God made a woman from part of the man's body. The man woke up. He recognized that this other human was the partner for him.

"We were made for each other," the first humans said. "We are part of each other." They thanked God for making sure they would not be alone.

—based on Genesis 2:5–24

Scripture Signpost

"It is not good for the man to be alone. I will make a suitable partner for him."

Genesis 2:18

Why do you think the first human needed a partner?

WE ARE INVITED
Open *Continued*

Working with the Text

- Read or summarize the first paragraph. Explain to the students that the Bible tells us God created everything. Use *The Language of Faith* below to further develop the highlighted term.
- Have volunteers read aloud the *We're Partners* Scripture Story. As you discuss the story, emphasize God's role in creating man and woman.

Working with the Pictures

Call attention to the pictures on these two pages.
What kinds of created things do the pictures show? (animals, birds, flowers, plants, people) **Who created all of them?** (God)

Scripture Signpost Read the Scripture verse aloud, and ask volunteers to respond to the caption question. (Possible answers: to avoid loneliness, to have someone who understood what it meant to be human.)

The Language of Faith

The word **created** comes from the Latin word *creatus*. The distinction between *created* and *made* is an important one. When a person *makes* something, the materials already exist and can be formed or shaped into something else. When God *creates*, someone or something is called into being from nothing, not from already existing materials.

Scripture Background

The second story of creation, as told in the **Book of Genesis**, reverses the order of creation, placing the creation of animals *after* the creation of the first man and for his benefit. Tell the students that the creation stories are not to be taken as scientific fact. Rather, the stories inspire us to think of how all creation began with God.

Teaching Tip

Handling sensitive topics The topic of creationism versus evolution is an issue of concern for many parents today. The Church takes a position of avoiding a too-literal approach to Scripture while recognizing God as the origin of all natural laws and processes. Emphasize to the students that *how* God made the first parents of all humans is not as important to us as Catholics as *that* God created humans and *why* he did. The Scripture Story tells us that people were created out of a desire to share God's life and love in a special way reserved only for humans.

We Explore
2. Build
Working with the Pictures

Talk about the shared experience that the priest and parishioners are having. Invite volunteers to respond to the caption questions. **(the Church community; to worship God)**

Working with the Text

- Read or summarize *Called Together*. Use *The Language of Faith* below to further discuss the term *community*.
- Remind the students that they all belong to the special group that God created—humans. Then ask volunteers to recall some of the other groups to which they belong. **(Girl Scouts, Boy Scouts, sports teams, and so on)**
  How are the groups you belong to communities? **(Their members come together for a common purpose.)**

Catholics Believe Explain to the students that it is God's plan for us not to be alone.

What kind of community is shown here? Why have these people come together?

Catholics Believe...
that God created humans to live in community.
Catechism, #1879

Called Together

Living with other people, sharing happy times and sad times, is not just a good thing. It's a human thing. God created us to be *related*, or connected, to others. From the time of the first humans right up to our own time, people have been drawn to one another. They have married and made families. They have made friends and formed partnerships. They have come together in neighborhoods, towns, and nations.

When people come together for a shared purpose, the group they form is called a **community**. The first humans formed the first community.

We belong to many different communities. A family is a community. So is a neighborhood. This year we will be looking closely at one very special community, the Church.

8 : We Explore

Resource Center

The Language of Faith
The word **community** suggests living in fellowship, or living in unity. Jesus understood the importance of living in fellowship when he called together the first community of believers—his disciples. Christians come to know Jesus best within the community of believers called the Church.

optional Link to the Family
Invite the students to work at home to create lists of ways their families live as communities. Schedule time in the next group meeting for them to share their lists. Tell the students that our family is the very first community to which we belong.

Notes: Building the Chapter

This year we will explore many definitions of Church. But most of all we will look at the Church as a community. We will explore what it means to be that community.

- **The word *Church* can mean many things. What do you think of when you hear this word?**

The word **Church** comes from two different words. One word means "a community called together." The other word means "belonging to the Lord." These meanings tell us that the Church is different from other communities. We don't just join the Church. God calls us to be part of this community.

Communities are human gatherings, but they are more than human, too. The need for community was created by God. Being together tells us something about God that we would never know if we were always alone. We meet God's love and share God's life in good communities, especially the Church.

The community of the Church is often compared to the community of a family. In both communities people share life and love.

WE EXPLORE : 9

WE EXPLORE
Build *Continued*
Working with the Text

- Read the introduction and the bulleted material aloud. Then invite volunteers to respond to the question about the word *Church*. **(Possible answers: a special building where Mass is celebrated; the pope, bishops, and priests; a group of people who share faith in God.)**
- Read or summarize the remaining text aloud.
  How is the Church community different from other communities? **(in its reason for gathering—to worship God, and in its goal—to promote the kingdom of God and to love and serve God and other people.)** Use *The Language of Faith* below to further develop the word *Church*.
- To focus on the Church as a special community, refer to the graphic organizer on page 5B. You may use the suggested activity or one of your own choosing.

Working with the Pictures

Point out that the family seems to be enjoying a special time together. Ask the students to compare the family community with the Church community pictured on page 8.

The Language of Faith

The **Church** is described in the New Testament with a variety of images. It is explained as God's building or temple, God's assembly, the assembly of the saints, and a family with God as our Father. The Church is also described as a new creation, a mother, and the Body of Christ. Christ refers to himself as the vine and to his followers as the branches who receive their life from him. All of these images give us a picture of what Jesus calls the Church to be.

Multicultural Link

To help the students develop an appreciation for the many cultures that make up our country and our Church, call attention once again to the family meal pictured on this page. Invite the students to describe the foods enjoyed by their own families, neighbors, and friends.

Link to Liturgy

Invite the students to identify the similarities between a family meal and the Mass. **(We greet one another; we share family stories; we share food together; we pray together and give thanks.)** Ask the students to recall special family meals they have shared. (Be sensitive to the fact that this may be difficult for students whose families don't eat together or share stories.)

WE REFLECT
Review

Recall Have volunteers share their answers to the questions. (a group that comes together for a shared purpose; God)

Think and Share Have the students think about the question carefully before responding. (Possible answers: lonely, boring, difficult.)

Continue the Journey Provide the students with the date and the correct spellings of your name and the name of your parish.

Alternative Encourage the students to design and complete their own Church membership cards at home and bring them to the next group meeting.

We Live Our Faith *At Home:* Brainstorm a few of the ways the students can show that they belong to their family communities (running an errand, helping plan an event, and so on). Remind the students that members of a community serve the other members willingly and without complaint. *In the Parish:* Tell the students that they might speak with the pastor or another parish leader to discover one new thing about their parish. Explain that the parish bulletin is another good source of information.

Faith Journal The students may begin pages 1–2 of their *Faith Journal* in class and complete them at home. As part of your own spiritual development, complete *Your Faith Journal* (page J2) for this chapter.

RECALL
What is a community? Who calls the community of the Church together?

THINK AND SHARE
What would life be like if there were no communities?

CONTINUE THE JOURNEY
Fill out the membership card.

Membership Card

FIRST NAME _____ LAST NAME _____

TEACHER'S NAME _____

PARISH NAME _____ DATE _____

WE LIVE OUR FAITH
At Home Show that you belong to your family community by doing an extra chore or helping a family member.

In the Parish Your parish is the first place in which you get to know the Church community. This week, find out one new thing about your parish.

10 : We Reflect

Resource Center

Meeting Individual Needs
Learners acquiring English Pair students acquiring English with students who can help them read and complete the membership card.

Link to the Faith Community
Help the students make a connection between Baptism and belonging to the Church community. Encourage the students to ask their families about the day they were baptized and the reasons their parents wanted them to belong to the Church community.

Faith Journal

10 : Chapter 1

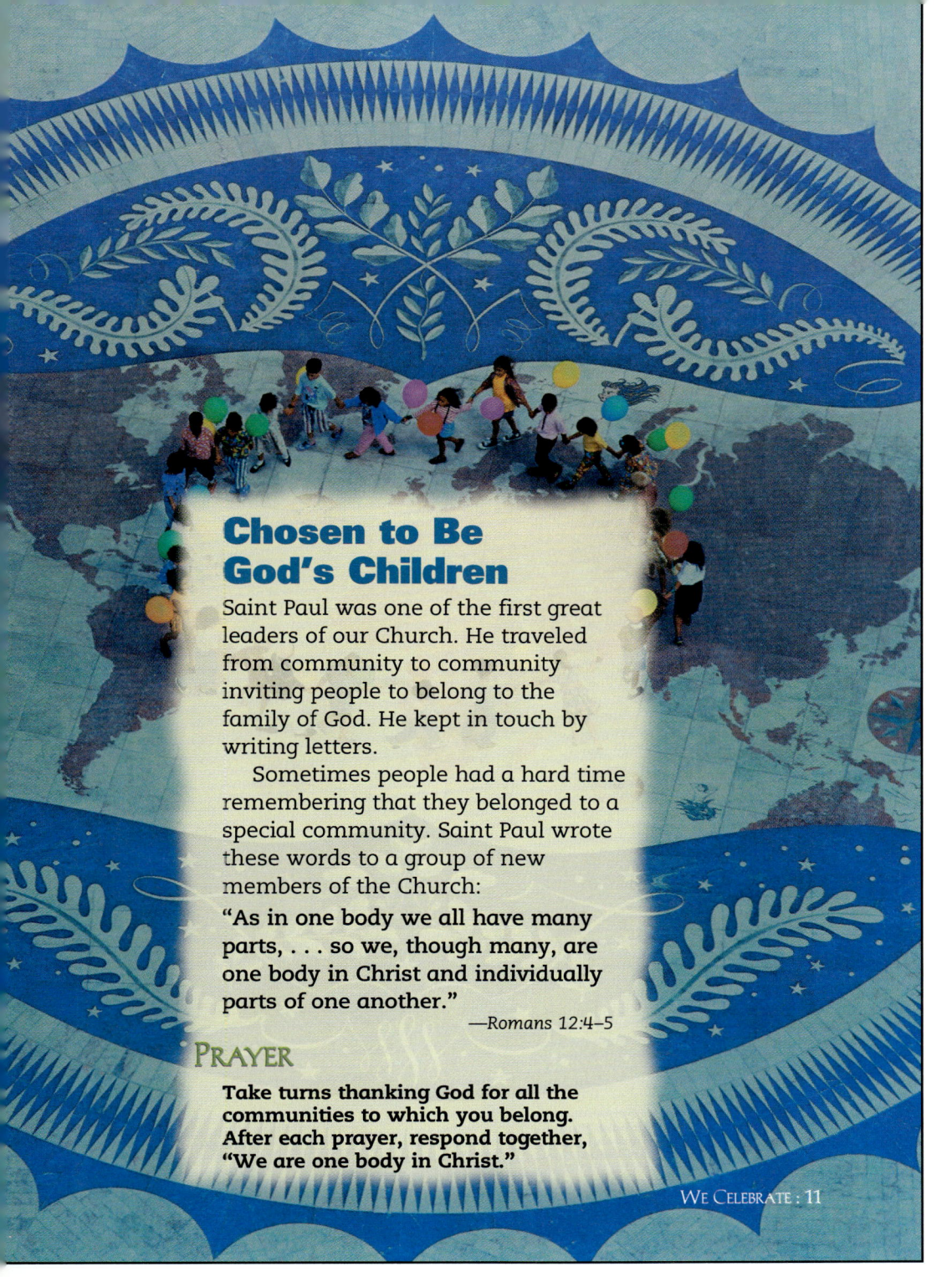

Chosen to Be God's Children

Saint Paul was one of the first great leaders of our Church. He traveled from community to community inviting people to belong to the family of God. He kept in touch by writing letters.

Sometimes people had a hard time remembering that they belonged to a special community. Saint Paul wrote these words to a group of new members of the Church:

"As in one body we all have many parts, . . . so we, though many, are one body in Christ and individually parts of one another."

—Romans 12:4–5

PRAYER

Take turns thanking God for all the communities to which you belong. After each prayer, respond together, "We are one body in Christ."

WE CELEBRATE : 11

WE CELEBRATE
3. Close

Working with the Pictures

- Call attention to the children in the picture.
  What are the children doing that shows they are a community? (playing together; holding hands; enjoying time together)
- Point out that there is a world map in the picture to show that we are a world community.

Working with the Text

Read or summarize the text. Explain to the students that people from every country are called by God and encouraged by Church leaders to belong to the Church community. Read aloud the words of Saint Paul in the text. Explain that "one body in Christ" is another way of referring to the whole Church and the community of people within it.

Prayer Close the chapter with prayer. If possible, have the students hold hands and spread out around the room in a circle like the children shown in the picture. After praying and responding together, invite the students to sing a closing song with you, such as "He's Got the Whole World in His Hands."

Scripture Background

Saint Paul is noted for his missionary journeys to the Christian communities that he established and also for the letters he wrote to encourage and exhort them. Today these inspired letters are considered revelatory to the Christian community at large. Of the thirteen letters in the New Testament generally attributed to Saint Paul, seven are considered to have been written by him: **1 Thessalonians**, **Galatians**, **1 and 2 Corinthians**, **Philippians**, **Philemon**, and **Romans**. The six remaining letters were written by other early Christians and attributed to Paul.

Link to the Family

To set the tone for the year and to involve your students' families in their religious education, send home the Unit One Family Letter from the Resource Package.

Notes: Closing the Chapter

Getting Ready: Chapter 2

The Family of Creation

Program Resources
Student Text, pp. 12–17
Student Faith Journal, pp. 3–4
Your Faith Journal, p. J3
Chapter 2 Transparency
Unit One Music and Liturgy Resources

Unit One (Creation)
Created for Community

Key Content Summary
We value the gifts of creation as symbols of God's love.

Planning the Chapter

	Pacing Guide *Suggested time/Your time*	Content	Objectives	Materials
Open	10–15 min./ _____ min.	*We Are Invited*, p. 12	• Discover signs of God's love.	• art materials
Build	20–25 min./ _____ min.	*We Explore*, pp. 13–15	• Develop a sense of responsibility to care for creation. • Discover that communities need all kinds of people. • Recognize sacramentals as sacred signs of God's presence.	• audiobook of Noah's Ark story, puppets, animal cutouts • Chapter 2 Transparency from the Resource Package
Review	15–20 min./ _____ min.	*We Reflect*, p. 16	• Demonstrate understanding of chapter concepts. • Apply learning through activity. • Practice faith at home and in the parish.	• art materials, magazines, scissors, glue • *Student Faith Journal*, pp. 3–4 • *Your Faith Journal*, p. J3
Close	10–15 min./ _____ min. *For additional suggestions, see Scheduling, pp. T35–T37.*	*We Celebrate*, p. 17	• Summarize the relatedness of the gifts of creation.	• Unit One Music and Liturgy Resources from the Resource Package

Catechism in Context

Doctrinal Foundation This chapter points out that everything in creation is interconnected. The Bible teaches us that all creatures come from God and exist to give him glory. Nature shows us how each creature is interdependent with others for its sustenance and growth. Despite what both the Bible and nature tell us, we often ignore our connection to other living things, indeed to all created things. When we ignore our interdependence, we fail to recognize our kinship with all creation. Saint Francis of Assisi, then, is a model for all of us. He perceived this relationship when he spoke of "Brother Sun," "Sister Moon," and "Mother Earth." His recognition of his connectedness to all creatures prompted him all the more to praise the Lord, who made them all.

See Catechism of the Catholic Church, #344.

One-Minute Retreat for Catechists

Read
"Study nature as the countenance of God."
—Charles Kingsley

Reflect
How can I encourage my students to care for God's creation?

Pray
May my students understand the importance of their responsibility, Lord. As they grow up, may their respect for all of God's creation grow stronger. Help them end the destruction of life and become servants of the world.

Visualizing the Lesson

Use this graphic organizer to help the students visualize how all parts of creation are related.

Redraw the graphic organizer on a sheet of paper, making the shapes large enough to cut out. Divide the class into small groups, and give each group a copy. Have the students cut out all of the shapes and use them to make mobiles. Have each group tape the shape for *God* at the top of a coat hanger and use yarn or string to attach the remaining shapes to the bottom of the coat hanger. Invite the students to add other parts of creation to the mobiles.

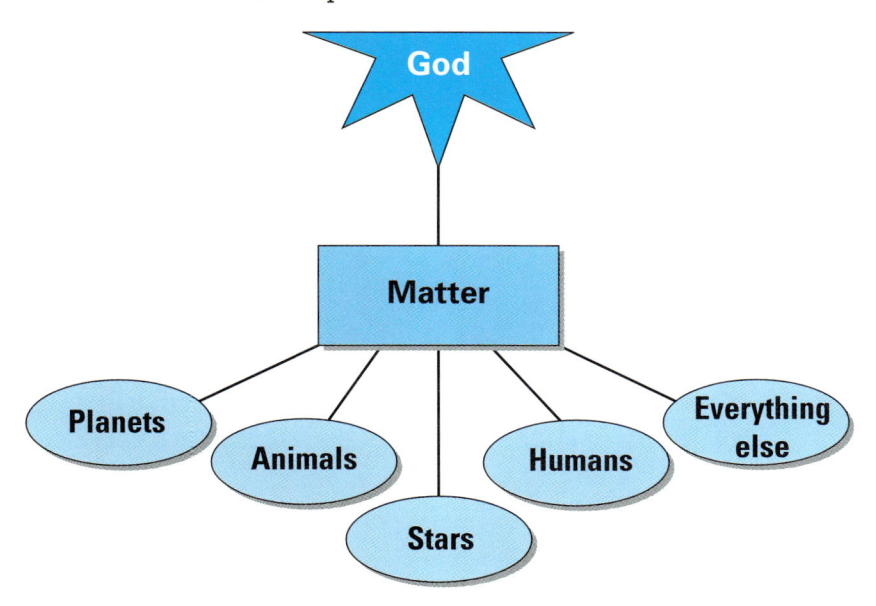

```
              God
               |
            Matter
   /    /    |    \    \
Planets Animals Humans Everything else
            Stars
```

Library Links

Books for Children
St. Francis of Assisi by Margaret and Matthew Bunson (Our Sunday Visitor, 1-800-348-2440).

The Bunsons tell the story of Saint Francis and his dedication to God's creation.

Books for Parents and Teachers
The Meaning of Sacramental Symbols—Answers to Today's Questions by Klemens Richter (The Liturgical Press, 1-800-858-5450).

This book deals with the origins, meanings, and present-day understanding of sacramentals for Christians.

Multimedia

For children:
God's Place for Me. Episode #4, "Caring for God's Creation" produced by the Archdiocese of St. Paul-Minneapolis (video) (BROWN-ROA, 1-800-922-7696).

Two young hosts take children to a school, store, food distribution center, and landfill, demonstrating choices about handling resources.

For parents and teachers:
Peace with God the Creator, Peace with All Creation (resource kit) (USCC Publishing Services, 1-800-235-8722).

This parish resource kit helps with the implementation of environmental justice.

Organizations
For further information about caring for creation, contact:

U.S. Bishops' Department of Social Development and World Peace
3211 Fourth Street NE
Washington, DC 20017
(1-202-541-3000)

Strengthening the Family Link

Here are some suggestions for reaching out to your students' families:

- Encourage the students to talk with family members about ways they can work together to take care of God's creation.
- Invite family members to join the class in praying the closing prayer, based on Saint Francis's "Canticle of the Sun."

Chapter 2 pages 12–17

Objectives
- Discover signs of God's love.
- Develop a sense of responsibility to care for creation.
- Discover that communities need all kinds of people.
- Recognize sacramentals as sacred signs of God's presence.

Gathering WE ARE INVITED
1. Open

Personal Experience Share with the students one of your most memorable experiences with nature, such as a visit to a beach. Encourage volunteers to do the same.

Prayer Ask a volunteer to lead the group in praying the opening prayer.

Working with the Pictures

Ask volunteers to describe what they see in the photographs on this and the next page.
What do all these photographs have in common? (They all show examples of God's creation, including people, plants, and animals.) Explain that sometimes we see signs of God's creation where we least expect them—in a sidewalk crack, for example.

Working with the Text
- Let the students look out the nearest window as you ask them the questions in *The Family of Creation*. Encourage all students to respond. As you read aloud the last sentence of the text, emphasize that God's love never leaves us.

  Give the students art materials for the activity. Invite students to share their drawings.

CHAPTER 2
The Family of Creation

PRAYER

We praise you, God, for your wonderful creation. Help us remember that we are related to all people and all things.

Look out the nearest window. How many signs of God's love can you see? How many did you see on the way to class today?

Signs of God's love are all around us in the world God made.

ACTIVITY
Draw a sign of God's love you see in creation.

12 : WE ARE INVITED

Resource Center

Link to Liturgy
Remind the students that during the preparation of the gifts at Mass, we thank God for creation. Encourage the students to listen closely for prayers that specifically give thanks to God the Creator.

Notes: Opening the Chapter

Sisters and Brothers

Everything we see in the world around us comes from God. Everything was made by God. All parts of creation are related, as all members of a family are related. Scientists tell us that everything in the universe is made up of the same basic stuff, called *matter*. Our bodies, the birds that fly, the tall trees, and the stars are all made of the same material.

As human members of the family of creation, we have responsibilities. A **responsibility**, or response to God, is a duty to act in ways that show respect and love. Family members have a responsibility to care for one another. We have a responsibility to care for the world God made, with all its wonders. We have a responsibility to show respect and love for all people. We are sisters and brothers to all creation.

● What is one way you can carry out your responsibility to care for creation?

Catholics Believe...
that all parts of creation are related. All creatures come from God and exist to give God glory.

Catechism, #344

WE EXPLORE : 13

WE EXPLORE
2. Build

Working with the Pictures

Have the students look at the people in the pictures on this and the previous page.
How are they showing responsibility toward creation? (feeding a calf, tending a garden, picking up trash from the beach, cheering on participants in a race)

Working with the Text

- As you read or summarize *Sisters and Brothers*, you may wish to use the graphic organizer on page 11B to help the students focus on the content. Use the suggested activity or one of your own choosing.

- Use *The Language of Faith* below to further explain the highlighted term.

- Lead the students to understand that we are connected to everything that God created.
Who has a responsibility to care for creation? (We do.)

- Read aloud the bulleted question, and encourage volunteers to respond.

Catholics Believe Help the students understand that we and all created things in the universe exist because of God. Encourage the students to praise God. Remind them that prayer is the perfect way to offer praise.

The Language of Faith
The word **responsibility** comes from a Latin word that means "a thing or person for which or whom one gives an explanation or an accounting." As persons of faith we are called by God to accept responsibility for God's creation. Because of our solidarity with others, we are accountable for the animals, the plants, and the earth, as well as for one another.

Link to the Faith Community
Remind the students that each time we are present at the Sunday liturgy, we are fulfilling our responsibility to come together in faith to support one another and to welcome one another as sisters and brothers of Jesus. Ask the students to practice showing their care for other members of the parish family by participating in the Sunday liturgy and other parish events.

Notes: Building the Chapter

We Explore
Build *Continued*

Working with the Text
- As you read or summarize the text, emphasize that differences among people are *good*. Explain that the Church welcomes people of every race and culture.
  How does our parish welcome people? (Possible answers: having ministers of hospitality welcome people at Mass, sending letters of welcome to families who move into the parish.)
- Use *The Language of Faith* below to discuss the highlighted word. You might want to tell the students about some of your own family customs. Then have volunteers respond to the bulleted question.

Saints Walk with Us Talk about the statue of Saint Francis of Assisi, which shows him wearing a simple robe. Then share the information in *Profile* below.

Landmark As you discuss the story of Noah's Ark, lead the students away from a literal interpretation of the Scripture Story. Stress that this story teaches us about God's promise of salvation.

Alternative If possible, play an audiobook version of the story of Noah. Have the students use puppets or animal cutouts to enact the story.

Saints Walk with Us
Saint Francis of Assisi
Feast Day: October 4

Saint Francis called all the gifts of creation *Sister* and *Brother*. He honored all people with respect.

You will often find statues of Saint Francis in gardens. He is the patron saint of those who care for creation.

The Church and Creation

Each of us has a duty to care for creation. But as members of the Church, we have a group responsibility, too. We are called to help all people learn to understand creation. By the way we live, people should be able to see signs of God's love everywhere.

One message the Church has to share about creation is that differences are good. This is a very important message in our world because people sometimes see differences as frightening. Creation needs whales and hummingbirds, lightning and sunshine. The human community needs all kinds of people. Our differences are like the differences in creation. They make us beautiful and interesting.

The Church shares this message by welcoming all people. We don't all speak the same language. We don't all live in the same place. But we are still related. We welcome many **customs**, or ways of living and celebrating. Different people's customs add to the beauty and interest of our Church community.

- **What are some of your family or parish customs?**

Landmark The story of Noah's Ark is found in the first book of the Bible *(Genesis 6:5–22)*. In the story the Ark was a boat that saved God's creatures from a great flood. The Church is sometimes compared to Noah's Ark because it offers all people the chance to be saved.

14 : We Explore

Resource Center

The Language of Faith
The word **custom** has special meaning when applied to the Church and its way of celebrating and experiencing faith. The Catholic Church is open to the customs of all people as long as they promote the gospel and enrich Christian life. The Church also has its own customs pertaining to liturgy and rituals, yet these customs differ among the different Rites, as well as within them. For example, in the Latin Rite it is the custom to make the Sign of the Cross by touching the left shoulder before the right shoulder. In the Byzantine Rite (and in the other Eastern Rite Churches) it is customary to make the Sign of the Cross by touching the right shoulder first. Both customs are accepted and respected by the Church. The Church encourages various customs that help different cultures express their faith.

Profile
Saint Francis of Assisi (1181–1226) Saint Francis was born in Assisi, the son of a wealthy merchant. He had everything he wanted; yet he was not happy. He began to notice that many people in his town did not have enough food or clothing and that some people were very sick. Francis of Assisi changed his way of life completely by living simply, owning few possessions, and begging for food. He began to see Jesus in the people around him, especially people who were poor, sick, and forgotten, whom he tried to help. Many men and women began to follow Saint Francis and his new way of living. Today we call these followers of Saint Francis *Franciscans*.

Another important message our Church shares is that creation itself is good. Sometimes people forget that God created all things out of love and goodness. Our Church community reminds people of the goodness of God's gifts by using created things in our celebrations and prayers. Some of these ways of using God's gifts are called **sacramentals**, or sacred signs.

The most common sacramental is blessing. A **blessing** asks God's protection for someone or something. It sets that person or thing apart for God's work. A blessing is usually made up of a prayer and a gesture, such as the Sign of the Cross.

The chart below shows some of the gifts of creation we use as part of our sacramentals.

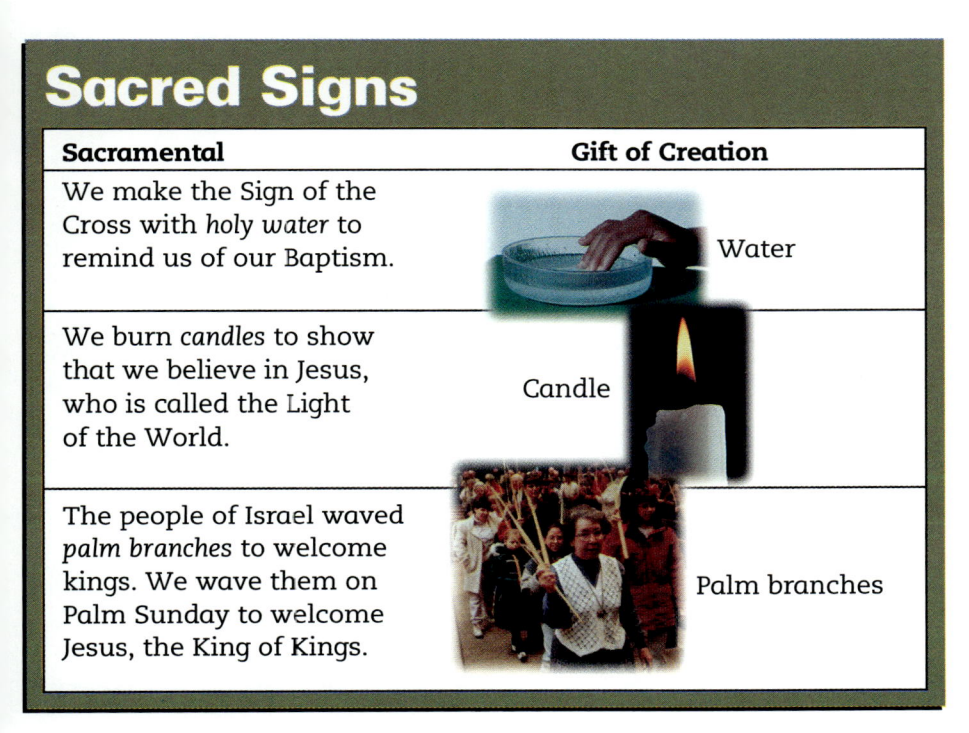

Sacred Signs

Sacramental	Gift of Creation
We make the Sign of the Cross with *holy water* to remind us of our Baptism.	Water
We burn *candles* to show that we believe in Jesus, who is called the Light of the World.	Candle
The people of Israel waved *palm branches* to welcome kings. We wave them on Palm Sunday to welcome Jesus, the King of Kings.	Palm branches

WE EXPLORE : 15

WE EXPLORE
Build *Continued*
Working with the Text

- As you continue to work with the text, use *The Language of Faith* below to discuss the meanings of the highlighted terms.
  What other sacramentals are you familiar with? (rosaries, medals, crucifixes, and statues of Jesus, Mary, and the saints)

- **What are some everyday uses of blessings?** (grace at meals, bedtime prayers) Point out that blessings are already a common part of our lives and a way of reminding us that God is always close to us.

- Refer to the *Sacred Signs* chart to show the use of holy water, candles, and palm branches as sacramentals. Explain that the Church uses these gifts of creation to point to God's presence in our lives.

Working with the Pictures

Have students study the photographs in the chart as you read about each sacramental. Ask the students to identify times and places they have seen these gifts of creation used within the Church community.

The Language of Faith

- The word **sacramental** is derived from the Latin word *sacer*, which means "sacred," or "holy." Sacramentals do not confer the grace of the Holy Spirit as the sacraments do but rather point to the presence of God in our midst. A sacramental is a sacred sign that is accompanied by a prayer and usually a gesture, such as the Sign of the Cross or the sprinkling of holy water.

- Among the sacramentals **blessings** are the most important. Every blessing praises God and asks for God's gifts. With blessings Christians ask God's favor on people, meals, objects, and places. Some blessings have a lasting importance because they consecrate persons to God or dedicate places or objects, such as an altar, for liturgical use.

Teaching Tip

Memorization To reinforce the teaching of blessings, pair the students up to practice praying the Blessing Before Meals and Thanksgiving After Meals on page 175.

We Reflect
Review

Recall Encourage volunteers to respond to the questions. *(because God is the Creator of all; a duty to act in ways that show respect and love)*

Think and Share Invite the students to share their responses. Then affirm their understanding that God wants us to know and appreciate the differences in all of creation. Explain to the students that a lack of respect for creation can lead to prejudice, pollution, violence, poverty, and the endangerment of animals.

Continue the Journey Give the students the opportunity to either draw pictures or cut out magazine pictures for the activity. Supply the necessary materials.

Alternative Have the students complete this activity at home. You may want to schedule time at your next group meeting for the students to share their artwork.

We Live Our Faith *At Home:* Ask the students to plan three things they might discuss with their families for this activity.
In the Parish: Invite the students to make their own lists, or brainstorm the list together.

Faith Journal The students may begin pages 3–4 of their *Faith Journal* in class and complete them at home. As a part of your own spiritual development, complete *Your Faith Journal* (page J3) for this chapter.

Recall
Why do we say that all parts of creation are related? What is a responsibility?

Think and Share
Why is it important for the Church to show people that differences are good and that all creation is good?

Continue the Journey
Draw a picture of one of your favorite gifts of creation. Give your picture a title that calls this gift *Brother* or *Sister*.

We Live Our Faith

At Home With your family, decide on one thing you can do to care for creation.

In the Parish Make a list of the ways you see the gifts of creation used at Mass. Look for flowers and plants decorating the altar, water used in Baptism, and other ways we use what God has given us.

16 : We Reflect

Resource Center
Multicultural Link

Tell the students that the Catholic Church as a whole is unified; it is also diverse in the way the local parishes bring the gospel message to the people. Remind the students that not all Catholics in the United States speak English, so the language used at Mass may differ from parish to parish according to the needs of the people in the parish. In some parishes in the United States, Spanish is the most common language, while in others, Polish is the main language. Point out to the students that although the message of Jesus is proclaimed in every language and in many unique ways, the message remains the same.

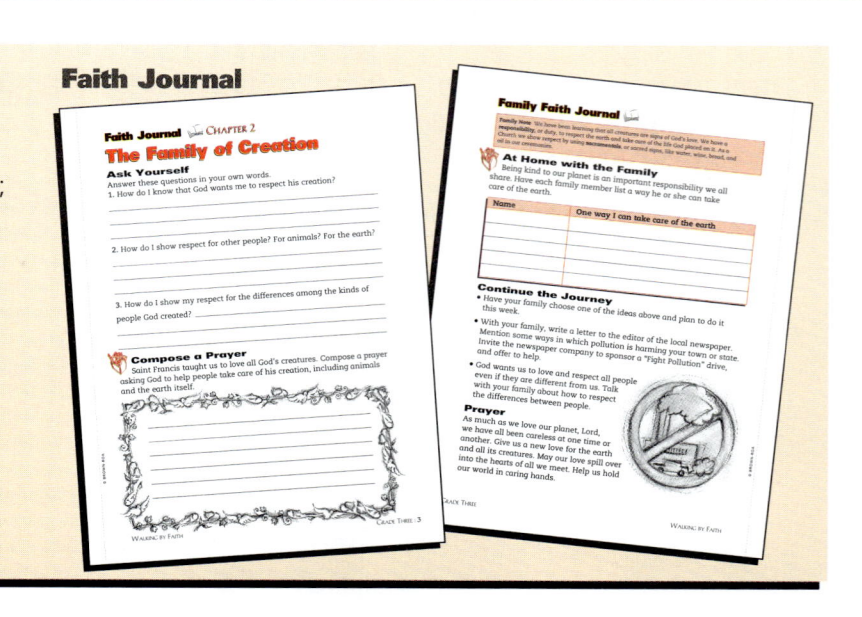

Faith Journal

For All Your Creatures

Saint Francis of Assisi wrote one of the first poems in the Italian language. His poem was a prayer called the "Canticle of the Sun." The word *canticle* means "song of praise." Francis wrote this prayer at a time in his life when he was sick and lonely. Just thinking about the wonders of creation made Francis feel better. He knew that God would care for him just as God cares for our brothers and sisters of creation.

Here is a prayer based on the "Canticle of the Sun."

PRAYER

Praise to you, O Lord our God,
 for all your creatures!
For our Brother Sun and our Sister Moon,
 we praise you!
For our Brother Wind and our Sister Water,
 we praise you!
For our Brother Fire and our Mother Earth,
 we praise you!
All creatures, praise God and give
 God thanks!

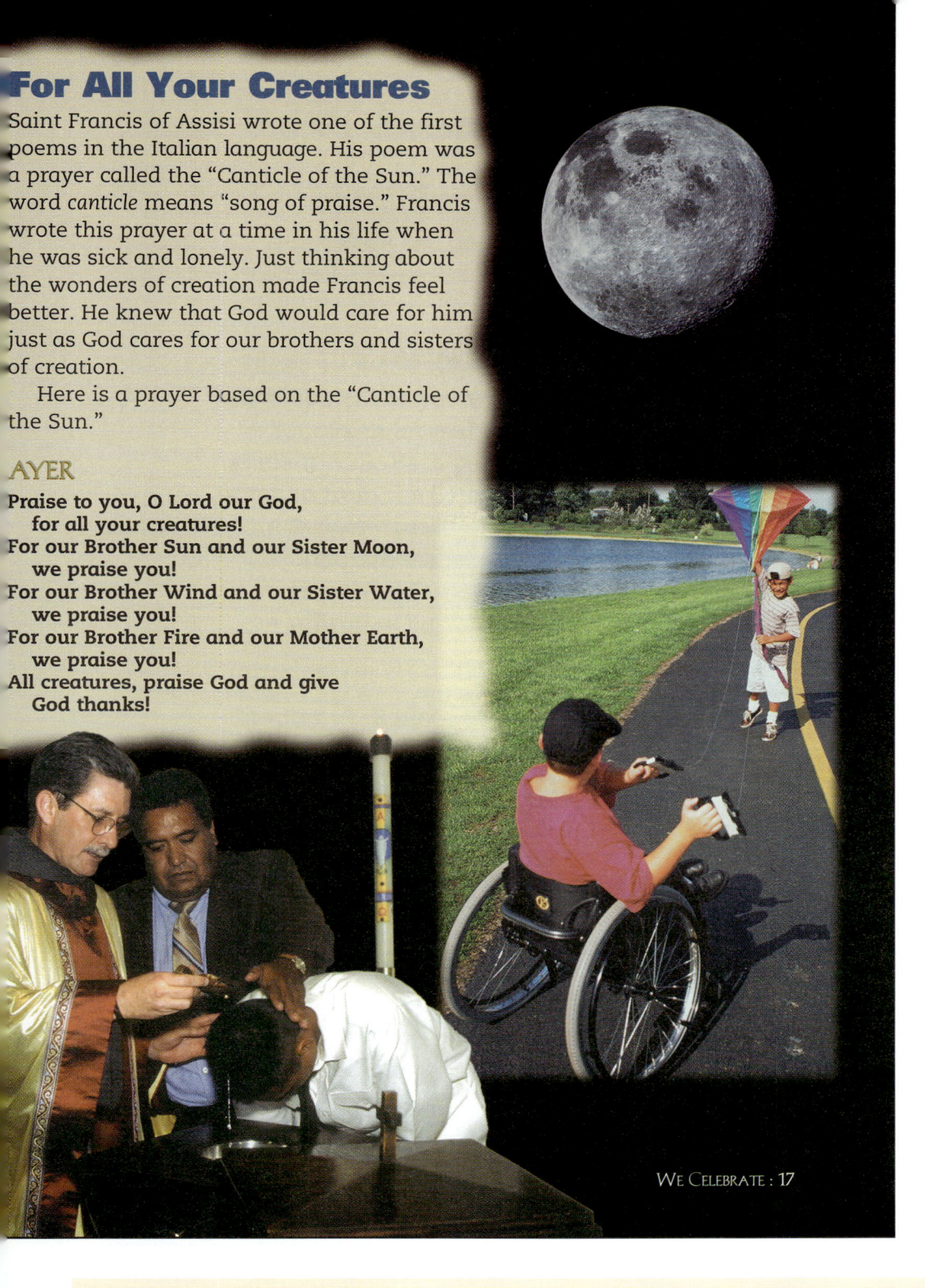

We Celebrate : 17

We Celebrate
3. Close

Working with the Text

After reading or summarizing *For All Your Creatures*, ask these questions about Saint Francis's song of praise.

How does Saint Francis's canticle show that he trusted God? (By praising God when he felt sick and lonely, Saint Francis showed his belief that God was with him in his illness and loneliness.)

Working with the Pictures

What are some gifts of creation that are shown in the photographs? (the moon and night sky, water, grass and trees, people)

What do the pictures on this page have to do with praising God? (They all show gifts of creation, which are good reasons for praising God.)

Prayer Bring the chapter to a close by praying the "Canticle of the Sun." If time permits, add gestures to the prayer. Also consider going outdoors to a grassy area where the students can celebrate the gifts of creation that surround them. Invite volunteers to take turns reading the lines aloud, with everyone joining in on the repeated refrains.

Link to the Family

Encourage the students to pray the "Canticle of the Sun" with their families this week. Ask them to share the story of Saint Francis of Assisi with their younger brothers and sisters. Above all, encourage the students to appreciate the diversity of gifts they see in themselves and in their family members.

Music and Liturgy Resources

To enhance your prayer and celebration, you may wish to use the Unit One Music and Liturgy Resources from the Resource Package.

Notes: Closing the Chapter

Parish : 17

Getting Ready: Chapter 3

Light of the World

Program Resources
Student Text, pp. 18–23
Student Faith Journal, pp. 5–6
Your Faith Journal, p. J4
Chapter 3 Transparency
Unit One Assessment

Unit One (Creation)
Created for Community

Key Content Summary
The Church is a sign and source of God's saving grace.

Planning the Chapter

Open	Pacing Guide *Suggested time/Your time*	Content	Objectives	Materials
	10–15 min./ _____ **min.**	*We Are Invited,* pp. 18–19	• Recognize that the world created by God is good but bad things happen. • Understand the concept of original sin.	

Build				
	20–25 min./ _____ **min.**	*We Explore,* pp. 20–21	• Identify grace as the life of God shared with us. • Discover that followers of Jesus are called to be a light to the world.	• art materials (to make bookmarks) • Chapter 3 Transparency from the Resource Package

Review				
	15–20 min./ _____ **min.**	*We Reflect,* p. 22	• Demonstrate understanding of chapter concepts. • Apply learning through activity. • Practice faith at home and in the parish.	• *Student Faith Journal,* pp. 5–6 • *Your Faith Journal,* p. J4 • Unit One Assessment from the Resource Package

Close				
	10–15 min./ _____ **min.** For additional suggestions, see Scheduling, pp. T35–T37.	*We Celebrate,* p. 23	• Realize that heaven is the happiness of being with God forever.	• live or recorded musical accompaniment to the song "This Little Light of Mine"

Catechism in Context

Doctrinal Foundation This chapter teaches that God freely gives us grace, the gift of his own life, in order to bring all creation back into a relationship of love with him. "But the gift is not like the transgression. For if by that one person's transgression the many died, how much more did the grace of God and the gracious gift of one person, Jesus Christ, overflow for the many" *(Romans 5:15)*. Indeed, "where sin increased, grace overflowed all the more." This grace is nothing less than the Holy Spirit, the Lord and giver of life. The Spirit has been given to us although we did not deserve this gift. If we cooperate with him, however, we will be made worthy of the promises of Christ. Jesus tells us to let the light of the Spirit shine forth in us and not to hide it under a bushel basket.

See Catechism of the Catholic Church, #1999.

One-Minute Retreat for Catechists

Read
"Sometimes a light surprises
The Christian while he sings;
It is the Lord who rises
With healing on his wings."
—William Cowper

Reflect
When did I first experience the light of God's love?

Pray
God of love, help me remember that your light is always with me. I pray that my students will follow where the light of your grace leads them and that they will see the importance of their relationship with you.

Visualizing the Lesson

Use this graphic organizer to help the students visualize the cause and effect of original sin. Draw the graphic organizer on the board or on chart paper, leaving out the words *original sin*. Ask the students to look at the lines connecting God and humans *Before* and *After* original sin.

What do you notice about the lines? *(The line is connected Before, and the line is broken After).* **What happened to cause this break?** *(original sin)* Fill in *original sin* as the students respond.

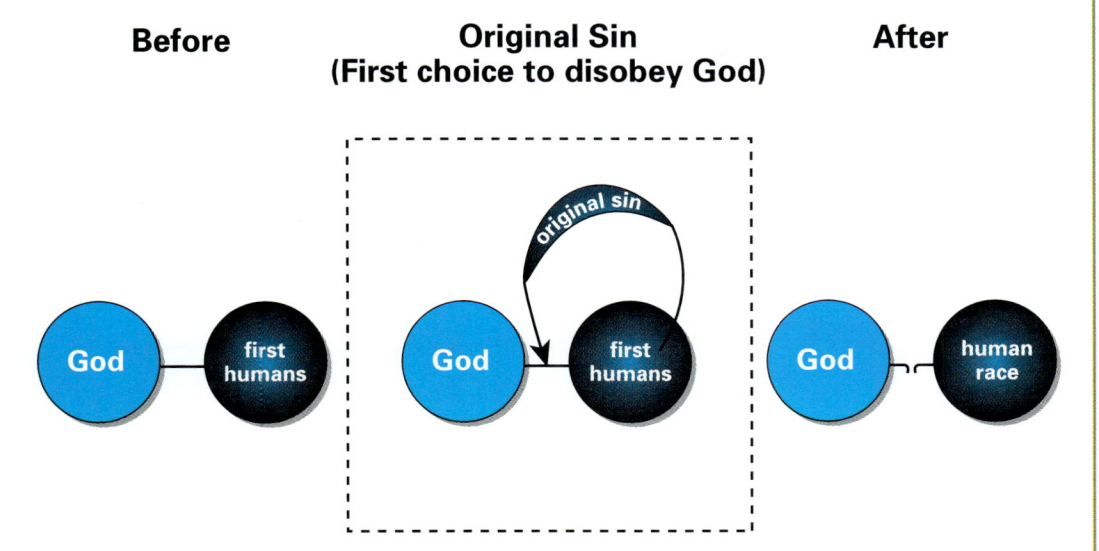

Before — God — first humans

Original Sin (First choice to disobey God) — God → first humans (original sin)

After — God --- human race

Library Links

Books for Children
Lucia, Child of Light by Florence Ekstrand (Music for Little People, 1-800-727-2233).
This book tells the Swedish legend of Saint Lucia, a symbol of light and hope for others.

Books for Parents and Teachers
Telling Stories, Compelling Stories by William J. Bausch (Twenty-Third Publications, 1-800-321-0411).
The author tells 35 stories of people of grace.

Multimedia
For children:
Joey (video) (Pauline Books & Media, 1-800-876-4463).
Learning about love helps a little boy change his life.
God's Place for Me. Episode #1, "We Are the Salt of the Earth" produced by the Archdiocese of St. Paul-Minneapolis (video) (BROWN-ROA, 1-800-922-7696).
God has given us gifts that are important to the world around us.
Glory Day, "Deep Down I Know" by David Haas (GIA Publications, 1-800-442-1358).
Use this song to make music a part of chapter material.

For parents and teachers:
Grace (video) (Paulist Press, 1-800-218-1903).
Grace is woven throughout our lives.

Organizations
For information about ways to let God's light shine through you to those in need, contact:
Catholic Network of Volunteer Service
4121 Harewood Road NE
Washington, DC 20017
(1-202-529-1100)

Strengthening the Family Link

Here are some suggestions for reaching out to your students' families:

- Encourage the students to talk with family members about ways to share God's grace with others.
- Invite family members to join the class in singing the song at the end of the chapter, "This Little Light of Mine."

PARISH : 17B

Chapter 3 pages 18–23

Objectives

- Recognize that the world created by God is good but bad things happen.
- Understand the concept of original sin.
- Identify grace as the life of God shared with us.
- Discover that followers of Jesus are called to be a light to the world.

Gathering WE ARE INVITED
1. Open

Personal Experience Invite the students to think about times when their families received good news.

Prayer Ask the students to keep their "good news" experiences in mind as you pray the prayer together.

Working with the Pictures

Point out that the boy and his family in the photograph look concerned. **Where do you think these people are? (in a hospital waiting area) Why might they be there? (Someone in the family might be seriously ill or injured.)**

Working with the Text

- As you read aloud or summarize the text, ask the students how hearing the good news was like a light being turned on in the darkness for Michael and his family. **(They no longer felt scared and alone; they felt hopeful that everything would turn out all right.)** Remind students that God is always with us in good times and in bad times, helping light our way.
- Ask the students to read and respond to the caption questions. **(Possible answers: Michael felt scared, upset, and sad *before*, and happy, excited, and relieved *after* hearing the good news.)**

CHAPTER 3
Light of the World

PRAYER

God, you created us to share your own life. We will share our light with the world so all creation will praise you.

Michael sat next to his grandmother in the hospital waiting room. It was late at night. Michael could hear Grandma and her friend from the parish praying softly.

They were waiting for news about Michael's brother Ray. A man had robbed the store where Ray worked. Ray had been badly hurt.

"It's not fair," Michael thought. "Ray works hard. He's not in a gang. He doesn't use drugs. Why did this happen to him?" Michael couldn't imagine life without his big brother.

The door opened and a doctor came in. The doctor smiled at Michael. "It's good news," the doctor said. "Ray will be all right. Someone found him and called 911 in time. You can come and see him now."

How do you think Michael felt before the doctor came in? How do you think he felt after hearing the doctor's good news?

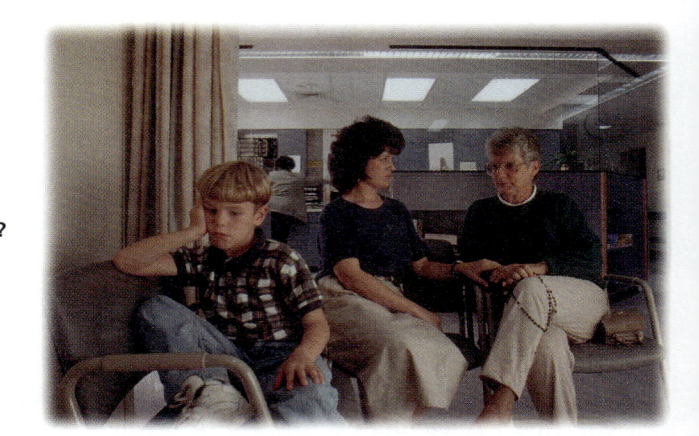

18 : We Are Invited

Resource Center

Teaching Tip

Handling sensitive topics Be aware that students who have had a recent death or illness in their families may be sensitive to the material on this page. To comfort them, let them express their feelings as freely as they wish. Also assure the students that God is always with them in times of trouble.

Link to Liturgy

Explain that during Mass, at the general intercessions, the reader may name people who are sick and ask the assembly to pray for them. A response that the people may give is "Lord, hear our prayer." You may want to have the students take turns spontaneously praying for people they know who are sick. The students can respond together to each prayer with "Lord, hear our prayer."

Notes: Opening the Chapter

A Broken Community

The world God created was good. God made men and women to live happily with one another and with God. But we know that bad things happen. We know that people do not always choose to act in loving ways.

The Bible tells a story to help us understand how creation lost its perfect goodness. In the story the first humans chose to disobey God. They turned away from the goodness God had made. They turned away from the goodness in themselves. They thought they could be happier on their own, without God. They were wrong (Genesis 3:1–24).

The choice to disobey God is called **sin**. Sin hurts relationships. We call the first choice to disobey God **original sin**. The word *original* means "first of all." Original sin hurt the relationships between God and people and between people and creation. Sickness, sadness, and death entered creation. Because of these effects of original sin, our world can sometimes be a scary place.

In the Bible story a beautiful garden called *Eden* is the sign of God's good creation. After they chose to disobey God, the first humans had to leave the garden.

Our Moral Guide

Like the first humans, we are free to choose. Sin is choosing to disobey God.

Catechism, #397

Why do you think God made people free to choose?

WE ARE INVITED : 19

WE ARE INVITED
Open Continued

Working with the Pictures

Use the caption information as a motivator for the students to discuss what life in a perfect place might be like. Be sure the students do not take the story literally. Focus on Eden as an example of perfect friendship with God.

Working with the Text

- As you read and discuss *A Broken Community*, use the *Language of Faith* below to discuss the highlighted terms. To discuss original sin, ask these questions: **Did anyone make the first humans turn away from God?** (No.) Explain that they themselves chose to disobey God. **Why did they make this choice?** (They thought they could be happier on their own without God.)
- Be sure the students understand the definition of the italicized word *original* in the third paragraph.
- Refer to the graphic organizer on page 17B to help the students understand original sin. Use the suggested activity or one of your own choosing.

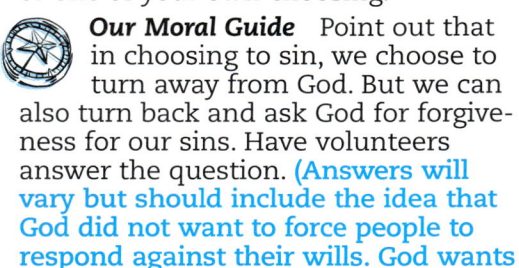

Our Moral Guide Point out that in choosing to sin, we choose to turn away from God. But we can also turn back and ask God for forgiveness for our sins. Have volunteers answer the question. (Answers will vary but should include the idea that God did not want to force people to respond against their wills. God wants all people to respond *freely* in love.)

The Language of Faith

- **Sin** is turning away from God. It is a choice freely made. In the Sacrament of Reconciliation, God forgives the sins of those who are baptized. The Church also celebrates forgiveness in Baptism, Eucharist, and Anointing of the Sick.
- **Original sin** is the sin committed by the first humans, who, according to the scriptural account, were expelled from the garden by God because they did not follow his word **(Genesis 3:1–24)**. This story shows how original sin broke the perfect friendship with God that humans once enjoyed. We believe that human nature continues to be affected by original sin.

Teaching Tip

Clarifying concepts Assure the students that people do not become ill because they have sinned. Jesus tells us in *John 9:1–41* that the blind man was not born blind because of his sin or the sin of his parents. When the Church teaches that sickness entered the world because of original sin, it means that we are born into a condition that is broken, no longer perfect. Sickness is one of the effects of our fallen human condition, *not* of the sins of individuals. However, we are called to avoid sinful practices and disrespect for our health, which may lead to illness.

Scripture Background

The story of the first humans' act of disobedience in **Genesis 3:1–24** is centered around God's command not to eat from the tree of knowledge of good and evil. In Hebrew the word for knowledge has more to do with experience and relationship than with intellectual understanding. Eating from this tree would change the relationship between God and the first humans and become an obstacle to what God intended them to be.

WE EXPLORE
2. Build
Working with the Text

- As you work with the text, talk about *grace* as a gift from God. Use *The Language of Faith* below to further explain the concept.
  When have you shared in the grace of God? (Answers will vary but might include while being in relationship with God; while praying, celebrating the sacraments, and helping others.)

- Explain that by dying on the cross, Jesus gave his life to save us from the power of sin and everlasting death and restore us to grace, a share in God's life. He did it freely, not as a reward but simply because he loves us. Remind the students that the message of God's grace is meant to be shared with others.

Working with the Pictures

- Call attention to the community of people in the photograph.
  How are the people lighting up a darkened world? (They are carrying candles in the darkness.)

- Use the caption and activity to emphasize the idea that we can be like a light that spreads the word of God. If time permits, provide the students with the necessary materials, and have them make bookmarks.

  Alternative Have the students work on their bookmarks at home and bring them to the next session.

  Catholics Believe Use this statement to point out that God is always willing to forgive sinners and restore their relationship with God and with others. Grace is a wonderful gift of God that helps restore our spiritual health.

Catholics Believe...
that God gives us grace, the free gift of God's own life, to bring all creation back into relationship with him.
Catechism, #1999

ACTIVITY
The Church is sometimes called "a light to all people." Make a bookmark in the shape of a candle. Let it remind you to share the message of God's grace with others.

Sharing God's Life

The first humans turned away from God. But God never turned away from people. God sent Jesus to us with good news. The good news is that creation is not too badly hurt to be saved. Sin will not win because Jesus freely gave his life to save us.

God's own life, called **grace**, is always there for us. Grace is a gift with no strings attached. It heals the community that sin hurts. We can do nothing to earn God's grace, but we can cooperate with it. We can be open to God's grace. We can be signs of grace to others.

Our Church community helps us share in the life of grace. When we pray together or care for each other or celebrate sacraments, we are sharing in grace. And because we have received this great gift of grace, we can be a sign of hope to the world. We can show by our actions that there is something more powerful than sin, stronger than death, and greater than ourselves. God's saving love is always with us.

Resource Center

The Language of Faith
Grace comes from the Latin word *gratia*, meaning "favor or thanks." God freely gives grace, a share in his life, because he loves us.

Link to the Family
Tell the students that most people first come to experience God's grace by being loved unconditionally. This means they are loved not because they did something that deserves a reward but just because they exist. Encourage the students to become more aware this week of the many different ways that grace is experienced in their lives through their families, friends, and neighbors.

Link to Liturgy
Tell the students that there is a special time in the celebration of Mass when we acknowledge our sins and rejoice in God's mercy and forgiveness. We call this part of the Mass the *penitential rite*. Ask the students to listen at the beginning of Mass for the penitential rite and join in on these responses: "Lord, have mercy; Christ, have mercy; Lord, have mercy."

Scripture Story
Share Your Light

One sunny afternoon Jesus spoke to a great crowd on a hillside. Jesus told his followers what the world needed from them.

"You are the light of the world," Jesus said. "Don't hide your goodness. Have you ever seen a city on a mountaintop with all its buildings lit up? No one can miss seeing a city like that, even on the darkest night! Be like that city."

Jesus went on. "You don't light a lamp and then put a basket over it, do you?"

The people laughed and shook their heads. That would be silly!

"Share your light, don't hide it," Jesus said. "Let people see you caring and loving. Then the world will see God's grace in what you do. All creation will praise God."

—based on Matthew 5:14–16

Jesus was not talking only to the people on the hillside. His words were meant for us, too. Our world needs the light we bring. Everyone needs to hear the message of God's saving grace.

Scripture Signpost

"You are the light of the world."
Matthew 5:14

What kind of light does our world need? How can we bring light?

We Explore
Build Continued

Working with the Text

Read or summarize the Scripture Story, *Share Your Light*. Be sure to emphasize that Jesus' words apply both to us and to the people of his time.

Working with the Pictures

Point out that Jesus used the example of a city on a hill, like the city in this illustration, because it was an example that he knew the people would understand. Like a light that shines forth, it cannot be hidden.

Scripture Signpost Explain that the light Jesus is speaking of is not the light from a lamp or flashlight but rather the light of God's saving grace that brings hope to the world. (Responses to the questions will vary but might include joy, hope, peace; acts of caring, love, forgiveness.)

Scripture Background

The writer of **Matthew 5:14–16**, in addressing former Jews who were being persecuted for their conversion to Christianity, used these sayings of Jesus to inspire the Christians to be proud of their Church membership. The purpose of Church is to be a sign of the kingdom. Its good works are not for our own glory, but for the glory of God.

Notes: Building the Chapter

WE REFLECT
Review

Recall Invite volunteers to respond to the questions. (original sin; God's own life)

Think and Share Allow the students sufficient time to ponder the questions before responding. (Answers will vary but should include selfishness and a feeling that they don't need God.)

Continue the Journey Have the students complete the activity and then share their responses. If time permits, have volunteers suggest other pictures for this activity.

Alternative Encourage the students to complete the activity at home. Then schedule time in your next group meeting for them to share their responses.

We Live Our Faith *At Home:* Tell the students about one way in which you experience God's grace in your life. Invite volunteers to suggest a thank-you prayer. *In the Parish:* If possible, provide information about the day and time your parish community celebrates the Sacrament of Reconciliation each week.

Faith Journal The students may begin pages 5–6 of their *Faith Journal* in class and complete them at home. As a part of your own spiritual development, complete *Your Faith Journal* (page J4) for this chapter.

RECALL
The first humans chose to disobey God. What do we call their choice? What is grace?

THINK AND SHARE
Why do you think people choose to turn away from God?

CONTINUE THE JOURNEY
Each picture shows a way the Church shares light. Tell what is happening in each picture.

1
2

1. _____
   _____

2. _____
   _____

WE LIVE OUR FAITH

At Home At mealtime, take turns sharing how you have experienced God's grace. Thank God together in prayer.

In the Parish Celebrate the Sacrament of Reconciliation to show that you choose to turn toward God.

22 : WE REFLECT

Resource Center

Assessment Tip
You may wish to copy the Unit One Assessment from the Resource Package in preparation for giving this test after completing Chapters 1–4.

Enrichment
Encourage the students to be on the lookout at home and in the neighborhood for people who are signs of God's grace as they do good deeds for others. During the next session, ask the students to share the good deeds they witnessed. Celebrate the good deeds together.

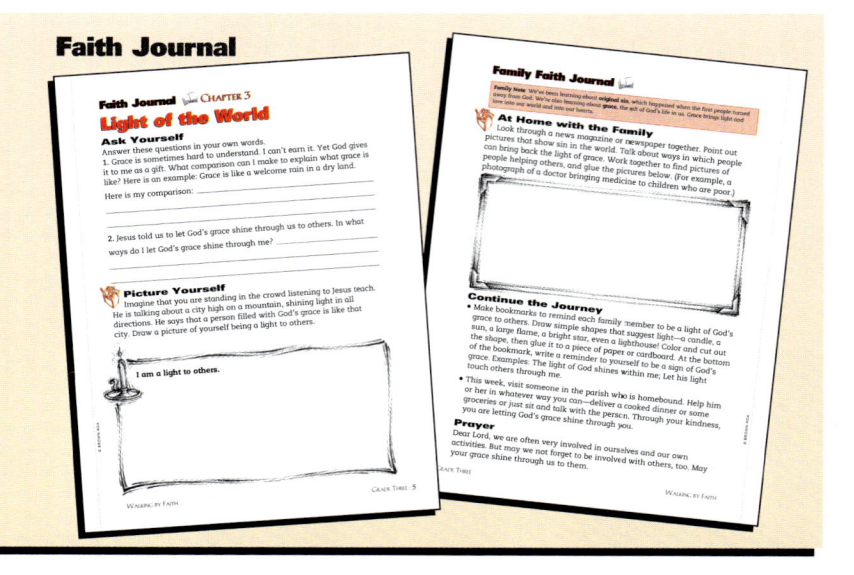

Let It Shine!

When the sun rises each morning, birds begin to sing. The light of the sun and the music of the birds are connected. Light and music are connected for people, too. Both light and music make us feel happy and hopeful. The Bible describes **heaven**, or being with God forever, as full of light and singing.

Singing can be a kind of prayer. When our Church community sings together, we are praising God in music. All creation joins in our song.

Prayer

Sing this song of light together:

This little light of mine, I'm gonna let it shine (3 times)
Let it shine, let it shine, let it shine.
All around my family, I'm gonna let it shine . . .
All around my neighborhood, I'm gonna let it shine . . .
All around the Church, I'm gonna let it shine . . .
All through God's creation, I'm gonna let it shine . . .

We Celebrate
3. Close

Working with the Text

- Read aloud or summarize *Let It Shine*. Explain to the students that when we "shine our lights" with prayer, song, and music, we are following the words of Jesus.
  What are we a sign of when we show God's love in this way? (grace)
- Use *The Language of Faith* to further explain the term *heaven*.

Working with the Pictures

What do you see in the photograph? (a sunrise, a parish choir singing) How do both pictures show that God is being praised? (The choir is praising God by singing, and the sun, like all creation, joins the song of praise.)

Prayer Bring the chapter to a close by praising God with the song "This Little Light of Mine." Remind the students that the Church community often uses songs as prayers to God. As the students prepare to sing, ask them to keep in mind people who are sick or injured and need the light of the Church community in their lives. Ask everyone to sing with joy and enthusiasm. You might provide live or recorded musical accompaniment. Encourage the students to clap their hands and march around the classroom as they sing the song.

The Language of Faith

Heaven is a state of perfect happiness in an afterlife with God. Happiness in heaven comes from sharing God's love for all eternity in a life of peace without struggle. Heaven is referred to in Scripture in a variety of ways, including the "Father's house" **(John 14:2)**. Heaven is not identical with the kingdom or reign of God, which will in its fullness bring forth a new heaven and a new earth **(Revelation 21:1)**.

Optional Multicultural Link

Remind the students that God's light shines throughout the world on all people. Lead the students in naming several different continents or countries around the world. Then add lines about those places to the song "This Little Light of Mine"; for example, "All around Africa, I'm gonna let it shine."

Notes: Closing the Chapter

Unit One Review

Objective
- Review the unit and assess progress.

Chapter Summaries

Use this information to reinforce key points before administering the review. These summaries will also help you assess students' responses to *Show How Far You've Come*, page 25.

Chapter 1
- God created us to be related, or connected, to others.
- When people come together for a shared purpose, the group they form is called a community.
- We belong to a special community called the Church.

Chapter 2
- As human members of the family of creation, we have responsibilities.
- The Church teaches us that differences in creation and among people are good.
- The Church uses some gifts of creation as sacramentals, or sacred signs, in our celebrations and prayers.

Chapter 3
- Through original sin sickness, sadness, and death entered creation.
- The choice to turn away from God is called sin.
- God's own life shared with us, called grace, can help us turn back to God and be a light for others.

Review

You may have the students work on the review in writing or work together to answer questions orally.

Fill in the Blanks Call attention to the word bank. Assign the exercise for the students to complete individually. Then invite volunteers to respond orally.

Matching Discuss any terms the students do not fully understand.

Share Your Faith Have students role-play their responses with partners.

Alternative Assign this exercise as written homework.

Unit One Checkpoint

Review

Fill in the Blanks Complete each sentence with the correct term from the word bank.

1. A group of people who come together for a shared purpose is called a __community__.
2. The word __Church__ means "a community called together, belonging to the Lord."
3. A response to God, a duty, is a __responsibility__.
4. The most common __sacramental__ is blessing.
5. The choice to disobey God is __sin__.

Word Bank

sin   sacramental   community   responsibility   Church

Matching Match each description in Column A with the correct term from Column B.

Column A

__c__ 1. Different ways of living and celebrating.

__a__ 2. God's own life, freely given to us.

__d__ 3. Being with God forever.

__e__ 4. Asking God's protection, or setting a person or thing apart to be used in God's work.

__b__ 5. The first humans' choice to disobey God.

Column B

a. grace
b. original sin
c. customs
d. heaven
e. blessing

Share Your Faith Imagine that someone says, "I don't need other people. I don't need God. I can be happy all by myself." Tell why you believe community is important.

Resource Center

Assessment Tips

Use one or more of the following strategies to assist you in assessing student progress:

- If you need a more detailed written review, you may give the Unit One Assessment from the Resource Package.
- Work as a class to assess progress by discussing the important concepts learned in this unit.
- Ask the students to think about what they have learned about God's grace in their lives. Invite them to tell how they have responded to the *We Live Our Faith* activities.

Show How Far You've Come Use the chart below to show what you have learned. For each chapter, write or draw the three most important things you remember.

Created for Community

Chapter 1	Chapter 2	Chapter 3
Made for Each Other	The Family of Creation	Light of the World
Look for answers reflecting the key points listed under Chapter Summaries.		

What Else Would You Like to Know?
List any questions you still have about God's creation and the Church community.

_____
_____
_____

Continue the Journey Choose one or more of the following activities to do on your own, with your class, or with your family.
- Look through your Faith Journal pages for Unit One. Choose your favorite activity, and share it with a friend or family member.
- Make your own book of the story of the first humans or Jesus' words about being the light of the world. Tell the story in your own words, and draw pictures to illustrate it.
- Make a poster showing some favorite customs of your class or parish.

REVIEW : 25

Show How Far You've Come You may want to brainstorm *Chapter Summaries* with the group. Pay attention to responses that differ widely from the key points of the chapters. Review any areas in which presentation of material was unclear and needs special attention. Discuss key concepts as needed. If time permits, extend the activity by asking the students to recall their favorite stories, pictures, or activities from the unit.

What Else Would You Like to Know? Have the students share their questions and vote on a class list of three questions for you to answer at the next session.

Continue the Journey If possible, provide time at a later session for the students to demonstrate how they have completed one or more of these activities. For example:
- Ask volunteers to tell the group how they shared *Faith Journal* activities at home.
- Use the posters the students created as a basis for discussing favorite customs.
- Write a class letter for the parish bulletin highlighting what was learned. Or sponsor coffee and doughnuts after one of the Masses, and display work from the class.

Prayer
Close your review time by gathering the students and praying spontaneous prayers of thanks for God's grace in their lives, especially during this part of their faith journey.

Reference Sources
For help in addressing students' questions about this unit's topics, see:
- *The HarperCollins Encyclopedia of Catholicism* (HarperCollins, 1995).

Good resources for third graders include:
- *You and God—Friends Forever* by Francine O'Connor (Liguori Publications, 1993).
- *Saints for Young Readers*, vol. 1 & 2 (Pauline Books & Media, 1995).

Your parish is another important resource. Priests, deacons, catechists, other staff members, godparents, sponsors, and members of religious communities are all good sources for answering students' questions.

Link to the Family
If possible, allow the students to take these pages home to share with family members.

PARISH : 25

Getting Ready: Chapter 4

Mother of the Church

Program Resources
Student Text, pp. 26–29
Student Faith Journal, pp. 7–8
Your Faith Journal, p. J5

Unit One (Creation)
Created for Community

Key Content Summary
Mary, our mother, shares God's saving love with all people.

Planning the Chapter

	Pacing Guide Suggested time/Your time	Content	Objectives	Materials
Open	10–15 min./ _____ min.	*We Are Invited*, p. 26	• Acknowledge Mary as the mother of Jesus and Mother of the Church.	
Build	20–25 min./ _____ min.	*We Explore*, p. 27	• Recognize Mary as Our Lady of Guadalupe.	• map showing Mexico and Mexico City • world map or globe (optional)
Review	15–20 min./ _____ min.	*We Reflect*, p. 28	• Demonstrate understanding of chapter concepts. • Apply learning through activity. • Practice faith at home and in the parish.	• *Student Faith Journal*, pp. 7–8 • *Your Faith Journal*, p. J5 • art materials (including colored paper, markers, pencils, clay, and glue) (optional)
Close	10–15 min./ _____ min.	*We Celebrate*, p. 29	• Celebrate Mary as Mother of the Americas.	• statues and pictures of Mary, music

For additional suggestions, see Scheduling, pp. T35–T37.

Catechism in Context

Doctrinal Foundation This chapter explains that the Virgin Mary, the Mother of God, is also called the Mother of the Church. As Jesus was dying on the cross, he commended to her the disciple whom he loved, "Woman, behold your son." And he commended her to him, "Behold your mother." The Church regards Mary as another mother to all Jesus' followers. We are, after all, members of the Body of Christ. As such our mother Mary continues to care for us, watch over us from heaven, and help us by her powerful prayers and matchless example. Although she is Mother of the whole Church, she is often invoked by particular titles throughout the world, for example, *Our Lady of Paris* and *Our Lady of Guadalupe*.

See Catechism of the Catholic Church, #969.

One-Minute Retreat for Catechists

Read
"The Savior of the world is our Brother.
Our God has become—through Mary—our Brother."
—Saint Anselm

Reflect
How can I emulate Mary?

Pray
To you, Mary, I owe great thanks. May your spirit inspire me, especially when I am with my students. May they sense your love and gentleness through me.

Visualizing the Lesson

Use this graphic organizer to help the students visualize Mary's many roles.

Draw the graphic organizer on the board or on chart paper, omitting all of the text except *Mary*. As you work with the text on page 26, help the students fill in the circles.

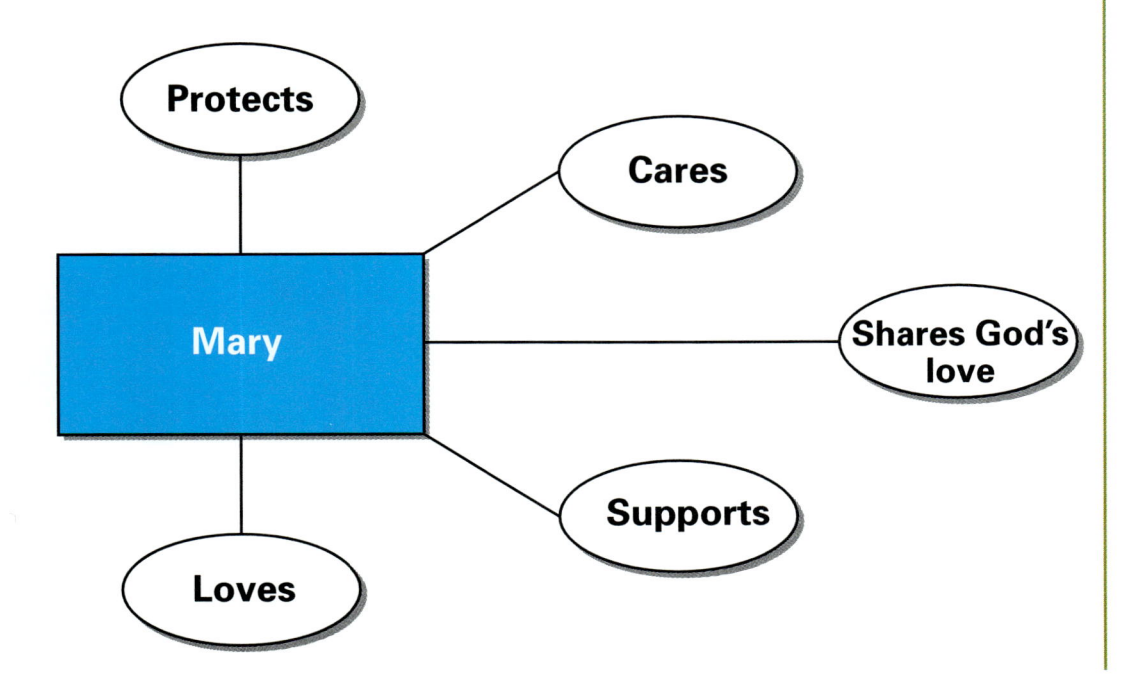

Mary: Protects, Cares, Shares God's love, Supports, Loves

Library Links

Books for Children
Our Lady of Guadalupe: Queen of the Americas by Joanne McPortland and Juanita Vaughan (Franciscan Communications, 1-800-488-0488).
Mary is important to the Americas.

Books for Parents and Teachers
Mary: Woman and Mother by Francis J. Moloney SDB (The Liturgical Press, 1-800-858-5450).
Mary loves all people.

Multimedia
For children:
Mary, the Mother of Jesus produced by Instructional TV, Archdiocese of New York (video) (Sheed & Ward, 1-800-333-7373).
The video tells the story of Mary as the mother of Jesus.
Glory Day, "Magnificat" by David Haas (GIA Publications, 1-800-442-1358).
Use this song to make music a part of chapter material.

For parents and teachers:
Behold Your Mother (video) (Don Bosco Multimedia, 1-914-576-0122).
Truths about Mary are presented from the bishops' pastoral letter.
Interlupe (http://www.spin.com/mx/~msalazar).
This World Wide Web home page is dedicated to Our Lady of Guadalupe.

Organizations
For further information about Mary, contact:
The Marian Library/International Marian Research Institute
University of Dayton
300 College Park
Dayton, OH 45469-1390
(1-937-229-4214)
(http://www.udayton.edu/mary)

Strengthening the Family Link

Here are some suggestions for reaching out to your students' families:

- Encourage the students to talk with family members about Mary and about her appearance at Guadalupe.
- Invite family members to join the class in praying to Mary.

Chapter 4 pages 26–29

Objectives
- Acknowledge Mary as the mother of Jesus and Mother of the Church.
- Recognize Mary as Our Lady of Guadalupe.
- Celebrate Mary as Mother of the Americas.

Gathering — We Are Invited
1. Open

Personal Experience Invite volunteers to name one quality that makes their mothers or caregivers special.

Prayer Ask the students to keep their mothers or caregivers in mind as they pray together the prayer to Mary.

Working with the Text
- Read aloud the question just below the prayer, and then invite volunteers to respond. (Possible answers: care for their children's daily needs, comfort them when they are sick or sad, encourage them.)
- Read or summarize the text. To help the students understand Mary's role, talk with them about her as the mother of Jesus, our mother, and the Mother of the Church. Explain that she cares for us as members of her family.
- To clarify Mary's role, refer to the graphic organizer on page 25B. Use the suggested activity or one of your own choosing.

Working with the Pictures
Have the students look at the photograph showing a mosaic of Our Lady of Guadalupe (gwah•dah•LOO•pay). Explain that this mosaic can be found in the National Shrine of the Immaculate Conception in Washington, DC.

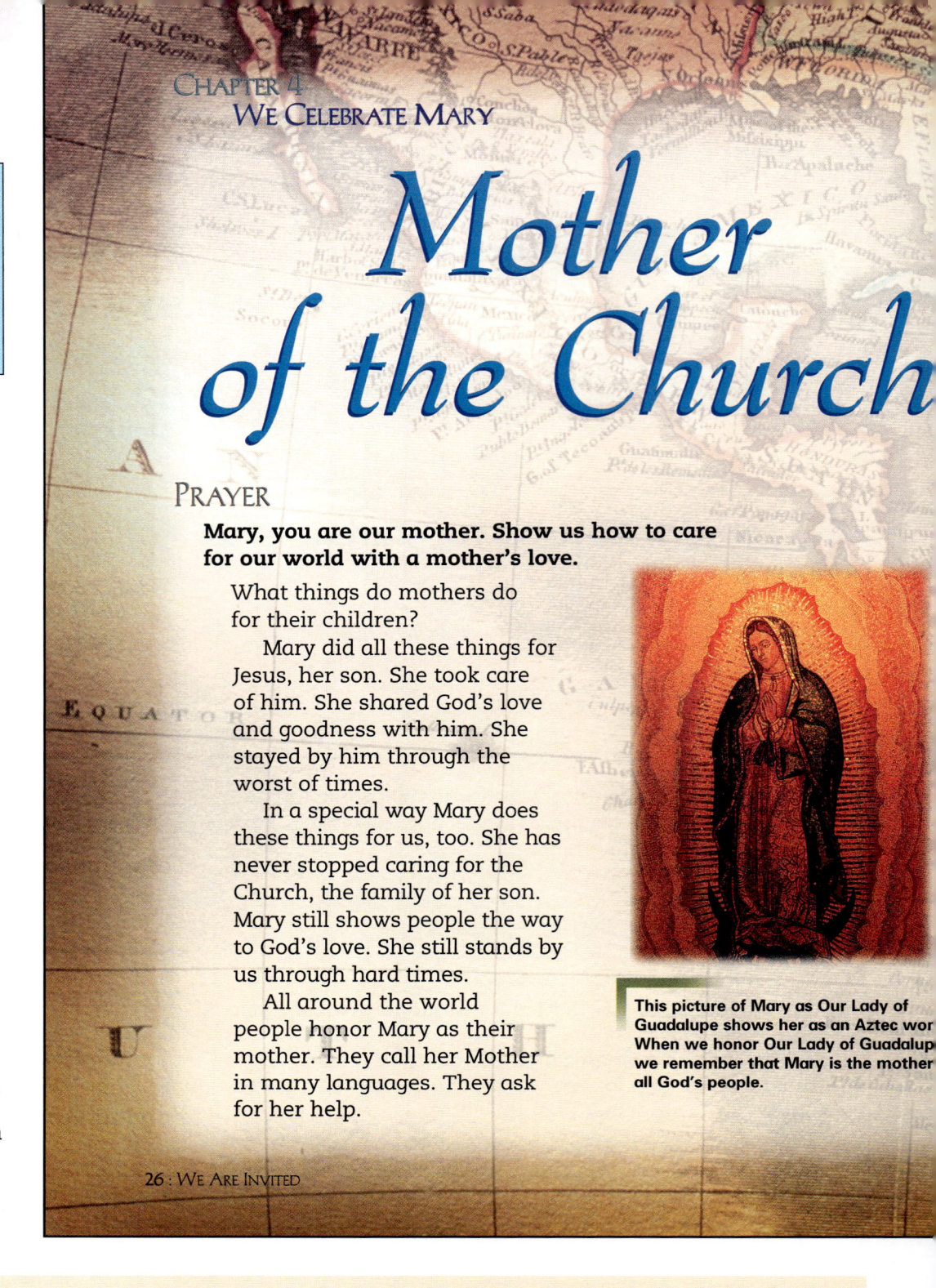

CHAPTER 4
WE CELEBRATE MARY

Mother of the Church

PRAYER

Mary, you are our mother. Show us how to care for our world with a mother's love.

What things do mothers do for their children?

Mary did all these things for Jesus, her son. She took care of him. She shared God's love and goodness with him. She stayed by him through the worst of times.

In a special way Mary does these things for us, too. She has never stopped caring for the Church, the family of her son. Mary still shows people the way to God's love. She still stands by us through hard times.

All around the world people honor Mary as their mother. They call her Mother in many languages. They ask for her help.

This picture of Mary as Our Lady of Guadalupe shows her as an Aztec wor[an]. When we honor Our Lady of Guadalupe we remember that Mary is the mother [of] all God's people.

26 : We Are Invited

Resource Center

Art Background
The mosaic in the photograph is a copy of the miraculous image of Our Lady of Guadalupe that appeared on Juan Diego's cloak. The cloak, made of rough cactus fiber, is displayed today in the Basilica of our Lady of Guadalupe at Tepeyac, near Mexico City. The image shows Mary with mixed Spanish and Aztec facial features. The colors and designs on her clothing were symbolic, to the Aztecs, of the mother of the creator god; Mary stands on a crescent moon, which, to the Catholic Spaniards, was a sign that she was the Immaculate Conception.

Notes: Opening the Chapter

"I Am Your Mother"

Long ago in Mexico, the Aztec Indian people needed help. Soldiers from Spain had taken over their country and made the people slaves. Some Aztecs had become Christians, and some Spanish people worked to help the Aztecs. But life was still very hard.

On a cold December morning, an Aztec Christian named Juan Diego met a beautiful Aztec woman. She wore a blue cloak shining with golden stars. The Lady called Juan Diego's name. She spoke in his own Indian language.

"Don't be afraid, my son," the Lady said. "I am your mother. I am the Mother of God, who gives life to all creatures. I will always be with your people. I will care for you and for all those who need God's love."

Through this event Mary came to be known as **Our Lady of Guadalupe**. By coming to Juan Diego, Mary showed that God's love belongs to everyone. She showed the Spanish people that the Aztecs were God's children, too. Today a large church stands on the spot near Mexico City where Blessed Juan Diego met the Lady. People from all over the world gather there to honor Mary, their mother.

Pilgrims gather at the shrine of Our Lady of Guadalupe.

Catholics Believe . . .
that Mary, the mother of Jesus, continues to care for us as Mother of the Church.
Catechism, #969

WE EXPLORE
2. Build

Working with the Text

- Before reading *I Am Your Mother*, point out Mexico and its capital, Mexico City, on a map. Explain that the story of Mary's visit to Juan Diego (HWAHN dee•AY•go), told on this page, happened in what is today the country of Mexico. Then read the story aloud.
- Ask the students to imagine how Juan Diego felt when Mary appeared to him. (Possible answers: surprised, frightened, confused, happy.) **Why did Mary appear to Juan Diego?** (She wanted to give the Aztec people hope and to show that all people are God's children; she wanted people to grow in love for her son, Jesus.)
- As you continue to work with the text, use *The Language of Faith* below to discuss the highlighted title.

Working with the Pictures

- Direct the students' attention to the photograph, and read the caption aloud. Explain that pilgrims are people who travel to religious shrines or sacred places to show their devotion. **What do you think the pilgrims in the pictures are doing?** (praying for Mary's intercession; singing hymns to her)
- Explain that each year millions of pilgrims visit the shrine of Our Lady of Guadalupe near Mexico City. Above the altar of the shrine, the cloak of Juan Diego containing the image of Mary is on display.
- **Catholics Believe** Emphasize that Mary cares for us through her love, compassion, and protection. Remind the students that they should pray for Mary's intercession. She is our mother in heaven.

The Language of Faith
Our Lady of Guadalupe—in Spanish *Nuestra Señora de Guadalupe* (nco•AYS•trah sayn•YOR•ah DAY gwah•dah•LOO•pay)—is the title under which Mary is honored in her miraculous visit to the people of Mexico. The title actually refers to an earlier title of honor in Spain; Guadalupe is an Arabic word meaning "hidden river" and refers to a place where an image of Mary was honored during the Moorish conquest of Spain.

Multicultural Link
Tell the students that Mary is honored in special shrine churches around the world. These include Lourdes, in France; Fatima, in Portugal; Knock, in Ireland; Montserrat, in Spain; and Czestochowa, in Poland. On a map or globe, point out each of these locations. Then point out that Mary is the Mother of the Church family throughout the world.

Notes: Building the Chapter

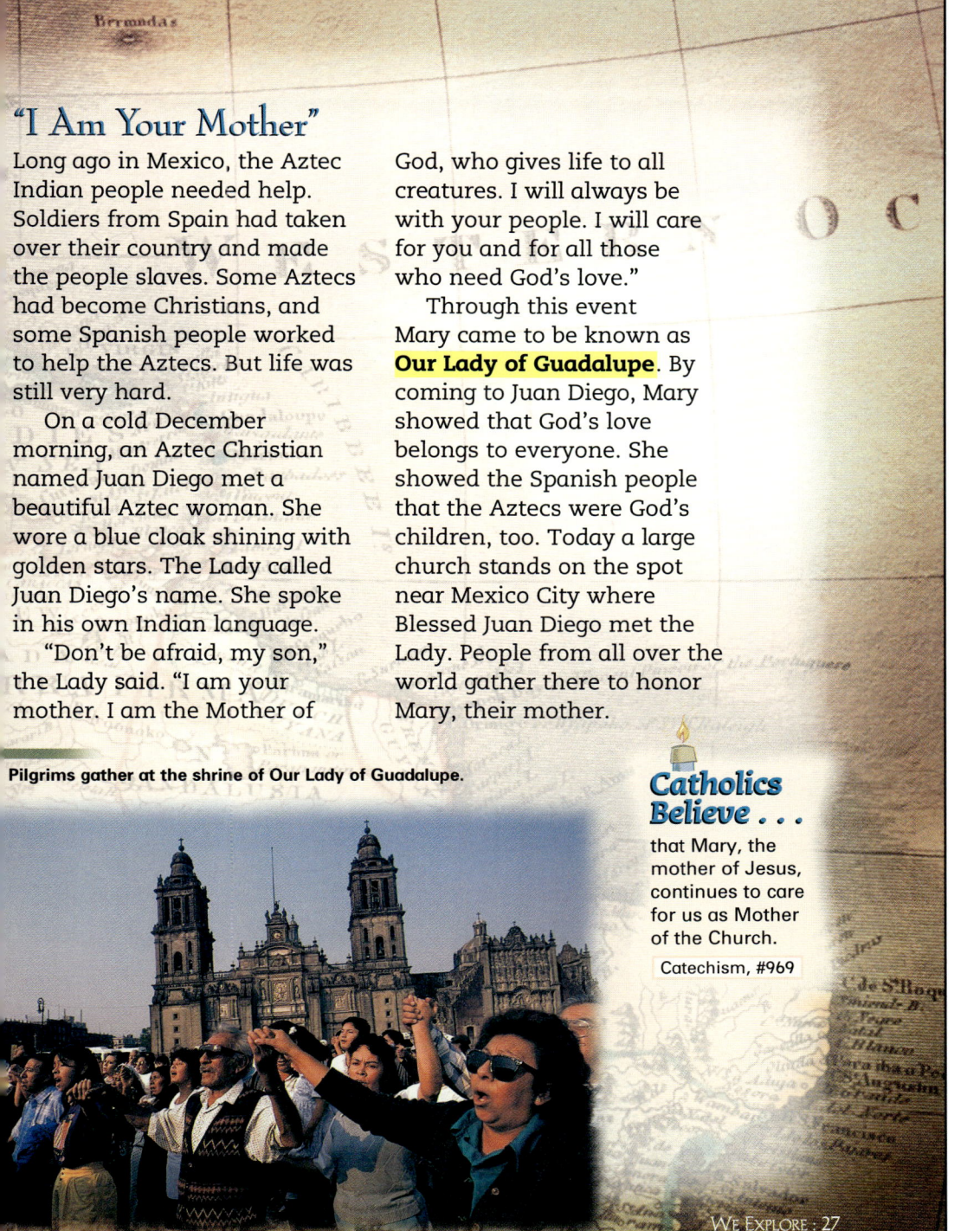

PARISH : 27

WE REFLECT
Review

Recall Ask volunteers to share their answers to the questions. (Jesus; Juan Diego)

Think and Share Ask the students to share their answers. Then tell them that *all* people need to hear Mary's message of love and care.

Continue the Journey Before the students write their prayers, you may want to brainstorm ideas together. If time permits, invite volunteers to share their completed prayers by reading them aloud.

We Live Our Faith *At Home:* Give the students some suggestions, such as making the beds, setting the table, or helping to fold and put away the family's laundry. *In the Parish:* You might want to suggest the names of some parish people the students can talk to about the titles for Mary.

Faith Journal The students may begin pages 7–8 of their *Faith Journal* in class and complete them at home. As a part of your own spiritual development, complete *Your Faith Journal* (page J5) for this chapter.

RECALL
Who was Mary's son? Who was the Aztec who met the Lady of Guadalupe?

THINK AND SHARE
The Aztec people of Mexico needed to hear Mary's message of love and care. Who are some people today who need to hear that message?

CONTINUE THE JOURNEY
Write a prayer asking Mary, Mother of the Church, to help us share God's love with our world.

WE LIVE OUR FAITH

At Home Do something special to say thank you to someone who cares for you as Mary cared for Jesus.

In the Parish Mexicans and Mexican Americans honor Mary by calling her *Nuestra Señora de Guadalupe* (Our Lady of Guadalupe). Find out some of the names by which the people of your parish community honor Mary.

28 : WE REFLECT

Resource Center

Optional Enrichment Activity
Invite the students to create their own images of Mary as a homework activity. They might create mosaics, paintings, statues, or drawings. Suggest a wide variety of materials, including colored paper, markers, pencils, clay, and glue. Tell the students that the images they create should be respectful and reverent.

Link to the Faith Community
Tell the students that the Church community has always honored Mary with many different devotions. The most popular devotion to Mary is the Rosary. Instructions for praying the Rosary can be found on page 182. Encourage the students to attend a parish recitation of the Rosary.

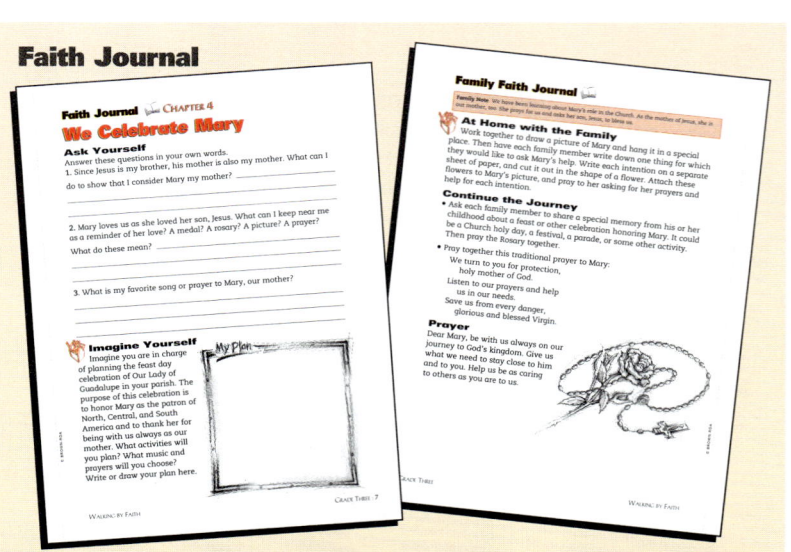

Mother of the Americas

As Our Lady of Guadalupe, Mary is honored as the patron saint of North, Central, and South America.

The feast day of Our Lady of Guadalupe is December 12. Many Mexican people celebrate this feast by waking up at sunrise to sing songs honoring Mary. They dance special dances. They decorate churches and homes with red roses, the flowers that were blooming when Juan Diego met the Lady. Everyone shares a feast-day breakfast of sweet bread and hot chocolate spiced with cinnamon.

Share the prayer you wrote to Mary, our mother. Then read together this prayer based on "Las Mañanitas," the morning song to Our Lady of Guadalupe.

PRAYER

These are the morning prayers
  King David used to sing.
Today, because it is your feast day,
  we sing them to you here.
Wake up, Mother Mary, wake up!
  Look, it's already dawn.
The birds are already singing. The
  moon has already gone down.
Here comes the day. The light of
  day is given to us.
Like Blessed Juan Diego, we greet
  you with heavenly music,
Our Mexican Mother, the Mother
  of all God's people!

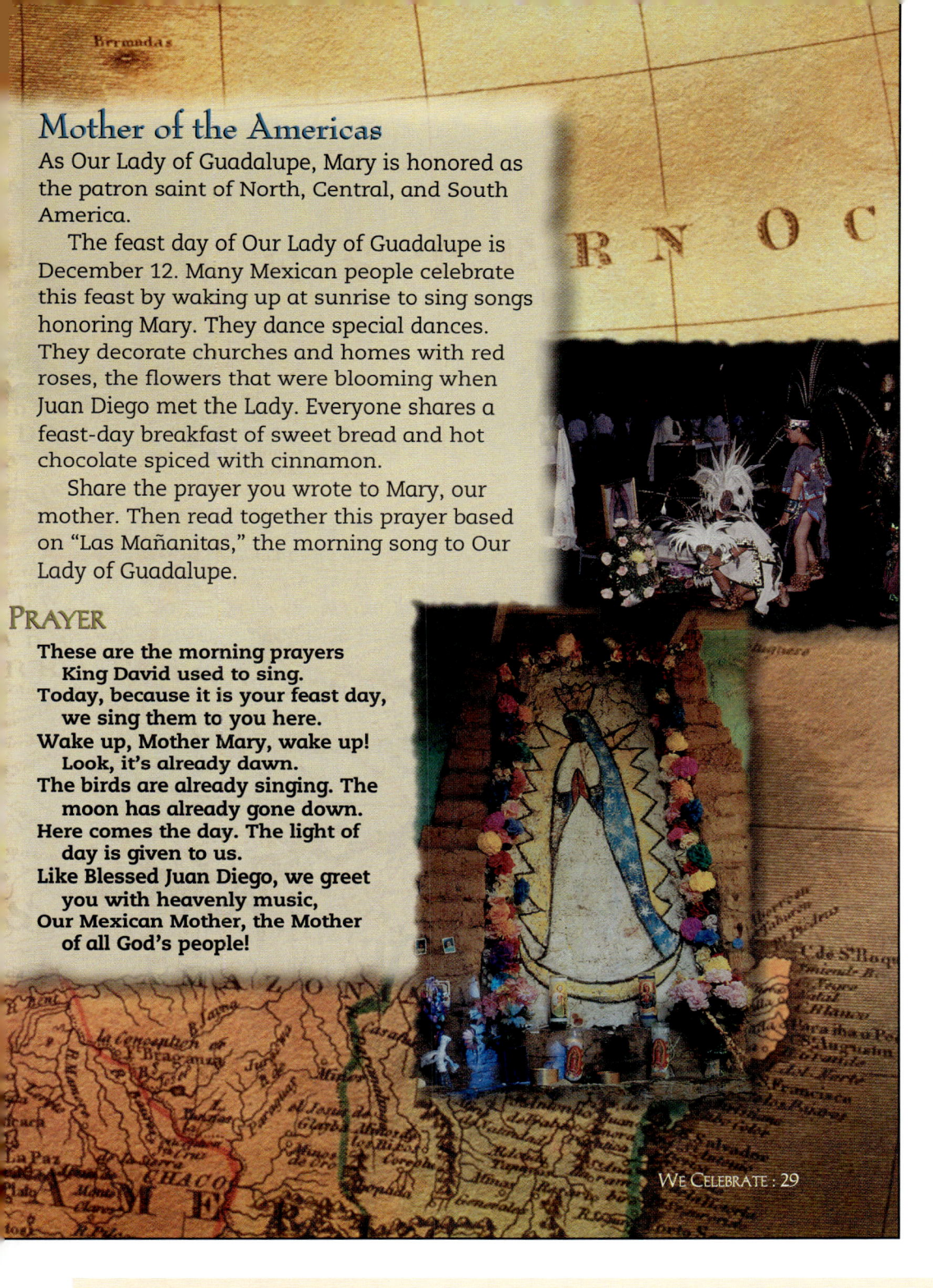

We Celebrate : 29

WE CELEBRATE
3. Close

Working with the Pictures

Have the students describe what they see in the photographs. (children in costumes honoring Mary; an image of Mary on a church wall surrounded by flowers)

Working with the Text

Read aloud or summarize *Mother of the Americas*. Be sure to emphasize the special way that Our Lady of Guadalupe is honored in Mexico and in many parts of the United States on her feast day. Invite volunteers to tell how they might share in the celebration.

Prayer Bring the chapter to a close by honoring Mary with prayer. If time permits, decorate an area with statues and pictures of Mary. Plan a celebration complete with music and dance. Gather the students at the prayer table with the prayers they wrote for the *Continue the Journey* activity. Allow those who wish to share their prayers to do so. Then pray together the morning prayer based on "Las Mañanitas" (las ma•nyah•NEE•tahs).

Art Background

The painting of Mary as Our Lady of Guadalupe was done by Ted DeGrazia and is located in the Mission in the Sun Church in Tucson, Arizona. Throughout the centuries artists have rendered many different images of Our Lady of Guadalupe, as well as others of Mary under other titles. The catacombs contain the very first images of Mary, which date back to the third century. Over the centuries a popular depiction of Mary is as a mother, holding Baby Jesus in her arms.

Link to the Family

Many families have a special devotion to Mary, such as praying the Rosary together during Advent, the months of May and October, and Lent. Encourage the students to attend a novena service with their families at their parish church. Encourage volunteers to share with the class how their families, friends, or neighbors honor Mary.

Notes: Closing the Chapter

Getting Ready: Chapter 5

We Believe in God

Program Resources
Student Text, pp. 30–35
Student Faith Journal, pp. 9–10
Your Faith Journal, p. J6
Chapter 5 Transparency
Unit Two Family Letter

Unit Two (God)
People of God

Key Content Summary
The great mystery of our faith is belief in the Holy Trinity.

Planning the Chapter

	Pacing Guide Suggested time/Your time	Content	Objectives	Materials
Open	10–15 min./ _____ min.	*We Are Invited,* p. 30	• Recognize that through the Sacrament of Baptism we become members of the Church.	
Build	20–25 min./ _____ min.	*We Explore,* pp. 31–33	• Describe the development of belief in one God. • Recognize that God reveals himself as Father, Son, and Spirit in the mystery of the Holy Trinity.	• index cards (optional) • art materials • drawing materials • Chapter 5 Transparency from the Resource Package
Review	15–20 min./ _____ min.	*We Reflect,* p. 34	• Demonstrate understanding of chapter concepts. • Apply learning through activity. • Practice faith at home and in the parish.	• *Student Faith Journal,* pp. 9–10 • *Your Faith Journal,* p. J6
Close	10–15 min./ _____ min.	*We Celebrate,* p. 35	• Demonstrate belief in the Holy Trinity through gesture and prayer.	• Unit Two Family Letter from the Resource Package

For additional suggestions, see Scheduling, pp. T35–T37.

Catechism in Context

Doctrinal Foundation   This chapter explores the mystery of God, which we profess in the Creed: "We believe in one God: the Father . . . , his only Son . . . , and the Holy Spirit. . . ." Faithful to our Jewish roots, we confess that there is only one God: "Hear, O Israel, Yahweh our God is Lord alone." But we have experienced this one God in the Persons of the Father, Son, and Spirit. The Father sent the Son to live among us and the Spirit to dwell in us. "But when the fullness of time had come, God sent his Son, born of a woman, born under the law, to ransom those under the law, so that we might receive adoption. As proof that you are children, God sent the spirit of his Son into our hearts, crying out, 'Abba, Father!'" (Galatians 4:4–6).

See Catechism of the Catholic Church, #234.

One-Minute Retreat for Catechists

Read

"Faith lights us through the dark to Deity; faith builds a bridge across the gulf of death, to break the shock that nature cannot shun, and lands thought smoothly on the farther shore."

—Edward Young

Reflect

How does faith help me throughout life?

Pray

Lord, my faith is a walking stick. Remind me, when I am on a steep hill, that it should be stronger. When I am on level ground, let me not put it away but carry it always. In the classroom I pray that my students will learn to fashion their own walking sticks—each beautiful and unique—out of love.

Visualizing the Lesson

Use this graphic organizer to help the students visualize God as Three Persons in one—God the Father, God the Son, and God the Holy Spirit.

On a sheet of paper, draw two copies of the graphic organizer without the text. Make copies for the students. Guide the students in filling in the text on the first graphic. Invite the students to write their names on the stem on the second graphic and include three of their own identities on the leaves (for example: Jen—sister, friend, daughter).

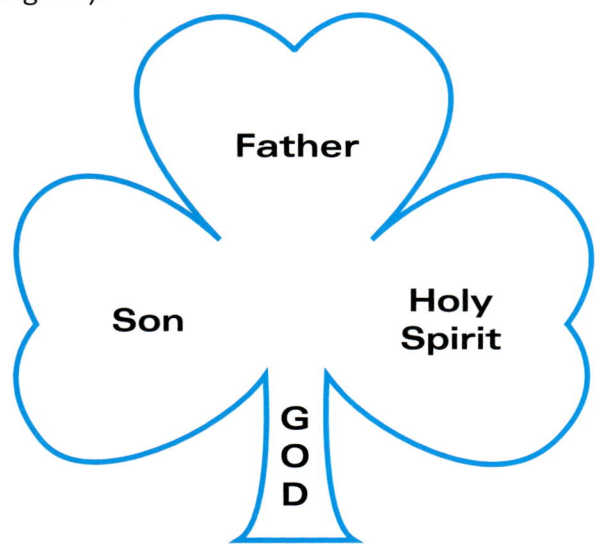

Library Links

Books for Children

Shamrocks, Harps and Shillelaghs: The Story of St. Patrick's Day Symbols by Edna Barth (Houghton Mifflin, 1-800-352-5455).

Barth describes the customs and symbols associated with St. Patrick's Day.

Books for Parents and Teachers

"We Believe . . ."—A Survey of the Catholic Faith by Oscar Lukefahr CM (Liguori Publications, 1-800-325-9521).

This overview of the faith includes questions and activities.

Multimedia

For children:

St. Patrick's Day produced by Colman Communications Corp. (video) (BROWN-ROA, 1-800-922-7696).

The video retells the legend of Saint Patrick.

Glory Day, "Without Seeing You" by David Haas (video) (GIA Publications, 1-800-442-1358).

Use this song to make music a part of the chapter material.

For parents and teachers:

Trinity from the Mystery of Faith series produced by Olive Branch Productions (video) (Paulist Press, 1-800-218-1903).

The doctrine of the Trinity is a central mystery of the Christian faith.

Organizations

For further information about the Holy Spirit in the life of the Church, contact:

National Service Committee of the Catholic Charismatic Renewal of the U.S., Inc.
P.O. Box 628
Locust Grove, VA 22508-0628

Strengthening the Family Link

Here are some suggestions for reaching out to your students' families:

- Encourage the students to talk with family members about the Holy Trinity and the symbols we use to describe the Trinity, such as the shamrock.
- Invite family members to join the class in making shamrocks as symbols of the Holy Trinity.

Chapter 5 pages 30–35

Objectives
- Recognize that through the Sacrament of Baptism we become members of the Church.
- Describe the development of belief in one God.
- Recognize that God reveals himself as Father, Son, and Spirit in the mystery of the Holy Trinity.

Gathering WE ARE INVITED
1. Open

Personal Experience Ask volunteers to describe times when they attended a Baptism.

Prayer Ask the students to keep in mind their experiences of the Sacrament of Baptism as you pray the prayer together.

Working with the Text
Read aloud or summarize the text on this page. Point out that each person in the story was baptized in the name of the Father, the Son, and the Holy Spirit. **What family have the newly baptized members joined?** (the Church family)

Working with the Pictures
- Call attention to the photograph. **How is this Baptism similar to the Baptism you attended?** (Possible answer: the person's family is gathered at the baptismal font with the priest and godparents.)
- Invite volunteers to respond to the caption question. Reinforce the belief that we become members of the Church community through the Sacrament of Baptism.

CHAPTER 5
We Believe in God

PRAYER

God of loving community, we believe that you love us and care for us. Help us come to know you better through your Church.

"John Paul, I baptize you in the name of the Father, and of the Son, and of the Holy Spirit."

Joan watched her little brother crinkle up his nose as Father Al poured the water. She smiled at her mother and took a deep breath. Now it was her turn.

Joan bent her head over the baptismal font. She heard Father Al's words clearly. "Joan Marie, I baptize you in the name of the Father, and of the Son, and of the Holy Spirit."

Joan stepped back with Aunt Thea, her sponsor. She watched as her father leaned over the water. "James Benedict, I baptize you . . ."

Everyone at Mass clapped. Joan's mother was crying happy tears. Now everyone in the family belonged to the Church family, too.

When did you become a member of the Church?

30 : WE ARE INVITED

Resource Center

Teaching Tip
Handling sensitive topics Be aware that there may be students in the class who have not yet been baptized. Without personalizing the situation, emphasize that God loves *all* people, whether or not they are baptized. In addition, point out that people are baptized at different ages, as shown by the opening story.

Link to the Faith Community
Remind the students that each time we enter a church and make the Sign of the Cross with holy water, we are remembering our Baptism. This prayerful gesture links us to all the members of the Church community and to Jesus, whose life we share through Baptism.

Notes: Opening the Chapter

One God

On the Sunday after their Baptism, Joan and her family went to Mass together. With the rest of the parish community, they stood to pray the Creed. The *Nicene Creed* is a statement of the beliefs we share as Christians. "We believe in one God," they began.

Long ago people believed in many gods or spirits. People saw the power of nature. They thought trees or rocks or storms had their own gods. Sometimes these gods were not much stronger or kinder than humans. According to the old stories, these gods often played cruel tricks on people.

But God wanted people to know and love him alone. So God began to **reveal** himself, or share himself with people. The people of Israel were the first to recognize the one true God. The Bible tells us what they learned about God. We know that God is one. God is all-powerful. God always was and always will be. And God is not cruel or mean but completely loving and just.

An ancient Jewish prayer begins, "Hear, O Israel! The Lord our God, the Lord is one." Jewish people sometimes display special cases like this one, containing the words of the prayer.

Catholics Believe...

in the mystery of the Holy Trinity: one God who is Father, Son, and Holy Spirit.

Catechism, #234

WE EXPLORE : 31

WE EXPLORE
2. Build

Working with the Text

- As you read aloud or summarize *One God*, use *The Language of Faith* below to develop further the term *reveal*.
- Explain that we receive our belief in the one true God from the Jewish people, the people of Israel, who are our ancestors in faith.
- Remind the students that Jesus and his human family were Jewish and believed in the same God we now believe in.
  How do you think Jesus learned about his Jewish faith? (from his family members and the teachers in the synagogue) **How do you learn about your faith?** (from family members, the Bible, the Church)

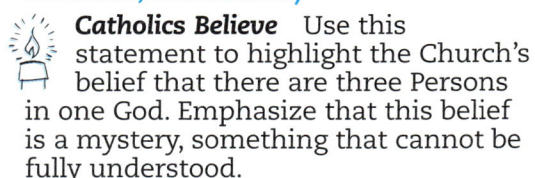

Catholics Believe Use this statement to highlight the Church's belief that there are three Persons in one God. Emphasize that this belief is a mystery, something that cannot be fully understood.

Working with the Pictures

Call attention to the Jewish prayer case shown on this page and identify it as a *mezuzah* (ma•zoo•zah). See *Art Background* below.

The Language of Faith

Reveal, from the Latin word *revelare*, literally means "to draw back the veil." When God reveals himself, he is making himself known to us. Out of love for us, God draws back the veil so that we can know God and his love for us. We believe that Jesus reveals most fully for us who God is.

Teaching Tip

Memorization As a homework assignment you may wish to have the students memorize the Apostles' Creed, which is found on page 176 of the student text. Assign a few lines of the Creed to each student, and have him or her copy the lines on index cards. Schedule time at the next meeting for the students to assemble their cards in sequence and practice praying the Creed.

Art Background

Many Jewish people display a mezuzah on an entrance doorway. As they enter or leave, they touch the mezuzah with the right hand and pray from memory the words of Scripture *(Deuteronomy 6:4–9)* written on a scroll inside the prayer case. The words of this central Jewish prayer, which is known as the *Shema* (sheh•MAH), profess the Jewish people's belief in the one true God.

We Explore
Build *Continued*
Working with the Text

- As you read aloud or summarize the text, use *The Language of Faith* below to develop further the meanings of the highlighted terms.
- Be sure the students understand the meaning of the word *trinity*. Point out the three relationships within the Holy Trinity—Father, Son, and Holy Spirit. To help the students understand the idea of "three in one," name three relationships that the students may have, such as son, brother, cousin; or daughter, sister, aunt.

    Scripture Signpost Explain that this greeting from Scripture expresses our belief in the Holy Trinity. Encourage volunteers to respond to the question. **(at Mass)**

Working with the Pictures

- Point out the two symbols on this page. **How does the shield show the Holy Trinity? (with a circle of three fish)**
- Point out that the second symbol uses a triangle and circle with an eye inside to show the Holy Trinity. The triangle stands for the three Persons in one God. The circle represents God's eternal nature. The eye is a symbol of the all-seeing God.

    Provide the students with art materials to create their own Trinity symbols.

    Alternative Have the students complete this activity as a homework assignment. Schedule time during the next meeting for volunteers to share their completed artwork.

Father, Son, and Holy Spirit

Scripture Signpost
"The grace of the Lord Jesus Christ and the love of God and the fellowship of the holy Spirit be with all of you."
2 Corinthians 13:13
Where do we hear these words?

It was Jesus who taught us the greatest truth about God. Jesus taught us about the one God who is at the same time three Persons: Father, Son, and Holy Spirit.

Jesus called God *Abba*, a word that means "Father" or "Daddy." Jesus taught us to call God our Father, too. By his actions Jesus also helped us see that he was the Son of God. Jesus was not just a very holy human. He was and is God the Son, who became human to save us. And Jesus asked his Father to send us the Holy Spirit, who is God's love and grace present with us.

We call this truth about God the mystery of the **Holy Trinity**. The word *trinity* means "a union of three." A **mystery** is a truth of our faith that we believe even though we cannot fully understand it. We continue to learn about the Trinity from the Church and from the people who love us. We are baptized in the name of the Father and of the Son and of the Holy Spirit.

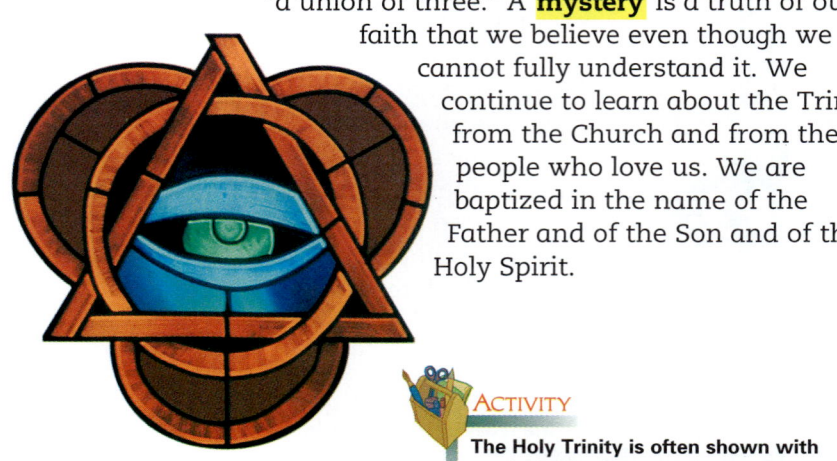

Activity
The Holy Trinity is often shown with symbols like the ones shown on this page. Make up your own symbol for the Holy Trinity.

Resource Center

The Language of Faith

- The doctrine of the **Holy Trinity** is a central Christian belief. After much reflection on God, the nature of God, and the Scriptures, the Church fathers declared that in the life of Jesus, God is revealed as Father, Son, and Spirit. The doctrine of the Trinity teaches us that God lives in *relationship*, and because we are created in the image of God, we are made to live in relationship with God and with one another.

- The word **mystery** comes from the Greek *mysterion*, which means "something closed, a secret." Our infinite God cannot be fully understood by our finite minds. God, who is a mystery, is revealed to us by faith. Faith complements reason, and the two work together to help us understand the mystery of God.

Notes: Building the Chapter

Three in One

This legend tells how one good storyteller tried to explain the Holy Trinity.

Bishop Patrick had a hard job. Patrick had come to Ireland to tell people about Jesus. He wanted to invite the Irish people to be baptized. But they had their own beliefs. They worshiped the sun and the earth as gods.

One day Bishop Patrick was sitting on a rock in a field, trying to tell people about God. "Why do you pray to three gods?" someone asked. "You pray to the Father, the Son, and the Holy Spirit. How can you say there is only one God?"

Patrick tried to think of a way to explain the Holy Trinity. He looked around. Next to the rock was a patch of clover, a small plant with three leaves on one stem. The Irish word for clover is *shamrock*. Bishop Patrick plucked a shamrock from the ground. He held it up.

"See," he said. "Even the plants of the field tell about God. The shamrock has three leaves but only one stem. Father, Son, and Holy Spirit are not three gods, but one God."

- How do you think the people felt about Bishop Patrick's story?

ACTIVITY
Draw a shamrock. Write *Father* on one leaf, *Son* on a second leaf, and *Holy Spirit* on the third leaf. Write *God* on the stem. Use your drawing to tell Bishop Patrick's story to a family member.

Our Moral Guide
Believing in God should make a difference in our lives. When our actions show that we believe in God, we are *witnessing* to our faith.

Catechism, #323

Name one way you can show by your actions that you believe in God.

WE EXPLORE
Build *Continued*

Working with the Text

- Read aloud or summarize the text. Point out that Patrick, as a bishop of the Church, taught the Christian faith to the people of Ireland. Explain that today the bishops of the Church continue teaching the Christian faith to people around the world.
- For more information about Saint Patrick, see *Background* below.
- Invite volunteers to answer the bulleted question. (Possible answers: happy to understand God better, grateful for an explanation.)

Our Moral Guide Be sure the students understand the word *witnessing*. Tell them that people who have real faith are *living* their faith through their actions each day: they are not just talking about it but are living it with their actions. Encourage volunteers to respond to the caption by thinking of how they might help out at home and at school. (Possible answers: helping younger siblings, being kind to someone who has no friends.)

To help the students visualize the concept of the Trinity, refer to the graphic organizer on page 29B. You may wish to do the suggested activity or one of your own choosing. Then provide drawing materials for the activity, and draw or show a picture of a shamrock.

Working with the Pictures

- Call attention to the illustration. **What is Bishop Patrick holding?** (a bunch of shamrocks)
- Encourage the students to use the shamrocks they made to describe the Trinity to their families.

Teaching Tip
Answering questions The students may ask whether Bishop Patrick and Saint Patrick are the same person. Tell the students that while Patrick was living in Ireland after his ordination, he was known to the Irish people as Bishop Patrick. It was only after his death, when the Church recognized Bishop Patrick's special holiness, that he was named a saint. He is now known as Saint Patrick.

Background
Saint Patrick was born c. 389 in Roman Britain. At the age of sixteen, he was sold into slavery and taken to Ireland. While in slavery Patrick turned to religion as a source of comfort and strength. Eventually Patrick escaped slavery and returned to Britain (and some say to Gaul, present-day France) to study for the priesthood. Patrick was determined to return to Ireland and teach the Irish people about the one true God. He did return to Ireland and was met with strong opposition by the leaders of the indigenous religions. However, Patrick continued his teaching and was made a bishop in 431. He died c. 461. Saint Patrick is the patron saint of Ireland, and his feast day is celebrated on March 17.

PARISH : 33

We Reflect
Review

Recall Encourage volunteers to respond to the questions. (the people of Israel; in the name of the Father, the Son, and the Holy Spirit)

Think and Share Allow the students to consider their answers before responding. (Possible answers: We know God loves us; we trust God; we know that God will continue to reveal himself to us as we grow in our faith.)

Continue the Journey You may want to work as a group to complete the activity.

Alternative Have the students complete the activity as a homework assignment. Schedule time during the next meeting for volunteers to share their prayers. Encourage the students to use their prayers to recall the Holy Trinity.

We Live Our Faith *At Home:* Share with the students one way you will live your faith this week in your home. *In the Parish:* Ask the students to be aware of the ways we address God as Father, Son, and Holy Spirit at Mass. Some examples include the Sign of the Cross and when the priest ends a prayer with these words: "Grant this through our Lord Jesus Christ, your Son, who lives and reigns with you and the Holy Spirit, one God, forever and ever."

Faith Journal The students may begin pages 9–10 of their *Faith Journal* in class and complete them at home. As a part of your own spiritual development, complete *Your Faith Journal* (page J6) for this chapter.

RECALL
Who were the first people to recognize that there is one true God? In whose name are we baptized?

THINK AND SHARE
Why do you think we believe in the mysteries of our faith even though we don't fully understand them?

CONTINUE THE JOURNEY
Finish each prayer in your own words.

God our Father, _____

Jesus, Son of God, _____

Holy Spirit, help us _____

WE LIVE OUR FAITH

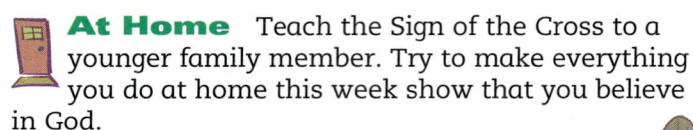

At Home Teach the Sign of the Cross to a younger family member. Try to make everything you do at home this week show that you believe in God.

In the Parish Listen at Mass for ways that we pray to the Holy Trinity. Join in these prayers.

34 : We Reflect

Resource Center

Optional Enrichment Activity
Invite the students to add to their shamrock drawings by writing descriptive phrases about each of the Persons of the Trinity on the appropriate leaves, such as *God the Father is kind and loving; Jesus the Son is our Savior; the Holy Spirit gives us the courage to do the right thing.*

Assessment Tip
Use the students' responses to the *Continue the Journey* activity to assess their progress in understanding the concept of the Holy Trinity and how it relates to their own lives.

Faith Journal

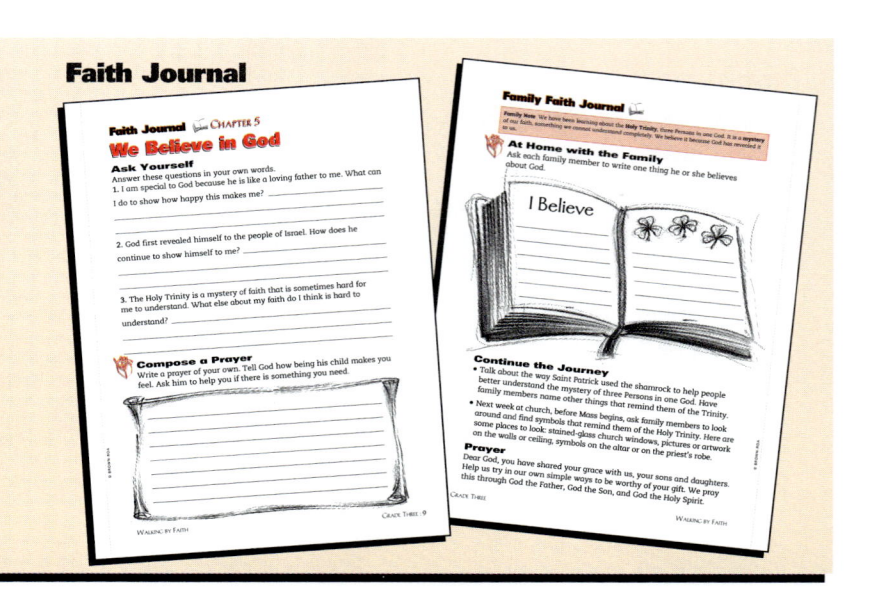

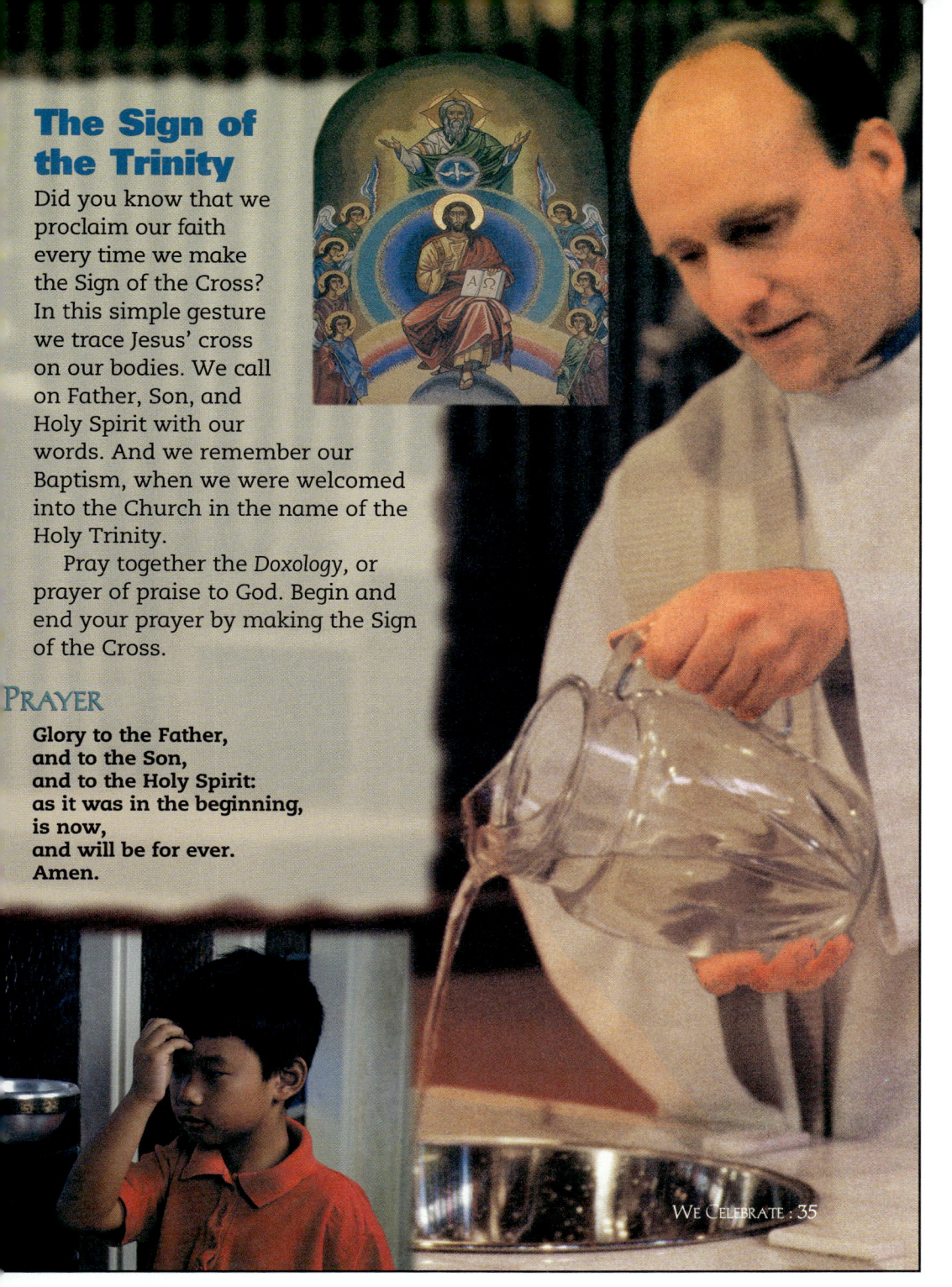

The Sign of the Trinity

Did you know that we proclaim our faith every time we make the Sign of the Cross? In this simple gesture we trace Jesus' cross on our bodies. We call on Father, Son, and Holy Spirit with our words. And we remember our Baptism, when we were welcomed into the Church in the name of the Holy Trinity.

Pray together the *Doxology*, or prayer of praise to God. Begin and end your prayer by making the Sign of the Cross.

Prayer

Glory to the Father,
and to the Son,
and to the Holy Spirit:
as it was in the beginning,
is now,
and will be for ever.
Amen.

We Celebrate
3. Close

Working with the Text

Explain that the word *doxology* means "words of glory." When we pray a doxology, we use words of praise and glory about the Father, the Son, and the Holy Spirit.

Working with the Pictures

- Call attention to the mosaic shown at the top of the page. Point out the depiction of God the Father as the older man, Jesus as the younger man, and the Holy Spirit as a dove. Explain that the picture is only a simple way of imagining the Trinity.

- Call attention to the two Greek letters shown on the book in the mosaic. Explain that these are the first and last letters of the Greek alphabet, symbolizing that Jesus Christ is the beginning and the end of all things.

- Invite volunteers to describe the remaining photographs, which show a priest at a baptismal font and a boy making the Sign of the Cross. **How do both of these photographs show faith in the Holy Trinity?** (The priest is preparing to baptize someone in the name of the Trinity; the boy is showing his faith in the Trinity by making the Sign of the Cross.)

Prayer Close the session by praising the Holy Trinity in gesture and prayer. Gather the students together. Begin the prayer experience by leading the class in making the Sign of the Cross. Then have the students bow slightly as you pray together the doxology. End the prayer by praying the Sign of the Cross together.

Link to Liturgy

At the end of the Eucharistic Prayer at Mass, the celebrant sings or says another form of the doxology: "Through him, with him, and in him, in the unity of the Holy Spirit, all glory and honor is yours, almighty Father, forever and ever." The people respond, "Amen." Invite the students to listen carefully for these words of praise the next time they attend Mass.

Link to the Family

To help your students' families stay connected with what you are exploring in religion class, send home the Unit Two Family Letter from the Resource Package.

Notes: Closing the Chapter

Getting Ready: Chapter 6

We Worship God

Program Resources
Student Text, pp. 36–41
Student Faith Journal, pp. 11–12
Your Faith Journal, p. J7
Chapter 6 Transparency
Unit Two Music and Liturgy Resources

Unit Two (God)
People of God

Key Content Summary
The Church responds to God's love in prayer and worship.

Planning the Chapter

	Pacing Guide *Suggested time/Your time*	Content	Objectives	Materials
Open	10–15 min./ _____ min.	*We Are Invited*, p. 36	• Explain that people come together to worship God.	• drawing materials
Build	20–25 min./ _____ min.	*We Explore*, pp. 37–38	• Identify community worship as an integral part of Catholic prayer. • Examine prayer as communication with God.	• Bibles • Chapter 6 Transparency from the Resource Package
		Stepping Stones, p. 39	• Explore different ways of praying.	
Review	15–20 min./ _____ min.	*We Reflect*, p. 40	• Demonstrate understanding of chapter concepts. • Apply learning through activity. • Practice faith at home and in the parish.	• copies of previous Sunday's parish bulletin • *Student Faith Journal*, pp. 11–12 • *Your Faith Journal*, p. J7
Close	10–15 min./ _____ min.	*We Celebrate*, p. 41	• Summarize ways of praying at Mass.	• Unit Two Music and Liturgy Resources from the Resource Package

For additional suggestions, see Scheduling, pp. T35–T37.

Catechism in Context

Doctrinal Foundation This chapter explores our duty and privilege to worship God through prayer and action. The culmination of our worship is the celebration of the Eucharist, the source and summit of the Christian life. When we do what Jesus told us to do in memory of him, we offer to God Christ's own sacrifice: Christ's body broken on the cross, his blood poured out for the forgiveness of sins. We do so in a sacramental way, with the priest blessing the bread, which becomes Christ's Body, and the wine, which becomes his Blood, through the power of the Holy Spirit. Christ's Passover prayer of blessing (praise, thanks, intercession, and petition) is the model for our Eucharistic Prayers at Mass. We make his prayer our own when we participate in it; we make his sacrifice our own when we share in it with our lives.

See Catechism of the Catholic Church, #752.

One-Minute Retreat for Catechists

Read
"Our prayer brings great joy and gladness to our Lord. He wants it and awaits it."
—*Julian of Norwich*

Reflect
How does prayer and worship of God bring me joy and happiness as well?

Pray
As my students learn about worship, Lord, help them see that it is a way of life. Let them recognize spiritual growth within themselves and in others, never seeking an end to the process. Through my lessons and my example, help them see that the Eucharist is the center of our life as a Church.

Visualizing the Lesson

Use this graphic organizer to help the students visualize the relationship between personal prayer, worship, and liturgy.

Draw the graphic organizer on the board or on chart paper, but omit the words *Personal Prayer*, *Worship*, and *Liturgy*. Write these words separately on the board. Ask the students to fill in the correct terms above their meanings.

Prayer
Communicating with God

- **Personal Prayer** — Private devotion, petition, and praise
- **Worship** — Honoring God in prayer and action
- **Liturgy** — Public, community worship (e.g., the Mass)

Library Links

Books for Children
I Can Pray the Mass by Mary Terese Donze ASC (Liguori Publications, 1-800-325-9521).

Donze retells the story of the first Mass and explains the actions and meanings of each part of today's Mass.

Books for Parents and Teachers
Dear God—Prayers for Families with Children by Kathleen Finley (Twenty-Third Publications, 1-800-321-0411).

Families can celebrate everyday events and Church feasts.

Multimedia
For children:
God Created Me. Episode #1, "Going Fishing" produced by the Archdiocese of St. Paul-Minneapolis (video) (BROWN-ROA, 1-800-922-7696).

A young girl's grandfather teaches her about prayer.

For parents and teachers:
What Is Prayer? (video) (Paulist Press, 1-800-218-1903).

The video presents insights into types of and reasons for prayer.

Organizations
For further information about worship, contact:
National Conference of Catholic Bishops
Liturgy Committee
3211 Fourth Street NE
Washington, DC 20017-1194
(1-202-541-3000)

Strengthening the Family Link

Here are some suggestions for reaching out to your students' families:

- Encourage the students to talk with family members about ways they can be more active in worship at Mass.
- Invite family members to join the class in writing special prayers of praise, thanks, intercession, and petition to God. After families write their prayers, pray them together.

Parish : 35B

Chapter 6 pages 36–41

Objectives
- Explain that people come together to worship God.
- Identify community worship as an integral part of Catholic prayer.
- Examine prayer as communication with God.
- Explore different ways of praying.

Gathering WE ARE INVITED
1. Open

Personal Experience Encourage volunteers to share their memorable experiences of Church. To spark ideas, share a memorable experience of your own.

Prayer Ask the students to think about their good experiences of Church as you pray the prayer together.

Working with the Text

- Explain that the word *Church* can mean both "a building" and "the people gathered." Emphasize that "the people gathered" is the more important meaning of *Church*.
- Provide the students with drawing materials. Display the students' completed artwork as a mural.

  Alternative Have the students complete this activity at home. Schedule time during the next meeting for volunteers to share their completed artwork.

Working with the Pictures

- Call attention to the photograph. **What game are the girls playing?** (a finger-play that makes a church building and shows the people inside the church)
- Invite the students to try the finger-play.

CHAPTER 6
We Worship God

PRAYER

Dear God our Father, we know that you love us. We want to return your love. We gather to honor you in prayer and action.

"Here is the church, here is the steeple. . . ."

You might have learned this finger-play game when you were younger. You build a church out of your folded hands. Do you remember how the rest of the rhyme goes? "Open the doors—and see all the people!"

There is an important truth hidden in that child's game. The Church is not only a building. It is also the people gathered. We gather in many kinds of buildings, all around the world. We speak different languages. But we all share the same reason for gathering. We come together in God's name.

ACTIVITY
Draw a picture of yourself at Mass. Put your picture together with your classmates' in a mural.

36 : We Are Invited

Resource Center

Link to the Faith Community

Help the students identify some members of the Catholic Church in the local community. Include the names of your local bishop and pastor, as well as other parish staff members and men and women religious. Include your name and the names of your students. Then invite the students to name a few other parishioners. Explain that everyone who belongs to the Church is related to all other Church members because we are all children of God.

Notes: Opening the Chapter

Honoring God

When we gather as Church, we come together to worship. **Worship** is honoring God in prayer and action. Worship is a way to return the love God shows us.

Prayer is communicating with God. When we pray, we talk to God, and we listen to God's message for us. We can pray by ourselves, but we are never really alone. Whenever we pray, the whole Church prays with us.

At Mass and in the sacraments, we pray as a community. This kind of public, community worship is called *liturgy*. Although Catholics have many ways to pray and worship, the Eucharist, or the Mass, is the most important. In the Eucharist the community joins with Jesus to worship God the Father.

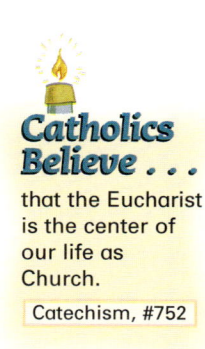

Catholics Believe... that the Eucharist is the center of our life as Church. Catechism, #752

How is Jesus with us in the Eucharist?

We Explore
2. Build

Working with the Text

- Read aloud or summarize *Honoring God*. Use *The Language of Faith* below to develop further the terms *worship* and *prayer*.
- To help the students visualize the relationship of prayer, worship, and liturgy, refer to the graphic organizer on page 35B. You may wish to do the suggested activity or one of your own choosing.
- Tell the students that Catholics all over the world are joined together by worshiping God.
- Be sure the students understand the meaning of the word *liturgy*. Liturgy means "the work of the people." Stress that liturgy happens when the community is gathered for worship. Ask for examples of liturgies the students have attended. (the Eucharist, sacramental celebrations)

   Catholics Believe Emphasize that everything we believe and do as the Church community is centered on our gathering for Eucharist.

Working with the Pictures

- Direct the students' attention to the photograph.
  How are the people in the picture worshiping God? (with words and actions)
- Invite volunteers to respond to the caption question. (Jesus is with us in the community gathered, in the Scriptures read, in the Eucharist shared, and in the priest presiding.)

The Language of Faith

- **Worship** is an element of most religions. Early Christian worship got its form from Jewish worship, which was composed of sacrifice and prayer, but worship for Christians took on new meaning because of Jesus. The Eucharist is a sacrifice and a sacred meal. The sacrifice offered in worship is now Jesus' sacrifice on Calvary. The meal we share nourishes us for our work as Christians. The Mass, our central form of worship, today includes our reenactment of the sacrifice of Jesus on Calvary (through which we have been redeemed), prayer, the proclamation of the Sacred Scriptures, and the sharing of the Body and Blood of Jesus. We gather in thanksgiving and go out to share the good news of God's love.

- It is with God's grace that we are called to **prayer**. God has already communicated with us, and we respond in prayer. The person who prays acts in faith and is led into a deeper relationship with God. Our prayer does not change God's mind or otherwise direct God into doing our will. Rather, *we* are changed by prayer. We become more trusting, more honest, and more open to the Holy Spirit working in our lives. God always hears our prayers. Through prayer we are healed and strengthened by the gift of grace.

We Explore
Build Continued
Working with the Text
- What are some reasons you pray? (Possible answers: to ask a favor of God for oneself or others, to thank God for something, to praise God, to complain to God.)
- As you read aloud or summarize *Forms of Prayer*, ask the students to think about times when they pray each type of prayer.
- **Landmark** Use *The Language of Faith* below to expand on the meaning of the word *psalm*. If time permits, have the students find the Book of Psalms in the Bible and see how long the book is.

Working with the Pictures
- Call attention to the handwritten, decorated page from the Book of Psalms. Point out that the picture shows King David, who may have written many of the psalms. Why do you think King David is shown playing a musical instrument? (because the Bible says David was a harpist and because the psalms were meant to be sung)
- Explain that the photograph shows an illuminated manuscript hand painted in France during the 1500s. Until the invention of the printing press in the 1400s, the books of the Bible were copied by hand. Monks handwrote and decorated the Scriptures as a way to glorify God. The beginning letter of the first word on the page was often enlarged and decorated. The gold, silver, and other bright colors helped light up, or *illuminate*, the page.

Forms of Prayer
Alone or together we pray for many reasons. At times we are moved to respond to the love and care God gives us. We return that love in prayers of blessing.

"Come, bless the Lord,
all you servants of the Lord. . . ."
—*Psalm 134:1*

Sometimes we are moved by God's greatness. So we pray prayers of praise.

"Give to the Lord, you families of nations,
give to the Lord glory and might;
give to the Lord the glory due his name!"
—*Psalm 96:7–8*

In times of need we ask God for help in a prayer of *petition*. When we do wrong or hurt someone we love, we say we are sorry. We ask forgiveness. When we sin, we ask God's forgiveness. We ask for God's mercy.

"Have mercy on me, God, in your goodness. . . .
For I know my offense;
my sin is always before me."
—*Psalm 51:1, 5*

We pray for other people, and we pray for the whole community. We pray prayers of *intercession*, asking for God's help.

"Do good, Lord, to the good,
to those who are upright of heart."
—*Psalm 125:4*

We don't always remember to thank God for the gifts we receive. God hears our prayers, answers our requests, and forgives our sins. So the kind of prayer we should pray most often is a prayer of thanksgiving.

"Give thanks to the Lord who is good,
whose love endures forever!"
—*Psalm 107:1*

Landmark A psalm is a prayer that can be sung to music. The Book of Psalms in the Bible contains 150 of these prayers.

38 : We Explore

Resource Center
The Language of Faith
The Book of **Psalms**, found in the Old Testament, has been central to Jewish worship for thousands of years. King David is often given credit as author, although modern Scripture scholars generally agree that David probably wrote only about 50 of the 150 psalms. Christianity shares this treasure-house of prayer with Judaism, and the psalms play a major role in the prayer life of the Church, as well as in the celebration of the Eucharist and the other sacraments.

Catechism Background
For information on other forms of prayer, see the *Catechism of the Catholic Church* (#2700–2724).

Notes: Building the Chapter

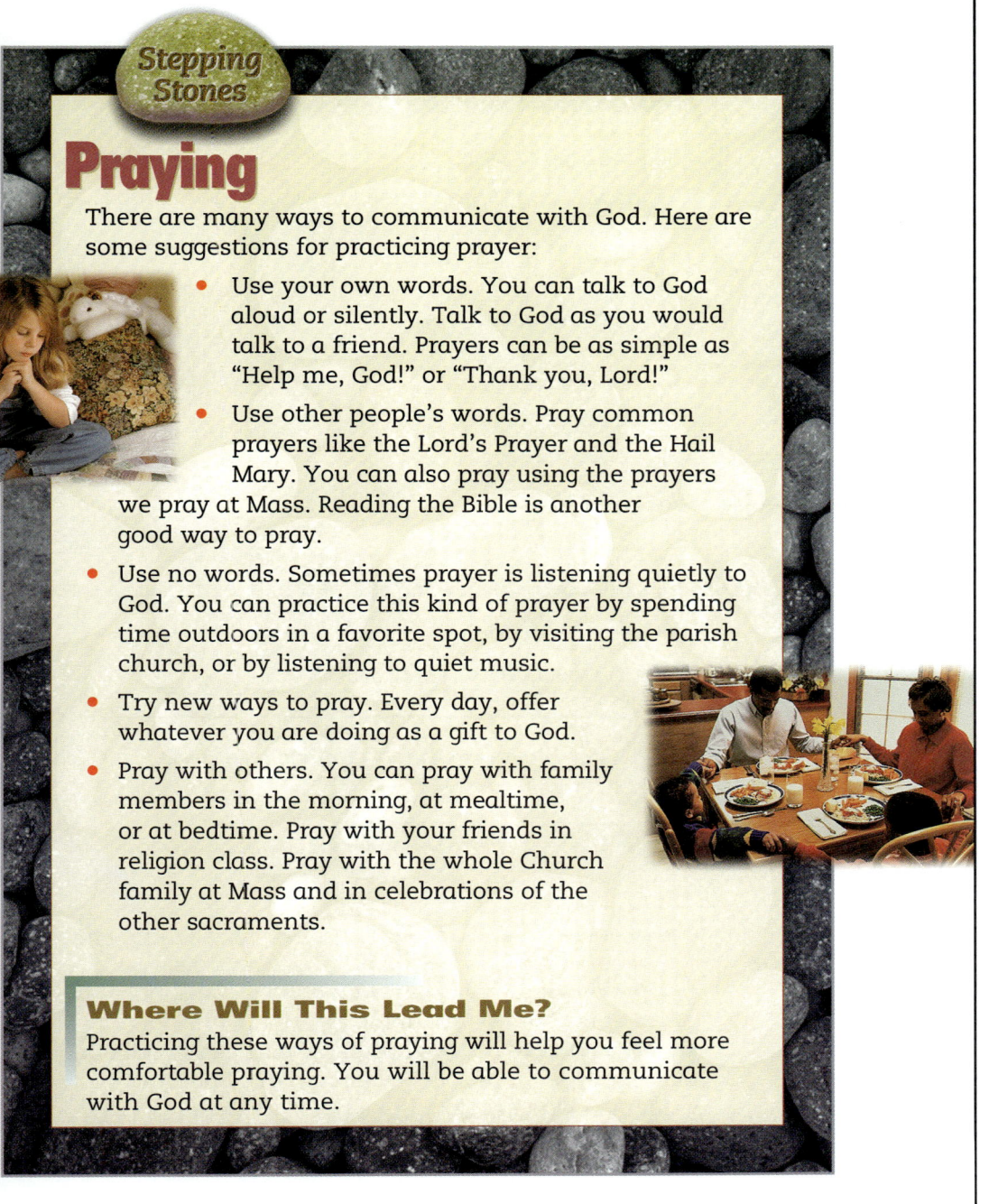

Stepping Stones

Praying

There are many ways to communicate with God. Here are some suggestions for practicing prayer:

- Use your own words. You can talk to God aloud or silently. Talk to God as you would talk to a friend. Prayers can be as simple as "Help me, God!" or "Thank you, Lord!"
- Use other people's words. Pray common prayers like the Lord's Prayer and the Hail Mary. You can also pray using the prayers we pray at Mass. Reading the Bible is another good way to pray.
- Use no words. Sometimes prayer is listening quietly to God. You can practice this kind of prayer by spending time outdoors in a favorite spot, by visiting the parish church, or by listening to quiet music.
- Try new ways to pray. Every day, offer whatever you are doing as a gift to God.
- Pray with others. You can pray with family members in the morning, at mealtime, or at bedtime. Pray with your friends in religion class. Pray with the whole Church family at Mass and in celebrations of the other sacraments.

Where Will This Lead Me?

Practicing these ways of praying will help you feel more comfortable praying. You will be able to communicate with God at any time.

WE EXPLORE : 39

WE EXPLORE
Build Continued

Stepping Stones

Working with the Pictures

Call attention to the two photographs. **What do the people in both photographs have in common?** (They are all praying.) **How are they different?** (The girl is praying alone, but the family is praying together.)

Working with the Text

- Read aloud or summarize each suggestion for practicing prayer. Emphasize that there are many ways to pray.
- Remind the students that prayer is available to us at any time and in any place.
- Read aloud *Where Will This Lead Me?*
- Encourage the students to look for new ways to pray each day and to pray often with others, especially with their families.

Practice If time permits, have partners practice praying aloud a few of the common prayers found on pages 174–177.

Multicultural Link

Tell the students that people of most religious faiths practice a form of prayer or meditation. In Islam the main form of prayer is a short worship service performed five times a day by Muslim men. The home and the synagogue are the main places for Jewish prayer. The weekly Sabbath and the holy days are important times for prayer. Many Hindus have home shrines, where they worship individually before physical images.

Assessment Tip

Observing the students during this prayer practice and during the remaining prayer experiences for this chapter can give you insight into their skill levels. Since praying is a subjective and personal experience, assess only those skills that can be taught and learned, such as the memorization of common prayers.

Teaching Tip

Maximizing success Some students may be unsure about trying some of the forms of prayer practiced on this page. Keep the prayer sessions short. Model the behaviors before asking individuals to respond. Compliment the students' efforts.

We Reflect
Review

Recall Invite volunteers to respond to the questions. *(honoring God in prayer and action; because the community joins with Jesus to worship God the Father)*

Think and Share Give the students sufficient time to consider their answers before responding. *(They need to be a part of the Church community.)*

Continue the Journey Work together as a group to complete this activity.

Alternative Have the students complete this activity as a homework assignment. Schedule time during the next meeting for volunteers to share their answers.

We Live Our Faith At Home: Encourage the students by sharing with them one way you pray at home with your family. (Also see *Link to the Family* below.) In the Parish: If possible, provide the students with copies of last Sunday's parish bulletin. Suggest that the students attend an upcoming celebration you think they would enjoy.

Faith Journal The students may begin pages 11–12 of their *Faith Journal* in class and complete them at home. As a part of your own spiritual development, complete *Your Faith Journal* (page J7) for this chapter.

Recall
What is worship? Why is the Eucharist the central worship of the Church?

Think and Share
Why do you think people need to gather to worship God?

Continue the Journey
Tell when you might use each form of prayer. Examples are given.

Blessing It's a beautiful day.
_____

Praise We are at Mass.
_____

Petition We are sorry for making fun of a new classmate.
_____

Intercession A classmate's parent is sick.
_____

Thanksgiving The big storm didn't damage our town.
_____

We Live Our Faith

At Home With your family, choose a time for regular family prayer. You may want to set up a prayer corner at home with a Bible, a rosary, and other things to help you pray.

In the Parish Look through your parish bulletin. Make a list of all the ways your parish community gathers to worship God. If possible, attend a celebration other than Sunday Mass, and tell your classmates about it.

Resource Center

Link to Liturgy
Remind the students that we pray at least part of one psalm at every Mass. During the Liturgy of the Word, we pray a *responsorial psalm*. The psalm is a response to the first reading. Ask the students to listen for and participate in the praying of the responsorial psalm or song at the next Mass they attend.

Link to the Family
Ask volunteers to talk about their family experiences of prayer. Encourage them to describe how families might pray together and as individuals. Invite volunteers to share with the class who in the family taught them how to pray.

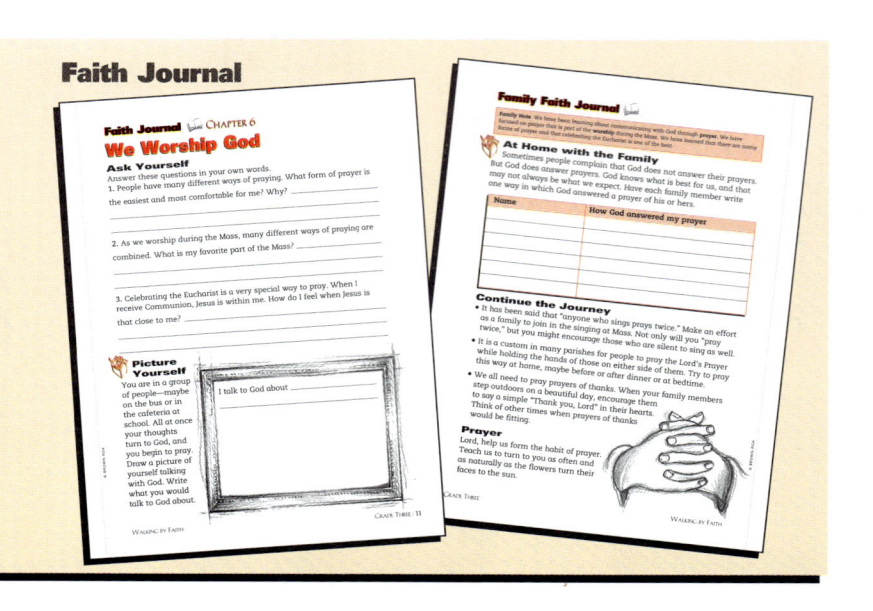

Glory to God

At Mass we pray in words and music. We pray with singing and silence. We even pray with our bodies as we stand, bow our heads, or fold our hands.

The words below are from a prayer we pray at Mass. Make up gestures to go with the words as you pray or sing this prayer together.

PRAYER

Glory to God in the highest,
and peace to his people on earth.
Lord God, heavenly King, almighty God
   and Father,
we worship you, we give you thanks,
we praise you for your glory.

We Celebrate : 41

WE CELEBRATE
3. Close

Working with the Text

- Read aloud or summarize *Glory to God*, emphasizing the many ways that we pray.
  How do we worship God at Mass? (with words, music, silence, gestures, and by sharing in the Eucharist)

- If time permits, invite students to make up accompanying gestures to the prayer. You may want to make some suggestions, such as arms upraised; arms outstretched; hands folded, opened, and raised.

Working with the Pictures

Call attention to the two photographs of prayer.
How are the people at Mass praying? (They are celebrating the Eucharist.)
How are the children praying? (They are using gestures and silent prayer.)

Prayer Gather the students in a circle. Then use words, gestures, and if possible, music to pray together the Glory to God. Begin the prayer experience with the Sign of the Cross. Use the gestures made up earlier in the session to sing or pray the prayer together. Add energy and enthusiasm to the words of the prayer to make it a prayer of praise. If time permits, you may want to pray the prayer several times before ending the experience with the Sign of the Cross.

Teaching Tip

Answering questions The idea that prayer is a way of having all our wishes come true is very common and can lead to frustration and a turning away from God. Explain that God does not always grant our wishes, but God is always with us when we ask for help.

🎵 Music and Liturgy Resources

To enhance your prayer and celebration, you may wish to use the Unit Two Music and Liturgy Resources from the Resource Package.

Notes: Closing the Chapter

Getting Ready: Chapter 7

We Belong to God

Program Resources
Student Text, pp. 42–47
Student Faith Journal, pp. 13–14
Your Faith Journal, p. J8
Chapter 7 Transparency
Unit Two Assessment

Unit Two (God)
People of God

Key Content Summary
We have a covenant relationship with God.

Planning the Chapter

	Pacing Guide Suggested time/Your time	Content	Objectives	Materials
Open	10–15 min./ _____ min.	*We Are Invited,* pp. 42–43	• Identify humans' universal need to belong.	
Build	20–25 min./ _____ min.	*We Explore,* pp. 44–45	• Explain that God gave the Ten Commandments as a sign of love. • Identify Jesus' death on the cross as a new covenant between God and all people.	• Chapter 7 Transparency from the Resource Package
Review	15–20 min./ _____ min.	*We Reflect,* p. 46	• Demonstrate understanding of chapter concepts. • Apply learning through activity. • Practice faith at home and in the parish.	• *Student Faith Journal,* pp. 13–14 • *Your Faith Journal,* p. J8 • video or books about synagogues (optional) • Unit Two Assessment from the Resource Package
Close	10–15 min./ _____ min.	*We Celebrate,* p. 47	• Identify the origin and purpose of the Magnificat.	

For additional suggestions, see Scheduling, pp. T35–T37.

41a : Chapter 7

Catechism in Context

Doctrinal Foundation This chapter teaches that the Church is a sign of God's covenant with all people. This new covenant is open to all nations and peoples. Those who believe in Christ and his teachings respond to the new covenant. It is an intimate covenant, being written on our hearts. The Ten Commandments of the old covenant are interpreted by Jesus, Paul, and the Church in terms of the Great Commandment to love God and neighbor. In the Beatitudes and the Sermon on the Mount, Jesus shows us how to read the commandments of the old law in the light of the new.

See Catechism of the Catholic Church, #781.

One-Minute Retreat for Catechists

Read
"I find the doing of the will of God leaves me no time for disputing His plans."
—George Macdonald

Reflect
How can I do the will of God in the classroom?

Pray
Lord, as you keep your promise to us, help us be faithful to your law. While it is in our nature to question things, help us accept your wishes for us. Let us not dispute, but embrace your words and your love.

Visualizing the Lesson

Use this graphic organizer to help the students visualize the covenants God made through Abraham, Moses, and Jesus.

Draw the graphic organizer on the board or on chart paper, but omit *Great family*, *Ten Commandments*, and *Eucharist* from the graphic organizer. Invite volunteers to supply the sign of each covenant.

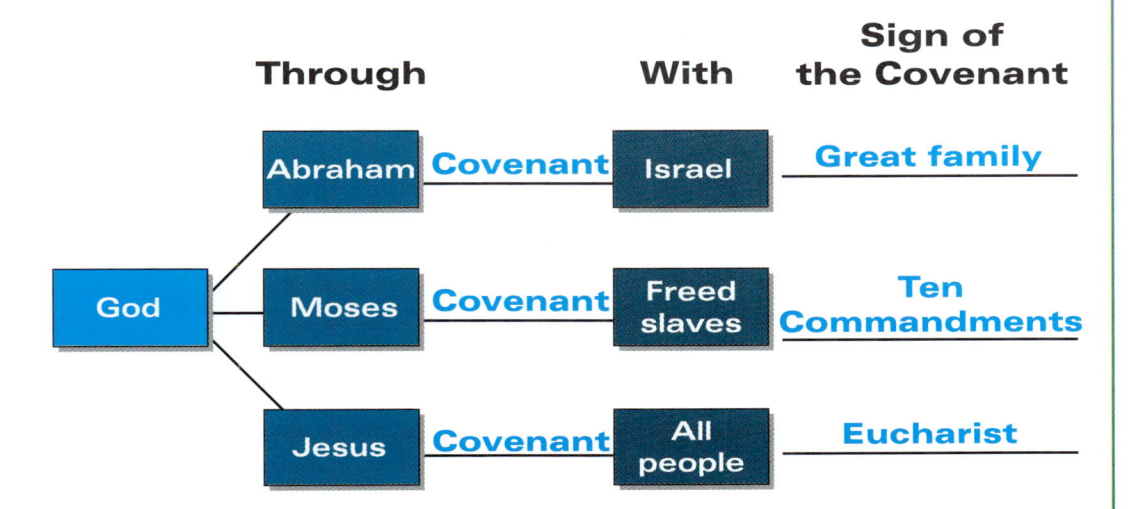

	Through		With	Sign of the Covenant
God	Abraham	Covenant	Israel	Great family
	Moses	Covenant	Freed slaves	Ten Commandments
	Jesus	Covenant	All people	Eucharist

Library Links

Books for Children
The Ten Commandments for Children by H.J. Richards (The Liturgical Press, 1-800-858-5450).

The Ten Commandments are explained in language children can understand.

Books for Parents and Teachers
You Can Know God—Christianity for Daily Living by Marilyn N. Gustin (Liguori Publications, 1-800-325-9521).

Gustin explores the action of God in our spiritual development.

Multimedia
For children:
The Commandments (video) (BROWN-ROA, 1-800-922-7696).

Each of the commandments is presented as being as relevant today as it was for the people of Israel.

Glory Day, "You Are Mine" by David Haas (video) (GIA Publications, 1-800-442-1358).

Use this song, featured in Haas's concert video or audio CD, to make music a part of the chapter material.

For parents and teachers:
The Ten Commandments (video) (commercial rental).

The life of Moses and the Ten Commandments are presented.

Organizations
For information about ways you can live the Great Commandment, contact:
Catholic Network of Volunteer Service
4121 Harewood Road NE
Washington, DC 20017
(1-202-529-1100)

Strengthening the Family Link

Here are some suggestions for reaching out to your students' families:

- Encourage the students to talk with family members about ways they can keep the Ten Commandments.
- Invite family members to join the class in praying the closing prayer based on the Magnificat.

PARISH : 41B

Chapter 7 pages 42–47

Objectives
- Identify humans' universal need to belong.
- Explain that God gave the Ten Commandments as a sign of love.
- Identify Jesus' death on the cross as a new covenant between God and all people.

Gathering WE ARE INVITED
1. Open

Personal Experience Share with the students the names of some groups to which you belong, such as your family or a club. Ask the students to name some of the groups to which they belong.

Prayer Invite the students to recall the groups to which they belong as you pray the prayer together.

Working with the Text

As you read aloud or summarize the story, be sure the students understand the meaning of the word *adoption*. Explain that this family chose Chan to become a member of their family.

Working with the Pictures

- Call attention to the photograph. **Why do you think this family wanted to celebrate?** (Possible answers: Bringing a new person into the family was a happy event; they knew how important it was to Chan to finally belong to a family.)
- Ask volunteers to respond to the caption question. (It feels happy, peaceful, safe.)

Chapter 7
We Belong to God

Prayer

We belong to you, O God. Thank you for choosing us and loving us. We will always be faithful to you.

Chan looked around the bedroom he shared with his brother, Greg. There was his bed, the top bunk. There were his books and toys on the shelf. Chan's backpack hung on a hook next to Greg's. On the wall there was room for a map of China, where Chan had been born.

He ran downstairs to join Greg, his sister, and Mom and Dad. They were going out for a picnic to celebrate Chan's *adoption*. Chan smiled. It had been a long time, but he finally belonged somewhere.

How does it feel to know that you belong?

Resource Center

Teaching Tip

Handling sensitive topics It is important that the students understand that an adopted child is as much a part of his or her family as a child who is born into a family. Emphasize how special it is to have been chosen for adoption. Explain that some families share this statement with their adopted children: "I wasn't expected, I was selected."

Link to the Faith Community

Remind the students that we belong to another family—our parish family. Our parish family makes us feel that we belong by inviting us to celebrate happy times and to be together in sad times. Our greatest celebration with our parish family is the Eucharist, when Jesus is with us in a special way.

Notes: Opening the Chapter

Scripture Story
I Will Be Your God

Abraham looked out at the darkness of the desert. He heard his wife, Sarah, lighting the lamp in their tent. Abraham sighed. He and Sarah were very old. They had no children, and they were lonely.

Abraham prayed. "God, you know how much we trust in you. You promised to give my family a wonderful land to live in. But what good will it do? We have no children. Soon we will die and be forgotten."

Then Abraham heard God speaking to him in his heart. "I know you are faithful," God said. "I am faithful, too. I keep my promises. Look up into the night sky." Abraham looked up. As far as he could see, thousands of stars sparkled.

"You will have children," God said. "Your family will outnumber the stars. They will be my very own people, and I will be their God. You and Sarah will be remembered forever. This is my **covenant**, my special holy agreement with you."

—based on Genesis 15:1–6, 17:1–8

Our Moral Guide

God's covenant is not a one-sided agreement. Being God's people means being faithful to what God wants for us. It means responding to God's love.

Catechism, #2062

How do we know what God wants us to do?

We Are Invited
Open Continued
Working with the Pictures
Point out the picture of Abraham and Sarah near their tent. Explain that Abraham raised sheep and lived in a tent so that he and Sarah could move on with the sheep as the sheep grazed. **What do you think life might have been like for Abraham and Sarah?** (Possible answer: Life was difficult due to the hard work and the moves from place to place.)

Working with the Text
- Read aloud or summarize *I Will Be Your God*.
- Emphasize that because Abraham trusted God, God rewarded him by promising him a place to belong and a large number of descendants.
- Use *The Language of Faith* below to further explain the highlighted term.

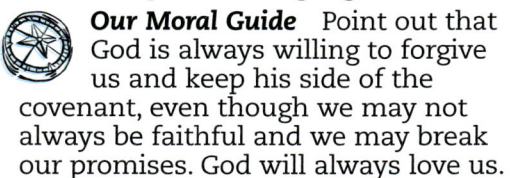

Our Moral Guide Point out that God is always willing to forgive us and keep his side of the covenant, even though we may not always be faithful and we may break our promises. God will always love us.

- Invite volunteers to answer the question. (Answers should include that we can follow the teachings of the Church.)

The Language of Faith
The word **covenant** is a translation of the Hebrew word *b'rith*, which means "testament," "agreement," or "pact." The covenant between God and Abraham was an unconditional promise or agreement. God promised Abraham that he would be with him in a special way. God asked Abraham only to believe. In the New Testament Jesus announces God's new covenant in word and action at the Last Supper **(Luke 22:20)**. Paul's Letter to the Corinthians **(2 Corinthians 3:6–18)** and the Letter to the Hebrews **(Hebrews 8:7–13, 9:15–16)** express the same teaching.

Scripture Background
According to **Genesis 17:1–8**, when Abram was ninety-nine years old, God entered into a covenant with him. God gave him the name *Abraham*, which is Hebrew for "father of a multitude." As father of the Jewish people, Abraham is the spiritual ancestor of all true believers. It is through Abraham that the Jewish people came to have faith in God's promises, a faith Christians now share with the Jewish people through Jesus.

We Explore
2. Build
Working with the Text

- To help the students visualize our covenant with God, refer to the graphic organizer on page 41B. You may wish to do the suggested activity or one of your own choosing.

- As you read or summarize *People of Promise*, use *The Language of Faith* below to further explain the Ten Commandments.
  How do we know that God kept his promise to Abraham? (Abraham and Sarah had a family that grew to be the people of Israel.) **What covenant did God give the people of Israel?** (the law, which includes the Ten Commandments) **What did God expect in return?** (faithfulness in keeping the commandments)

- Point out the great love God showed for us when he sent his own Son into the world as a new covenant with all people.

- **Catholics Believe** Use this statement to point out the continuing covenant God makes with us.

Working with the Pictures

- Point out the photograph of Pope John Paul II meeting with the Chief Rabbi of Rome.
- Read aloud the caption question, and invite volunteers to respond. (because we are all God's children, because we can work together to keep our promises to God)

Catholics Believe...
that the Church is a sign of God's new covenant with all people.
Catechism, #781

People of Promise

Abraham and Sarah did have a child and grandchildren as God had promised. Their family grew to be the people of Israel. Over and over again God reminded the people how much he loved and cared for them. God remained faithful to the covenant.

When the people of Israel were slaves in Egypt, God led them to freedom. God renewed the covenant with the people. Through their leader, Moses, God gave the people of Israel the **Ten Commandments**. The commandments are ways for people to show their faithfulness in return for God's love.

Jesus, God's own Son, was born into the people of Israel. Through the death of Jesus, God made a new covenant with all people. Jesus' followers became the Church, a new sign of God's loving promise.

All Jews and Christians are children of Abraham and Sarah. We are God's people.

God is faithful to us. We keep our promises to God.

Why is it important to remember what we share with people of other faiths?

44 : We Explore

Resource Center

The Language of Faith
The **Ten Commandments** sum up the moral code given by God to Moses on Mount Sinai. These ten distinct commandments are also called the *Decalogue*. The first three commandments deal with the love and worship of God. The remaining commandments deal with love for others.

Link to Justice
Tell the students that the fourth through the tenth commandments give us many ways to treat people justly, giving them what is their due. Have students choose one commandment this week and discuss how they will live it in a positive way that brings justice to someone.

Notes: Building the Chapter

We still follow the commandments God gave to the people of Israel. This chart shows the Ten Commandments and tells how we can keep them.

The Ten Commandments

1. I am the Lord, your God. You shall not have strange gods before me.
   - Love God above all things.
   - Trust in God, not in magic or luck.
2. You shall not take the name of the Lord your God *in vain*.
   - Show respect for God.
   - Don't swear or use bad language.
3. Remember to keep holy the Lord's day.
   - Participate in Mass and the other sacraments.
   - Take time for rest and prayer, and avoid unnecessary work.
4. Honor your father and your mother.
   - Obey, respect, and love family members.
   - Obey all good rules.
5. You shall not kill.
   - Respect all life.
   - Do not fight or use violence.
6. You shall not commit *adultery*.
   - Show respect for God's gift of *sexuality*.
   - Honor and support marriage and family life.
7. You shall not steal.
   - Don't take anything that doesn't belong to you.
   - Be careful with other people's things.
8. You shall not *bear false witness* against your neighbor.
   - Tell the truth.
   - Don't *gossip*.
   - Keep your good promises.
9. You shall not *covet* your neighbor's wife.
   - Be faithful to family members and friends.
   - Don't be *jealous*.
10. You shall not *covet* your neighbor's goods.
    - Make sure all people have what they need.
    - Don't be greedy or *envious*.

WE EXPLORE : 45

WE EXPLORE
Build *Continued*
Working with the Text
- Read aloud the first paragraph, which introduces the Ten Commandments and the suggestions for their application. Be sure the students understand the italicized words. See *Teaching Tip* below for suggested definitions.
- Point out that people of all ages are called by God to obey the commandments. By obeying the commandments, we show God that we love him and want to be faithful to him.

Working with the Pictures

Call attention to the photographs of a girl playing the piano with her grandfather and three children enjoying time together as friends. **How are the people in both photographs obeying the Ten Commandments?** (The girl is honoring the fourth commandment by spending time with her grandfather; the children are honoring the ninth commandment by being faithful to each other as friends.)

Teaching Tip
Clarifying concepts Consider using the following definitions to explain the italicized words in the chart.

in vain: in a disrespectful way; for no reason

adultery: unfaithfulness in marriage by sharing the special love meant for a husband or wife with someone else

sexuality: everything about us that makes us male or female

bear false witness: to tell lies about another person; to accuse someone of something they did not do

gossip: to spread information about others that might harm them

covet: to want something that belongs to another

jealous: holding too tightly to relationships

envious: desiring the relationships or possessions of others

Assessment Tip
Encourage students to read the chart on this page frequently. Encourage them to keep private records of the many ways they keep the commandments.

WE REFLECT
Review

Recall Invite volunteers to share their responses to the questions. *(a special, holy agreement between God and God's people; Abraham and Sarah)*

Think and Share Allow the students to think about their answers before responding. *(Responses should include the idea that by keeping the commandments we are demonstrating our love for God by honoring him and respecting others.)*

Continue the Journey Allow the students to work independently on the activity. If time permits, ask volunteers to read their promissory statements aloud.

Alternative Have the students complete this activity as a homework assignment. Schedule time during the next meeting for volunteers to share their promissory statements.

We Live Our Faith *At Home:* Brainstorm a list of ways the students can follow this commandment. You may want to have the students make reminders to post somewhere at home. *In the Parish:* If possible, contact a teacher at the Hebrew school, and explain the project. Ask that the Hebrew-school students respond to your class letter. If there is no Hebrew school in your vicinity, try contacting one via the Internet.

Faith Journal The students may begin pages 13–14 of their *Faith Journal* in class and complete them at home. As a part of your own spiritual development, complete *Your Faith Journal* (page J8) for this chapter.

RECALL
What is a covenant? To whom did God promise a great family?

THINK AND SHARE
Choose one of the Ten Commandments. How does keeping this commandment show love for God?

CONTINUE THE JOURNEY
You became part of God's people at Baptism. Renew your promise by filling out the form.

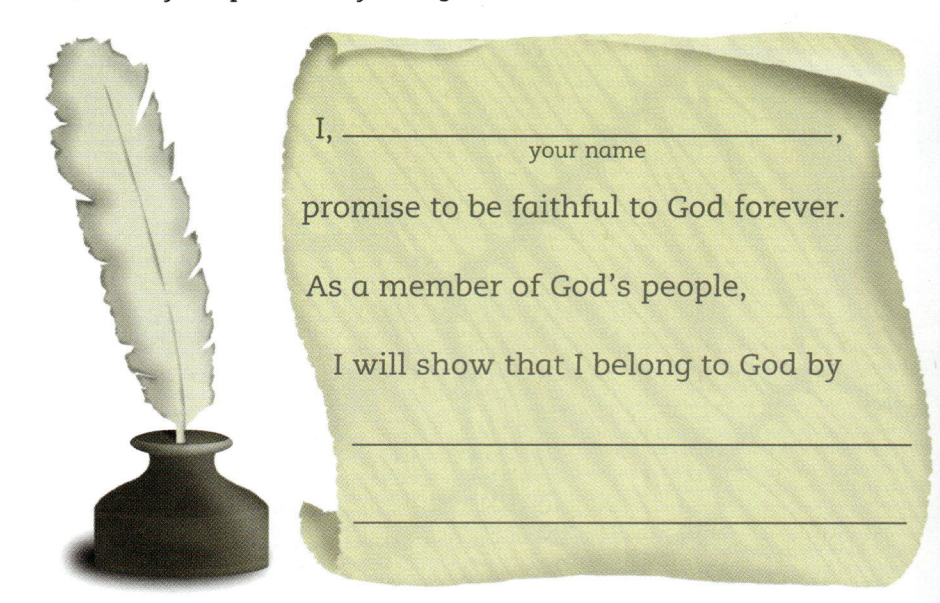

I, _____, your name
promise to be faithful to God forever.
As a member of God's people,
I will show that I belong to God by
_____
_____

WE LIVE OUR FAITH

At Home Find one way to keep the fourth commandment. Share your idea with a family member who can help you stick to it.

In the Parish As a class, write a letter to third graders who attend Hebrew school at a local temple or synagogue.

46 : WE REFLECT

Resource Center

Enrichment
optional Activity

Make arrangements for the group to visit a local synagogue or temple. Ask the rabbi to conduct a short tour and explain the significance of what the students see in the worship space. Ask the rabbi to emphasize, while conducting the tour, the beliefs that Jews and Christians share. Allow the students to ask appropriate questions. If a tour is not possible, you may want to show the students a video or bring in books about synagogues.

Assessment Tip
You may wish to copy the Unit Two Assessment from the Resource Package in preparation for giving the test after completing Chapters 5–8.

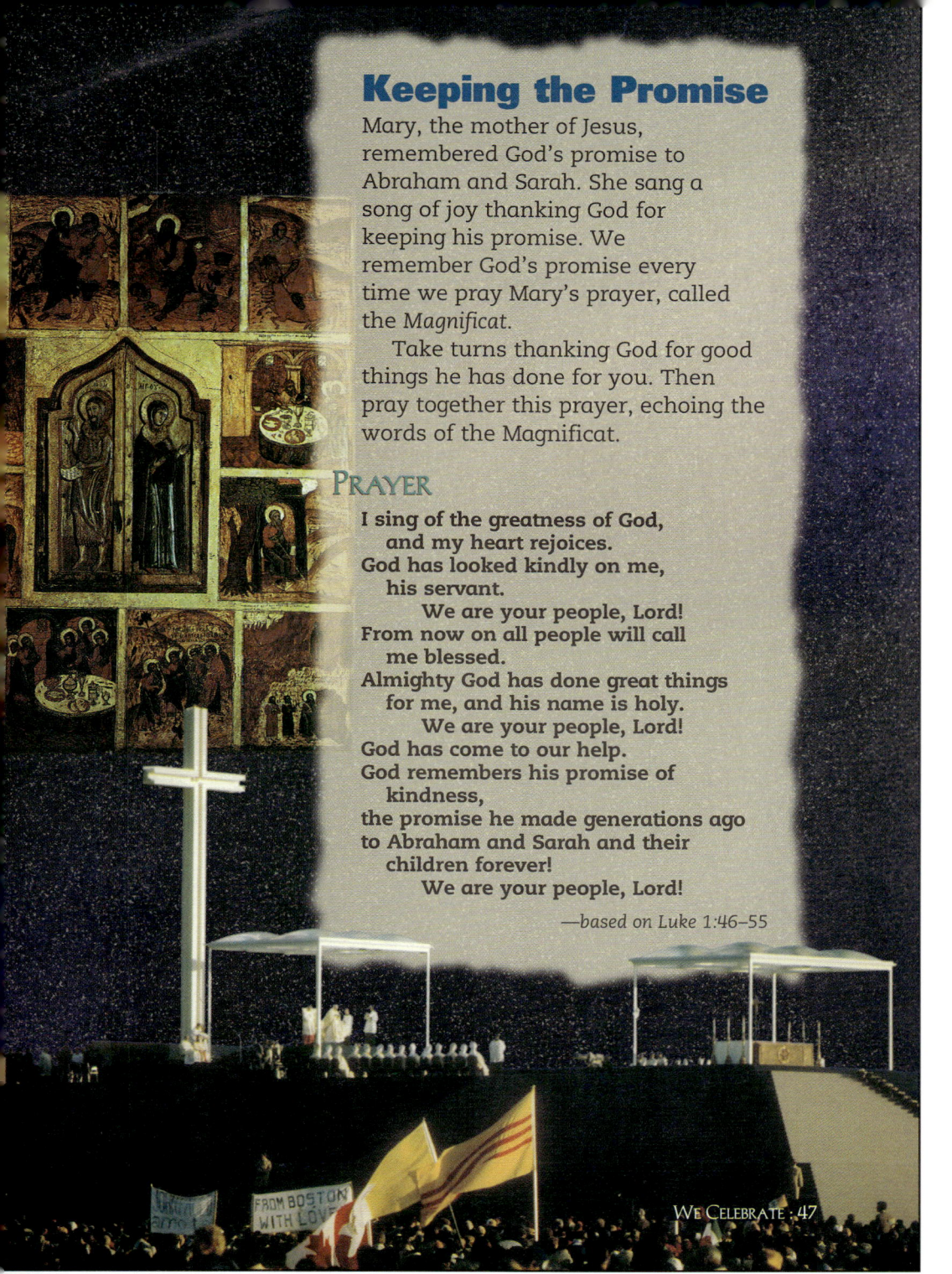

Keeping the Promise

Mary, the mother of Jesus, remembered God's promise to Abraham and Sarah. She sang a song of joy thanking God for keeping his promise. We remember God's promise every time we pray Mary's prayer, called the *Magnificat*.

Take turns thanking God for good things he has done for you. Then pray together this prayer, echoing the words of the Magnificat.

Prayer

I sing of the greatness of God,
  and my heart rejoices.
God has looked kindly on me,
  his servant.
    We are your people, Lord!
From now on all people will call
  me blessed.
Almighty God has done great things
  for me, and his name is holy.
    We are your people, Lord!
God has come to our help.
God remembers his promise of
  kindness,
the promise he made generations ago
to Abraham and Sarah and their
  children forever!
    We are your people, Lord!

—*based on Luke 1:46–55*

We Celebrate
3. Close

Working with the Text

- Read aloud or summarize the first paragraph of *Keeping the Promise*. Be sure the students understand the term *Magnificat*. Explain that *magnificat* comes from the Latin *magnificare*, which means "to magnify" or "to glorify." **What did Mary's prayer glorify?** (God, who promised Abraham and Sarah that they would become a great nation)
- Point out that Mary also glorified God for his promise to make her the mother of Jesus, who is God's own Son.

Working with the Pictures

- Point out the icon at the top of the page. Explain that this icon shows the story of Abraham and Sarah and their family. Have the students find Abraham and Sarah in the center of the icon. For more information, see *Art Background* below.
- Call attention to the photograph of Pope John Paul II celebrating an outdoor Mass in Boston. Explain that the people are celebrating the Eucharist as a sign of unity. **How do both pictures relate to this line of the prayer: "We are your people, Lord!"?** (The members of Abraham and Sarah's family as well as the Church family are children of God.)

Prayer Read aloud the second paragraph of *Keeping the Promise*. Then pray together the prayer based on Mary's Magnificat. You might want the students to pray the prayer as an antiphon—one half of the class prays the first two sentences. All respond "We are your people, Lord!" The other half of the class prays the next two sentences, and so on.

Teaching Tip

Memorization You might have the students refresh their memories of the Hail Mary, found on page 174, or memorize the Ten Commandments. Pair the students and allow time for practice.

Art Background

The Russian icon on this page depicts scenes from the life of Abraham and Sarah and their family. You might describe what is happening in a few of the scenes. Among the stories depicted in the panels of the icon are the angels' visit to Abraham and Sarah, the sacrifice of Isaac, and the destruction of Sodom.

Notes: Closing the Chapter

Unit Two Review

> **Objective**
> • Review the unit and assess progress.

Chapter Summaries
Use this information to reinforce key points before administering the review. These summaries will also help you assess the students' responses to *Show How Far You've Come*, page 49.

Chapter 5
- We become members of the Church through the Sacrament of Baptism.
- We believe in one God, who reveals himself to us as Father, Son, and Holy Spirit.
- We call one God in three Persons the Holy Trinity.

Chapter 6
- Prayer is communication with God.
- Community worship is an integral part of Catholic prayer.
- The Eucharist is our most important community worship, or liturgy.

Chapter 7
- God made a covenant with the Jewish people through Abraham and Moses as a sign of love and faithfulness.
- God gave the Ten Commandments to Moses as a sign of God's covenant with the people of Israel.
- Through Jesus' death and resurrection, God made a new covenant with all people.

Review
You may have the students work on the review in class or assign the exercises as homework to be completed with family members.

Which Words Don't Fit? Invite a volunteer to explain why the word *Mary* does not belong with the other words in group A. Then work through the rest of this exercise orally with the students.

Matching Review the students' answers as a class. If time permits, you may want to have the students use their glossaries to verify their responses.

Share Your Faith Have the students respond orally to this exercise as if they were on a Christian radio or TV talk show.

Unit Two Checkpoint
Review

Which Words Don't Fit? Circle the term in each group that does not belong.

A	B	C
1. Holy Spirit	1. prayer	1. adoration
2. Son	2. worship	2. (commandment)
3. (Mary)	3. liturgy	3. petition
4. Father	4. (sin)	4. intercession

D	E
1. (covet)	1. Patrick
2. covenant	2. shamrock
3. agreement	3. Trinity
4. promise	4. (England)

Matching Match the terms in Column B with their correct meanings in Column A.

Column A

_d_ 1. A statement of the beliefs we share as Christians.

_e_ 2. A song prayer from the Bible.

_a_ 3. The Mass.

_b_ 4. One God who is Father, Son, and Holy Spirit.

_c_ 5. A truth of our faith that we believe even though we do not understand it fully.

Column B

a. Eucharist
b. Holy Trinity
c. mystery
d. Nicene Creed
e. psalm

Share Your Faith Tell why you think prayer and worship are important in our lives.

48 : Review

Resource Center
Assessment Tips
Use one or more of the following strategies to assist you in assessing student progress:
- If you need a more detailed written review, you may give the Unit Two Assessment from the Resource Package.
- Ask the students to assess their own progress by listing the important ideas they learned in this unit. Then invite the students to share their lists with the group.
- Ask the students to consider ways that they are living the Ten Commandments, as well as ways they can do even more. Have volunteers share their responses.

Show How Far You've Come

Use the chart below to show what you have learned. For each chapter, write or draw the three most important things you remember.

People of God

Chapter 5 We Believe in God	Chapter 6 We Worship God	Chapter 7 We Belong to God
Look for responses that reflect the key points listed under Chapter Summaries.		

What Else Would You Like to Know?

List any questions you still have about the Holy Trinity, worship, or covenant.

_____

_____

_____

Continue the Journey

Choose one or more of the following activities to do on your own, with your class, or with your family.

- Look through your Faith Journal pages for Unit Two. Choose your favorite activity, and share it with a friend or family member.
- Plan a prayer celebration for your class or your family.
- Make a poster or bulletin board showing how to follow the Ten Commandments.

REVIEW : 49

Show How Far You've Come Use *Chapter Summaries* to evaluate the students' responses. Pay attention to responses that differ greatly from the key points of the chapters. Look for responses that indicate areas where presentation was unclear and needs additional attention. Review key concepts as needed. If time permits, extend this activity by asking the students to recall their favorite stories, activities, or pictures from this unit.

What Else Would You Like to Know? Encourage the students to share their questions and vote on a class list of three questions for you to explore together further.

Continue the Journey Schedule time during a later session for the students to demonstrate how they have completed one or more of these activities. For example:
- Ask volunteers to report about sharing *Faith Journal* entries.
- Discuss plans for the prayer celebration.
- Have the students view the posters or bulletin boards on display. Encourage the students to talk about some of the ways suggested for following the Ten Commandments.

Prayer

Gather the students into a circle to pray a prayer of thanks. Lead them in a spontaneous prayer of thanks for what they have learned about the Holy Trinity and worship in this part of their faith journey.

Reference Sources

For help in addressing the students' questions about this unit's topics, see:
- *The HarperCollins Encyclopedia of Catholicism* (HarperCollins, 1995).
- *The Modern Catholic Encyclopedia* (The Liturgical Press, 1994).
- *This Is Our Faith: A Catholic Catechism for Adults* by Michael Francis Pennock (Ave Maria Press, 1989).

Good resources for third graders include:
- *The Collins Dove Dictionary for Young Catholics* by Laurie Woods (Collins Dove, 1990).

Your parish community is another important resource. Priests, deacons, other staff members, catechists, godparents, sponsors, and members of religious communities are all good reference sources for answering the students' questions.

Link to the Family

If possible, allow students to take these pages home to share with family members.

PARISH : 49

Getting Ready: Chapter 8

Honoring Their Memory

Program Resources
Student Text, pp. 50–53
Student Faith Journal, pp. 15–16
Your Faith Journal, p. J9

Unit Two (God)
People of God

Key Content Summary
The witness of the saints builds the Church.

Planning the Chapter

	Pacing Guide Suggested time/Your time	Content	Objectives	Materials
Open	10–15 min./ _____ min.	We Are Invited, p. 50	• Identify Bishop Polycarp as a saint and martyr of the Church.	• world map or globe
Build	20–25 min./ _____ min.	We Explore, p. 51	• Explain why the Church honors saints and martyrs.	
Review	15–20 min./ _____ min.	We Reflect, p. 52	• Demonstrate understanding of chapter concepts. • Apply learning through activity. • Practice faith at home and in the parish.	• *Student Faith Journal*, pp. 15–16 • *Your Faith Journal*, p. J9
Close	10–15 min./ _____ min.	We Celebrate, p. 53	• Recognize All Saints' Day as an occasion to honor all the saints.	

For additional suggestions, see Scheduling, pp. T35–T37.

49A : CHAPTER 8

Catechism in Context

Doctrinal Foundation This chapter tells how and why we commemorate the saints. The earliest saints to be honored in the Church were martyrs, "witnesses" who were put to death by the Roman Empire because of their Christian faith, which forbade them to worship false gods or the emperor. It became customary to celebrate the Eucharist on the martyrs' tombs, in recognition of their share in Christ's sacrifice. The martyrs were remembered and honored primarily because of the example of their witness to Christ, even unto death.

See Catechism of the Catholic Church, #957.

Because they bore such a striking witness, their prayers, in the communion of saints, were sought. Later, "confessors" (any saints not martyrs who nevertheless witnessed to Christ in a memorable way) were also honored as saints and commemorated on their feast days. Honoring the saints inspires us to grow in faith: "Therefore, since we are surrounded by so great a cloud of witnesses, let us rid ourselves of every burden and sin that clings to us and persevere in running the race that lies before us, while keeping our eyes fixed on Jesus, the leader and perfecter of our faith. For the sake of the joy that lay before him he endured the cross, despising its shame, and has taken his seat at the right hand of the throne of God" (*Hebrews 12:1–2*).

One-Minute Retreat for Catechists

Read
"A man can be as truly a saint in a factory as in a monastery, and there is as much need of him in one as in the other."
—Robert J. McCracken

Reflect
In what ways can I imitate the saints in my daily life?

Pray
Lord, help me make my life more saintly. Let my students see that becoming a saint is not an impossible goal and that sainthood is achieved by forming habits of goodness.

Visualizing the Lesson

Use this graphic organizer to help the students visualize the relationship between *Christians*, *saints*, and *martyrs*.

Draw the graphic organizer on the board or on chart paper. Explain to the students that not all Christians are saints and not all saints are martyrs. Ask them to name one example of each. (Possible responses: Christian—myself, Saint—Saint Patrick, Martyr—Saint Polycarp.) Write in the examples they suggest.

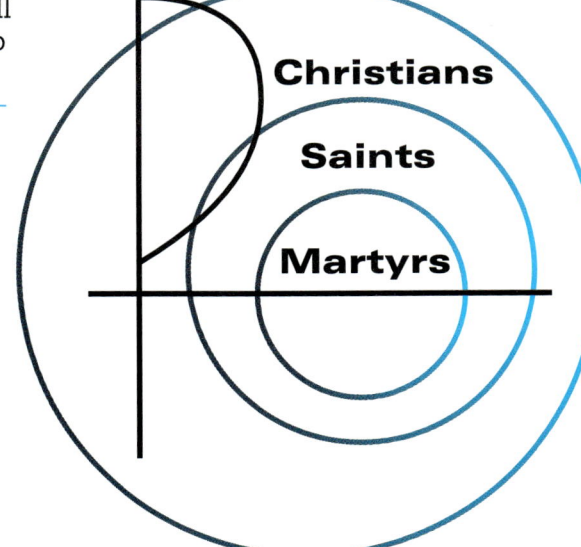

Library Links

Books for Children
The One-Year Book of Saints by Clifford Stevens (Our Sunday Visitor, 1-800-348-2440).
Saints inspire us all year long.

Books for Parents and Teachers
Roots, Deep and Strong—Great Men and Women of the Church by Mary Penrose OSB (Paulist Press, 1-800-218-1903).
This book contains short biographies of major figures of the Church.

The Saints and Our Children by Mary Reed Newland (TAN Books & Publishers, 1-800-437-5876).
A mother of seven children relates the lessons of the saints to the everyday lives of children.

Multimedia
For children:
An Empire Conquered (video) (BROWN-ROA, 1-800-922-7696).
This docudrama tells part of the story of the early Christian Church by reenacting the lives of some of the martyrs.

For parents and teachers:
Monsieur Vincent: St. Vincent de Paul (video) (Franciscan University Press, 1-614-283-3771).
The video tells the story of the Apostle of Charity.

Organizations
For information about ways to minister to others, contact:
National Association for
Lay Ministry
5420 S. Cornell Avenue
Chicago, IL 60615
(1-773-241-6050)

Strengthening the Family Link

Here are some suggestions for reaching out to your students' families:

- Encourage the students to talk with family members about ways they can become saints.
- Invite family members to join the students in choosing a patron saint for the class. Provide background information for several saints, including your parish's name saint, and have the students and their guests work together to choose the patron.

Chapter 8 pages 50–53

Objectives
- Identify Bishop Polycarp as a saint and martyr of the Church.
- Explain why the Church honors saints and martyrs.
- Recognize All Saints' Day as an occasion to honor all the saints.

Gathering
WE ARE INVITED
1. Open

Personal Experience Invite volunteers to name people in their own lives whom they believe to be holy persons.

Prayer Have the students think about these people as you pray the prayer together.

Working with the Text
- Tell the students that they will read about a bishop named Polycarp (PAHL•ee•kahrp), who was a very holy man.
- Read or summarize the text.
- For more information about Bishop Polycarp, see *Background* below.

Working with the Pictures
- Call attention to the stained-glass representation of Bishop Polycarp. Invite volunteers to describe the bishop's clothing and staff. For detailed information, see *Art Background* below.
- Read the caption aloud. If possible, show the students on a world map or globe where the present-day country of Turkey is located.

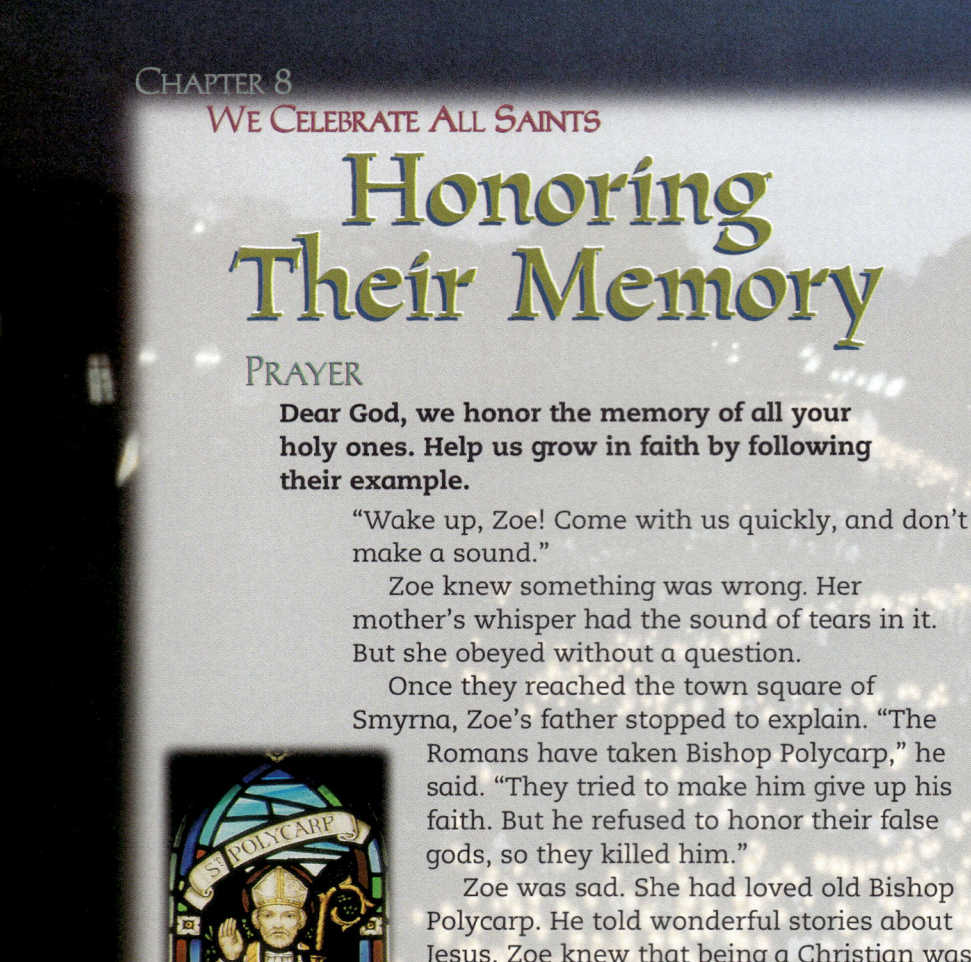

CHAPTER 8
WE CELEBRATE ALL SAINTS

Honoring Their Memory

PRAYER

Dear God, we honor the memory of all your holy ones. Help us grow in faith by following their example.

"Wake up, Zoe! Come with us quickly, and don't make a sound."

Zoe knew something was wrong. Her mother's whisper had the sound of tears in it. But she obeyed without a question.

Once they reached the town square of Smyrna, Zoe's father stopped to explain. "The Romans have taken Bishop Polycarp," he said. "They tried to make him give up his faith. But he refused to honor their false gods, so they killed him."

Zoe was sad. She had loved old Bishop Polycarp. He told wonderful stories about Jesus. Zoe knew that being a Christian was against the Roman law. But she had never thought they would bother the old bishop, who was so kind to everyone.

"Will they come for us, too?" Zoe asked.

Her father hugged her. "I hope not," he said. "But if they do, I hope we will be as strong in our faith as Bishop Polycarp."

Saint Polycarp was the bishop of Smyrna, in what is today the country of Turkey. He may have been a student of Jesus' friend and apostle, Saint John.

50 : We Are Invited

Resource Center

Background
Saint Polycarp (d.156) faced many difficulties in Smyrna because Christians were a minority there. At the age of eighty-six, he was arrested by Roman soldiers who demanded that he renounce Christ. When Bishop Polycarp refused, he was burned at the stake. February 23 is the feast day of Saint Polycarp.

Art Background
In this stained-glass window, Saint Polycarp wears a *miter* (a tall, pointed hat) and a *cope* (a cloak). He carries a tall staff called a *crosier*. These are signs used by the artist to show that Polycarp was a bishop.

Notes: Opening the Chapter

"But why are we here?" asked Zoe.

Her mother pointed to a corner of the square, where a small group of Christians had gathered. "The Romans left Bishop Polycarp's body in the street," she said. "We have come to honor him by burying his body."

Zoe was a little frightened as her family drew close to the bishop's body. She had never seen a dead person. But Bishop Polycarp did not look scary. He seemed to be sleeping peacefully. There was a smile on his face.

Every year from then on, Zoe's family and the other Christians met at the grave of Bishop Polycarp. They celebrated the Eucharist, using his tomb as an altar. They called him a **saint**, a person of great holiness. By remembering Saint Polycarp, the Christians of Smyrna strengthened their own faith. It was as if the old bishop were still with them, teaching and caring.

Catholics Believe...
that honoring the memory of the saints is a way to grow in faith.

Catechism, #957

In early pictures martyrs are shown wearing white robes and carrying crowns as signs of their victory over death. In the background are palm branches, another sign of victory.

We Remember Saints

The first saints honored by the Church were martyrs like Saint Polycarp. A **martyr** is someone who remains a faithful *witness* even when it means giving up his or her life. The first saints' feast days were like the gatherings at Saint Polycarp's grave.

Not all saints are martyrs. There are many ways to be faithful and to live a holy life. But all saints are like Bishop Polycarp in one important way. When we honor them, they help us grow in faith. Their prayers help us on our journey.

We Explore : 51

We Explore
2. Build
Working with the Text

- To help the students visualize the relationship of saints, martyrs, and Christians with God, refer to the graphic organizer on page 49B. You may wish to do the suggested activity or one of your own choosing.

- As you continue reading or summarizing the text, use *The Language of Faith* below to further explain the terms *saint* and *martyr*.

- **Who are some other saints and martyrs you know?** (Possible answers: Saint Patrick, Saint Francis of Assisi, Saint Joan of Arc.)

- **Catholics Believe** Explain that retelling the stories of the saints is a way we can follow Jesus more closely.

Working with the Pictures

Point out the mosaic, which depicts a procession of saints, and read the caption aloud. Encourage volunteers to describe what they see in the mosaic. For further information about this art, see *Art Background* below.
How are all the saints and martyrs victorious over death? (They live on forever with God.)

The Language of Faith
- The Church teaches that all holy men and women who have followed the teachings of Jesus faithfully in life are counted among the **saints**. Canonization, the process of formally recognizing the sanctity of a person's life, admits the saint to the Church's calendar of feasts.
- A **martyr**, which means "witness," is a person who gives his or her life for the faith. The first recognized saints were martyrs.

Art Background
The mosaic called "Procession of Martyrs" is from Ravenna, Italy. The churches of Ravenna contain some of the finest examples of early Christian art in the form of mosaics. Each mosaic is a picture or decorative design made by setting small pieces of colored glass or marble into plaster.

Notes: Building the Chapter

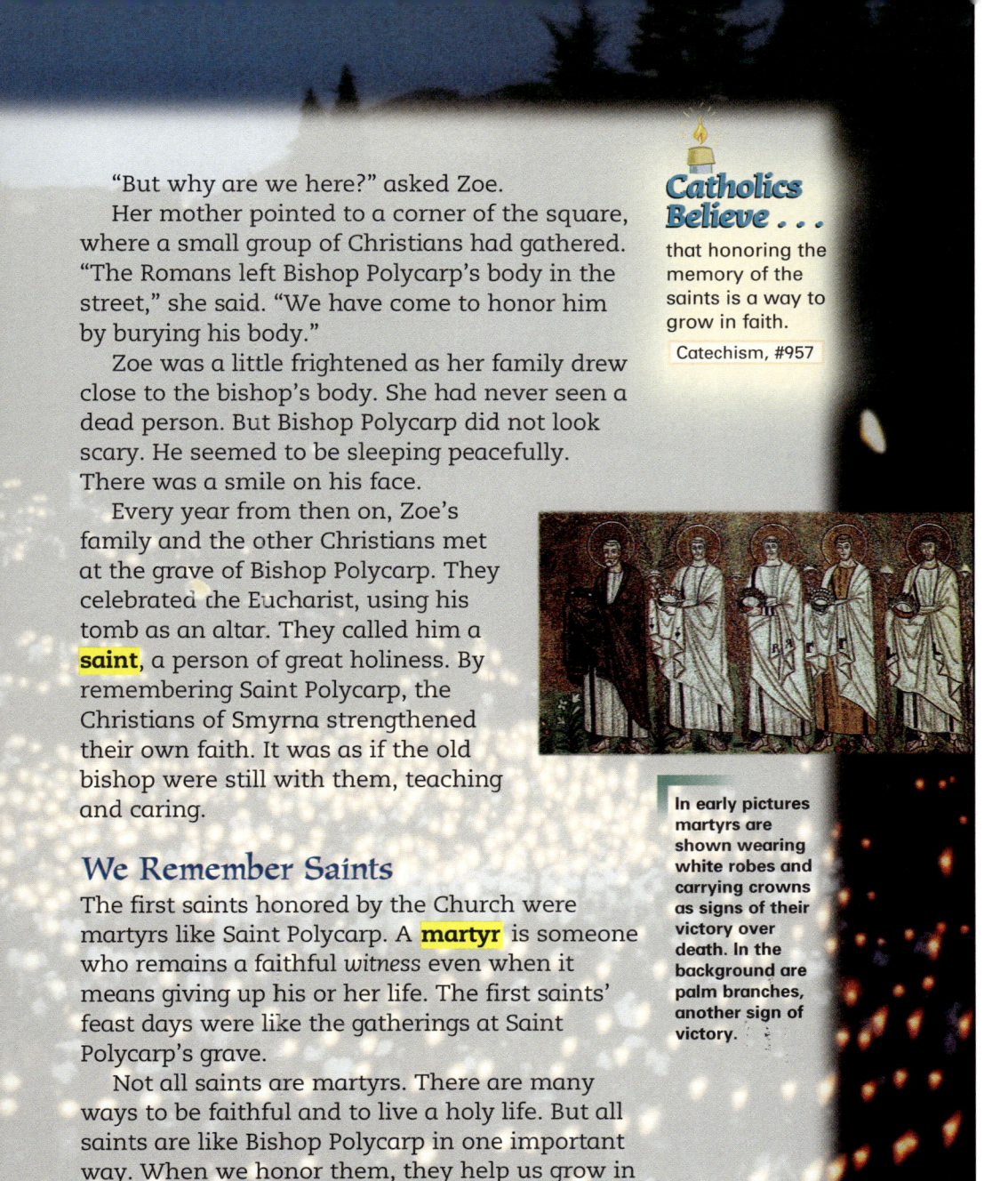

WE REFLECT
Review

Recall Invite volunteers to respond to the questions. (because he continued to show his belief in God; a witness who remains faithful even when it means giving up his or her life)

Think and Share Allow the students to consider their answers before responding. (Possible answers: People would live in fear for their lives; our parish community could not exist.)

Continue the Journey To spark ideas you might want to talk about someone who has helped you grow in your faith. Encourage volunteers to do the same.

Alternative Have the students complete this activity as a homework assignment. Encourage them to mail or deliver the thank-you notes in person.

We Live Our Faith *At Home:* Encourage the students to write down a few of the stories told by their family members so they can share them at a later session. *In the Parish:* When your class has decided on how it would like to celebrate All Saints' Day, ask your pastor or parish administrator for help in advertising the celebration in the parish bulletin.

Faith Journal The students may begin pages 15–16 of their *Faith Journal* in class and complete them at home. As a part of your own spiritual development, complete *Your Faith Journal* (page J9) for this chapter.

RECALL
Why was Bishop Polycarp killed? What is a martyr?

THINK AND SHARE
What do you think it would be like if being a Christian were against the law today?

CONTINUE THE JOURNEY
Bishop Polycarp helped Zoe and her family grow in faith. Write a thank-you note to someone who helps you grow in faith.

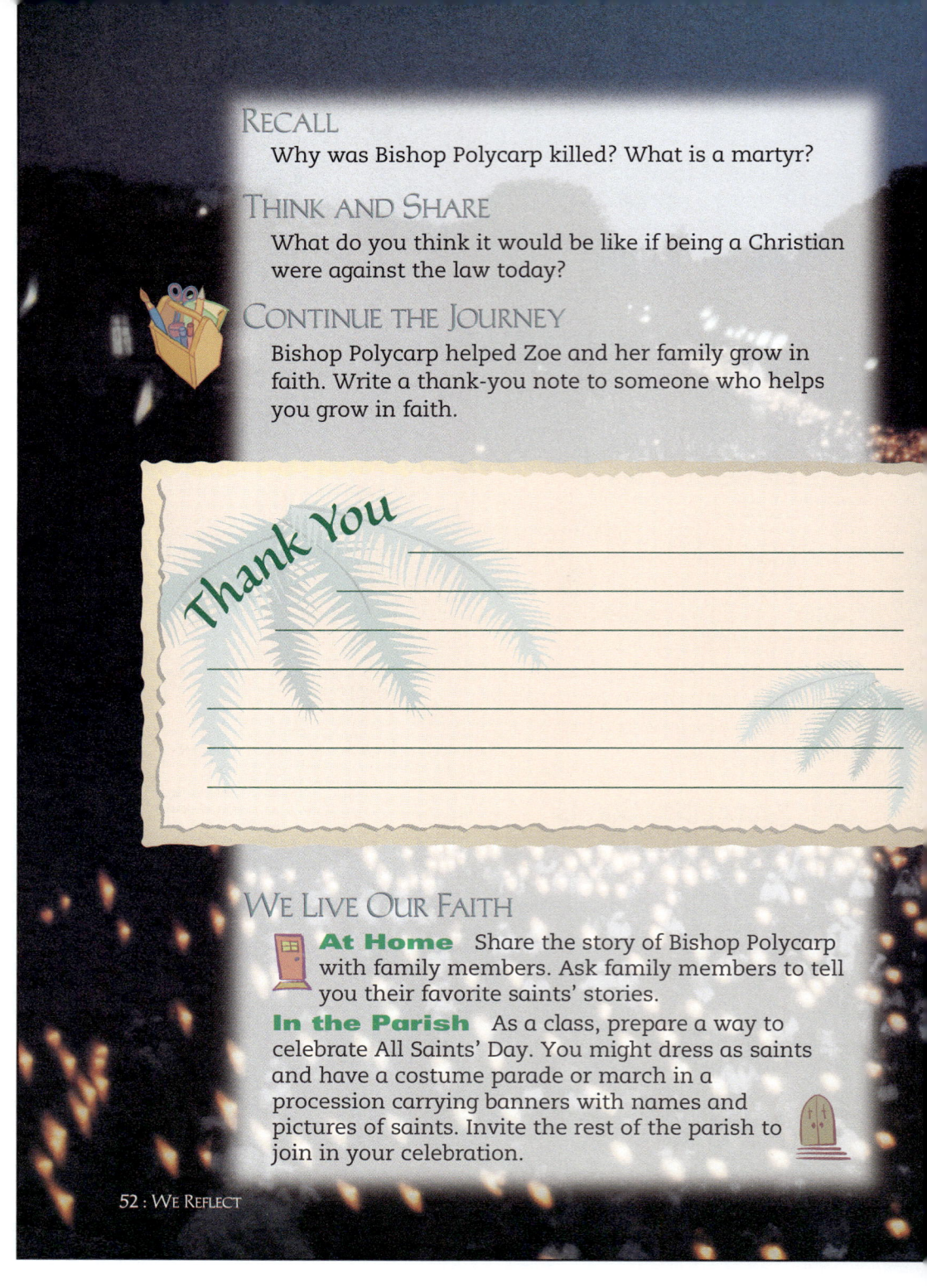

Thank You

WE LIVE OUR FAITH

At Home Share the story of Bishop Polycarp with family members. Ask family members to tell you their favorite saints' stories.

In the Parish As a class, prepare a way to celebrate All Saints' Day. You might dress as saints and have a costume parade or march in a procession carrying banners with names and pictures of saints. Invite the rest of the parish to join in your celebration.

52 : WE REFLECT

Resource Center
Multicultural Link

Many countries and ethnic groups honor certain saints as a part of their cultural and religious heritage. Japanese Christians honor Saint Paul Miki and Companions for their brave Christian witness as martyrs. The people of Peru revere Rose of Lima and Martín de Porres as native saints. Mary, as Our Lady of Guadalupe, is honored by the people of Mexico and the United States.

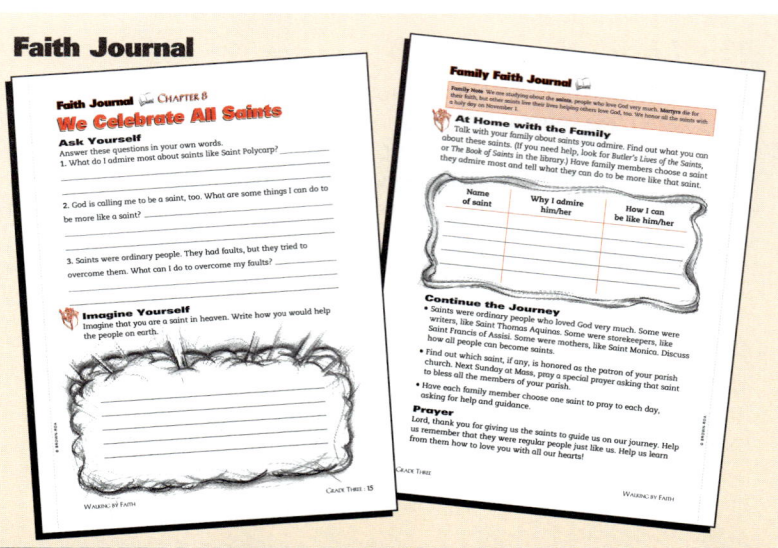

52 : CHAPTER 8

A Festival of Saints

...me saints have feast days in the Church calendar. But many ...ly women and men do not have feast days of their own. So we ...t aside one day every year to honor the memory of *all* the ...ints. We call this festival of saints **All Saints' Day**, and we ...elebrate it as a *holy day* on November 1.

Pray together this prayer from the Mass of All Saints' Day.

...YER

Let us all rejoice in the Lord
and keep a festival in honor of all the saints.
Let us join with the angels in joyful praise to the Son of God.

...t us pray.
...ther, all-powerful and ever-living God,
... day we rejoice in holy men and women of every time and place.
... ay their prayers bring us your forgiveness and love.
...e ask this through our Lord Jesus Christ, your Son,
...ho lives and reigns with you and the Holy Spirit,
...e God, for ever and ever.
...men.

We Celebrate : 53

WE CELEBRATE
3. Close

Working with the Text

- As you read aloud or summarize *A Festival of Saints*, use *The Language of Faith* below to further develop the meaning of *All Saints Day*. Explain that on this day the Church honors all people, living and dead, who have led holy lives.

- Explain that *a holy day* is a day set aside by the Church to celebrate a holy person, such as Mary, or a holy event, such as the birth of Jesus. The Church obliges us to attend Mass on holy days.

Working with the Pictures

Call attention to the photographs. **In what special way are the people in the photographs celebrating All Saints' Day?** (The children are dressed in costumes of the saints; the community members are holding lighted candles.)

Prayer If time permits, teach the students the song "When the Saints Go Marchin' In," and have them march around the room while singing the song. Then invite volunteers to pray aloud the lines of the prayer labeled 1 and 2. Pray aloud the remaining section together. End the celebration with the Sign of the Cross.

The Language of Faith

All Saints' Day is a holy day set aside to celebrate the entire communion of saints. The communion of saints is the union of all those, living and dead, who share a relationship with God through Jesus Christ.

Optional Link to the Family

The names of saints are popularly used to name people and places with a Catholic population. As a homework assignment, have the students work with family members to list people and places in their community that are named after particular saints. Schedule time during the next meeting for volunteers to share their lists.

Notes: Closing the Chapter

Getting Ready: Chapter 9

Jesus Brings Good News

Program Resources
Student Text, pp. 54–59
Student Faith Journal, pp. 17–18
Your Faith Journal, p. J10
Chapter 9 Transparency
Unit Three Family Letter

Unit Three (Jesus Christ)
The Body of Christ

Key Content Summary
Jesus was sent to bring the news of God's kingdom, of which the Church is a sign.

Planning the Chapter

	Pacing Guide Suggested time/Your time	Content	Objectives	Materials
Open	10–15 min./ _____ min.	*We Are Invited*, pp. 54–55	• Explain that good news is to be shared with others. • Affirm that God sent his Son to bring good news to all people.	• art materials • information about people who made a difference (optional)
Build	20–25 min./ _____ min.	*We Explore*, p. 56 *Stepping Stones*, p. 57	• Describe the good news that Jesus shared. • Recognize the responsibility to share the good news. • Apply the steps for hearing the good news of the Gospels.	• missalettes • copies of next Sunday's readings (optional) • Chapter 9 Transparency from the Resource Package
Review	15–20 min./ _____ min.	*We Reflect*, p. 58	• Demonstrate understanding of chapter concepts. • Apply learning through activity. • Practice faith at home and in the parish.	• art materials • *Student Faith Journal*, pp. 17–18 • *Your Faith Journal*, p. J10
Close	10–15 min./ _____ min.	*We Celebrate*, p. 59	• Plan ways to put the words of the Lord's Prayer into action.	• Unit Three Family Letter from the Resource Package

For additional suggestions, see Scheduling, pp. T35–T37.

Catechism in Context

Doctrinal Foundation This chapter tells how Jesus announced the coming of God's kingdom. Like John the Baptist, Jesus proclaimed, "Repent!" This word means to turn around (from evil to good), to convert, to change our minds. Jesus added "and believe the gospel." The gospel is the good news that he preached and that he is. Jesus prefaced this proclamation with the words, "This is the time of fulfillment. The kingdom of God is at hand." In him the fullness of time has come. The kingdom is so near that he also told his followers that the kingdom of God was in their midst. The king has come; therefore the kingdom has been ushered in. But the Messiah's kingdom, which he will present to his Father, is an eternal and universal kingdom. It is a "kingdom of truth and life, a kingdom of holiness and grace, a kingdom of justice, love and peace" *(Preface for the Feast of Christ the King)*. If this kingdom is not evident in the world, then Christians must cooperate more completely with the Holy Spirit, not to "bring it about" but to remove the obstacles that keep Christ's dominion from reaching everyone for whom he died. At the end of time, the kingdom will be revealed in its fullness.

See Catechism of the Catholic Church, #763.

One-Minute Retreat for Catechists

Read
"Wherever God rules over the human heart, there is the kingdom of God established."
—Paul W. Harrison

Reflect
When did I first experience the kingdom of God?

Pray
Lord, as my students hear your good news, help them recognize signs of your kingdom in themselves and in others. Let each of us open our hearts to your reign, so that we can teach others how to love and be loved.

Visualizing the Lesson

Use this graphic organizer to help the students understand the concept of sharing the good news.

Draw the graphic organizer on the board or on chart paper. Have the students explain how the good news of God is shared. Then brainstorm with the students specific ways they can spread the good news through their words and actions. *(by reading Scripture, by forgiving others, by loving others, by praying)*

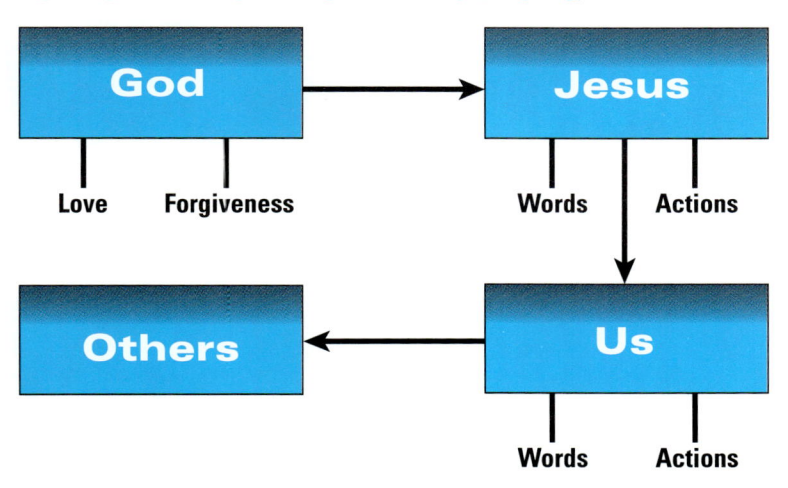

```
        God  →  Jesus
         |       |
    Love Forgiveness  Words Actions
         |       |
       Others ← Us
                 |
              Words Actions
```

Library Links

Books for Children
Did Jesus Wear Blue Jeans? by Betsy Rosen Elliot (Standard Publishing Co., 1-800-543-1353).
   The author addresses questions about Jesus.

Books for Parents and Teachers
My Galilee, My People: Jesus Stands in Solidarity by John Wijngaards (Paulist Press, 1-800-218-1903).
   This book explores Jesus' life in Galilee.

Multimedia
For children:
The Parable of the Great Feast: King Bird's Big Bash produced by Twenty-Third Publications (video) (BROWN-ROA, 1-800-922-7696).
   King Gandy, the bird king, invites all the birds in the kingdom to a party.

For parents and teachers:
The Gospels (CD-ROM) (Pauline Books & Media, 1-800-876-4463).
   This multimedia software brings the Gospels to life.

Organizations
For more information about ways the good news of Jesus is spread in the world today, contact:

Cursillo Movement
National Cursillo Center
P.O. Box 210226
Dallas, TX 75211

Strengthening the Family Link

Here are some suggestions for reaching out to your students' families:

- Encourage the students to talk with family members about ways the kingdom of God is present and how they can be signs of the kingdom of God to others.

- Invite family members to join the class in a discussion about the parable of the mustard seed and the kingdom of God. Start by having a volunteer read the parable aloud *(Matthew 13:31–32)*. Then have the students share their responses for the *Continue the Journey* activity—what they think this parable tells about the kingdom of God.

PARISH : 53B

Chapter 9 pages 54–59

Objectives
- Explain that good news is to be shared with others.
- Affirm that God sent his Son to bring good news to all people.
- Describe the good news that Jesus shared.
- Recognize the responsibility to share the good news.
- Apply the steps for hearing the good news of the Gospels.

Gathering — We Are Invited
1. Open

Personal Experience Invite volunteers to share some good news they have.

Prayer Pray the opening prayer together.

Working with the Text
After you have read aloud or summarized the text, point out that people usually share their good news.
Why do you share good news with other people? (Our happiness is greater when we share it with others; our good news makes other people happy, too.)

Working with the Pictures
- Call attention to the photograph. **How do you think the girl in the photograph feels?** (happy, proud) **Why do you think she feels that way?** (Accept all reasonable suggestions.)

   Distribute art materials, and have the students work on their drawings. If time permits, allow volunteers to show and explain their pictures to the rest of the class.

Alternative Have the students complete this activity as homework. You may want to schedule time during the next meeting for volunteers to share their completed artwork.

Chapter 9

Jesus Brings Good News

Prayer
Jesus, you bring us wonderful news about your Father's kingdom. Help us share this happy news with others.

"Guess what!"

Maybe your pet dog had puppies. You got a good grade on a test. You learned how to dive off the diving board at the pool. Whatever good news you have, you can't wait to share it.

In fact, the best part of having good news is sharing it. The more people who know about your happiness, the better. Joy gets bigger when we share it.

Activity
Draw a picture that stands for some good news you have. Share your good news by showing and explaining the picture.

54 : We Are Invited

Resource Center

Enrichment
Give information about well-known people today or in the past who made a difference in other people's lives—for example Abraham Lincoln, Florence Nightingale, Archbishop Desmond Tutu, Harriet Tubman, and Mohandes Gandhi. Focus on the good news these people shared with others.

Notes: Opening the Chapter

Scripture Story
Jesus' Good News

It was the *Sabbath* day in Nazareth. Everyone had gathered for worship. Jesus, the son of Joseph the carpenter, had come back to his hometown. Today he was going to read from the Scriptures.

Jesus opened the Book of Isaiah. He began to read the words that described the one God promised to send.

"The spirit of the Lord is upon me," Jesus read. "God has sent me to bring good news to the poor. I have come to set people free and to bring sight to the blind. I have come to announce a time of blessings from God."

The people of Nazareth knew these words by heart. But they were very surprised at what they heard next. Jesus closed the Book of Isaiah and said, "Today, right here, these words of promise have come true!"

—based on Luke 4:16–22

Christians believe that Jesus is the one promised in the Book of Isaiah. He is the **Messiah** sent to save all people.

Scripture Signpost

"I must proclaim the good news of the kingdom of God, because for this purpose I have been sent."
Luke 4:43

How can we share Jesus' good news with others?

We Are Invited
Open *Continued*
Working with the Text

- As you work with the text, be sure the students understand the meaning of *Sabbath*—the day of the week set aside for worship and rest, rooted in the story that God created the world in six days and rested on the seventh day. Explain that the Sabbath day for Jewish people is Saturday and begins at sundown on Friday. The day of worship for Christians is Sunday, the day Jesus rose from the dead.

- Use *The Language of Faith* below to explain further the term *Messiah*. **What good news did Jesus bring?** (Jesus said that a time of God's blessings had arrived.) **Why were people surprised by Jesus' words?** (They had not recognized Jesus as the one the prophet Isaiah had spoken about.)

- For more information about the Book of Isaiah, see *Scripture Background* below.

Working with the Pictures

As you call attention to the illustration, explain that in Jesus' time, books were handwritten on long sheets of cloth or paper and rolled up into scrolls. **What is Jesus doing in this illustration?** (Jesus is reading from the Scriptures.)

Scripture Signpost Encourage volunteers to consider the question before responding. (by sharing our talents with others, by being good friends to others, by helping our family members, by celebrating our faith with others, and so on)

The Language of Faith

The word **messiah** comes from a Hebrew word meaning "the Anointed One." In Greek the word is *Christos*, from which the word *Christ* is derived. The people of Israel waited thousands of years for the messiah but did not always agree on what type of person the messiah would be. In Jesus' time some believed that he would be a warrior whose army would overthrow the ruling Romans. Others believed that he would be a king, like David, who would rule over the Jewish people with justice and mercy. Jesus' humble status did not conform to either of these expectations.

Scripture Background

The Book of Isaiah is a collection of writings by at least three prophets. Prophets are called by God to speak for him about the problems in society, to preserve religious tradition, and to caution about the future consequences of sin. When Christians read the Book of Isaiah, they see Jesus in the references to the anointed one. It is from this biblical book that Jesus read prophetic words in the synagogue in Nazareth and applied them to himself **(Luke 4:16–21)**.

We Explore
2. Build

Working with the Text

- As you read aloud or summarize the text, use *The Language of Faith* below to clarify the terms *kingdom of God* and *parables*.
- Emphasize that Jesus' purpose was to bring us the good news of God's kingdom, which would free everyone from sin and sorrow.
- Stress that Jesus expects all of us to do what he did—share the good news of God's kingdom with others in words and actions. To help the students visualize how we share the good news of God's kingdom, refer to the graphic organizer on page 53B. You may wish to do the suggested activity or one of your own choosing.
- **Catholics Believe** Reinforce the Christian belief that Jesus was the Messiah who came to free us all from sin and sadness.

Working with the Pictures

Invite volunteers to answer the caption question regarding the photographs. (The man is sharing the good news of God's kingdom by reading Scriptures; the children are singing to cheer up people who are elderly; and the sister is helping mothers take good care of their children.)

Catholics Believe...
that Jesus announced the coming of God's kingdom.

Catechism, #763

Sharing Good News

The good news Jesus shared was that God loves us and saves us from sin. In the Bible we read how God invites us to a new life in the **kingdom of God**. God's kingdom is not a place or a time. It is a way of being in relationship with God.

The words Jesus read from Scripture give us some hints for recognizing God's kingdom. The poor hear joyful news. No one is imprisoned or enslaved by sin and sadness. Sick people are healed.

Jesus used words and actions to show us even more about God's kingdom. He told stories, called **parables**, describing the kingdom. He healed sick people. He set people free from loneliness, sorrow, and sin.

Just as Jesus shared good news with us, we pass it on to others. As Jesus was sent by God, we are sent by Jesus. The work of the Church community is to share the good news in words and actions. We are sent to invite the whole world into God's kingdom.

How is each picture a sign of the kingdom of God?

56 : We Explore

Resource Center

The Language of Faith

- The **kingdom of God** exists in two dimensions—the beginning of the kingdom, brought to the world by Jesus and experienced now, and the fulfillment of the kingdom, which God will bring about at the end of time. The kingdom is both "in our midst" and yet to come. All followers of Jesus are called through Baptism to be signs of God's kingdom through their words and actions.

- A **parable** is a story that teaches a lesson. The storyteller uses familiar situations—lost sheep, for example—to symbolize and clarify things that may be difficult to grasp. Jesus used parables to explain the kingdom of God.

Notes: Building the Chapter

Stepping Stones

Hearing Good News

Another word for good news is **gospel**. We give the name *Gospels* to the four books of the Bible that tell about Jesus' life and teachings. We read from the Gospels and from other parts of the Bible at every Mass. It is important to learn how to hear this good news from God.

Here are steps to follow:

- If you can, study the gospel and the other Scripture readings before Mass. The readings are usually in a special section of the *missalette*. They are printed in order by date.

- During the readings, sit quietly and listen carefully. Do not try to read along with the readers. If the gospel reading is a parable, imagine you are listening to Jesus telling the story.

- Pay close attention to the *homily*, the explanation that follows the readings. The priest or deacon can help you understand the Scripture readings.

- After Mass, talk with family members or classmates about the readings and the homily. Ask questions and share your ideas.

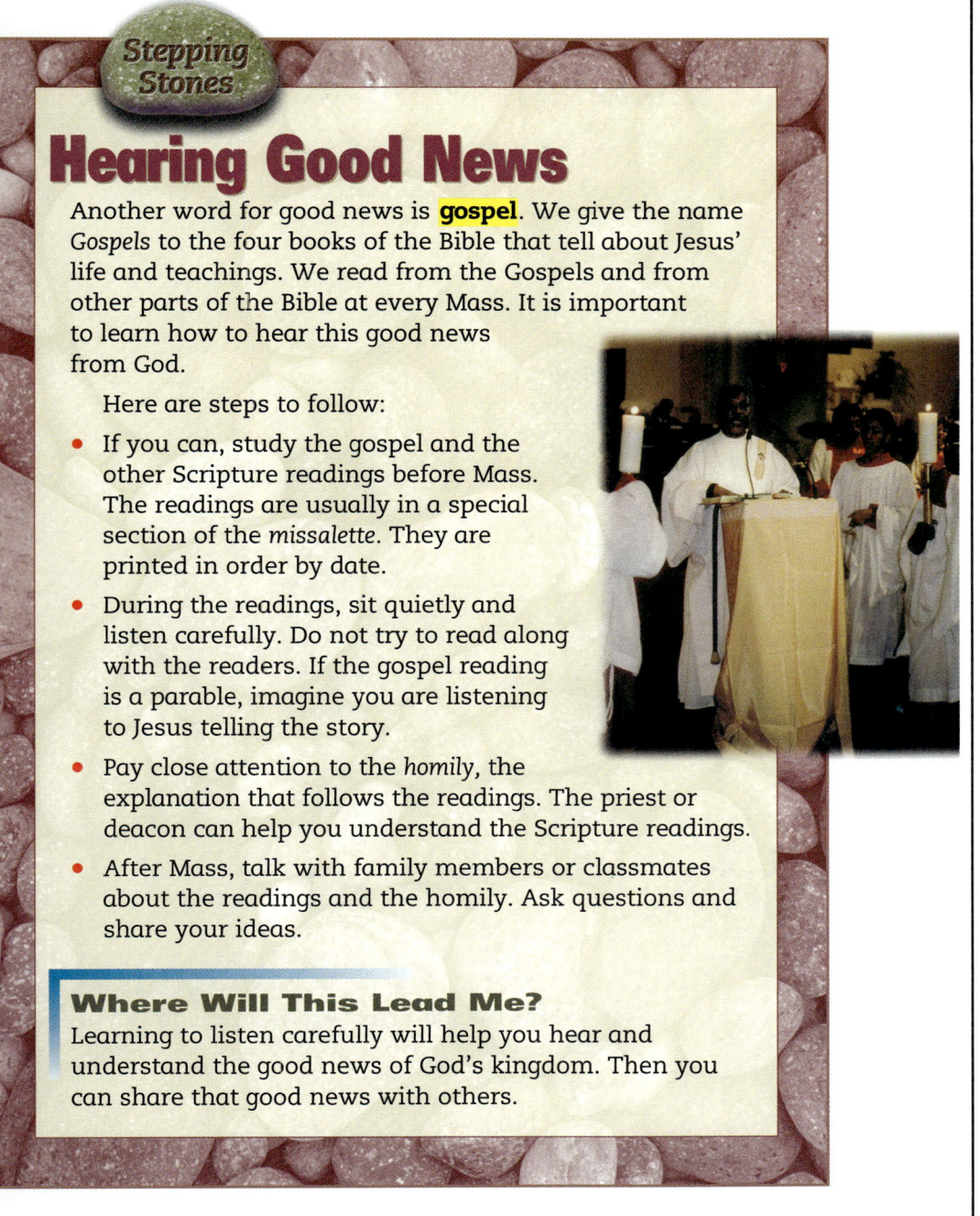

Where Will This Lead Me?
Learning to listen carefully will help you hear and understand the good news of God's kingdom. Then you can share that good news with others.

WE EXPLORE
Build Continued
Stepping Stones
Working with the Text

- After you have read the steps aloud, discuss how they help us hear and understand Jesus' good news.

- You may want to use *The Language of Faith* below to clarify the term *gospel*. Be sure the students understand the meaning of each italicized word. **Why is the homily an important part of the readings?** (It helps us understand the Scripture passage's meaning and helps us apply it to today.)

Working with the Pictures

Ask the students to imagine that they are attending the service shown in the photograph and to identify the step that is pictured. (the second step, listening to the Scripture readings)

Practice If appropriate, be sure the students know how to use a missalette. If time allows, provide missalettes, and help the students find next Sunday's readings.

The Language of Faith
The word **gospel** comes from the Anglo-Saxon *godspell*, or "good word." The Greek form of "good news" is *evangel*, from which we get the word *evangelist*, a term for the Gospel writers.

Link to the Family
Encourage the students to prepare for the Sunday readings at home with their families. Consult a lectionary or missalette for next Sunday's readings. Send this information home with students so they can read the readings from the family Bible before attending Sunday Mass.

Assessment Tip
Use their performance while discussing the steps as a means of assessing how well the students understand the process of active listening and their ability to learn from the Scriptures.

Multicultural Link
Tell the students that the Scripture readings and homily are delivered in many different languages throughout the world.

Link to the Faith Community
Explain that the Church is a sign of the kingdom of God in many ways. Suggest that the students talk with parish members or read the parish bulletin to learn about ways in which their parish community acts to share the good news with others.

We Reflect
Review

Recall Invite volunteers to respond to the questions. (God loves us, forgives our sins, and invites us to new life in the kingdom of God; *gospel* means "good news.")

Think and Share Allow the students to reflect on the question before responding. (Possible answer: Many people have forgotten the good news or have never heard it.)

Continue the Journey Distribute art materials, and have the students complete the activity. If time permits, have volunteers share their explanations and drawings.

Alternative Have the students complete this activity as a homework assignment. Encourage them to share their completed work with family members or friends. Schedule time during the next meeting for volunteers to share their work.

We Live Our Faith *At Home:* Help the students think of specific ways they can share good news at home. *In the Parish:* Encourage the students also to describe the homily to family members.

Faith Journal The students may begin pages 17–18 of their *Faith Journal* in class and complete them at home. As a part of your own spiritual development, complete *Your Faith Journal* (page J10) for this chapter.

Recall
What good news did Jesus come to share? What does the word *gospel* mean?

Think and Share
Why do you think we still need to share good news today?

Continue the Journey
Read the Parable of the Mustard Seed (Matthew 13:31–32). In your own words, explain what the story tells us about God's kingdom. Draw a picture to go with the story.

God's Kingdom Is Like . . .

We Live Our Faith

At Home Share good news with your family. In words or actions, be a sign of God's kingdom at home.

In the Parish Listen carefully to the gospel. In your own words, tell the story to someone else.

Resource Center

Enrichment (optional Activity)
Remind the students that Jesus spread the good news that our sins will be forgiven. As a homework assignment, ask the students to make and decorate bookmarks with the words *Be at peace. You are forgiven!* Encourage the students to use the bookmarks in their Bibles.

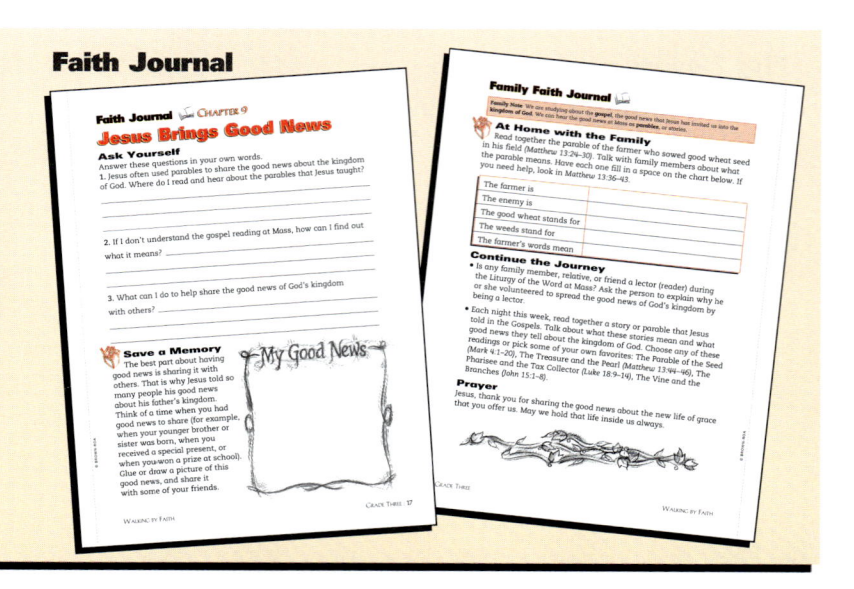

Faith Journal

Praying for the Kingdom

The words of the Lord's Prayer remind us of what it is like to live in the kingdom of God. We have what we need to eat. We forgive one another. We turn away from sin and evil. We do **God's will**, what God wants for us. We are saved. That's good news!

Pray the Lord's Prayer together. Think about what the words mean. How can you put them into action?

PRAYER

Our Father, who art in heaven,
hallowed be your name;
your kingdom come;
your will be done
on earth as it is in heaven.
Give us this day our daily bread;
and forgive us our trespasses
as we forgive those who trespass
against us;
and lead us not into
temptation,
but deliver us from evil.
Amen.

WE CELEBRATE
3. Close

Working with the Pictures

Call attention to the photographs. **How do all of these pictures show signs of the kingdom of God here on earth?** (The breaking of the Eucharistic bread shows that God shares his love with the parish community; the teacher and students praying together shows communication with God; the mountain scene shows the awesomeness of God's creation.)

Working with the Text

- Read aloud or summarize the first paragraph of *Praying for the Kingdom*.
- You may want to use *The Language of Faith* below to clarify the new term. **How can we live the Lord's Prayer in words and actions?** (Possible answers: forgiving others when they have hurt us, helping people in need, avoiding people or situations that might lead us to sin, living as brothers and sisters of one Father.)

Prayer Close the chapter by having a volunteer lead the class in praying the Lord's Prayer, which Jesus taught to his disciples. Ask the students to think carefully about the words as they pray.

Explain that this prayer combines praising God, expressing sorrow for our sins, and asking for his help. We praise God when we pray "hallowed be your name" and "your will be done." We confess our sins when we pray "forgive us our trespasses as we forgive those who trespass against us." We ask God for help when we pray "Give us this day our daily bread . . . and lead us not into temptation, but deliver us from evil." Then repeat the prayer with the class. If time permits, sing the prayer to a familiar melody.

The Language of Faith

God's will is God's intention for us—that we love and serve God in this life and enter into eternal union with God after death. Each of us learns through prayer, the desires and longings of our hearts, the Church, the sacraments, and the guidance of other people how to live in accord with God's will. Doing what God wants us to do sometimes involves making difficult choices. However, these choices lead to our ultimate happiness.

Link to the Family

To help your students' families stay connected with your exploration of this unit, send home the Unit Three Family Letter.

Notes: Closing the Chapter

Getting Ready: Chapter 10

New Life in Jesus

Program Resources
Student Text, pp. 60–65
Student Faith Journal, pp. 19–20
Your Faith Journal, p. J11
Chapter 10 Transparency
Unit Three Music and Liturgy Resources

Unit Three (Jesus Christ)
The Body of Christ

Key Content Summary
The Church was born from the saving actions of Jesus.

Planning the Chapter

	Pacing Guide Suggested time/Your time	Content	Objectives	Materials
Open	10–15 min./ ___ min.	*We Are Invited*, p. 60	• Explain that from death can come new life.	
Build	20–25 min./ ___ min.	*We Explore*, pp. 61–63	• Explain that Jesus sacrificed his life for all people. • Describe the events of the Last Supper.	• art materials • Bible (optional) • Chapter 10 Transparency from the Resource Package
Review	15–20 min./ ___ min.	*We Reflect*, p. 64	• Demonstrate understanding of chapter concepts. • Apply learning through activity. • Practice faith at home and in the parish.	• drawing materials • *Student Faith Journal*, pp. 19–20 • *Your Faith Journal*, p. J11
Close	10–15 min./ ___ min.	*We Celebrate*, p. 65	• Proclaim belief in the Paschal mystery.	• Unit Three Music and Liturgy Resources from the Resource Package

For additional suggestions, see Scheduling, pp. T35–T37.

Catechism in Context

Doctrinal Foundation This chapter explains that Jesus' love for us was so great that he sacrificed his life for us: he "always loved those who were his own in the world, and when the time came for him to be glorified by you, his heavenly Father, he showed the depth of his love" *(Eucharistic Prayer IV)*. And "no one has greater love than this, than to lay down one's life for one's friends." That Jesus should consider us his friends, despite our sins, is overwhelming. That he should die for us when our sins nailed him to the cross can only be grasped by faith. "What wondrous love is this, that caused the Lord of bliss to bear the dreadful curse for my soul?" ("Wondrous Love")

See Catechism of the Catholic Church, #609.

One-Minute Retreat for Catechists

Read
"Christ is not valued at all unless he be valued above all."
—Saint Augustine

Reflect
What does it mean to value Christ above all?

Pray
Jesus, help me be unselfish as you are unselfish. Help me explain your covenant to my students, so that each of them can explore what it means to him or her. I pray that each of them will one day seek to renew that covenant with you.

Visualizing the Lesson

Use this graphic organizer to help the students understand the Paschal mystery.

Redraw the graphic organizer on a sheet of paper, but omit all of the text except *Paschal mystery*. Distribute copies to the students. Then invite pairs of students to fill in the text and describe the Paschal mystery to each other in their own words.

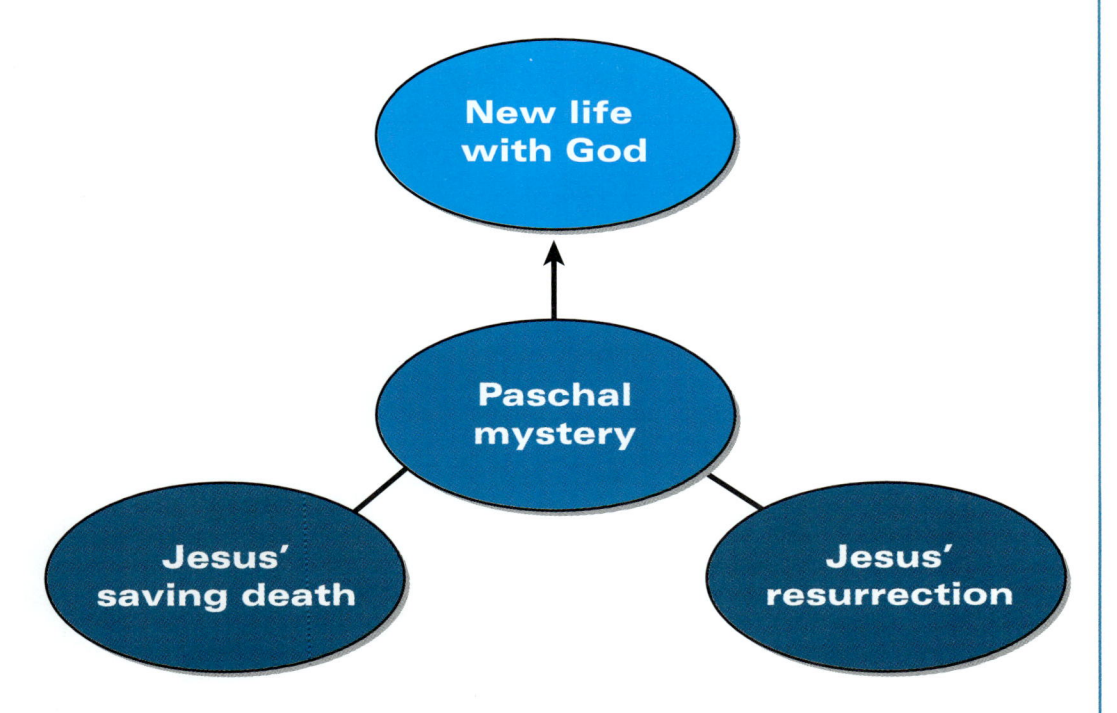

- New life with God
- Paschal mystery
- Jesus' saving death
- Jesus' resurrection

Library Links

Books for Children
We Say Thanks by Corinne Hart (Franciscan Communications, 1-800-488-0488).

Hart helps children understand and participate more fully in the Mass.

Books for Parents and Teachers
Loaves and Fishes: From Faith Experience to Empowered Community by Virginia A. Blass (Paulist Press, 1-800-218-1903).

We grow in faith and the new covenant.

Multimedia
For children:
The Grain of Wheat (video) (BROWN-ROA, 1-800-922-7696).

An African American family considers its role in spreading love, truth, and kindness.

To Climb a Mountain (video) (Paulist Press, 1-800-218-1903).

A young boy learns that the desire to give of oneself can supersede the desire to win.

For parents and teachers:
Offer It Up: What Does It Mean? (video) (Franciscan University Press, 1-800-783-6357).

We offer all we are to do God's will.

Organizations
For information on ways to show our love for others, contact:
Campaign for Human Development
3211 Fourth Street NE
Washington, DC 20017
(1-202-541-3000)

Strengthening the Family Link

Here are some suggestions for reaching out to your students' families:

- Encourage the students to talk with family members about the importance of making sacrifices for others as a way of showing our love.
- Invite family members to join in planting a classroom flower box. Reflect together on the process of the seeds, appearing to die in order to sprout new life, and relate this to Jesus' sacrifice for us.

Chapter 10 pages 60–65

Objectives
- Explain that from death can come new life.
- Explain that Jesus sacrificed his life for all people.
- Describe the events of the Last Supper.

Gathering — WE ARE INVITED
1. Open

Personal Experience Tell the students about a time when someone was very generous with his or her time, money, or talents. Then invite volunteers to share similar experiences.

Prayer Invite the students to pray the opening prayer together.

Working with the Text
As you read aloud or summarize the text, point out that we can discover important truths about our faith from small things in creation such as flower seeds.

Working with the Pictures
- Call attention to the photographs of the sunflower seeds and flowers.
- Ask volunteers to answer the caption questions. *(the seed; the flower)*

CHAPTER 10

New Life in Jesus

PRAYER

Loving Father, your Son, Jesus, gave his life so that we could be with you forever. Help us be as generous as Jesus.

Have you ever looked closely at a flower seed? It is so small it fits on your fingertip. But it can grow into a beautiful flower.

If you plant the seed, something wonderful happens. Deep in the ground the seed seems to die. But then one day it sprouts! Tiny green stems push up into the sunlight. When the plant is tall and strong, a flower forms.

The flower will not last forever. It will die. But before it dies, the flower will make new seeds. New life will begin.

What seems to die so the flower can grow? What makes new seeds before it dies?

60 : WE ARE INVITED

Resource Center

Multicultural Link
Tell the students that in Japan on April 29 plant life is celebrated. This day of celebration is called *Greenery Day (Midori-no-hi)* in honor of former Emperor Hirohito's great interest in and love for plants. Originally celebrated as the emperor's birthday, this celebration became a national holiday following his death in 1989.

Link to the Family
Family members sometimes receive flowers or plants as gifts for special occasions. Explain to the students that these gifts can be signs of new life, as at the birth of a new baby; or signs of continuing life, as at a birthday celebration.

Notes: Opening the Chapter

A Loving Choice

Sometimes, something has to die or be given up so something else can grow. It is only after the seed seems to die that the flower grows. We sometimes give up something good for the sake of something better.

When we give up something or do something difficult out of love, it is called a **sacrifice**. It is not easy to make a sacrifice. It takes a lot of love and courage. Making a sacrifice means being unselfish. No one can force us to do it.

Jesus chose to make the greatest sacrifice of all. He gave up his life so we could be saved from sin and everlasting death. No one forced Jesus to die on the cross. He freely gave up his life so we would have new life with God forever.

God rewarded Jesus for his loving choice. Through God's loving power Jesus overcame death. He rose to new life. We call his rising the **resurrection**. We celebrate Jesus' sacrifice and his resurrection at every Mass.

Catholics Believe...
Jesus' love for us was so great that he sacrificed his life to save us.

Catechism, #609

People have always offered sacrifices to God in worship. In the Eucharist we celebrate Jesus' offering of himself.

WE EXPLORE
2. Build

Working with the Text
- As you read aloud or summarize the text, use *The Language of Faith* below to clarify the highlighted terms.
- Stress that by dying on the cross, Jesus willingly gave up his life for us. **How did God the Father reward Jesus for his sacrifice?** (by raising him to new life) **How do we benefit by the sacrifice that Jesus made?** (We are saved from the power of sin and everlasting death.)

Catholics Believe Use the statement to remind the students that all people benefit from Jesus' loving sacrifice. Suggest that the students remember the sacrifice of Jesus each time they attend Mass.

Working with the Pictures
What is the priest doing in the photograph? (holding up the host and chalice at Mass) Read the caption aloud. Point out that we receive the Body and Blood of Jesus Christ at Mass.

The Language of Faith
- **Sacrifice**, the act of making offerings to God, was a common practice in Jesus' time. The Jewish people sacrificed the season's first lambs, kid goats, birds (usually doves), or fresh fruits and vegetables. They believed these sacrifices would please God. Their hope was that God would forgive their sins and bless them. Jesus' sacrifice was not the sacrifice of an animal's life but rather the sacrifice of his own life.

- The **resurrection**, Jesus' victory over death, is the basis for the Christian belief in life with God after death. Through Baptism into the death and resurrection of Jesus, the faithful obtain deliverance from sin and the promise of resurrection to eternal life.

Link to the Faith Community
Remind the students that by attending Mass they are joining with the faith community in celebrating the sacrifice that Jesus made for us.

WE EXPLORE
Build *Continued*
Working with the Text

- Explain that this Scripture Story focuses on a meal that Jesus had with his friends.
- As you read or summarize *The New Covenant* aloud, use *The Language of Faith* below to clarify the meanings of *Passover* and *new covenant*.
  What was the bread Jesus shared? (his Body) **What was the wine?** (his Blood)
- Help the students connect the Last Supper to the celebration of the Eucharist.
  When do we hear the words "This is my Body" and "This is my Blood"? (at Mass)
- **Scripture Signpost** Ask the students to compare the grain of wheat to the sunflower seed that produces a new plant.
  When the grain of wheat and the sunflower seed seem to die, what do they produce? (new life)
- Invite responses to the question. (Jesus' sacrifice was the single grain that made the fruit of the Church grow.)

Working with the Pictures

- Ask the students to compare this picture with the picture on page 61.
  What do both pictures show? (bread and wine, the symbols for Jesus' sacrifice on the cross)
- Provide art materials for the activity. If time permits, have volunteers explain the symbols they used in their artwork.
  Alternative Have the students work on their projects at home and share their artwork at the next meeting.

SCRIPTURE STORY
The New Covenant

Scripture Signpost

"Unless a grain of wheat falls to the ground and dies, it remains just a grain of wheat; but if it dies, it produces much fruit."
—*John 12:24*

In what way is the Church like the fruit that grows from the single grain?

Jesus and his friends gathered on the night before he died. They met to celebrate the Jewish feast of **Passover**. This feast remembers how God led the people of Israel out of slavery in Egypt.

After the meal was over and the songs were sung, Jesus took a piece of bread. He blessed it and broke it into pieces. He gave the bread to his friends, saying, "This is my Body, which will be given for you. Do this to remember me."

Then Jesus took a cup of wine. He prayed the blessing. He passed the cup to his friends. "This is the cup of the **new covenant**, the new holy agreement God makes with people," he said. "This is my own Blood, which is poured out for you."

—based on Luke 22:14–20

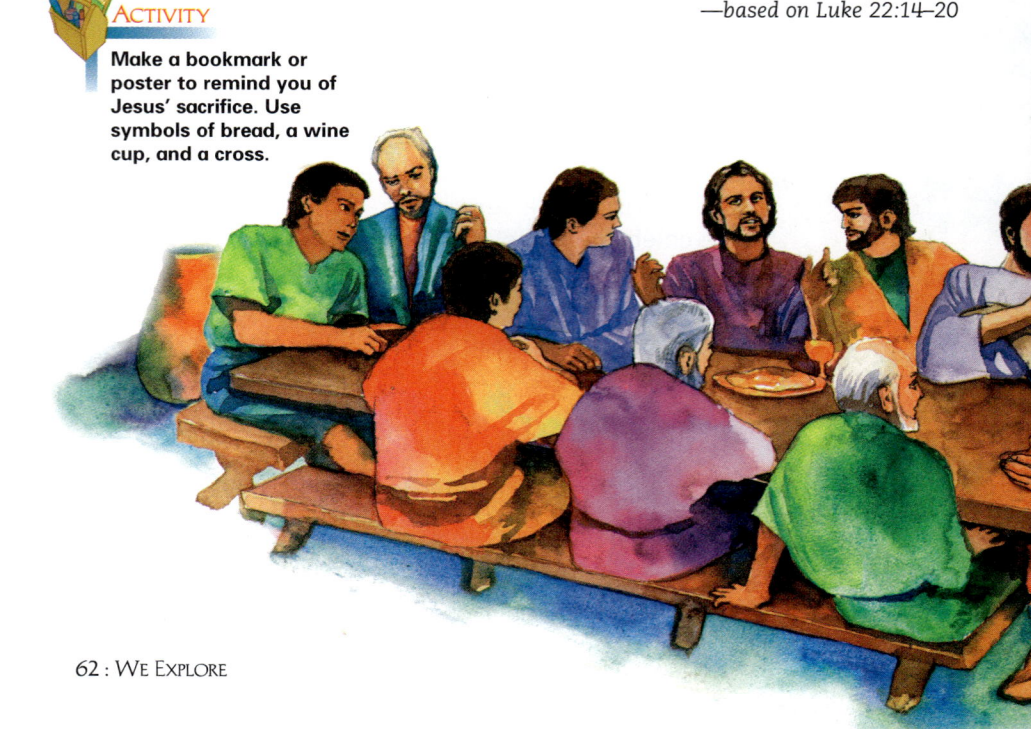

ACTIVITY

Make a bookmark or poster to remind you of Jesus' sacrifice. Use symbols of bread, a wine cup, and a cross.

62 : WE EXPLORE

Resource Center

The Language of Faith

- According to the Scriptures **Passover**, a solemn Jewish feast, is to be observed in the spring by every generation. By celebrating this feast the Jewish people remember how God freed their ancestors from slavery in Egypt.
- The **new covenant**, made by Jesus' dying on the cross, began a new relationship between God and all people. Christians see the new covenant as the fulfillment of the covenant God has made with his people. Through Jesus all people can be saved from the power of sin and everlasting death.

Enrichment

Read **Luke 22:14–20** to the students. Note the similarity between this passage and the words of consecration at Mass.

Notes: Building the Chapter

Jesus' Last Supper with his friends was the First Eucharist. When we celebrate the Mass, we celebrate Jesus' passover. Jesus "passed over" from death to new life. He offered himself to free us from the slavery of sin.

Jesus' saving death and resurrection make up the **Paschal mystery**. This truth of our faith gets its name from *Pesach*, the Hebrew word for "Passover." The Mass, the sacraments, and all our liturgical celebrations are ways of living out this great mystery. This chart shows the connections between Passover and the Eucharist.

The Paschal Mystery

	Passover	The Eucharist
The people of . . .	Israel	the Church
Set free from . . .	slavery	sin
Led by . . .	Moses	Jesus
Through . . .	the waters of the sea	death
To . . .	a new land promised by God	new life with God forever
Offer in sacrifice . . .	the Paschal lamb	Jesus, the Lamb of God
Share a ritual meal . . .	the Seder	the Mass

We Explore : 63

We Explore
Build *Continued*
Working with the Text

- As you continue to read the text, use *The Language of Faith* to develop further the highlighted term.
- To help the students visualize the concept of the Paschal mystery, refer to the graphic organizer on page 59B. You may wish to do the suggested activity or one of your own choosing.
- Point out that Jesus' death and resurrection is the most important mystery of our faith. We don't completely understand Jesus' sacrifice and his victory over death, but we believe that these events truly happened and truly bring about our salvation.
- As you read the chart together, compare Passover to the Eucharist.

Working with the Pictures

- Point out the picture that shows Moses leading the people of Israel through the Red Sea to a new land.
- Have a volunteer point out the sacrificial lamb in the bottom picture. As you point out the angels and members of the clergy in traditional religious clothing, invite the students to find them in the picture. For more information, see *Art Background* below.

The Language of Faith
The **Paschal mystery**—Jesus' suffering, death, and resurrection—is the most important mystery of our faith. Because Jesus offered his life for us, we can now live with God forever. Sin and death are not the end for God's people. All sins have been made up for through Jesus' sacrifice on the cross.

Link to Liturgy
Remind the students that we remember the Passover of the Lord each time we pray these words at Mass: "Lord, by your cross and resurrection you have set us free. You are the Savior of the world." Encourage the students to listen for these words at Mass. Explain that these words are not used at every liturgy. They are one of four choices known as the *memorial acclamation*.

Art Background
In "Adoration of the Mystic Lamb," a famous Flemish altarpiece (from Northern Belgium) of the fifteenth century by Hubert and Jan van Eyck, Christ is represented as the lamb whose sacrifice redeemed the world. From a radiant sun the Holy Spirit looks down on the pastoral scene. Angels surround the altar of the sacrificial lamb. The apostles are shown kneeling at the lower right. The people in the painting represent a community of all nations and languages.

Parish : 63

WE REFLECT
Review

Recall Have the students respond to the questions. *(We sacrifice when we give up something or do something difficult out of love; Jesus sacrificed his life for all people.)*

Think and Share Allow the students to consider the question before answering. *(Possible answer: attend Mass.)*

Continue the Journey Discuss signs of new life in nature, such as a seed sprouting, an egg hatching, or a tree budding. If time permits, allow the students to share their drawings and writings.

We Live Our Faith *At Home:* Share with the students one sacrifice you will make this week. *In the Parish:* Remind the students to listen for the words we sometimes pray together at Mass—*Christ has died. Christ is risen. Christ will come again.* Suggest that in church the students look for the stations of the cross and the crucifix, which remind us of Christ's sacrifice.

Faith Journal The students may begin pages 19–20 of their *Faith Journal* in class and complete them at home. As a part of your own spiritual development, complete *Your Faith Journal* (page J11) for this chapter.

RECALL
What is a sacrifice? What sacrifice did Jesus make?

THINK AND SHARE
How can we share in Jesus' sacrifice?

CONTINUE THE JOURNEY
Draw or write about a sign of new life that you have seen.

WE LIVE OUR FAITH

At Home Thank family members for the sacrifices they make for you. Make a loving sacrifice for the good of someone in your family.

In the Parish Look for signs of Jesus' loving sacrifice and resurrection in your parish church.

64 : We Reflect

Resource Center
Link to Justice

Remind the students that Jesus calls us to bring justice to all people. Sometimes bringing justice means sacrificing our time and using our talents to help others. Have the students discuss the sacrifices they see family members, friends, and neighbors making for others. Talk about the love and courage these sacrifices show.

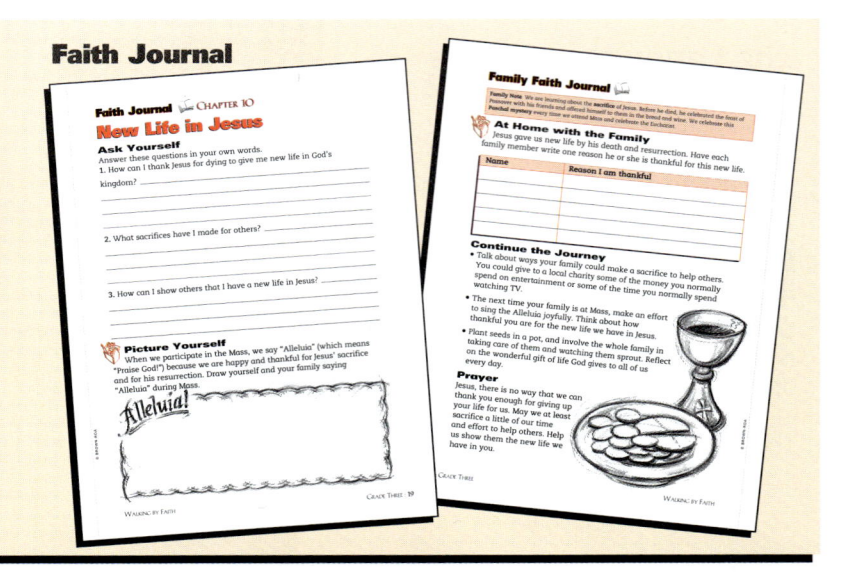

Faith Journal

64 : Chapter 10

Alleluia!

At Easter time and before the gospel at Mass, we sing or pray a shout of joy. The word *Alleluia* comes from the Hebrew for "Praise God!" We are happy because we know we will share in Jesus' resurrection. Saint Augustine said, "We are Easter people, and Alleluia is our song."

We praise God for sending us Jesus. During the Mass we proclaim our belief in the Paschal mystery.

The following prayer combines our statement of faith with our joyful "Alleluia."

Prayer

Let us proclaim the mystery of our faith:
Christ has died, Alleluia!
Christ is risen, Alleluia!
Christ will come again, Alleluia!

We Celebrate : 65

We Celebrate
3. Close

Working with the Pictures

Invite volunteers to describe what they see pictured on this page.
How do all the pictures show God being praised? (The Mass procession is in honor of Jesus, who is risen; the flowers are signs of new life in Jesus; and the stained-glass window of Jesus on the cross praises God for sending his Son to be our Savior.)

Working with the Text

When reading the text, make sure that the students understand the meaning of *Alleluia*. You may want to remind them that after Lent is over the Church community uses the word *Alleluia* again, beginning with the Easter Vigil.
Why is Easter a good time to sing, pray, or shout Alleluia? (It is the time of year when we celebrate Jesus' resurrection.)

Prayer Close the chapter by praising God in song and prayer. Choose a sung version of the Alleluia. Gather the students into a circle to sing the Alleluia song and then pray the prayer together.

Explain to students that the word *Alleluia* is heard most often during the Easter Season, but it is used throughout the liturgical year as well. It occurs in the psalms, the heavenly liturgy of *Revelation 19:1–8*, at Mass before the gospel, as antiphons before and after the psalms, and in the psalms of the Liturgy of the Hours. It is not used during Lent because Lent is a time of penance rather than rejoicing. Conclude by having the students tell what the Easter celebration means to them.

Art Background

"The Crucifixion" on this page is by the Russian artist Marc Chagall. Chagall was commissioned to design stained-glass windows for a number of French churches, including Rheims Cathedral, where this stained-glass window is located.

Assessment Tip

Use their responses about the celebration of Easter to assess the progress the students have made in recognizing and proclaiming the mystery of faith.

Music and Liturgy Resources

To enhance your prayer and celebration, you may wish to use the Unit Three Music and Liturgy Resources from the Resource Package.

Notes: Closing the Chapter

Parish : 65

Getting Ready: Chapter 11

Jesus Works Through Us

Program Resources
Student Text, pp. 66–71
Student Faith Journal, pp. 21–22
Your Faith Journal, p. J12
Chapter 11 Transparency
Unit Three Assessment

Unit Three (Jesus Christ)
The Body of Christ

Key Content Summary
Jesus continues to work in our world through us, his Body.

Planning the Chapter

	Pacing Guide Suggested time/Your time	Content	Objectives	Materials
Open	10–15 min./ _____ min.	*We Are Invited*, p. 66	• Explain that all people have been given gifts to use in service to others.	
Build	20–25 min./ _____ min.	*We Explore*, pp. 67–69	• Identify the Church as the Body of Christ on earth. • Examine the call to serve Jesus by serving one another.	• art materials • Chapter 11 Transparency from the Resource Package
Review	15–20 min./ _____ min.	*We Reflect*, p. 70	• Demonstrate understanding of chapter concepts. • Apply learning through activity. • Practice faith at home and in the parish.	• parish bulletins • *Student Faith Journal*, pp. 21–22 • *Your Faith Journal*, p. J12 • Unit Three Assessment from the Resource Package
Close	10–15 min./ _____ min. *For additional suggestions, see Scheduling, pp. T35–T37.*	*We Celebrate*, p. 71	• Explain ways to love and serve.	

Catechism in Context

Doctrinal Foundation This chapter explains that we who are members of the Church are members of the Body of Christ on earth: "For as in one body we have many parts, and not all the parts have the same function, so we, though many, are one body in Christ, and individually parts of one another" *(Romans 12:4–5)*. We are called to serve and to share our gifts with one another. "Since we have gifts that differ according to the grace given to us, let us exercise them: if prophecy, in proportion to faith; if ministry, in ministering; if one is a teacher, in teaching; if one exhorts, in exhortation; if one contributes, in generosity; if one is over others, with diligence; if one does acts of mercy, with cheerfulness" *(Romans 12:6–8)*. We are called to develop the gifts we have been given, to respect the gifts not granted to us but bestowed on others, and to work together so that our gifts combine with theirs for the benefit of all and redound to the glory of God.

See Catechism of the Catholic Church, #794.

One-Minute Retreat for Catechists

Read
"Earth grows into heaven, as we come to live and breathe in the atmosphere of the incarnation. Jesus makes heaven wherever He is."
—Frederick William Faber

Reflect
How can I work toward heaven?

Pray
Lord, as your hands on earth, help me be less clumsy. With one tool—your love—and steady hands, may I leave your mark everywhere with acts of kindness, faith, hope, charity, and service.

Visualizing the Lesson

Use this graphic organizer to help the students visualize how the Church is the Body of Christ.

Draw the graphic organizer on the board or on chart paper, leaving all but the middle box blank. As you work with the text on page 69, fill in the boxes. Invite volunteers to name specific examples from their own lives for as many boxes as they can.

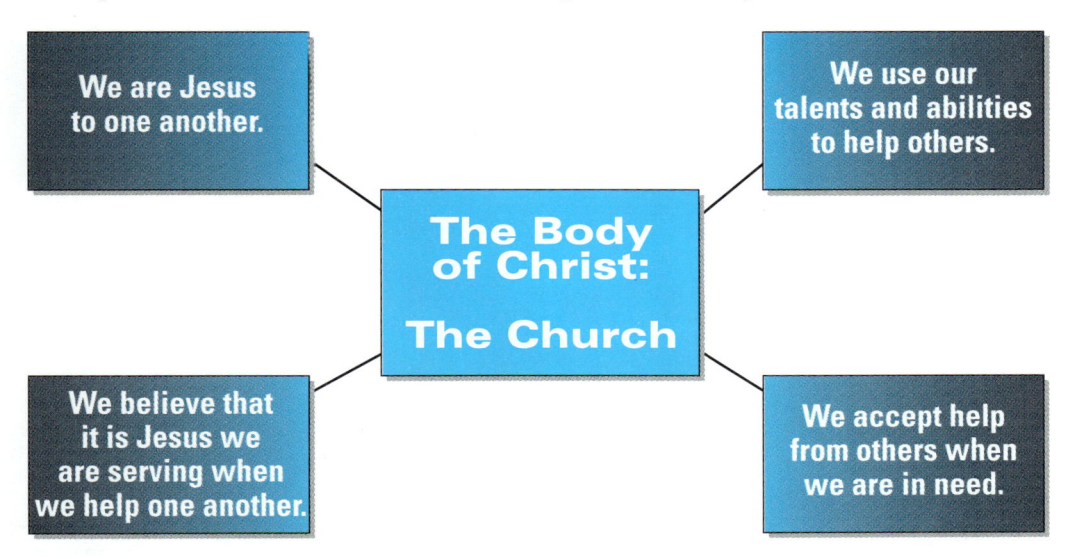

- We are Jesus to one another.
- We use our talents and abilities to help others.
- **The Body of Christ: The Church**
- We believe that it is Jesus we are serving when we help one another.
- We accept help from others when we are in need.

Library Links

Books for Children
The Legend of Nine Talents by Joan Hutson (Pauline Books and Media, 1-800-876-4463).

Being faithful to his own talents helps a little boy bring his family together.

Books for Parents and Teachers
The Church Today: Belonging and Believing by Anthony T. Padovano (Franciscan Communications, 1-800-488-0488).

Our culture and our beliefs affect our belonging to the Church.

Multimedia
For children:
God Helps Me. Episode #1, "Gifts to Share" produced by the Archdiocese of St. Paul-Minneapolis (video) (BROWN-ROA, 1-800-922-7696).

People are all created to be different and have different gifts.

Glory Day, "Prayer for Peace" by David Haas (GIA Publications, 1-800-442-1358).

Use this song, featured in Haas's concert video or audio CD, to make music a part of chapter material.

For parents and teachers:
My Soul Proclaims: Voices of Catholic Women (video) (USCC Publishing Services, 1-800-235-8722).

Women who minister in the Church share their experiences.

Organizations
For more information about being Christ's hands on earth, contact:
National Christ Child Society
5101 Wisconsin Ave. NW, Suite 304
Washington, DC 20016
(1-202-363-9516)

Strengthening the Family Link

Here are some suggestions for reaching out to your students' families:

- Encourage the students to talk with family members about ways they can use their talents to serve.
- Invite family members to join the class in making a poster. Have each person trace his or her hand on a sheet of paper, cut the handprint out, and attach it to a poster titled *Our Hands Are Jesus' Hands*.

Chapter 11 pages 66–71

Objectives
- Explain that all people have been given gifts to use in service to others.
- Identify the Church as the Body of Christ on earth.
- Examine the call to serve Jesus by serving one another.

Gathering — WE ARE INVITED
1. Open

Personal Experience Invite volunteers to share times when someone needed their help.

Prayer Have the students think about their helping experiences as you pray the opening prayer together.

Working with the Text
As you read or summarize the text, emphasize that everyone needs help sometimes.
How did Jaime help his family? (He got a towel for his mother, took care of his baby brother, and helped his sister sort laundry.)

Working with the Pictures
- Point out the photograph.
What can you tell about Jaime by looking at this picture? (He seems responsible, loving, caring, and patient.)

Brainstorm this list with the students. Then encourage them to use the suggestions to help their families at home.

CHAPTER 11

Jesus Works Through Us

PRAYER
Thank you, God, for the many gifts you have given us. Help us use them to serve other people.

Jaime's baby brother Nando was only a month old. Jaime was eight and a half, and his mother always needed his help.

Just yesterday Jaime helped her by getting a towel for Nando's bath. Then he rocked Nando while their mother was busy. And then he had to help his older sister sort the laundry.

Last night his whole family had dinner together. Jaime's mother told his father, "I don't know what I would have done today without Jaime. He was like an extra set of hands and feet for me."

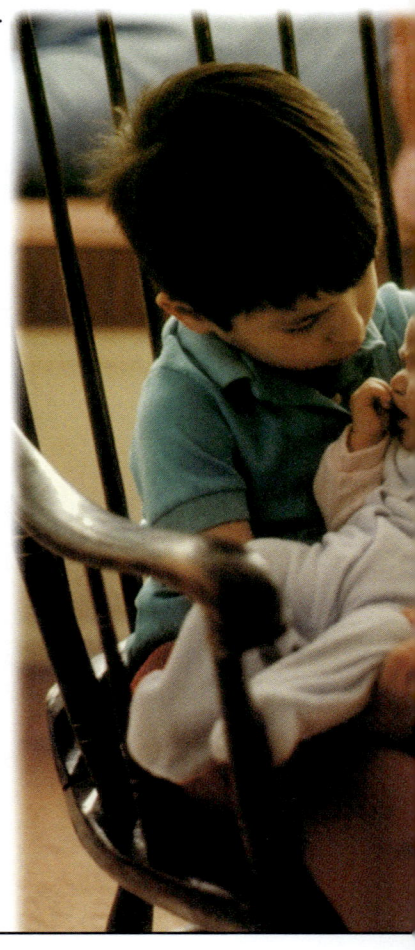

ACTIVITY
List some things you do to help your family.

66 : We Are Invited

Resource Center

Link to the Faith Community
Invite the leader of a parish service ministry to speak to the students about the group's work, such as preparing and delivering meals for families in mourning or driving people who are elderly or have disabilities to a doctor or a food store. Ask the speaker to focus on *why* the group's members help people in this way.

Teaching Tip
Handling sensitive topics Be mindful of any students in your class whose families are in conflict or are coping with separation or divorce. Assure the students that whatever the family situation, there are always words we can say and actions we can do that will help a family member who is sad, disappointed, worried, or upset.

Notes: Opening the Chapter
_____
_____
_____
_____
_____
_____

How is this person doing Jesus' work?

Doing Jesus' Work

Every family has times when members have to help each other a little more than usual. For example, we all pitch in when someone's not there to do his or her usual jobs.

When we were baptized, we became members of the Church family. We're all God's children, and Jesus is our brother. When Jesus was here with us, he did God's work. He served many people. Jesus has returned to his Father in heaven, but his work goes on. We all pitch in to do what is needed.

As the Church we aren't just standing in for Jesus. We *are* Jesus to one another. One name for the Church is the **Body of Christ**. This name reminds us that we are all one, as the parts of a body are one. It also reminds us that we belong to Jesus. We use our hands and feet, mouths and ears, minds and hearts to do what Jesus does.

Catholics Believe . . .
that we are members of the Body of Christ. We share our gifts and serve one another.
Catechism, #794

We Explore : 67

WE EXPLORE
2. Build

Working with the Pictures
- Call attention to the pictures of a stained-glass window showing Jesus healing someone and a man carrying a child with disabilities off a school bus.
- For additional information, see *Art Background* below.
- Ask volunteers to respond to the caption question. **(by helping someone in need, as Jesus did)**

Working with the Text
- As you read aloud or summarize the text, use The *Language of Faith* below to explain further *Body of Christ*.
- Emphasize that as members of the Church community, we, like Jesus, have a responsibility to love all people.
- **Catholics Believe** Explain that as Christians we are united in a special way and are responsible to serve one another as sisters and brothers.

The Language of Faith

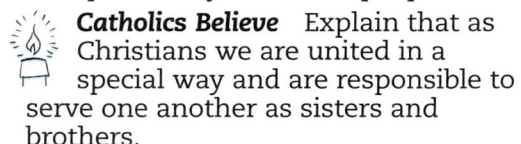

The **Body of Christ** as an image of the Church community is found in Paul's epistles, or letters, written to the Christian communities that he began. Paul used this image to help the first Christians understand their special relationship to Jesus and to one another. To be a Christian in Paul's time and in ours means to recognize that Baptism connects us with Jesus and with one another in much the same way parts of a body are connected.

Art Background

The stained-glass window pictured on this page is located in Notre-Dame-du-Cap in Quebec, Canada. Many artists who created images of Jesus for churches chose to show him helping people by healing them of illness.

Multicultural Link

Emphasize that the Body of Christ, the Church, is made up of people of many races, ethnic groups, nationalities, and cultures; yet we are all one family. The members of Jesus' family are joined together because Jesus lives in *every* one of them.

We Explore
Build Continued
Working with the Pictures

- As you call attention to the illustration, explain that it shows some of the first Christians. Invite volunteers to describe the specific actions shown.
  How are all these actions alike?
  (Someone is helping another person.)

  Distribute art materials, and have the students complete the activity. If time permits, encourage volunteers to share their drawings.

  Alternative Have the students complete this activity at home. Schedule time during the next meeting for volunteers to share their completed artwork.

Working with the Text

- Read aloud or summarize *Serving the King*. Explain to the students that by telling this story, Jesus helped his followers understand how to serve one another.
  Why were the people surprised by the king's words? (They did not know they were serving the king when they helped other people.)

- Encourage volunteers to consider their answers before responding to the bulleted question. **(By helping anyone who needs help; by using our talents to serve others; the students may also mention specific actions.)**

  Our Moral Guide Read the statement aloud. Then ask volunteers to respond to the question.
  (Jesus gave us the responsibility to care for others.)

ACTIVITY
Draw a picture of yourself serving Jesus.

Our Moral Guide
We are known as Jesus' followers by the way we serve the poor.

Catechism, #2443

Why does the Church have a special mission to care for people in need?

SCRIPTURE STORY
Serving the King

Jesus told his followers this story:

At the end of time, the king will call all people before him. To some people, the king will say, "Enter into the kingdom and be joyful! When I was hungry, you fed me. You gave me water when I was thirsty and clothes when I needed them. When I was in prison, you visited me."

The people will be puzzled. "Lord," they will ask, "when did we do these things for you?"

The king will smile and say, "Whenever you did these things for anyone in need, you did them for me."

—based on Matthew 25:31–40

- How can we serve Jesus today?

68 : We Explore

Resource Center

Scripture Background

In **Matthew 25:31–40** Jesus explains what will happen at the last judgment. He makes it clear that his followers will be judged not on how well they followed ritual laws and ceremonies but rather on how well they loved him by loving others. It is from this Scripture passage that the Church has identified specific Corporal Works of Mercy: feed the hungry, give drink to the thirsty, shelter the homeless, clothe the naked, and visit the sick and imprisoned.

Link to Justice

Have the students choose one of the actions that Jesus included in his story and decide how they as a class or as individuals could carry out that action in their own lives.

Notes: Building the Chapter

Every Gift Is Needed

God gave each of us special gifts, or talents. A *talent* is something you enjoy doing and can do well. We are called to use our talents to serve others.

Everyone's talents are different. But when we put our talents together and work as the Body of Christ, we can do more than any of us can do alone.

Each of us has needs, too. Part of learning to be the Body of Christ is learning to accept help. As the Church, we serve and we are served.

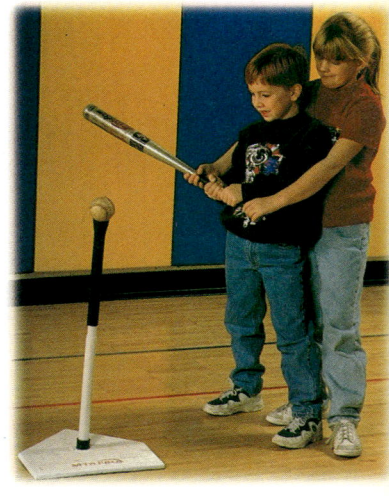

What are these children's talents? How are they using their talents to help others?

Saints Walk with Us
Saint Teresa of Avila
Feast Day: October 15

Teresa used her gifts of writing, speaking, leading, and laughing to serve the whole Church.

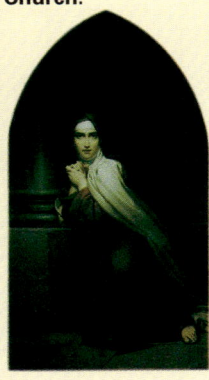

Saint Teresa told the sisters she lived with that "Christ has no hands but your hands, no feet but your feet."

We Explore
Build *Continued*

Working with the Text

- Describe someone using a talent to serve others; for example, a good cook preparing a meal for a parish fund-raising supper. Invite volunteers to make other suggestions.
- Emphasize that *everyone* needs help at times. For example, a student who is usually good in math might need help learning long division. Ask the students to think of other examples.
- To help the students visualize the Church as the Body of Christ, refer to the graphic organizer on page 65B. You may wish to do the suggested activity or one of your own choosing.

Working with the Pictures

- Be sure the students understand who is helping and who is being helped in each picture. **(The older girl is helping the younger boy; the children are helping others who are not shown.)**
- Ask the students to respond to the caption questions. **(The girl knows how to play T-ball; she is teaching the younger boy how to play; the children can walk long distances; they are walking to collect money to help others.)**

Saints Walk with Us Explain that learning about the saints' lives helps us discover ways we can use our own talents to help others.
What did Teresa mean when she said, "Christ has no hands but your hands, no feet but your feet"? (The sisters were acting as Jesus when they did good works for other people.)

WE EXPLORE : 69

Profile

Saint Teresa of Ávila (1515–1582) Teresa grew up in Ávila, Spain, in the early 1500s. When she was a teenager, her mother died. Teresa decided to become a nun and joined a Carmelite convent. Saint John of the Cross taught her how to pray devotedly. She learned that she could talk with Jesus as her best friend. Teresa wrote much about God, Jesus, and prayer. Her writings are still read and respected today. She is a doctor of the Church.

WE REFLECT
Review

Recall Invite responses to the question. (We are all one, as there are many parts in one body.)

Think and Share Allow time for the students to think about the question before responding. (Possible answer: Different people have different needs so many different talents are needed.)

Continue the Journey Invite students to work on the activity independently or in pairs. If time permits, ask volunteers to share their ideas.

Alternative Have the students work on this activity at home. Schedule time during the next meeting for sharing completed activities.

We Live Our Faith *At Home:* Ask the students to think about their family members' needs as well as their own talents. *In the Parish:* Make copies of parish bulletins available to the students.

Faith Journal The students may begin pages 21–22 of their *Faith Journal* in class and complete them at home. As a part of your own spiritual development, complete *Your Faith Journal* (page J12) for this chapter.

RECALL
Why is the Church called the Body of Christ?

THINK AND SHARE
Why do you think God gave us all different talents?

CONTINUE THE JOURNEY
Write about how you will use your talents to help someone. Then write about how someone could use his or her talents to help you.

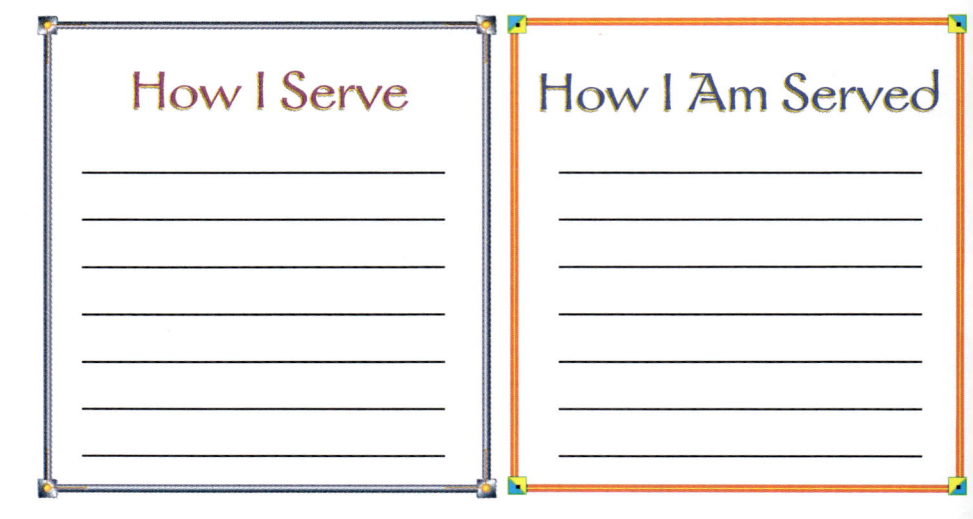

How I Serve

_____
_____
_____
_____
_____
_____

How I Am Served

_____
_____
_____
_____
_____
_____

WE LIVE OUR FAITH

At Home Use one of your talents to help a family member feel happier.

In the Parish Find a way to help your parish community carry out Jesus' work. What are the needs of people in your parish? What are your talents? How can you put needs and talents together?

Resource Center

Enrichment
Discuss with the students the different groups of people who serve your community: police officers, firefighters, doctors, nurses, and teachers. Discuss the specific needs that each group fulfills.

Assessment Tip
You may wish to copy the Unit Three Assessment from the Resource Package in preparation for giving this test after completing Chapters 9–12.

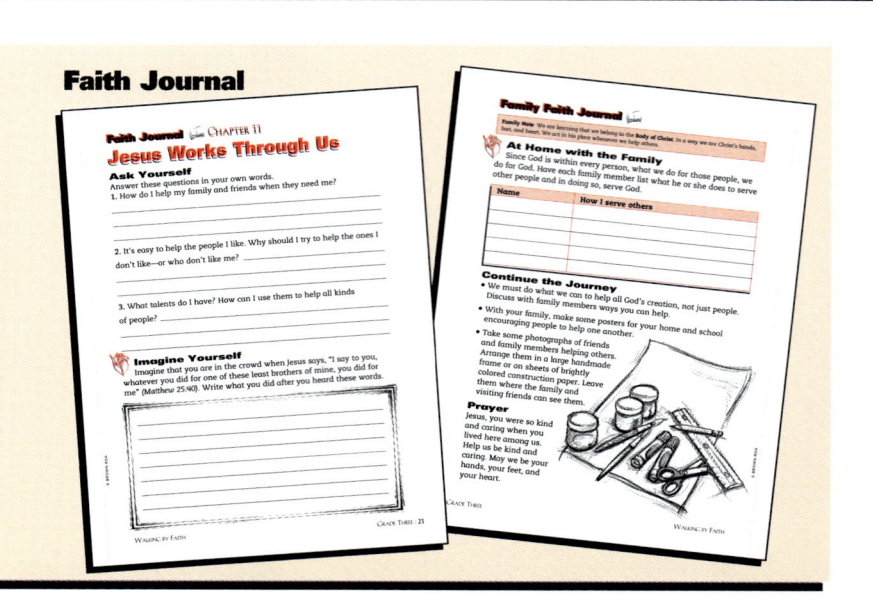

We Love and Serve

At the end of Mass, we go forth to do Jesus' work in the world. The priest or deacon blesses us and says, "Go in peace to love and serve the Lord!" We love and serve the Lord by loving and serving all God's people.

Take turns praying the numbered lines. All join in the response.

Prayer

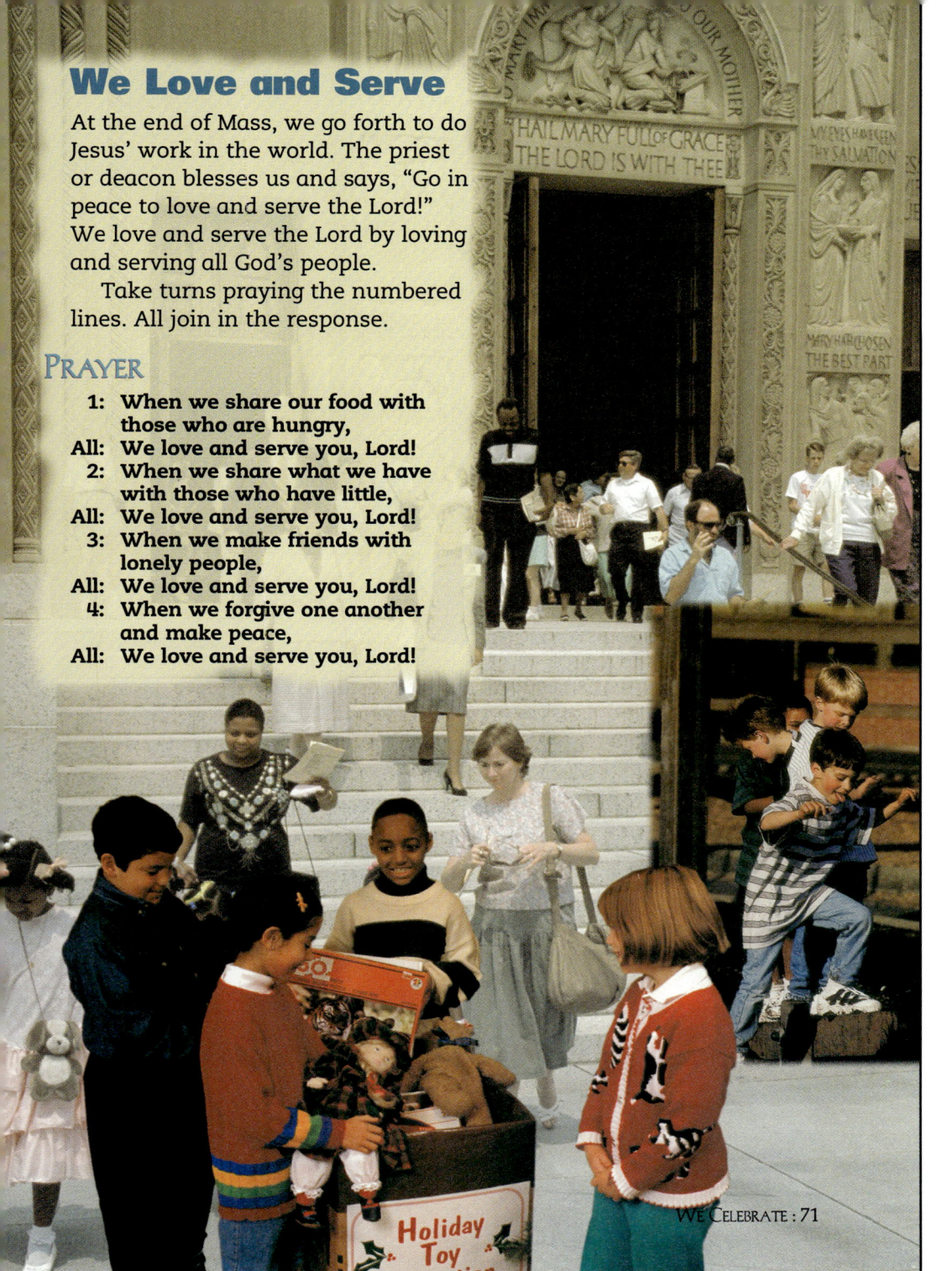

1: When we share our food with those who are hungry,
All: We love and serve you, Lord!
2: When we share what we have with those who have little,
All: We love and serve you, Lord!
3: When we make friends with lonely people,
All: We love and serve you, Lord!
4: When we forgive one another and make peace,
All: We love and serve you, Lord!

WE CELEBRATE
3. Close

Working with the Text

Read aloud or summarize *We Love and Serve*. Discuss the responsibility we take with us when we leave Mass and return to our homes, schools, and neighborhoods.

Working with the Pictures

How are the people in the picture serving Jesus? (by making friends with others, by attending Mass with friends and family members, and by giving freely to those in need) Explain that people serve Jesus in different ways according to their talents and abilities.

Prayer Before you begin the prayer, brainstorm as a group some promises of service; for example, a promise to be friendly to a new class member. Then have the class follow the instructions for praying the prayer aloud. End the celebration with a favorite hymn.

Link to Liturgy

Ask the students to identify people who serve the parish community at Sunday Mass, such as the altar servers, the lectors, the music minister, and the choir members. Explain that all or most of these parishioners are volunteers who give of their time and talents so that the parish family can celebrate the Eucharist more prayerfully and joyfully. Encourage the students to take special notice of these and other liturgical ministers at Sunday Mass.

Notes: Closing the Chapter

Unit Three Review

Objective
- Review the unit and assess progress.

Chapter Summaries

Use this information to reinforce key points before administering the review. These summaries will also help you assess the students' responses to *Show How Far You've Come*, page 73.

Chapter 9
- God sent his Son to bring good news to all God's people.
- The good news that Jesus shared was that God loves all people and saves us from sin.
- Understand that Jesus used parables to teach about the kingdom of God.

Chapter 10
- Jesus sacrificed his life on the cross for all people.
- Jesus' resurrection makes possible new life with God forever.
- The celebration of the Eucharist is a celebration of the Passover of Jesus, his death on the cross, and his resurrection to new life.

Chapter 11
- The Church is the Body of Christ on earth.
- We are called to serve Jesus by serving one another.
- We serve God by using the talents and abilities he gave us.

Review

You may have the students work on the review in class or assign the exercises as homework to be completed with family members.

Fill in the Blanks Read the sentences and the words in the word bank aloud. You might do the first sentence together. Allow the students to complete the sentences individually. If time permits, review their answers as a class.

Matching Review the students' answers as a class. If time permits, brainstorm together other important terms from the chapter.

Share Your Faith Pair the students for this activity. If time permits, invite volunteers to share their responses with the class.

Alternative Encourage the students to complete this activity at home.

72 : UNIT THREE

Unit Three Checkpoint Review

Fill in the Blanks Complete each sentence with the correct term from the word bank.

1. Jesus is the ____**Messiah**____, the one God promised.
2. Jesus came to share the good news of the ____**kingdom**____ of God.
3. We celebrate Jesus' sacrifice and ____**resurrection**____ at every Mass.
4. We are called to use our ____**talents**____ to do Jesus' work.
5. One name for the ____**Church**____ is the Body of Christ.

Word Bank
Church kingdom Messiah resurrection talents

Matching Match the definitions in Column A with the correct terms in Column B.

Column A	Column B
_b_ 1. Another name for good news.	a. Alleluia
_d_ 2. Stories Jesus told about God's kingdom.	b. gospel
_e_ 3. Jesus' saving death and resurrection.	c. sacrifice
_a_ 4. A Hebrew shout of joy, praising God.	d. parables
_c_ 5. To give something up or do something difficult out of love.	e. Paschal mystery

Share Your Faith Tell someone how the Eucharist is like the Passover celebration.

72 : REVIEW

Resource Center

Assessment Tips

Use one or more of the following strategies to assist you in assessing student progress:

- If you need a more detailed written review, you may give the Unit Three Assessment from the Resource Package.
- Ask the students to assess their own progress by working in pairs or small groups to identify the important ideas they learned in this unit.
- Ask the students to consider how they can better live out the Corporal Works of Mercy (page 179) in their own lives. Invite volunteers to share their responses.

Show How Far You've Come Use the chart below to show what you have learned. For each chapter, write or draw the three most important things you remember.

The Body of Christ

Chapter 9 Jesus Brings Good News	Chapter 10 New Life in Jesus	Chapter 11 Jesus Works Through Us
Look for responses that reflect the key points listed under Chapter Summaries.		

What Else Would You Like to Know?
List any questions you still have about Jesus and the Church.

_____
_____
_____

Continue the Journey Choose one or more of the following activities to do on your own, with your class, or with your family.

- Look through your Faith Journal pages for Unit Three. Choose your favorite activity, and share it with a friend or family member.
- Make a book of the life of Jesus. Draw pictures to illustrate your book.
- Act out one of Jesus' parables.
- Choose one of the Works of Mercy from the list on page 179. Do this work for someone who needs it.

REVIEW : 73

Show How Far You've Come Use *Chapter Summaries* to evaluate the students' responses. Particularly note any responses that differ greatly from the key points of the chapters. These responses may indicate areas where presentation was unclear and needs additional attention. If time permits, extend this activity by asking the students to recall their favorite stories, activities, or pictures from this unit.

What Else Would You Like to Know? Have the students share their questions and vote on a class list of three questions for you to answer at the next session.

Continue the Journey If possible, provide time at a later session for the students to demonstrate how they have completed one or more of these activities. For example:

- At the beginning of the next session, ask volunteers to share one of their *Faith Journal* entries.
- Display the students' books where the entire class can enjoy them.
- Provide time for the students to role-play the parables they have chosen.
- At the beginning of the next session, ask volunteers to talk about the works of mercy they chose and how they performed them.

Prayer

Close the review by leading the class in praying together. Begin the prayer with this petition: "Jesus, help us follow your lead and help others by . . ." Invite spontaneous responses. Then have the class pray "Lord, hear our prayer."

Reference Sources

For help in addressing the students' questions about this unit's topics, see:

- *The HarperCollins Encyclopedia of Catholicism* (HarperCollins, 1995).
- *Our Sunday Visitor's Catholic Encyclopedia* (Our Sunday Visitor, Inc., 1991).

Good resources for third graders include:

- *The Collins Dove Dictionary for Young Catholics* by Laurie Woods (Collins Dove, 1990).

Your parish community is another important resource. Priests, deacons, other staff members, catechists, godparents, sponsors, and members of religious communities may be able to answer students' questions or provide additional information.

Link to the Family

If possible, allow students to take these pages home to share with family members.

PARISH : 73

Getting Ready: Chapter 12

A Time to Remember

Program Resources
Student Text, pp. 74–77
Student Faith Journal, pp. 23–24
Your Faith Journal, p. J13

Unit Three (Jesus Christ)
The Body of Christ

Key Content Summary
During Advent the Church looks back to the Old Testament faith in God's promise and forward to Jesus' second coming.

Planning the Chapter

	Pacing Guide Suggested time/Your time	Content	Objectives	Materials
Open	10–15 min./ _____ min.	*We Are Invited*, p. 74	• Realize that every person belongs to a family that is connected through the generations.	• family photographs brought in by the students (optional)
Build	20–25 min./ _____ min.	*We Explore*, p. 75	• Identify the purpose of Advent.	• Bible (optional)
Review	15–20 min./ _____ min.	*We Reflect*, p. 76	• Demonstrate understanding of chapter concepts. • Apply learning through activity. • Practice faith at home and in the parish.	• Advent calendar • *Student Faith Journal*, pp. 23–24 • *Your Faith Journal*, p. J13
Close	10–15 min./ _____ min. *For additional suggestions, see Scheduling, pp. T35–T37.*	*We Celebrate*, p. 77	• Identify our ancestors in faith represented on the Jesse tree.	• Jesse tree or other Advent symbol

73a : CHAPTER 12

Catechism in Context

Doctrinal Foundation This chapter focuses on the Season of Advent, the season of preparation for Christmas. When we celebrate the first coming, or advent, of Christ, we anticipate his second coming in glory. In other words, the Church challenges us to remember a past event (Christ's birth two thousand years ago) in such a way that "we wait in joyful hope for the coming of our savior, Jesus Christ." His first coming makes his second coming a certainty. The day of the Lord will come "like a thief in the night," but it will come. And it is drawing ever closer: "our salvation is closer now than when we first accepted the faith." Only if we look forward as well as backward during the Advent and Christmas Seasons can we see clearly that the present moment is also graced: "To discover how to be living now is the reason I follow this star" (W. H. Auden).

See Catechism of the Catholic Church, #524.

One-Minute Retreat for Catechists

Read
"In darkness there is no choice. It is light that enables us to see the differences between things; and it is Christ that gives us light."
—Mrs. C. T. Whitmell

Reflect
How do I let Christ be my light?

Pray
As I search for hope throughout my life, Lord, may I always be aware of your guidance. Especially during the holidays, when many people feel lonely, may I be a mirror, reflecting your love and your light for all the world to see. Let no one despair when there is so much joy to be shared.

Visualizing the Lesson

Use this graphic organizer to help the students visualize the meaning of Advent.

Draw the graphic organizer on the board or on chart paper, omitting the words *Past*, *Present*, and *Future*. Ask the students to fill in these words by having volunteers explain the three-fold purpose of Advent.

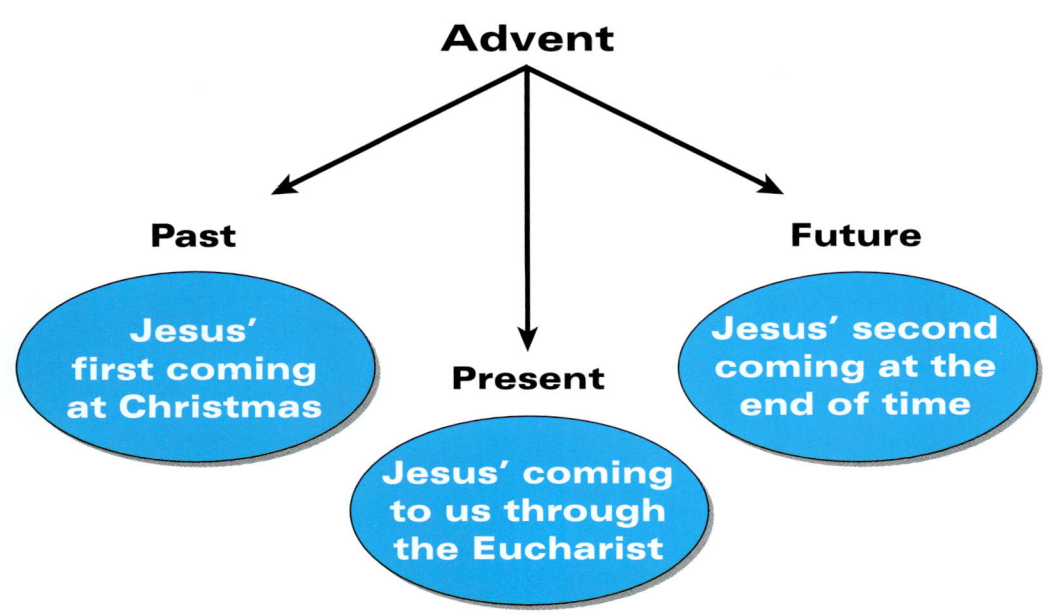

Advent
- **Past:** Jesus' first coming at Christmas
- **Present:** Jesus' coming to us through the Eucharist
- **Future:** Jesus' second coming at the end of time

Library Links

Books for Children
Tree of Hope by Joanne McPortland (St. Anthony Messenger Press, 1-800-488-0488).

McPortland explains customs of Advent and the Jesse tree.

Books for Parents and Teachers
God Is with Us—Daily Reflections for Advent by John J. McIlhon (The Liturgical Press, 1-800-858-5454).

A reading and a reflection are presented for each day of Advent.

Multimedia

For children:
Multicultural Christmas produced by Colman Communications (video) (BROWN-ROA, 1-800-922-7696).

The video shows five families of different ethnicity during the Advent Season.

For parents and teachers:
It's a Wonderful Life (video) (commercial rental).

At Christmas time a man learns the importance of life.

Organizations
For information about ways to bring Christ's light of hope to others, contact:
Amnesty International
322 Eighth Avenue
New York, NY 10001
(1-212-807-8400)
(http://www.igc.apc.org/amnesty/index.html)

Strengthening the Family Link

Here are some suggestions for reaching out to your students' families:

- Encourage the students to talk with family members about ways they will prepare for the coming of Jesus at Christmas.
- Invite family members to join the class in decorating the Jesse tree. Make paper ornaments, each with the name of one of Jesus' ancestors listed in the closing prayer. On either a small tree in your classroom or a tree drawn on a poster board, attach each ornament at the appropriate time while praying the closing prayer.

Chapter 12 pages 74–77

Objectives
- Realize that every person belongs to a family that is connected through the generations.
- Identify the purpose of Advent.
- Identify our ancestors in faith represented on the Jesse tree.

Gathering WE ARE INVITED
1. Open

Personal Experience Have volunteers share favorite family stories.

Prayer Encourage the students to think about their family stories as you pray the opening prayer together.

Working with the Text
- As you read or summarize the text, lead the students to understand that family pictures help us know who we are and give us a feeling of belonging.
- You might want to explain the meaning of *generation*, each age group in a family: children, parents, grandparents, great-grandparents, and so forth.

Working with the Pictures
- What are the child and older family member in the photograph doing? (Looking at a family tree; perhaps the older person is sharing a favorite story about someone in the family.)

  Read the activity directions aloud, and ask the students to complete the activity with a family member or friend at home.

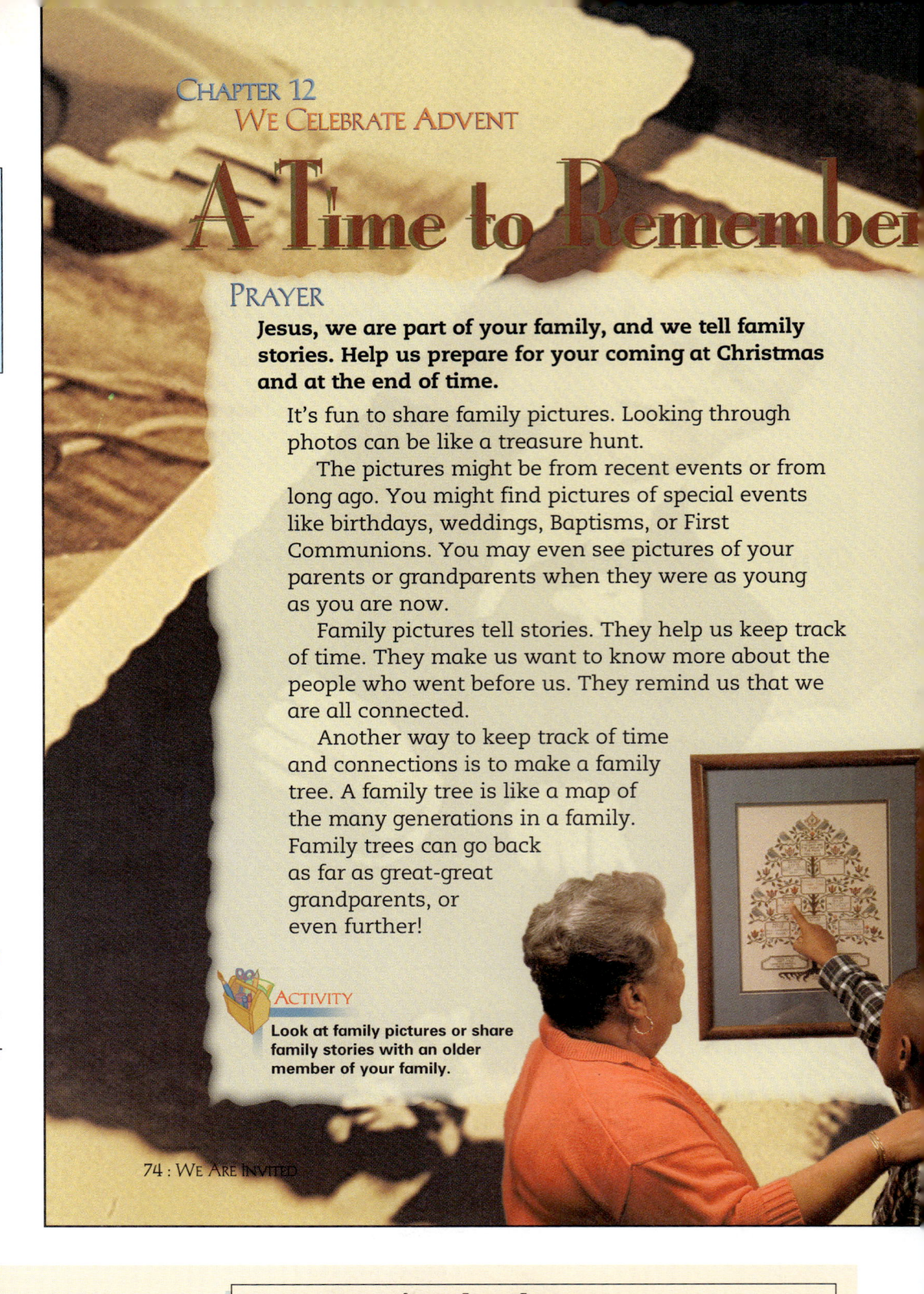

CHAPTER 12
WE CELEBRATE ADVENT

A Time to Remember

PRAYER

Jesus, we are part of your family, and we tell family stories. Help us prepare for your coming at Christmas and at the end of time.

It's fun to share family pictures. Looking through photos can be like a treasure hunt.

The pictures might be from recent events or from long ago. You might find pictures of special events like birthdays, weddings, Baptisms, or First Communions. You may even see pictures of your parents or grandparents when they were as young as you are now.

Family pictures tell stories. They help us keep track of time. They make us want to know more about the people who went before us. They remind us that we are all connected.

Another way to keep track of time and connections is to make a family tree. A family tree is like a map of the many generations in a family. Family trees can go back as far as great-great grandparents, or even further!

ACTIVITY
Look at family pictures or share family stories with an older member of your family.

74 : We Are Invited

Resource Center

Optional Link to the Family

Invite the students to bring in family photographs that they would like to share with the class. Assure them that the pictures will be handled carefully and returned to them to take home again at the end of the class. Allow time for brief descriptions of the photographs.

Teaching Tip

Handling sensitive topics As you discuss families throughout this chapter, keep in mind that for various reasons some students may not be able to trace their family heritages. Assure these students that even if we don't know a lot about our families' histories, we all have people who love us and care for us. Members of a family are not necessarily related by blood. We are members of our Church family.

Notes: Opening the Chapter

74 : CHAPTER 12

There were no photo albums in Jesus' time. But there were family stories and family trees. From generation to generation people passed along the story of God's love. They kept alive their hope in God's promise to send a messiah.

Landmark A family tree showing the generations before Jesus is known as a *Jesse tree*. Jesse was the father of King David, from whose family Jesus came. The Jesse tree shows people from the Old Testament who believed in God's promise.

A Time to Look Ahead

During the four weeks before Christmas, our Church family looks back together. We remember the family tree of Jesus. We share family stories from Scripture. But we look ahead, too. We prepare to celebrate Jesus' birth at Christmastime. And we prepare to welcome Jesus when he returns at the end of time.

We call this time of preparation **Advent**, which means "coming." Advent begins the Church's special calendar, a way of keeping time based on celebrations. During Advent we remember that we are connected to all those before us who believed in God's promise. And we look forward to the time when that promise will come true forever.

Catholics Believe...
that we celebrate Advent to renew our hope for the second coming of Jesus at the end of time.
Catechism, #524

WE EXPLORE : 75

WE EXPLORE
2. Build
Working with the Pictures

Landmark Read aloud or summarize the *Landmark* caption. Then call attention to the family tree shown in the photograph on the previous page. **How are these two family trees alike?** (They both show family members back through generations.) **What is so special about the Jesse tree?** (It is Jesus' family tree.)

Point out the other photographs on the page. Invite volunteers to figure out what the photographs are. (pictures from a family album)

Working with the Text

- Before you read or summarize *A Time to Look Ahead*, remind the students that people of Jesus' time relied on word of mouth to pass on and remember important stories. Most did not read or write, and they did not have the technological means we have today.

- Emphasize that Advent reminds us that Jesus will return again in glory. **Who promised to send Jesus again?** (God the Father)

- Use *The Language of Faith* below to clarify the highlighted term.

- To help the students visualize the concept of Advent, refer to the graphic organizer on page 73B. You may wish to do the suggested activity or one of your own choosing.

- **Catholics Believe** Explain that we do not know when Jesus' second coming will happen or exactly what it will be like. But we believe that Jesus will come in great majesty and bring all people who believe in God's promise and live by his teachings into the fullness of his kingdom.

The Language of Faith
The Season of **Advent** has a three-fold meaning for Christians. During this period we recall the coming into history of the eternal Son of God. We also think about how Jesus comes into our lives every day, especially through his special presence in the Eucharist. Finally, we remember Jesus' promise to return in glory at the end of time.

Enrichment
The genealogy of Jesus, as described in **Matthew 1:1–17**, includes 42 generations from Abraham to Jesus. If time permits, read aloud or summarize part of this Bible passage. Emphasize that Matthew wanted us to know who Jesus was.

Notes: Building the Chapter

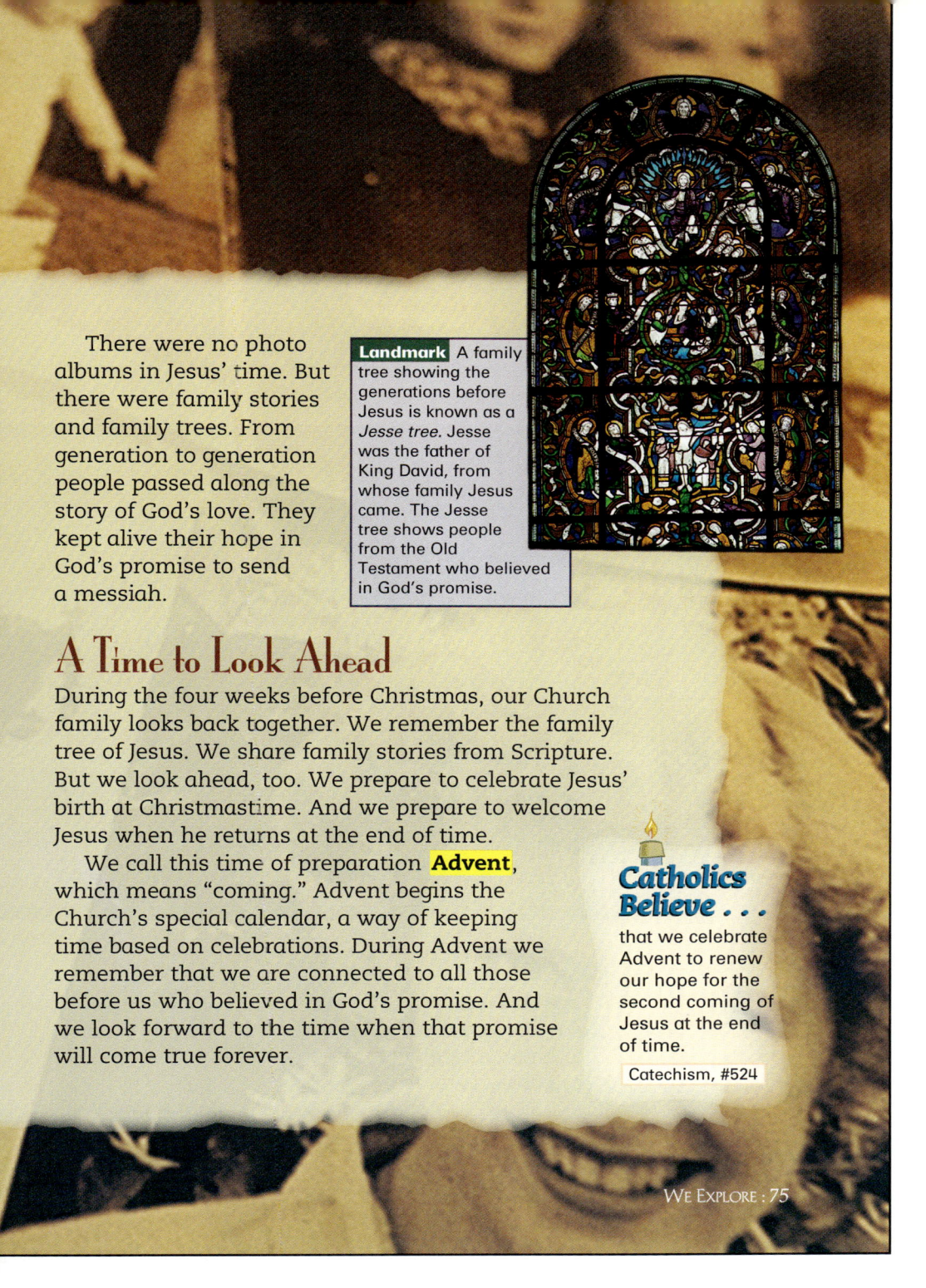

WE REFLECT
Review

Recall Invite responses to the questions. *(a time of preparation for Christmas; the Jesse tree)*

Think and Share Allow the students to consider the question before responding. *(The stories reminded people of God's promise.)*

Continue the Journey Encourage the students to write as many family members' names as they know on the family tree. As a homework assignment, ask the students to work with family members to add more names.

We Live Our Faith *At Home:* If possible, provide an example of an Advent calendar. *In the Parish:* Make the students aware of the parish's scheduled Reconciliation services.

Faith Journal The students may begin pages 23–24 of their *Faith Journal* in class and complete them at home. As a part of your own spiritual development, complete *Your Faith Journal* (page J13) for this chapter.

RECALL
What is Advent? What do we call the family tree of Jesus?

THINK AND SHARE
How did telling family stories help people continue to believe in God's promise?

CONTINUE THE JOURNEY
Add the names of your family members to the family tree. Decorate the family tree.

WE LIVE OUR FAITH
At Home Make a family calendar for the days of Advent. Each day, look at a family picture or share a family story.

In the Parish Participate in a parish celebration of the Sacrament of Reconciliation to prepare for Jesus' coming.

76 : We Reflect

Resource Center

Link to Liturgy
During Advent the solemn blessing in the concluding rite speaks about our longing for Jesus to return again in glory. Ask the students to listen for these words near the end of Mass on the First Sunday of Advent:

"You believe that the Son of God once came to us;
you look for him to come again.
May his coming bring you the light of his holiness
and his blessing bring you freedom."

Assessment Tip
Give the students an opportunity to assess their learning by having them complete a simple chart with these two headings: *What I Knew About Advent* and *What I Learned About Advent*.

Our Family of Faith

Some parishes and families use a Jesse tree to count the days of Advent. Each member of Jesus' family tree has a special sign. These signs are made into ornaments. One ornament is placed on the Jesse tree each day of Advent. This custom reminds us of the faithful people who believed in God's promise.

We can remember these people in prayer, too. Pray this prayer together as part of your Advent celebration.

PRAYER

Dear God our Father, we are part of your family.
As we look forward to celebrating the birthday of your Son, Jesus, we remember
Noah's family, who saw your rainbow in the sky;
Abraham and Sarah, whose children are as countless as the stars;
Jacob, who made peace with his brother;
Joseph, who was lost and found again;
Moses and Joshua, who led your people into the Land of Promise;
Ruth, who was faithful;
Jesse, who was the father of kings;
David, who taught us to sing your praise;
and all the members of your family who believed.
Keep us faithful to your promise until the end of time,
when Jesus comes again.

We Celebrate : 77

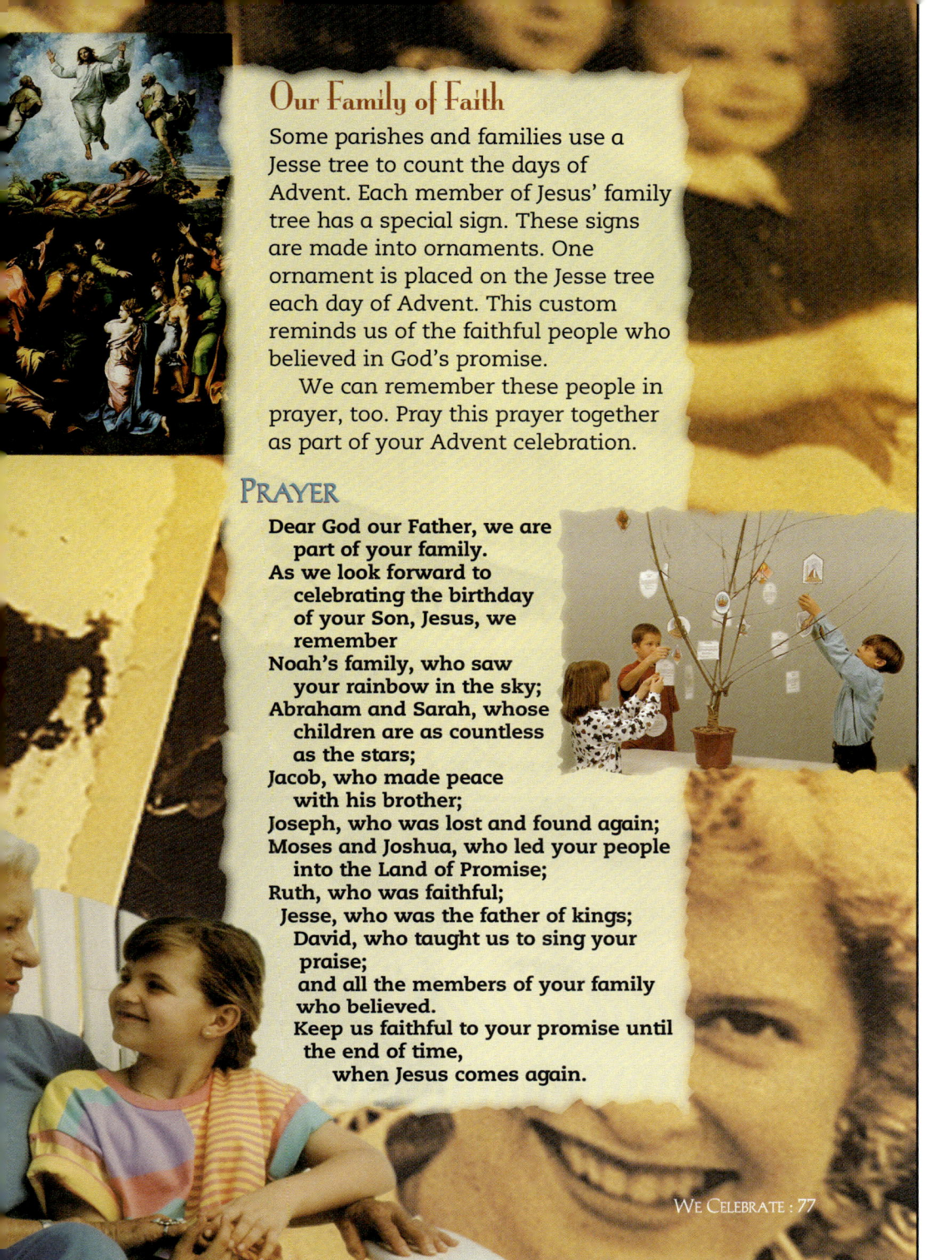

WE CELEBRATE
3. Close

Working with the Pictures

- Call attention to the painting at the top of the page, and invite volunteers to describe it. Tell the students this is a picture of Jesus' transfiguration, described in *Matthew 17:1–2* and *Mark 9:2–3*.
- Refer to Art Background below for additional information.
- Point out the picture of three children decorating a Jesse tree.
- Ask the students to examine the rest of the pictures on this page.
  What do all the people in the pictures have in common? (They all belong to God's family.)

Working with the Text

Read aloud or summarize *Our Family of Faith*. Discuss the Jesse tree the children are shown making.
What do some parishes and families use to count the days of Advent? (the Jesse tree)

Prayer If possible, gather the students around a Jesse tree or other Advent symbol. Pray the first two stanzas of the prayer aloud yourself; then have a student pray aloud each of the following nine stanzas, which name members of Jesus' family. Pray the final stanza together. Allow time for the students to offer silent prayers for members of their families. You may want to close the celebration by singing a familiar Advent hymn, such as "O Come, O Come, Emmanuel."

Art Background

The painting of Jesus' transfiguration was done by Raphael in the sixteenth century. The two men shown on either side of Jesus are Moses and Elijah. Moses was the prophet asked by God to lead the people of Israel out of slavery into the Promised Land. He was also the one to whom God gave the Law. Elijah, another prophet, constantly called the people of Israel away from the worship of idols (false gods) and to a belief in one true God.

Notes: Closing the Chapter

PARISH : 77

Getting Ready: Chapter 13

The Church Works Together

Program Resources
Student Text, pp. 78–83
Student Faith Journal, pp. 25–26
Your Faith Journal, p. J14
Chapter 13 Transparency
Unit Four Family Letter

Unit Four (The Church)
Guided by the Holy Spirit

Key Content Summary
The Church is a structured organization with leaders who serve.

Planning the Chapter

Open	Pacing Guide *Suggested time/Your time*	Content	Objectives	Materials
	10–15 min./ _____ **min.**	*We Are Invited*, pp. 78–79	• Discover that the Church community has a mission that Jesus sent us to carry out.	• art materials

Build				
	20–25 min./ _____ **min.**	*We Explore*, pp. 80–81	• Understand that the Church is an organized institution. • Recognize the need for Church leaders.	• world map or globe • state or regional map (optional) • Chapter 13 Transparency from the Resource Package

Review				
	15–20 min./ _____ **min.**	*We Reflect*, p. 82	• Demonstrate understanding of chapter concepts. • Apply learning through activity. • Practice faith at home and in the parish.	• *Student Faith Journal*, pp. 25–26 • *Your Faith Journal*, p. J14

Close				
	10–15 min./ _____ **min.**	*We Celebrate*, p. 83	• Participate in a prayer of intercession.	• recording of instrumental music • Unit Four Family Letter from the Resource Package

For additional suggestions, see Scheduling, pp. T35–T37.

77A : CHAPTER 13

Catechism in Context

Doctrinal Foundation This chapter explains that all members of the Church make up the Body of Christ. As the people of God, we are all equal in dignity, and we all have unique gifts, or talents, to contribute to the well-being of the Church and to build up the Body of Christ. As Paul wrote, "If the whole body were an eye, where would the hearing be? If the whole body were hearing, where would the sense of smell be? But as it is, God placed the parts, each one of them, in the body as he intended. If they were all one part, where would the body be? But as it is, there are many parts, yet one body" (1 Corinthians 12:17–20). Just as it is necessary for all the parts of the human body to cooperate with one another for the benefit of the whole body, so all the members of the Body of Christ—lay men and women, religious men and women, deacons, priests, bishops, and the pope—are to work together to carry on the work of God in the world. Each is called to use his or her talents, working with the other members, to perform particular functions in the Body of Christ.

See Catechism of the Catholic Church, #872.

One-Minute Retreat for Catechists

Read
"They serve God well who serve his creatures."
—Caroline Newman

Reflect
How can I serve others?

Pray
As my students learn about their spiritual duties, help them find their special roles. Help me instill in them a sense of respect for humanity, for animals, and for the earth. Through our service, let us worship you and show our gratitude for creating us.

Visualizing the Lesson

Use this graphic organizer to help the students understand ordained Church leadership.

Draw the graphic organizer on the board or on chart paper, leaving out the words *Pope, Bishop,* and *Pastor*. Have volunteers use the diagram to tell who heads the Church worldwide, a(n) (arch)diocese, and a parish. Discuss with the students ways these ordained ministers both lead and serve.

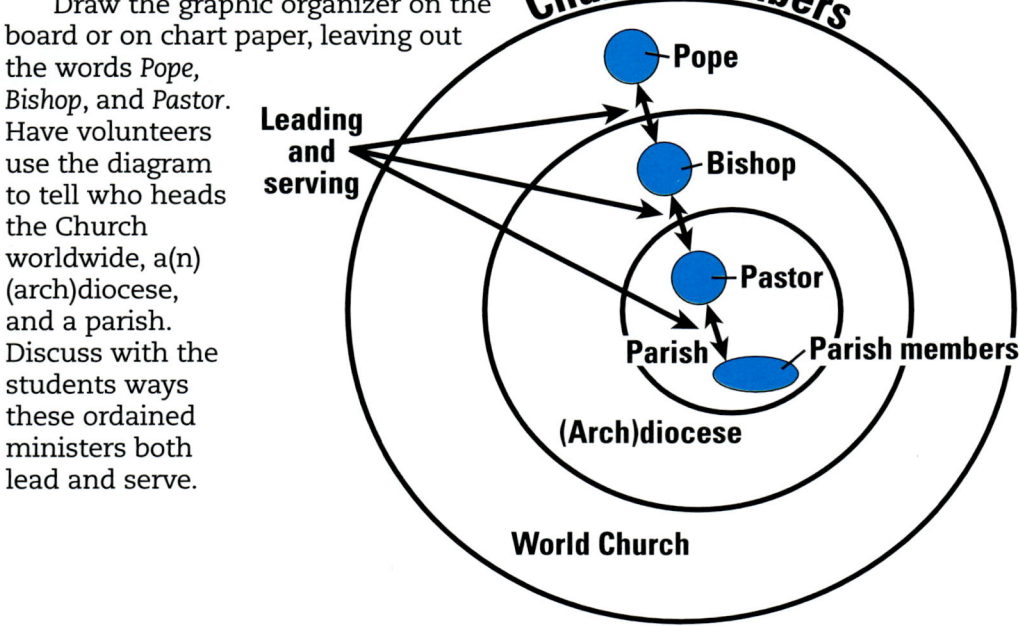

Library Links

Books for Children
I Am a Roman Catholic by Brenda Pettenuzzo (Franklin Watts, 1-212-686-7070).
The Catholic tradition is told in photographs and easy-to-read text.

Books for Parents and Teachers
What It Means to Be Catholic by Joseph Champlin (Franciscan Communications, 1-800-488-0488).
Our actions reflect our Catholic faith.
Pontiffs: Popes Who Shaped History by John Jay Hughes (Our Sunday Visitor, 1-800-348-2440).
This book tells stories of eleven popes.

Multimedia
For children:
Rome: In the Footsteps of Peter and Paul. Episode #1, "In the Beginning" produced by Heart of the Nation (video) (BROWN-ROA, 1-800-922-7696).
Simon Peter meets Jesus.
Glory Day, "E Na Lima Hana" (The Working Hands) by David Haas (GIA Publications, 1-800-442-1358).
Use this song to reinforce chapter material with music.

For parents and teachers:
And There Came a Man (video) (commercial rental).
This is a biography of Pope John XXIII.

Organizations
For information about ways to use one's talents to help build up the Body of Christ, contact:
Jesuit Volunteer Corps
Eighteenth and Thompson Streets
Philadelphia, PA 19121

Strengthening the Family Link

Here are some suggestions for reaching out to your students' families:
- Encourage the students to talk with family members about ways they can help build up the Body of Christ by using their special talents.
- Invite family members to join the class in decorating a poster or bulletin board about the Body of Christ.

Parish : 77B

Chapter 13 pages 78–83

Objectives
- Discover that the Church community has a mission that Jesus sent us to carry out.
- Understand that the Church is an organized institution.
- Recognize the need for Church leaders.

Gathering WE ARE INVITED
1. Open

Personal Experience Ask the students to think about positive experiences they have had working on projects with others.

Prayer Ask the students to keep those experiences in mind as they pray the opening prayer together.

Working with the Text

Read aloud or summarize the text. **What difficulty did the friends have the first time they set up the stand?** (They didn't have the right supplies because they didn't have a plan or a leader.)

Working with the Pictures

Call attention to the picture. Invite the students to speculate about what will happen now that the group has a plan and a leader.

Resource Center

Link to the Family
Tell the students about a time when your family took on a project such as cleaning out the garage or doing spring cleaning. Tell them who the leader was and what the plan was to complete the project. Then invite volunteers to share similar experiences.

Meeting Individual Needs
Learners acquiring English Group these students with English-proficient students who can help them understand the story as they read it aloud. You might ask knowledgeable students to explain the practice of setting up a lemonade stand to earn money—what it involves and why youngsters do it.

CHAPTER 13

The Church Works Together

PRAYER

Bless your Church, dear God, as we work together to do your work on earth.

Katie and her friends wanted to raise money for their class field trip. One hot Saturday morning they decided to set up a lemonade stand.

"We need supplies," Katie said. So everyone went home to get something. Katie, Robert, and Sean all brought back water. Sarah brought cups, but she didn't bring enough.

Katie's friends laughed. "We need a plan," Katie said. "We need to work together." Katie knew what to do. "I'll ask my mom to squeeze lemons for us," she said. "Robert, can you bring sugar?"

"Sure," Robert answered. "And I can paint a sign for our stand, too."

Notes: Opening the Chapter

"We have cups at home, too," said Sean. "But how will we carry everything?"

"I'll get my wagon," Sarah said. "We'll bring everything. Then we can use the wagon for the stand!"

By the end of the afternoon, the friends had raised the money they needed. And there was enough lemonade left for each of them to enjoy a cool, refreshing drink.

A Mission and a Structure

Katie and her friends gave themselves a task. In order to carry it out, they needed a leader to guide them and a plan to direct their action. They needed everyone's contributions.

The Church, too, has a task. But the task of the Church has been given to us by Jesus. It is our **mission**, the work we were sent to do. In order to carry it out, we need leaders. We need some kind of structure that allows everyone to share time, talent, and treasure.

Scripture Signpost
"In one body we have many parts, and all the parts do not have the same function."
Romans 12:4

What would happen if everyone in our Church community had the same gifts and did the same thing?

ACTIVITY
Draw or write about a time when you worked with others to carry out a task.

WE ARE INVITED : 79

WE ARE INVITED
Open *Continued*

Working with the Pictures

- Point out both photographs. **What two things helped the group organize their lemonade stand?** *(choosing a leader and making a plan)*

  Supply the necessary art materials for the activity. Encourage volunteers to share their work.

  Alternative Have the students complete this activity as a homework assignment.

Working with the Text

- After you have finished reading the story, ask the students if it turned out the way they had predicted.
- Read aloud or summarize *A Mission and a Structure*, using *The Language of Faith* below to further develop the term *mission*.
- Stress that Jesus' work on earth depends on each of us using our talents and abilities to serve others.

  Scripture Signpost Ask volunteers to respond to the question. *(The work Jesus sent us to do would not get done because it requires a variety of talents and roles.)* For additional information, see *Scripture Background* below.

The Language of Faith

Mission, from the Latin *missio*, means "to be sent out." Jesus has sent us out as the Body of Christ to announce the good news of God's love for all people. The Church is called to preach the good news of the gospel, celebrate God's love in the liturgy and the sacraments, and provide an example of God's love in action by performing works of charity.

Scripture Background

In Paul's time Rome was the center of the world for travel and commerce, and many people visited the city. Paul was a citizen of Rome. His **Letter to the Romans** is a powerful exposition of his teaching that Christ is the source of salvation. He tells the Roman Christians that they are not saved by following a code of law. Yet faith in Christ does not mean there is lawlessness. They must follow the life and example of Christ, who saves them.

Link to the Faith Community

Tell the students that many parishes have mission statements describing how the parish community will carry out Jesus' work. If time permits, invite a member of the parish staff to explain your parish's mission statement to the class.

WE EXPLORE
2. Build

Working with the Pictures

- Direct the students' attention to the picture of St. Peter's Basilica.
- Explain that the Vatican in Rome is the center of the Catholic Church's worldwide activities.

Landmark Point out Rome on a world map or globe. Explain to the students that the Basilica of St. Peter, the Vatican Palace, and the surrounding gardens and official buildings make up Vatican City. The Vatican includes libraries and museums containing invaluable manuscripts, books, and works of art, such as the Sistine Chapel and Michelangelo's *Pieta*.

Working with the Text

- As you read *The Call to Serve*, explain that an *institution* is an organized group working toward a common goal. The Church works as an institution to carry out Jesus' mission.
- As you work with the Scripture Story, share *Scripture Background* below.
- Elicit student responses to the bulleted question. **(Jesus was giving Peter the responsibility to lead the Church.)**
- Make sure the students understand that Jesus did not literally hand Peter a set of keys. Rather, he used the idea of "the keys of the kingdom" to help Peter understand that he was being entrusted with something very important—the Church community, the beginning of the kingdom of God on earth.

Catholics Believe Emphasize that Christ is the life force of the Church.

Landmark This picture shows St. Peter's Basilica in the Vatican, an independent country in Rome, Italy. Tradition says that the main altar is built over Saint Peter's tomb.

The Call to Serve

The Church is not a lemonade stand. It is not a club or a team or a business. It is a community called by God. But because it is a community of humans, the Church needs a structure or form. That is why we say that the Church is an *institution* as well as a community.

The Church's leaders are not bosses or kings. They are called to serve others, not to have power over them. They are called to care for people as shepherds care for the sheep.

SCRIPTURE STORY
Jesus Chooses Peter

One day Jesus asked the apostles, "Who do you think I am?"

Simon said, "You are the Christ, the Son of the living God."

Jesus looked at Simon and said, "Simon, no one told you to say that. God told you to say that. Your name is now Peter." (*Peter* means "rock.") "Upon this rock I will build my Church. Evil will never overpower it."

Then Jesus continued, "Peter, I will give you the keys to the kingdom of heaven. Whatever you bind on earth will be bound in heaven. And whatever you loose on earth will be loosed in heaven."

—based on Matthew 16:15–19

- **What do you think Jesus meant by giving Peter the "keys to the kingdom of heaven"?**

Catholics Believe... that we all help build the Body of Christ by using our special talents and abilities.
Catechism, #872

80 : WE EXPLORE

Resource Center

Scripture Background

Matthew 16:15–19 tells us that when his earthly mission was almost completed, not long before his crucifixion and death, Jesus asked his apostles, "Who do people say that I am?" Jesus realized that there was still much about him and the reason for his coming into the world that his disciples did not understand. He was encouraged when Peter answered that Jesus was the Messiah *and* the Son of God. It was therefore to Peter that Jesus entrusted the Church and its authority—he was God's instrument to reveal Christ as the Messiah and the Son of God, who alone could save all people.

Notes: Building the Chapter

Leading and Serving

Peter was chosen by Jesus to be the first leader of the Church. The other apostles shared in his mission to carry out the work of Jesus. Today our Church continues to be led by bishops, who are ordained to serve God's people. The word *bishop* means "overseer." A bishop usually oversees, or leads and serves, an area called a **diocese**.

Dioceses are made up of many parishes. Each parish has leaders, too. The **pastor** is a priest who has been given the authority to lead a parish community. He celebrates the sacraments and works with other ministers and staff members to serve the people of the parish.

Tradition calls Peter the first pope. The word **pope** comes from an Italian word for "Father." The pope is the Bishop of Rome. The pope and the bishops are pastors, too. Together they lead and inspire the whole Catholic Church in doing Jesus' work.

Saints Walk with Us
Pope John XXIII

This twentieth-century pope has not been officially canonized. But he was loved by people all over the world for the way in which he led and served the Church.

Pope John XXIII gathered the world's bishops for the Second Vatican Council. This great meeting helped the Church bring Jesus' good news to the modern world.

ACTIVITY
In a small group, make a list of good qualities you think Church leaders should have. Compare your list with those from other groups.

WE EXPLORE : 81

WE EXPLORE
Build *Continued*

Working with the Text
- As you read aloud or summarize the text, use *The Language of Faith* below to further explain the terms *diocese*, *pastor*, and *pope*.
  What is the sacrament in which a priest is ordained? (the Sacrament of Holy Orders)
- Point out that the pope is ordained first as a deacon, second as a priest, and third as a bishop.
- To clarify the Church's organization, use the graphic organizer on page 77B. You may wish to do the suggested activity or one of your own choosing.

  Brainstorm this list together with the students.

  Alternative Ask the students to complete this activity at home with the help of adult family members.

- *Saints Walk with Us* Tell the students that very few popes had as strong an impact on the Church and the world as John XXIII—even though he was pope for only five years (1958–1963). See *Profile* below for more information.

Working with the Pictures
How is the bishop in the picture serving the people of this parish? (He has helped the parishioners celebrate a sacrament; he is getting to know the parish members and their needs.)

The Language of Faith
- A ***diocese*** is the specific territory in which a bishop has authority over the Church members. Each diocese is made up of several parishes. Use a state or regional map to show the students the boundaries of their own diocese.
- A ***pastor*** is a priest who has been assigned by the bishop of the diocese to lead one or more parishes in a diocese. The word *pastor* means "shepherd."
- The ***pope*** is the bishop of Rome and the leader of all Church members throughout the world.

Profile
Pope John XXIII *(1881–1963)* Pope John XXIII was a pope who brought renewal to the Church. Only 100 days after his election, Pope John XXIII called for a general council, a special meeting of all the Church's leaders. This meeting, called the *Second Vatican Council*, attempted to invigorate the spiritual life of the Church and to encourage fuller involvement of all Catholics in spreading the gospel message.

We Reflect
Review

Recall Ask volunteers to respond. **(Peter; a diocese)**

Think and Share Have the students consider the question before responding. **(Leaders help people use their talents to assist in the Church's mission; they make plans for doing Jesus' work.)**

Continue the Journey Complete this activity orally with the students. You might explain the difference between a diocese and an archdiocese. **(An archdiocese is a diocese of some significance, such as size or age, with an archbishop or cardinal as its leader.)** Supply names of Church leaders as necessary.

We Live Our Faith *At Home:* Discuss various ways to show thanks to family members. *In the Parish:* The parish bulletin is a good source of this information.

Faith Journal The students may begin pages 25–26 of their *Faith Journal* in class and complete them at home. As part of your own spiritual development, complete *Your Faith Journal* (page J14).

Recall
To whom did Jesus give the keys to the kingdom of heaven? What is the name of an area overseen by a bishop?

Think and Share
Why do you think the Church needs leaders?

Continue the Journey
Fill in the blanks to show how you belong to the community of the Church.

My name is _____.

I am a member of _____ parish

in the (Arch)Diocese of _____.

Our pastor is _____.

Our (arch)bishop is _____.

Pope _____ leads our Church.

We Live Our Faith

At Home Make a list of what each family member does to serve your family. Thank each member for his or her contribution.

In the Parish Find out who leads and serves your parish. Write a thank-you note to these people.

82 : We Reflect

Resource Center
Assessment Tip
As the students share their responses to *Think and Share*, look for an understanding that Church leaders have a mission to fulfill following in the footsteps of Peter and the other apostles.

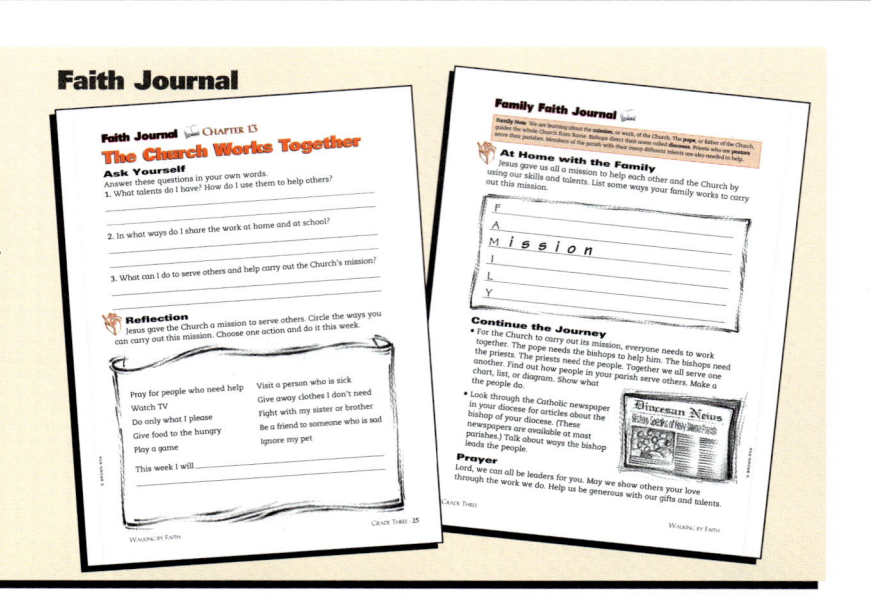

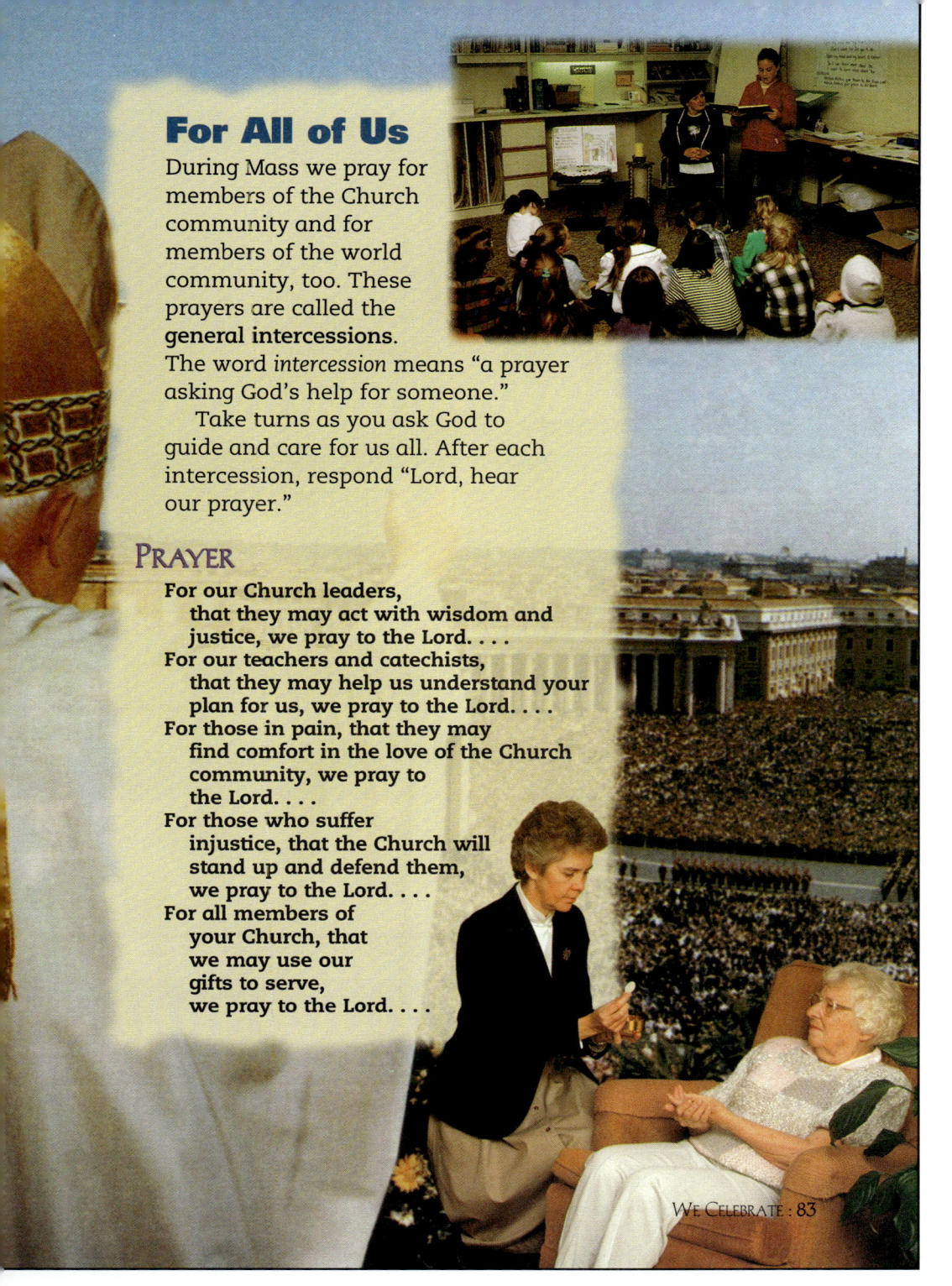

For All of Us

During Mass we pray for members of the Church community and for members of the world community, too. These prayers are called the **general intercessions**.

The word *intercession* means "a prayer asking God's help for someone."

Take turns as you ask God to guide and care for us all. After each intercession, respond "Lord, hear our prayer."

PRAYER

For our Church leaders,
   that they may act with wisdom and
   justice, we pray to the Lord. . . .
For our teachers and catechists,
   that they may help us understand your
   plan for us, we pray to the Lord. . . .
For those in pain, that they may
   find comfort in the love of the Church
   community, we pray to
   the Lord. . . .
For those who suffer
   injustice, that the Church will
   stand up and defend them,
   we pray to the Lord. . . .
For all members of
   your Church, that
   we may use our
   gifts to serve,
   we pray to the Lord. . . .

We Celebrate : 83

WE CELEBRATE
3. Close

Working with the Pictures

Call attention to the photographs.
   How does the pope serve the Church community? (The pope is the leader of the entire Church.)
   How does a catechist serve the Church community? (A catechist teaches people about Jesus and the Church, training them in the Church's beliefs and practices.)
   How does a Eucharistic minister serve the Church community? (A Eucharistic minister helps distribute Communion and brings the Eucharist to Church members who cannot attend Mass.)

Working with the Text

- As you read or summarize *For All of Us*, use *The Language of Faith* below to clarify the term *general intercessions*.
- Stress that all members of the Church community are called to serve others. One important way we serve others is by praying for them.
- **Prayer** Close the chapter by celebrating prayer as a way of serving others. You might play a recording of instrumental music as you gather the students into a circle. Invite the students to hold hands. Ask volunteers to take turns praying the intercessions, with the class responding "Lord, hear our prayer" after each one. If time permits, close the prayer celebration by singing a favorite hymn together.

The Language of Faith

The **general intercessions** prayed at Mass are prayers that ask for God's help for others and for ourselves as a Church community. They are prayed in faith, knowing that God our loving Father always listens to our prayers. Jesus has promised that when the community gathers for prayer, he is in our midst. We offer our intercessions to God our Father in Jesus' name. We trust that our prayers will be heard and answered if it is God's will. The general intercessions are always prayed at Sunday Mass. They follow the Creed and are part of the Liturgy of the Word. These prayers help us recognize that there are needs beyond the local community.

Link to the Family

To keep family members involved with what the students are learning in this unit, copy and distribute the Unit Four Family Letter from the Resource Package.

Notes: Closing the Chapter

PARISH : 83

Getting Ready: Chapter 14

One and Holy

Program Resources
Student Text, pp. 84–89
Student Faith Journal, pp. 27–28
Your Faith Journal, p. J15
Chapter 14 Transparency
Unit Four Music and Liturgy Resources

Unit Four (The Church)
Guided by the Holy Spirit

Key Content Summary
Marks of the Church are signs by which the Church's authenticity is recognized.

Planning the Chapter

	Pacing Guide *Suggested time/Your time*	Content	Objectives	Materials
Open	10–15 min./ _____ min.	*We Are Invited,* pp. 84–85	• Realize that the Mass is an experience common to all Catholics.	
Build	20–25 min./ _____ min.	*We Explore,* pp. 86–87	• Identify the four marks of the Church. • Recognize the unity and holiness of the Church.	• Chapter 14 Transparency from the Resource Package
Review	15–20 min./ _____ min.	*We Reflect,* p. 88	• Demonstrate understanding of chapter concepts. • Apply learning through activity. • Practice faith at home and in the parish.	• missalettes or hymnals • *Student Faith Journal,* pp. 27–28 • *Your Faith Journal,* p. J15
Close	10–15 min./ _____ min.	*We Celebrate,* p. 89	• Recognize and meditate on the Holy Spirit's presence in our lives.	• Unit Four Music and Liturgy Resources from the Resource Package

For additional suggestions, see Scheduling, pp. T35–T37.

83A : CHAPTER 14

Catechism in Context

Doctrinal Foundation This chapter explores the Church's unity and holiness. The Church is and must be *one*. To be an effective sign of God's redemptive work in Christ, it must be a community of reconciliation. It must bring its members together into a communion of faith, trust, and mutual concern. In doing so, it reverses the effects of sin, which have alienated people from God, from one another, and from themselves. The various communions make up the Church, which is the People of God, one Body of Christ, one Temple of the Spirit. The Church is one, despite all human divisions, because of the work of the Holy Spirit.

See Catechism of the Catholic Church, #813.

The Church, by the power of God's grace, is and must be *holy*. Its life and its unity are from above. Animated by the Holy Spirit, it constantly calls its members out of their sinful, broken existence, so that while remaining in the world, they are no longer of it. The Church is the *communion of saints*.

One-Minute Retreat for Catechists

Read
"When people surrender themselves to the Spirit of God, they will learn more concerning God and Christ and the Atonement and Immortality in a week, than they would learn in a lifetime, apart from the Spirit."

—Henry Ward Beecher

Reflect
How have I learned from the Holy Spirit?

Pray
Holy Spirit, help me contribute to the unity of our Church. Help my students recognize the marks of our Church. May they continue to learn and grow in God's love.

Visualizing the Lesson

Use this graphic organizer to help the students visualize Church unity.

Draw the graphic organizer on the board or on chart paper, leaving the outer circles blank. Have the students use the diagram to name the ways in which the Church is one, and fill in their responses. Discuss each of these common elements with the students.

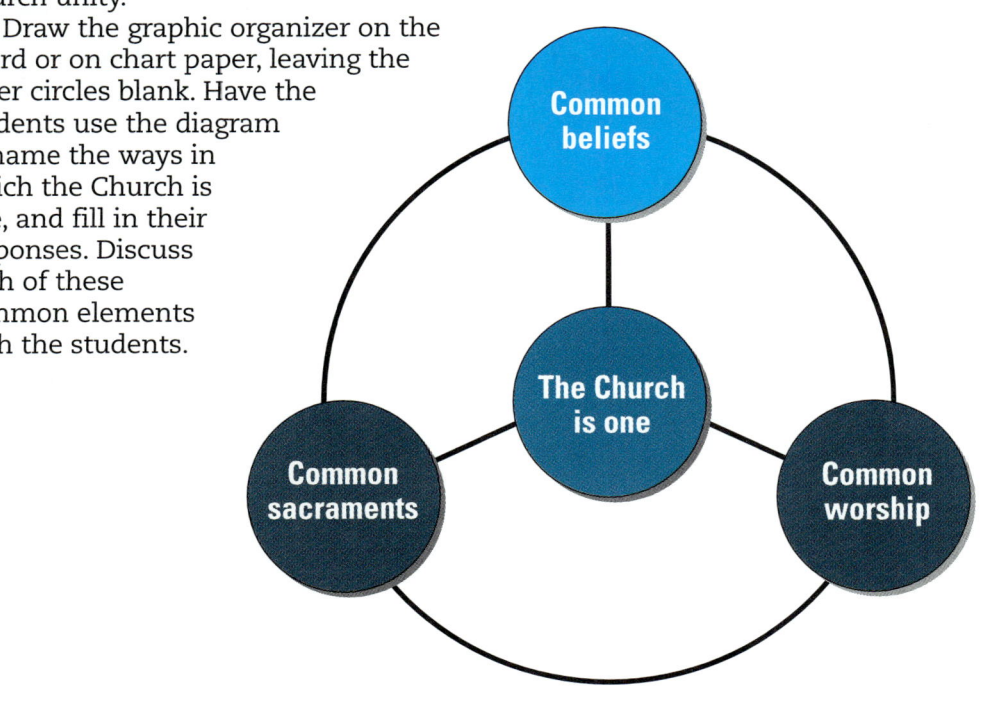

- The Church is one
  - Common beliefs
  - Common sacraments
  - Common worship

Library Links

Books for Children
Let's Learn About the Church and Celebrate Its Message by Mary Cay Senger (The Liturgical Press, 1-800-858-5450).

Senger gives an overview of the Church and its traditions.

Books for Parents and Teachers
The Church We Believe In: One, Holy, Catholic and Apostolic by Francis A. Sullivan (Paulist Press, 1-800-218-1903).

This book explains the beliefs of the Catholic Church.

Multimedia
For children:
Together in Faith (video) (BROWN-ROA, 1-800-922-7696).

This presentation offers a brief overview of the community of the Catholic Church.

Glory Day, "We Are One in the Lord" by David Haas (GIA Publications, 1-800-442-1358).

Use this song, featured in Haas's concert video or audio CD, to reinforce chapter material with music.

For parents and teachers:
Church from the Mysteries of Faith series produced by Fisher Productions (video) (Paulist Press, 1-800-218-1903).

This video explores the meaning of Church and its presence in today's world.

Organizations
For further information about the marks of the Catholic Church, contact:

Committee on the *Catechism of the Catholic Church*
National Conference of Catholic Bishops
3211 Fourth Street
Washington, DC 20017-1194
(1-202-541-3000)
(http://www.nccbuscc.org)

Strengthening the Family Link

Here are some suggestions for reaching out to your students' families:

- Encourage the students to talk with family members about Pentecost and how the Holy Spirit helps the Church.
- Invite family members to join the class in the prayer to the Holy Spirit.

PARISH : 83B

Chapter 14 pages 84–89

Objectives
- Realize that the Mass is an experience common to all Catholics.
- Identify the four marks of the Church.
- Recognize the unity and holiness of the Church.

Gathering — WE ARE INVITED
1. Open

Personal Experience Invite volunteers to share experiences of attending Mass in a Catholic church other than their own.

Prayer Ask the students to reflect on those experiences as you pray the prayer together.

Working with the Text
- Read aloud or summarize the text.

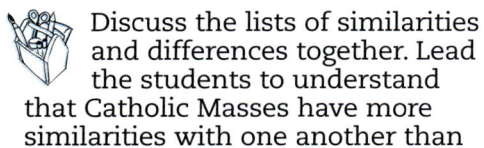

Discuss the lists of similarities and differences together. Lead the students to understand that Catholic Masses have more similarities with one another than they have differences.

Working with the Pictures
Call attention to the photographs. **What do these buildings have in common?** (All have spires or towers, and most have one or more crosses.)

CHAPTER 14
One and Holy

PRAYER

Dear Holy Spirit, thank you for the unity and holiness you give to the Church.

Dear Mom,
  California is lots of fun. Uncle Frank and Aunt Nancy have been really nice to me. They took Cousin Meggie and me swimming and to lots of other places.
  Yesterday we went to church. I was excited. It looked different. The building was round! I could look past the altar and see people facing me!

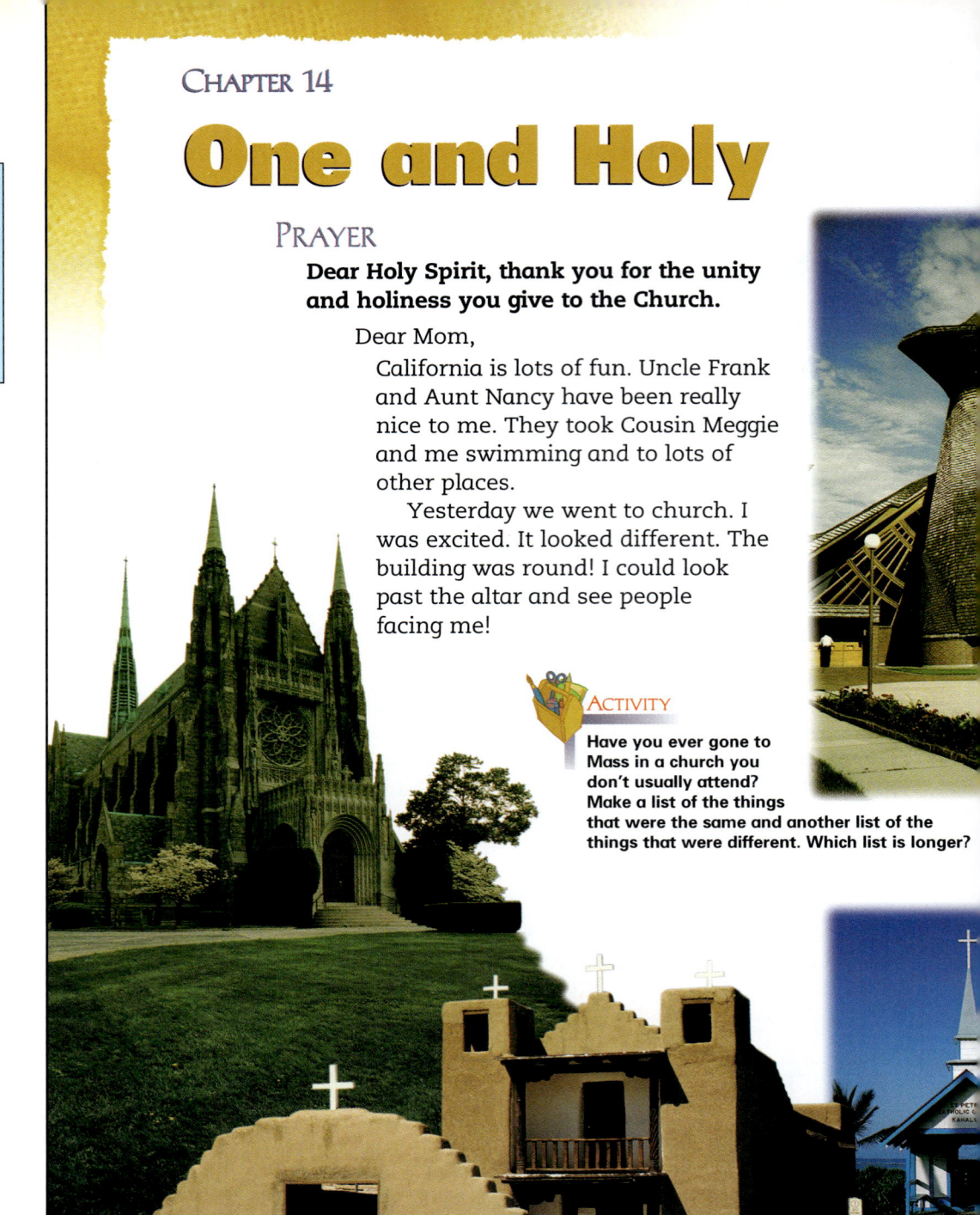

ACTIVITY
Have you ever gone to Mass in a church you don't usually attend? Make a list of the things that were the same and another list of the things that were different. Which list is longer?

84 : We Are Invited

Resource Center

Background
Tell the students that church architecture—the "look" of a church and how it is built—has changed over time. Many early Catholic churches were round, square, or in the shape of a cross, with the altar in the center where the Mass could be the focus of what took place there. Many modern churches have returned to this early style. A high, domed ceiling was used to remind people of heaven. Later, stained-glass windows and spires that seemed to reach up to heaven were added. People believed that churches should be beautiful in order to give glory and praise to God. The design of a church helps people worship God in a space set aside as sacred because God and people meet there in a special way.

Notes: Opening the Chapter

Then Mass started. Suddenly I felt right at home. The priest was praying the words I knew from New York. There were Scripture readings, just like at home. The songbook had a different cover, but I knew some of the songs. Mass was the same.

Our churches are so much alike. My religion teacher was right when she said that the building doesn't matter. What people believe and how they honor God is what makes this our Church.

Tomorrow we go to the beach again. I can't wait to tell you all about my adventures when I get home. I'm having fun, but I miss you. See you soon!

Love,
Jackie

- **What are some things that all Catholics believe?**

The parts of the Mass are always the same, but the celebrations can look different.

WE ARE INVITED : 85

We Are Invited
Open Continued
Working with the Pictures
- Call attention to the photographs.
- Emphasize that we can go into *any* Catholic church and feel at home, even though the building and the celebration itself may look unfamiliar. The most important parts of the Mass are the same wherever Mass is celebrated in the world.

Working with the Text
- Read aloud or summarize the rest of the letter.
  What are some of the things that Jackie's home church had in common with the one he or she visited? (Scripture readings, songs, the Mass)
- Encourage volunteers to respond to the bulleted question. (Answers will vary. Listen for items mentioned in the Creed.)

Multicultural Link
Point out to the students that the Catholic Church in the United States is made up of a wide diversity of people with different origins, cultures, customs, and traditions. Church buildings often reflect these differences. For example, Mexican Americans may display pictures of Our Lady of Guadalupe in their churches, while Eastern Rite Catholics adorn their churches with icons. Ask volunteers to name art objects or church furnishings that are signs of your parish's history or tradition.

WE EXPLORE
2. Build
Working with the Text

- As you read or summarize the text, use *The Language of Faith* below to further develop the term *marks of the Church*.
How is the Church like God?
(It is loving, caring, compassionate, forgiving, merciful, and so on.)

- To illustrate the ways in which the Church is one, refer to the graphic organizer on page 83B. You may wish to do the suggested activity or one of your own choosing.

- **Catholics Believe** Lead the students to understand that God's work would not be done without the help of the Holy Spirit.

Working with the Pictures

- Call attention to the photographs. **What do all these pictures have in common?** (All show practices of Catholics throughout the world.)

- Ask volunteers to respond to the caption question. (Catholics share common beliefs, worship, and sacraments.)

Catholics Believe...
that the Church is unified because of the work of the Holy Spirit.
Catechism, #813

Our Unified Church

There are four **marks of the Church** we use to recognize the Church begun by Jesus. Jesus' Church is one, holy, catholic, and apostolic. The Catholic Church shares these marks of the one true Church.

Jackie recognized the oneness of the Church when she participated at Mass. All over the world Catholics share common beliefs, worship, and sacraments.

We know that the Church is holy, or Godlike, because it is loved by Christ. The Church works to show this love to the world by following Jesus' teachings. And the Church knows that all followers of Jesus share in this holiness.

The Holy Spirit keeps the Church unified and holy. Through the Church and its people, God's work is done.

What do Catholics all over the world share?

86 : WE EXPLORE

Resource Center

The Language of Faith

The **marks of the Church** have been used to identify the Church of Jesus Christ ever since the First Council of Constantinople in 381 C.E. At that meeting these four characteristics were used in writing the Nicene Creed, in which we pray: "We believe in one holy catholic and apostolic Church." These four identifying marks remind us of who we are as Church.

Notes: Building the Chapter

Scripture Story
The Feast of Pentecost

Fifty days after Easter the followers of Jesus were together in a house in Jerusalem. Suddenly the house was filled with the sound of wind. A tongue of fire came to rest on each one in the room. All were filled with the Holy Spirit. They began to speak in strange languages as they told the good news of Jesus.

There were people from all over the world in Jerusalem that day. They heard the noise and gathered in front of the house. They heard the apostles preaching. They were amazed that they could understand the preaching of people from Galilee.

—based on Acts 2:1–12

Scripture Signpost

"One Lord, one faith, one baptism . . ."
Ephesians 4:5

Why is oneness so important to our Church?

The Church is sometimes called the temple, *or holy dwelling place, of the Holy Spirit. The Spirit lives in the Church community and in each individual member.*

We Explore
Build *Continued*

Working with the Text

- Read or summarize *The Feast of Pentecost*.
- Point out that the symbols of wind and fire are used to describe the Holy Spirit. Explain that the Holy Spirit can be as gentle as a breeze or as powerful as a strong wind, bringing God's message of love to everyone.
  How is the Holy Spirit like fire? (Possible answer: The Holy Spirit lights up our lives and warms our hearts.)

- **Scripture Signpost** Elicit responses to the question. (Jesus wants us to be united so we can continue his work.)

Working with the Pictures

- As you point out the illustration, explain that it shows the apostles being filled with the Holy Spirit.
  Why were other people amazed? (Even though the people spoke different languages, they all understood the message of the apostles.)
- Read the caption aloud. Point out that through Baptism, all Christians become temples of the Holy Spirit.

Scripture Background

- Jesus' ascension, his return to the Father, occurred 40 days after Easter. Pentecost is the fiftieth day after Easter. The story of Pentecost is found in **Acts 2:1–12**, in the New Testament book that describes how the first Christians lived. People from many countries visited Jerusalem. When the Holy Spirit filled the apostles, their message was understood by people who spoke many different languages. The disciples spoke Aramaic; yet all the people visiting Jerusalem were able to understand them. The Holy Spirit made it possible for the message of Jesus to be preached to all people of the world.
- The author of **Ephesians 4:5** wrote this letter to the people of the city of Ephesus, but it applies to the entire Church. The letter expressed the concern that the Church fulfill the mission that Jesus entrusted to it.

WE REFLECT
Review

Recall Have volunteers give examples of unity. (beliefs, worship, and sacraments)

Think and Share Ask the students to consider their answers before responding. (The Holy Spirit prompts us to feed the hungry, care for the sick, provide shelter for the homeless, and so on.)

Continue the Journey Have the students complete this activity. You might use these prayers in the closing prayer celebration for this chapter.

Alternative Have the students complete this activity as a homework assignment. Schedule time during the next meeting for volunteers to pray their prayers aloud.

We Live Our Faith *At Home:* Brainstorm with the students a list of ways to honor the Holy Spirit. *In the Parish:* If possible, distribute missalettes or hymnals, and have the students identify hymns and prayers that mention the Holy Spirit.

Faith Journal The students may begin pages 27–28 of their *Faith Journal* in class and complete them at home. As part of your own spiritual development, complete *Your Faith Journal* (page J15).

RECALL
Give some examples of unity as shown in the Catholic Church.

THINK AND SHARE
How do you think the Holy Spirit helps us do God's work today?

CONTINUE THE JOURNEY
Write a prayer to the Holy Spirit. Ask the Spirit to help you and the whole Church grow in holiness.

WE LIVE OUR FAITH
At Home Talk with your family about the feast of Pentecost, and decide on a special way to honor the Holy Spirit.

In the Parish Listen for mentions of the Holy Spirit in the prayers and songs at Mass.

88 : WE REFLECT

Resource Center

Link to the Faith Community
Invite a member of the parish to speak to the students about the Holy Spirit's presence in his or her life. Ask the speaker to describe how he or she prays to the Holy Spirit and experiences the gifts of the Spirit. Encourage the students to ask questions.

Assessment Tip
Use the students' written prayers from *Continue the Journey* to assess their understanding of the Holy Spirit's gifts of unity and holiness.

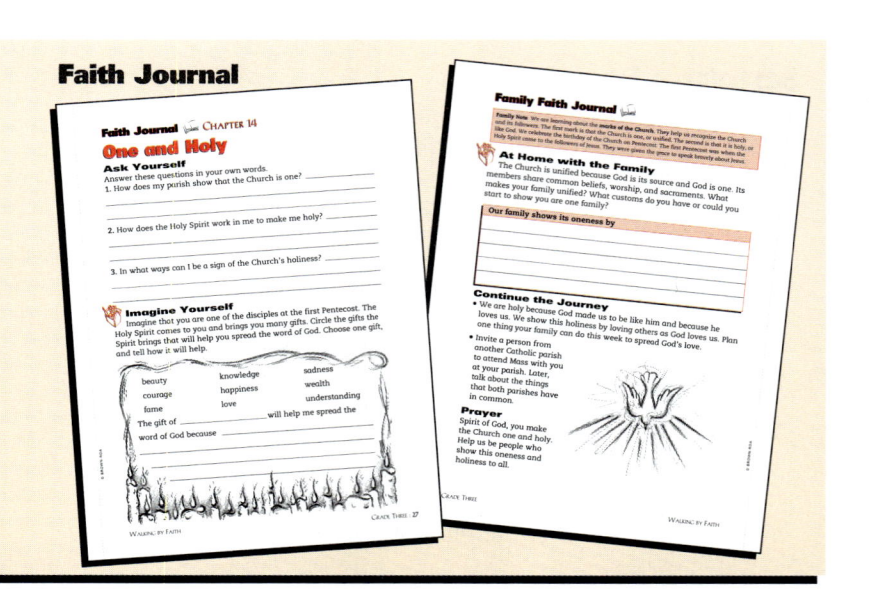

The Church's Birthday

Pentecost, the feast 50 days after Easter, is sometimes celebrated as the birthday of the Church. On that day we celebrate the Holy Spirit's coming to the followers of Jesus. When we pray to the Holy Spirit, we ask for help in doing God's work.

Read together this prayer to the Holy Spirit. Then close your eyes, breathe slowly, and think about what you prayed.

PRAYER

Come, Holy Spirit, fill the hearts of your faithful,
and light in them the fire of your love.
Send forth your Spirit, and we will be created,
and you will renew the face of the earth.
Lord, by the light of the Holy Spirit, you have taught the hearts of your faithful.
In the same Spirit, help us choose what is right and always rejoice in your kindness.
We ask this through Christ our Lord. Amen.

WE CELEBRATE : 89

WE CELEBRATE
3. Close

Working with the Pictures

You may want to explain that symbols such as wind, flames, and doves are used to help us visualize the Holy Spirit.

Working with the Text

- Remind the students that the Father, Son, and Holy Spirit make up the Holy Trinity.
  When we pray to the Holy Spirit, to whom are we praying? (God)

- You may want to clarify the difference between Jesus' *disciples* and his *apostles*. The apostles were missionaries and messengers sent by Jesus to proclaim the good news of the kingdom of God in New Testament times. The Twelve were apostles, but not all apostles were part of the Twelve. Other apostles include Paul, Barnabas, Andronicus, and Junia. The bishops of today are considered the apostles' successors. Jesus' disciples were all those who followed his teachings. All Christians today are disciples and followers of Jesus.

Prayer Elaborate on the prayer celebration by adding music. Lead the students in singing a familiar hymn. Then invite them to begin their prayer with the Sign of the Cross. If the students wrote prayers, pray them now. Then pray the prayer on this page. If time allows, have the students close their eyes and think about the words of the prayer as you repeat it aloud. End the prayer celebration with another hymn.

Link to the Family

Encourage the students to retell the story of Pentecost to their family members. Suggest that they add a prayer to the Holy Spirit to their family prayer at meals this week.

Music and Liturgy Resources

To enhance your prayer and celebration, you may wish to use the Unit Four Music and Liturgy Resources from the Resource Package.

Notes: Closing the Chapter

PARISH : 89

Getting Ready: Chapter 15

Catholic and Apostolic

Program Resources
Student Text, pp. 90–95
Student Faith Journal, pp. 29–30
Your Faith Journal, p. J16
Chapter 15 Transparency
Unit Four Assessment

Unit Four (The Church)
Guided by the Holy Spirit

Key Content Summary
We are sent by Jesus to bring the good news to everyone, everywhere.

Planning the Chapter

	Pacing Guide *Suggested time/Your time*	Content	Objectives	Materials
Open	10–15 min./ ____ min.	*We Are Invited,* pp. 90–91	• Describe Paul's instructions to the early Christians.	• art materials
Build	20–25 min./ ____ min.	*We Explore,* pp. 92–93	• Discover what is meant by *catholic* and *apostolic*.	• age-appropriate reference materials on popes, poster board • Chapter 15 Transparency from the Resource Package
Review	15–20 min./ ____ min.	*We Reflect,* p. 94	• Demonstrate understanding of chapter concepts. • Apply learning through activity. • Practice faith at home and in the parish.	• *Student Faith Journal,* pp. 29–30 • *Your Faith Journal,* p. J16 • art materials to make greeting cards (optional) • Unit Four Assessment from the Resource Package
Close	10–15 min./ ____ min.	*We Celebrate,* p. 95	• Demonstrate our unity as Christians by praying the Apostles' Creed.	• background music

For additional suggestions, see Scheduling, pp. T35–T37.

Catechism in Context

Doctrinal Foundation This chapter explores the catholic and apostolic nature of the Church. The Church is and must be *catholic*. Since Jesus died and rose for the whole human family, his Church sacramentally expresses the universality of his redemptive love. It is not a religious sect with an elite or exclusive membership; it embraces all humanity: women and men, young and old, learned and unlearned, saints and sinners—people of every race, language, and condition. The Church is catholic because Jesus commissioned his apostles to proclaim the good news of God's love throughout the world. The Church is also for all time until Jesus returns, when God's reign of justice, love, and peace will be complete.

This means that the Church is also essentially *apostolic*. It remains, and must continue to remain, in visible continuity with its own origins, with unbroken faith. "This faith comes to us from the apostles in the continual celebration of the sacraments and in the ministry of bishops who are the successors of the apostles."

See Catechism of the Catholic Church, #857.

One-Minute Retreat for Catechists

Read

"What we have done for ourselves alone dies with us. What we have done for others and the world remains and is immortal."
—Albert Pine

Reflect

How much have I done for others and can I yet do?

Pray

Thank you, dear Jesus, for bringing us the good news. Help me impress upon my students the need to spread that good news. Inspire us as you did the apostles to bring love and kindness to others.

Visualizing the Lesson

Use this graphic organizer to help the students visualize how the gospel message reaches the Church community.

Redraw the graphic organizer on a sheet of paper, omitting the words *Church community*, and make copies for students.

Where on this chart do we belong? Invite the students to add their initials to this part of the diagram. Then ask the students to add the names of several popes and apostles to the diagram.

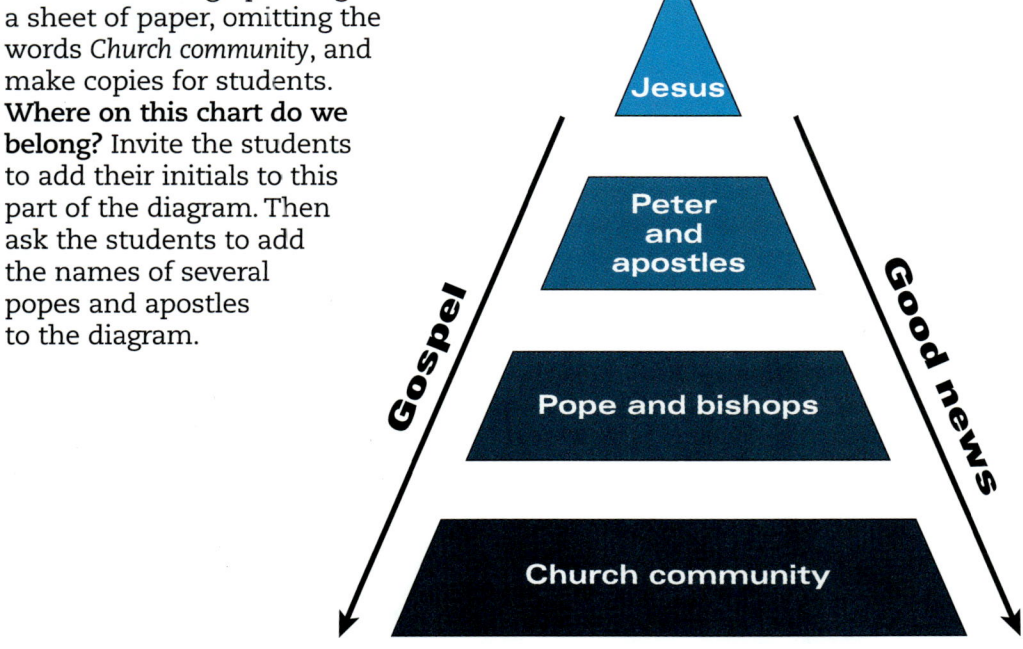

Pyramid diagram (top to bottom): Jesus / Peter and apostles / Pope and bishops / Church community. Left side labeled "Gospel"; right side labeled "Good news".

Library Links

Books for Children

What Christians Believe by Hubert J. Richards (The Liturgical Press, 1-800-858-5450).

The beliefs of the Church have been handed down through the teachings of the apostles.

Books for Parents and Teachers

The Creed by Bernard L. Marthaler (Twenty-Third Publications, 1-800-321-0411).

This study of the Creed links the past and the present.

Multimedia

For children:

Rome: In the Footsteps of Peter and Paul. Episode #2, "The Early Church" produced by Heart of the Nation (video) (BROWN-ROA, 1-800-922-7696).

This video explores the link between Peter and Paul and the Christian faith still alive and celebrated today.

Glory Day, "Blest Are They" by David Haas (GIA Publications, 1-800-442-1358).

Use this song, featured in Haas's concert video or audio CD, to reinforce chapter material with music.

For parents and teachers:

The Gospel in History (video) (Paulist Press, 1-800-218-1903).

This video tells the gospel story through the centuries and shows how it has shaped the Church.

Organizations

For information on carrying on the apostolic mission of the Church, contact:

Society for the Propagation of the Faith
366 Fifth Avenue
New York, NY 10001

Strengthening the Family Link

Here are some suggestions for reaching out to your students' families:

- Encourage the students to talk with family members about ways they can share the good news of Jesus with others.
- Invite family members to join the class in praying the Apostles' Creed.

Chapter 15 pages 90–95

Objectives
- Describe Paul's instructions to the early Christians.
- Discover what is meant by *catholic* and *apostolic*.

Gathering — WE ARE INVITED
1. Open

Personal Experience Invite volunteers to share experiences of receiving a phone call or letter from a friend or relative who lives far away.

Prayer Pray the opening prayer together.

Working with the Text
- As you read aloud or summarize the text, emphasize that a *Christian* is someone who follows Jesus Christ. **Why do you think the people were excited to receive a letter from Paul?** (He was a special person, one of the Church leaders; it put them in touch with Christians in other places.)
- Explain that Paul often used letters to teach Jesus' message.

Working with the Pictures
- Call attention to the illustration of the early Christians gathered together. Explain that in the time of the early Christians, people sat either on the floor or on low wooden benches. The only sources of light to read by were candles and oil lamps. Messages were written on scrolls—paper or cloth that was rolled up.
- After you read the caption aloud, be sure the students understand that Paul did not make up his own message but repeated and explained a message from Jesus' teachings.

Chapter 15
Catholic and Apostolic

Prayer

Holy Spirit, send us to share God's word just as you sent the apostles.

Tobias sat with his father in their home in Ephesus. It was his family's turn to host the early followers of Christ. These *Christians* were gathering for the breaking of the bread.

Tonight was extra special, though. There was a new letter from Jesus' follower Paul for everyone to hear. Tobias glowed with pride as his father read in the quiet room.

Paul's letter said, "From now on, tell the truth to each other because we are all parts of one another. Do not sin, even if you are angry. Do not let the sun go down on your anger."

The early Christians gathered in homes to hear God's message—the same message that we now hear at Mass.

90 : We Are Invited

Resource Center
Teaching Tip

Clarifying concepts Be sure the students understand that "the breaking of the bread" is the name the early Christians used for the celebration of the Eucharist. The central Eucharistic action of breaking the one loaf is a sign of Christ's sacrifice. Today the presider still breaks the large consecrated host before Communion.

Notes: Opening the Chapter

Paul's letter continued, "If you have been a thief, stop stealing. Get an honest job so you can share with people in need. Watch your language. Use words to help others. Don't disappoint the Holy Spirit, who has chosen you to be set free" (based on Ephesians 4:25–30).

Tobias thought about his own life. He had been angry with his sister Martha for playing with his toys without asking. If he wanted to follow Paul's teachings, he had to do something.

Before they went to sleep that night, Tobias sat down with Martha. "I'm sorry I got so mad at you today. Let's find a way to enjoy my toys together."

Martha said, "I was wrong, too. I should have asked before I took your toys."

Tobias felt better. He wasn't angry any more. He had learned something important from Paul's words.

Activity

Draw a picture of yourself using Paul's message in your life. Share your drawing with the class.

WE ARE INVITED : 91

WE ARE INVITED
Open Continued
Working with the Text

Continue to read aloud or summarize the rest of the story. Point out that the story has been told from the point of view of a boy listening to Paul's letter. **How did Paul's message change Tobias's behavior and feelings?** (He apologized to his sister and talked with her about ways to share his toys. He was not angry anymore.)

Working with the Pictures

- Direct the students' attention to the picture of Tobias and Martha after they have made up.
- You might tell the students that long ago children often played with simple toys such as marbles and wooden tops.
- Provide art materials for the activity. If time permits, allow volunteers to share their drawings.

Alternative Have the students complete the activity at home. Schedule time during the next meeting for volunteers to share their completed artwork.

Link to Liturgy

Explain that we share God's word during the part of the Mass called the Liturgy of the Word. This part of the Mass consists of a reading from the Old Testament, a song or prayer from the **Psalms**, and a reading from the **Acts of the Apostles** or the letters found in the New Testament. During the Easter Season the first reading is from the Acts of the Apostles. The priest or deacon then reads the gospel and gives the homily, a short talk about the meaning of the Scriptures in our lives. We then profess our faith by praying the Creed. The Liturgy of the Word concludes with the general intercessions.

PARISH : 91

We Explore
2. Build
Working with the Text

- As you work with the text, use *The Language of Faith* below to further develop the terms *catholic*, *apostolic*, and *apostolic succession*. Point out that an *apostle* is someone chosen by Jesus to bring his message to others.
- Explain that the Holy Spirit helps the entire Church, guided by the bishops and the pope, understand and spread Jesus' message today.
- To clarify the meaning of *apostolic succession*, refer to the graphic organizer on page 89B. You may wish to do the suggested activity or one of your own choosing.

Catholics Believe Emphasize the importance of the apostles, who received God's message directly from Jesus.

Working with the Pictures

- Call attention to the pictures of the three popes.
  What do all three of these popes have in common? (They all led the Church in spreading Jesus' message.)

  Provide age-appropriate reference materials for the students' research. If time permits, have volunteers present their posters.

  Alternative Have the students complete this activity at home with the help of adult family members or friends. You might schedule time during the next meeting for volunteers to share their work.

Catholics Believe...
that the whole Church is apostolic because it is founded on the apostles.
Catechism, #857

The Church Across Time

We say that our Church is **catholic** because it is meant for all people for all time. The word *catholic* means "universal," or "everywhere." This means that the beliefs Paul taught Tobias and his community are the same beliefs that the Church teaches around the world today. Follow Jesus. Forgive one another. Share what you have. Bring others to God.

The word *apostle* means "sent forth." Jesus sent the apostles, including Paul, throughout the world to share his message of love. We say that our Church is **apostolic** because it is built on the foundation of the apostles.

Bishops today continue the work of the apostles. We call this **apostolic succession**. Over time Christ continues to lead the Church through the pope and the bishops, who are the successors of Peter and the apostles.

Pope Leo XIII

ACTIVITY
Since the time of Peter, the Church on earth has had leaders. Work with a partner to look up one of these popes in an encyclopedia or other reference book. Create a poster telling why this particular pope was important.

Pope Gregory I

Pope

Resource Center

The Language of Faith

- The word **catholic** (lowercase *c*) as a mark of the Church means that the Church welcomes all people.
- **Apostolic** refers to the apostles. The Church is built on the foundation of the apostles. The word also refers to the mission the apostles received from Jesus—to share his message with all people. We can be apostolic by sharing the good news Jesus gave to the apostles through our words and actions.
- The term **apostolic succession** reminds us that it was Jesus who started the Church and entrusted it to his apostles. In turn, the apostles passed on their work to their successors. The pope and the bishops are their successors today.

Notes: Building the Chapter

We Go Forth

Catholics all over the world gather for Mass. As Mass ends, they are sent forth to share Jesus' message by working in their communities.

Our Moral Guide

We obey Jesus by sharing the good news with people of all nations.

Catechism, #849

Why do you think Jesus wants all people to hear the good news?

Slovakia

Mexico

China

WE EXPLORE : 93

WE EXPLORE
Build Continued

Working with the Text

Read aloud *We Go Forth*.
- After Mass what are Catholics sent forth to share with other people? (Jesus' message)

Working with the Pictures

Point out the photographs.
- What do all of the Catholics celebrating Mass in these pictures have in common? (They all share the same form of worship, the same beliefs and sacraments, and the same responsibility to share the good news with others.)
- *Our Moral Guide* Encourage volunteers to respond to the question. (Possible answers: Jesus came to save *all* people; everyone must be given the opportunity to accept and follow Jesus.)

Link to the Family

Encourage the students to suggest to their families that they read a short passage from the New Testament each evening at dinner, in addition to praying the meal blessing. Ask them to think about how they and their family members could take that message with them when they go to school or work each day.

Multicultural Link

Discuss the work of missionaries. Explain that missionaries carry Jesus' message to people who have never heard of him and his love. Missionaries may be ordained ministers, members of religious communities, or laypersons. Missionaries not only teach people about Jesus and the Church but also help them by building schools, showing people how to improve farming and other work, caring for people in hospitals and clinics, and doing other good works. If possible, invite a representative of a missionary religious community or a lay mission organization to speak to the class about the mission's work.

PARISH : 93

We Reflect
Review

Recall Encourage volunteers to respond to the question. (The Church is universal, everywhere, and meant for all people for all time; apostolic succession refers to the Church's being built on the foundations of the apostles.)

Think and Share Allow the students to think about their answers before responding. (The pope serves the Church community, and each Church member is called to serve others.)

Continue the Journey Work with the students to brainstorm words for this activity.

Alternative Have the students complete the activity at home. Invite volunteers to share their work during the next meeting.

We Live Our Faith *At Home:* Provide the necessary Scripture reference for this activity—*Mark 3:14–19*. *In the Parish:* You might suggest that the students write letters to the bishop thanking him for serving the people of your diocese.

Faith Journal The students may begin pages 29–30 of their *Faith Journal* in class and complete them at home. As part of your own spiritual development, complete *Your Faith Journal* (page J16).

Recall
Why do we call our Church *catholic*? What is apostolic succession?

Think and Share
One of the pope's titles is "Servant of the Servants of God." What do you think that means?

Continue the Journey
Describe our Church with words beginning with the following letters. The first one is done for you.

THE CATHOLIC CHURCH IS...

C hristian
H
U
R
C
H

We Live Our Faith

At Home With your family, find out who the apostles are.

In the Parish Look for your bishop's picture in a parish building.

94 : We Reflect

Resource Center

Optional Activity: Enrichment
You might have the students make welcome cards for new parish members who were recently baptized or confirmed in the Church community or who moved into the parish. Encourage the students to tell the new members why they are happy to welcome them into the parish family. If possible, arrange for the cards to be made available to new parish members at Mass and other services.

Assessment Tip
You may wish to copy the Unit Four Assessment from the Resource Package in preparation for giving this test after completing Chapters 13–16.

Faith of the Apostles

A **creed** is a statement of faith. The word *creed* comes from the Latin word for "I believe." The Apostles' Creed is a statement shared by Christians around the world.

The apostles did not make up this statement. It began to be used hundreds of years after they died. But we call this the Apostles' Creed because it sums up the faith of the apostles.

When we recite the Apostles' Creed, we show that we are united in faith with followers of Jesus everywhere, in every time.

PRAYER

With your classmates, recite the Apostles' Creed prayerfully. If you do not know this creed by heart, you can find the words on page 176.

We Celebrate : 95

WE CELEBRATE
3. Close

Working with the Text

As you read or summarize the text, use *The Language of Faith* below to further explain the term *creed*.

Working with the Pictures

Direct the students' attention to the pictures.
What do all of these pictures have in common? (All show our unity as followers of Jesus, our acceptance of all people, and our apostolic faith.)

- **Prayer** Gather the students into a circle. Begin the celebration with a familiar hymn. Then lead the students in praying the Apostles' Creed. You might play background music during the prayer. End the prayer celebration with the Sign of the Cross.

The Language of Faith

Creed comes from the Latin *credo*, meaning "I believe." The early Christians used simple expressions of faith to describe their beliefs. For example, the words accompanying the Sign of the Cross state the Christians' belief that they should live "in the name of the Father, and of the Son, and of the Holy Spirit." The Apostles' Creed is another, more detailed statement of faith that describes Christians' beliefs.

Teaching Tip

Clarifying concepts Explain the difference between a prayer and a creed. A prayer is a way of communicating with God. In prayer we both listen to God speaking to our hearts and talk to God. In a creed we express what we believe about God, Jesus, and the Church. Explain that we can also use a creed as a prayer.

Notes: Closing the Chapter

PARISH : 95

Unit Four Review

Objective
- Review the unit and assess progress.

Chapter Summaries
Use this information to reinforce key points before administering the review. These summaries will also help you assess the students' responses to *Show How Far You've Come*, page 97.

Chapter 13
- The Church has a mission, work Jesus has given us to do.
- The Church is an institution as well as a community.
- Jesus entrusted the Church to Peter and the apostles and, through them, to the popes and bishops who followed them.

Chapter 14
- The Church's four marks are one, holy, catholic, and apostolic.
- The common beliefs, worship, and sacraments of Catholics are signs of the Church's oneness and holiness.
- The coming of the Holy Spirit at Pentecost was the beginning of the Church.

Chapter 15
- The early Christians heard the same message from God that we hear at Mass.
- The Church is *catholic*, open to the whole world.
- The Church is *apostolic*, based on the teachings of the apostles.

Review
You may have students work on the review in writing or work together with them to answer the questions orally.

Matching Review the students' answers together. Explain any concepts the students do not understand.

Which Is Correct? Invite volunteers to respond. Review any unclear concepts.

Share Your Faith Allow partners to brainstorm their responses and help each other refine their explanations.

96 : UNIT FOUR

Unit Four Checkpoint

Review

Matching Match each description from Column A with the correct term from Column B.

Column A		Column B
_c_	1. For all people for all time.	a. apostle
_e_	2. Fifty days after Easter.	b. diocese
_b_	3. Area led by a bishop.	c. catholic
_a_	4. A messenger sent by Jesus.	d. one
_d_	5. Sharing common beliefs.	e. Pentecost

Which Is Correct? Circle the correct term to complete each sentence.
1. The successors of the apostles are the (**bishops**, saints).
2. The "rock" on whom Jesus built the Church is (Saint Thomas, **Saint Peter**).
3. On Pentecost the apostles received (Holy Communion, **the Holy Spirit**).
4. An early statement of the Church's beliefs is called the (**Apostles' Creed**, apostolic succession).
5. Because Christ loves the Church, it is (catholic, **holy**).

Share Your Faith Explain the four marks of the Church in your own words.

96 : REVIEW

Resource Center

Assessment Tips
Use one or more of the following strategies to assist you in assessing student progress:

- If you need a more detailed written review, you may give the Unit Four Assessment from the Resource Package.
- Have the students assess their own progress by asking partners to identify and explain to each other the important ideas they learned in this unit.
- Ask the students to suggest ways in which they can share the message of the apostles with others at home, in school, and in their neighborhoods.

Show How Far You've Come

Use the chart below to show what you have learned. For each chapter, write or draw the three most important things you remember.

Guided by the Holy Spirit

Chapter 13 The Church Works Together	Chapter 14 One and Holy	Chapter 15 Catholic and Apostolic
Look for answers reflecting the key points listed under Chapter Summaries.		

What Else Would You Like to Know?

List any questions you still have about the Church.

_____
_____
_____

Continue the Journey

Choose one or more of the following activities to do on your own, with your class, or with your family.

- Look through your Faith Journal pages for Unit Four. Choose your favorite activity, and share it with a friend or family member.
- Ask your pastor, deacon, another staff member, or a parish council member about how decisions are made in your parish.
- Choose one of the marks of the Church, and draw a poster showing what it means to you.

REVIEW : 97

Show How Far You've Come Use *Chapter Summaries* to evaluate students' responses. Pay particular attention to responses that differ greatly from the key points of the chapters. These responses may indicate areas where your presentation was unclear and needs additional review. If time permits, extend this activity by asking the students to recall their favorite stories, activities, or pictures from this unit.

What Else Would You Like to Know? Have the students share their questions and vote on a class list of three questions for you to answer at the next session.

Continue the Journey Provide time at a later session for the students to demonstrate how they have completed one or more of these activities. For example:
- Ask volunteers to share favorite *Faith Journal* entries.
- Let the students report their findings in written summaries (for homework) or oral summaries (in class).
- Allow the students to show and explain their posters.

Prayer

Close the review by gathering the students into a circle. Lead them in praying a prayer of intercession asking God's blessing on Church leaders.

Reference Sources

For help in addressing the students' questions about this unit's topics, see:
- *The Church We Believe In: One, Holy, Catholic, and Apostolic* by Francis A. Sullivan (Paulist Press, 1988).
- *The Story of the Church* by Alfred McBride O. Praem. (accompanying videos available) (St. Anthony Messenger Press, 1996).
- *What It Means to Be Catholic* by Joseph Champlin (St. Anthony Messenger Press, 1986).

Good resources for third graders include:
- *I Am a Roman Catholic* by Brenda Pettenuzzo (Franklin Watts, 1987).
- *What Christians Believe* by Hubert J. Richards (The Liturgical Press, 1992).

Your parish community is another important resource. Priests, deacons, other staff members, catechists, catechumens, godparents, sponsors, and members of religious communities are all good reference sources for answering students' questions.

Link to the Family

If possible, have students take these pages home to share with their families.

Getting Ready: Chapter 16

The First Nativity Scene

Program Resources
Student Text, pp. 98–101
Student Faith Journal, pp. 31–32
Your Faith Journal, p. J17

Unit Four (The Church)
Guided by the Holy Spirit

Key Content Summary
Francis of Assisi set up the first nativity scene, a custom honoring the birth of Jesus.

Planning the Chapter

	Pacing Guide *Suggested time/Your time*	Content	Objectives	Materials
Open	10–15 min./ _____ min.	*We Are Invited,* p. 98	• Recognize Francis of Assisi as the originator of the nativity crèche	
Build	20–25 min./ _____ min.	*We Explore,* p. 99	• Discover that a nativity scene depicts Christ's birth.	
Review	15–20 min./ _____ min.	*We Reflect,* p. 100	• Demonstrate understanding of chapter concepts. • Apply learning through activity. • Practice faith at home and in the parish.	• art materials • *Student Faith Journal,* pp. 31–32 • *Your Faith Journal,* p. J17
Close	10–15 min./ _____ min.	*We Celebrate,* p. 101	• Pray a prayer that is a reminder of Jesus' birth.	

For additional suggestions, see Scheduling, pp. T35–T37.

97a : CHAPTER 16

Catechism in Context

Doctrinal Foundation This chapter discusses the importance of Christmas, the celebration of Christ's birth. This feast recalls that the Son of God, in taking on a human nature, became a citizen of this world, related to all creation. Christmas reminds us that Jesus came into the world in a very humble way: he was born in a stable. This simple beginning made the knowledge of his true greatness all the more great: "your eternal Word has brought to the eyes of faith a new and radiant vision of your glory" (*Christmas Preface #1*). Jesus later told us that we must humble ourselves, be born from above, and become children of God. Only then will Christ be fully formed in us, and only when we are fully formed in him will the mystery of Christmas be fulfilled in us.

See Catechism of the Catholic Church, #525.

One-Minute Retreat for Catechists

Read
"Trumpets! Lightnings! The earth trembles! But into the virgin's womb thou didst descend with noiseless tread."
—Agathias Scholasticus

Reflect
How am I affected by the story of Jesus' birth?

Pray
Help us rejoice in your birth, O Lord. Like the magi, may my students come to you with their humble gifts of themselves. We thank you, Lord, for your birth, life, death, and resurrection.

Visualizing the Lesson

Use this graphic organizer to help the students understand the significance of the nativity scene.

Draw the graphic organizer on the board or on chart paper, but leave out the words in parentheses. Have the students tell whom the shepherds and kings symbolize. Explain to the students that these parts of the nativity scene show that Jesus came for all people, rich and poor alike.

The Nativity

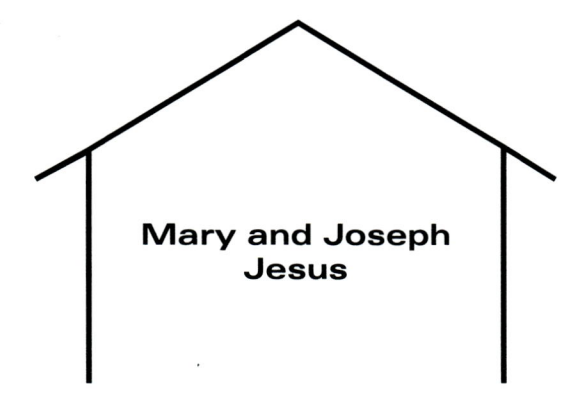

- Mary and Joseph, Jesus
- The Shepherds (all people/the poor)
- The Kings (all nations/the rich)

Library Links

Books for Children
Saint Francis by Brian Wildsmith (Eerdmans, 1-800-253-7521).
This beautifully illustrated book retells the story of Saint Francis.

The Nativity by Julie Vivas (Harcourt Brace, 1-800-543-1918).
This retelling of Jesus' birth is also available in Spanish.

Books for Parents and Teachers
The Mystery of Christmas by Raniero Cantalamessa OFM Cap. (The Liturgical Press, 1-800-858-5450).
This book discusses the three canticles of Luke's Christmas story.

Multimedia
For children:
The Perfect Present produced by Robert Blaskey (video) (BROWN-ROA, 1-800-922-7696).
A little girl dreams that she is at the first Christmas.

The Legend of the Christmas Flower (video) (Music for Little People, 1-800-727-2233).
This video tells the classic tale of the poinsettia.

For parents and teachers:
Incarnation from the Mysteries of Faith series produced by Fisher Productions (video) (Paulist Press, 1-800-218-1903).
The birth of Jesus tells us much about God as well as humanity.

Organizations
For information on ways to spread the true meaning of Christmas, contact:

Catholic Charities USA
1731 King Street, Suite 200
Alexandria, VA 22314
(1-703-549-1390)
(http://www.catholiccharitiesusa.org)

Strengthening the Family Link

Here are some suggestions for reaching out to your students' families:

- Encourage the students to talk with family members about ways they can share the true meaning of Christmas with others.
- Invite family members to come watch the class put on a live nativity scene. Invite other classes to join you as well.

Chapter 16 pages 98–101

Objectives
- Recognize Francis of Assisi as the originator of the nativity crèche.
- Discover that a nativity scene depicts Christ's birth.
- Pray a prayer that is a reminder of Jesus' birth.

Gathering WE ARE INVITED
1. Open

Personal Experience Ask volunteers to describe nativity scenes they have seen.

Prayer Pray the opening prayer together.

Working with the Text
As you read aloud or summarize the text, emphasize that in his nativity scene, Francis used real people and animals rather than statues. Explain that Francis is honored today as Saint Francis of Assisi.

Working with the Pictures
Call attention to the picture of the nativity scene.
How is the nativity scene on this page similar to the one Francis of Assisi created? (It also uses live people and animals.)

Landmark Explain that *crèche* is a French word meaning "manger" or "crib."

Chapter 16
We Celebrate Christmas

The First Nativity Scene

PRAYER
Jesus, we welcome you into our hearts. We rejoice in the hope you bring of peace on earth.

Roberto and Paolo were so excited. This was the big night! The shepherd brothers were on their way to be in a play.

Their friend Francis from Assisi wanted their entire village to see what the first Christmas looked like. To do this, he needed people, animals, a manger, and some hay. Francis had many friends who were happy to lend him these things.

Roberto and Paolo were leading some lambs up a hill to Francis. The brothers saw their neighbor Amelia and her husband, Nino, and their baby waiting with Francis.

Landmark Saint Francis of Assisi set up the first nativity scene, or *crèche,* in Greccio, Italy, on Christmas Eve in 1223. All of the nativity scenes we have now came from Francis's idea.

98 : We Are Invited

Resource Center
Link to the Faith Community
Invite a member of the parish to speak to the students about some of the traditional ways in which the parish celebrates the nativity. Ask the visitor to point out any cultural traditions that are incorporated into the celebrations and the background of those traditions. Also encourage the visitor to explain the history of the parish's crèche.

Notes: Opening the Chapter

As the brothers drew closer, they understood Francis's idea. Amelia and Nino had put the baby in the manger. They were looking at the baby with wonder and joy. A donkey and an ox were nearby, quietly enjoying some hay on the moonlit hillside. Roberto and Paolo felt as if they were the shepherds who had walked into Bethlehem so long ago to see the newborn Jesus!

People from their town came to the hillside to see what Francis and his friends were doing. As the townspeople walked up the hill, they stopped chattering. They gazed thoughtfully at the baby, the parents, the animals, and the shepherds. They understood the gift of the Christ Child, too.

Francis's display was called a *nativity scene*. The word **nativity** means "birth." Another name for Christmas is the Feast of the Nativity of Our Lord. Many nativity scenes have been made since Saint Francis's time. Each is different, but they all tell the same wonderful story.

Catholics Believe . . .
that the Son of God was born in a stable in Bethlehem.
Catechism, #525

ACTIVITY
With two or three classmates, list some of the differences among these nativity scenes. What do those differences tell you about the people for whom they were made?

WE EXPLORE : 99

WE EXPLORE
2. Build
Working with the Text

- Finish reading or summarizing the text. Refer to *The Language of Faith* below to further develop the meaning of *nativity*.
  Why do you think Francis created the nativity scene? (Possible answer: He thought it would help people understand and feel the joy of Jesus' birth.)

- To help the students fully understand the significance of the nativity scene, refer to the graphic organizer on page 97B. You may wish to do the suggested activity or one of your own choosing.

Working with the Pictures

- Point out how different the nativity scenes shown are—for example, the complex painting compared with the simple but eloquent carvings.

  Brainstorm this list together. Lead the students to understand that each scene reflects the time and place in which it was created.

  Catholics Believe Explain that no one knows what Jesus' birthplace looked like. It may have been a wooden shed, a stone building, or even a cave.

The Language of Faith
Nativity comes from the Latin *nativitas*, meaning "birth." Although Christians around the world celebrate Jesus' birth on December 25, the exact date of his birth is unknown. December 25 almost coincides with the winter solstice—the day with the fewest hours of daylight. From that day on the days lengthen and light increases. On Christmas we celebrate the coming of the Son of God, the Light of the World, into a world where there is sin and selfishness.

Multicultural Link
Explain that the carved crèche figures shown at the top of this page were made in Africa. Although the human Jesus was born into a Jewish family who did not look like these figures, people around the world often make images of the Holy Family that look like themselves. These images tell us that the Son of God came for *all* people.

Notes: Building the Chapter

WE REFLECT
Review

Recall Invite volunteers to respond to the questions. (Francis of Assisi; in a stable in Bethlehem)

Think and Share Encourage the students to think about their answers before responding. (Possible answers: People like to see what the first Christmas was like, to see the Holy Family as people like themselves.)

Continue the Journey Supply art materials, and ask the students to complete this activity. If time permits, allow them to share their drawings.

Alternative Have the students complete the activity at home. Schedule time during the next meeting for volunteers to present their nativity scenes.

We Live Our Faith At Home: Help the students summarize the story on pages 98–99.
In the Parish: Encourage the students to compare the parish's crèche with the ones shown on pages 98–99.

Faith Journal The students may begin pages 31–32 of their *Faith Journal* in class and complete them at home. As part of your own spiritual development, complete *Your Faith Journal* (page J17).

RECALL
Who set up the first nativity scene? Where was Jesus born?

THINK AND SHARE
Why do you think people like nativity scenes and other ways of showing Jesus' birth?

CONTINUE THE JOURNEY
Draw your own nativity scene. Include yourself, your friends, and family.

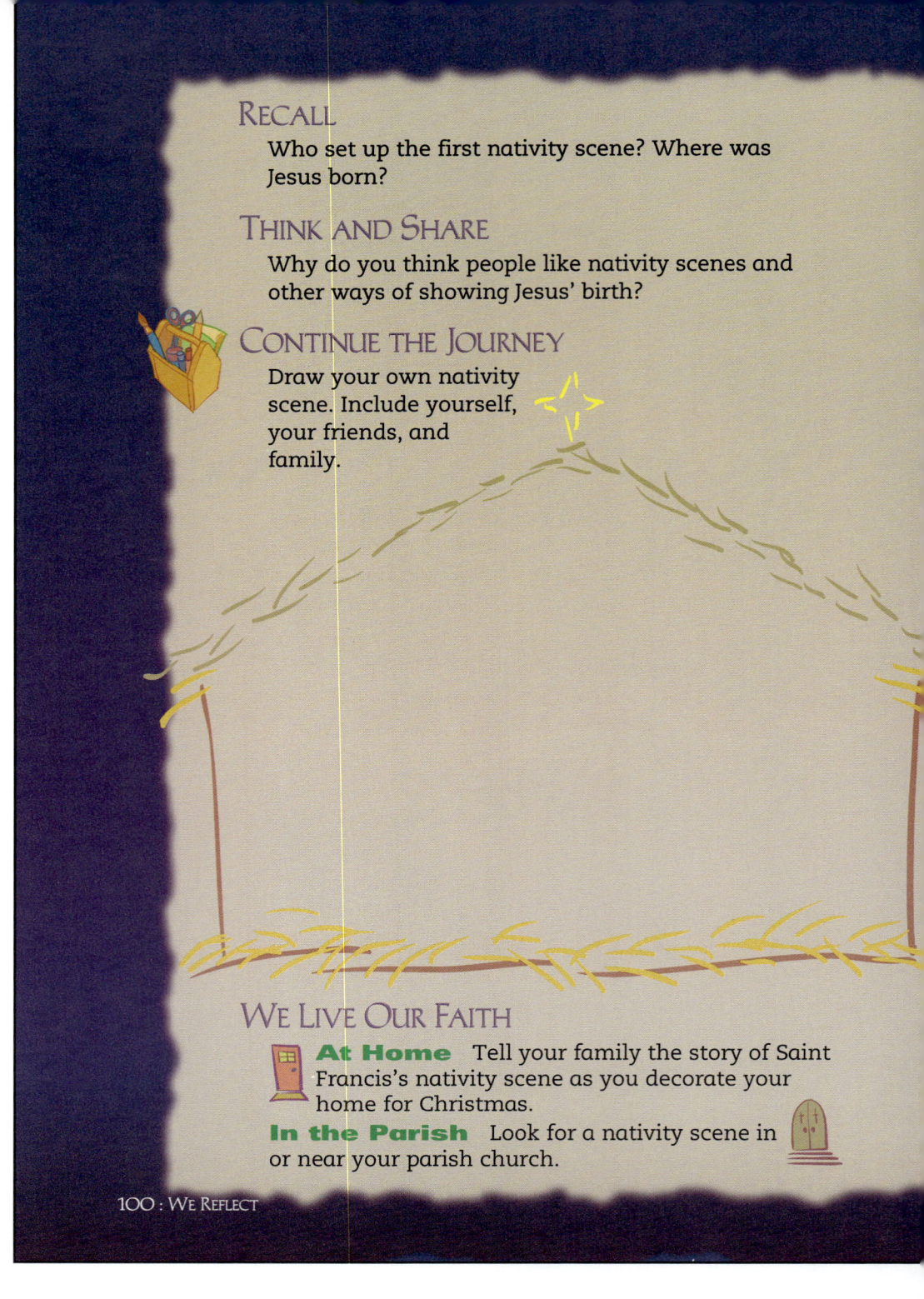

WE LIVE OUR FAITH
At Home Tell your family the story of Saint Francis's nativity scene as you decorate your home for Christmas.

In the Parish Look for a nativity scene in or near your parish church.

100 : We Reflect

Resource Center

Link to the Family
Ask the students to list the ways in which their families remember the nativity, such as with Christmas trees, lights, wreaths, and other decorations. Point out that although many traditions are the same or similar among families, each family has its own way of celebrating this holy season.

Assessment Tip
Use the students' artwork from the *Continue the Journey* activity to assess their understanding of the nativity. Some students may know that, according to the account in Matthew's Gospel, three *magi*, or wise men (sometimes shown as kings), also visited the newborn Jesus.

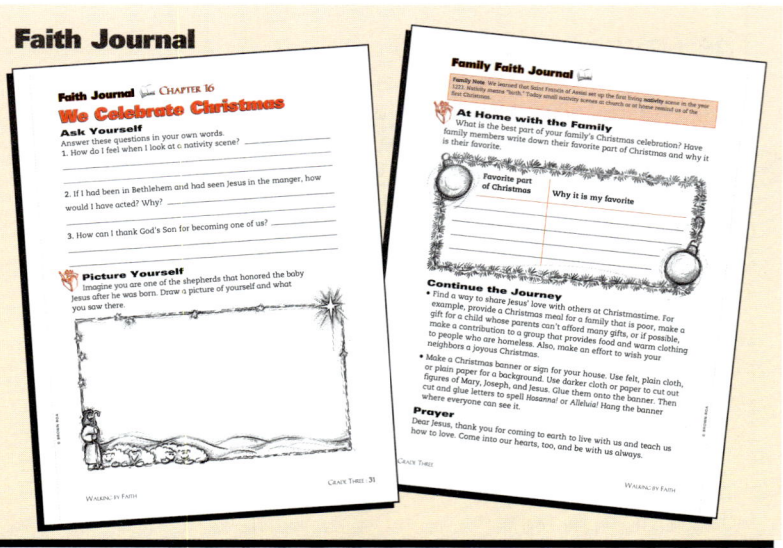

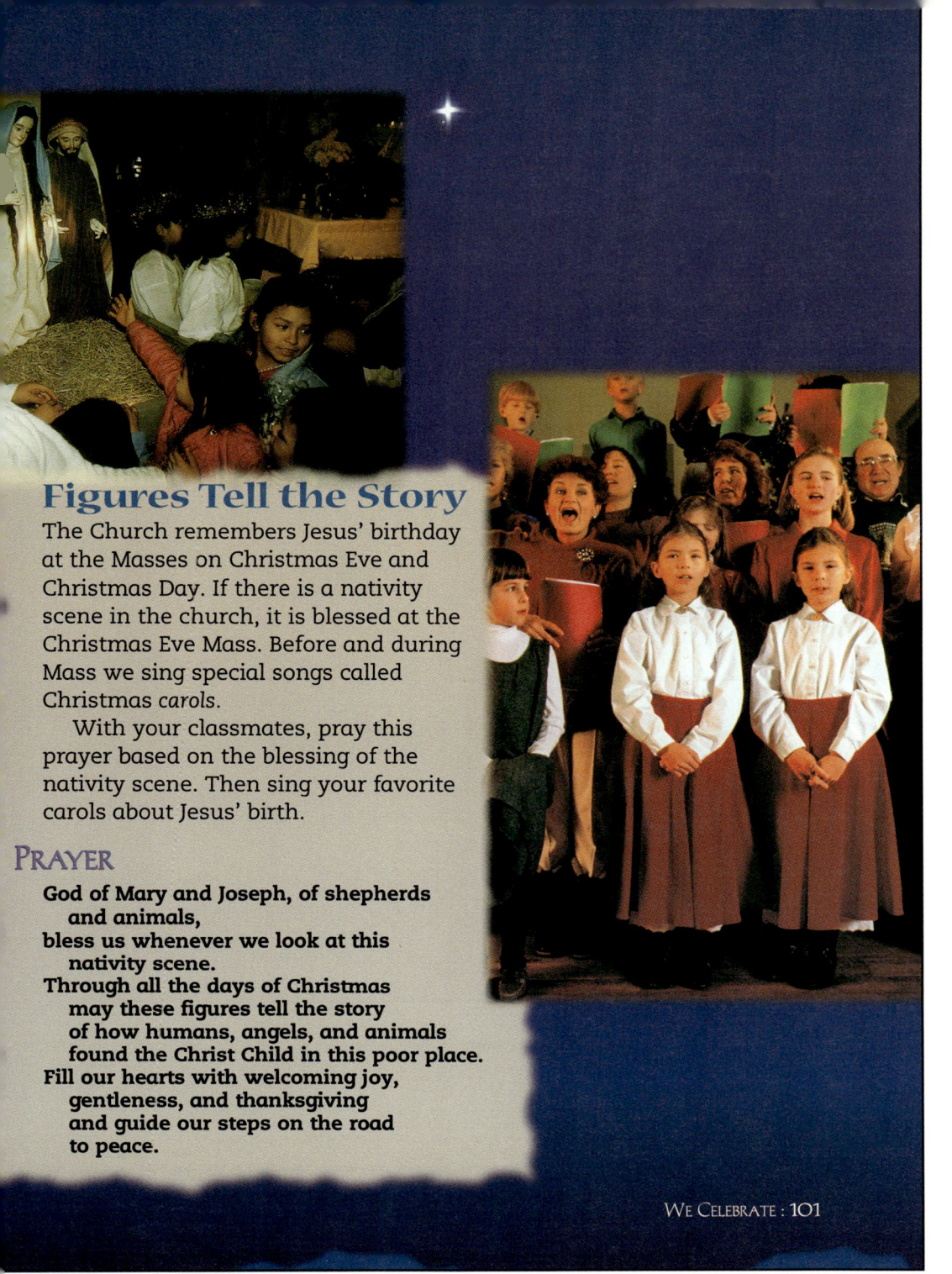

Figures Tell the Story

The Church remembers Jesus' birthday at the Masses on Christmas Eve and Christmas Day. If there is a nativity scene in the church, it is blessed at the Christmas Eve Mass. Before and during Mass we sing special songs called Christmas *carols*.

With your classmates, pray this prayer based on the blessing of the nativity scene. Then sing your favorite carols about Jesus' birth.

Prayer

God of Mary and Joseph, of shepherds and animals,
bless us whenever we look at this nativity scene.
Through all the days of Christmas may these figures tell the story of how humans, angels, and animals found the Christ Child in this poor place.
Fill our hearts with welcoming joy, gentleness, and thanksgiving and guide our steps on the road to peace.

We Celebrate : 101

We Celebrate
3. Close

Working with the Pictures
Call attention to the photographs. Ask the students to think about what happens in their parish church on Christmas Eve and Christmas Day.

Working with the Text
As you read or summarize *Figures Tell the Story*, emphasize the joy we feel when we celebrate Jesus' birth.

- **Prayer** Close the chapter with prayer. If time permits, sing a favorite Christmas carol. Then begin with the Sign of the Cross, and pray the prayer together. Sing another carol to close the prayer celebration.

Link to Liturgy
Tell the students that many parishes celebrate a children's Mass on Christmas Eve or Christmas Day. During this Mass children act out the gospel story of the first Christmas. If this tradition is celebrated in your parish, encourage your students to participate. Also prompt the students to listen closely to the gospel reading when they attend Mass on the Feast of the Nativity.

Notes: Closing the Chapter

Getting Ready: Chapter 17

Jesus' Law of Love

Program Resources
Student Text, pp. 102–107
Student Faith Journal, pp. 33–34
Your Faith Journal, p. J18
Chapter 17 Transparency
Unit Five Family Letter

Unit Five (Christian Morality)
Temple of the Holy Spirit

Key Content Summary
Jesus' law of love sums up everything we must do as members of the Church.

Planning the Chapter

	Pacing Guide Suggested time/Your time	Content	Objectives	Materials
Open	10–15 min./ _____ min.	*We Are Invited,* p. 102	• Recognize that we have the ability to make good decisions.	
Build	20–25 min./ _____ min.	*We Explore,* pp. 103–105	• Recognize that the Church can help us make the right choices. • Acknowledge Jesus' law of love as a guide for making good choices. • Realize that loving one's neighbor means caring for all people.	• Chapter 17 Transparency from the Resource Package
Review	15–20 min./ _____ min.	*We Reflect,* p. 106	• Demonstrate understanding of chapter concepts. • Apply learning through activity. • Practice faith at home and in the parish.	• *Student Faith Journal,* pp. 33–34 • *Your Faith Journal,* p. J18
Close	10–15 min./ _____ min. For additional suggestions, see Scheduling, pp. T35–T37.	*We Celebrate,* p. 107	• Pray a prayer asking for Jesus' help in following his law of love.	• Unit Five Family Letter from the Resource Package • recording of "Day by Day" from the musical *Godspell* (optional)

101a : Chapter 17

Catechism in Context
Doctrinal Foundation This chapter teaches that we are called to follow Jesus' law of love. This law has two parts, both taken from the Old Testament: "You shall love the Lord your God with all your heart, and with all your soul, and with all your strength, and with all your mind" *(Deuteronomy 6:4)* and "you shall love your neighbor as yourself" *(Leviticus 19:18)*. In his law of love, Jesus joined these two commandments together in a new way, so that they are two sides of the same coin. Loving God is not the same thing as loving our neighbor, but we cannot do one fully without doing the other. Raising the joined commandments above all others as the greatest is also new, as is the way Jesus defined our neighbor as anyone in need (see the parable of the good Samaritan). This two-fold Great Commandment actually implies another love: the love of self, for he commands us to love our neighbor *as* we love ourselves. We cannot really love our neighbor unless we love ourselves, and we can only love ourselves because "while we were still in our sins, God loved us first."

See Catechism of the Catholic Church, #1970.

One-Minute Retreat for Catechists
Read
"There is no love which does not become help."
—Paul Tillich

Reflect
What would life be like without love?

Pray
Lord, help us give comfort and strength to others through loving actions. Through my lessons, help me teach my students the power of love. May they cultivate that power, so that they contribute what they can to the world. Be it through a poem, a kind word, or a friendly smile—may all of us give the best of ourselves.

Visualizing the Lesson
Use this graphic organizer to help the students visualize Jesus' law of love.

Draw the graphic organizer on the board or on chart paper. Ask the students to point out on the diagram how sharing their love with others is also sharing God's love. Invite volunteers to give examples from their own lives.

Library Links
Books for Children
The Beatitudes for Children by Hubert J. Richards (The Liturgical Press, 1-800-858-5450).

This book presents the Beatitudes in a simple manner.

Books for Parents and Teachers
God's Passion, Our Passion—The Only Way to Love . . . Every Day by Pierre Wolff (Triumph Books, 1-800-325-9521).

Wolff discusses Jesus' ministry of love.

Multimedia
For children:
God's Plan for Me. Episode #1, "The Beatitudes" produced by the Archdiocese of St. Paul-Minneapolis (video) (BROWN-ROA, 1-800-922-7696).

This is a dramatization of three of the Beatitudes.

The Parable of the Good Samaritan: Sammy, the Good Neighbor produced by Twenty-Third Publications (video) (BROWN-ROA, 1-800-922-7696).

Blue Fish lies wounded, but Sammy Squid stops to care for him.

For parents and teachers:
Making Friends with Yourself (audiocassette) (Paulist Press, 1-800-218-1903).

This is a guide to following the Great Commandment.

Organizations
For information about ways to follow Jesus' law of love, contact your local chapter of Big Brothers-Big Sisters, or their

National Office
230 N. Thirteenth Street
Philadelphia, PA 19107
(1-215-567-7000)

Strengthening the Family Link
Here are some suggestions for reaching out to your students' families:
- Encourage the students to talk with family members about Jesus' law of love.
- Invite family members to join the class to watch one of the suggested videos.

Parish : 101B

Chapter 17 pages 102–107

Objectives
- Recognize that we have the ability to make good decisions.
- Recognize that the Church can help us make the right choices.
- Acknowledge Jesus' law of love as a guide for making good choices.
- Realize that loving one's neighbor means caring for all people.

Gathering WE ARE INVITED
1. Open

Personal Experience Ask volunteers to share stories or movies about someone who did something wrong and then regretted it.

Prayer Pray the opening prayer together.

Working with the Text
- Read aloud or summarize the text. **What do we call our inner moral guide?** (our conscience)
- Invite responses to the bulleted question. (Possible answers: Nathan needs to apologize to William; he should stick up for William the next time.)

Working with the Pictures
- Point out the pictures on this and the next page and have the students describe what they see happening.
  Invite volunteers to respond. (Accept all reasonable suggestions for positive alternatives.)

Chapter 17
Jesus' Law of Love

Prayer

Dear Jesus, teach your Church how to live out your law of love.

Nathan had a whole conversation with himself on the way home from school. He kept remembering everything that had happened at lunchtime.

"I'm so confused," Nathan thought. "I know why I did what I did, but I don't like myself for doing it. Sure, William is the new kid in our class, and he's shy. But I walked home with him one day, and I thought he was all right. Today when those kids started making fun of him on the playground, I should have told them to stop. But I didn't. I just walked away because I didn't want them to make fun of me. William looked so hurt. He's walking home by himself today. Now what should I do?"

● What do you think Nathan should do?

ACTIVITY Think of how you act on the playground. List three loving choices you can make when you play.

102 : We Are Invited

Resource Center

Link to the Family
Tell the students that our families can help us make good choices when we find ourselves in difficult situations. If time permits, share a family experience of your own as an example. Encourage volunteers to explain how family members have helped them make good decisions.

Teaching Tip
Clarifying concepts Explain that *all* people sometimes need help making good decisions. Discuss how others are hurt by our unloving or selfish decisions. Stress that when we make bad choices, we can always ask God's forgiveness and the forgiveness of the people we have hurt. However, God's willingness to forgive is never an excuse for making bad choices.

Notes: Opening the Chapter

Tough Choices

We make choices every day. Some are easy, like whether to have toast or cereal for breakfast. Other choices are harder. Like Nathan, we sometimes find ourselves choosing between two uncomfortable situations. How can we know what to do?

One way God has given us help in making good choices is through the Church. At Mass we hear readings from the Old Testament about how God gave the Ten Commandments to Moses and the people. When you prepare for the Sacrament of Reconciliation, you use the commandments to examine your conscience.

But sometimes we're like Nathan. He didn't do anything to hurt William. But he didn't help William when the others were making fun of him. Like Nathan, we sometimes sin by not doing something we know is right.

Catholics Believe...
that we are called to follow Jesus' law of love.
Catechism, #1970

WE EXPLORE : 103

WE EXPLORE
2. Build
Working with the Text
- Read or summarize *Tough Choices*.
- If time permits, review the Ten Commandments with the students. Remind them that the commandments teach us how to love and honor God as well as how to love and respect other people.
- Emphasize that each one of us has the free will to choose to follow the commandments. We also have the help of the Church.
  What sacrament celebrates God's forgiveness when we fail to follow the Ten Commandments and are sorry? (the Sacrament of Reconciliation)

Catholics Believe Stress that love helps us make the right choices.

Link to the Faith Community
Remind the students that our parish family can also help us make good decisions. We can discuss difficult decisions with a priest during the Sacrament of Reconciliation, and parish leaders are also available for us to discuss any problems we may be trying to solve. Explain that Jesus gives us the strength we need to make loving choices. Each time we come together to pray with our parish family, we grow stronger.

Notes: Building the Chapter

We Explore
Build *Continued*
Working with the Text
- As you work with the text, use *The Language of Faith* below to further develop the terms *Beatitudes* and *law of love*.
- To illustrate the law of love, refer to the graphic organizer on page 101B. You may wish to do the suggested activity or one of your own choosing.

Scripture Signpost Be sure the students understand that Jesus never stops loving us. When we do not love others as Jesus loves us, we are not following his commandment. Elicit responses to the question. **(Possible answers: by collecting food for a local food pantry, starting a thrift shop, providing child care for parishioners during Mass.)** See *Link to Justice* below for additional ideas.

Working with the Pictures
- Direct the students' attention to the photographs.
  How did the older child follow Jesus' law of love? **(She helped the frustrated child as Jesus would have done.)**
- Read aloud and discuss the caption question.

Scripture Signpost
"If you keep my commandments, you will remain in my love."
— John 15:10

How can our Church family live by the Beatitudes and the law of love?

The Church Teaches Love

We read about Jesus' teaching in Scripture. Through the Church we also receive Jesus' command to love. In the **Beatitudes** Jesus taught us how to make loving choices. In these teachings he showed us what real happiness and holiness mean. Followers of Jesus share the sadness of others. They are not afraid to suffer for what is right. They are people who are kind and gentle. They show mercy and work for justice and peace (Matthew 5:3–11).

But how can Nathan, and all members of the Church family, remember all these ways to act? Jesus gave us a **law of love** that is simple enough for everyone to remember. He said, "This is my commandment: love one another as I love you" (John 13:34).

As the Church we live by Jesus' law of love. Many parishes have groups of volunteers who feed hungry people, build houses, and teach people to read. They work for peace and justice in the community around them.

How can you show God's love?

104 : We Explore

Resource Center

The Language of Faith
- The **Beatitudes**, which are some of Jesus' teachings, ask us to go beyond the level of simple obedience to the Ten Commandments. When we live the Beatitudes, we show love to others as Jesus would. We apply the commandments as broadly as possible.
- Jesus' **law of love** tells us to treat other people lovingly and respectfully. When we follow this one simple law, we are also following the Beatitudes and the Ten Commandments.

Scripture Background
John's Gospel speaks often of Jesus' relationship with his Father. By asking us, in **John 13:34**, to keep his commandment of love, Jesus is assuring us that we will stay connected to him and to God our Father. Jesus loves us with the same love with which God the Father loves him, and we in turn are called to love others.

Link to Justice
Have the students brainstorm a list of injustices they have noticed in their own school or community—for example, limiting access for people with disabilities, treating one group differently, excluding someone because of race or gender. Talk about why these are injustices.

Scripture Story
The Good Samaritan

A man asked Jesus, "What should I do to have eternal life?" Jesus answered with another question. "What is the law?" Jesus asked. The man quoted the **Great Commandment**: "Love God, and love your neighbor as yourself." Jesus said, "Keep that law."

But the man wanted to be clear about what Jesus meant. So he asked, "Who is my neighbor?" This story was Jesus' reply.

"A Jewish traveler was beaten, robbed, and left on the side of the road. A religious leader saw him and left him there. Later another important person passed by without helping. Finally, a Samaritan saw the wounded man. The Samaritans and Jews were usually enemies, but the Samaritan felt sorry for the traveler. He bandaged his wounds, took him to an inn, and cared for him. When he had to leave, he gave the innkeeper money to care for the injured man. Which man was the traveler's neighbor?"

Surprised, the man answered, "The third man." Jesus said, "Then be like him."

—based on Luke 10:25–37

Why was the Samaritan an especially good example of being a good neighbor?

We Explore
Build Continued
Working with the Text

- As you read aloud the Scripture Story, refer to *The Language of Faith* below to clarify the term *Great Commandment*.
- Lead the students to understand that Jesus was teaching an important lesson with this story: He was telling us how to be a good neighbor. We must be willing to go out of our way to help others, even those we sometimes view as strangers or enemies.

Working with the Pictures

- Point out the scene pictured on this page.
  How do you think the injured man felt when the Samaritan stopped and helped him? (surprised and thankful)
- Encourage volunteers to respond to the caption question. (The Samaritan helped someone who was not only a stranger to him but who was also considered to be his enemy.)

The Language of Faith
The **Great Commandment**—quoted by the man who questioned Jesus—comes from the Books of Deuteronomy and Leviticus in the Old Testament. This was not a new law but was well known to the Jewish people of Jesus' time. Jesus assures the man that he will live forever with God if he keeps the Great Commandment. But Jesus adds a new dimension to the way in which the law is understood: We are a neighbor to others when we help anyone who is in need.

Assessment Tip
Ask the students to check their knowledge of the Ten Commandments and see how many they can recall. Have them turn to page 178 to check their lists.

Multicultural Link
Help the students recognize that people often discriminate against others. Point out that through the story of the Good Samaritan, Jesus teaches us that we must act lovingly toward *all* people, not just those who are like us. Elicit from the students reasons people discriminate. Talk about these.

Teaching Tip
Handling sensitive topics Point out that being a Good Samaritan can mean asking an adult to help someone. Young children should not attempt to help strangers by themselves but should always seek help for them. You may mention that some states have Good Samaritan laws that protect people who give assistance to strangers.

PARISH : 105

We Reflect
Review

Recall Invite volunteers to respond to the questions. *(Love one another as I love you; love God and love your neighbor as yourself.)*

Think and Share Ask the students to consider their answers before responding. *(Possible answer: by asking ourselves "What would Jesus do in this situation?")*

Continue the Journey Brainstorm this list with the students.

Alternative Have the students complete this list at home with an adult family member.

We Live Our Faith *At Home:* Discuss with the students simple actions that would express love and care for a family member or neighbor.
In the Parish: If time permits, help the students identify people in their school, parish, or neighborhood who would welcome a friendly gesture.

Faith Journal The students may begin pages 33–34 of their *Faith Journal* in class and complete them at home. As part of your own spiritual development, complete *Your Faith Journal* (page J18).

RECALL
What is Jesus' law of love? What is the Great Commandment?

THINK AND SHARE
How can we use Jesus' law of love to make decisions?

CONTINUE THE JOURNEY
List people who are your "neighbors." Next to each one, write a way of showing love.

WE LIVE OUR FAITH

At Home Surprise a family member or a neighbor with a loving action.

In the Parish Go outside your usual circle of friends. Make a new friend or spend time with someone who is lonely.

106 : We Reflect

Resource Center

Link to Justice

Talk about the Big Brother and Big Sister associations that link young children with adult volunteers who can provide them with friendship and guidance. Discuss how the volunteers are following the law of love by helping care for others.

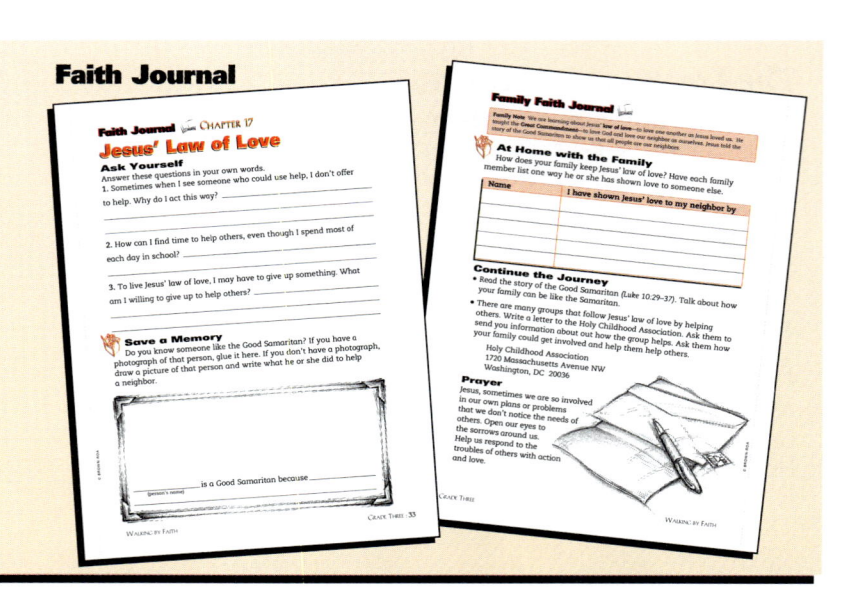

106 : Chapter 17

Following Jesus

Living the law of love is really living like Jesus. We do this when we come to know Jesus better and follow him more closely. Then the love we have for Jesus will be shared with all people.

This prayer was written by Saint Richard of Chichester. Saint Richard was an English bishop who tried to follow Jesus' law of love in every action. Pray this prayer together.

PRAYER

Thanks to you, O Lord Jesus Christ,
 for all that you have given us.
O most merciful Redeemer, Friend,
 and Brother,
may we know you more clearly,
love you more dearly,
and follow you more nearly
day by day.

We Celebrate
3. Close

Working with the Text

- Read or summarize *Following Jesus*.
- Explain that saints such as Richard of Chichester help us live like Jesus through their prayers and by examples they have set.

Working with the Pictures

- Have the students study the background picture. Explain that this twelfth-century stone panel was carved for the Cathedral of the Holy Trinity in Chichester, England, where Richard served as bishop. The panels show the story of the raising of Lazarus. Originally, the panels were painted bright colors, and precious stones were set into the eyes.
- Call attention to the photographs. **How does each photograph show Jesus' law of love being lived?** (The girl is spending time with an older person; children are reading the Scriptures to learn about Jesus.)

Prayer Close the session with prayer. Gather the students into a circle to pray Saint Richard's prayer together. Encourage the students to hold hands, and then repeat the prayer. Conclude the prayer celebration by singing "Day by Day" from the play *Godspell*.

Background
Saint Richard of Chichester (1197–1253) was a farmer's son who became a priest and eventually was named bishop of the diocese of Chichester, England. He was compassionate to those who came to him to confess their sins and was known for his generosity to those with financial problems.

Link to the Family
To keep family members involved with what the students are learning in this unit, copy and distribute the Unit Five Family Letter from the Resource Package.

Notes: Closing the Chapter

Getting Ready: Chapter 18

The Church Helps

Program Resources
Student Text, pp. 108–113
Student Faith Journal, pp. 35–36
Your Faith Journal, p. J19
Chapter 18 Transparency
Unit Five Music and Liturgy Resources

Unit Five (Christian Morality)
Temple of the Holy Spirit

Key Content Summary
Our Church family helps us follow the law of love.

Planning the Chapter

	Pacing Guide *Suggested time/Your time*	Content	Objectives	Materials
Open	10-15 min./ ____ min.	*We Are Invited*, pp. 108–109	• Recognize that Christians are called to do the right thing when faced with difficult choices.	• magazines, newspapers, scissors, glue, drawing materials, poster board (optional)
Build	20-25 min./ ____ min.	*We Explore*, p. 110	• Identify how the Church helps us develop our conscience. • Explore the role of the Sacrament of Reconciliation in forming a good conscience.	
		Stepping Stones, p. 111	• Identify the steps in an examination of conscience.	• Chapter 18 Transparency from the Resource Package
Review	15-20 min./ ____ min.	*We Reflect*, p. 112	• Demonstrate understanding of chapter concepts. • Apply learning through activity. • Practice faith at home and in the parish.	• *Student Faith Journal*, pp. 35–36 • *Your Faith Journal*, p. J19
Close	10-15 min./ ____ min.	*We Celebrate*, p. 113	• Discover God's forgiveness and rejoice in his mercy.	• instrumental music • Unit Five Music and Liturgy Resources from the Resource Package

For additional suggestions, see Scheduling, pp. T35–T37.

Catechism in Context

Doctrinal Foundation This chapter explains that the Holy Spirit, the word of God inspired by the Spirit, and the teachings of the Church, the Temple of the Holy Spirit, all help us make good choices. The "law of the Spirit of Christ Jesus has freed you from the law of sin and death" (Romans 8:2). The promptings of the Spirit enliven our conscience and give us the strength to resist temptations. The word convicts us of sin but assures us of the possibility of forgiveness even as it indicates the way in which we should walk. The Church, a long-time expert in human nature and guided into all truth by the Spirit, spells out the implications of the word for our own time and place. And the Church ministers reconciliation to us when we fail to make the right choices.

See Catechism of the Catholic Church, #1785.

One-Minute Retreat for Catechists

Read
"He will easily be content and at peace whose conscience is pure."
—Thomas à Kempis

Reflect
When has my conscience been most at peace?

Pray
Lord, please forgive me when I take wrong paths along my spiritual journey. When I am tempted and blinded by my own weakness, may I feel your presence. Help me turn to your love.

Visualizing the Lesson

Use this graphic organizer to help the students visualize what helps us make good decisions.

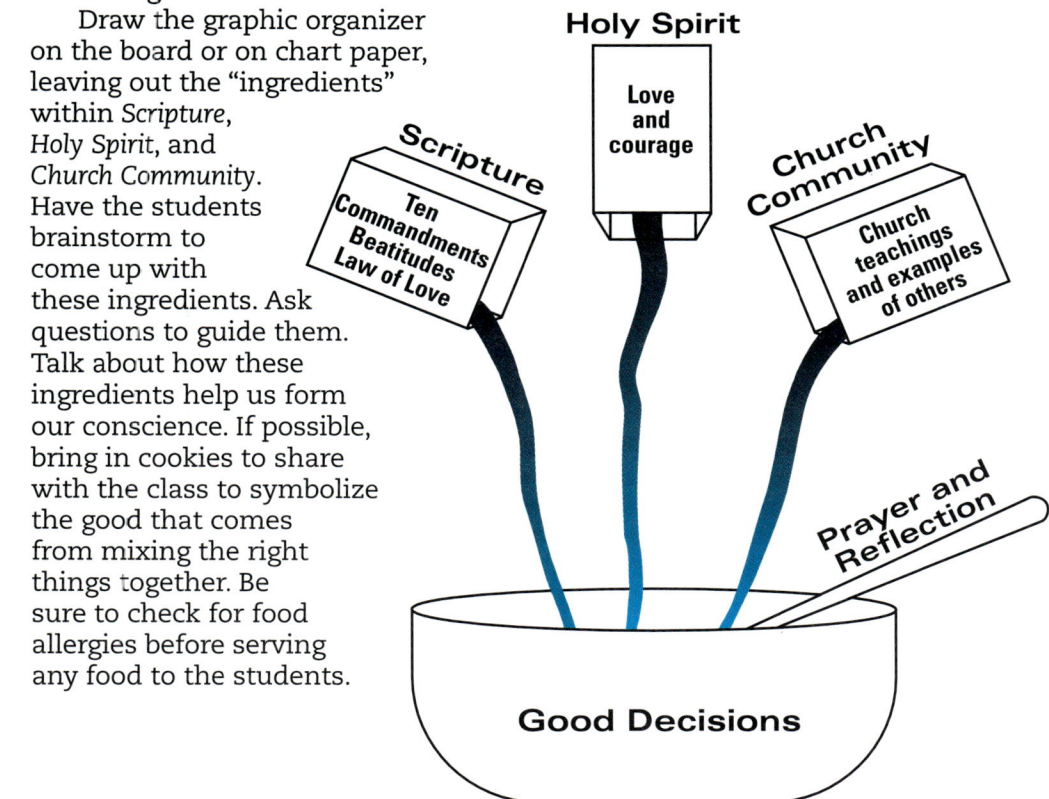

Draw the graphic organizer on the board or on chart paper, leaving out the "ingredients" within *Scripture*, *Holy Spirit*, and *Church Community*. Have the students brainstorm to come up with these ingredients. Ask questions to guide them. Talk about how these ingredients help us form our conscience. If possible, bring in cookies to share with the class to symbolize the good that comes from mixing the right things together. Be sure to check for food allergies before serving any food to the students.

Library Links

Books for Children
The "I Confess" for Children by Hubert J. Richards (The Liturgical Press, 1-800-858-5450).
This book helps children learn about forgiveness.

Books for Parents and Teachers
Conscience in Conflict—How to Make Moral Choices by Kenneth R. Overberg SJ (St. Anthony Messenger Press, 1-800-488-0488).
Overberg presents a decision-making process for contemporary situations.

Whatever Happened to Sin?—The Truth about Catholic Morality by Charles E. Bouchard OP (Liguori Publications, 1-800-325-9989).
Our understanding of conscience, sin, virtue, liturgy, and friendship shapes our moral lives.

Multimedia
For children:
Kevin's Temptation produced by Twenty-Third Publications (video) (BROWN-ROA, 1-800-922-7697).
Kevin is tempted to do things he knows are wrong.

For parents and teachers:
Reconciliation from the Mysteries of Faith series produced by Fisher Productions (video) (Paulist Press, 1-800-218-1903).
This sacrament helps us live the truth in our relationship with God.

Organizations
For more information about how the Church helps us, contact:
Secretariat for Family, Laity, Women, and Youth
USCC
3211 Fourth Street NE
Washington, DC 20017
(1-202-541-3040)
(http://www.nccbuscc.org)

Strengthening the Family Link

Here are some suggestions for reaching out to your students' families:

- Encourage the students to talk with family members about ways to make good choices.
- Invite family members to join the class for a Reconciliation service. Ask your parish priest to hold a Reconciliation service for your class or all the classes in your program.

PARISH : 107B

Chapter 18 pages 108–113

Objectives

- Recognize that Christians are called to do the right thing when faced with difficult choices.
- Identify how the Church helps us develop a conscience.
- Explore the role of the Sacrament of Reconciliation in forming a good conscience.
- Identify the steps in an examination of conscience.

Gathering   WE ARE INVITED
1. Open

Personal Experience Invite volunteers to share times when they had problems and needed help.

Prayer Remind the students that we can ask the Holy Spirit for help. Then pray the opening prayer together.

Working with the Text

- Explain that these two pages continue the story of Nathan and William from the previous chapter. Then read aloud or summarize the text.
- Invite the students to predict what might happen next.

Working with the Pictures

- Call attention to the photograph. **How is Nathan's mother showing him that she wants to help?** (She is sitting and listening to Nathan, holding his hand, and asking questions.)

  Be sure the students understand that we should go to people we trust whenever we need help. Encourage volunteers to share their lists.

CHAPTER 18

The Church Helps

PRAYER

Holy Spirit, thank you for the strength and support we find in the Church.

Nathan was still upset about William. He was having an after-school snack, but he was very quiet.

"Nathan, is something bothering you?" his mother asked.

He told her what happened with William on the playground. "That is a bad situation. How would you feel if you were William? How would you want to be treated?"

Nathan thought for a while. "I would feel lonely. I would want people to be nice to me and be my friends."

"Then you know what you have to do, don't you?" his mother said.

ACTIVITY
Sometimes we need help making the right choice. Make a list of people you can talk to when you need help.

108 : We Are Invited

Resource Center

Link to the Family
Invite the students to think of family members they can turn to for help with difficult decisions—for example, an older brother or sister, a favorite aunt or uncle, or a grandparent. Suggest that they perform acts of kindness to express their thanks for these people's help.

Optional   Enrichment
Have the students create poster montages about acceptance, friendship, and having the courage to do the right thing. Tell them they can use pictures and headlines cut from magazines and newspapers as well as pictures they have drawn. Let them work in pairs or small groups to create the montages. Display the completed posters in the classroom.

Notes: Opening the Chapter

_____
_____
_____
_____
_____
_____

"But what if the other kids make fun of me?" Nathan was sure that that would happen.

"Remember your religion lesson from last week? What did Jesus say about loving people?" Nathan's mother asked.

"We should love everyone the way he loves us. So I shouldn't care what the mean kids think?" Nathan asked.

His mother answered, "I know that's hard, but you will be happy with yourself for doing the loving thing. And you will be teaching the other kids how they should treat others."

Nathan got up from the table. "Where are you going?" his mother asked.

"I'm going to invite William over to play, if that's all right. I want him to feel like he has a friend."

Our Moral Guide

The Holy Spirit helps us make good choices.

Catechism, #1830

When have you had to make a difficult choice? How has the Holy Spirit helped you?

WE ARE INVITED : 109

WE ARE INVITED
Open Continued

Working with the Pictures

Point out the photograph.
> How can you tell that the boys are friends? **(They are having a good time together; Nathan is smiling.)**

Working with the Text

Read aloud or summarize the rest of the story. Emphasize that Nathan knows he must do what is right even if others make fun of him.

Our Moral Guide Point out that the Holy Spirit is always there to listen to our prayers. Encourage the students to pray to the Holy Spirit whenever they need help. Invite volunteers to share their responses to the questions. **(Accept all reasonable responses.)**

Teaching Tip

Handling sensitive topics Be aware of students in your class who find it difficult to make and keep friends. The story of William and Nathan may make these students feel uncomfortable. Emphasize that through Nathan's caring words and actions he has found a new friend in William. Also stress that we should make an effort to get to know someone before we decide whether we want to be good friends with that person.

We Explore
2. Build
Working with the Text

- As you read or summarize the text, refer to *The Language of Faith* below to clarify the highlighted term.
  How can the Scriptures help us form our conscience? (Possible answer: They reveal Jesus' teachings about how to love God and our neighbor.)
- To show how we are helped to make good decisions, refer to the graphic organizer on page 107B. You may wish to do the suggested activity or one of your own choosing.
- **Catholics Believe** Explain that the Church's teachings are based on the word of God, which is revealed through Scripture.

Working with the Pictures

- Direct the students' attention to the photograph.
- Ask volunteers to respond to the caption question. (Possible answers: Scripture, my family's advice, what I learned in religion class, my conscience.)

Catholics Believe...
the Holy Spirit, the word of God, and the teachings of the Church help us make good choices.

Catechism, #1785

The Church Helps Us Choose Wisely

Nathan's mother asked questions that helped him make a loving choice. She tried to help him form a good **conscience**. Your conscience is your inner knowledge of what is right and wrong. Your conscience will help you make good decisions.

Nathan's mother was like the Church. The Church helps us form our conscience through its teachings and laws, which are based on Scripture. To find the right way to do something, you can talk with family members, teachers, or catechists. You can read and think about Scripture. You can pray to the Holy Spirit for help.

Through the Sacrament of Reconciliation, the Church gives us a chance to look at what we have done, to seek forgiveness when we have sinned, and to change our behavior.

What helps you decide between right and wrong?

110 : We Explore

Resource Center

The Language of Faith

Conscience comes from a Latin word meaning "knowledge within." Our conscience gives us the inner knowledge to judge a situation and then act in a way that shows love and respect for ourselves and others. Our conscience also informs us when we have done wrong.

Notes: Building the Chapter

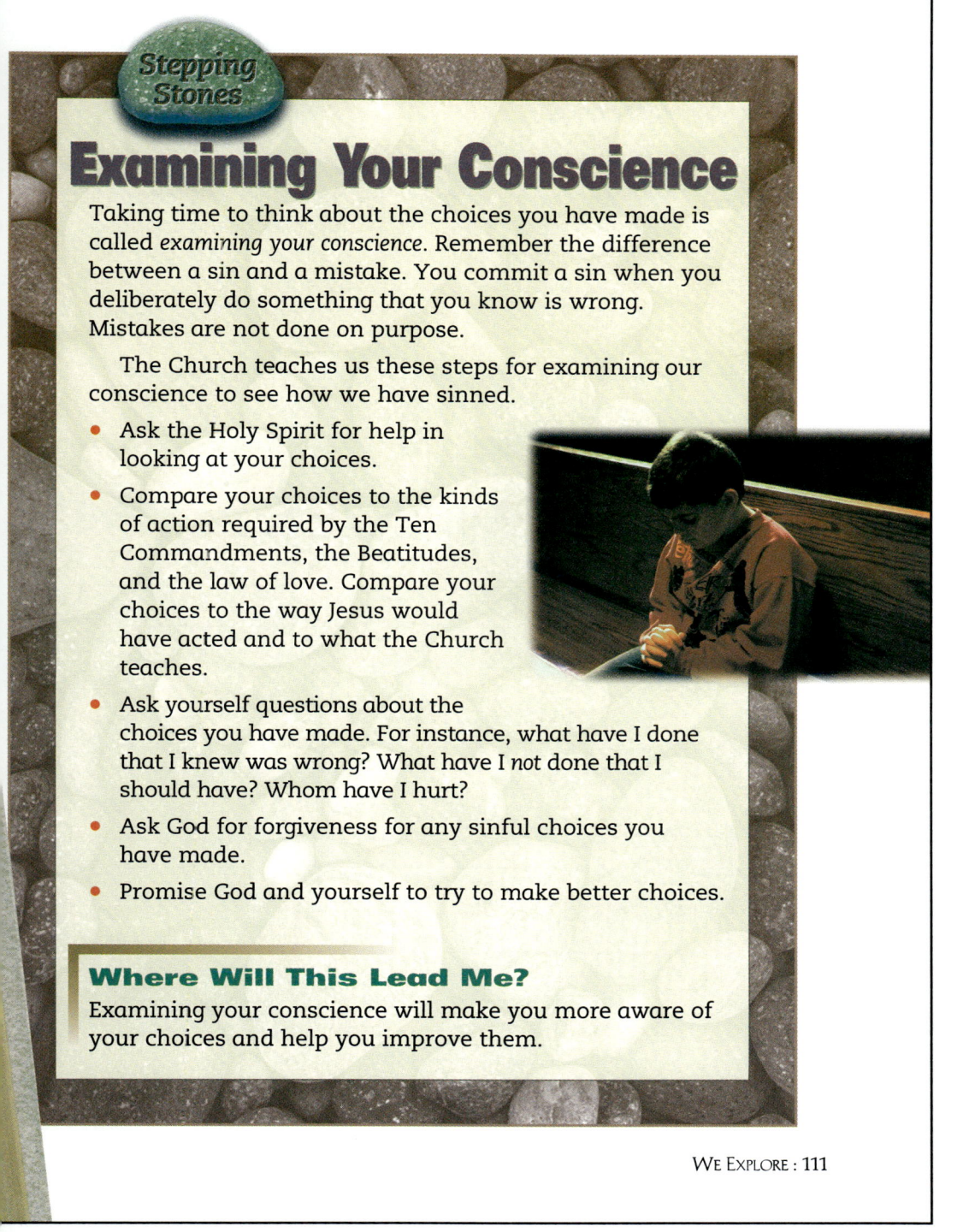

Stepping Stones

Examining Your Conscience

Taking time to think about the choices you have made is called *examining your conscience*. Remember the difference between a sin and a mistake. You commit a sin when you deliberately do something that you know is wrong. Mistakes are not done on purpose.

The Church teaches us these steps for examining our conscience to see how we have sinned.

- Ask the Holy Spirit for help in looking at your choices.
- Compare your choices to the kinds of action required by the Ten Commandments, the Beatitudes, and the law of love. Compare your choices to the way Jesus would have acted and to what the Church teaches.
- Ask yourself questions about the choices you have made. For instance, what have I done that I knew was wrong? What have I *not* done that I should have? Whom have I hurt?
- Ask God for forgiveness for any sinful choices you have made.
- Promise God and yourself to try to make better choices.

Where Will This Lead Me?

Examining your conscience will make you more aware of your choices and help you improve them.

WE EXPLORE
Build Continued
Stepping Stones
Working with the Text

- Read aloud or summarize the steps in *Examining Your Conscience*. Be sure the students understand what the term *examining your conscience* means.
- Point out that even though we examine our conscience before the Sacrament of Reconciliation, it is a good idea to examine our conscience at other times, too, such as at night before going to sleep.

Working with the Pictures

Explain that through the Sacrament of Reconciliation, our sins are always forgiven if we are truly sorry.
How is the boy in the picture preparing for this sacrament? (He is examining his conscience.)

Practice Ask the students to carry out each step as you read each one aloud.

Alternative Have the students turn to page 177 in their texts and pray the Act of Contrition together.

Link to Justice

Tell the students that when we examine our conscience, we need to think about how we have treated other people. Have we behaved justly toward others, treating them with the respect all people deserve as children of God? Remind the students that we can pray for people who suffer from injustice even if we are not able to help them directly.

Link to the Faith Community

Tell the students that most parish communities come together a few times a year—usually during the Seasons of Advent and Lent—to communally celebrate the Sacrament of Reconciliation. The community members pray together, listen to Scripture readings, and participate in an examination of conscience. Individuals who want to confess their sins to a priest and receive absolution privately are invited to do so. To conclude the sacrament, the assembly prays the Lord's Prayer and sings a song of praise together.

WE REFLECT
Review

Recall Invite volunteers to respond. (our inner knowledge of right and wrong; by following the Church's teachings, reading Scripture, talking with others, and praying to the Holy Spirit)

Think and Share Encourage the students to consider their answers before responding. (The first case is an example of a mistake or accident. The second case is an example of a sin—deliberately doing something you know is wrong.)

Continue the Journey Praise the students for their efforts in developing a conscience. Suggest that they use their reminders every day.

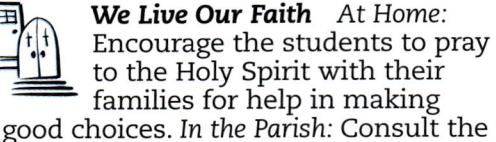

We Live Our Faith *At Home:* Encourage the students to pray to the Holy Spirit with their families for help in making good choices. *In the Parish:* Consult the parish bulletin for the date of the next communal celebration.

Faith Journal The students may begin pages 35–36 of their *Faith Journal* in class and complete them at home. As a part of your own spiritual development, complete *Your Faith Journal* (page J19).

RECALL

What is your conscience? How can you form a good conscience?

THINK AND SHARE

Here are two situations: (1) A child trips and falls and spills a pitcher of milk. (2) A child has been reminded to do homework but still refuses to do it. Are both of these actions sins? Why or why not?

CONTINUE THE JOURNEY

Make a reminder to ask for the Holy Spirit's help in making good choices.

REMINDER

_____
_____
_____
_____
_____
_____
_____
_____

WE LIVE OUR FAITH

At Home Talk with family members about how they make important choices. Ask the Holy Spirit to help your family follow Jesus.

In the Parish Find out when there will be a communal celebration of the Sacrament of Reconciliation.

112 : WE REFLECT

Resource Center

Background

The *Sacrament of Penance* is the official name for the sacrament of forgiveness. Over the years the sacrament has been known by unofficial titles that reflected the emphasis of the times. Some adults may remember calling it *Confession*, which emphasized the confessing of sins. The name most often used today is the *Sacrament of Reconciliation*. This name emphasizes the reconciliation of the penitent with God and with those whom the penitent has injured through words or actions.

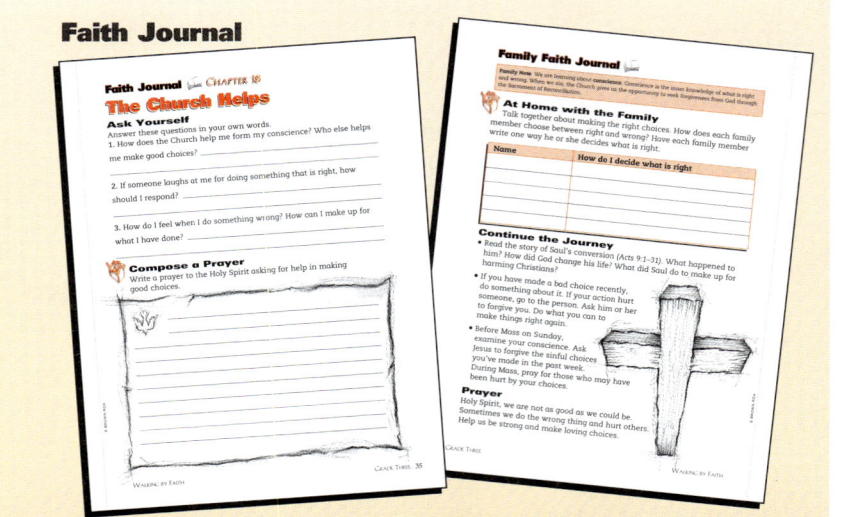

We Ask for Forgiveness

We take part in the Sacrament of Reconciliation because we know we have hurt other people and God through our actions and *neglect*. The following prayer asks God for forgiveness.

Prayer

After each statement, respond, "But you love us and come to us."

Sometimes we have not behaved as your children should. . . .

We have given trouble to our parents and teachers. . . .

We have quarreled and called each other names. . . .

We have been lazy at home and in school and have not been helpful to our parents (brothers, sisters, friends). . . .

We have thought too much of ourselves and have told lies. . . .

We have not done good to others when we had the chance. . . .

—*from the Rite of Penance*

We Celebrate : 113

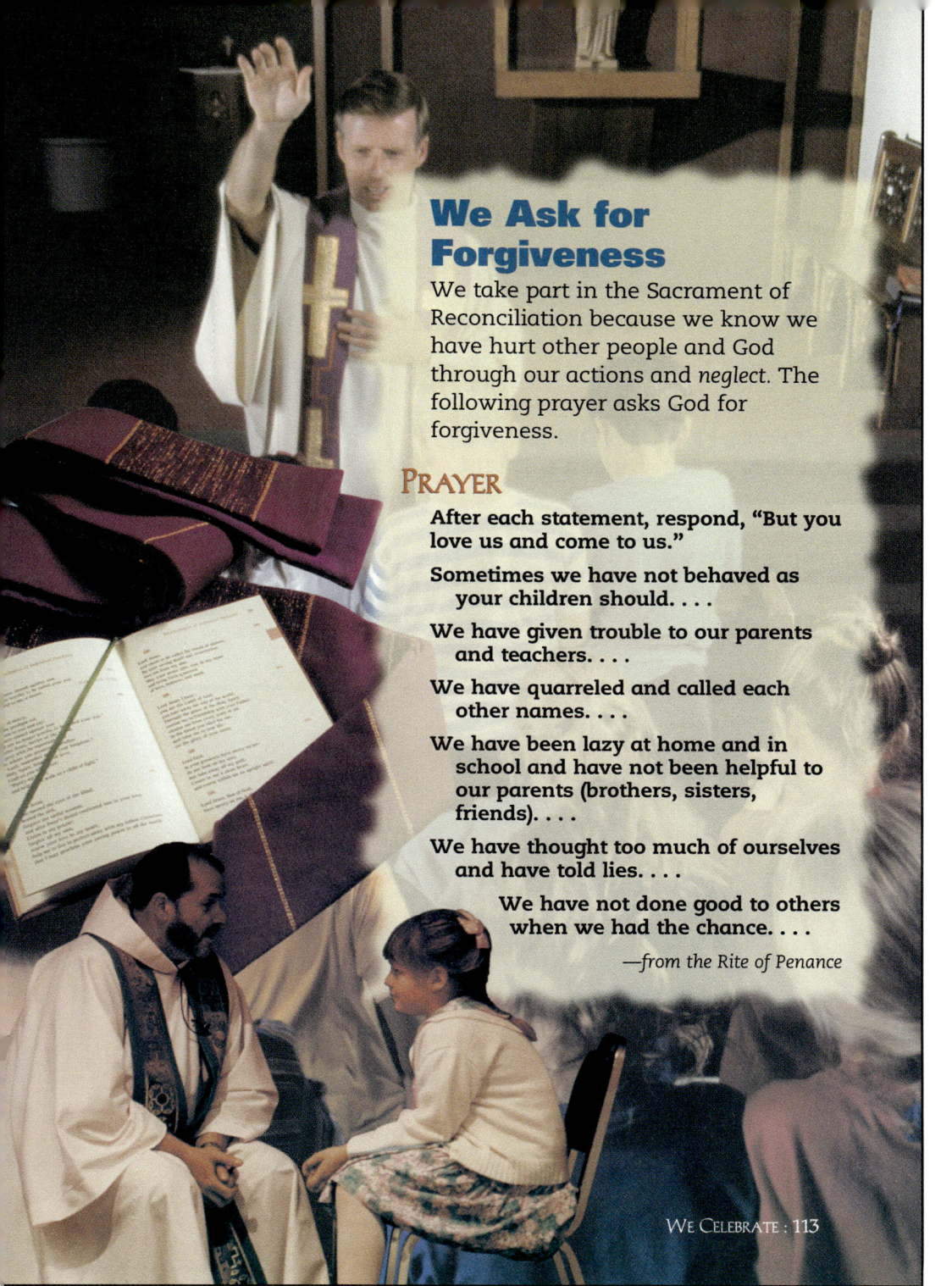

We Celebrate
3. Close

Working with the Text

Read or summarize *We Ask for Forgiveness*. You might explain that *neglect* means not doing something we know we should do.
  What are some things that people your age might neglect to do?
  (Accept all reasonable answers.)

Working with the Pictures

Point out the photograph.
  What did the young girl do before meeting with the priest?
  (She examined her conscience.)

Prayer Explain that the prayer on this page will help the students examine their conscience. Gather the students in a circle, and lead them in singing a favorite hymn about forgiveness. If possible, play instrumental music in the background. Conclude the prayer with the Sign of the Cross.

Link to Liturgy

Tell the students that the Eucharist is a celebration of our reconciliation with God. Sins that are not serious can be forgiven through our participation in the Eucharist. One prayer used in the penitential rite begins, "I confess to almighty God, and to you, my brothers and sisters, that I have sinned through my own fault. . . ." Ask the students to listen for this prayer and participate in the penitential rite when they attend Mass.

Music and Liturgy Resources

To enhance your prayer and celebration, you may wish to use the Unit Five Music and Liturgy Resources from the Resource Package.

Notes: Closing the Chapter

Parish : 113

Getting Ready: Chapter 19

Faith, Hope, and Love

Program Resources
Student Text, pp. 114–119
Student Faith Journal, pp. 37–38
Your Faith Journal, p. J20
Chapter 19 Transparency
Unit Five Assessment

Unit Five (Christian Morality)
Temple of the Holy Spirit

Key Content Summary
The virtues help us live as members of the Church.

Planning the Chapter

	Pacing Guide Suggested time/Your time	Content	Objectives	Materials
Open	10–15 min./ _____ min.	We Are Invited, p. 114	• Recognize actions that demonstrate love and courage.	
Build	20–25 min./ _____ min.	We Explore, pp. 115–117	• Recognize that virtues help us share God's love. • Discover that faith, hope, and love must be practiced in our lives. • Identify the precepts of the Church.	• Chapter 19 Transparency from the Resource Package
Review	15–20 min./ _____ min.	We Reflect, p. 118	• Demonstrate understanding of chapter concepts. • Apply learning through activity. • Practice faith at home and in the parish.	• art materials • Student Faith Journal, pp. 37–38 • Your Faith Journal, p. J20 • Unit Five Assessment from the Resource Package
Close	10–15 min./ _____ min.	We Celebrate, p. 119	• Summarize the theological virtues through prayer.	• recording of favorite hymn

For additional suggestions, see Scheduling, pp. T35–T37.

Catechism in Context

Doctrinal Foundation This chapter describes the virtues of faith, hope, and love. These virtues, called the theological virtues, are gifts from God. They are the foundation of Christian moral life, giving our daily lives vitality and character. Paul tells us: "So faith, hope, and love remain, but the greatest of these is love" (1 Corinthians 13:13). Faith is not only believing in God and all that he has revealed but trusting in God as well. By faith we commit ourselves to God. With hope we wait in anticipation for the reign of God to be fulfilled and rejoice that it has already begun. Hope inspires our activities so that we keep our lives focused on God, our relationship with him, and what he has promised us.

See Catechism of the Catholic Church, #1813.

The virtue of love enables us to love God above all else and to love our neighbor as ourselves. For Christians Jesus is the perfect example of love. If we were to replace the word "love" with the name "Jesus" in Saint Paul's wonderful description in *1 Corinthians 13*, it would ring absolutely true: "Jesus is patient; Jesus is kind; Jesus is not jealous, pompous, inflated, or rude. He does not seek his own interests; he is not quick tempered; he does not rejoice in wrongdoing, but rejoices in the truth. Jesus bears all things, believes all things, hopes all things, endures all things." Would it ring as true if we replaced his name with our own?

One-Minute Retreat for Catechists

Read
"It is strange that men will talk of miracles, revelations, inspiration, and the like, as things past, while love remains."
—Henry David Thoreau

Reflect
How can love be miraculous, revealing, and inspirational?

Pray
Help me recognize when I am spiritually hungry, O Lord. May I not blindly starve but reach out for the sustenance that is always available for the taking. Help me always remember that faith, hope, and love are the most perfect and fulfilling foods.

Visualizing the Lesson

Use this graphic organizer to help the students understand how God's gift of the virtues and the Church's precepts help us grow closer to God.

Redraw the graphic organizer on a large sheet of paper, and make copies for the students. Ask students to explain the symbolism of the virtues as the wheels and precepts as road signs. Have volunteers recall the precepts of the Church and write key words on their diagrams below each sign. Have them decorate their diagrams and keep them as reference.

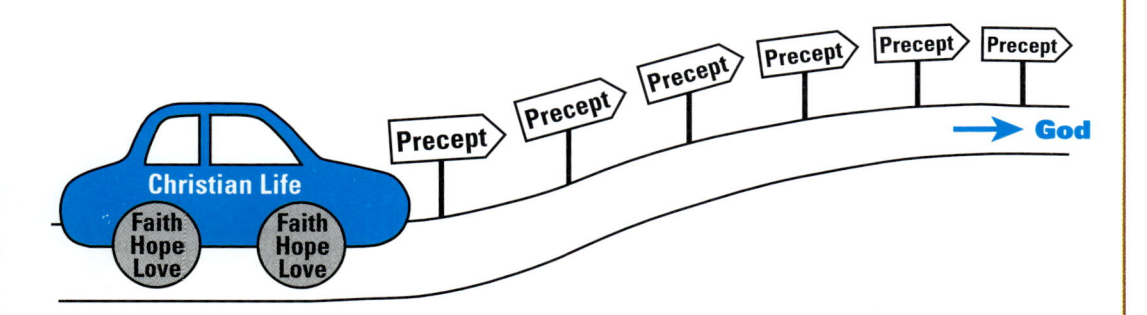

Library Links

Books for Children
A Child's First Book of Virtues by Emily Hunter (Doubleday, 1-800-688-4442).
   Children discover the virtues.

The Book of Virtues for Children by William J. Bennett (Simon & Schuster, 1-800-223-2336).
   This collection of stories and poems teaches virtues. (Audiotape available.)

Books for Parents and Teachers
The Book of Virtues by William J. Bennett (Simon & Schuster, 1-800-223-2336).
   Well-known literary works are presented to teach virtues. (Audiotape available.)

Multimedia
For children:

The Parable of the Two Sons: Pete, the Sorry Son produced by Twenty-Third Publications (video) (BROWN-ROA, 1-800-922-7696).
   Pete refuses to help his father. His brother Peabody agrees to help but changes his mind. Pete decides to help and turns out to be the more responsible son.

The Magic Fishbowl produced by Oblate Media and Communication (Sheed & Ward, 1-800-333-7373).
   Change works with faith.

Glory Day, "Increase Our Faith" by David Haas (GIA Publications, 1-800-442-1358).
   Use this song to make music a part of chapter material.

Organizations
For further information about living the virtues, contact:
Pax Christi USA
532 W. Eighth Street
Erie, PA 16502
(1-814-453-4955)

Strengthening the Family Link

Here are some suggestions for reaching out to your students' families:

- Encourage the students to talk with family members about making the virtues a habit.
- Invite family members to join the class for a review of the Church's precepts. Have the precepts displayed, and ask volunteers to explain how each precept guides us.

PARISH : 113B

Chapter 19 pages 114–119

Objectives
- Recognize actions that demonstrate love and courage.
- Recognize that virtues help us share God's love.
- Discover that faith, hope, and love must be practiced in our lives.
- Identify the precepts of the Church.

Gathering WE ARE INVITED
1. Open

Personal Experience Ask volunteers to share times when they chose to act in a loving way.

Prayer Ask the students to think about these loving choices as they pray the opening prayer together.

Working with the Text
- Read aloud or summarize the letter from Mr. Jackson.
- Ask volunteers to respond to the bulleted question. (Possible answers: Nathan's yelling would only have made the other children tease them more; the other children would have become angry at Nathan and been unwilling to get to know William.)

Working with the Pictures
Call attention to the photograph. **Why do you think Nathan feels happy with the choice he made?** (Possible answer: Nathan knows he did the right thing; he stopped caring what other people thought, which brought him peace.)

CHAPTER 19
Faith, Hope, and Love

PRAYER
Dear God, show us how to live in faith, hope, and love every day.

Dear Mr. and Mrs. Davis,
I wanted to share with you what happened on the playground today. Nathan was playing with William. Some of the other children started to tease them. Nathan said to them, "William is a nice kid. He likes a lot of the things you like. He's told me neat stories about where he used to live. I hope you'll get to know him and stop teasing us."

A few of the teasers walked away. But some of them stayed and talked to William. Your son did the right thing, and you should be very proud of him.
    Sincerely,
    Mr. Jackson, Third Grade Teacher

- **What do you think would have happened if Nathan had yelled at the other kids and tried to make them feel guilty?**

Nathan made the loving choice and was happy with it.

114 : WE ARE INVITED

Resource Center

Assessment Tip
Have the students think about how they might have responded to the children who were teasing William. How might Jesus have responded?

Teaching Tip
Making connections Point out that making a choice we *know* is right makes us feel good about ourselves. In turn, doing things that make us feel good about ourselves makes us healthier mentally and emotionally. Ask the students to suggest examples of situations in which people their age must make difficult decisions and to describe the right (and healthy) choice in each situation.

Notes: Opening the Chapter

Using Faith, Hope, and Love

Think about how Nathan talked to his friends. He made it clear that he believed the other kids would like William. He hoped they would get to know him. He cared about William. He used the **virtues**, or good qualities, of faith, hope, and love to convince the others to stop being mean. God gave us these virtues as a way of sharing his love for us and helping us remember that God is with us always.

In the past Nathan had seen children getting along. Nathan believed, or had faith, that William and the other children could care for one another. As followers of Jesus we believe in what we have seen. But we also believe in things we haven't seen and don't understand. True faith is believing in God and all that God has revealed. We can believe because Jesus, in whom we trust fully, taught us how to live. The Church today teaches us how to be faith-filled.

Catholics Believe...
God gives us the virtues of faith, hope, and love to help us live as he wants us to live.
Catechism, #1813

Jesus' follower Thomas didn't believe that Jesus had been given new life until he saw him. Jesus said to him, "Blessed are those who have not seen and have believed" *(John 20:29)*.

We Explore
2. Build
Working with the Text
- Read aloud or summarize *Using Faith, Hope, and Love.*
- Refer to *The Language of Faith* below to clarify the term *virtue*.
  What does faith mean? (Faith helps us believe in things that our minds cannot fully understand and in things that our eyes have not seen.) **What are some things you believe in but don't fully understand or haven't seen?** (Possible answers: the existence of other planets, the way a seed sprouts and grows.)
- **Catholics Believe** Emphasize that the virtues of faith, hope, and love do not originate with us.
  Who gives us the gifts of faith, hope, and love? (God) Explain that God gives us these gifts to help us follow Jesus.

Working with the Pictures
- Point out the artwork of Thomas touching the wounds of the risen Christ. This wood carving is found in the Church of St. Cunibert in Cologne, Germany.
- Read the caption aloud.
  What did Jesus mean when he said, "Blessed are they who have not seen and have believed"? (People who have faith are blessed.)

The Language of Faith

The term **virtue** comes from the Latin word for "strength." The virtues of faith, hope, and love are strengths within us—given to us by God—to help us act in believing, trusting, and generous ways. When we practice these virtues, we grow in our knowledge of God, anticipate the coming of God's kingdom in its fullness, and share in the loving life of the Trinity.

Scripture Background

The story in **John 20:24–29** of "Doubting Thomas" is found only in the Gospel of John. It tells us how one of Jesus' closest companions came to have faith in the risen Christ. Thomas had a hard time believing what he hadn't seen for himself. From Thomas we know that it is human to have questions. The gift of faith helps us believe in God's word even when it may not make sense to us. For us, like Thomas, faith is the strength we rely on to help us follow Jesus more closely.

Notes: Building the Chapter

We Explore
Build Continued
Working with the Text

- Read aloud or summarize the text.
  What three gifts has everyone been given? (faith, hope, and love)
  What gift helps us not to lose heart, even when life becomes difficult? (hope)

  Scripture Signpost Explain that Paul, a follower of Jesus, wrote these words in a letter to the Corinthians, one of the early Christian communities. See *Scripture Background* below for more information.

- Ask volunteers to respond to the question. (Possible answers: We can practice faith by believing more in the goodness of others; have hope that things can be better for everyone at home, at school, and in the world; practice love by respecting ourselves and others.)

Working with the Pictures

Point out the picture of the children visiting two women.
How are these children practicing the virtue of love? (by spending time with people who are lonely)

Scripture Signpost
"So faith, hope, love remain, these three; but the greatest of these is love."
1 Corinthians 13:13

How can you practice faith, hope, and love?

Nathan hoped that the other children would get to know William. Hope is the virtue that looks to the future. The Church hopes for a world that is closer to God's kingdom than our present world. Nathan was looking forward to a more peaceful playground.

When Nathan spoke, he showed love for William. We show our love for God by loving other people. We protect people. We listen to friends who have problems. We do kind things. The Church wants us to show love for God by treating everyone with kindness and respect.

Faith, hope, and love are all gifts from God. But we must bring them into our lives by practicing them. It's like playing the piano. Having one in your home is not enough. You have to take lessons and practice if you want to play well. You have to develop the habit.

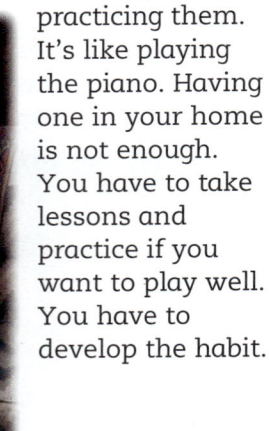

Visiting people who may be lonely is one way to share love.

116 : We Explore

Resource Center

Scripture Background
In **1 Corinthians 13:13** Paul addresses one of the most serious concerns of the Christian community at Corinth. The people had been fighting among themselves about which of God's gifts was the most important. Paul explains that all of God's gifts are necessary for the Church's survival but that the most important gift is love. With love all other gifts given to the Church community gain life and purpose. When God's kingdom comes in its fullness and we share in the heavenly life of God, faith in and hope for union with God will no longer be necessary. Only love remains.

Link to Justice
Remind the students that groups as well as individuals practice the virtues of faith, hope, and love by bringing relief to those who are suffering from injustice, hunger, homelessness, and other social ills. Talk with the students about a group that works to change unjust structures—for example, Oxfam America or Pax Christi. Encourage the students to think of ways that they can help people who suffer from various forms of oppression.

Guides for Life

The Church has many guides to help us live lives of virtue. Some of the guiding teachings, or **precepts**, of the Church are listed here.

Precepts of the Church

Precept	How It Guides Us
1. Take part in the Mass on Sundays and holy days. Keep these days holy and avoid unnecessary work.	Makes sure we take time to be with Jesus and our faith community. Allows us time to strengthen our faith by attending Mass, resting our bodies, and enjoying the world God has given us.
2. Receive the Sacrament of Reconciliation at least once a year if we have committed mortal sin.	Helps us look at our lives, see where we need to change, and improve our actions.
3. Receive Holy Communion at least once a year during the Easter Season.	Strengthens our faith and makes us one with Jesus.
4. Fast and abstain from meat on the days the Church sets apart for **penance**, or making up for sin.	Helps us share in the sacrifice of Jesus, train ourselves spiritually, and experience the hungers of the world's poor people.
5. Give of our time, talents, prayers, and money to support the Church.	Encourages us to support the Church and participate in its works.

WE EXPLORE : 117

WE EXPLORE
Build Continued

Working with the Text

- As you read aloud *Guides for Life*, point out to the students that all of the precepts are things that even children their age can follow. Use *The Language of Faith* below to clarify the highlighted words.
  Why does the Church give us these precepts? (Precepts give us concrete ways to practice the virtues we are given by God.)
- To help students visualize how the virtues and the Church's precepts help us become closer to God, use the graphic organizer on page 113B. You may wish to do the suggested activity or one of your own choosing.

Working with the Pictures

Have volunteers match the two pictures with the precepts that describe them. (eating a spare or light Lenten meal, precept 5; donating money, precept 6)

The Language of Faith

- The **precepts** of the Church are guidelines of behavior defined by the Church for all Catholics to follow. Precepts 1 through 4 call for specific actions; precept 5 is more general, allowing people to choose their own specific actions. By carrying out these actions in their everyday lives, Catholics grow in faith, show their hope for the coming of God's kingdom in its fullness, and practice love for others.
- Prayers or actions we do to make up for sins are called **penance**. The priest gives us a penance in the Sacrament of Reconciliation. We also do works of penance during Lent to prepare for Easter.

Link to the Family

Explain that just as a family has basic rules its members are expected to follow, our Church family has basic rules that make us more active members of the Church. Ask the students to think about some of the basic rules their families have and how these rules help family life go smoothly.

Teaching Tip

Clarifying concepts Make sure the students understand that the precepts of the Church are distinct from the Ten Commandments. We do not find the precepts in the Bible. Over the centuries the Church has attempted to set down some minimal guidelines that all Catholics need to follow in order to be more active in showing their faith, hope, and love. From time to time the number of precepts changes according to the Church's needs.

We Reflect
Review

Recall Elicit student responses. (faith, hope, and love; a rule that the Church gives us to guide us in living lives of virtue)

Think and Share Ask the students to consider the question before responding. (Possible answers: Love will last forever; we are called to love others just as we are loved by God.)

Continue the Journey Provide art materials, and have the students complete the activity.

Alternative Have the students complete the activity at home. Encourage them to share their drawings with friends or family members.

We Live Our Faith *At Home:* Encourage the students by sharing with them one thing you hope for in the future.
In the Parish: You may need to name some people and explain how each shows the virtues. The parish bulletin is also a good source of names.

Faith Journal The students may begin pages 37–38 of their *Faith Journal* in class and complete them at home. As part of your own spiritual development, complete *Your Faith Journal* (page J20).

Recall
Name the three special virtues God gives us. What is a precept?

Think and Share
Why do you think love is called the greatest virtue?

Continue the Journey
Draw a picture of yourself following one of the precepts of the Church.

We Live Our Faith

At Home Ask a family member what hopes he or she has for the future. Encourage him or her to fulfill those hopes.

In the Parish Think of a person in your parish who shows a lot of faith, hope, or love. Write that person a thank-you note for setting a good example.

118 : We Reflect

Resource Center

Assessment Tips
Allow time for the students to reflect on which precepts they actively follow and which ones they need to follow more closely.

You may wish to copy the Unit Five Assessment from the Resource Package in preparation for giving this test after completing Chapters 17–20.

Link to the Faith Community
Help the students understand that each time the parish community celebrates the Eucharist, it is practicing the virtue of faith. Point out that the parish exists because of its hope that the Church community through its parishioners' lives will witness to the kingdom of God in its fullness. A parish's social ministries are also ways in which the people show love for others.

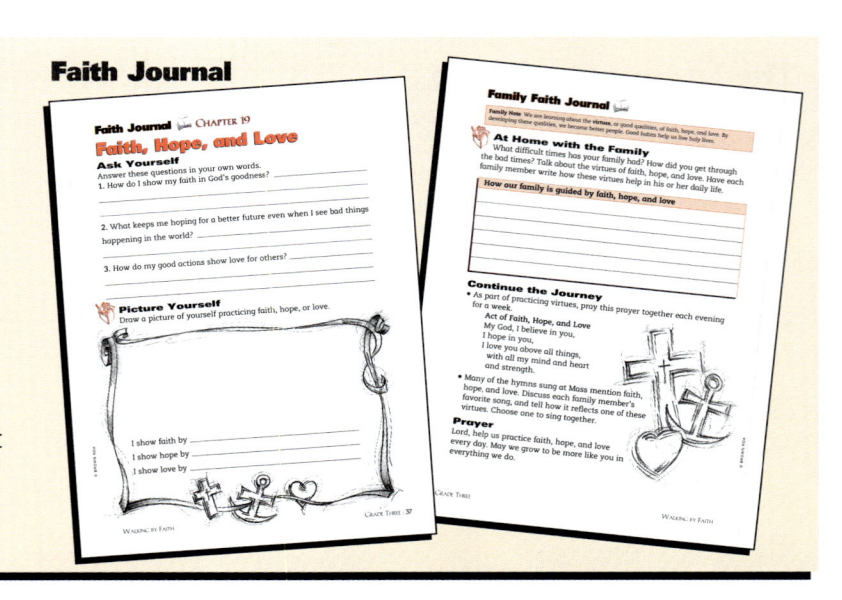

Praying for Virtues

The Church treasures the virtues of faith, hope, and love. You may see symbols of these virtues in church artwork. The cross is a sign of faith. The *anchor*, which holds a boat safely in a harbor through a storm, is a sign of hope. And the rose is a sign of love, or *charity*. Sometimes all three signs are combined into one design to show that the virtues cannot exist without each other.

Pray this Act of Faith, Hope, and Love with your classmates.

PRAYER

My God, I believe in you,
 hope in you,
 love you above all things,
with all my mind and
 heart and strength.

We Celebrate : 119

We Celebrate
3. Close

Working with the Text

Read *Praying for Virtues* aloud.
  What is the symbol of faith? (a cross)
  What is the symbol of hope? (an anchor)
  What is the symbol of charity, or love? (a flower)

Working with the Pictures

- Point out the photograph of Nathan, William, and the other children praying together in religion class.
- Encourage the students to identify the symbols of faith, hope, and love shown in the photograph.

Prayer Begin the prayer celebration with song. You might play a recording or sing a favorite hymn together. Pray the Act of Faith, Hope, and Love together. End with the Sign of the Cross.

Teaching Tip

Memorization You might have the students memorize the Act of Faith, Hope, and Love. Pair the students for practice in praying the prayer from memory.

optional **Multicultural Link**

Activity Encourage the students to consult other people—family members, friends, neighbors, and other students in your school—to learn the words for *faith*, *hope*, and *love* in various languages, including American Sign Language.

Notes: Closing the Chapter

Parish : 119

Unit Five Review

> **Objective**
> • Review the unit and assess progress.

Chapter Summaries
Use this information to reinforce key points before administering the review. These summaries will also help you assess the students' responses to *Show How Far You've Come*, page 121.

Chapter 17
- Jesus' law of love sums up everything we must do as members of the Church.
- In the Beatitudes and the Great Commandment, Jesus taught us how to make loving choices.

Chapter 18
- Our Church family helps us follow the law of love.
- The Holy Spirit, the word of God, and the teachings of the Church help us make good choices.
- We examine our conscience before taking part in the Sacrament of Reconciliation.

Chapter 19
- God gives us the virtues of faith, hope, and love to help us follow Jesus.
- The Church's laws, or precepts, help us practice faith, hope, and love.
- Love is the greatest virtue.

Review
You might have the students complete the review in writing or work together to answer questions orally.

Which Terms Don't Belong? Do set A aloud with the students. Make sure they understand why the term *holy days* does not belong with the other three terms. **(The Ten Commandments, the Beatitudes, and the law of love are guides for behavior given in the Bible, but holy day observance is a precept of the Church.)** Let the students do sets B and C on their own. Discuss why *mistake* and *sin* do not belong in those sets.

Complete the Sentence As you review the answers with the students, discuss any difficult sentences.

Share Your Faith Pair the students for this activity. If time permits, invite volunteers to share their responses.

UNIT FIVE CHECKPOINT
Review

Which Terms Don't Belong? Circle the term that does not belong with the others in each group.

A	B	C
1. Ten Commandments	1. conscience	1. hope
2. Beatitudes	2. Holy Spirit	2. (sin)
3. law of love	3. (mistake)	3. love
4. (holy days)	4. grace	4. faith

Complete the Sentence Circle the correct term to complete each sentence.

1. "Love God, and love your neighbor as yourself" is ((the Great Commandment), the Beatitudes).
2. The greatest virtue is (penance, (love)).
3. A Church teaching that guides us is called a (conscience, (precept)).
4. One of the precepts of the Church tells us to take part in the Mass on Sundays and (weekdays, (holy days)).
5. We are called to (worship, (form)) our conscience.
6. The Holy Spirit helps us make (perfect, (good)) choices.
7. ((Mistakes), Sins) are not done on purpose.

Share Your Faith Someone says that following rules like the Ten Commandments and the Beatitudes is not necessary for Catholics. What do you say?

Resource Center

Assessment Tips
Use one or more of the following strategies to assist you in assessing student progress:

- If you need a more detailed written review, you may want to give the Unit Five Assessment from the Resource Package.
- Let the students assess their own progress by discussing the unit's important ideas with partners.
- Invite volunteers to list two ways that they could practice the virtues of faith, hope, and love at home, in school, and in the parish community.

Show How Far You've Come Use the chart below to show what you have learned. For each chapter, write or draw the three most important things you remember.

Temple of the Holy Spirit

Chapter 17 Jesus' Law of Love	Chapter 18 The Church Helps	Chapter 19 Faith, Hope, and Love
Look for answers reflecting the key points listed under Chapter Summaries.		

What Else Would You Like to Know?
List any questions you still have about how laws, precepts, and virtues help us follow Jesus.

_____
_____
_____

Continue the Journey Choose one or more of the following activities to do on your own, with your class, or with your family.

- Look through your Faith Journal pages for Unit Five. Choose your favorite activity, and share it with a friend or family member.
- Make up a list of hints and suggestions for third graders who want to follow the law of love. Make your suggestions practical.
- Draw your own symbols for the virtues of faith, hope, and love. Explain your symbols.

Show How Far You've Come Use *Chapter Summaries* to evaluate students' responses. Note responses that differ greatly from the key points of the chapters. These responses may indicate areas where your presentation was unclear and needs additional attention. You might extend this activity by asking the students to recall their favorite stories, activities, or pictures from this unit.

What Else Would You Like to Know? Have the students share their questions and vote on a class list of three questions for you to answer at the next session.

Continue the Journey Provide time at a later session for the students to demonstrate how they have completed one or more of these activities. For example:
- Ask volunteers each to share one of their *Faith Journal* entries.
- Remind the students to refer to their lists when they need help in following the law of love.
- If time permits, allow the students to show and explain their symbols.

Prayer
Close the review with prayer. Encourage the students to complete this statement: "Jesus, help us follow your law of love by . . ."

Reference Sources
For help in addressing the students' questions about this unit's topics, see:
- *Conscience in Conflict—How to Make Moral Choices* by Kenneth Overberg SJ (St. Anthony Messenger Press, 1994).
- *Jesus' Plan for a New World: The Sermon on the Mount* by Richard Rohr with John Bookser Feister (St. Anthony Messenger Press, 1996).

Good resources for third graders include:
- *The ABC's Lessons of Love* by Francine O'Connor (Liguori Publications, 1991).
- *The "I Confess" for Children* by Hubert J. Richards (The Liturgical Press, 1992).

Your parish community is another important resource. Priests, deacons, other staff members, catechists, catechumens, godparents, sponsors, and members of religious communities are all good reference sources for answering students' questions.

Link to the Family
If possible, have the students take these pages home to share with their families.

Getting Ready: Chapter 20

Strength Through Practice

Program Resources
Student Text, pp. 122–125
Student Faith Journal, pp. 39–40
Your Faith Journal, p. J21

Unit Five (Christian Morality)
Temple of the Holy Spirit

Key Content Summary
Our Lenten practices train us to follow Jesus every day.

Planning the Chapter

	Pacing Guide *Suggested time/Your time*	Content	Objectives	Materials
Open	10–15 min./ _____ min.	*We Are Invited,* p. 122	• Recognize the benefits of spending some time alone.	• art materials (optional)
Build	20–25 min./ _____ min.	*We Explore,* p. 123	• Discover that the Season of Lent is a special time for growing in faith.	• chart paper
Review	15–20 min./ _____ min.	*We Reflect,* p. 124	• Demonstrate understanding of chapter concepts. • Apply learning through activity. • Practice faith at home and in the parish.	• *Student Faith Journal,* pp. 39–40 • *Your Faith Journal,* p. J21
Close	10–15 min./ _____ min.	*We Celebrate,* p. 125	• Identify with Jesus by praying a prayer based on a psalm.	• crucifix, Bible, recording of a psalm • art materials (optional)

For additional suggestions, see Scheduling, pp. T35–T37.

Catechism in Context

Doctrinal Foundation This chapter stresses that Lent is a time for spiritual exercise—penance. It is also a time of preparation for Baptism. By participating in the traditional observances of fasting, prayer, and almsgiving for the 40 days of Lent, we prepare ourselves for the 50 days of Easter joy. We fast from food on Ash Wednesday and Good Friday and abstain from meat on these days and all the Fridays of Lent in a gesture of self-denial. In other words, we fast from our own needs, in a way, from ourselves, in order to free ourselves from ourselves, so that we may love God and our neighbor more effectively.

We show our love for God especially in prayer. And we prove our love for our neighbors by coming to their aid when they are in need, particularly through almsgiving or acts of charity.

See Catechism of the Catholic Church, #1438.

One-Minute Retreat for Catechists

Read
"When Jesus Christ utters a word, He opens His mouth so wide that it embraces all Heaven and earth, even though that word be but in a whisper."

—Martin Luther

Reflect
How can spiritual exercise bring me closer to God?

Pray
Whether you whisper or shout, Jesus, help me hear you. As you help me train my students, may they train others. We celebrate through learning and loving.

Visualizing the Lesson

Use this graphic organizer to help the students understand the Church's Lenten practices.

Draw the graphic organizer on the board or on chart paper, omitting the words on the tree. As the students discuss the Lenten practices, have them add the words to the diagram. Then discuss how the practices they named help us grow in faith.

Growing in Faith

(Tree diagram with words: Pray, Fast, Abstain, Sacrifice, Perform works of charity; trunk: Lenten practices; ground: Church)

Library Links

Books for Children
The Stations of the Cross for Children—A Dramatized Presentation by Rita Coleman (The Liturgical Press, 1-800-858-5450).

Children of Jesus' era tell the story of their friend who loved them. They follow Jesus on his road to Calvary.

Books for Parents and Teachers
Forty Days Plus Three—Daily Reflections for Lent and Holy Week by Monsignor John J. McIlhon (The Liturgical Press, 1-800-858-5450).

This book discusses human dignity and the Paschal mystery.

Multimedia
For children:
The Temptation (video) (BROWN-ROA, 1-800-922-7696).

While Jesus is in the desert, he is tempted by the devil, but he refuses to forsake God's way to please himself.

For parents and teachers:
Were You There? (video) (Paulist Press, 1-800-218-1903).

Six individuals are challenged to become disciples along Jesus' way of the cross.

Organizations
For further information about ways to train for Lent, contact:
Catholic Network of Volunteer Services
4121 Harewood Road NE
Washington, DC 20017
(1-202-529-1100)

Strengthening the Family Link

Here are some suggestions for reaching out to your students' families:

- Encourage the students to talk with family members about ways to practice growing in faith during Lent.
- Invite family members to join the class for the Way of the Cross. Go over to the church together, and walk from station to station. Talk about what happened at each station and why we reflect on Jesus' suffering during Lent.

Chapter 20 pages 122–125

Objectives
- Recognize the benefits of spending some time alone.
- Discover that the Season of Lent is a special time for growing in faith.
- Identify with Jesus by praying a prayer based on a psalm.

Gathering WE ARE INVITED
1. Open

Personal Experience Invite volunteers to tell where they go when they want to be alone.

Prayer Pray the opening prayer together.

Working with the Text
As you read aloud or summarize the text, ask the students to think about times when they may have gone to a quiet place to be alone. Reassure them that wanting to be alone at times is a normal and healthy feeling.

Working with the Pictures
- Call attention to the girl in the photograph.
- Invite volunteers to respond to the caption question. (It gives the children some quiet time to calm down, think about what they did, and think of better ways to behave.)

CHAPTER 20
WE CELEBRATE LENT

Strength Through Practice

PRAYER
Dear Jesus, you went to the desert to pray and prepare. Help us use this Lent well.

Where do you go when you need some time alone? Children (adults, too!) often go away to a bedroom or another quiet place when they are angry or sad or need to think about things. Sometimes being by yourself helps you give more attention to a problem. You can think more clearly about how to solve it. And sometimes you just need to be away from things that are bothering you.

Children often are sent to their rooms if they have been quarreling or fighting. How does that help them change the way they act?

122 : We Are Invited

Resource Center

Optional — Link to the Family
Suggest that the students make "Quiet Time—Please Do Not Disturb" signs at home to use when they need some time alone. Encourage them to lend the signs to other family members when they need quiet time, too. Remind the students to respect others' need for quiet time, just as they want others to respect their need for it.

Enrichment
Ask the students to think of special quiet places where they could be alone and picture themselves sitting quietly there. Have them close their eyes and create the places in their minds. Caution the children about being alone in unsafe places, especially outdoors, or places where others would not know where to find them.

Notes: Opening the Chapter

Becoming Like Jesus

Jesus sometimes needed time to be alone, too. Before he began to preach God's message, he went into the desert by himself to pray and to **fast**, which means "to eat little or no food."

Throughout **Lent**, the 40 days before Holy Thursday, we try to become more like Jesus by doing some of the things he did. Members of the Church community pray, give alms, and perform acts of penance to make up for our sins. Adults in good health are asked to fast. Those 14 years old and older are asked to **abstain** from, or go without eating, meat on certain days.

Like Jesus' time in the desert, Lent gives us time to practice growing in faith. We train ourselves by choosing what to eat and what to do. Our Lenten practice can include going without certain treats. Giving things up is a way to practice sacrifice. Giving alms can help us recall the needs of people who have very little.

Lenten practice can be positive action, too. Instead of giving something up, we can choose to go out of our way to do something good. Acts of **charity**, or loving care for those in need, are especially good ways to grow in faith during Lent.

Catholics Believe . . .
Lent is a time of spiritual exercise.
Catechism, #1438

Activity
Athletes train their bodies for competition. During Lent we train ourselves, body and spirit, to follow Jesus. With your class, make a list of things you can do to train during Lent.

We Explore
2. Build
Working with the Text

- As you work with the text, use *The Language of Faith* below to further develop the terms *fasting, Lent, abstain,* and *charity*.
- Explain that giving *alms* means giving money to people in need. You might talk about donating canned food or clothing to those in need.
- Point out that sacrifice can also mean doing something difficult, such as giving up play time to read to a family member.
  What would be a sacrifice for you?
  (Accept all reasonable responses.)

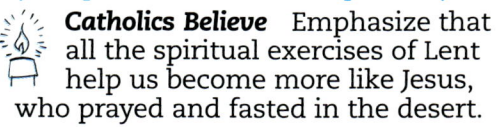

  Catholics Believe Emphasize that all the spiritual exercises of Lent help us become more like Jesus, who prayed and fasted in the desert.

- To focus on Lenten practices, refer to the graphic organizer on page 121B. You may wish to do the suggested activity or one of your own choosing.

Working with the Pictures

Direct the students' attention to the photograph of the runner.
How does running every day help this athlete get ready for competition?
(It makes her heart, lungs, and muscles stronger.)

Brainstorm the list together.

The Language of Faith

- **Fasting** helps us gain better control over our appetites. In the Church today fasting means that healthy adults should eat only one full meal each day, a small amount of food at the other meals, and nothing between meals.
- The word **Lent** comes from the old Anglo-Saxon word *lencten*, meaning "springtime" (death to new life).
- To **abstain** means to not eat particular foods, such as meat. All Catholics age 14 and older are obliged to abstain from eating meat on Ash Wednesday, Good Friday, and the other Fridays during Lent.
- **Charity**, from the Latin word *caritas*, meaning for "love, care," traditionally has meant donating food, clothing, or money to those in need. However, charity can also consist of performing acts of loving service, such as taking on extra chores at home or visiting someone who is lonely or sick.

Notes: Building the Chapter

We Reflect
Review

Recall Ask volunteers to respond. (He went alone into the desert to fast and pray; the 40 days that lead up to Easter.)

Think and Share Ask the students to carefully consider the question before responding. (Possible answer: Jesus needed time to think about his difficult task and ask for his Father's help.)

Continue the Journey You may want to work as a class to complete this list.

Alternative Have the students complete this list as homework with the help of adult family members. Schedule time during the next meeting for volunteers to share their lists.

We Live Our Faith *At Home:* Brainstorm with the students some ideas for simple family practices during Lent, such as praying certain prayers together. *In the Parish:* If possible, take the students to the church for a few minutes of quiet prayer.

Faith Journal The students may begin pages 39–40 of their *Faith Journal* in class and complete them at home. As part of your own spiritual development, complete *Your Faith Journal* (page J21).

RECALL
What did Jesus do before he started to preach God's word? When is Lent?

THINK AND SHARE
Why would Jesus want to go into the desert and pray before he started to preach?

CONTINUE THE JOURNEY
Make up your own Lenten training plan.

Athlete's Training
1. Eat healthy meals.
2. Get lots of rest.
3. Exercise every day.
4. Practice running long distances.

Lenten Training
1. _____
2. _____
3. _____
4. _____

WE LIVE OUR FAITH

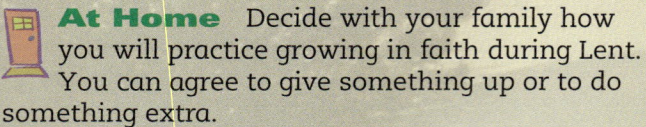

At Home Decide with your family how you will practice growing in faith during Lent. You can agree to give something up or to do something extra.

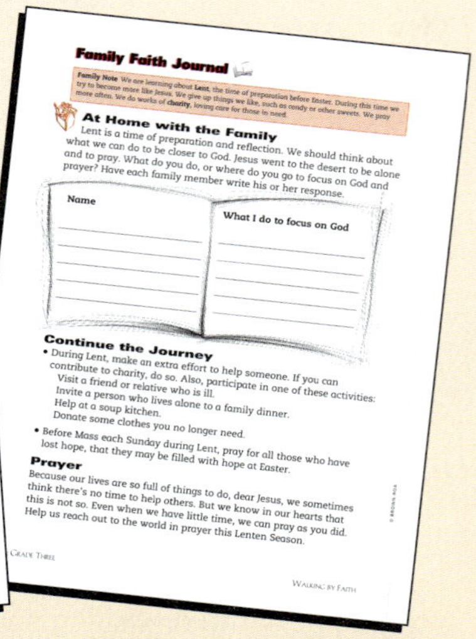

In the Parish Spend some quiet time in the church with a family member or your class. Think about how Jesus prepared for his preaching life in a quiet place.

124 : We Reflect

Resource Center
Multicultural Link

Tell the students that, like Christianity, other religions have special times set aside for prayer and fasting. For example, in the religion of Islam, Muslims eat only a meal at sundown and a small meal before sunrise during the holy month of Ramadan. For Jewish people Yom Kippur is a day of atonement (asking forgiveness for sins), prayer, and fasting.

raying as Jesus Prayed

hen Jesus was growing up, he learned to
cite the psalms. The Jewish people of Jesus'
ne used the psalms for daily prayers as
ll as for special occasions. Jews and
ristians still follow this practice of praying
e psalms. The following prayer is based on
alm 119.

YER

er each statement, all respond:
RD, teach us the ways of your laws;
we shall observe them with care."

D, give us wisdom to see your teaching,
to keep it with all our hearts. . . .

d us in the path of your commands,
for that is our joy. . . .

rn our hearts toward your teachings. . . .

rn our eyes away from worthless things. . . .

 how we long for your precepts;
in your justice, give us life. . . .

en.

—based on Psalm 119:33–40

We Celebrate : 125

We Celebrate
3. Close

Working with the Text

- Read aloud or summarize *Praying as Jesus Prayed*.
- Explain that the Church uses the psalms often in its liturgy and other prayer celebrations.

Working with the Pictures

Point out that the monk is praying the psalms.
How are the monk and the children imitating Jesus? (They have gone to quiet places to pray.)

- **Prayer** Gather the students in a circle. Remind them that God is close to them during this holy time. Place a crucifix and a Bible opened to the Book of Psalms on the prayer table. If possible, play a recording of a psalm. Then pray the prayer together. Close the celebration with a few moments of silent prayer.

Link to Liturgy
Remind the students that the psalms are part of the Liturgy of the Word at Mass. We sing or pray a responsorial psalm after the first reading. During Lent we may replace familiar hymns with psalms of God's mercy and love. Invite the students to pay special attention to the psalms that are prayed and sung at Sunday Mass.

optional Enrichment

Activity — Have the students create a class banner for use with the Lenten liturgy or prayer service. Provide art materials. Have the students decorate their banner with Christian symbols such as the cross, an anchor, and a dove.

Notes: Closing the Chapter

_____

_____

_____

_____

_____

_____

Parish : 125

Getting Ready: Chapter 21

We Become Part of the Church

Program Resources
Student Text, pp. 126–131
Student Faith Journal, pp. 41–42
Your Faith Journal, p. J22
Chapter 21 Transparency
Unit Six Family Letter

Unit Six (Sacraments)
Belonging, Healing, Serving

Key Content Summary
The Sacraments of Initiation welcome us into the Church.

Planning the Chapter

	Pacing Guide *Suggested time/Your time*	Content	Objectives	Materials
Open	10–15 min./ _____ min.	*We Are Invited*, pp. 126–127	• Describe the Sacrament of Baptism.	
Build	20–25 min./ _____ min.	*We Explore*, pp. 128–129	• Identify Baptism, Confirmation, and Eucharist as the Sacraments of Initiation. • Compare the actions and effects of the Sacraments of Initiation.	• Chapter 21 Transparency from the Resource Package
Review	15–20 min./ _____ min.	*We Reflect*, p. 130	• Demonstrate understanding of chapter concepts. • Apply learning through activity. • Practice faith at home and in the parish.	• art materials • list of names of candidates in your parish • *Student Faith Journal*, pp. 41–42 • *Your Faith Journal*, p. J22 • video of Confirmation rite (optional)
Close	10–15 min./ _____ min.	*We Celebrate*, p. 131	• Renew the baptismal promises through prayer.	• bowl of holy water • Unit Six Family Letter from the Resource Package

For additional suggestions, see Scheduling, pp. T35–T37.

Catechism in Context

Doctrinal Foundation This chapter explores the Sacraments of Initiation: Baptism, Confirmation, and Eucharist. These sacraments lay the foundations of Christian life. Baptism is the basis of this life, for it is through Baptism that we enter into life in the Holy Spirit. Through water and the Holy Spirit, we are reborn and welcomed into the Church. In Confirmation we are sealed with the Holy Spirit, symbolized by the anointing with chrism. This sacrament binds us closer to the Church and reinforces the gifts of the Spirit so that we may be strengthened as true witnesses of Christ. The Eucharist completes our Christian initiation. Through this sacrament Christ gives us his Body and Blood—the Bread of life and the Cup of eternal salvation—to nourish us on our spiritual journey. As Paul says, these sacraments give us the courage we need to walk by faith.

See Catechism of the Catholic Church, #1212.

One-Minute Retreat for Catechists

Read
"The spiritual virtue of the sacrament is like light. . . ."
—*Saint Augustine*

Reflect
How can I use the light of the sacraments to guide others?

Pray
God, as I join with you and the Church in the sacraments, may my heart greet your light with joy. May I dwell not on the darkness of life on earth but on the bountiful light of heaven. Help my students understand that hope comes when they open their eyes to divine reality.

Visualizing the Lesson

Use this graphic organizer to help the students remember the effects of the Sacraments of Initiation.

Draw the graphic organizer on the board or on chart paper. Include the headings *Baptism*, *Confirmation*, and *Eucharist*, but leave each block blank. As you work through the lesson, have the students tell what each sacrament does for us. Use their responses to complete the graphic organizer.

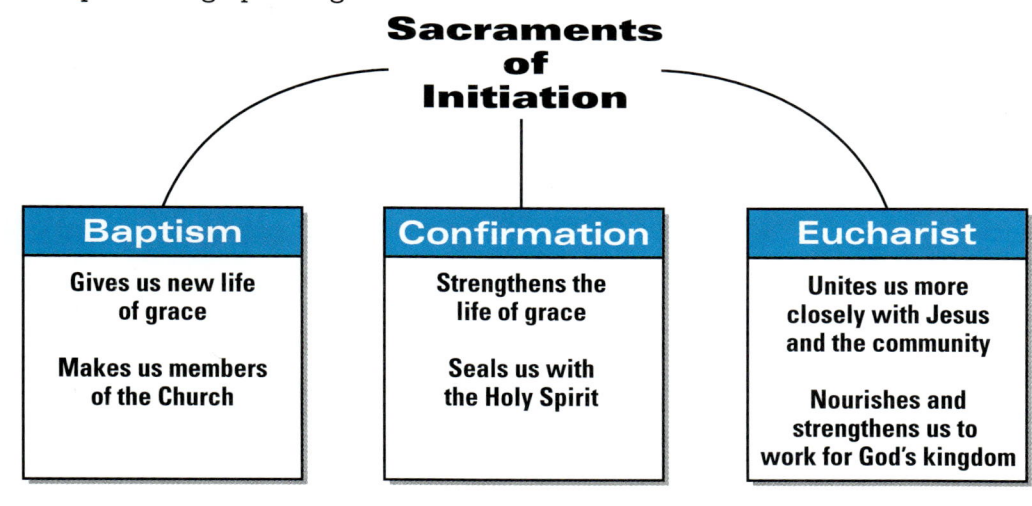

Sacraments of Initiation

Baptism
- Gives us new life of grace
- Makes us members of the Church

Confirmation
- Strengthens the life of grace
- Seals us with the Holy Spirit

Eucharist
- Unites us more closely with Jesus and the community
- Nourishes and strengthens us to work for God's kingdom

Library Links

Books for Children
Initiation Customs by Lucy Rushton (Thomas Learning, 1-800-880-4253).

Initiation customs from world religions are compared and contrasted.

Books for Parents and Teachers
The Church Speaks About Sacraments with Children: Baptism, Confirmation, Eucharist, Penance with commentary by Mark Searle (Liturgy Training Publications, 1-800-933-1800).

This collection of liturgical and catechetical documents is introduced by Mark Searle in a way that helps clarify the meaning and direction of each sacrament.

Multimedia

For children:
The Mass and Me, a Robert Blaskey Production (video) (BROWN-ROA, 1-800-922-7696).

This video follows two students as they prepare for First Eucharist. It also includes interviews with a variety of children answering the question "What does the Mass mean to you?"

For parents and teachers:
Through Water and the Holy Spirit (Paulist Press, 1-800-218-1903).

The Sacrament of Baptism is explained using Scripture, Christian traditions, and daily life.

Strengthening the Family Link

Here are some suggestions for reaching out to your students' families:

- Encourage the students to talk with family members about the Sacraments of Initiation and about how the sacraments have helped them on their faith journey.
- Invite family members to join the class for a discussion about the actions and effects of the Sacraments of Initiation (see page 129). End the discussion by praying together the closing prayer, based on our baptismal promises.

PARISH : 125B

Chapter 21 pages 126–131

Objectives
- Describe the Sacrament of Baptism.
- Identify Baptism, Confirmation, and Eucharist as the Sacraments of Initiation.
- Compare the actions and effects of the Sacraments of Initiation.

Gathering WE ARE INVITED
1. Open

Personal Experience Ask the students to think about how their families welcome new people to their homes. Invite a volunteer to share his or her experience.

Prayer Remind the students that our Church family welcomes new members, too. Then invite the students to pray the opening prayer with you.

Working with the Text
- Read the story aloud. Explain that the Easter Vigil is a special liturgy celebrated on Holy Saturday evening, the night before Easter Sunday. The Easter Vigil is special because at this liturgy, adults and children are sometimes baptized and the entire community renews its baptismal promises.
- Point out that *candidates* are people who are preparing to join the Church family.

Working with the Pictures
- Draw the students' attention to the photograph. Explain that the picture shows a new candidate being baptized in a baptismal pool.
- Read the caption aloud. Emphasize that water is a sign that we are given new life in Jesus.

CHAPTER 21
We Become Part of the Church

PRAYER
Holy Spirit, thank you for making us part of the Church through the sacraments.

Noah yawned as he helped clear the Easter dinner dishes from the table. He was sleepy but happy. The night before Noah had stayed up late for the Easter *Vigil* celebration. With his whole family he had stood by as Uncle Mike became a member of the Church.

Noah's mom had explained everything to him during the ceremony. Uncle Mike and the other *candidates* had celebrated three sacraments. First, they were baptized in the parish's baptismal pool. Then Father Gardiner anointed them in the Sacrament of Confirmation. Finally, they received Holy Communion for the first time.

Noah joined the rest of the family in the den. They were watching the videotape from the night before. Noah's mom had the family photo album out, too.

"Look, Noah," his mom said. "Here are the pictures we took when you were baptized. And here are your First Eucharist pictures."

Water is one of the signs of Baptism. The baptismal pool or font is the place where we are born into a new life as members of the Church.

126 : We Are Invited

Resource Center

Link to the Family
Invite the students to talk about Baptisms they have celebrated with their families, such as the Baptism of a younger brother or sister or another family member. Encourage the students to share their feelings about the liturgical celebration.

Link to the Faith Community
Invite a knowledgeable parish member to speak to the class about the different ways in which the Sacrament of Baptism is celebrated in the parish, both for infants and for older children and adults. If time permits, take the class to the church baptismal pool or font for the talk. Encourage the students to be attentive when a Baptism is celebrated at the Sunday liturgy. At a later session, talk with them about what they saw and heard.

Notes: Opening the Chapter

Landmark White clothing and lighted candles are used in the celebration of Baptism. The white clothing or robe is a sign of the new life in Christ that the person has put on. The lighted candle is a sign of Christ, the Light of the World.

Some things about the pictures and the videotape were different. Noah had been baptized as a baby. He had received Communion for the first time in second grade. He hadn't celebrated Confirmation yet. Noah had been baptized at the baptismal font, while Uncle Mike had stepped into the baptismal pool. Baby Noah had worn a white baptismal gown, while Uncle Mike was given a white robe to put on after his Baptism.

But some things were the same. Noah's godfather was Uncle Mike's sponsor, too. Father Gardiner had baptized both Noah and Uncle Mike. In both the pictures and the videotape, Noah's parents were happy. Noah's family had a party after his First Eucharist, just like this Easter party they were having for Uncle Mike.

Noah's mom said, "Now we're not only related as a family—we're all members of the same Church family, too."

Scripture Signpost

"So then you are no longer strangers and *sojourners,* but you are fellow citizens with the holy ones and members of the household of God."

Ephesians 2:19

Which sacraments make us "members of the household of God"?

WE ARE INVITED : 127

WE ARE INVITED
Open *Continued*
Working with the Pictures

Draw the students' attention to the photograph. Point out that the woman on the right is the other woman's sponsor. Explain that a sponsor is a Church member who agrees to help a new member grow in faith.
What kind of person does a sponsor need to be? (someone who has a strong faith; is able to share that faith with others; and practices the virtues of faith, hope, and love in daily life)

Landmark Invite a volunteer to read the caption aloud. List the signs of Baptism on the board or on chart paper, and include *washing with water* in the list. Ask volunteers to explain what each sign means.

Working with the Text

Read the text aloud. Point out that parishes throughout the world baptize new members of the Church family at the Easter Vigil. All baptized Catholics belong to the same Church family.

Scripture Signpost Invite a volunteer to read the Scripture passage aloud. Explain that a *sojourner* is a wanderer, a person who moves from place to place and has no home. When we are baptized, we are no longer sojourners and strangers but are joined together in Jesus' family and have a new home in the Church. Invite responses to the question. **(Baptism, Confirmation, and Eucharist)**

Multicultural Link

In some cultures—including Hispanic, Creole, and Haitian—the role of godparent has significant cultural implications. Consider inviting a godparent who belongs to such a culture to speak to the class about the ways in which the culture honors the role of godparent. Ask the visitor to describe the responsibilities of a godparent and the special relationship that may exist between a child and his or her godparent. In the Greek Orthodox faith, the role of godparent is very important. The best man at a couple's wedding automatically becomes the godfather of their first-born child. Likewise, the maid of honor very often becomes the godmother. If the godparent is Greek Orthodox, he or she does the actual christening of the baby during the Baptism.

Teaching Tip

Clarifying concepts As you present the Sacraments of Initiation, you might want to point out the elements common to all seven sacraments:

- The sacraments all have their origins in the words or actions of Jesus of Nazareth.
- The sacraments are special signs through which God's grace is shared with us as a Church community and as individuals.
- The sacraments make Jesus present to us now in a special way.
- The sacraments are actions of the Holy Spirit, uniting us as a Church and making us better able to represent Jesus to others.
- The sacraments are all acts of worship.

PARISH : 127

WE EXPLORE
2. Build
Working with the Text

- Read aloud or invite volunteers to read aloud *A Special Relationship*. Use *The Language of Faith* below to clarify the highlighted terms.
  What club do you know about or belong to that has a welcoming ceremony before someone becomes a full member? (Answers might include the Boy or Girl Scouts, 4-H, and so on.)
- Explain that the Church community is *not* a club but rather a special community that invites new members to celebrate the Sacraments of Initiation.

Catholics Believe Emphasize that the Sacraments of Initiation join us to Jesus and the Church community and strengthen us with the presence of the Holy Spirit.

Working with the Pictures

- Draw the students' attention to the photograph. Point out that the bishop is marking each person's forehead with oil. Explain that the oil used in the Sacrament of Confirmation is called *chrism*.
- Ask a volunteer to read the caption aloud. Emphasize that Confirmation strengthens our relationship with Jesus and with the entire Church community.

Catholics Believe...
the Sacraments of Initiation are the basis of every Christian life.
Catechism, #1212

A Special Relationship

Uncle Mike celebrated three sacraments at the Easter Vigil. **Sacraments** are signs and celebrations of grace, God's life in us. Through the power of the Holy Spirit, Jesus works in and through the sacraments. Members of the Church community are changed through the celebration of the sacraments.

Uncle Mike celebrated the Sacraments of Baptism, Confirmation, and First Eucharist. These three sacraments make us members of the Church. They bring us into a special relationship with God and the Church community. These sacraments are known as the **Sacraments of Initiation**. *Initiation* means "beginning." We are beginning our membership in the Church.

Sacraments of Initiation can be celebrated by people of any age. Most Catholics are baptized as babies, celebrate First Eucharist at about the age of seven, and are confirmed later. But the three Sacraments of Initiation may be celebrated all at once, as they are at the Easter Vigil liturgy, by adults and by children.

Confirmation seals and completes Baptism. In this sacrament the gifts of the Holy Spirit are strengthened in us.

128 : WE EXPLORE

Resource Center

The Language of Faith

- **Sacraments** are religious ceremonies through which we share in God's grace. Through the sacraments Christ is present in our lives, providing us with the help and strength we need in order to follow in his footsteps.

- The three **Sacraments of Initiation** make us full members of the Church community. The first sacrament, Baptism, unites us to Jesus and his Church, frees us from sin, and gives us new life as adopted children of God. Confirmation completes Baptism and seals us with the Holy Spirit. It celebrates our commitment to live as Christians, with the responsibility to proclaim the gospel in our everyday lives. Eucharist nourishes us so that, united to Christ and one another, we can do Jesus' work in the world.

Notes: Building the Chapter

In each of the Sacraments of Initiation, we see the actions and hear the words of the minister. But it is the Holy Trinity who is acting. The Son shares with us the love of the Father through the power of the Holy Spirit. Each Sacrament of Initiation changes us in some way. We are changed as individuals and as a whole community.

This chart outlines the actions and effects of the Sacraments of Initiation.

The Sacraments of Initiation

Sacrament	Baptism	Confirmation	Eucharist
Action of the Minister	Priest or deacon pours water on or immerses the person, saying, "I baptize you in the name of the Father, and of the Son, and of the Holy Spirit."	Bishop or priest lays hands over the person's head and then anoints him or her with chrism, saying, "Be sealed with the Gift of the Holy Spirit."	Priest prays the Eucharistic Prayer, consecrating bread and wine; shares Christ's Body and Blood with the community.
Action of the Holy Spirit	Removes original sin, forgives personal sin, and gives new life in Christ; marks the person as a member of Christ's Body.	Seals and completes Baptism and strengthens the life of grace; marks the person as a member of the Church.	Makes Christ truly present in the word and in the sacrificial meal.
Effect on the Individual	Gives new life of grace; makes a member of Christ's Body, the Church.	Increases gifts of the Spirit; unites more fully with Christ; strengthens in living the faith.	Unites more closely with Christ and the Church community; forgives venial sin and increases grace.
Effect on the Church Community	Unites all Christians as brothers and sisters.	Increases the community's ability to carry out its mission of proclaiming the good news.	Unites all who share at the table of the Word and the table of the Eucharist into the one Body of Christ.

WE EXPLORE
Build Continued
Working with the Text
- Read the introductory paragraph aloud. Emphasize that when we celebrate a sacrament, the Holy Trinity acts in the entire Church community and in each of us individually.
- Before working with the chart, invite the students to identify some actions and their possible effects—for example, doing a chore at home: a happier family. Explain that in a similar way, the actions in the sacramental ceremonies produce certain effects or results.
- Read the chart, sacrament by sacrament. Explain the meanings of any words that may be unfamiliar to the students.
- To summarize the major effects of these sacraments, use the graphic organizer on page 125B. You may want to do the suggested activity or one of your own.

Working with the Pictures
Ask the students to look carefully at the photograph. Be sure they recognize it as a picture of a Baptism. Remind the students that washing with water is a sign of our new life in Christ.

WE EXPLORE : 129

Background
The earliest Christian symbols were inherited from ancient Hebrew traditions. Symbols such as water and palm branches, for example, came from the Jewish Feast of Tabernacles, or Booths. They symbolized a new era that Jews awaited and that Christians believed had been ushered in by Jesus. However, Christians soon created their own symbols. The cross is the best known and most widely used, dating back to the fifth century. During times of persecution the cross could not be displayed in public without serious consequences for those who displayed it. Therefore, it was often disguised as an anchor or as a combination of the two Greek words *chi (X)* and *rho (P)*. The symbol of the dove has come to represent the Holy Spirit. The sacraments, too, have their own symbols. For example, wavy lines suggest the waters of Baptism, and grapes and wheat suggest the Eucharist. These symbols bring to mind the meanings behind these two sacraments.

Assessment Tip
If time permits, you might want to assess the students' understanding of the Sacraments of Initiation and their actions and effects by inviting volunteers to restate the material on the chart in their own words. Listen for any responses that may stray from the main concepts.

PARISH : 129

We Reflect
Review

Recall Call on volunteers to share their responses. *(signs and celebrations of grace, God's life in us; becoming a member; Baptism, Confirmation, and Eucharist)*

Think and Share Read the question aloud, and invite the students to respond. *(Answers should mention the value of regularly nourishing our unity with Jesus and the faith community.)*

Continue the Journey Divide the class into small groups of four or five. Distribute art materials. Ask the groups to create symbols for each of the three Sacraments of Initiation. *(Possible symbols for Baptism: water, oil, white garment, baptismal candle; for Confirmation: dove or flames of Holy Spirit, bishop, chrism; for Eucharist: altar, community, bread, wine, chalice.)*

Alternative Let the students complete the activity at home. Allow time at the beginning of the next session to review their work.

We Live Our Faith *At Home:* Encourage the students to follow through with the activity by telling them that you will ask volunteers to share family stories at the beginning of the next session.
In the Parish: Provide the students with the names of the candidates in your parish. Encourage them to bring their letters to the next session so you can arrange to have them delivered.

Faith Journal The students may begin pages 41–42 of their *Faith Journal* in class and complete them at home. As part of your own spiritual development, complete *Your Faith Journal* (page J22) for this chapter.

Recall
What are sacraments? What does initiation mean? Name the Sacraments of Initiation.

Think and Share
Baptism and Confirmation can be celebrated only once in a person's lifetime. But we are encouraged to celebrate the Eucharist frequently. Why do you think this is so?

Continue the Journey
Draw symbols for the Sacraments of Initiation.

We Live Our Faith

At Home Talk with family members or godparents about the celebration of any Sacraments of Initiation you have already celebrated. Ask family members to share memories of their own celebrations of these sacraments.

In the Parish Write a letter to someone in your parish who is preparing for one or more of the Sacraments of Initiation. Welcome him or her into the Church community.

Resource Center
Link to the Faith Community

Consult the parish staff or the Sunday bulletin to find out when the parish will next celebrate the Sacrament of Confirmation. If possible, arrange for your class to attend. Be sure to talk with the students about their experiences at the beginning of the next session. If attending a parish Confirmation is not possible, ask your parish's director of religious education to help you locate a video that shows and explains the Confirmation rite.

Remembering Our Promises

We make special promises of faith when we celebrate Baptism. If we are baptized as babies, our parents and godparents make these promises for us. In Confirmation we renew these promises. In the Eucharist we are nourished to live our faith every day.

This prayer is based on the baptismal promises. Renew your promises as you pray with your classmates.

Prayer

We believe in God our Father.
We believe in Jesus Christ, the only Son of God.
We believe in the Holy Spirit.
We believe in the holy catholic Church and all it teaches.
We believe in the forgiveness of sins, the resurrection of the body, and life everlasting.
This is our faith. This is the faith of the Church. We are proud to profess it, in Christ Jesus our Lord.
Amen.

We Celebrate : 131

WE CELEBRATE
3. Close

Working with the Pictures

Help the students identify the pictures: people praying together during an Easter Vigil; a baptismal font; a bishop and priest leading a liturgical celebration.
What sacraments have most of these people celebrated? (the Sacraments of Initiation)

Working with the Text

Read aloud *Remembering Our Promises*. Point out that we have many opportunities to renew our baptismal promises in our daily lives.
What are some ways you can renew your baptismal promises? (by celebrating the Eucharist frequently, praying every day, treating others as Jesus would, and so on)

Prayer Place a bowl of holy water on a small table. Gather the students in a circle near the bowl of water. Begin the prayer celebration by singing a favorite hymn. Pray the prayer aloud together, pausing afterward to allow the students to think about the words. Invite the students to dip their fingers into the holy water and make the Sign of the Cross. Close the celebration with another hymn.

Link to Liturgy

Tell the students that during the Easter Season, many parishes include the Rite of Blessing and Sprinkling with Holy Water in the Mass in place of the penitential rite and Lord, Have Mercy. During this rite we renew our baptismal promises. Encourage the students to watch and listen for this rite at Mass during the Easter Season.

Link to the Family

To keep family members involved with what the students are learning in this unit, distribute the Unit Six Family Letter from the Resource Package.

Notes: Closing the Chapter

Getting Ready: Chapter 22

The Church Celebrates Healing

Program Resources
Student Text, pp. 132–137
Student Faith Journal, pp. 43–44
Your Faith Journal, p. J23
Chapter 22 Transparency
Unit Six Music and Liturgy Resources

Unit Six (Sacraments)
Belonging, Healing, Serving

Key Content Summary
The Sacraments of Healing restore us to health of soul and body.

Planning the Chapter

	Pacing Guide *Suggested time/Your time*	Content	Objectives	Materials
Open	10–15 min./ _____ min.	*We Are Invited*, pp. 132–133	• Describe ways to comfort people who are sick or lonely. • Identify the two Sacraments of Healing.	• art materials, list of parish members who are homebound or ill
Build	20–25 min./ _____ min.	*We Explore*, pp. 134–135	• Analyze a scriptural example of Jesus' forgiving sins and healing the sick. • Compare the signs of the two Sacraments of Healing.	• Chapter 22 Transparency from the Resource Package
Review	15–20 min./ _____ min.	*We Reflect*, p. 136	• Demonstrate understanding of chapter concepts. • Apply learning through activity. • Practice faith at home and in the parish.	• drawing materials • list of parish members who are sick or injured • *Student Faith Journal,* pp. 43–44 • *Your Faith Journal,* p. J23 • prayer cards (optional)
Close	10–15 min./ _____ min.	*We Celebrate*, p. 137	• Pray together a prayer of healing.	• small dish of olive oil or baby oil • Unit Six Music and Liturgy Resources from the Resource Package

For additional suggestions, see Scheduling, pp. T35–T37.

Catechism in Context

Doctrinal Foundation This chapter explores the Sacraments of Healing: Reconciliation and the Anointing of the Sick. When a baptized person sins and therefore rejects the grace that he or she has received from God, the Church has the authority to minister forgiveness to that person. Jesus, physician of our souls and bodies, preached a Baptism of repentance for the forgiveness of sins and commanded his disciples to baptize. He also forgave sins personally without baptizing and gave his apostles the authority to forgive sins independently of Baptism: "Amen, I say to you, whatever you bind on earth shall be bound in heaven, and whatever you loose on earth shall be loosed in heaven" *(Matthew 18:18)*. Through the Sacrament of Reconciliation, then, our sins are forgiven, and we are healed and reconciled to the community of faith through the ministry of the Church.

The Anointing of the Sick—another Sacrament of Healing—primarily addresses physical illness. Jesus laid hands on the sick, and they were healed. James wrote that people who were sick should call the priests of the Church, who would pray over them, anointing them in the name of the Lord. "The prayer of faith will save the sick person, and the Lord will raise him up. If anyone has committed any sins, he will be forgiven" *(James 5:15)*.

See Catechism of the Catholic Church, #1421.

One-Minute Retreat for Catechists

Read
"The Church should be the society of the forgiven and forgiving."
—*William George Spencer*

Reflect
How have I felt the healing power of reconciliation?

Pray
Lord, help me feel the power of your forgiveness. Help me never turn away from you and the community of the Church in shame. Instead, may I choose to turn to you and to others for forgiveness, love, healing, and guidance.

Visualizing the Lesson

Use this graphic organizer to help the students recognize the Sacraments of Healing.

You might want to have the students create posters based on the graphic organizer to summarize the information about these sacraments. Or redraw the graphic organizer on a sheet of paper, leaving blank the boxes labeled *Action* and *Effect*. Distribute copies of the graphic organizer, and have partners work together to describe the actions and effects.

Sacraments of Healing	
Sacrament of Reconciliation	**Sacrament of Anointing of the Sick**
ACTION: Extending hand in blessing	ACTION: Anointing with oil on head and hands
EFFECT: Forgiveness of sin and reconciliation with God and Church community	EFFECT: God's healing, peace, and comfort

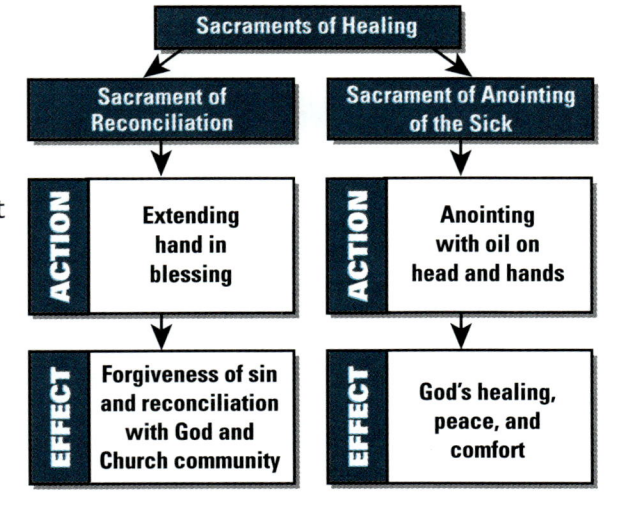

Library Links

Books for Children
We Ask Forgiveness—A Young Child's Book for Reconciliation by Corinne Hart (Franciscan Communications, 1-800-488-0488).

This book offers an examination of conscience and helps students prepare for Reconciliation.

Books for Parents and Teachers
The Forgiving Family—First Steps to Reconciliation by Carol Luebering (St. Anthony Messenger Press, 1-800-488-0488).

Discussion and suggestions for families to use in the everyday reconciling of family life events are presented.

Multimedia
For children:
Reconciliation: Closing the Gap (video) (BROWN-ROA, 1-800-922-7696).

Viewers make the connection between conflicts in their lives and the need to celebrate the Sacrament of Reconciliation.

For parents and teachers:
Reconciliation from the Mystery of Faith series produced by Fisher Productions (video) (Paulist Press, 1-800-218-1903).

The power of this sacrament is needed for living in relationship with God and others.

Organizations
For information on comforting those who are terminally ill, contact:

Hospice Foundation of America
2001 South Street NW, Suite 300
Washington, DC 20009
(1-202-638-5419)

Strengthening the Family Link

Here are some suggestions for reaching out to your students' families:

- Encourage the students to talk with family members about the ways the Sacraments of Reconciliation and Anointing of the Sick heal us.
- Invite family members to join the class in reading the Scripture Story on page 134.

Chapter 22 pages 132–137

Objectives
- Describe ways to comfort people who are sick or lonely.
- Identify the two Sacraments of Healing.
- Analyze a scriptural example of Jesus' forgiving sins and healing the sick.
- Compare the signs of the two Sacraments of Healing.

Gathering WE ARE INVITED
1. Open

Personal Experience Invite the students to think about times when they were injured or sick and family members or friends visited with them. Have a volunteer share his or her experience.

Prayer Pray the opening prayer together.

Working with the Text
- Read aloud the story of Toni and Keesha, or invite two volunteers to read the dialogue.
- Read the bulleted question aloud, and invite a volunteer to respond. (worried, sad, frightened, and so on)

Working with the Pictures
- Draw the students' attention to the picture.
  How did other people make Toni feel loved and remembered while she was in the hospital? (The parish priest came to visit her; her classmates sent get-well cards.)
- Ask volunteers to describe what Father Jim is doing in the picture. (anointing Toni with oil)
  What else is included in the Sacrament of Healing? (Special prayers are prayed.)

CHAPTER 22
The Church Celebrates Healing

PRAYER
For the comfort we find in the Sacraments of Healing, we thank you God.

"I'm glad you came to visit me. I've been so lonely!" Toni said to Keesha. "I want to get back to school to see everybody."

"Were you scared in the hospital?"

"I was nervous before the operation. But my parents were with me. Father Jim came in, too."

"Why was he there?"

"He said some prayers and put oil on my head and hands," Toni answered. "It's a special sacrament for sick people. He said the whole parish would be praying for me to get better."

"Well, I know our whole class has been," Keesha said. "We miss you."

- How do you feel when someone close to you is sick or injured?

Resource Center

Teaching Tip
Clarifying concepts Emphasize that there are many different kinds of healing. Sometimes people need to be healed from physical illnesses or injuries. People also need to be healed from hurt feelings, anger, and loneliness. And sometimes people need to be healed from sin. Point out that *everyone* needs healing at various times in his or her life.

Link to the Faith Community
Help the students explore how the parish brings help and healing to people who are hungry, homeless, lonely, or ill. With the assistance of a parish staff member or by consulting your parish's Sunday bulletin, list the groups or individuals who help people in need. Make the connection between these ministries and the ways that healing takes place.

Notes: Opening the Chapter

"So, how's school going?" Toni asked her friend.

Keesha shook her head. "School is all right, but I wish I hadn't done something dumb. I told Carlos that Mary took his new ruler. She found out, and they both got mad at me. And you're still not in school, so now I feel like I don't have any friends. What should I do?"

Toni thought a minute. "You could talk to Father Jim about it in Reconciliation. God will forgive you, and Carlos and Mary will, too. Don't worry. We'll all be back together soon."

Toni and Keesha were feeling the loneliness of being apart from their friends. We've all felt that way at times. It hurts! But through the **Sacraments of Healing**—Reconciliation and the Anointing of the Sick—we can feel the love and strength of our Church community.

Our Moral Guide

The new law Jesus gave is a law of love, grace, and freedom.

Catechism, #1972

How does the Sacrament of Reconciliation give us freedom?

ACTIVITY

Make a greeting card for someone who can't come to Mass this week.

WE ARE INVITED : 133

WE ARE INVITED
Open *Continued*
Working with the Text

- Finish reading the story aloud, but stop before the final paragraph.
- Ask volunteers to describe the different kinds of healing that Toni and Keesha need. (Toni: physical healing from her operation; Keesha: healing from the hurt she caused Carlos and Mary)
- Read the last paragraph aloud. Use *The Language of Faith* below to clarify the highlighted term.

  Our Moral Guide Emphasize that Jesus' law calls us to live as he lived. Invite a volunteer to respond to the question. (Accept all reasonable responses, such as that the sacrament frees us from sin, helps us love God and others in the future, helps us learn from our mistakes, and if needed, reunites us with God and the Church community.)

Working with the Pictures

- Invite a volunteer to name the Sacrament of Healing that Father Jim and Toni are celebrating together. (Anointing of the Sick)
- Point out that the anointing is an important part of this sacrament. It represents God's healing touch and is a symbol of the Holy Spirit's presence.

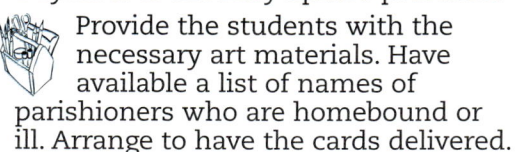

  Provide the students with the necessary art materials. Have available a list of names of parishioners who are homebound or ill. Arrange to have the cards delivered.

  Alternative Have the students work together to create a large get-well card for someone in the parish who is in the hospital or homebound. Arrange to have the class card delivered.

The Language of Faith
The **Sacraments of Healing** are based on Jesus' work of healing and forgiving. In the Sacrament of Reconciliation, God forgives our sins, and we are reunited with him and the Church community. In the Sacrament of Anointing of the Sick, Jesus gives strength to a person who is sick and restores health or bestows the grace to accept the illness. The Church community is always ready to offer us love and healing when we are hurting. Both sacraments help heal, although in different ways.

Link to the Family
Point out that we usually experience Jesus' healing power for the first time within our own families. When we are sick, our family members take care of and support us with their presence and love. Encourage the students to identify ways they have experienced healing within their families. List their responses on the board or on chart paper. Emphasize that these healing experiences at home are similar to the healing experiences we share with our Church family.

We Explore
2. Build
Working with the Text

- Tell the students that the Sacraments of Healing are a continuation of Jesus' own healing words and actions. This Scripture Story gives us an example.
- Read the Scripture Story aloud. Then ask the bulleted question. Call on a volunteer to respond. *(Jesus knew the power to heal and to forgive sins came from God; Jesus wanted the people to see that he had God's power of forgiveness on earth.)*
  Why do you think faith is important when a person asks for healing? *(Faith opens us up to being healed by the power of God.)*
- Share information in *Scripture Background* below.

  Catholics Believe Emphasize that in addition to continuing Jesus' work through the Sacraments of Healing, the Church is involved in other ministries of reconciliation and healing.

Working with the Pictures

Invite a volunteer to identify the part of the Scripture Story that is shown in the picture. Be sure the students recognize that Jesus is healing the paralyzed man. **What is Jesus doing in the picture?** *(putting his hand on the man's forehead, healing the man)* **How is this like the Sacrament of Anointing of the Sick that we celebrate today?** *(The priest also puts his hand on the person's head.)*

Catholics Believe...
Jesus wants the Church to continue his work of healing in the Sacraments of Reconciliation and Anointing of the Sick.

Catechism, #1421

Scripture Story
Jesus Forgives and Heals

One day some men were trying to bring a paralyzed man to Jesus. But the house Jesus was in was too crowded. The men went up on the roof and took some tiles off. They lowered the man on a stretcher so that he was in front of Jesus. Seeing their faith, Jesus said, "Your sins are forgiven."

Jesus knew that some people in the room were wondering how he could forgive sins. He asked them, "Which is easier to do, to forgive sins or make a paralyzed man walk?" Then he turned to the paralyzed man and said, "Get up, pick up your stretcher, and go home." The man stood up, picked up his stretcher, and walked home praising God. Everyone in the room was amazed and said, "We have seen astonishing things today."

—based on Luke 5:17–26

- Why do you think Jesus asked whether forgiving sins or making a paralyzed man walk was easier?

Resource Center
Scripture Background

The Gospel of Luke relates many stories of healing. **Luke 5:17–26** combines healing and forgiveness. Jesus both astonished and angered some of the people gathered around him. They knew that some holy people had the power to heal but that the power to forgive sins belonged only to God. The men who lowered the paralyzed man into the house believed that God's power was with Jesus. Jesus rewarded their faith by forgiving the sins of the paralyzed man and healing him.

Notes: Building the Chapter

Sacraments of Healing

Sin and sickness are different in a very important way. Sickness may separate us from others, but it is not a choice. When we sin, however, we make the choice to turn away from God and the community, and we are responsible for our decision.

The effects of sin and sickness can be similar. Both make us feel separated from those we love. The forgiveness of sin and the healing of sickness are similar, too. Both give us a chance to celebrate God's healing love. Both give the community a chance to share sorrows and joys.

Like all sacraments, the Sacraments of Healing use words and actions to communicate God's love. This chart shows the signs of the Sacraments of Healing.

Signs of Healing

	Action	Words
Reconciliation	The priest extends his hand in blessing.	"I absolve you from your sins in the name of the Father, and of the Son, and of the Holy Spirit."
Anointing of the Sick	The priest anoints the head and hands of the sick person with oil.	"Through this holy anointing may the Lord in his love and mercy help you with the grace of the Holy Spirit. May the Lord who frees you from sin save you and raise you up."

WE EXPLORE : 135

WE EXPLORE
Build Continued
Working with the Text

- Read aloud *Sacraments of Healing*. Emphasize that sin always involves a choice. We can choose to love ourselves and others as Jesus loves us, or we can choose to be hurtful and neglectful.
- Stress that sin hurts the entire community and weakens our relationship with one another and with God. Remind students that we can sin both by what we do or say and by what we do *not* do or say.
- Point out that no matter how we have sinned, we can always ask God's forgiveness and receive his mercy. God wants to heal us both from sinfulness and from sickness of every kind.
- To summarize the two sacraments' actions and effects, use the graphic organizer on page 131B. You may want to do one of the suggested activities or one of your own.

Working with the Pictures

- Ask the students to look carefully at the pictures.
  Why do you think both of these sacraments use gestures and touch to express forgiveness and healing? (Accept all reasonable responses, such as that the priest imitates Jesus' touching those he healed and forgave.)
- Point out the priest's stole in the first picture. Explain that the stole is a sign that the priest is acting in the name of Jesus and the Church.

Link to Liturgy

- Remind the students that the Mass includes opportunities for us to celebrate God's forgiveness and mercy and to recall our sins. At the beginning of the celebration of the Eucharist, the penitential rite celebrates God's willingness to forgive our sins and bring us peace. When we pray the Lord's Prayer and the Lamb of God, we again ask God's forgiveness and celebrate his mercy. Encourage the students to listen closely for these parts of the Eucharistic celebration and to participate in them when they attend Mass.
- In a communal celebration of the Sacrament of Reconciliation, Church members meet together to read Scripture and make a general examination of conscience. Next, they confess their sins individually to a priest and receive absolution and penance. Finally, they come together again to celebrate the mercy and forgiveness of God.

Teaching Tip

Answering questions Students may wonder why we need to celebrate the Sacrament of Reconciliation, since we can always ask God's forgiveness in our private prayers. Explain that we can and should ask forgiveness in prayer, but the Sacrament of Reconciliation lets us *hear* words of forgiveness and *feel* God's forgiveness and mercy. By celebrating the sacrament we also show other Church members that we want to be reunited with God and with the faith community.

WE REFLECT
Review

Recall Ask volunteers to share their answers. **(Reconciliation and Anointing of the Sick; Anointing of the Sick)**

Think and Share Encourage the students to think about the question carefully before responding. Call on a volunteer to respond. **(Possible answers: The sacrament honors God's healing love; in sharing others' sorrows and joys, we draw closer to them and to God.)**

Continue the Journey Allow the students to work in pairs or small groups to create the picture stories. **(Sample situation: children throwing a snowball or baseball, breaking a window on purpose, then apologizing and offering to pay for the window.)** Discuss accountability and reparation even when an action is not intentionally destructive. Clarify that carelessness is not usually sin.

Alternative Invite the students to complete the activity at home and be prepared to share their work at the next session.

We Live Our Faith *At Home:* Guide the students in brainstorming ways to show others that we forgive them.
In the Parish: Provide each student with the name of a parishioner who is sick or injured. Encourage the students to write prayers for these people and pray those prayers daily.

Faith Journal The students may begin pages 43–44 of their *Faith Journal* in class and complete them at home. As part of your own spiritual development, complete *Your Faith Journal* (page J23) for this chapter.

RECALL
Name the Sacraments of Healing. In which Sacrament of Healing is oil used?

THINK AND SHARE
How do you think the Anointing of the Sick honors God and helps the Church community?

CONTINUE THE JOURNEY
Draw a picture story of a third grader who causes some pain or damage on purpose but then helps heal or repair it.

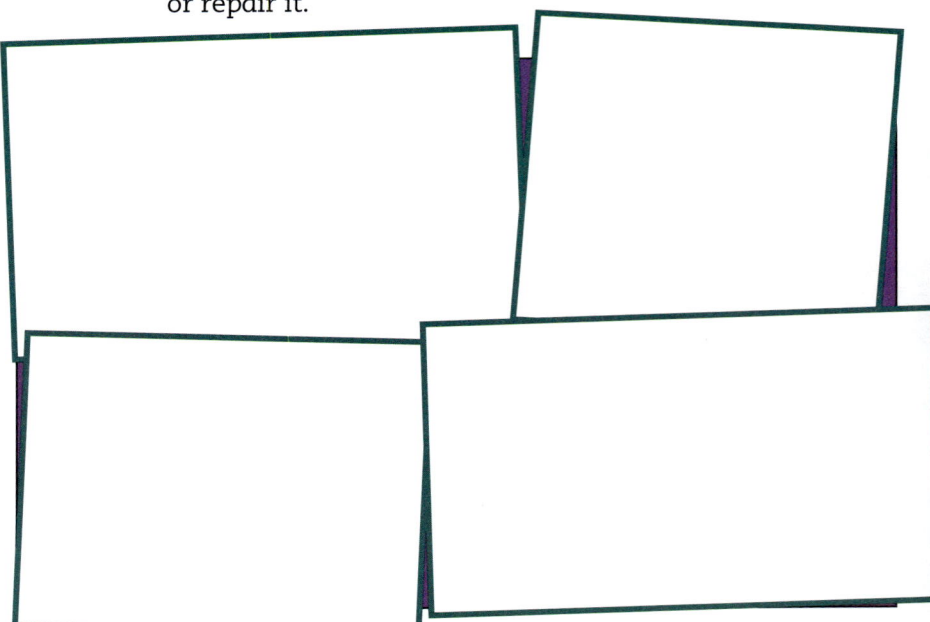

WE LIVE OUR FAITH

At Home Show God's love by forgiving someone who has hurt you.

In the Parish Find out the name of a parish member who is sick or injured, and write a prayer for him or her.

136 : WE REFLECT

Resource Center

Assessment Tip
Listen carefully to the students' responses to the *Think and Share* question, and examine their drawings for the *Continue the Journey* activity. In both responses, look for a basic understanding of healing and forgiveness and the role of the Sacraments of Healing.

Teaching Tip
Memorization You may want to have the students memorize an act of contrition, such as the prayer on page 177. Before the session, prepare "prayer cards" with this prayer on them for the class. Encourage the students to take the prayer cards home and put them in a place where they will see them every day. Ask the students to pray the prayer daily until they have learned it by heart.

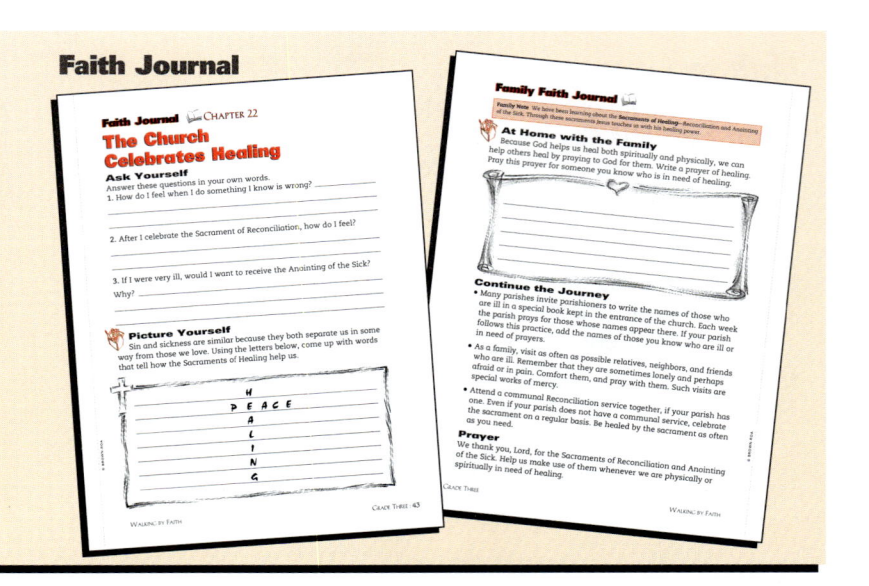

Healing Through Prayer

Everyone needs to be healed at some time. That is why Jesus gave us the Sacraments of Healing. Pray the following prayer, which is based on a prayer from the Sacrament of the Anointing of the Sick.

Prayer

Loving God,
you take every family under your care
and know our physical and spiritual
    needs.
Strengthen us with your grace
so that we may grow in faith and love.
We ask this through our Lord Jesus
    Christ, your Son,
who lives and reigns with you and the
    Holy Spirit,
one God, for ever and ever.
Amen.

We Celebrate : 137

We Celebrate
3. Close

Working with the Pictures

- Ask the students to look carefully at the pictures. Be sure they recognize what is shown: Jesus healing a man, a priest's stole worn in the Sacrament of Reconciliation, and a small container of oil used in the Sacrament of Anointing of the Sick.
  Who is Jesus healing in the picture? (a blind man) **How can you tell?** (Jesus is touching the man's eyes.)

- Share information in *Art Background* below.

Working with the Text

Read the text aloud. Point out that Jesus knows all our needs and wants to fill them.
What other physical and spiritual needs besides healing does Jesus fill? (Answers will vary but might include the need for love, for acceptance by others, for strength to do what is right.)

Prayer Gather the students in a circle, and place a small dish of olive oil or baby oil on a table or on the floor in the center. Then lead the class in praying the prayer aloud. Anoint each student's hands lightly with oil as you pray the following prayer: "May your hands be used to heal and help others." Invite the student to respond "I thank you, Jesus." Explain that this anointing is not a sacrament because it is not done by a priest. It is a gesture to show the Holy Spirit's healing presence in our lives.

Art Background

Christ Healing the Blind of Jericho by Nicholas Poussin (1594–1665) is based on Matthew's account of the two blind men whose sight was restored **(Matthew 20:29–34)**. The Gospels of Mark and Luke also refer to this event, but they tell of only one man being healed—Mark says his name was Bartimaeus **(Mark 10:46–52)**. This story contrasts physical blindness with spiritual blindness. Although the man could not see Jesus, he believed that Jesus had the power to heal him. Others in the crowd around him were blind to the fact that Jesus had God's power to heal and forgive.

Music and Liturgy Resources

To enhance your prayer and celebration, you may wish to use the Unit Six Music and Liturgy Resources from the Resource Package.

Notes: Closing the Chapter

Getting Ready: Chapter 23

Sacraments of Service

Program Resources
Student Text, pp. 138–143
Student Faith Journal, pp. 45–46
Your Faith Journal, p. J24
Chapter 23 Transparency
Unit Six Assessment

Unit Six (Sacraments)
Belonging, Healing, Serving

Key Content Summary
Sacraments of Service help us share our talents in the service of others.

Planning the Chapter

	Pacing Guide *Suggested time/Your time*	Content	Objectives	Materials
Open	10–15 min./ ____ min.	*We Are Invited,* pp. 138–139	• Give examples of using one's talents to serve others. • Identify the two Sacraments of Service.	• drawing materials
Build	20–25 min./ ____ min.	*We Explore,* pp. 140–141	• Describe how a married man and woman serve their family. • Compare the actions and effects of the two Sacraments of Service.	• Chapter 23 Transparency from the Resource Package
Review	15–20 min./ ____ min.	*We Reflect,* p. 142	• Demonstrate understanding of chapter concepts. • Apply learning through activity. • Practice faith at home and in the parish.	• large sheet of paper • *Student Faith Journal,* pp. 45–46 • *Your Faith Journal,* p. J24 • drawing materials (optional) • Unit Six Assessment from the Resource Package
Close	10–15 min./ ____ min.	*We Celebrate,* p. 143	• Pray together for married people and priests.	

For additional suggestions, see Scheduling, pp. T35–T37.

Catechism in Context

Doctrinal Foundation This chapter explores the Sacraments of Service: Matrimony and Holy Orders. When a baptized man and woman pledge themselves to love one another as long as both live, their pledge is regarded by the Church as a sacrament. Their pledge or vow is a covenant, which God blesses with the grace to fulfill it. Jesus is present through his Spirit in a sacramental marriage, enabling the couple to serve one another, their children, and others in his name.

See Catechism of the Catholic Church, #1534.

In the three-fold Sacrament of Holy Orders, men whose call to ministry has been verified by the Church are ordained by laying on of hands and by prayer. That is, they are admitted to one of three orders of ministry in the Church: the order of deacons, the order of priests, or the order of bishops.

A bishop's primary task is to proclaim the word of God in preaching and teaching. The bishop is the ordinary minister of all the sacraments except marriage. The bishop also oversees the ministries of all others who serve in his diocese. Because the bishop cannot be in all places within his diocese at the same time, priests have been delegated by their ordination to preach in the bishop's name and to celebrate the sacraments (with the exception of ordinations and, in some instances, Confirmation) on his behalf. A deacon is primarily a minister of charity, delegated by the bishop to assist the priests in giving help to those in need. At Mass the deacon proclaims the gospel and may be asked to preach. He is also the primary minister of the chalice at Communion, although he may be asked to distribute the host. Deacons may also witness marriages and baptize.

One-Minute Retreat for Catechists

Read

"The Church is a workshop . . . and every Christian man and woman is bound to help in the common cause."

—Alexander MacLaren

Reflect

How can I join in the common cause of the Church?

Pray

God, when opportunities to serve others present themselves, make me a willing servant. Whatever form that service takes, help me be faithful to my commitments. Help my students understand that their expression of love for others through service is a testimony of their love for you.

Visualizing the Lesson

Use this graphic organizer to help the students remember the effects of the Sacraments of Service on the Church community.

Draw the graphic organizer on the board or on chart paper, leaving all but the top circle blank. Have volunteers complete the graphic organizer as you work through the lesson.

Sacraments of Service → Matrimony, Holy Orders → Service to Church and the world

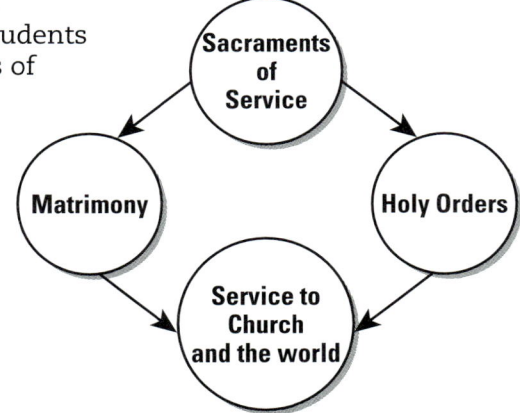

Library Links

Books for Children

Ten Catholics: Lives to Remember by Kenneth Christopher (HarperCollins, 1-800-242-7737).

These stories show the many ways to answer God's call.

Books for Parents and Teachers

Understanding the Sacraments Today by Lawrence E. Mick (The Liturgical Press, 1-800-858-5450).

The sacraments are explained in a comprehensive way for the faith community.

Multimedia

For children:

God Blessed Me. Episode #5, "Answering God's Call" produced by the Archdiocese of St. Paul-Minneapolis (video) (BROWN-ROA, 1-800-922-7696).

The concepts of vocation are explored as a calling to use gifts and talents in service to others.

Organizations

For information about the vocation of marriage, contact:

Worldwide Marriage Encounter
1908 E. Highland Avenue, Suite A
San Bernardino, CA 92404
(1-800-367-0343)
(http://www.scri.fsu.edu/~sollohub/wwme)

For information about the vocation of the priesthood, contact:

National Conference of Catholic Bishops
Office of Priestly Life and Ministry
3211 Fourth Street NE
Washington, DC 20017
(1-202-541-3000)
(http://www.nccbuscc.org)

Strengthening the Family Link

Here are some suggestions for reaching out to your students' families:

- Encourage the students to talk with family members about friends or other family members who have celebrated the Sacrament of Holy Orders.
- Invite family members to join the class for a question-and-answer session about ways married people and ordained ministers serve God and others.

Chapter 23 pages 138–143

Objectives
- Give examples of using one's talents to serve others.
- Identify the two Sacraments of Service.
- Describe how a married man and woman serve their family.
- Compare the actions and effects of the two Sacraments of Service.

Gathering — We Are Invited
1. Open

Personal Experience Ask the students to think about people they know who use their talents to help others. Call on one or more volunteers to describe the people they selected.

Prayer Tell the students that using our talents to help others is called *service*. Pray the opening prayer together.

Working with the Text
- Read the text aloud.
  What are some other talents that people your age might have?
  (Accept all reasonable answers.)
- Read the bulleted question aloud, and invite volunteers to respond.
  (Accept all reasonable answers.)

Working with the Pictures
- Draw the group's attention to the photograph of Jill reading the Scriptures. **How did Jill's reading aloud serve the Church community?** (She encouraged others to participate actively by clearly proclaiming God's word so all could hear.)

Provide the necessary drawing materials. If the students have difficulty thinking of a talent, review the talents discussed in *Working with the Text* above.

Chapter 23

Sacraments of Service

Prayer

Dear Jesus, help those who have celebrated the Sacraments of Service be faithful to their calling.

Mrs. Brown was getting ready for a prayer service. "Jill, we need someone to read Scripture today. You've got a clear voice and you read well. Would you do it?"

"Mrs. Brown, I've never done that before. I'd be nervous reading in front of all the parents and students. What if I mess up? Can't someone else do it?"

"Jill, of course someone else could read. But I picked you because of your talents. You'll have time to practice. You might be nervous, but don't worry about making mistakes. Please give it a try."

● What would you do if you were Jill?

Activity
Jill used her talents to serve her Church community. Draw a picture of yourself using one of your talents to serve others at home, in your neighborhood, or in your church.

138 : We Are Invited

Resource Center

Link to Liturgy
Remind the students that the Mass includes a special time when we listen to God's word proclaimed in the Scriptures. We call this special time the *Liturgy of the Word*. Point out that at the Sunday liturgy, a lector (usually a layperson) reads the first two readings. The cantor and the assembly sing together a psalm. Then the priest (presider) or deacon reads the gospel. Reading God's word at Mass is a special honor and responsibility. Invite the students to consider how they will serve the parish community now and as adults.

Assessment Tip
Use the students' drawings to assess their understanding of the meaning of Christian service as well as their understanding of their own talents and gifts.

Notes: Opening the Chapter

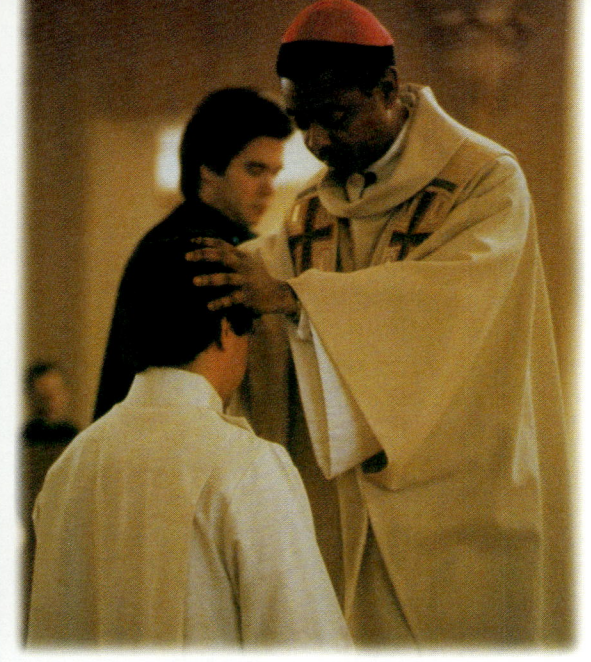

After many years of preparation, a man becomes a priest. He receives Holy Orders from a bishop at a special ceremony called *ordination*.

Serving God's People

Like Jill, we are sometimes asked to serve others by sharing our talents. The Church celebrates two **Sacraments of Service**. They are Holy Orders and Matrimony.

Holy Orders is the sacrament that men receive to become deacons, priests, or bishops so that the Church can continue to grow. Their commitment is to share God's message of love and celebrate the sacraments. Once a man receives Holy Orders, he is a priest forever. He shares in the ministry of Jesus in a special way.

Let's look at a typical day of a pastor. Father Miguel gets up and says his morning prayers. Then he goes to church to celebrate Mass for his parishioners. He meets with his staff to make decisions about parish business. He visits and anoints sick parishioners, and he teaches people about the Catholic faith. He gives advice to people who are uncertain about what God wants them to do. It's a big job, but it can be very fulfilling.

- How does your pastor serve the children in your parish?

Catholics Believe...
Holy Orders and Matrimony are directed toward helping other people find God.

Catechism, #1534

WE ARE INVITED : 139

WE ARE INVITED
Open *Continued*

Working with the Pictures
- Draw the students' attention to the photograph. Explain that the man being ordained is kneeling as a sign of his reverence for and obedience to God.
- Read the caption aloud. Point out that only a bishop can ordain a new priest or deacon.

Working with the Text
- Read aloud *Serving God's People*. Use *The Language of Faith* below to clarify the meaning of the highlighted term.
- Explain that the men who are called to serve the Church family as deacons, priests, and bishops dedicate their entire lives to this service. Stress that only some men receive this special calling, but *everyone* is called to serve God and the faith community.
- Read the bulleted question aloud. Invite volunteers to respond. **(Answers will vary.)** If the students do not know what your pastor does, explain his pastoral responsibilities.

Catholics Believe Use the statement to emphasize the selflessness of Matrimony and Holy Orders. Emphasize that although the lives of married people and ordained men are very different, both serve others.

The Language of Faith
The **Sacraments of Service**—unlike the Sacraments of Initiation and of Healing discussed in the two previous chapters—are administered only to adults. The Sacrament of Matrimony is a source of holiness and a symbol of the union between Christ and his Church. God shares his grace with the married couple so they can help and comfort each other and be open to having children. The Sacrament of Holy Orders continues Jesus' priestly work on earth and his proclamation of the good news. Through this sacrament God calls men to leadership in the Church and to be his representatives in forgiving sins and changing bread and wine into the Body and Blood of Jesus. Like Jesus, these men live lives dedicated to serving others.

Teaching Tip
Answering questions Students may ask why only men can be ordained as bishops, priests, and deacons in the Catholic Church. Explain that this rule is based on Jesus' choice of only men as the Twelve, who are also called *apostles*, to carry on his ministry in a special way.

WE EXPLORE
2. Build
Working with the Text
- Read aloud *Serving One Another*. Use *The Language of Faith* below to clarify the meaning of the word *vows*. Tell the group that religious priests, brothers, and sisters also take vows.
- Encourage volunteers to share their own ideas about ways a married couple serves the family.

Working with the Pictures
- Draw the students' attention to the picture. Ask a volunteer to describe how the *children* in the family shown could serve other family members. (Accept all reasonable responses, such as by doing household chores, helping a younger sibling with schoolwork, and so on.)
- Brainstorm responses to this activity as a class. List the students' responses on the board or on chart paper.

Saints Walk with Us Point out that Isidore and Maria are honored as saints because of their faith in God and their love for others. For more information about Saint Isidore and his wife, see *Profile* below.
How can you tell that Saint Isidore is the patron saint of farmers?
(He is shown plowing a field.)

Saints Walk with Us
Saint Isidore the Farmer
Feast Day: May 15
Saint Isidore and his wife, Maria, were never rich or famous. They loved God, each other, and all God's creation.

Saint Isidore is the patron of farmers. In Spain, where he and his wife lived, Maria is also honored as a saint.

Serving One Another
Married people have received a Sacrament of Service, too. A man and a woman who love each other may decide that they want to be together for the rest of their lives. In the presence of a priest and witnesses, they make promises, called **vows**, to each other. They promise to serve God by loving and serving each other and any children they may have.

How do married people serve each other? David and Kathleen work at their jobs so that their family will have money for food, clothing, and a home. At home they share work so that no one person has too much to do. They play with their children and help them with their homework. They also make decisions together about what is best for their family. When the family prays and attends church, they ask God for help with all their responsibilities.

ACTIVITY
God asks priests and married people to serve others in special ways. List some of the ways priests and married couples serve others.

140 : We Explore

Resource Center
The Language of Faith
Vows are sacred promises made to God and/or to other people. In both Matrimony and Holy Orders, the promises are made for life, and the Holy Spirit bestows the strength to keep them.

Profile
Saint Isidore (c. 1070–1130) Saint Isidore and Saint Maria de la Cabeza (d. 1175) are one of the few married couples the Church has canonized as saints. They had one son, who died when he was young. Isidore and Maria were not priests or religious brothers or sisters, and they held no place of honor in society. They worked their entire lives as farmers. Yet their love for God, each other, other people, and even their farm animals showed us what it means to live a holy life. By seeing God in all creation, this couple demonstrated God's love to everyone.

Notes: Building the Chapter

Answering the Call to Serve

Both Holy Orders and Matrimony involve lifetime commitments. After a man has been ordained a priest or permanent deacon, he remains a priest or deacon for the rest of his life. As part of the Sacrament of Matrimony, marriage partners promise to remain faithful to each other until one partner dies.

Not all members of the Church are called to the Sacraments of Service. However, through Baptism and Confirmation we are all called to use our talents in service to God's people. In whatever way we answer that call, we strengthen the Church community.

The chart below describes the Sacraments of Service and their effects on the participants and the Church.

Sacraments of Service

Matrimony 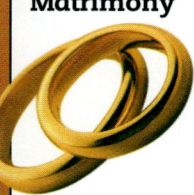	In front of a priest or deacon and other witnesses, a woman and man promise to love each other and work for each other's growth in faith and for positive change in the world.	The man and woman become husband and wife. The community is stronger because a new family is formed.
Holy Orders (ordination to the priesthood)	A bishop lays his hands on the man to be ordained and prays to the Holy Spirit. 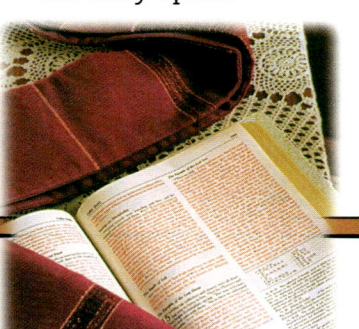	The man becomes a priest, with the authority to lead within the Church community. In the name of Jesus, he forgives sins and consecrates bread and wine, which become the Body and Blood of Jesus.

We Explore : 141

We Explore
Build Continued
Working with the Text

- Read aloud or invite volunteers to read *Answering the Call to Serve*. Point out that the Sacraments of Service are meant to be lifelong commitments. Emphasize that the entire Church community is called to service.

- Read through the chart, sacrament by sacrament. Explain that deacons and bishops are also ordained. **Why do you think the Church views marriage and ordination as sacraments?** (Answers will vary but might include that both states of life strengthen the Church community and make God's love present to others.)

- To highlight the effects of the Sacraments of Service, use the graphic organizer on page 137B. You may want to do the suggested activity or one of your own.

Working with the Pictures

Draw the students' attention to the wedding rings and the priest's stole and Bible in the pictures.
Why do you think a new husband and wife exchange rings? (to symbolize their vows to each other and to God)
What do you think a priest's stole represents? (that he acts in the name of Jesus)

Teaching Tip
Handling sensitive topics Students whose parents are separated or divorced may be confused by the text statement that marriage involves a lifetime commitment. Emphasize that all married couples experience difficulties from time to time and that sometimes the difficulties are too great to overcome. Point out that although a marriage may end, God's love for the man and woman and their children *never* ends.

Link to Liturgy
Discuss the different roles of a priest and a permanent deacon in the celebration of Mass. Be sure the students understand that a priest is a *presider:* he oversees and directs the liturgy. The deacon *assists* the priest: he may read the gospel, distribute Holy Communion, give the homily, invite the faithful to exchange the greeting of peace, and dismiss them at the conclusion of the liturgy. The deacon is a reminder that the Church is called to service. Remind the students that they, too, have a role in the celebration: to actively participate in the prayers, hymns, Liturgy of the Word, and Liturgy of the Eucharist.

Parish : 141

WE REFLECT
Review

Recall Invite volunteers to respond to the questions. (A man becomes a deacon, priest, or bishop; Matrimony.)

Think and Share Encourage the students to think about their answers before responding. Invite a volunteer to respond. (They are called *Sacraments of Service* because through them a person or couple is asked to serve other people. A priest shares in Jesus' work by presiding at Mass with the Church community and forgiving people's sins in the name of God. Married people help each other and their children grow in faith.)

Continue the Journey Have the students compose a class letter to your pastor or another priest of their choice. As the students dictate the sentences, write them on a large sheet of paper. Have each student sign the letter. Arrange to have the letter delivered.

We Live Our Faith *At Home:* Encourage the students by telling them about your marriage ceremony or the ceremony of a married couple in your family. *In the Parish:* If a parish priest or deacon is not available, consider asking a retired priest from your diocese to speak to the class.

Faith Journal The students may begin pages 45–46 of their *Faith Journal* in class and complete them at home. As part of your own spiritual development, complete *Your Faith Journal* (page J24) for this chapter.

RECALL
What happens through the Sacrament of Holy Orders? Which sacrament joins a man and a woman into a new family?

THINK AND SHARE
Why does the Church call Holy Orders and Matrimony *Sacraments of Service?*

CONTINUE THE JOURNEY
Write a letter to your pastor or a priest you know, thanking him for serving your Church community.

WE LIVE OUR FAITH

At Home Ask a married family member about the marriage ceremony.

In the Parish Invite a parish priest or deacon to describe his ordination ceremony.

142 : WE REFLECT

Resource Center

Meeting Individual Needs
Learners acquiring English If these students are not capable of or comfortable with contributing to the class letter verbally, invite them to contribute by decorating it with appropriate drawings. Take time to read the completed letter aloud slowly, adding gestures for meaning when necessary.

Assessment Tip
You may wish to copy the Unit Six Assessment from the Resource Package in preparation for giving this test after completing Chapters 21–24.

Faith Journal

Celebrating Service

People who have received the Sacraments of Service have agreed to help other people. But they need our support. It is good to remember priests and married people in our prayers and ask God to help them with their service to others. Pray the following litany with your classmates.

PRAYER

1: For priests, who lead us to God, we pray . . .
All: Lord, hear our prayer.
2: . . . who forgive us in God's name, we pray . . .
3: . . . who teach us about God, we pray . . .
4: For married people, who lead one another to God, we pray . . .
5: . . . who are willing to say I'm sorry, we pray . . .
6: . . . who teach one another and their children about God, we pray . . .

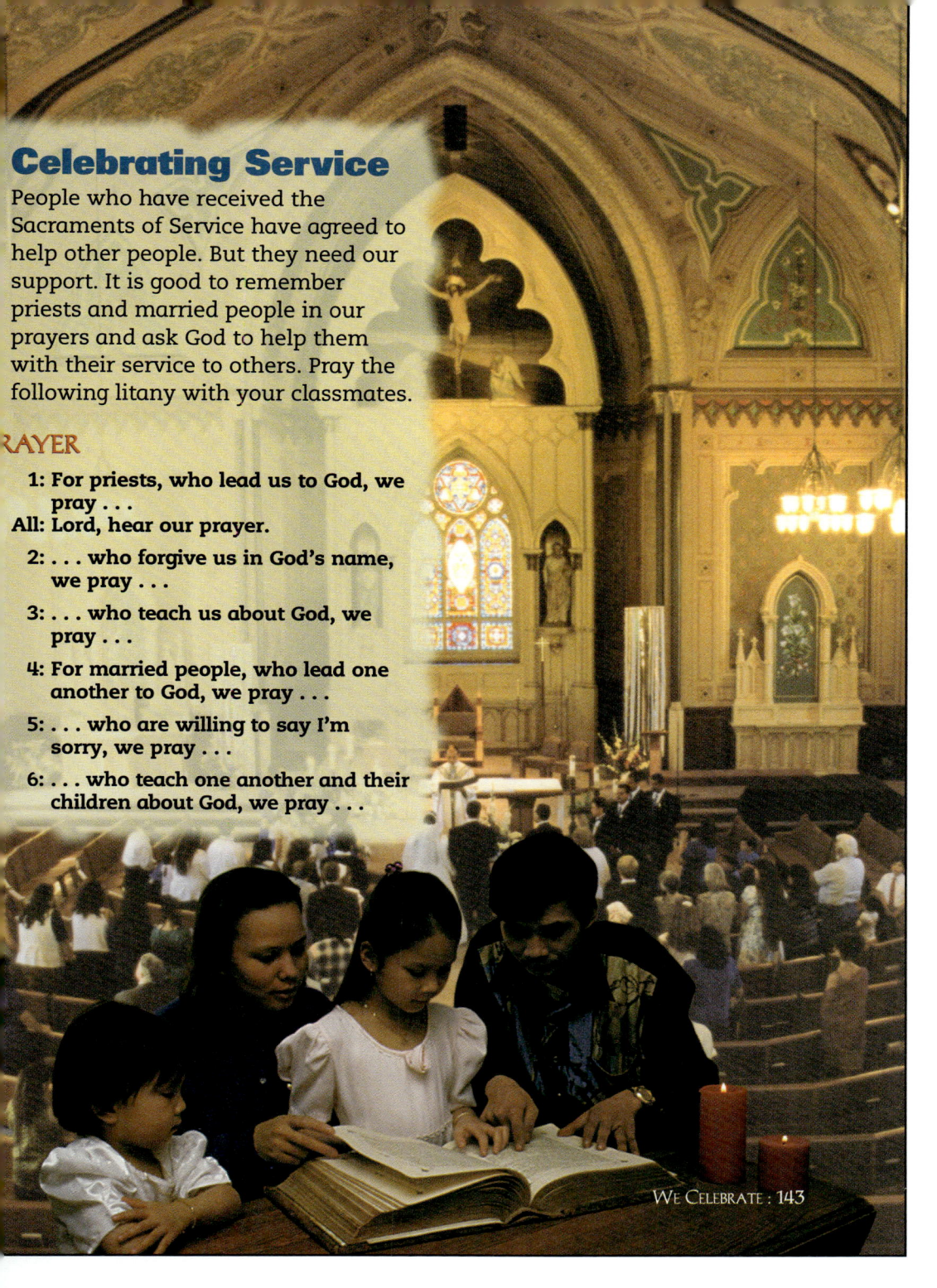

WE CELEBRATE : 143

WE CELEBRATE
3. Close

Working with the Pictures

Draw attention to the photographs. Invite a volunteer to describe what is shown in each. (a marriage ceremony; parents reading the Bible with their children)
What does each picture show about serving others? (In the marriage ceremony the man and woman *promise* to serve others. In their daily lives they *act* to serve others.)

Working with the Text

- Read aloud *Celebrating Service*, or invite a volunteer to do so. Point out that just as our bodies need food and water, our souls need spiritual food—the Eucharist, God's word in the Scriptures, and prayer.
- Emphasize that everyone needs to pray for others and to be prayed for by others.

Prayer Gather the students in a semicircle. Choose six volunteers to pray the intercessions aloud. Ask the remaining students to bow their heads, and invite the readers to begin. Join the students in praying or singing the response after each intercession. To conclude the prayer celebration, lead the class in singing a favorite hymn.

Link to the Family

Suggest that the students talk with at least one married couple in their families this week—perhaps their parents, grandparents, or an aunt and uncle—to find out what marriage means to them. Encourage the students to ask the couples to explain how their marriages have helped them serve each other, God, and other people.

optional Link to the Faith Community

Activity Point out that our faith community is made up of people who are living many different types of lives: married people, single people, ordained ministers, and men and women who are members of religious communities. Challenge the students to list the special gifts that each of these groups brings to the faith community. Invite the students to think about how the parish would be different if we did not have each group to help us on our journey of faith.

Notes: Closing the Chapter

_____
_____
_____
_____
_____
_____
_____

PARISH : 143

Unit Six Review

Objective
- Review the unit and assess progress.

Chapter Summaries
Use this information to reinforce key points before administering the review. These summaries will also help you assess the students' responses to *Show How Far You've Come*, page 145.

Chapter 21
- The sacraments are signs and celebrations of God's life in us.
- We become members of the Church through the three Sacraments of Initiation: Baptism, Confirmation, and Eucharist.

Chapter 22
- Through the Sacraments of Healing—Reconciliation and the Anointing of the Sick—we experience the Church community's love and strength.
- Jesus calls us to continue his mission of healing and forgiveness.

Chapter 23
- Holy Orders and Matrimony are Sacraments of Service.
- Holy Orders and Matrimony are lifelong commitments of service to others.

Review
Have the students work on the review in writing or work together to answer the questions orally.

Matching Review the answers as a group. Discuss any missed responses to make sure the students understand the correct answers.

Which Is Correct? Discuss any questions with which the students had difficulty.

Share Your Faith The students may work in pairs or small groups. Have them share their responses with the rest of the class.

Unit Six Checkpoint
Review

Matching Match each description in Column A with the correct term from Column B.

Column A	Column B
_e_ 1. These make us part of the Church.	a. deacon, priest, bishop
_c_ 2. These continue Jesus' work of forgiving and curing.	b. vows
_d_ 3. These help others find God.	c. Sacraments of Healing
_a_ 4. These are ordained men.	d. Sacraments of Service
_b_ 5. These are sacred promises.	e. Sacraments of Initiation

Which Is Correct? Circle the term that best completes each sentence.
1. The sacrament that seals and completes Baptism is (Reconciliation, **Confirmation**).
2. The sacrament that nourishes our faith every day is (**Eucharist**, Holy Orders).
3. All the sacraments are celebrated by the power of the (**Holy Spirit**, priest).
4. The sacrament that gives special grace for marriage and family life is (Baptism, **Matrimony**).
5. Reconciliation and Anointing of the Sick are sacraments of (Initiation, **Healing**).

Share Your Faith Someone tells you that the sacraments help people only as individuals. Explain how the sacraments affect the whole Church community.

Resource Center

Assessment Tips
Use one or more of the following strategies to assist you in assessing student progress:
- If you need a more detailed written review, administer the Unit Six Assessment from the Resource Package.
- Have the students assess their own progress by discussing with partners the important ideas they learned in this unit.
- Invite volunteers to suggest ways in which they can prepare now to live lives of service to others.

Show How Far You've Come Use the chart below to show what you have learned. For each chapter, write or draw the three most important things you remember.

Belonging, Healing, Serving

Chapter 21 We Become Part of the Church	Chapter 22 The Church Celebrates Healing	Chapter 23 Sacraments of Service
Look for answers reflecting the key points listed under Chapter Summaries.		

What Else Would You Like to Know?
List any questions you still have about the sacraments.

_____
_____

Continue the Journey Choose one or more of the following activities to do on your own, with your class, or with your family.

- Look through your Faith Journal pages for Unit Six. Choose your favorite activity, and share it with a friend or family member.
- Make a mural or booklet on the sacraments. Use words and pictures to show what you have learned about the Sacraments of Initiation, Healing, and Service.
- Attend parish celebrations of the sacraments. Write a report about what you see and hear.
- Interview parish members about how they see themselves living their baptismal promises. Share what you learn with your class.

Show How Far You've Come Compare the students' responses with *Chapter Summaries* on page 144. Note and correct any responses that differ widely from the key chapter concepts. Review key concepts as needed. If time permits, extend this activity by asking students to reread any portions of the chapters they did not understand.

What Else Would You Like to Know? Have the students share their questions and vote on a class list of three questions for you to answer at the next session.

Continue the Journey Provide time at a later session for the students to demonstrate how they have completed one or more of these activities. For example:

- Ask volunteers to share their favorite *Faith Journal* entries.
- Display the students' booklets or murals in the classroom. Allow time for them to explain their work.
- Encourage the students to share their reports and what they learned in the interviews.

Prayer

Gather the students at the prayer table. Pray the following prayer aloud: "God, thank you for blessing our Church community with the gifts of the sacraments." Have the students respond "Amen."

Reference Sources

For help in addressing the students' questions about this unit's topics, see:

- *Catechism of the Catholic Church* (United States Catholic Conference, 1994).
- *Life in Christ* by Revs. James Killgallon and Gerard Weber, revised by Revs. Michael Place and Sammie Maletta (ACTA Publications, 1995).

Good resources for third graders include:

- *Children's Catholic Catechism* (BROWN-ROA, 1990).
- *ABC's of the Sacraments . . . for Children* by Francine O'Connor (Liguori Publications, 1989).

Your parish community is another important resource. Encourage the students to discuss any questions they may have about this unit with priests, deacons, other staff members, catechists, and members of religious communities.

Link to the Family

If possible, have students take these pages home to share with their families.

Getting Ready: Chapter 24

Hosanna!

Program Resources
Student Text, pp. 146–149
Student Faith Journal, pp. 47–48
Your Faith Journal, p. J25

Unit Six (Sacraments)
Belonging, Healing, Serving

Key Content Summary
The celebrations of Holy Week teach us about Jesus' passion.

Planning the Chapter

	Pacing Guide Suggested time/Your time	Content	Objectives	Materials
Open	10–15 min./ _____ min.	We Are Invited, p. 146	• Identify Palm Sunday as the Church's celebration of Jesus' entry into Jerusalem.	• blessed palm branches (optional)
Build	20–25 min./ _____ min.	We Explore, p. 147	• Describe the Palm Sunday Mass. • Sequence the events honored during Holy Week.	
Review	15–20 min./ _____ min.	We Reflect, p. 148	• Demonstrate understanding of chapter concepts. • Apply learning through activity. • Practice faith at home and in the parish.	• drawing materials • large sheets of art paper • Student Faith Journal, pp. 47–48 • Your Faith Journal, p. J25
Close	10–15 min./ _____ min.	We Celebrate, p. 149	• Celebrate Jesus' arrival in Jerusalem with prayer, a procession, and music.	• small instruments (bells, small cymbals), palms (or paper streamers or evergreen branches), recordings of hymns appropriate to Palm Sunday

For additional suggestions, see Scheduling, pp. T35–T37.

Catechism in Context

Doctrinal Foundation This chapter discusses Holy Week. The drama of Holy Week is astounding: from the enthusiastic crowds who welcomed Jesus to Jerusalem with "Hosanna!" on Palm Sunday through his last Passover to the mob howling for his death on Good Friday, pleading with Pilate to "Crucify him!" On the night before Jesus died, he was betrayed by one of his own disciples. Another would deny him. And yet at that last meal, he showed the depth of his love by giving himself for us and to us.

See Catechism of the Catholic Church, #559.

The events of the last days of Jesus' life have long been celebrated not primarily for their historical interest but for what they mean for Christians of every age. We welcome Jesus into our lives, yet we betray him by our sins. Our celebration highlights this inner conflict in order to "spur us on to victory." We have already accepted Christ, but our acceptance of him needs to be made complete. By facing the realities of sin and death liturgically during Holy Week, we can draw closer to the one who has conquered them both, Jesus Christ, our risen Lord.

One-Minute Retreat for Catechists

Read
"God has two dwellings: one in heaven, and the other in a meek and thankful heart."

—Izaak Walton

Reflect
How have I shown my thanks to Jesus for his sacrifice?

Pray
Jesus, when I carry palms, help me imagine myself on the streets of Jerusalem, hailing you as my Messiah. Help my students know that you still walk through the streets and through our homes, for you are with us always. Through our faith, help us honor you every day as you have honored us.

Visualizing the Lesson

Use this graphic organizer to help the students remember the meaning and sequence of the celebrations during Holy Week.

Redraw the graphic organizer on a sheet of paper, and make copies for the students. After discussing the drawing with the students, distribute art materials. Have them draw symbols for each of the three days. *(Possible symbols: Palm Sunday—palms; Holy Thursday—bread, wine, grapes; Good Friday—cross, crown of thorns.)*

Holy Week

Palm Sunday	Holy Thursday	Good Friday
Jesus entered Jerusalem.	Jesus gave himself in the Eucharist.	Jesus suffered and died for us.

Library Links

Books for Children
Hosanna to You, Jesus—A Palm Sunday Experience by Marisa Mignolli (Pauline Books & Media, 1-800-876-4463).

A simple presentation of the events of Palm Sunday helps children more fully understand the Paschal mystery.

Books for Parents and Teachers
The Crucified Jesus Is No Stranger by Sebastian Moore (Paulist Press, 1-800-218-1903).

Biblical reflections and discussions on the crucifixion of Jesus help bring an understanding of its purpose in contemporary life.

Multimedia
For children:
The Story of Benjamin Burro produced by the Archdiocese of St. Paul-Minneapolis and Rogerdin Productions (video) (BROWN-ROA, 1-800-922-7696).

The story of Jesus' last days is told as seen through the eyes of the burro that carried him through Jerusalem.

Organizations
For information about ways to "die to self" and give to others in preparation for Easter, contact:
Catholic Charities USA
1731 King Street, Suite 200
Alexandria, VA 22314
(1-703-549-1390)
(http://www.catholiccharitiesusa.org)

Strengthening the Family Link

Here are some suggestions for reaching out to your students' families:

- Encourage the students to talk with family members about what we celebrate on Palm Sunday and why we read the Passion on that day.
- Invite family members to join the class in reading from Scripture about Jesus' entry into Jerusalem (Matthew 21:1–11). Work together to make a poster or banner titled *Hosanna to the Son of David!*

Chapter 24 pages 146–149

Objectives
- Identify Palm Sunday as the Church's celebration of Jesus' entry into Jerusalem.
- Describe the Palm Sunday Mass.
- Sequence the events honored during Holy Week.
- Celebrate Jesus' arrival in Jerusalem with a prayer, a procession, and music.

Gathering — We Are Invited
1. Open

Personal Experience Invite the students to recall how their families welcome special guests to their homes. Ask volunteers to share their experiences.

Prayer Encourage the students to keep their families' welcoming celebrations in mind as you pray the opening prayer together.

Working with the Text
- Read the story text aloud and with great excitement.
  How did the people feel about Jesus' arrival? **(happy, joyful, excited)**
  Why do you think they felt that way? **(Jesus was a very special person to those who knew him; some thought he was the Messiah and that he could save them.)**
- Read the bulleted question aloud. **(We are recalling Jesus' entry into Jerusalem, and we are praising him for saving us.)**

Working with the Pictures
- Ask the students to name the kind of tree that is shown in the background picture. **(a palm tree)** Explain that palm trees were common where Jesus lived.
- Invite a volunteer to read the caption aloud.

Resource Center

Link to the Faith Community
Ask the students to recall Palm Sunday services they have attended in the past. Remind them that the blessed palm is a sacramental symbol that should be handled and treated with respect.

Optional Enrichment
Provide each student with a blessed palm from your parish. Have the students make crosses by braiding the palms. There are several different techniques that can be used, utilizing two, three, or four strands. If necessary, consult an art teacher for assistance. Let the students take the crosses home to display in a place of honor.

Notes: Opening the Chapter

CHAPTER 24
We Celebrate Holy Week

HOSANNA!

Prayer
Dear Jesus, lead us to understand the first Palm Sunday and celebrate your love now.

"He's coming! I can see Jesus now!" Elizabeth was running to her father's shop, calling her brother Seth. "You have to come right away!"

Seth and Elizabeth ran out into the street. Some people were waving palm branches in the air and praising Jesus. Others were putting their cloaks down in front of the donkey Jesus was riding.

Seth and Elizabeth had heard Jesus teaching and had seen some of his miracles. They were happy Jesus would be in Jerusalem for Passover.

- The people praised Jesus with "Hosanna," which means "Save us!" Why do we use the same word during the Mass?

Every year on Palm Sunday, Christians around the world remember Jesus' entry into Jerusalem.

146 : We Are Invited

WE CELEBRATE PALM SUNDAY

Like Elizabeth and Seth, we think of Jesus as a teacher and a miracle worker. We also believe that Jesus is God.

The Church recalls Jesus' entry into Jerusalem on Palm Sunday, which is also called *Passion Sunday*. **Palm Sunday** marks the beginning of **Holy Week**, the week before Easter.

The Palm Sunday Mass begins with the blessing of palms. The gospel reading is called the **Passion**, which is a reading about the suffering and death of Jesus. At the end of Mass, we take home blessed palms to honor Jesus as he was honored long ago in Jerusalem. Any palms left from Palm Sunday are burned to make the ashes for the next Ash Wednesday.

The readings of Holy Week tell how Jesus showed his love for us. On Palm Sunday he willingly entered Jerusalem. On Holy Thursday he gave himself in the Eucharist. On Good Friday he suffered and died for us.

Catholics Believe...

that children and God's poor honored Jesus as he entered Jerusalem bearing witness to the coming of God's kingdom.

Catechism, #559

Activity

The palms that are blessed and given out on Palm Sunday remind us how Jesus was loved and honored when he entered Jerusalem. On Palm Sunday, take a blessed palm home and put it in a place of honor.

We Explore : 147

WE EXPLORE
2. Build

Working with the Text

- Read aloud *We Celebrate Palm Sunday*. Use *The Language of Faith* to clarify the highlighted terms.
- To highlight the important days of Holy Week as they are mentioned in the text, use the graphic organizer on page 145B. You may want to do the suggested activity or one of your own.
- **Catholics Believe** Point out that when God's reign comes, those who are "least" in our world, such as children and those who are poor, will be the greatest.

Working with the Pictures

- Ask the students to study the pictures carefully. Point out the picture of the priest blessing palms before Mass. **What is the family doing with the palms they have?** (displaying them behind a crucifix) **Where did the family probably get the palms?** (at Mass on Palm Sunday) **Where do you put the palm you receive on Palm Sunday?** (Answers will vary.)
- Tell the students that some people braid the palms into crosses for display in their homes.
- Read the caption aloud. Encourage the students to display their palms in a place of honor at home.

The Language of Faith

- **Palm Sunday**, the liturgical celebration of Jesus' entry into Jerusalem, begins with the blessing of the palms, often held outdoors. From that area the presider, other ministers, and the assembly enter the church in a joyful procession, carrying blessed palms and singing songs.
- **Holy Week** is the most sacred period in the Church year. During this time we commemorate Jesus' last days on earth.
- The **Passion**, the Scripture reading that recalls Jesus' suffering and death, is first read on Palm Sunday. The word *passion* means "suffering."

Notes: Building the Chapter

WE REFLECT
Review

Recall Invite volunteers to share their responses. *(Jesus' entry into Jerusalem for Passover; because we read the Passion, the story about how Jesus showed his love for us, on Palm Sunday, Holy Thursday, and Good Friday)*

Think and Share Give the students sufficient time to consider their responses before answering. *(to recall Jesus' suffering and death during Holy Week)*

Continue the Journey Distribute the necessary art materials. Invite the students to work independently.

Alternative Divide the class into small groups, and assign one of the following days to each group: Palm Sunday, Holy Thursday, Good Friday. Have each group draw a picture on a large sheet of paper. You could also assign the art project to be completed at home.

We Live Our Faith *At Home:* Tell the students that these readings for Holy Week can be found in a missalette. *In the Parish:* Inform the class of the dates and times of the parish celebrations.

Faith Journal The students may begin pages 47–48 of their *Faith Journal* in class and complete them at home. As part of your own spiritual development, complete *Your Faith Journal* (page J25) for this chapter.

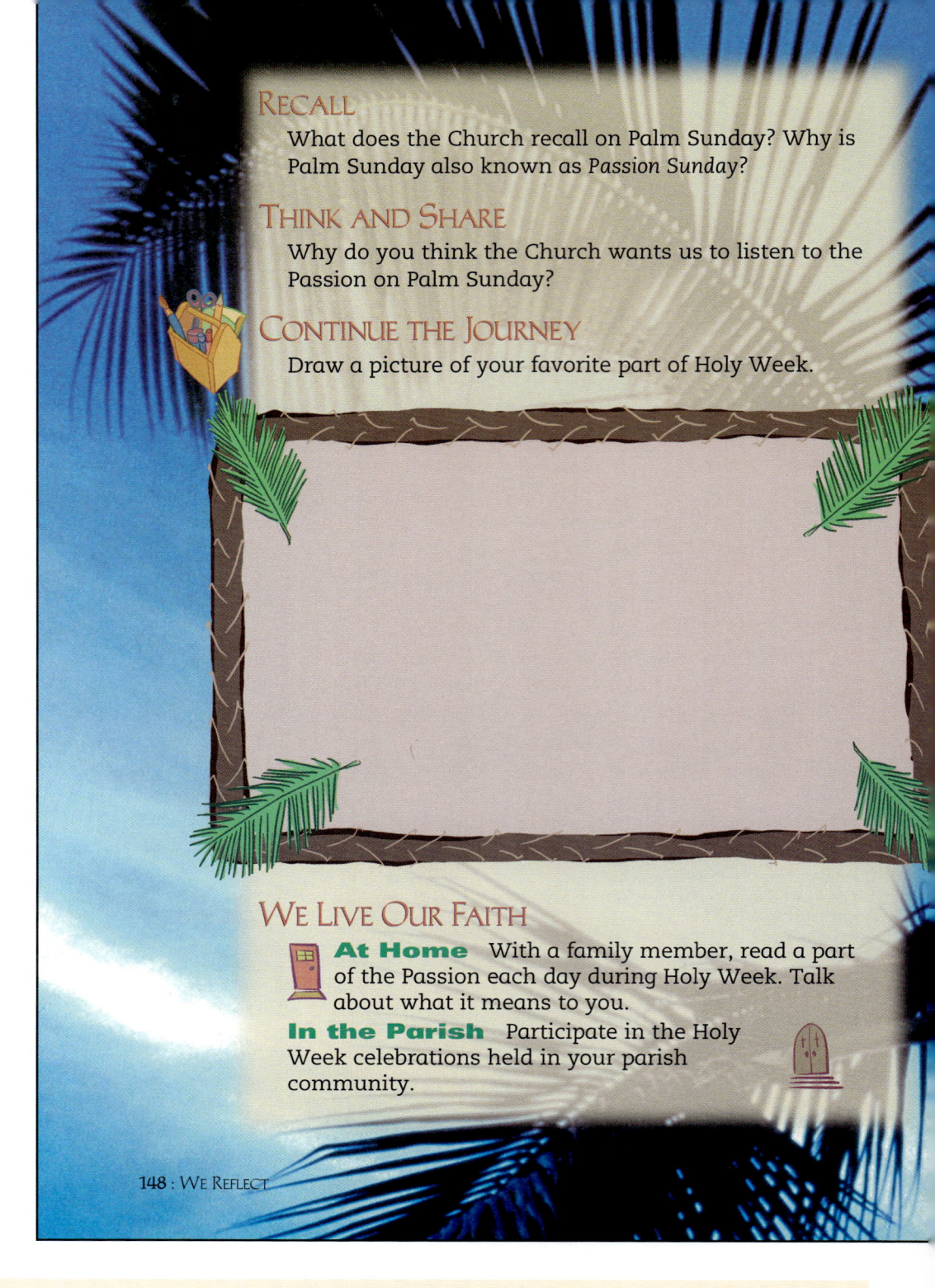

RECALL
What does the Church recall on Palm Sunday? Why is Palm Sunday also known as *Passion Sunday?*

THINK AND SHARE
Why do you think the Church wants us to listen to the Passion on Palm Sunday?

CONTINUE THE JOURNEY
Draw a picture of your favorite part of Holy Week.

WE LIVE OUR FAITH

At Home With a family member, read a part of the Passion each day during Holy Week. Talk about what it means to you.

In the Parish Participate in the Holy Week celebrations held in your parish community.

148 : WE REFLECT

Resource Center

Assessment Tip
Use the students' drawings and their responses to the review questions to determine their level of understanding of the main concepts presented in this chapter. Review any areas of instruction that may not have been thoroughly presented.

Link to the Family
Invite volunteers to describe their families' ways of observing Holy Week. Also suggest that they ask older family members to tell them how they observed Palm Sunday and Holy Week when they were younger. Ask the students to discuss with their families ways that they could observe Holy Week this year.

148 : CHAPTER 24

BLESSED IS HE WHO COMES!

We celebrate Jesus' arrival in Jerusalem on Palm Sunday. With your class, pray this prayer based on the Palm Sunday Mass.

Prayer

Reader: The children of Jerusalem welcomed Christ the King.

All: Hosanna to the Son of David.

Reader: They carried olive branches, spread their cloaks before him, and loudly praised the Lord:

All: Hosanna to the Son of David!

Reader: Blessed is he who comes in the name of the Lord!

All: Hosanna to the Son of David!

We Celebrate : 149

We Celebrate
3. Close

Working with the Pictures

- Ask the students if they have ever seen large palm branches like those in the larger picture. Explain that most parishes distribute individual palm blades rather than entire branches.
- Point out the halo around Jesus' head in the painting.
  Why do you think the artist included the halo around Jesus' head?
  (to show that Jesus was holy)
- Share the information in *Art Background* below. Draw the students' attention to how the artist crowded many people into the painting to portray the excitement of Jesus' arrival.

Prayer Make the prayer celebration joyous by including a procession, songs, hand clapping, and small percussion instruments such as bells or small cymbals, if available. If real palms are not available, substitute paper streamers or evergreen branches. Choose appropriate hymns for the students to sing, or play recordings of the hymns. Pray the prayer aloud yourself, or choose three students to do so. Lead the procession around the room and to the prayer table. Have the class joyfully call out the response after each verse. End the celebration with another procession and song.

Link to Liturgy

Remind the students that the joyful calls of "Hosanna!" on Palm Sunday are also prayed every time Mass is celebrated. At the beginning of the Eucharistic Prayer, we pray or sing "Hosanna" as part of the Holy, Holy, Holy Lord. Encourage the students to listen for and participate in this special prayer of praise at Mass.

Art Background

This painting of Jesus riding into Jerusalem is only one scene on a wooden panel measuring 9 by 15 feet. This panel, entitled *Maestà*, is the masterpiece of Duccio di Buoninsegna (c. 1255–1315). It contains paintings on both sides. On one side is a painting of Mary and the Child Jesus. On the other side is the painting shown on this page, along with 25 other scenes showing Jesus' suffering, death, and resurrection.

Notes: Closing the Chapter

Parish : 149

Getting Ready: Chapter 25

Connected to the Past

Program Resources
Student Text, pp. 150–155
Student Faith Journal, pp. 49–50
Your Faith Journal, p. J26
Chapter 25 Transparency
Unit Seven Family Letter

Unit Seven (Salvation History)
Yesterday, Today, and Tomorrow

Key Content Summary
Our Church has roots in the past.

Planning the Chapter

	Pacing Guide Suggested time/Your time	Content	Objectives	Materials
Open	10–15 min./ _____ min.	We Are Invited, pp. 150–151	• Summarize and explain the Church's past.	• Jesse tree ornaments (optional)
Build	20–25 min./ _____ min.	We Explore, pp. 152–153	• Explore the meaning of Church as a community of people. • Observe examples of the Church's history worldwide.	• Chapter 25 Transparency from the Resource Package
Review	15–20 min./ _____ min.	We Reflect, p. 154	• Demonstrate understanding of chapter concepts. • Apply learning through activity. • Practice faith at home and in the parish.	• drawing materials • Student Faith Journal, pp. 49–50 • Your Faith Journal, p. J26
Close	10–15 min./ _____ min.	We Celebrate, p. 155	• Affirm our Church connection with people of all times and nations.	• globe, cross • Unit Seven Family Letter from the Resource Package

For additional suggestions, see Scheduling, pp. T35–T37.

Catechism in Context

Doctrinal Foundation This chapter explores our heritage of faith. Thousands of years ago God called Abraham and promised him descendants as numerous as the stars in the sky or the grains of sand in the sea, and a land of his own. Abraham believed in God's promises and was rewarded in his old age with a son, Isaac, and with the land of Canaan (Israel). From Abraham, through Isaac, were descended the people known first as *Hebrews*, then as *Israelites* (sons of Israel, that is, Jacob, son of Isaac and Rebekah), and finally as *Jews* (that is, *Judeans*, or people of Judah).

See Catechism of the Catholic Church, #759.

From these people, the People of God, came Jesus, the Messiah. However, he came not only for them but for all who would accept him. The early Church, made up at first of Jewish followers of Jesus, soon came to realize that all people, Jew and Greek, that is, Jew and Gentile (non-Jew), male and female, slave and free, are one in Christ, the Savior of the world. As Christians we trace our family of faith back to Abraham, our father in faith. Our family history goes back nearly four thousand years and is peopled with great heroes, patriarchs and prophets, apostles and martyrs, men and women of such faith and holiness that they are called saints. We look forward to joining the other members of our family, the People of God, when God's kingdom is fulfilled.

One-Minute Retreat for Catechists

Read
"The Church must be a very strong and righteous thing, for it has survived every enemy it ever had."
—Eddie Cantor

Reflect
How can reflecting on the work of early Christians strengthen my faith?

Pray
God, help me recognize the importance of the sacrifices made by early Christians. Through their stories, help me see how I can work to help build the Church today. May I find inspiration in the Church's history and hope for its future.

Visualizing the Lesson

Use this graphic organizer to help the students visualize the Church's history.

Draw the graphic organizer on the board or on chart paper. Point out the dates on the time line, and have the students help you read the descriptions of the events associated with them. Tell the students that the biblical dates are approximate.

1800 B.C.E. God makes a covenant with Abraham and the people of Israel.

0 – 30 C.E. Jesus organizes the apostles to help him spread God's word.

2000 C.E. The Church continues today.

Library Links

Books for Children
Christians Throughout the Ages—Around the World by John Drane (Lion Publishing/Chariot Books, 1-800-437-4337).

This book tells the story of Christianity throughout the world and of the many people who live and practice their Christian faith.

Books for Parents and Teachers
Impressions of a Life by Denis McBride CSSR (Liguori Publications, 1-800-325-9521).

Fifteen people of the Gospels share their impressions of Jesus to help us understand Jesus and his message.

Multimedia
For children:
Rome: In the Footsteps of Peter and Paul, Part III produced by Heart of the Nation (video) (BROWN-ROA, 1-800-922-7696).

Part III describes Church history from the Renaissance to today and surveys the masterpieces and structures created during that period. Rediscovery of the catacombs shows their important link between our Church today and the "Rock of Peter."

For parents and teachers:
Jewish/Christian Dialogue: Jewish Feasts (video) (Alba House Communications, 1-800-533-2522).

Discussion and visuals help explain the Jewish feasts.

Organizations
For more information about the history of the Church, contact:
Catholic Historical Society
The Catholic Center
1011 First Avenue
New York, NY 10022
(1-800-225-7999)
(http://www.catholic.org/uschs)

Strengthening the Family Link

Here are some suggestions for reaching out to your students' families:

- Encourage the students to talk with family members about our connection to the people of Israel whose story is told in the Old Testament.
- Invite family members to join the class in watching all or part of the video *Rome: In the Footsteps of Peter and Paul* listed above.

Chapter 25 pages 150–155

Objectives
- Summarize and explain the Church's past.
- Explore the meaning of Church as a community of people.
- Observe examples of the Church's history worldwide.

Gathering WE ARE INVITED
1. Open

Personal Experience Talk with the students briefly about your family history. Refer to your grandparents as your "ancestors."

Prayer Tell the students that the Church also has a family history. Then pray the opening prayer together.

Working with the Text

- Read the text aloud. Be sure the students understand that the term *ancestors* means those in our family who have lived before us. Help the students make the connection that our ancestors *in faith* are all those people who lived before us and passed on their faith to us.
  Why do we call the Jewish people our ancestors in faith? (Jesus and his family were descendants of Abraham and Sarah.)

- To highlight our Church history, use the graphic organizer on page 149B. You may want to do the suggested activity or one of your own choosing.

- If time permits, recall with the students the story of Abraham and Sarah (see page 43). Explain that this story is found in the Old Testament.

- Point out that a *synagogue* is a place where Jewish people meet to worship and learn about their faith.

Chapter 25
Connected to the Past

PRAYER

Jesus our Brother, be with us as we learn about your Church's past. Help us remember that we are united with Christians in every time and place.

You have a history. The story of your life begins long before your birth. Your personal history goes back through all your family's generations. It goes back to the earliest *ancestors* anyone can remember.

As a Catholic you have an even greater history. You are part of the story of the Church. The Church's history goes back before its birth, too. It is a story thousands of years long. It takes place in every country on earth.

The Church's history really begins with the people of Israel. Their story is told in the Old Testament of the Bible. It is our story, too. It is a story of how God shows his love for humans and for the world he created.

Jesus and his first followers were Jews, the people of Israel. The Church was born in the Jewish *synagogues*, or religious meeting places. There Jesus preached and taught and prayed.

The first Christians gathered in homes and synagogues. In time some of these were made into churches.

150 : WE ARE INVITED

Resource Center

Link to Liturgy
The Eucharistic Prayer of the Mass is the prayer of the whole Church that recalls the story of Jesus' life, death, and resurrection. It remembers Church members who have died as well as those throughout the world who are living. In Eucharistic Prayer I we celebrate the Church's connection to the Israelites by asking God to accept our gifts as he once accepted the offerings of Abraham, our father in faith.

Teaching Tip
Making connections Remind the class that the Jesse tree is a "family tree" showing the Church's ancestors. If you used a Jesse tree during Advent, use its ornaments now to help the students recall stories about some of our ancestors in faith.

Notes: Opening the Chapter

150 : Chapter 25

Landmark During times of persecution in Rome, Christians met secretly in underground tombs called **catacombs**. They sometimes celebrated Mass using the tomb of a martyr as an altar.

After Jesus returned to his Father, his friends and followers continued to meet at the synagogues for Jewish prayer. But they also gathered in their homes to celebrate the Eucharist. Gradually the good news of Jesus spread to people who were not Jews. These *Gentiles* were baptized. The followers of Christ became known as *Christians*. They no longer saw themselves as Jews, but as a new people, the Church.

Christians brought their faith to other lands throughout the Roman Empire. The Church came to be known as *catholic*, or universal.

The early years of the Church were not easy. There were times of *persecution*, when Christians were punished by *imprisonment* or death. But even in hard times, the followers of Jesus remembered his words "And behold, I am with you always. . . ."

—Matthew 28:20

Scripture Signpost

"Jesus Christ is the same yesterday, today, and forever."
Hebrews 13:8

Why is it important to learn about Christians of the past?

WE ARE INVITED : 151

WE ARE INVITED
Open *Continued*
Working with the Text

- As you continue to read the text aloud, focus first on how the followers of Jesus became known as Christians. **Where does the word *Christian* come from?** (the word *Christ*)

- Be sure the students understand that people who are not Jewish are called *Gentiles*.

- Explain that some people did not want to hear the good news about Jesus. They made laws against the practice of the Christian faith. These were hard times for the early Church. Be sure the students understand that the term *persecution* means "to treat in a cruel or harsh way because of one's beliefs or ideas." Explain that *imprisonment* means "to be kept in jail or prison."

- Remind the class that Jesus promised to be with his followers always. That promise gave the first Christians comfort and hope through hard times.

Working with the Pictures

Direct the students' attention to the photograph that shows an underground room in the catacombs that the early Christians of Rome used for burial.

Landmark Read the caption aloud. Remind the students that a *martyr* is a faithful witness to Jesus who dies for his or her faith. If time permits, share the information about the catacombs from *The Language of Faith* below.

Scripture Signpost Read the Scripture passage aloud. Invite responses to the question. (The followers of Jesus in all times and all places believed the same things we believe. They are our Christian ancestors in faith.)

The Language of Faith

The **catacombs** were a network of underground tunnels built by the Romans for waterworks. After the waterworks were abandoned, the tunnels began to be used for burials. The dead were placed on ledges along both sides of the narrow walkways. The catacombs were used as cemeteries until the early fifth century.

Scripture Background

- In **Matthew 28:20** Jesus promises to be with his Church, echoing God's covenants with Abraham and with Moses **(Genesis 12:1–9)**. Through these words Jesus connects the apostolic Church with its ancestors, the people of Israel.

- The author of **Hebrews 13:8** tells Christians not to lose faith because their original Church leaders have died. Instead, Christians are to imitate the faith of these leaders, for Christ still lives in the Church and always remains the same.

Link to the Faith Community

Explain that the Church in Rome initially consisted mostly of people who were poor. However, by the third century a number of wealthy people had also converted to Christianity. Their large homes became the first Church centers. Large numbers of Christians could gather in these centers to celebrate the Eucharist and the sacraments, receive religious instruction, and assist those in need. Today some groups of parishioners still meet in one another's homes for prayer or Scripture study. Find out if your parish has such groups. If it does, ask a representative to visit your class and explain what his or her group does.

WE EXPLORE
2. Build
Working with the Text
- Read aloud *The Church Through Time*; then read the bulleted question. Invite volunteers to respond. **(Responses will vary but may include questions about the first churches in America.)**
- Remind the students that *we* are the Church but that church buildings can teach us much about our Church family. For example, the name of the church will remind us of Jesus, Mary, or a specific saint; if the church has stained-glass windows, they might depict stories about Jesus, Mary, and other saints who are in our Church family.
- **Catholics Believe** Read the statement aloud. Remind the students that God is always with the Church, from one generation to another.

Working with the Pictures
- Invite the students to study the pictures of the churches carefully. **How are the churches alike?** (bell towers, crosses, arches, and so on)
- Point out that the differences between the churches tell about the times in which they were built and the people who built them.
- Read aloud or invite volunteers to read the captions. You may want to share the information about the church buildings in *Art Background* below. Refer to *The Language of Faith* to discuss the term *cathedral*.

Catholics Believe...
the "family of God" is formed according to God's plan through the years of human history.

Catechism, #759

The Church Through Time
The Church is not a building. The Church is people gathered to worship God and to follow Jesus. But we can learn a lot about the history of the Church by looking at church buildings. The picture story on these pages shows some snapshots from the history of the Church in many lands.

- What time or place in the Church's history would you like to know more about?

The finest artists and craftspeople in Europe designed and built great churches called cathedrals. A **cathedral** is the home church of a bishop. *Cathedra* means "bishop's chair." Cathedrals like this one in France took hundreds of years to complete.

The Church came to the American Southwest with Spanish missionaries like Blessed Junipero Serra and Padre Eusebio Kino. This mission church in Arizona is known as "the white dove of the desert." Its walls are made of mud bricks called *adobe*.

152 : WE EXPLORE

Resource Center

The Language of Faith
A **cathedral** is literally the church in each diocese in which the bishop's chair is present. The chair, which is reserved for the bishop when he presides at liturgy, is a symbol of his authority.

Link to the Family
In recent times Church leaders have described the Christian family as "the domestic Church" or "Church of the home." We learn how to be Church, the family of Jesus, through our own families. Brainstorm with the students some practical ways that loving family members can be "Church" to one another. Help the class see that such relationships include patience and forgiveness, concern for one another, and the willingness to help and protect one another.

Art Background
- The Church of San Xavier del Bac (hahv•YAIR dail BAHK) is located just south of Tucson, Arizona. The mission, which is a graceful blend of Moorish, Byzantine, and late Mexican Renaissance architectures, was built between 1783 and 1797 by the Tohono O'ohdam Indians (Papagos).
- Chartres (SHAHR•truh) Cathedral, a magnificent Gothic church, was built over the ruins of an eleventh-century cathedral that had been destroyed by fire. Another fire necessitated further building, which accounts for the different styles in the two spires.

Saints Walk with Us

Saint Bede
Feast Day: May 25

Saint Bede was a British monk who wrote a history of the Church in England. Although he included many legends, much of what we know about early Christianity comes from Bede's book.

Saint Bede is the patron saint of Church historians.

When Rome was attacked by raiders from the north, Christians in Ireland and Scotland kept the gospel message alive in monasteries like this. Saints like Patrick, Brigid, Kevin, and Columba carried on the Church's mission.

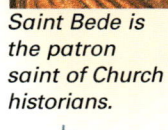

The Christians of Ethiopia were the first Africans outside of Egypt to follow Jesus. Ethiopian Catholic churches and liturgies include a mix of Egyptian, Syrian, and Jewish traditions.

WE EXPLORE : 153

WE EXPLORE
Build *Continued*

Working with the Pictures

- Draw the students' attention to the top left photograph, which shows the interior of a church in Ireland. Have volunteers describe the interior and compare it with their own parish church.

- Read this photograph's caption aloud. If time permits, use the information in *Background* below to increase the students' knowledge of the saints mentioned.

- Have the class look carefully at the other church pictured on this page. Read the caption aloud.

Saints Walk with Us Read the text aloud. Invite a volunteer to describe Saint Bede to the rest of the class. **Why do you think the Church has honored Saint Bede as the patron saint of Church historians?** (He wrote the history of the Church in England.) Tell the students that Saint Bede the Venerable (673–735) was a scholarly priest who wrote *Ecclesiastical History of the English People* (c. 731). He also wrote descriptions of the Church as God's kingdom and family, based on Old Testament passages about kings.

Background

- **Saints Patrick** (390–461), **Brigid** (450–525), **Kevin** (d. 618), and **Columba** (521–597) are associated with the Irish Church, although Patrick was a British missionary to Ireland and Columba evangelized the Picts of Scotland.

- **Blessed Junipero Serra** (1713–1784), a Franciscan, established nine missions in what would later become California. **Padre Eusebio Kino** (1645–1711), a Swiss-born Jesuit, worked among the native peoples of northern Mexico. He established missions in what would later become Arizona and New Mexico.

Catechism Background

For more information about the Church's history, you may wish to read *Catechism of the Catholic Church* (#758–769).

Notes: Building the Chapter

PARISH : 153

WE REFLECT
Review

Recall Invite responses to the questions. (Old Testament; underground tombs in Rome where Christians gathered in times of persecution)

Think and Share Ask the students to think carefully about their responses before answering. (faith in God, belief in Jesus, sacraments, worship, Scripture, a desire to serve others)

Continue the Journey In discussing the question, look for an understanding of Church as a family of people who worship together and help one another. Be sure the students write the current year below their drawings.

Alternative Allow the students to complete their drawings at home this week. Provide time at the beginning of the next session to comment on their work and to have volunteers explain their drawings.

We Live Our Faith *At Home:* Invite volunteers to bring their family histories to the next session to share with the rest of the class. Encourage the students to ask their family members for help in this assignment. *In the Parish:* Before the next session, find out some basic historical dates and events of your parish, and begin the next session by sharing your information with the class.

Faith Journal The students may begin pages 49–50 of their *Faith Journal* in class and complete them at home. As part of your own spiritual development, complete *Your Faith Journal* (page J26) for this chapter.

RECALL
Where do we find the history of the people of Israel? What are catacombs?

THINK AND SHARE
What are some things we have in common with members of the Church in all times and places?

CONTINUE THE JOURNEY
Draw your parish church. Fill in today's date on the frame. What do you think Catholics in the future could learn about your faith community from seeing a picture of your church?

CATHOLICS IN THE YEAR _____

WE LIVE OUR FAITH

At Home Make a book or tape of your family history with help from other family members.

In the Parish Learn about the history of your parish. When did it begin? Who are the people it has served through the years?

154 : WE REFLECT

Resource Center

Assessment Tip
As the students progress through this chapter, look for a growing appreciation of the Church's history as well as an understanding that we can learn from people who have preceded us in faith.

Link to Justice
Numerous Church documents have spoken out about the dignity of people in all lands and the need to respect and learn from different cultures. The Church is truly catholic, or universal, which also means that the Church is multicultural. Christians are called to accept all people as family members in Christ and to reach out to include them. Explain that as Church we are to support multicultural education, social events, and liturgies.

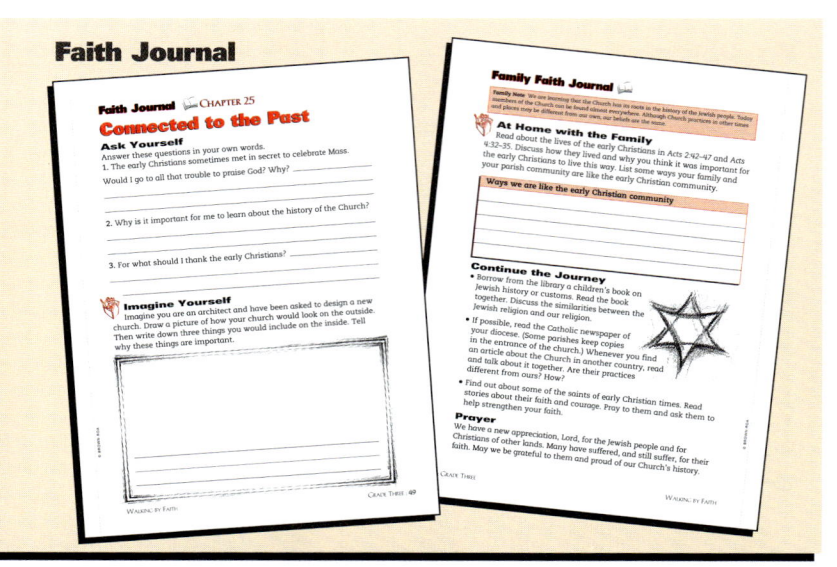

We Are Your People

Many great saints lived during the early years of the Church. Some of them are mentioned in the First Eucharistic Prayer. Saint Clement was a pope and martyr. This prayer is based on one that he wrote. Pray with your classmates.

PRAYER

We beg you, Lord, to help and defend us.
Raise those who have fallen,
show yourself to the needy,
heal the sick, feed the hungry,
lift up the weak,
and take off prisoners' chains.
May every nation realize
that you are God,
that Jesus Christ is
your Child,
and that we are your
people. Amen.

WE CELEBRATE
3. Close

Working with the Pictures

- Draw the students' attention to the ancient map in the background. Explain that the Christian message has spread to almost all parts of the world.
- Draw the students' attention to the picture of the children with their arms raised.
  What do you think the children are doing? (singing, praying) **How do they remind you of the Church?** (The Church is made up of people who pray together.)
- Tell the students that the bottom picture is a painting found in a catacomb in Rome. See *Art Background* below for more information to share with the students.

Working with the Text

Read aloud *We Are Your People*. Explain that the Eucharistic Prayer is prayed between the Preparation of Gifts (Offertory) and the Lord's Prayer at Mass. If time permits, share the information about Saint Clement in *Profile* below.

Prayer Display a globe and a cross. Remind the students that our faith connects us to people throughout the world. When we pray, we join our prayers with the prayers of every person of faith, living and dead. Then invite the students to raise their arms high above their heads or in front of them as you pray the prayer aloud. Have the students repeat each line after you. Conclude the prayer celebration by singing a familiar hymn.

Art Background
The woman with outstretched hands and palms up (the attitude of prayer known as the *orante*) is the central figure in a fresco called *The Veiling* that covers the back wall of a small room in the Catacombs of Priscilla in Rome. The figure, which shows a woman's soul in eternal glory, dates from the second half of the third century.

Background
Saint Clement (d. 101) was the fourth pope, serving from 91 to 101. His feast day is November 23.

Link to the Family
To keep family members involved with what the students are learning in this unit, copy and distribute the Unit Seven Family Letter from the Resource Package.

Notes: Closing the Chapter

Getting Ready: Chapter 26

The Church Today

Program Resources
Student Text, pp. 156–161
Student Faith Journal, pp. 51–52
Your Faith Journal, p. J27
Chapter 26 Transparency
Unit Seven Music and Liturgy Resources

Unit Seven (Salvation History)
Yesterday, Today, and Tomorrow

Key Content Summary
The Church offers us guidance for meeting the problems of today.

Planning the Chapter

	Pacing Guide Suggested time/Your time	Content	Objectives	Materials
Open	10–15 min./ _____ min.	*We Are Invited*, p. 156	• Give examples of ways the Church is called to make the world better.	• Bibles
Build	20–25 min./ _____ min.	*We Explore*, pp. 157–158	• Describe the Church's role in hastening God's kingdom.	• world map or globe
		Stepping Stones, p. 159	• Explore practical steps for giving witness to God's kingdom.	• Chapter 26 Transparency from the Resource Package • copies of a local newspaper
Review	15–20 min./ _____ min.	*We Reflect*, p. 160	• Demonstrate understanding of chapter concepts. • Apply learning through activity. • Practice faith at home and in the parish.	• drawing materials • copies of parish bulletin • *Student Faith Journal*, pp. 51–52 • *Your Faith Journal*, p. J27
Close	10–15 min./ _____ min.	*We Celebrate*, p. 161	• Develop the gift of imagination in helping solve the world's problems.	• Unit Seven Music and Liturgy Resources from the Resource Package

For additional suggestions, see Scheduling, pp. T35–T37.

Catechism in Context

Doctrinal Foundation This chapter discusses the Church as it exists in the world today. Those of us who are alive at this moment belong to the communion of saints, which includes those who have "gone before us marked with the sign of faith." We are in communion with all believers who have walked this earth in the past; we have a relationship with them. United with them, we face the problems and crises of this world. Strengthened by their example, we try to apply the message of the gospel to these problems and crises. Fortified by their prayers, we strive to be signs of the kingdom of God established by Jesus Christ.

We who make up the Church on earth have long been called the "Church Militant." This phrase does not mean that we are warlike or aggressive, but that we are actively engaged in the struggle against evil and for good. We are bold in our proclamation of the good news and brave in our fight for justice and our efforts for peace.

See Catechism of the Catholic Church, #2046.

One-Minute Retreat for Catechists

Read

"If you do not wish God's kingdom, don't pray for it. But if you do, you must do more than pray for it; you must work for it."

—John Ruskin

Reflect

How am I working for God's kingdom?

Pray

Through your grace and mercy, O Lord, you give me the strength to witness to my faith in you. Help me rely on your strength so that I may work with love to make things better for those around me and thus help bring your kingdom in its fullness.

Visualizing the Lesson

Use this graphic organizer to help the students visualize the practical steps they can take to live their faith every day.

Redraw the graphic organizer on a sheet of paper, omitting the steps. Distribute copies to the students, and have them fill in the steps as you work with page 159.

Steps for Giving Witness

- **I** Get **I**nformation.
- **W** Know the **W**ords of Jesus.
- **I** Pray for **I**deas.
- **T** **T**hink of a plan.
- **N** **N**ote what others say.
- **E** **E**nact your plan.
- **S** **S**eek others' help.
- **S** Be **S**trong.

Library Links

Books for Children

Thistle by Walter Wangerin Jr. (Cokesbury Good Books, 1-800-672-1789).

This parable about a young girl who saves her family shows the power of compassion.

Books for Parents and Teachers

The Church Today: Believing and Belonging from the Catholic Home Library series by Anthony Padovano (Franciscan Communications, 1-800-488-0488).

This book gives an in-depth explanation of the faith and traditions of the Catholic Church today.

Multimedia

For children:

Making Peace produced by Jan Phillips (multimedia slide show) (Sheed & Ward, 1-800-333-7373).

People around the world are shown celebrating the unity and diversity we share as a human family.

For parents and teachers:

Needle's Eye produced by Paulist Productions/Insight Films (video) (Paulist Press, 1-800-218-1903).

Two friends struggle with the dream of the good life and the reality of suffering in the world.

Organizations

For information about the Church working in other parts of the world today, contact:

Maryknoll
Catholic Foreign Mission Society of America
Maryknoll, NY 10545
(1-914-941-7590)
(http://www.maryknoll.org/society)

Strengthening the Family Link

Here are some suggestions for reaching out to your students' families:

- Encourage the students to talk with family members about sharing the good news of Jesus every day through their words and actions.
- Invite family members to join the class in discussing ways to give witness to our faith. (See *Practice* on page 159.)

Chapter 26 pages 156–161

Objectives
- Give examples of the ways the Church is called to make the world better.
- Describe the Church's role in hastening God's kingdom.
- Explore practical steps for giving witness to God's kingdom.

Gathering WE ARE INVITED
1. Open

Personal Experience Invite the students to join you in devising a class list of some of today's problems, such as violence, drugs, and homelessness.

Prayer Tell the students that we can always ask the Holy Spirit to help us solve the world's problems. Pray the opening prayer together.

Working with the Text
- Read the text aloud, or invite several volunteers to read the text as a dialogue.
- Read the bulleted question aloud, and invite the class to respond. **(Accept all reasonable responses.)**

Working with the Pictures
- Invite a volunteer to describe some ways peace is shown in the picture. **(Accept all reasonable answers.)** If time permits, share the information in *Art Background* below.
- Read the caption aloud. Before reading *Isaiah 11:1–9* aloud, ask the students to listen to what the prophet tells us we should do for the world.
  What are we as Church called to do?
  (love others; live in peace)
- Share information in *Scripture Background* below.

Resource Center

Scripture Background
Isaiah 11:1–9 describes the loving relationships between all creatures in the peaceful kingdom of God. God's kingdom will be ruled by a leader filled with the wisdom and power of God's spirit.

Art Background
The Peaceable Kingdom was painted by Edward Hicks (1780–1849), an American preacher. In the foreground the wild beasts, the domestic animals that ordinarily would be their prey, and the children live together in peace. In the background William Penn signs a treaty with indigenous peoples. The message is clear: In God's kingdom all creatures will live in peace and love.

CHAPTER 26
The Church Today

PRAYER
God of wisdom, help your Church find solutions to the world's problems. Send your Spirit to guide and inspire us.

"Imagine you have the power to solve just one problem in the world," Sister Lorraine said. "Which problem would you choose?"

The members of the third-grade religion class were silent for a minute. Then they started to call out suggestions.

"I would end wars," Ernesto said.

"I would make sure nobody was poor," Anna said.

Other students named other problems. "Guns." "Drugs." "Gangs."

"I'd find a way to cure cancer or AIDS," said Lauren.

"I would make people get along and not hate each other because of their race or the way they talk," said Ian.

● Which problem would you solve?

This artist's view of a world without problems is based on a vision of the prophet Isaiah (Isaiah 11:1–9). Read these words to find out what we as Church are called to do.

156 : WE ARE INVITED

Notes: Opening the Chapter

Right Here, Right Now

Our world has many problems. And no person has the power to end even one of these problems overnight. But every time we try to change things for the better, we get a little hint of the kingdom of God in its fullness. Every time we feed a hungry person, or stop a fight, or give someone hope, we are sharing the good news of Jesus.

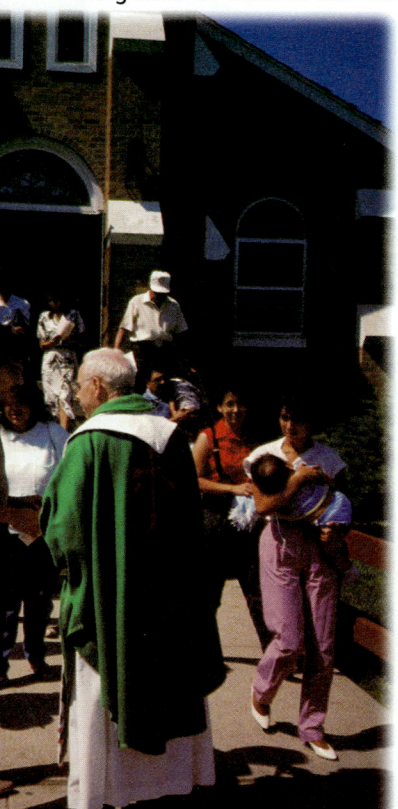

Some people think religion is only about the faraway past or some future heaven. Those people don't understand. We live in the present. Right here, right now is the only chance we get to be the Church.

Being Catholic is not just something we do on Sunday mornings. We are called to work for God's reign of justice, love, and peace in every minute of every day.

Catholics Believe...
that the kingdom of God in its fullness will come more quickly when we work with love to make the present better for everyone.
Catechism, #2046

At the end of Mass, we are sent forth to make a difference in the world. The words of the dismissal remind us: "Go in peace to love and serve the Lord."

WE EXPLORE : 157

WE EXPLORE
2. Build
Working with the Text

- Read aloud *Right Here, Right Now*. Emphasize that the Church is called to be a leader in working for solutions to the world's problems. Because *we* are the Church, we must be signs of the kingdom of God in our world *today*.
- Share some examples of people at home, in the neighborhood, or in the community who are working for a better world. Invite the students to do the same. Ask them to take notice of other examples in everyday life of people who take time to make a difference.

Working with the Pictures

- Invite a volunteer to identify what is shown in the picture. (people leaving church after Mass) How are the people in the picture living their faith? (They worship and pray at church, they greet one another, they try to be good parents and children, and so on.)
- Read the caption aloud. How can we be signs of God's kingdom when we leave church and go home to our families, our neighborhoods, and our schools? (by loving and helping others, by being friendly)

  Catholics Believe Read the statement aloud. Emphasize that we cannot make the world perfect, but we can help make it better.

Teaching Tip
Clarifying concepts Explain that we need God's help to make the world a more just and peaceful place. God gives us this help through the Holy Spirit and through the support of other Church members. It is God who brings the kingdom.

Link to the Family
Have the students brainstorm practical actions they can take to make life better for their family members. Some examples are helping them with chores, not fighting with them, and saying "please" and "thank you." Emphasize that when we do these things, we act as Church and are signs of God's kingdom on earth.

Notes: Building the Chapter

PARISH : 157

We Explore
Build *Continued*

Working with the Text

- Read aloud *People of the Kingdom*. Use *The Language of Faith* below to clarify the meanings of the highlighted terms. **Why is it important that we follow the example of Jesus?** (We need to act on our faith and help others in the world.)
- Tell the students that the following groups work every day to help solve world problems: Pax Christi (which works to end wars), Amnesty International (which protects human rights around the world), and the Society of St. Vincent de Paul (which helps those who are poor). Explain that when we join together with others, we can help hasten God's kingdom.
- Remind the students that we are the Body of Christ. That makes all people our brothers and sisters, regardless of their race, religion, or nationality.
- **Saints Walk with Us** Read the text about Jean Donovan aloud. It might be helpful to bring a world map or globe to the session so the class can see where El Salvador is located in relation to the United States. If time permits, share the information in *Profile* below.

Working with the Pictures

- Draw the students' attention to the large picture. Invite a volunteer to describe what is shown. (Catholic volunteers providing health care to mothers and their children)
- Tell the students that there are many Catholic volunteer groups who work with people in this country and in countries around the world, trying to bring God's kingdom into its fullness. Some of those groups are the Medical Missionary Sisters, Maryknoll, and Glenmary Home Missioners.

Saints Walk with Us
Jean Donovan

Jean was a lay missionary from the United States who worked with poor children in El Salvador. She shared her gifts of laughter, music, and love with them. She gave them hope that their future would be better.

Jean Donovan and three religious sisters were killed for living their Catholic faith. We remember their courage and example.

People of the Kingdom

The mission of the Church in today's world is to share the good news of the kingdom of God. When we do this, we make our world better today. We give people hope for the future. And we **witness** to, or show clearly by our actions, God's lasting justice, love, and peace.

As the Church we work together to solve all the problems listed by Sister Lorraine's class. We work to end war and violence between individuals and nations. We work for the basic human rights of every person. We care for those who are poor, ill, and lonely.

We do all these things because we follow the example of Jesus. We do them because all people, especially those most in need, are our sisters and brothers. This belief that we are all united in one family of God is called **solidarity**.

Catholic volunteers help care for our brothers and sisters around the world.

Resource Center

The Language of Faith

- To **witness** means to act on one's religious beliefs. All Christians are called to witness to the gospel and its values of justice, peace, and love. We give witness whenever we do works of mercy and follow Jesus' command to love others.
- **Solidarity**, or oneness with others, is a Christian virtue that calls for the sharing of both spiritual and material goods. We care about others as members of God's family.

Profile

Jean Donovan (1953–1980) This lay volunteer worked tirelessly with Sisters Dorothy Kazal, Maura Clarke, and Ita Ford to provide people in El Salvador with food, clothing, medical care, and hope. The four women were killed by a government-backed death squad because some powerful people in El Salvador did not want missionaries to help those who were poor join together and work for a better life.

Stepping Stones

Giving Witness

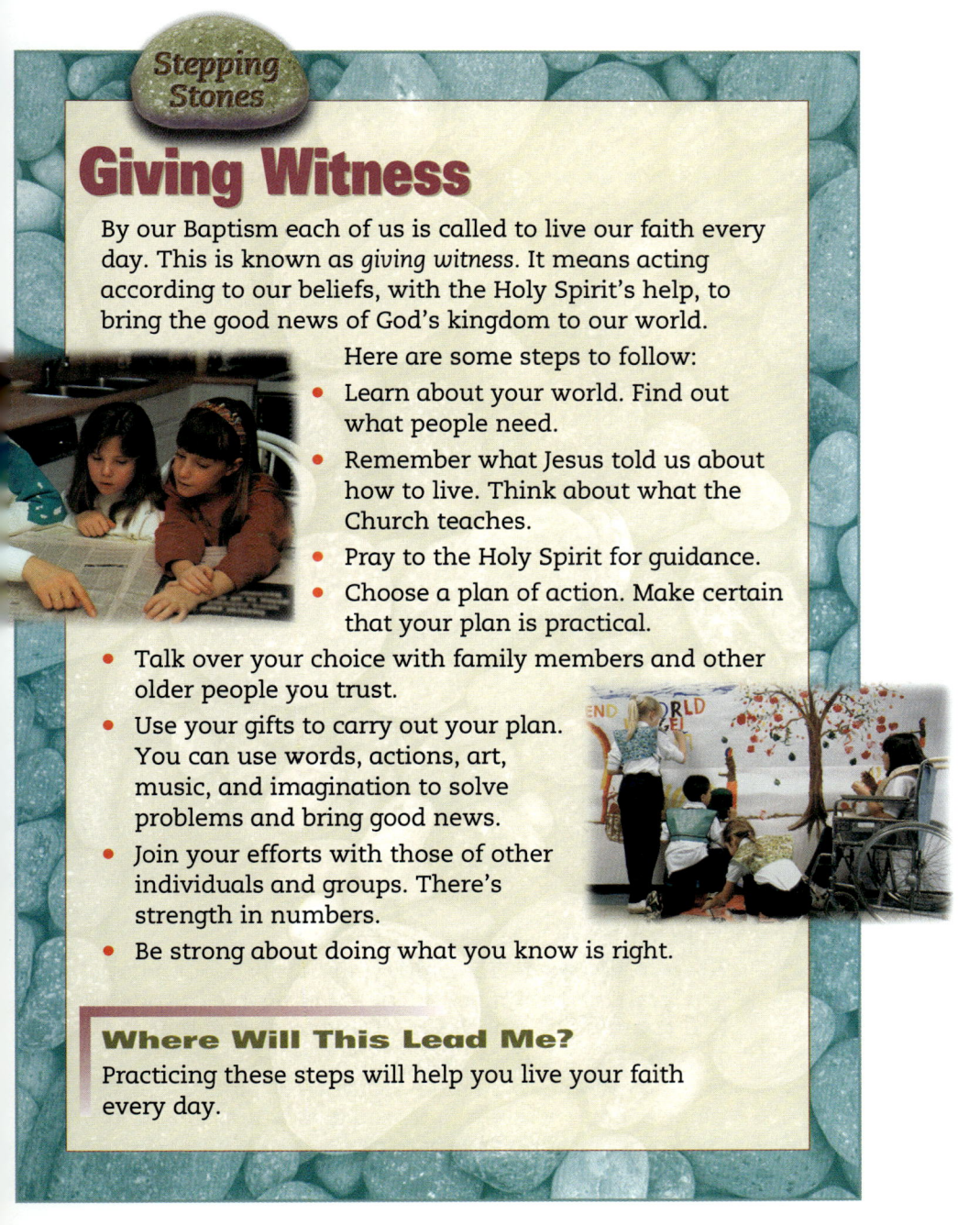

By our Baptism each of us is called to live our faith every day. This is known as *giving witness*. It means acting according to our beliefs, with the Holy Spirit's help, to bring the good news of God's kingdom to our world.

Here are some steps to follow:

- Learn about your world. Find out what people need.
- Remember what Jesus told us about how to live. Think about what the Church teaches.
- Pray to the Holy Spirit for guidance.
- Choose a plan of action. Make certain that your plan is practical.
- Talk over your choice with family members and other older people you trust.
- Use your gifts to carry out your plan. You can use words, actions, art, music, and imagination to solve problems and bring good news.
- Join your efforts with those of other individuals and groups. There's strength in numbers.
- Be strong about doing what you know is right.

Where Will This Lead Me?

Practicing these steps will help you live your faith every day.

WE EXPLORE : 159

WE EXPLORE
Build *Continued*
Stepping Stones
Working with the Text

- Read the text, and answer any questions the students may have.
- To help the students remember the eight steps in giving witness, use the graphic organizer on page 155B. You may want to do the suggested activity or one of your own.

Working with the Pictures

- Draw the students' attention to the photograph on the left.
  Which step in giving witness are the girls practicing? (the first step, learning about their world)
- Have the class look at the second picture.
  What are the students in this picture doing? (making other people aware of a problem)
- **Practice** If time permits, distribute copies of a local newspaper, or invite a parishioner to speak to the class about local needs. (See *Link to the Faith Community* below.) Guide the students in selecting needs that they can do something about. Encourage the students to ask their families for help in practicing the witnessing steps this week. At the beginning of the next session, ask the students to describe how they practiced the steps of giving witness.

Background

Some of the first Christian witnesses of God's kingdom were martyrs—people who died for their faith. (*Martyr* is the Latin word for "witness.") While martyrdom is the ultimate way to give witness to one's faith, the Church today emphasizes the call of all Christians to give witness to the gospel through daily living.

Link to the Faith Community

Most parishes have committees that actively work to meet community needs. For example, parishioners may work with a social justice committee, condolence committee, soup kitchen, food pantry, or homeless shelter. Find out how the students could help out with these ministries. Make that information available to interested volunteers in the class.

We Reflect
Review

Recall Invite the students to respond to the questions. (the belief that we are all united in one family of God; to act according to our beliefs, with the Holy Spirit's help)

Think and Share Allow sufficient time for the students to consider their answers before you call on volunteers to respond. (Jesus said to love others; all people in the world are our brothers and sisters; following Jesus' example of caring for the needs of those around us shows our faith in God and hope in his kingdom.)

Continue the Journey Let the students work individually or in pairs. Ask volunteers to show and explain their drawings.

Alternative Have the students work on a class mural over the course of the next few sessions. Provide some time during each of those sessions for the students to add to their mural. When the mural is completed, ask permission to display it in the parish hall or center.

We Live Our Faith *At Home:* Encourage the students by sharing with them some ideas you and your family will consider this week. *In the Parish:* Provide copies of the parish bulletin, or arrange for an involved parishoner to address the class.

Faith Journal The students may begin pages 51–52 of their *Faith Journal* in class and complete them at home. As part of your own spiritual development, complete *Your Faith Journal* (page J27) for this chapter.

Recall
What is solidarity? What does it mean to give witness?

Think and Share
Why should the Church be concerned with the problems of this world?

Continue the Journey
Draw your vision of a world without problems. How does your picture give witness to the kingdom of God?

We Live Our Faith
At Home Talk with your family about what you can do to meet the needs of people in your community. Choose one thing to do together this week.

In the Parish Find out how your parish helps people live their faith and give witness to the kingdom of God every day.

160 : We Reflect

Resource Center

Link to Justice
Explain to the students that in their pastoral letter *Brothers and Sisters to Us*, the U.S. bishops speak of the racial solidarity to which Christ calls us. We are challenged to treat others with justice and fairness, regardless of their race. We are also challenged to help those of all races who lack life's necessities, since they are our brothers and sisters.

Multicultural Link (Optional Activity)
Encourage the students to read about one of the following Catholics and how he or she witnessed to the gospel: Pierre Toussaint, Kateri Tekakwitha, Lorenzo Ruiz, Henriette Delille, Andrew Dung-Lac, or Andrew Kim.

Renew the Earth

One of the best gifts that we bring to the task of solving the world's problems is our imagination. We can ask the Holy Spirit to *inspire* us, or fill us with creative energy.

Guided meditation is a way to pray using our imagination. Your teacher will lead you in a guided meditation. Then form two groups and pray this prayer to the Holy Spirit.

PRAYER

1: Come, Holy Spirit, fill our hearts.

2: Let the fire of your love burn in us.

1: God our Father, send us your Spirit and we will be a new creation.

2: And you will renew the earth.

WE CELEBRATE

3. Close

Working with the Pictures

Ask the students to study the three photographs carefully.
What is the same about all of these photographs? (all deal with peace and love, are images of God's kingdom, and so on)

Working with the Text

- Read aloud *Renew the Earth*. Explain that *inspire* means "to breathe in"—to be filled with new ideas, hope, and energy.

- If time permits, lead the students in the guided meditation given below or another of your choice. Keep the meditation time short for children of this age.

Prayer Divide the class into two groups. Ask the students to close their eyes and imagine themselves with Jesus in a beautiful place. After a few minutes, lead the two groups in praying the prayer to the Holy Spirit. End the prayer celebration with a familiar hymn or the Sign of the Cross.

Enrichment

Guided meditation Invite the students to meditate with their eyes closed, like the students shown in the photograph. Read aloud the following meditation: *Imagine that you are inside on a cold, stormy day. Now you hear a knock on the door. Your friend Jesus has come and invites you to walk outside with him. "I have something to show you," he says. You follow him outside. The storm begins to clear. Everything is calm and peaceful and happy. Jesus says, "The world becomes like this each time you witness to your faith." He asks, "Will you witness to love and peace each day?" You nod your head yes. Then you walk with Jesus through the rest of the day.*

Music and Liturgy Resources

To enhance your prayer and celebration, you may wish to use the Unit Seven Music and Liturgy Resources from the Resource Package.

Notes: Closing the Chapter

Getting Ready: Chapter 27

Hope for the Future

Program Resources
Student Text, pp. 162–167
Student Faith Journal, pp. 53–54
Your Faith Journal, p. J28
Chapter 27 Transparency
Unit Seven Assessment

Unit Seven (Salvation History)
Yesterday, Today, and Tomorrow

Key Content Summary
The Church will meet the challenges of the future.

Planning the Chapter

	Pacing Guide Suggested time/Your time	Content	Objectives	Materials
Open	10–15 min./ _____ min.	We Are Invited, pp. 162–163	• Explain why Christians always have hope for the future.	
Build	20–25 min./ _____ min.	We Explore, pp. 164–165	• Explore the Church's teaching about Jesus' second coming and the last judgment. • Realize that Jesus is always present.	• art materials or premade Alpha and Omega symbols and tape or safety pins • missalettes (optional) • Bibles (optional) • Chapter 27 Transparency from the Resource Package
Review	15–20 min./ _____ min.	We Reflect, p. 166	• Demonstrate understanding of chapter concepts. • Apply learning through activity. • Practice faith at home and in the parish.	• *Student Faith Journal*, pp. 53–54 • *Your Faith Journal*, p. J28 • missalettes (optional) • Unit Seven Assessment from the Resource Package
Close	10–15 min./ _____ min.	We Celebrate, p. 167	• Summarize what has been learned in religion class this year.	• rhythm instruments

For additional suggestions, see Scheduling, pp. T35–T37.

Catechism in Context

Doctrinal Foundation This chapter discusses the future to which we are called. Jesus Christ promised his disciples—including us today—a glorious future in his kingdom, which will have no end. That kingdom has already begun on earth, although it is not yet complete. When it is complete, there will be a new heaven and a new earth. We are promised a share in Christ's reign over this kingdom and a place at the table of his heavenly banquet. "How blessed are they who are called to the wedding feast of the Lamb." His promise gives rise to our hope.

See Catechism of the Catholic Church, #1042.

Our faith is grounded in God's mighty deeds for his people throughout history, and our love in his love for us. So, too, our hope is rooted in his promises, for he is trustworthy and we know that he will keep his word. Our hope in the future and in God's promises must be kept pure and undefiled by the two great sins against hope—presumption and despair. When we do not live up to our responsibilities but put God to the test, expecting him to do our part, then we presume that he will be merciful. When we try to do it all, to save ourselves, we fail, and failing, we despair when we should let God help us. By keeping our eyes fixed on Jesus, we can stay on the road of hope and arrive one day at our goal.

One-Minute Retreat for Catechists

Read
"I live on hope and that, I think, do all
Who come into this world."
—Robert Bridges

Reflect
How does hope affect my life decisions?

Pray
Lord, help me have hope. As I confront misfortune, remind me that all problems are temporary. Give me the wisdom to see that hope is often born out of suffering.

Visualizing the Lesson

Use this graphic organizer to help the students visualize the Church's good news about the future.

Redraw the graphic organizer on the board or on chart paper. Have the students use the drawing to explain how our actions and God's judgment will affect the life of the world to come. **How do we receive God's judgment?** (through Jesus) **Why should we look forward to God's judgment?** (because we will be invited to everlasting life with God if we have lived good lives and asked God's forgiveness when we failed)

```
From:
God
God's Kingdom                    Jesus

         To: All People
             P.O. Box 777
             Earth
```

God's Judgment

Library Links

Books for Children
You and God: Friends Forever by Francine O'Connor (Liguori Publications, 1-800-325-9521).

This book tells of the relationship with God and inspires children in the ways of the Catholic faith.

Books for Parents and Teachers
Called and Gifted for the Third Millennium (USCC Publishing Services, 1-800-235-8722).

The laity of the Catholic Church is asked to accept the call of holiness, community, ministry, and Christian maturity.

God Will Tell You Stories by Jane Wolford Hughes (St. Mary's Press, 1-800-533-8095).

Inspirational stories can be found in everyday news.

Multimedia
For children:
God Blessed Me. Episode #1, "Psalm 139" produced by the Archdiocese of St. Paul-Minneapolis (video) (BROWN-ROA, 1-800-922-7696).

As a mime performs the psalm, he becomes more aware of God's knowledge of him and closes with an exuberant acceptance of God's guidance.

For parents and teachers:
Reign of God with Father Richard Rohr (video) (Paulist Press, 1-800-218-1903).

Responding to our loving God is more authentic if we open ourselves to the message of the gospel.

Strengthening the Family Link

Here are some suggestions for reaching out to your students' families:

- Encourage the students to talk with family members about hope for the second coming of Jesus.
- Invite family members to join the class in making the *Alpha* and *Omega* badges suggested in the activity on page 165. Talk about the meaning and significance of the *Alpha* and *Omega* symbols. After making the badges, pray the closing prayer, and encourage volunteers to add their own verses to the litany.

PARISH : 161B

Chapter 27 pages 162–167

Objectives
- Explain why Christians always have hope for the future.
- Explore the Church's teaching about Jesus' second coming and the last judgment.
- Realize that Jesus is always present.

Gathering WE ARE INVITED
1. Open

Personal Experience Ask the students to think about movies, cartoons, or television shows that tell about the future.

Prayer Point out that we have hope for the future because we believe that God has been with us in the past, is with us now in the present, and will continue to be with us in the future. Then pray the opening prayer together.

Working with the Text
- Read the opening question aloud. Invite volunteers to share their ideas about the future.
- Read the text aloud. Encourage the students to focus on *positive* possibilities.
  What is the good news that the Church brings? (Possible answers: God loves us and will always be with us; we are called to be happy with God forever.)

Working with the Pictures
- Invite the students to look carefully at the artist's drawing of a space shuttle docked at a space station high above the earth.
- Read the caption question aloud. (Accept all reasonable responses.)

CHAPTER 27
Hope for the Future

PRAYER
Lord Jesus, you will come in glory at the end of time. Help your Church live in love and hope now so that we will one day be welcomed into your glorious kingdom.

What will the future bring?

It's fun to daydream about a future world. In daydreams we might travel through space. We might have robots for pets. We might live in glass-bubble cities at the bottom of the ocean or in towering skyscrapers above the clouds.

Even with all the wonderful possibilities, we know that the future holds challenges and problems, too. Our human world will never be perfect. The Church will still be called to bring good news.

What do you think the Church will be like in the world of the future?

162 : We Are Invited

Resource Center

Link to the Family
Encourage the students to talk with older family members about hopes for the future they had when they were young. How did the world change during their lifetimes? What do they think will happen in the future? At the next session, invite group sharing if time permits.

Teaching Tip
Clarifying concepts Some students may be fearful about the future or worry that the world will end at any moment. Throughout the session, emphasize God's love for us and Jesus' promise to be with us always. No matter what the future brings, we can count on the Holy Spirit to help us.

Notes: Opening the Chapter

Scripture Story
New Heaven, New Earth

Long ago a man named John was sent to prison for following Jesus. John's prison was on a lonely, rocky island. John spent his time praying for the Christians he had left behind. He wanted to share with them a message of hope.

God gave John a message in the form of a **vision**, a dream of what would come. In the vision John saw the end of time. He saw that God's promise of everlasting justice, love, and peace would come true. Jesus would come again to bring the kingdom of God in glory.

"I saw a new heaven and a new earth," John wrote to his friends. "The old creation had passed away. I saw a holy city coming out of the sky. It was like a new Jerusalem. And I heard God's voice saying that there would be no more tears or sadness, no more suffering or death."

—based on Revelation 21:1–4

Scripture Signpost

"May the eyes of your hearts be enlightened, that you may know what is the hope that belongs to his call."
Ephesians 1:18

What are your hopes for the future?

We Are Invited
Open *Continued*

Working with the Pictures

- Invite a volunteer to describe what is shown in the picture. (a city surrounded by a wall)
- Explain that the picture shows one person's dream of God's kingdom. Point out that the wall has 12 gates, which represent the 12 apostles. We enter God's kingdom by following the teachings of Jesus, passed on to us through the apostles.

Working with the Text

- Read aloud the Scripture Story *New Heaven, New Earth*, or invite a volunteer to read it. Use *The Language of Faith* below to clarify the term *vision*. **Why did John have hope while he was in prison?** (He saw a better world and heard God's voice.) **How did John describe the city in his vision?** (It was a holy city with no more tears, sadness, suffering, or death.)
- Explain that the "new Jerusalem" John speaks of will not be a real city. Instead, it is a symbol that stands for God's kingdom. John's new city is a way of helping people imagine what God's kingdom will be like.
- If time permits, share the information about *Revelation 21:1–4* in *Scripture Background* below.

Scripture Signpost Read aloud the Scripture quotation and the question that follows it. Invite volunteers to share their responses. (Accept all reasonable responses.) If time permits, share the information about *Ephesians 1:18* in *Scripture Background* below.

The Language of Faith

A **vision** is a type of intuitive seeing that brings insight, understanding, and clarity about God's activity and presence. Christians believe that the goal of human life is to see God directly, face to face, after death. Throughout life we get only glimpses of this vision. We "walk by faith, not by sight" **(2 Corinthians 5:7)**.

Catechism Background

For more information about the relationship between faith, vision, and beatific vision, you may want to read *Catechism of the Catholic Church* (#163–165 and #2548–2550).

Scripture Background

- The writer of **Revelation 21:1–4** is in exile and longs for Jerusalem, which has recently been destroyed. The writer has no hope that Jerusalem will be restored in his lifetime; instead, he looks forward to the end of time, when a new Jerusalem will be God's dwelling place. This vision of a new Jerusalem stems from biblical tradition found in **Isaiah 52:1–3** and **65:17–25**.

- The author of **Ephesians 1:18** prays that the grace of Baptism may blossom in the lives of the readers. The author points to the great blessing we have received in our calling to be God's children. This call carries with it a hope beyond hopes—eternal life and happiness.

WE EXPLORE
2. Build
Working with the Text

- Read aloud *The Church's Future*. Use *The Language of Faith* below to clarify the highlighted terms.
- Invite the students to think about how they might feel when Jesus returns. **How do you think you will recognize Jesus?** Focus on answers that move beyond physical recognition to recognition based on the way Jesus acts.
- Explain that through the person of Jesus, God invites us to live our lives as members of his kingdom. It is up to each person to respond to God's invitation. God will judge us on how we respond.
- To help the students visualize the idea of the last judgment at the second coming, refer to the graphic organizer on page 161B. You may want to do the suggested activity if time permits.

Working with the Pictures

- Ask the students to describe the photograph. **(People have assembled for a funeral Mass; the bishop is blessing the casket.)**
- Read the caption aloud. Explain that the white cloth, called a *pall*, covering the casket is a reminder of the white garment worn at Baptism. The pall represents our rising to new life with Christ.

  Catholics Believe Ask the students when they think the end of time will come. Then read the faith statement aloud. Point out that the Bible does not tell us when this event will take place. Reassure the students that if they live as God's children, the coming of Jesus in glory will be a wonderful time, not a time to fear.

Catholics Believe...
that the Church will reach its full perfection when Jesus Christ comes in glory at the end of time.
Catechism, #1042

The Church's Future

As members of the Church, we look forward to the future with hope. But the future we look forward to is not just the future of the world. We look forward to the future coming of God's kingdom in its fullness.

In the Nicene Creed at Mass, we proclaim that we believe Jesus

"will come again in glory to judge the living and the dead, and his kingdom will have no end."

We don't look at Jesus' **second coming** and the **last judgment** with fear. We live in hope that our loving actions in this life will lead us to everlasting life in God's love.

We can hardly imagine a future that is counted in years. It is much more difficult to imagine eternity. But that is what we do whenever we work for love, peace, and justice. As the Church we are signs of God's timeless kingdom.

We know that not even death can put an end to God's love. We believe that all faithful people will rise to new life at the end of time. We do not know what that life will be like. But we know that it will be better than anything we can imagine because it will be life with God. And so we end the creed with a statement of joyful hope:

"We look for the resurrection of the dead, and the life of the world to come."

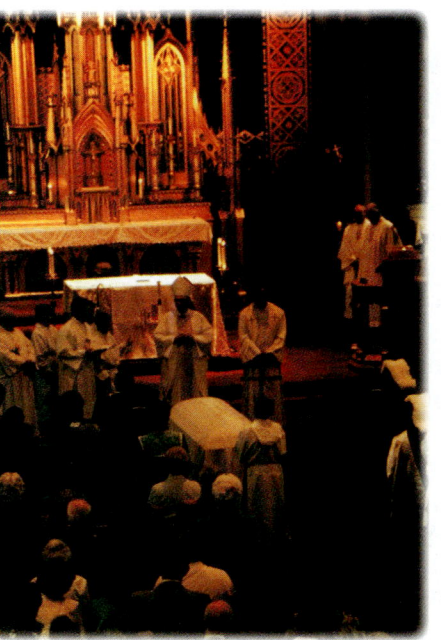

Our faith tells us that death is not the end. We will rise to new life with Jesus at the end of time.

164 : WE EXPLORE

Resource Center
The Language of Faith

- Christians believe that Jesus will return at the end of time to judge the living and the dead. This return is called the **second coming** to differentiate it from Jesus' birth and life on earth.
- Catholic doctrine teaches that there are two separate judgments after death. The first (particular judgment) occurs immediately after a person's death. People who have built a relationship with God through prayer and action and who have asked God's forgiveness for what they have done wrong will live forever with God in heaven. At the end of the world, Christ will come again in a **last judgment** (general judgment) of both the living and the dead. Resurrection of the body will occur at this time, as well as the fullness of God's kingdom.

Notes: Building the Chapter

ACTIVITY

Make a badge with the Alpha and Omega symbols as a reminder that Jesus is always with us.

The Beginning and the End

The Bible, God's word, begins and ends with stories of creation. In the Book of Genesis, the first book of the Bible, we hear how God created all things out of love. The last book of the Bible, the Book of Revelation, ends with John's vision of a new creation. This new creation is God's everlasting kingdom.

The ruler of all creation is Christ the King. The Son of God was present at the beginning of all things. He will be present at the end of time. In John's vision, Jesus says, "I am the Alpha and the Omega, the first and the last, the beginning and the end" (Revelation 22:13). *Alpha* and *Omega* are the first and last letters of the alphabet in Greek. By giving himself this title, Jesus reminds us that he is with us always.

Our Moral Guide

We are called to live every moment of our lives with our eternal future in mind.

Catechism, #1036

Why is it important to make choices based on the future God has prepared for us?

WE EXPLORE : 165

WE EXPLORE
Build Continued

Working with the Text

- Read aloud *The Beginning and the End*, and share information from *Scripture Background* below. Write the words *Alpha* and *Omega* on the board or on chart paper, along with their Greek letters (A and Ω). Explain that Jesus was in effect saying, "I am the A and the Z."
  What does this mean to you? (Accept all reasonable answers.)

- Ask the students to think about how the new creation might be different from the present creation. Invite volunteers to share their ideas.
  What kind of king do you think Jesus will be? (Responses will vary but should reflect an understanding that Jesus will be kind, loving, and just.)

Working with the Pictures

- Invite the students to look carefully at the stained-glass window of Jesus. Point out the Alpha and Omega symbols.
  Why do you think the artist included these two Greek letters? (to show that Jesus is the beginning and the end of all things)

  Distribute art materials, and have the students work individually. Provide tape or safety pins so the students can attach the badges to their clothing. If time is limited, prepare the Alpha and Omega symbols for the students beforehand. Show them how to overlap the two symbols (Alpha on top of Omega) to create a badge.

  Our Moral Guide Read aloud the statement and the question that follows it. Call on a volunteer to respond. (Possible answer: As Christians we choose to be good because we love God and want to live forever with him in the fullness of his kingdom.)

Scripture Background

Revelation 22:13 is typical of a literary genre known as *apocalyptic*—the telling of revealed secrets about heaven or the future in highly symbolic imagery. The description of the end of time symbolizes the victory of God's love and mercy over chaos and death.

Link to Liturgy

We profess our faith in the second coming of Christ at the memorial acclamation after the consecration at Mass. Distribute missalettes, and have the students find out how this belief is worded in each of the forms of the acclamation.

optional Enrichment

The Feast of Christ the King is celebrated in late November, on the last Sunday of the Church year before Advent begins. Distribute Bibles, and help the students find and read **Matthew 25:31–46**, the gospel from the Feast of Christ the King. Discuss the reading's description of Christ as a loving and just ruler.

PARISH : 165

We Reflect
Review

Recall Invite the students to respond to the questions. *(Jesus' return at the end of time; the letters that begin and end the Greek alphabet remind us that the Son of God was present at the beginning of all things and will return at the end of time.)*

Think and Share Ask the students to think carefully about their answers before they respond. Encourage them to evaluate their faith journeys this year in light of their hopes and dreams for the future and their growth as members of the Church. Look for a deeper appreciation of the Church and a desire to continue acting as good Church members.

Continue the Journey Have the students work independently or in pairs to write the prayers. Consider using some of these prayers during the prayer celebration.

Alternative Have the students compose a class prayer as you record it on the board or on chart paper. Consider using this prayer during the prayer celebration.

We Live Our Faith *At Home:* Caution the students to remember where they put the time capsules so they will be able to find them again in the future. *In the Parish:* If time permits, allow some class time for the students to write their notes.

Faith Journal The students may begin pages 53–54 of their *Faith Journal* in class and complete them at home. As part of your own spiritual development, complete *Your Faith Journal* (page J28) for this chapter.

RECALL
What is the second coming? Why are the Greek letters Alpha and Omega a sign of Jesus?

THINK AND SHARE
How has your religion class this year made you a stronger member of the Church? How has it prepared you for the future?

CONTINUE THE JOURNEY
Make up your own prayer of hope for the future—both for the future of the world and for the coming of God's eternal kingdom.

WE LIVE OUR FAITH

At Home Make a family time capsule. Put symbols of your family life, including your faith life, in a box. Write notes to yourselves in the future. Seal the box and mark it with the date. Decide how long you will wait before opening your time capsule.

In the Parish Write a thank-you note to your parish community for supporting you in your journey of faith this year.

166 : We Reflect

Resource Center

Link to the Faith Community
Optional Activity

Distribute missalettes, and direct the students to turn to the Nicene Creed. Read the creed together. Remind the students that the beliefs they have been studying this year come from this creed. Encourage the students to pray the Nicene Creed with the other parishioners at Mass.

Assessment Tip
You may wish to copy the Unit Seven Assessment from the Resource Package in preparation for giving this test after completing Chapters 25–28.

Hope and Joy

The next-to-last verse in the Bible is a prayer: "Amen! Come, Lord Jesus!" (*Revelation 22:20*). This is the Church's prayer for the future. It is our hope and joy.

PRAYER

Make up your own litany of thanks for the religion class you have shared this year. Include your hopes and prayers for the future, too. After each intercession, respond together "Amen! Come, Lord Jesus!"

WE CELEBRATE
3. Close
Working with the Pictures

- Draw the students' attention to the painting of Jesus. Point out that Jesus is blessing the children. If time permits, share information in *Art Background* below.
  Why do you think Jesus said that the greatest members of God's kingdom are like little children? *(Like children, they have faith, joy, and hope.)*

- Have a volunteer describe the background image of people at a joyful Church gathering.
  Why do you think the people are holding hands? *(Accept all reasonable responses, such as that they are a community, they care for one another.)*

Working with the Text

Ask a volunteer to read *Hope and Joy* aloud. If time permits, share the information about the word *amen* in *Background* below.

Prayer Invite the students to recall events from the year for which they are grateful and mention things they hope for in the future. Invite the group to respond "Amen! Come, Lord Jesus!" after each prayer of thanks. Pray the group prayer together, or invite volunteers to pray their individual prayers aloud. End the prayer celebration by singing a joyful hymn together. You might want to include a procession around the room. If rhythm instruments are available, invite volunteers to play them during the procession.

Art Background

Christ with the Children is the creation of French painter Maurice Denis (1870–1943), whose work resembles that of the impressionist Paul Gauguin. A deeply devout Christian, Denis painted many religious pictures, including this scene from **Mark 10:13–16**, in which Jesus blesses little children. Denis's paintings were a chief force in the revival of sacred art in France.

Background

The word *amen* comes from a Hebrew word meaning "It is true" or "So be it." When we say *amen*, we commit ourselves to what has just been spoken. Both Jews and Christians use the word as a formal conclusion to liturgical prayer so all those assembled can join in the official worship of God and express their faith. The Great Amen during Mass concludes the Eucharistic Prayer.

Notes: Closing the Chapter

Unit Seven Review

Objective
- Review the unit and assess progress.

Chapter Summaries
Use this information to reinforce key points before administering the review. These summaries will also help you assess the students' responses to *Show How Far You've Come*, page 169.

Chapter 25
- Studying Church history helps us appreciate today's Church.
- The Church is "the family of God," not a building.
- The Church is universal—present throughout the world.

Chapter 26
- We are called to work for a more peaceful and loving world.
- Baptism calls us to live our faith every day.

Chapter 27
- We have hope for the future because we believe God loves us.
- We believe Jesus will come again to judge everyone.
- As Church our vision of the future affects our present actions.

Review
Have the students work on the review in writing or work together to answer the questions orally.

Who Am I? Review the answers as a group. Discuss any missed responses to make sure the students understand the correct answers.

Multiple Choice Review the answers in the session to make sure the students understand them.

Share Your Faith Ask volunteers to explain why Church members have hope for the future.

168 : Unit Seven

Unit Seven Checkpoint
Review

Who Am I? Match each description in Column A with the correct person from Column B.

Column A

_c_ 1. I had a vision of the New Jerusalem.

_a_ 2. I was a pope and martyr of the early Church.

_e_ 3. I was an Irish monk who carried on the Church's mission.

_b_ 4. I gave my life helping the children of El Salvador.

_d_ 5. I am the patron saint of Church historians.

Column B

a. Saint Clement
b. Jean Donovan
c. John
d. Saint Bede
e. Saint Columba

Multiple Choice Circle the letter of the term that correctly completes each sentence.

1. The home church of a bishop is called a (a) synagogue **(b)** cathedral (c) catacomb.
2. Acting according to our beliefs, with the Holy Spirit's help, is called: (a) Catholicism (b) second coming **(c)** giving witness.
3. The belief that we are all united in the family of God is called **(a)** solidarity (b) vision (c) hope.
4. A name for Jesus that means he is our beginning and our end is (a) Christ **(b)** Alpha and Omega (c) King.
5. The Christians of Rome sometimes gathered in underground tombs called (a) ashrams (b) Gentiles **(c)** catacombs.

Share Your Faith Someone says there is no reason to hope for the future. Things will never get any better. What do you say?

168 : Review

Resource Center
Assessment Tips
Use one or more of the following strategies to assist you in assessing student progress:
- If you need a more detailed written review, administer the Unit Seven Assessment from the Resource Package.
- Ask the students to evaluate their attitudes and understanding throughout the unit. Ask them to think of ways they can improve their learning.
- Encourage the students to explain how they have put into practice what they have learned in this unit. Invite volunteers to describe their actions in response to the *We Live Our Faith* activities.

Show How Far You've Come Use the chart below to show what you have learned. For each chapter, write or draw the three most important things you remember.

Yesterday, Today, and Tomorrow

Chapter 25 Connected to the Past	Chapter 26 The Church Today	Chapter 27 Hope for the Future
Look for answers reflecting the key points listed under Chapter Summaries.		

What Else Would You Like to Know?
List any questions you still have about the Church.

_____

_____

_____

Continue the Journey Choose one or more of the following activities to do on your own, with your class, or with your family.

- Look through your Faith Journal pages for Unit Seven. Choose your favorite activity, and share it with a friend or family member.
- Design your own church building. Decide what you would include and where each item would go.
- Find out more about one of the saints or holy men and women mentioned in this unit. Share what you learn in the form of a booklet, a report, or a play.

REVIEW : 169

Show How Far You've Come Compare the students' responses with *Chapter Summaries* on page 168. Note and correct any responses that differ widely from the key chapter concepts. Review key concepts as needed. If time permits, extend this activity by asking the students to reread any portions of the chapters they did not understand.

What Else Would You Like to Know? Have the students share their questions. Try to answer any remaining questions before the final class session.

Continue the Journey Suggest that the students undertake one of the projects as a way of growing in faith over the summer. Working together can help students maintain positive friendships. Consider scheduling a summer gathering to share experiences.

Prayer

Gather the students for prayer. Encourage them to mention ways in which the Church helps us move forward on our journey of faith. Then lead the students in a spontaneous prayer of thanks for the progress they have made this year along their journeys of faith.

Reference Sources

For help in addressing the students' questions about the Church of the past, present, and future, see:

- *The Mystery of Death: A Catholic Perspective* by Janie Gustafson, Ph.D. (BROWN-ROA, 1994).
- *Catholic Source Book* edited by Rev. Peter Klein (BROWN-ROA, 1990).

Good resources for third graders include:

- *St. Patrick's Day* (video, 10 min.) (BROWN-ROA).
- *The Raising of Lazarus* (video, 10–15 min.) (BROWN-ROA).
- *Children's Catholic Catechism* (BROWN-ROA, 1991).
- *Christians Throughout the Ages—Around the World* by John Drane (Lion Publishing/Chariot Books, 1994).

Your parish community is another important resource. Encourage the students to discuss any questions they may have about the unit with parish priests, deacons, other staff members, catechists, and members of religious communities.

Link to the Family

If possible, have the students take these pages home to share with their families.

Getting Ready: Chapter 28

Signs of New Life

Program Resources
Student Text, pp. 170–173
Student Faith Journal, pp. 55–56
Your Faith Journal, p. J29

Unit Seven (Salvation History)
Yesterday, Today, and Tomorrow

Key Content Summary
We are Easter people.

Planning the Chapter

	Pacing Guide Suggested time/Your time	Content	Objectives	Materials
Open	10–15 min./ _____ min.	*We Are Invited*, p. 170	• Give examples of Easter symbols that recall Jesus' resurrection.	
Build	20–25 min./ _____ min.	*We Explore*, p. 171	• Explore the Easter customs of various cultures.	• pictures cut from magazines, catalogs, newspapers (optional)
Review	15–20 min./ _____ min.	*We Reflect*, p. 172	• Demonstrate understanding of chapter concepts. • Apply learning through activity. • Practice faith at home and in the parish.	• drawing materials • *Student Faith Journal*, pp. 55–56 • *Your Faith Journal*, p. J29
Close	10–15 min./ _____ min.	*We Celebrate*, p. 173	• Express Easter joy through prayer.	• a flower for each student

For additional suggestions, see Scheduling, pp. T35–T37.

Catechism in Context

Doctrinal Foundation This chapter discusses Easter, the central feast and central irony of our faith. Christ's death results in life for him, and more ironically, for us, for whose sins he died. In the upper room the risen Lord greeted his apostles—one of whom had denied him and all but one of whom had abandoned him in his suffering—not with reproach but with "Shalom," the greatest blessing in the Hebrew tradition: peace, health, the fullness of God's blessings. By appearing to his frightened apostles, Jesus strengthened them. With his Spirit he empowered them to preach the gospel without fear.

See Catechism of the Catholic Church, #638.

We can see ourselves in these men: sinful, mortal, and frightened; yet we are forgiven our sins, raised to new life, and transformed into bold proclaimers of the gospel by the Spirit of the crucified and risen Lord, who died but now reigns, nevermore to die.

One-Minute Retreat for Catechists

Read
"Easter is not a passport to another world; it is a quality of perception for this one."

—W. P. Lemon

Reflect
How does Easter affect my perception of the world?

Pray
Lord, help me see the promise of the resurrection in everything. As nature awakens around me, may I feel hope. Help me experience the promise of new life in every new day.

Visualizing the Lesson

Use this graphic organizer to help the students understand the meanings of common Easter symbols.

Redraw the graphic organizer on a sheet of paper, omitting all entries under the heading *Symbols*. After the students have read pages 170–171, distribute copies to the students, and have them work in small groups to fill in the symbols.

Symbols of Jesus' Resurrection

Symbols	What They Symbolize
Baby animals	Jesus' new life
Spring flowers	Life returning after death
Eggs	Jesus coming out of his tomb
Easter foods	The end of Lenten fasting
New clothes	The new life put on in Baptism
Fireworks	Jesus, the Light of the World

Library Links

Books for Children
Lilies, Rabbits and Painted Eggs: The Story of the Easter Symbols by Edna Barth (Houghton Mifflin, 1-800-225-3362).

Barth identifies Christian origins of many of the celebrations and symbols associated with Easter.

Books for Parents and Teachers
Praying at Easter by Donal Neary SJ (The Liturgical Press, 1-800-858-5450).

This book of guided meditations includes prayers, Scripture, and reflections for the weeks of the Easter Season.

Multimedia
For children:
Celebrating the Church Year for Children: Easter by Gaynell Cronin and Jack Rathschmidt OFM Cap. (video) (Paulist Press, 1-800-218-1903).

This video helps students understand the celebration of new life at Easter.

Glory Day, "I Know That My Redeemer Lives" by David Haas (GIA Publications, 1-800-442-1358).

Use this song to make music a part of chapter material.

For parents and teachers:
Rolling Back the Rock—The Religious Meaning of Holy Week by John Shea (video) (ACTA, 1-800-397-ACTA).

John Shea shares insights and reflections based on the Gospels on the true meaning of the Easter Triduum.

Easter Season: A Time to Remember by Dr. Kathleen Chesto (video) (Twenty-Third Publications, 1-800-321-0411).

Dr. Chesto presents families with ideas and suggestions to help remember the past while connecting it with the present.

Strengthening the Family Link

Here are some suggestions for reaching out to your students' families:

- Encourage the students to talk with family members about special Easter customs their families have and the meanings behind those customs.
- Invite family members to join the class in decorating Easter eggs.

Chapter 28 pages 170–173

Objectives
- Give examples of Easter symbols that recall Jesus' resurrection.
- Explore the Easter customs of various cultures.
- Express Easter joy through prayer.

Gathering WE ARE INVITED
1. Open

Personal Experience Invite the students to brainstorm ways the world comes alive again in spring, such as flowers budding and blooming, plants sprouting, baby birds hatching, and animals being born.

Prayer Remind the students that Jesus brought us new life through his resurrection. Pray the opening prayer together.

Working with the Text
Read the text aloud. Pause to allow the students to answer the questions in the second paragraph.

Working with the Pictures
- Invite the students to look at the background photograph.
Why are spring flowers a good symbol of Easter? (They are signs of new life after winter.)
- Have the students look carefully at the bottom picture.
Why are lambs a good symbol of Easter? (They are signs of new life and rebirth.) Point out that the lamb is also a symbol of Easter because Jesus is called the *Paschal Lamb* or the *Lamb of God*; he offered up his own life for us so we could be reconciled with God and have eternal life.

CHAPTER 28
WE CELEBRATE EASTER

Signs of New Life

PRAYER
Dear Jesus, we explore the mystery of your new life as we celebrate Easter.

The signs of Easter are everywhere. At Easter we celebrate Jesus' resurrection. Because God gave Jesus new life, we have hope for eternal life with God.

But what do baby chicks and bunnies and lambs have to do with Jesus' resurrection? What about Easter eggs and Easter lilies? Why do we eat sweet treats and cook special meals for Easter? Why do people wear new clothes to Easter Mass?

Easter falls in springtime, when new baby animals are born. Baby chicks and bunnies are signs of new life that remind us of Jesus' new life. Lilies and other flowers that bloom in the springtime are also signs of life returning after the death of winter.

Eggs are a special sign of new life. Out of eggs, baby birds are hatched. They must break through the tough eggshells. Long ago people saw this as a sign of Jesus' coming forth from his tomb.

170 : We Are Invited

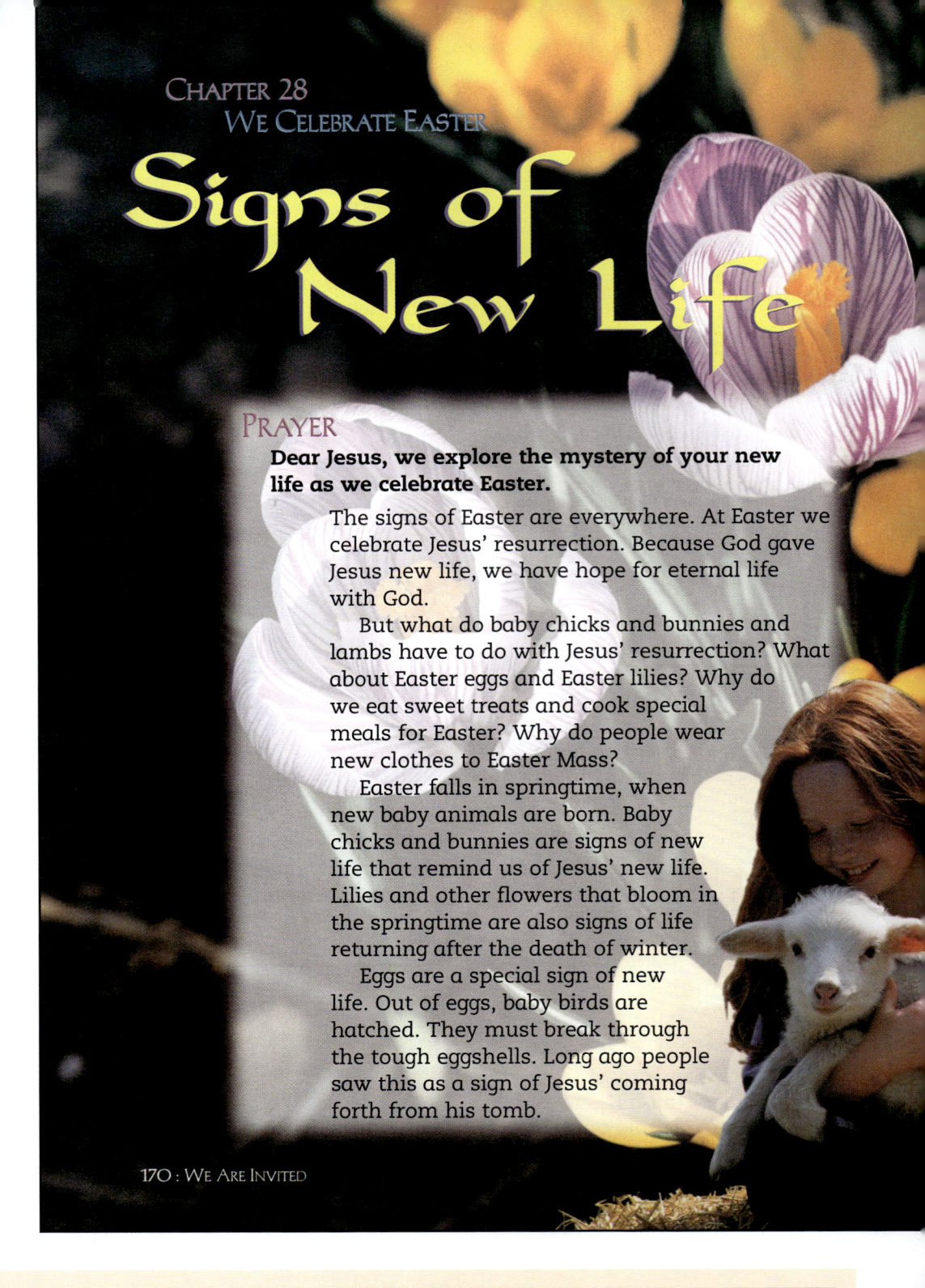

Resource Center

Link to the Family
Encourage the students to ask adult family members about Easter customs they participated in as children. Invite volunteers to describe those customs in the next session. Pay particular attention to any customs that are unfamiliar to the other students.

Background
Easter (the word means "dawn"), a movable feast that falls between March 22 and April 25, was established by the Council of Nicaea (325 C.E.). The exact date of Easter is the first Sunday following the first full moon after the vernal (spring) equinox. Eastern and Western Christians calculate the date differently because they follow different calendars.

Notes: Opening the Chapter

170 : Chapter 28

Activity

Ordinary things are made special for Easter celebrations. Make a list of your family's special Easter customs.

Easter meals and Easter candy remind us that Lent has ended. Our time of fasting and penance is over, and we can celebrate by enjoying all the gifts of God's creation.

The new clothes that many people wear on Easter Sunday are another sign of new life. They remind us of the new white robes worn by those who are baptized at the Easter Vigil. In Baptism we die and rise with Jesus.

Everyone Celebrates!

Every Church community has special ways of showing its joy at Jesus' new life. In Ukraine Easter eggs called *pysanky* are decorated with many colors. Using wax, dyes, and special tools, artists draw Easter symbols on the eggs. In Polish homes, a special lamb made of butter sits on the Easter table. It reminds us of Jesus, the Lamb of God.

In Italy, Spain, and Mexico, fireworks are used in Easter celebrations. They recall Jesus, the Light of the World. Christians in Iraq gather wild tulips to decorate their homes. The flowers come out of rocky ground, reminding people that Jesus came out of the tomb.

No matter how we celebrate, Jesus' new life is the center of our joy.

Catholics Believe...

the resurrection of Jesus from the dead is the central truth of our Church community.

Catechism, #638

We Explore : 171

We Explore

2. Build

Working with the Pictures

- Call attention to the boy in the picture who is decorating an Easter egg. Invite volunteers to relate their own experiences decorating Easter eggs.

  Complete this activity as a group. Elicit from the students their family Easter customs, and list them on the board or on chart paper.

Working with the Text

- Read aloud the top portion of the text. Use the graphic organizer on page 169B to help the students summarize the Easter symbols described on these two pages. You may want to do the suggested activity if time permits.

- Read *Everyone Celebrates!* aloud. Point out the *pysanky* (pee•SAHN•kee) in the picture. Ask the students if they have ever seen a person decorate eggs in this special way.

- Point out that all Christians throughout the world celebrate Easter with great joy and special customs.
  How are all Easter celebrations alike? (They celebrate the new life we have because Jesus rose from the dead.)

  Catholics Believe Read the statement aloud. Emphasize that Easter, not Christmas, is the most important feast day in the Church year.

Multicultural Link

Tell the students the following Ukrainian folktale: *A poor peddler named Simon was going to the marketplace to sell a basket of eggs. On the way he met Jesus struggling to carry his heavy cross to Calvary. Simon left his basket by the roadside and hurried to help Jesus carry his cross. When Simon returned, he found that the eggs in his basket had been transformed with bright colors and beautiful designs.* The eggs in the story have become a symbol of new life for all people.

Meeting Individual Needs

Learners acquiring English The text on this page includes English words and terms that may be difficult and unfamiliar for these students. Consider using several pictures cut from magazines, catalogs, and newspapers (in addition to the photographs on this page) to illustrate each Easter custom.

Notes: Building the Chapter

Parish : 171

We Reflect
Review

Recall Invite volunteers to respond to the questions. (Jesus' new life; eggs—Jesus coming out of the tomb; butter in the shape of a lamb—Jesus, the Lamb of God; fireworks—Jesus, the Light of the World; flowers—Jesus coming to new life)

Think and Share Invite the students to reflect on their answers before they respond. (Accept all reasonable answers.)

Continue the Journey Distribute drawing materials. Suggest that the students include some of the following symbols commonly used to decorate pysanky: fish (Jesus Christ, Son of God, our Savior), triangle (the Trinity), line encircling the egg without a beginning or end (eternal life).

Alternative Suggest that the students complete this drawing at home during the week and return to the next session prepared to share their drawings with the group.

We Live Our Faith *At Home:* Encourage the students to use their own words in their prayers and to pray them at family meals. *In the Parish:* At the next session, discuss the signs of new life that the students noted.

Faith Journal Have the students begin pages 55–56 of their *Faith Journal* in class and complete them at home. As part of your own spiritual development, complete *Your Faith Journal* (page J29) for this chapter.

Recall
What is the center of our Easter joy? Name some of the Easter symbols from around the world, and explain what they stand for.

Think and Share
How can we be a sign of new life to others at Easter time?

Continue the Journey
Decorate the egg with symbols of our new life in Jesus.

We Live Our Faith

At Home Make up a special prayer for your family to say before your Easter meal.

In the Parish See how many signs of new life you can find in your church on Easter.

172 : We Reflect

Resource Center

Catechism Background
For more information about Catholic beliefs regarding the resurrection, you may want to read *Catechism of the Catholic Church* (#638–658).

Assessment Tip
Look for an understanding of the main concepts being taught, particularly Jesus' resurrection and the great joy it brings to Christians throughout the world. The students' responses to the *Think and Share* question should give you an idea of whether they are able to personalize the resurrection experience and apply the new life won for us by Jesus to their own lives.

Easter Joy

The Easter liturgy is filled with prayers that show our joy. The following prayer is used to begin Easter Mass. Pray it with your classmates.

PRAYER

Leader: Let us pray that the risen Christ will raise us up and renew our lives.

All: Alleluia!

Leader: God our Father,
by raising Christ your Son,
you conquered the power
of death
and opened for us the way to
eternal life.

All: Alleluia!

Leader: Let our celebration today
raise us up and renew our lives
by the Spirit that is within us.

All: Amen, Alleluia!

We Celebrate : 173

WE CELEBRATE
3. Close

Working with the Pictures

- Explain that the top picture shows traditional Ukrainian and Polish foods for Easter. The foods are placed in baskets, covered with linen cloths, and taken to church on Holy Saturday to be blessed. In some cases a priest may visit homes to bless the Easter baskets. **What foods are shown in the baskets?** (eggs, bread, butter, meats)

- Ask a volunteer to identify the event shown in the sculpture. (Jesus emerging from his tomb) If time permits, discuss the artist with the group, using the information in *Art Background* below.

Working with the Text

Read the introductory paragraph aloud, or invite a volunteer to read it. Emphasize that when we celebrate Easter each year, we return to the most important belief of our faith: Jesus' resurrection.

Prayer Gather the students outside to pray the prayer together. You may want to select different volunteers to read the *Leader* parts. All should respond joyfully with "Alleluia." Then lead the group in singing an Easter song. To conclude the prayer celebration, you may want to give each student a flower as a symbol of new life.

Art Background

The Resurrection, a terra cotta relief by Luca della Robbia (1399–1482), reflects the artist's distinctive style. Sculpting in durable earthenware, della Robbia used glazes that outlasted paint. His figures, as here, are notable for their graceful forms and very human expressions. The background glaze—a color so associated with the artist that it is known as *della Robbia blue*—is intended to symbolize the glory of heaven.

Link to Liturgy

Tell the students that *Alleluia* is not said or sung during Lent. One of the changes that takes place in the Easter liturgy is the restoration of the *Alleluia!* before the gospel reading. Encourage the students to listen for this *Alleluia!* during Mass on Easter.

Notes: Closing the Chapter

PARISH : 173

Catholic Prayers and Resources

This section is a compendium of traditional Catholic prayers and important information. Refer to this section throughout the year when you need to introduce the students to Catholic prayers and practices. The lesson plan pages for *Catholic Prayers and Resources* provide strategies for building religious literacy and background for your own reference.

The Sign of the Cross
- Always begin and end classroom prayer with the Sign of the Cross to reinforce its significance.
- Take the students to the parish church and have them make the Sign of the Cross with holy water from the baptismal font or holy water container.

The Lord's Prayer
- Remind the students to listen for the Lord's Prayer at Mass and to join in praying it.
- Have the students suggest simple gestures to accompany the phrases of the prayer.

The Hail Mary
- Play various musical settings of this prayer, including some classical settings of the *Ave Maria*, for the students.
- Remind the students that the Hail Mary is part of popular devotions such as the Rosary, the *Angelus*, and the *Regina Coeli*.

Glory to the Father
- You might wish to review this prayer in combination with the Sign of the Cross to reinforce the Trinitarian formula.
- Use the phrase "as it was in the beginning, is now, and will be for ever" to remind the students that God is eternal.

CATHOLIC PRAYERS AND RESOURCES

The Sign of the Cross
In the name of the Father, and of the Son, and of the Holy Spirit. Amen.

The Lord's Prayer

Traditional/Liturgical
Our Father,
 who art in heaven,
hallowed be thy name;
thy kingdom come;
thy will be done on earth
 as it is in heaven.
Give us this day our daily bread;
and forgive us our trespasses
as we forgive those who
 trespass against us;
and lead us not into
 temptation,
but deliver us from evil. (Amen.)
For the kingdom,
the power, and the glory
 are yours,
now and for ever.

Contemporary
Our Father in heaven,
 hallowed be your name,
 your kingdom come,
 your will be done,
 on earth as in heaven.
Give us today our daily bread.
Forgive us our sins
 as we forgive those who sin
 against us.
Save us from the time of trial
 and deliver us from evil.
For the kingdom, the power,
 and the glory are yours,
 now and for ever.
Amen.

Hail Mary
Hail, Mary, full of grace,
the Lord is with you!
Blessed are you among women,
and blessed is the fruit of your womb, Jesus.
Holy Mary, Mother of God,
pray for us sinners,
now and at the hour of our death.
Amen.

Glory to the Father *(Doxology)*
Glory to the Father, and to the Son, and to the Holy Spirit.
As it was in the beginning, is now, and will be for ever. Amen.

Resource Center

Background

The Sign of the Cross Tracing the cross on one's own body or the forehead of another has been a common Christian gesture since the early centuries of the Church. Making the Sign of the Cross with holy water on entering or leaving a church is a reminder of Baptism, when we were marked with the cross in the name of the Holy Trinity.

The Lord's Prayer This prayer has its roots in Scripture. In the Gospels of Matthew **(Matthew 6:9–13)** and Luke **(Luke 11:2–4)**, Jesus teaches a form of this prayer to his disciples. Catholics have traditionally referred to this prayer as the *Our Father*, from its first words. The Lord's Prayer is prayed at Mass and in the Rosary.

The Hail Mary The first part of this prayer was used as an antiphon in the Little Office of Our Lady, a form of the Liturgy of the Hours prayed during the Middle Ages. The antiphon combines the Archangel Gabriel's greeting at the annunciation **(Luke 1:26–28)** with Elizabeth's words of praise for Mary's motherhood **(Luke 1:42)**. The second part of the prayer (from "Holy Mary" on) was added as devotion to Mary grew.

Glory to the Father This ancient prayer is known as a *doxology*, or "words of praise." It is part of the Rosary and is traditionally used to conclude the praying or chanting of a psalm in the Liturgy of the Hours.

Catechism Background
For more on the significance of the Lord's Prayer, see the *Catechism of the Catholic Church* (#2777–2865).

Prayer to the Guardian Angel

Angel sent by God to guide me,
be my light and walk beside me;
be my guardian and protect me;
on the path of life direct me.

Morning Prayer

Almighty God,
you have given us this day.
Strengthen us with your power
and keep us from falling into sin,
so that whatever we say or think or do
may be in your service
and for the sake of your kingdom.
We ask this through Christ our Lord.
Amen.

Evening Prayer

Lord, watch over us this night.
By your strength, may we rise at daybreak
to rejoice in the resurrection of Christ, your Son,
who lives and reigns for ever.
Amen.

Blessing Before Meals

Bless us, O Lord, and these your gifts
which we are about to receive from
   your goodness.
Through Christ our Lord.
Amen.

Thanksgiving After Meals

We give you thanks for all your gifts, almighty God,
living and reigning now and for ever.
Amen.

Prayer to the Guardian Angel

- If necessary, use information in *Background*, below, to introduce the students to the concept of the guardian angel.
- Have the students make prayer cards with the words of this prayer to take home and use as a night prayer.

Morning Prayer
Evening Prayer

- Review these prayers with the students by using them occasionally to begin or end a class session.
- Invite the students to compose their own morning and evening prayers.

Blessing Before Meals
Thanksgiving After Meals

- Teach these prayers and reinforce their use in conjunction with nutrition breaks and lunchtime.
- Libraries and bookstores carry many collections of meal prayers and graces from around the world. Introduce the students to meal prayers from other cultural traditions. Invite the students to share with the class their own families' meal prayers.
- Have the students compose their own meal prayers. You might try setting the students' prayers to familiar tunes and singing them.

Background

Prayer to the Guardian Angel Belief in the presence of a guardian spirit entrusted with the care of each person, though not a part of formal Catholic teaching, is a strong tradition in the Church. Scriptural references **(Matthew 18:10** and **Acts 12:15)** indicate that this belief may predate Christianity. Prayers to the guardian angel have been a part of the spiritual life of children and families for centuries. The Church celebrates the Feast of Guardian Angels on October 2. In teaching this prayer, explain to the students that God sends angels—spiritual beings—to care for creation as a sign of his love and protection.

Morning Prayer, Evening Prayer These prayers are rooted in the Church's oldest traditions of public prayer. Early Christians gathered for prayer in the morning and at nightfall. They read the Scriptures, sang psalms, and prayed. Morning prayer came to be known as *Lauds*, or "praise." Evening prayer was known as *Vespers*, after the Latin name of the evening star. When monastic communities began to form in the fifth century, they added formal prayer at other times of the day and night. These were known as the canonical hours. This cycle of prayers developed into the *Liturgy of the Hours*, or Divine Office, and is still prayed in an adapted form today by priests, deacons, religious, and some lay people.

Blessing Before Meals, Thanksgiving After Meals
These two traditional prayers are part of a single movement of praise and gratitude to God for his gifts. The Christian custom of meal prayers has its roots in Jewish practice. Jesus followed the Jewish formula of blessing when he instituted the Eucharist. At Mass, we hear echoes of the Jewish meal blessings in the Prayer over the Gifts and the Eucharistic Prayer. Although family meal blessings (popularly known as *grace*, from the Latin word for "thanksgiving") have declined in popularity as families spend less time together at table, there is good reason to revive the custom, adapting it to the needs of families today.

The Apostles' Creed
- Have the students make booklets or a mural illustrating each phrase of this creed.
- Review this creed with the students as part of your review of the Rosary. (See page 182.)

Act of Faith, Hope, and Love
- Use this prayer to begin or end class sessions on a regular basis.
- Help the students develop gestures to accompany the prayer.
- Remind the students to listen at Mass for the Creed, which is an extended profession of faith.

The Apostles' Creed

I believe in God, the Father almighty,
   creator of heaven and earth.
I believe in Jesus Christ, his only Son, our Lord.
   He was conceived by the power of the Holy Spirit
      and born of the Virgin Mary.
   He suffered under Pontius Pilate,
      was crucified, died, and was buried.
   He descended to the dead.
   On the third day, he rose again.
   He ascended into heaven,
      and is seated at the right hand of the Father.
   He will come again to judge the living and the dead.
I believe in the Holy Spirit,
   the holy catholic Church,
   the communion of saints,
   the forgiveness of sins,
   the resurrection of the body,
   and the life everlasting. Amen.

Act of Faith, Hope, and Love

My God, I believe in you,
I hope in you,
I love you above all things,
with all my mind and heart and strength.

Resource Center

Background

The Apostles' Creed This profession of faith received its name from the popular legend that it was composed by the apostles. However, the earliest reference to this creed appears in fourth-century writings, and the earliest text dates from the eighth century. The name is still appropriate because the Apostles' Creed certainly can be said to reflect the teachings of the early Church. Like the Nicene Creed, the Apostles' Creed is Trinitarian in structure, and flows from the baptismal formula. Charlemagne ordered its use throughout his empire. This creed is approved for use in place of the Nicene Creed in children's Masses.

Act of Faith, Hope, and Love This prayer is a simplified combination of three traditional prayers centered on the theological virtues. The word *act* in the title of the prayer comes from the Latin word for "doing"; as with the traditional Act of Contrition, it refers to prayer rooted in practice.

The Jesus Prayer

Lord Jesus Christ,
Son of God,
have mercy on me, a sinner.
Amen.

Act of Contrition

My God, I am sorry for my sins with
 all my heart.
In choosing to do wrong
and failing to do good,
I have sinned against you
whom I should love above all things.
I firmly intend, with your help,
to do penance,
to sin no more,
and to avoid whatever leads me to sin.
Our Savior Jesus Christ
suffered and died for us.
In his name, my God, have mercy.

I Confess

I confess to almighty God,
and to you, my brothers and sisters,
that I have sinned through my own fault
in my thoughts and in my words,
in what I have done,
and in what I have failed to do;
and I ask blessed Mary, ever Virgin,
all the angels and saints,
and you, my brothers and sisters,
to pray for me to the Lord our God.

CATHOLIC PRAYERS AND RESOURCES : 177

The Jesus Prayer
- Teach the students to pray this prayer meditatively, as it was prayed by Greek and Russian mystics in the Middle Ages. Have the students sit quietly, close their eyes, and time their silent repetition of the prayer to their breathing this way:

  Lord Jesus Christ, *(breathe in)*
  Son of God, *(breathe out)*
  have mercy on me, *(breathe in)*
  a sinner. *(breathe out)*

- Have the students make bookmarks with the text of this prayer.

Act of Contrition
- Have the students make prayer cards with the text of this prayer to use as reminders when celebrating the Sacrament of Reconciliation.
- Teach the students some other forms of the prayer of contrition. (See the *Rite of Penance*, #85–92.) The Jesus Prayer is one of these alternate forms.

I Confess
- Review this prayer with the students as part of your weekly preparation for Mass.
- Incorporate this prayer into classroom penitential prayer services.

Background

The Jesus Prayer This prayer, the text of which is based on the supplication of the blind beggar in **Luke 18:38**, has its roots in Greek and Russian spirituality. It is associated with a form of contemplative prayer called *Hesychasm* (from the Greek word for "stillness" or "peace"), or prayer of the heart. In the Middle Ages Hesychasts developed a tradition of coordinating their breathing with the phrases of the prayer, which was prayed silently over and over in an attempt to follow literally Paul's advice to "pray without ceasing" **(1 Thessalonians 5:17)**. The Orthodox Christian spiritual classic *Philokalia* and the Russian Orthodox account *The Way of a Pilgrim* are based on the Jesus Prayer. The prayer is used frequently by contemporary Orthodox Christians, but without the Hesychast associations to breathing.

Act of Contrition This form of the prayer of the penitent is part of the revised *Rite of Penance* (1974). The students' parents and grandparents may be more familiar with the traditional Act of Contrition, which begins "O my God, I am heartily sorry. . . ." The word *act* in the title of the prayer refers to a prayer of intention, in which prayer and action are combined.

I Confess This prayer is more commonly known by its Latin name, *Confiteor*. It is one of the forms of prayer that make up the penitential rite of the Mass. In former times the priest prayed this prayer in the name of the assembly. Today the assembly expresses its sorrow for sin in a communal prayer, set in the first person to remind us that sin is an individual choice.

The Great Commandment

- Review this central commandment with the class as Jesus might have heard the Scriptures reviewed in the synagogue. Pronounce each phrase slowly and meaningfully, and have the students repeat it after you.
- Have the students make their own mezuzahs by stapling together two index cards, leaving one short side open. Have the students decorate one side of the mezuzah. Have the students copy the Great Commandment onto scrolls (on parchment paper, if possible) to roll or fold up and place in the mezuzahs. Encourage the students to hang their mezuzahs at home near a doorway. Share with them the Jewish custom of touching the mezuzah when entering or leaving the house, praying a brief prayer to be faithful to the law.

The Ten Commandments

- Review the commandments frequently. Be sure the students know what the commandments require of us.
- Have the students make tablets from papier-mâché or plastic foam sheets such as meat trays from the supermarket. Help the students write the commandments on the tablets.
- Have the students compose an examination of conscience based on the Ten Commandments.

The Beatitudes

- Review the Beatitudes frequently.
- Ask the students to search newspapers, magazines, and reference books to find examples of people who live the Beatitudes.
- Have the students role-play situations in which young people are called upon to live by the values of the Beatitudes.

The Great Commandment

"You shall love the Lord your God with all your heart, with all your soul, with all your strength, and with all your mind; and your neighbor as yourself."

—Luke 10:27

The Ten Commandments

1. I am the Lord your God. You shall not have strange gods before me.
2. You shall not take the name of the Lord your God in vain.
3. Remember to keep holy the Lord's day.
4. Honor your father and your mother.
5. You shall not kill.
6. You shall not commit adultery.
7. You shall not steal.
8. You shall not bear false witness against your neighbor.
9. You shall not covet your neighbor's wife.
10. You shall not covet your neighbor's goods.

The Beatitudes

Blessed are the poor in spirit,
   for theirs is the kingdom of heaven.
Blessed are they who mourn,
   for they will be comforted.
Blessed are the meek,
   for they will inherit the land.
Blessed are they who hunger and thirst for righteousness,
   for they will be satisfied.
Blessed are the merciful,
   for they will be shown mercy.
Blessed are the clean of heart,
   for they will see God.
Blessed are the peacemakers,
   for they will be called children of God.
Blessed are they who are persecuted for the sake of righteousness,
   for theirs is the kingdom of heaven.

—Matthew 5:3–10

Resource Center

Background

The Great Commandment In answer to questions about the most important law to follow, Jesus either stated or had his questioner state the summary of the law we call the Great Commandment. This account appears in slightly different forms in both Matthew's and Luke's Gospels **(Matthew 22:37–39** and **Luke 10:27)**; the version given here is Luke's. The Great Commandment was stated in **Deuteronomy 6:4** and **Leviticus 19:18** and was an honored part of Jewish teaching.

The Ten Commandments Also known as the *Decalogue*, or "ten words," the Ten Commandments sum up the duties of the covenant relationship between God and his people. The wording and numbering of the commandments given here is traditional to Catholic and Lutheran communities, originating with Saint Augustine.

The Beatitudes Christians traditionally give the title Beatitudes to the eight teachings of Jesus presented in **Matthew 5:3–10**. The formula "Blessed is the one who . . ." occurs often in Old Testament wisdom literature; in using this style to describe the values of God's kingdom, Jesus was following a tradition familiar to his Jewish listeners.

Catechism Background

For background on the Great Commandment, see the *Catechism of the Catholic Church* (#2055). Part III, Section Two of the Catechism is devoted to an exploration of the Ten Commandments. For background on the place of the Beatitudes in Christian morality, see the *Catechism of the Catholic Church* (#1716–1729).

Precepts of the Church

1. Take part in the Mass on Sundays and holy days. Keep these days holy and avoid unnecessary work.
2. Celebrate the Sacrament of Reconciliation at least once a year if there is serious sin.
3. Receive Holy Communion at least once a year during Easter time.
4. Fast and abstain on days of penance.
5. Give your time, gifts, and money to support the Church.

Works of Mercy

Corporal *(for the body)*
Feed the hungry.
Give drink to the thirsty.
Clothe the naked.
Shelter the homeless.
Visit the sick.
Visit the imprisoned.
Bury the dead.

Spiritual *(for the spirit)*
Warn the sinner.
Teach the ignorant.
Counsel the doubtful.
Comfort the sorrowful.
Bear wrongs patiently.
Forgive injuries.
Pray for the living and the dead.

The Sacraments

Sacraments of Initiation
Baptism
Confirmation
Eucharist

Sacraments of Healing
Reconciliation
Anointing of the Sick

Sacraments of Vocation and Service
Matrimony
Holy Orders

CATHOLIC PRAYERS AND RESOURCES : 179

The Precepts of the Church
- Review this list with the students frequently.
- Have the students create a mural illustrating the precepts in action.
- Help the students look through the parish bulletin or diocesan newspaper for examples of people and groups who are living the precepts of the Church.

Works of Mercy
- Review these lists with the students frequently.
- Have the class refer to these lists for ideas when planning service projects or prayer services.
- Illustrate the works of mercy with examples taken from your parish bulletin, diocesan newspaper, and other media.

The Sacraments
- During the year, direct the students to this list and discuss any sacramental celebrations planned for your parish community. Ask the students to share what they see and hear when participating in sacramental celebrations for themselves, family members, and friends.
- Ask a priest, deacon, or parish liturgical minister to share with the students some of the objects, symbols, gestures, and prayers used in various sacramental celebrations. If possible, take the students on a tour of the parish baptismal font or pool, Reconciliation room or confessional, and the sanctuary area.
- Have the students create booklets, posters, or murals illustrating the rites and symbols of the sacraments.

Background

The Precepts of the Church These "commandments of the Church," as they are sometimes called, have existed in some form since the fourth century. The number and content of the *precepts* (a word that means "teachings") has varied throughout the years, and different lists are honored in different countries. Saints Peter Canisius and Robert Bellarmine contributed most to the version we know today, outlining matters of Church discipline and practice as part of the internal reforms undertaken by the Church in response to the Protestant Reformation. The precepts of the Church, which apply to all Catholics, have never been given the status of law.

Works of Mercy These actions on behalf of those in physical, spiritual, and emotional need are rooted in Scripture and in the Church's practice. They are closely related to action for justice, but where justice obligates us to give others what they need, mercy moves beyond obligation to give freely. Although tradition specifies seven Corporal Works of Mercy and seven Spiritual Works of Mercy, the intent of these practices is not to limit ourselves to specific actions but to open ourselves compassionately to others in need.

The Sacraments The sacraments are signs and celebrations that have their root in Jesus' actions. In the sacraments the saving actions of God are celebrated through the Church. Sacraments enrich and deepen the loving relationship with God that we call *grace*. The Church's theology and practice of the sacraments have developed through the centuries, but though certain aspects of the celebrations may change over time, the essential meaning and elements of the sacraments remain the same. Since the Council of Trent in the sixteenth century, the Catholic Church has recognized seven sacraments, usually grouped by their functions into Sacraments of Initiation, Healing, and Service.

Order of the Mass

- Refer to these pages throughout the year when taking the students through their weekly preparation for Mass.
- Have the students illustrate the order of the Mass.
- Use missalettes to help the students review the prayers, responses, and postures of the assembly.
- Ask your pastor or members of the parish liturgical team to go through the order of the Mass with the students, answering any questions they may have.

Order of the Mass

Introductory Rites
1. Entrance Song
2. Greeting
3. Rite of Blessing and Sprinkling with Holy Water *or* Penitential Rite
4. Glory to God
5. Opening Prayer

Liturgy of the Word
6. First Reading *(usually from the Old Testament)*
7. Responsorial Psalm
8. Second Reading *(from New Testament Letters)*
9. Gospel Acclamation *(Alleluia)*
10. Gospel
11. Homily
12. Profession of Faith *(Creed)*
13. General Intercessions

Liturgy of the Eucharist
14. Offertory Song *(Presentation of the Gifts)*
15. Preparation of the Bread and Wine
16. Invitation to Prayer
17. Prayer over the Gifts
18. Preface
19. Acclamation *(Holy, Holy, Holy Lord)*
20. Eucharistic Prayer with Acclamation
21. Great Amen

Communion Rite
22. Lord's Prayer
23. Sign of Peace
24. Breaking of the Bread
25. Prayers Before Communion
26. Lamb of God
27. Holy Communion
28. Communion Song
29. Silent Reflection or Song of Praise
30. Prayer after Communion

Concluding Rite
31. Greeting
32. Blessing
33. Dismissal

180 : CATHOLIC PRAYERS AND RESOURCES

Resource Center

Background

The Order of the Mass The basic structure of the Mass has remained the same since the second century. Based in part on the synagogue service familiar to the first Jewish Christians, the earliest celebrations of the Eucharist included Scripture readings and psalms, preaching, the people's offering of bread and wine accompanied by the presider's prayer of praise and thanksgiving, and the sharing of Holy Communion. Each of these basic parts of the Eucharistic liturgy has been elaborated on over the centuries. The most recent and widespread liturgical reform was begun by the Second Vatican Council in the latter part of the twentieth century.

Catechism Background

Part II of the *Catechism of the Catholic Church* is devoted to the sacraments and their celebration. This section includes material on the Eucharistic liturgy.

Holy Days
(observed in the United States)

Christmas, the Nativity of the Lord	December 25
Solemnity of Mary the Mother of God	January 1
Ascension of the Lord	40 days after Easter
Assumption	August 15
All Saints' Day	November 1
Immaculate Conception	December 8

Receiving Holy Communion

To receive Holy Communion, you must be free from mortal sin. You must be sorry for any venial sin committed since your last confession. The penitential rite at the beginning of Mass is an opportunity to express your sorrow.

To honor the Lord, we fast for one hour before receiving Holy Communion. Fasting means going without food and drink, except water and medicine.

Catholics are required to receive Holy Communion at least once a year during Easter time. But it is important to receive Holy Communion often—if possible, at every Mass.

Catholics are permitted to receive Holy Communion more than once a day within Mass.

The Sacrament of Reconciliation

Communal Rite of Reconciliation
1. Greeting
2. Reading from Scripture
3. Homily
4. Examination of Conscience with Litany of Contrition and the Lord's Prayer
5. Individual Confession, Giving of a Penance, and Absolution
6. Closing Prayer

Individual Rite of Reconciliation
1. Welcome
2. Reading from Scripture
3. Confession of Sins and Giving of a Penance
4. Act of Contrition
5. Absolution
6. Closing Prayer

CATHOLIC PRAYERS AND RESOURCES : 181

Holy Days
- Review this list with the students as needed.
- Have the students mark the holy days on their personal calendars. Other feasts (such as the students' patron saints' days) and liturgical seasons may also be noted.
- Have the students form groups. Assign each group a holy day that occurs during the school year. Ask each group to plan a class celebration in honor of its assigned holy day.

Receiving Holy Communion
- Review these reminders with the students regularly.
- Ask a Eucharistic minister and an usher to walk the students through a typical Communion procession in your parish.
- Invite those who bring the Eucharist to those who are sick or homebound to speak to the class about their ministry. Have the students write notes to those who are sick or homebound, to be delivered by the Eucharistic ministers.

The Sacrament of Reconciliation
- Frequently review with the students the steps in celebrating this sacrament.
- Once the students have celebrated First Reconciliation, arrange for them to celebrate the sacrament (either individually or as part of a communal parish celebration) on a regular basis. Encourage frequent participation while respecting students' privacy of conscience.
- Invite the pastor or another parish priest to role-play the celebration of the sacrament with the students as it is customarily celebrated in your parish. Ask the priest to go through the *Rite of Penance* with the students, explaining the various options for prayers.

Background

Holy Days These are major feasts of the Church to which the Sunday obligation also applies. The *Code of Canon Law* lists ten holy days, but bishops' conferences in various countries have the right to amend this list. The United States Catholic Bishops have removed the obligation from the Feasts of Saint Joseph (March 19) and Saints Peter and Paul (June 29). They have transferred the obligation for the Feasts of Epiphany and Corpus Christi to the nearest Sunday and have dispensed with the obligation for the Solemnity of Mary, the Assumption, and All Saints' Day when these feasts fall on a Saturday or Monday.

Receiving Holy Communion These rules for receiving Holy Communion are based on canon law. Although Eucharistic practice has varied throughout the years, the Church today emphasizes the importance of frequent Communion in strengthening our union with Christ and with one another. Holy Communion may be received a second time if the second reception takes place within a Mass.

The Sacrament of Reconciliation This sacrament has undergone profound changes throughout the centuries of its development; yet at its heart has always been the gospel call to conversion. The revisions of the *Rite of Penance* begun by the Second Vatican Council raised many questions and affected popular practice. Today the Church reminds us that we are to understand this sacrament only in context: Christ is our central sacrament of reconciliation, working through the Church, whose mission is also to reconcile.

Catechism Background

For more on the significance of Holy Communion, read the *Catechism of the Catholic Church* (#1382–1405). For more on the Sacrament of Reconciliation (Penance), read the *Catechism of the Catholic Church* Part II, Section II, Chapter Two, Article 4.

Praying the Rosary

- Review this page with the students frequently.
- Have the students follow with their own rosaries as you demonstrate how to pray the Rosary.
- Pray a decade of the Rosary occasionally as part of class prayer.
- Have the students make rosaries for themselves, family members, or members of the parish community who are sick or homebound. Encourage the students to be creative in their choice of materials, which might include premade wooden or glass beads, homemade clay beads, buttons, and the like.

Mysteries of the Rosary

- Have the students research the scriptural or traditional foundations for each of the mysteries of the Rosary.
- Invite the students to illustrate the mysteries.
- Have the students create reminder cards with the steps for praying the Rosary listed on one side and the mysteries of the Rosary listed on the other.

Praying the Rosary

1. Hold the crucifix, and pray the Apostles' Creed.
2. Pray the Lord's Prayer when holding each single bead.
3. Pray the Hail Mary on each bead in a group of three or ten. A group of ten Hail Marys is called a *decade* of the Rosary. Think of one mystery as you pray each decade.
4. After every group of Hail Marys, pray Glory to the Father.
5. Close the Rosary by praying Hail, Holy Queen.

> Hail, holy Queen, mother of mercy,
> hail, our life, our sweetness, and our hope.
> To you we cry, the children of Eve;
> to you we send up our sighs,
> mourning and weeping in this land of exile.
> Turn, then, most gracious advocate,
> your eyes of mercy toward us;
> lead us home at last
> and show us the blessed fruit of your womb, Jesus:
> O clement, O loving, O sweet Virgin Mary.

Mysteries of the Rosary

Joyful Mysteries
1. The Annunciation
2. The Visitation
3. The Nativity
4. The Presentation
5. Finding Jesus in the Temple

Sorrowful Mysteries
1. The Agony in the Garden
2. The Scourging
3. Crowning with Thorns
4. Carrying the Cross
5. The Crucifixion

Glorious Mysteries
1. The Resurrection
2. The Ascension
3. The Coming of the Holy Spirit
4. The Assumption
5. The Coronation of Mary as Queen of Heaven

Resource Center

Background

The Rosary The name for this most popular of Catholic devotions comes from the Latin for "rose garden," a phrase used in medieval times to designate a collection of spiritual writings or prayers. Popular tradition associates the name with a title given to Mary in the Litany of Loreto—*Mystical Rose*—and sees the Rosary as a garland of prayers offered to her. Legend attributes the inspiration for the Rosary to Saint Dominic, but although the Dominicans did much to standardize and popularize this devotion, aspects of the Rosary both precede and follow Saint Dominic's time. The practice of reciting numbers of prayers, often counted off on strings of beads, goes back beyond the first Christian monks. (Our English word *bead* comes directly from this practice, as it derived from *bede*, meaning "blessing" or "prayer.") During the Middle Ages, lay people imitated the monastic custom of reciting the 150 psalms in the Liturgy of the Hours by reciting 150 common prayers, such as the Lord's Prayer or the Hail Mary. A full Rosary, of all 15 mysteries, contains 150 Hail Marys. The prayer Hail, Holy Queen (*Salve, Regina*), customarily added to the Rosary, is a Marian antiphon for Night Prayer in the Liturgy of the Hours. It was composed in the eleventh century.

The Language of Faith

A

absolution The forgiveness of sin we receive from God through the Church in the Sacrament of Reconciliation. The word *absolve* means "to wash away."

abstain To go without something. Catholics 14 years old and older are asked to abstain from eating meat on certain days as a sign of penance.

Advent The four weeks before Christmas. We use this time of waiting to get ready to celebrate the birth of Jesus. The word *advent* means "coming." The Season of Advent is the beginning of the Church year.

All Saints' Day The holy day set aside to honor the memory of all the saints. The Church celebrates the Feast of All Saints on November 1.

Alpha and Omega The first and last letters of the Greek alphabet. The Book of Revelation in the Bible uses these letters as a title for Jesus, to show that he is with us always, from the beginning of all things to the end of time.

altar The table around which we gather to celebrate the Eucharist.

anoint To mark or rub with oil. Anointing is a sign of God's friendship and the presence of the Holy Spirit. It also means healing and strengthening. Anointing is part of the Sacraments of Baptism, Confirmation, Anointing of the Sick, and Holy Orders.

Anointing of the Sick The sacrament that celebrates the healing of body and spirit by Jesus. The Sacrament of Anointing can be celebrated anytime a person is seriously ill or weakened by age.

apostles The twelve special friends and followers of Jesus. The word *apostle* means "one who is sent."

apostolic Built on the foundation of the apostles. The Church is apostolic, which is one of its marks, or signs of the presence of the Holy Spirit.

apostolic succession The process by which bishops in every time continue to carry out the work of the apostles.

ascension Jesus' return to his Father in heaven after his resurrection. We celebrate the Feast of the Ascension as a holy day 40 days after Easter. The word *ascension* means "rising."

B

Baptism The first sacrament we celebrate. Baptism makes us children of God and members of the Church by making us members of the Body of Christ. It takes away original sin and all personal sin. The word *baptism* means "bath." Baptism is celebrated by pouring water on a person or placing the person in water and praying "I baptize you in the name of the Father, and of the Son, and of the Holy Spirit."

Beatitudes Sayings of Jesus (Matthew 5:3–10) that sum up the way to live in God's kingdom and that show us the way to true happiness. The word *beatitude* means "blessedness." The Beatitudes are one of the standards for measuring the morality of our actions and choices.

Bible God's word written down by humans; the Church's holy book, also called *Scripture*. The Bible is made up of two parts, the Old Testament and the New Testament. There are many different books collected in the Bible. The word *bible* means "library."

The Language of Faith

- Throughout the year, refer to this section when necessary to help the students understand key Catholic vocabulary.
- Invite the students to draw their own illustrations for the terms listed here.
- Link your work with these terms to other language arts exercises. Have the students make up sentences using the terms, or use the terms in poems or prayers.
- Invite the students to make up crossword puzzles and hidden-word squares using terms from the glossary.
- Keep a class list of new religious vocabulary not listed in the glossary. Encourage the students to research the meanings of these terms.

The Language of Faith

The importance of a common "language of faith" cannot be underestimated. As the *Catechism of the Catholic Church* reminds us, we do not believe in formulas or definitions but in the reality expressed by the terms. Yet that expression is vital for understanding and religious literacy. The glossary section of *Walking by Faith* Two has been designed to help you support the students' growth in religious understanding, so that they and their families can feel comfortable talking about their faith, passing it on, celebrating it in the Christian community, and making it a fundamental part of their lives. Toward these ends, memorization is only the first step. The students will "grow into" the language of faith on many levels as they grow to religious maturity.

Catechism Background

For more on the importance of a shared Catholic vocabulary, see the *Catechism of the Catholic Church* (#170–171).

bishop A man ordained to lead and teach the followers of Jesus. The bishops are successors of the apostles. A bishop or *archbishop* usually leads a group of parishes called a *diocese* or *archdiocese*. The word *bishop* means "overseer."

blessing Praising God and calling on him to continue to send his gifts. People and things that are blessed are made holy or set aside to do God's work.

Body of Christ A name for the Church that tells how closely we are joined with one another and with Jesus. The priest or Eucharistic minister also speaks these words when offering us the consecrated host at Holy Communion.

C

catholic A word that means "universal" or "everywhere." The Church is catholic because it is open to all people.

charity Actions of loving service, caring, and sharing. The word *charity* means "love."

Christians People who follow Jesus Christ. Christians are baptized in the name of the Father, the Son, and the Holy Spirit. The word *Christian* comes from *Christ*, which means "anointed one."

Christmas The holy day that celebrates the birth of Jesus, the Son of God who became human to save us from the power of sin and everlasting death. The name *Christmas* comes from the words "Christ's Mass." We celebrate Christmas on December 25.

Church The community of all baptized people who believe in God and follow Jesus. The word *church* comes from two different words. One means "a community called together." The other means "belonging to the Lord." We belong to the Catholic Church, which is led by the pope and the bishops. A *church* is also the name of the building where we gather to worship God.

community A group of people who share time and space and who have common beliefs, activities, and goals. A family, a neighborhood, a school, and a parish are all examples of communities.

confess To tell our sins to the priest in the Sacrament of Reconciliation. What we confess to the priest is private.

Confirmation The Sacrament of Initiation that seals and completes Baptism. In Confirmation we are sealed with the Holy Spirit.

conscience The gift from God that helps us know the difference between right and wrong and choose what is right. We must form our conscience properly through prayer and study. We *examine*, or check, our conscience in preparation for the Sacrament of Reconciliation.

consecrate To make holy by the power of the Holy Spirit. At Mass the bread and wine are consecrated. They become the Body and Blood of Jesus Christ.

contrition Sorrow for sin and willingness to do better. Contrition is our first step toward forgiveness.

covenant A sacred promise or agreement joining God and humans in relationship. God made a covenant with the people of Israel and renewed it often. Jesus' sacrifice established the new and everlasting covenant, open to all who do God's will.

created Made from nothing. God created our world and everything in it, including each of us.

creation Everything God made. Creation includes things we can see, such as people and animals, and things we can't see, such as angels.

creed A statement of what we believe. The word *creed* means "I believe." The two most familiar creeds are the Apostles' Creed and the Nicene Creed, which we proclaim at Mass.

customs Ways of living and celebrating. The Church is made up of people with many different customs.

D

deacon A man who is ordained to serve the Church by baptizing, proclaiming the gospel, preaching, witnessing marriages, and doing works of charity.

diocese The area overseen by a bishop. A diocese is usually made up of a number of parishes. A large diocese may be known as an *archdiocese*, overseen by an archbishop.

disciple A person who follows Jesus and learns from his teachings and actions. The word *disciple* means "one who learns from a master."

E

Easter The Feast of the Resurrection of Jesus Christ, our greatest holy day. In the northern hemisphere, Easter is celebrated in the springtime. The exact date changes every year.

Eucharist The sacrament of Jesus' presence under the form of bread and wine. We receive Jesus' own Body and Blood as Holy Communion during the Eucharistic celebration. The Mass is a sacrifice and a holy meal. We join with Jesus to offer him and ourselves to God our Father. The word *Eucharist* means "thanksgiving."

Eucharistic Prayer The great prayer of thanksgiving prayed by the priest at Mass. During the Eucharistic Prayer the gifts of bread and wine are consecrated by the power of the Holy Spirit. They become the Body and Blood of Jesus Christ.

F

faith The gift from God that helps us seek him. Through faith we believe in God and we believe all that God teaches us through the Church.

fast To go without food or eat only a small amount of food. Adult Christians fast during Lent and at other times to show sorrow for sin. To show respect for the Eucharist, we fast for one hour (taking only water or medicine) before receiving Holy Communion.

feast days Days when the Church community celebrates in worship and prayer. Feast days help us remember events in the life of Jesus, his mother, Mary, and the saints.

free will The ability to choose between good and evil. God gave us the gift of free will. God does not force us to do what is right.

G

general intercessions A litany of prayers at Mass in which we ask God to care for the needs of all people. The word *intercession* means "a prayer asking God's help for someone."

God The one, true, divine Being whom we worship. Jesus taught us that God is the Holy Trinity of Father, Son, and Holy Spirit. God created us and loves us.

godparent A person who agrees to sponsor someone who is to be baptized. For a child the family and godparents are responsible for helping the child grow in his or her Catholic faith.

Good Friday The Friday before Easter. On this day we remember that Jesus died for us. We honor the cross, the sign of Jesus' saving love.

gospel A word that means "good news." The gospel message is the good news of God's reign and saving love. In the New Testament, the four stories of Jesus' teachings are called the *Gospels*.

grace God's free, unlimited, loving gift of his own life, friendship, and help to humans. Grace is not a thing, but a relationship. We grow in grace by participating in the sacraments and living faithful, loving, and holy lives.

Great Commandment The rule that sums up all God's laws. The Great Commandment tells us to love God above all things and to love our neighbors as we love ourselves.

H

heaven Being with God forever. Heaven is not a place but a state of being. Through God's grace heaven is our destined home.

hell Being separated from God forever. Hell is the result of choosing to live in mortal sin, turning away from God's love and forgiveness.

holy days Special feast days of the Church. We celebrate holy days just as we do Sundays, by participating at Mass and by setting aside time to rest and pray.

Holy Orders The sacrament by which men are ordained to serve God and the Church as deacons, priests, or bishops.

Holy Spirit The third Person of the Holy Trinity. The Holy Spirit is God's own love and holiness present with us in the Church. Jesus promised that the Holy Spirit would help his followers. The Holy Spirit is one with the Father and the Son.

Holy Trinity Our name for the three Persons in one God. The word *trinity* means "a union of three." The Father, the Son, and the Holy Spirit are the Holy Trinity. We praise the Holy Trinity when we make the Sign of the Cross.

Holy Week The week before Easter. During Holy Week, we remember and celebrate how Jesus gave his life for us. Holy Week begins with Palm (Passion) Sunday and includes the celebrations of the sacred *Triduum*—Holy Thursday, Good Friday, and Holy Saturday.

J

Jesus A name that means "God saves." This is the name Mary gave to her son, who is the Son of God. We believe that Jesus is both God and human. He taught us about God, his Father. He suffered, died, and was raised from death to save us from the power of sin and everlasting death.

justice The virtue of giving each person what he or she is due. The justice of God's kingdom is more than simple fairness. Justice is an obligation, or duty, that flows from our baptismal commitment.

K

kingdom of God A way of being in relationship with God, marked by true justice, love, and peace. God invites everyone to live in his kingdom. The kingdom of God was begun by Jesus. It will come in fullness at the end of time. The kingdom of God is also called God's *reign*.

L

last judgment When Jesus will return at the end of time to judge all people, living and dead.

law of love Jesus' new commandment, given to his friends on the night before he died. "I give you a new commandment: love one another" (John 13:34).

Lent The 40 days of preparation for Easter. The Season of Lent is a time of prayer, penance, and acts of charity. Lent begins with Ash Wednesday.

liturgy Our public worship of God in the Mass and the other sacraments.

M

marks of the Church The signs of the Holy Spirit's presence in the Church. The Church is one, holy, catholic, and apostolic.

martyr A person killed for following Jesus. The word *martyr* means "witness." By being faithful even when faced with death, martyrs give witness to what they believe.

Mary The mother of Jesus. God chose Mary to be the mother of his Son. We believe that Mary was free from original sin and all personal sin from the very beginning of her life. We believe that she remained a virgin throughout her life. And we believe that God took her to be with him forever, body and soul, at the time of her death. Jesus told us to call Mary our mother, too. She is the Mother of the Church.

Mass Our celebration of the Eucharist. At Mass Jesus is present in the community, in the priest, in the word of God, and in Holy Communion.

Matrimony The sacrament that joins a man and a woman in Christian marriage.

messiah A Hebrew title that means "the anointed one" or "the one chosen by God." Christians believe that Jesus is the Messiah. *Christ* is the Greek form of this title.

mission The work the Church is sent to do. The whole Church shares the mission of Jesus, which is to announce the good news of God's kingdom. A *mission* can also mean a church built by a missionary.

missionaries People who are sent to bring the good news of God's kingdom to people in other places or distant lands.

moral Having to do with the way we put our beliefs into action. Christian moral life means making choices and acting according to Jesus' law of love, the Beatitudes, the Great Commandment, and the Ten Commandments.

mystery A truth of our faith that we cannot fully understand but that we believe because God has shown it to us in Scripture, in the life of Jesus, or in the teaching of the Church. The Holy Trinity is a mystery.

N

nativity A word that means "birth." The Feast of the Nativity is the Church's name for Christmas, the holy day that celebrates the birth of Jesus. We do not know exactly when Jesus was born, but we celebrate the Feast of the Nativity on December 25.

new covenant The new holy agreement God made with all people through the saving actions of his Son, Jesus Christ.

New Testament The second part of the Bible. The New Testament is the story of Jesus and his followers. It has four accounts of Jesus' life and teachings. These stories are called *Gospels*.

O

Old Testament The first part of the Bible. The Old Testament tells the story of the Jewish people before Jesus was born. It tells many stories of God's love.

ordained Called forth to serve God and the Church in a special way through the Sacrament of Holy Orders. Deacons, priests, and bishops are ordained men. The Church includes both lay people and ordained men.

original sin The human condition of weakness and tendency toward sin that resulted from the first humans' choice to disobey God. Only Jesus, the Son of God, and Mary, his mother, were free of original sin. Baptism restores the relationship of loving grace in which all people were created by God. But the temptation remains to choose what we want rather than what God wants.

Our Lady of Guadalupe A title by which Mary is honored in Mexico and the United States. Mary called herself by this name when she appeared to Blessed Juan Diego with a message of hope and God's love. As Our Lady of Guadalupe, Mary is honored as the patron of the Americas. The Church celebrates the Feast of Our Lady of Guadalupe on December 12.

P

Palm Sunday The Sunday before Easter. On this day we remember Jesus' joyful entry into Jerusalem. We listen to the reading of the *Passion*, the Gospel story of Jesus' suffering and death.

parable A special kind of teaching story Jesus used to describe the kingdom of God and to tell people how to live in the kingdom. Parables often have surprise endings.

parish A community of Catholics who gather at the same church for Mass, the sacraments, religious education, and other activities. Usually a parish is made up of people who live in the same neighborhood. The leader of a parish is called a *pastor*, which means "shepherd." Many parishes together make up a diocese or archdiocese.

Paschal mystery The saving mystery of Jesus' suffering, death, and resurrection. We celebrate the Paschal mystery at every Eucharist.

Passion The Gospel reading that tells the story of Jesus' suffering and death. The word *passion* means "suffering."

Passover The Jewish holy day that celebrates how God led the Israelites out of slavery and death in Egypt. According to the Gospels of Matthew, Mark, and Luke, Jesus' Last Supper with his friends was a celebration of the Passover meal.

pastor The priest who leads a parish. The word *pastor* means "shepherd." If no priest serves a parish full time, the parish may be led by an administrator who is a deacon or a lay person.

penance Prayers or actions we do to make up for our sins. The priest gives us a penance in the Sacrament of Reconciliation. We also do works of penance during Lent to prepare for Easter.

pope The visible leader of the Catholic Church on earth. The pope is the bishop of Rome. He follows in the footsteps of Saint Peter, whom Jesus chose to lead his followers. The pope acts with the bishops to teach and guide the Church in service to the word of God.

prayer Communicating with God. The five reasons for prayer are blessing and adoration, petition, intercession, thanksgiving, and praise. There are many ways to pray.

precepts of the Church Some of the important duties of Catholics. The word *precept* means "teaching" or "guidance."

priest A man who is ordained to serve God and the Church by celebrating the sacraments, preaching, and presiding at Mass.

prophet A person called by God to speak God's message to humans. Every baptized Christian is called to share in the ministry of the prophet.

psalms Prayers that can be sung. There are 150 of these prayers in the Book of Psalms in the Bible. Jews and Christians use the psalms in prayer and worship. We sing or pray a psalm in response to the first reading at Mass.

R

Reconciliation The sacrament that celebrates God's forgiveness of sin through the Church. This sacrament is also known as *Penance*. The word *reconciliation* means "coming back together" or "making peace."

religious communities Groups of men or women who make promises to serve God and the Church through lives of prayer and action. Members of religious communities are known as religious priests, sisters, nuns, brothers, monks, or friars.

responsibility A response to God or to someone else to whom we owe obedience. A responsibility is a duty to act in ways that show respect and love.

resurrection The mystery of Jesus being raised from death by God's loving power. We celebrate the Feast of the Resurrection at Easter.

reveal To show forth. We are able to know and believe in God because he reveals himself to us.

Rosary A form of prayer to Mary. We pray the Rosary by praying numbers of Hail Marys, usually counting off the prayers on a circle of beads. While we pray we keep in mind important events in the lives of Jesus and his mother. We call these events *mysteries of the Rosary*. The word *rosary* means "rose garden," because the prayers are like a bouquet we offer to Mary. The circle of beads used to pray the Rosary is also called a *rosary*.

S

sacraments Celebrations that are signs and sources of God's grace. In the sacraments Jesus joins with the community in special words and actions. The Catholic Church celebrates seven sacraments. They are Baptism, Confirmation, Eucharist, Reconciliation, the Anointing of the Sick, Matrimony, and Holy Orders.

sacramentals Sacred signs. Sacramentals are special ways the Church has of using God's gifts. The most common sacramental is blessing. Using holy water to make the Sign of the Cross, burning candles as signs of Jesus, and waving palms on Palm Sunday are other examples of sacramentals.

Sacraments of Healing Reconciliation and the Anointing of the Sick. These sacraments celebrate the power of God's love to forgive sin and to heal sickness of body and spirit.

Sacraments of Initiation Baptism, Confirmation, and Eucharist. These sacraments celebrate our being joined to Christ as members of his Church. The word *initiation* means "beginning" or "coming to belong."

Sacraments of Service Matrimony and Holy Orders. These sacraments celebrate people's commitment to serve God and the community as a married couple or as an ordained man. These sacraments are also known as *Sacraments of Vocation*, because they celebrate ways to answer God's vocation, or call.

sacrifice To give up something for a greater good. The religious meaning of *sacrifice* is "something precious offered completely to God." Jesus offered himself as a sacrifice on the cross to save us from the power of sin and everlasting death.

saint A holy person who lived a good life and loved God. Saints are happy forever with God in heaven. Each of us is called to be a saint.

second coming When Jesus will come again in glory at the end of time, to judge the living and the dead and to bring the kingdom of God in fullness.

sin The choice to disobey God. Sin can be serious (mortal) or less serious (venial). Sin is a deliberate choice, not a mistake or an accident. God forgives sin when we are truly sorry and promise to do better.

solidarity Our belief that all humans are united in one family of God. We practice solidarity when we share others' joys and sorrows.

synagogues Jewish houses of prayer and study. Jesus taught in the synagogues of his land.

T

Ten Commandments Some of God's laws. The Ten Commandments tell us how to make loving choices. They help us show love for God and others. God gave the Ten Commandments to the people of Israel as a sign of the covenant.

V

virtues Good qualities or habits of goodness. The *theological virtues* of faith, hope, and love are gifts from God. The *cardinal virtues* of prudence, justice, fortitude, and temperance are habits that help us grow in holiness.

vision A dream or understanding of what will come, sent by God as a message of hope or warning. This kind of vision is knowledge that is beyond our human senses.

vows Sacred promises. Christians make vows in the Sacraments of Baptism, Holy Orders, and Matrimony. Members of religious communities also make vows.

W

witness To show clearly what we believe, through our words and actions.

works of mercy Actions that show justice, love, and peace, as Jesus did. The Corporal Works of Mercy are actions that care for the physical needs of others. The word *corporal* means "for the body." The Spiritual Works of Mercy are actions that care for the spiritual needs of others.

worship Praising and honoring God in prayer and liturgy.

Index

A
Abraham, 43–44, 47
abstain, **123**
adultery, 45
Advent, 74–77, **75**
All Saints' Day, 52–**53**
Anointing of the Sick, Sacrament of, 133–137
apostles, 50, 80, 90, 92, 95
Apostles' Creed, 95
apostolic, **92**
apostolic succession, **92**
Ash Wednesday, 147
Augustine, Saint, 65

B
Baptism, Sacrament of, 32, 67, 126–128, 141
   at Easter Vigil, 30, 171
   faith and, 131, 159
   holy water as reminder of, 15–16
Beatitudes, **104**, 111, 178
Bede, Saint, 153
Bible, 14, 39, 57, 165, 167
   Old Testament of, 75, 103, 150
   people of Israel's lessons in, 31
   as Scripture, 55, 110
   story of creation in, 7, 19
bishop, 81, 92, 129
   Holy Orders, 139, 141
   home church of, 152
blessing, **15**, 55, 147
Blood of Christ, 129, 141
Body of Christ, **67**, 69, 129, 141
Brigid, Saint, 153

C
candles, 15, 20, 127
catacombs, **151**
cathedral, 152
catholic, **92**, 151
Catholic Church   *See* Church
charity, **123**
choices, 61, 103, 110
Christ   *See* Jesus Christ
Christians, early, 50–51, 90–92, 151
Christmas, 98–101
   preparing for, 74–75
Church, **9**, 67, 89, 152
   as community, 8–10, 15, 20, 56, 80, 123, 133
   future of, 164
   good news from, 162
   healing by, 132–137
   helping us, 108–113
   history of, 150–154
   law of love for, 102, 104
   leaders of, 80–81, 92
   marks of the, **86**
   members of, 14, 126–131
   mission of, 79
   precepts of, **117**
   today, 156–161
   working together, 78–83
Clement, Saint, 155
Columba, Saint, 153
Communion   *See* Eucharist, Sacrament of; Holy Communion
community, **8**, 19
   Church as, 8–10, 15, 20, 56, 80, 123, 133
confession   *See* Reconciliation, Sacrament of
Confirmation, Sacrament of, 126–131, 141
conscience, **110**
   examining your, 103, 111
consecration, 129
covenant, **43**–44, 46
created, **7**
creation
   Church and, 14–15
   family of, 12–17
   gifts of, 15
   story of, 7, 19
crèche, **98**
Creed, 31, **95**, 164
cross, 119
customs, **14**

D
David, King, 75
deacon, 71, 129, 141
death
   end to, 163–164
   entering creation, 19
   Jesus', 61
   Paschal mystery and, 63
diocese, **81**
Donovan, Jean, 158
Doxology, **35**

E
Easter, 170–173
   "Alleluias" at, 65
Easter Vigil, 126, 128, 171
Eden, 19
eternal life, 164–165
Eucharist, Sacrament of, 37, 129, 151
   First, 63, 128
   See also Holy Communion
everlasting life, 164–165
evil, 59, 80
examinination of conscience, 103, 111

F
faith, 35, 87, 114–119
   growing in, 51, 159
   our family of, 77
   history of, 154
fast, **123**, 171
Father, 32, 67, 129   *See also* God; Holy Trinity
First Eucharist, 63, 128
forgiveness, 111, 113, 134–135
Francis of Assisi, Saint, 14, 17, 98–99
future, 162–167

G
general intercessions, **83**
Genesis, 7, 14, 43, 165
God, 13, 20, 39
   belief in, 30–35
   belonging to, 42–47
   as Creator, 6–9, 12, 15, 18–19
   family of, 152
   kingdom of, 54, **56**–57, 59, 147, 157–158, 160, 163–164
   new life with, 63
   worshiping, 36–41
   See also Father; Holy Spirit; Holy Trinity; Jesus Christ
godparents, 130
God's will, **59**
Good Friday, 147
good news, 20, 54–59, 93, 158, 162
Good Samaritan, 105
gospel, **57**
grace, **20**, 32, 129
Great Commandment, **105**, 178
greed, 45
Gregory I, Pope, 92
guided meditation, 161

H
Hail Mary, 39
Healing, Sacraments of, 132–137, **133**
heaven, **23**, 67, 80, 163
holiness, 84, 86
Holy Communion, 117, 126, 181
   See also Eucharist, Sacrament of
holy days, 53, 117
Holy Orders, Sacrament of, 139, 141
Holy Spirit, 32, 87, 88, 159
   celebrating sacraments through, 128, 129
   prayer to, 89, 161
   strength and support from, 108–111
   unity and holiness from, 84, 86
Holy Thursday, 123, 147
Holy Trinity, 31–33, **32**, 35, 129
   See also Father; God; Holy Spirit; Jesus Christ
holy water, 15–16
Holy Week, 146–149, **147**
homily, **57**
hope, 114–119, 162–167
Hosanna, 146

I
immortality, 164–165
Initiation, Sacraments of, **128**–130
intercession, **38**, 83
Isaiah, 156
Isidore the Farmer, Saint, 140
Israel, people of, 31, 44–45, 62–63, 105, 125, 150–151, 154

J
Jerusalem, 147, 149
   new, 163
Jesse tree, 75, 77
Jesus Christ, 11, 21, 104
   becoming like, 123
   birth of, 98–101
   Body and Blood of, 67, 69, 129, 141
   followers of, 115, 151
   forgiveness and healing of, 134
   good news of, 20, 54–59
   new covenant of, 44
   new life in, 60–65
   resurrection of, 170–173
   second coming of, 164
   as Son of God, 32, 98–101, 129, 165
   titles for, 15, 63, 171
   working through us, 66–71

Boldfaced numbers refer to pages on which the terms are defined.

Jewish people, 31, 44–45, 62–63, 105, 125, 150–151
John, Saint, 163, 165
John XXIII, Pope, 81
Juan Diego, Blessed, 27, 29
Judaism *See* Jewish people
justice, 104, 157–158

K
Kevin, Saint, 153
kingdom of God, 54, **56**–**59**, 157
    coming of, 147, 163–164
    giving witness to, 160
    people of, 158
Kino, Padre, 152

L
Lamb of God, 63
Las Mañanitas, 29
last judgment, **164**
Last Supper, 62–63
law of love, 102–107, **104**, 111
lay person, 158
Lent, 122–125, **123**, 171
light of the world, 18–23, 171
litany, 143, 167
liturgy, **37**, 173, 180 *See also* Eucharist, Sacrament of; Mass
Lord *See* God; Jesus Christ
Lord's Prayer, 39, 59
love, 61, 114–119, 157–158
    law of, 102–107, 111

M
Magnificat, 47
marks of the Church, **86**
marriage *See* Matrimony, Sacrament of
martyr, **51**, 151, 155
Mary, Mother of God, 26–29, 47
Mass, 16, 61, 117, 180
    "Allelulias" at, 65
    commonalities in Catholic, 85–86
    end of, 71, 93, 157
    Holy Spirit during, 88
    homily at, 57
    Palm Sunday, 147–149
    prayers during, 34, 37, 39–40
Matrimony, Sacrament of, 139, 141
meditation, 161
mercy, 104, 179
Messiah, **55** *See also* Jesus Christ
mission, 68, **79**
missionary, 158
mission church, 152
morality, 19, 33, 43, 68, 93, 109, 133, 165
mortal sin, 117, 181
Moses, 63, 103
mystery, **32**
    of Holy Trinity, 31
    of new life, 170
    Paschal, **63**, 65

N
nativity, **99**
nativity scene, 98–100
new covenant, 44, **62**
new life, 127, 129, 170–173
    in Jesus Christ, 60–65
Nicene Creed, 31, 164
Noah's Ark, 14

O
Old Testament, 75, 103, 150
ordination, **139**
original sin, **19**, 129
Our Lady of Guadalupe, 26–29, **27**

P
palm branches, 15, 51, 147
Palm Sunday, 15, 146–149, **147**
parables, 56
parish, 10, 81–82
    history of, 154
    Jesus' work in, 70
    volunteers from, 104
    worship in, 40
Paschal mystery, **63**, 65
Passion, **147**–148
Passover, 62–63
pastor, **81**, 139
Patrick, Saint, 33, 153
Paul, Saint, 11, 90–91
peace, 104, 157–158
penance, **117**, 171 *See also* Reconciliation, Sacrament of
Pentecost, 87–89
Peter, Saint, 80–81, 92
petition, prayers of, **38**
Pius X, Pope, 92
Polycarp, Saint, 50–52
pope, **81**, 92
    as "Servant of the Servants of God," 94
    See also names of individual popes
prayer, **37**–39, 119
    healing through, 137
    See also individual prayers, 174–177, 182
precepts of the Church, 117, 179
priest as presider, 129
    Sacraments of Initiation and, 129
    Sacraments of Healing and, 135
    Sacraments of Service and, 139–141
prophet, 156
psalms, 38, 125

R
Reconciliation, Sacrament of, 22, 76, 103, 110, 112–113, 117, 133–135, 181
responsibility, **13**, 140
resurrection, **61**, 164
reveal, **31**
Revelation, Book of, 163, 165
Richard of Chichester, Saint, 107
Rome, 80–81, 151, 153

S
Sabbath, 55
sacramentals, **15**
sacraments, **128**, 179 *See also* individual sacraments
sacrifice, **61**, 64
sadness, 19, 56, 104, 163
saint, **51**, 155
Sarah, 43–44, 47
Scripture, 55, 110 *See also* Bible
second coming, **164**, 166
Second Vatican Council, 81
Serra, Blessed Junipero, 152
Service, Sacraments of, 138–143, **139**
shamrock, 33
sickness, 19, 56, 135
Sign of the Cross, 15, 34–35
Simon *See* Peter, Saint
sin, **19**, 56, 59, 63, 90, 111
    effects of, 135
    forgiveness of, 134
    mortal/venial, 117, 181
solidarity, **158**, 160
Son of God, 32, 98–101, 129, 165
sorrow, 56
suffering, 163
synagogue, 46, **150**

T
talent, **69**, 139, 141
temple, 46, 87
Ten Commandments, 44–46, 103, 111, 178
Teresa of Avila, Saint, 69
thanksgiving, prayers of, 38
Thomas the Apostle, Saint, 115
truth, 90

U
unity, 86

V
Vatican, 80
venial sin, 181
virtues, **115**, 119
vision, **163**, 165
vows, **140**

W
water, 126
    holy, 15
witness, 33, 51, **158**–159
world, 116, 159, 162
    light of the, 18–23, 171
    problems of, 156–157
worship, 36–41, **37**

BROWN-ROA
A Division of Harcourt Brace & Company

Our Mission

The primary mission of BROWN-ROA is to provide the Catholic and Christian markets with the highest quality catechetical print and media resources.
The content of these resources reflects the best insights of current theology, methodology, and pedagogical research.
The resources are practical and easy to use, designed to meet expressed market needs, and written to reflect the teachings of the Catholic Church.

Program Consultants

Rev. Dennis Colter
Theology

Sr. Jude Fitzpatrick CHM
Pedagogy

Rev. Robert Vogl
Scripture

Rev. Douglas K. Clark
Catechism in Context

Program Music and Liturgies by
David Haas
Robert W. Piercy Jr.

We wish to acknowledge the contributions of the pastoral staff, teachers, and catechists of Saint Joseph the Worker Parish, Dubuque, Iowa, to the development of this program.

Photography Credits

Art Resource, NY: 150; Erich Lessing: 47, 69, 75; Giraudon: 38, 137; Jewish Museum: 31; Scala: 51, 63, 77, 92, 99, 149, 151, 155, 173; **Associated Press:** World Wide Photos: 44; Arturo Mari: 83; Bruno Mosconi: 80; The Sun News, Jessica Tefft: 98; **Catholic News Service:** Gene Plaisted: 139; **Comstock:** 65; David Lokey: 12; **Corbis-Bettmann:** 158; **John Crook:** 107; **Gene Plaisted/The Crosiers:** 15, 26, 29, 32, 35, 50, 56, 63, 65, 67, 84, 89, 92, 95, 99, 102, 113, 115, 127, 128, 129, 131, 135, 147, 153, 155, 157, 165; **Bob Daemmrich:** 85, 101, 167; **FPG, Int'l:** 92, 146, 149; Dennie Cody: T9; Fara: 81; Gerald French: 122, 125, NASA 1986: 89; Michael Keller: 15; Miguel S. Salmeron: 141; Gail Shumway: 59; Telegraph Colour Library: 162; **Gamma Liaison:** 153; J. Chatin: 125; Steve Liss: 22; Guy Van de Berg: 86; **Jack Holtel:** 6, 14, 18, 30, 39, 56, 69, 71, 74, 86, 102, 104, 107, 108, 109, 110, 113, 114, 116, 117, 119, 126, 132, 137, 140, 141, 147, 159, 161; **Image Bank:** P. Ridenour: 74; **Index Stock Photography, Inc.:** 143; Myrleen Ferguson: 54; **Museum of American Folk Art:** 140; **PhotoEdit:** Paul Conklin: 8, 71; Deborah Davis: 23; Myrleen Ferguson: 35, 42, 45, 113, 125; Tony Freeman: 14, 81; Stephen McBrady: 149; Michael Newmann: 17, 61, 78; Jonathan Nourok: 19; Alan Oddie: 37, 59; James Shaffer: 164; David Young-Wolff: 66, 107; **The Picture Cube:** Kindra Clineff: 101; Robert Finken: 122; Tom McCarthy: 77; **James L. Shaffer:** 29, 53, 65, 83, 86, 89, 95, 119, 143, 146; **Stock Boston:** Dave Bartruff: 99; Bob Daemmrich: 67, 161; J. Dun: 170, 173; John Eastcott & Yva Mormatiuk: 93; John Elk III: 153; Owen Franken: 93; Michael J. Howell: 84; William Johnson: 161; A. Rancey: 56; Miro Vintoniv: 41, 173; **The Stock Market:** David Ball: 84; Ed Bock: 170; Frank Fournier: 50, 53; Mark Gamba: 71; Gabe Palmer: 12; Simon Wolfe: 84; **Tony Stone Worldwide:** 93; Lori Adamski: T10; Arruza: 20; Ken Biggs: 3; Kim Blaxland: 60; Myrleen Cate: 22; Robert E. Daemmrich: 23; Nick Dolding: 27, 29; Charles Gupton: 39; Alan Hicks: 45; George Hunter: 153; David Madison: 123; Mark McLane: 153; Lawrence Migdale: 9; Kevin R. Morris: 12; Adrian Neal: 95; Greg Pease: 11; Andy Sachs: 171; Don Smetzer: 17; World Prospective: 17; Robert Yager: 27; **SuperStock:** 57; Museum of Art, Pennsylvania: 156; Private Collection, Giraudon, Paris: 167; **U.S. Army Chaplain Center & School:** 85; **Jim Whitmer:** 138, 158; **Christie Wilson:** 15, 36, 41, 59, 60, 69, 77, 117; **Bill Wittman:** 13, 35, 47, 83, 111, 131, 159

Illustration Credits

Jeanine Kicheloe: 7, 21, 33, 43, 55, 62, 68, 87, 90, 91, 105, 134, 163

Notes

Walking by Faith gives teachers and catechists practical support in their ministry with young people.

Idea Files

The following pages contain information on ten topics of significance to catechists. Each Idea File contains a number of practical hints and successful strategies to assist you in your ministry as a catechist. The topics are:

Idea File #1: Establishing Group Atmosphere
Suggestions for gathering and classroom management

Idea File #2: Building Faith Community
Suggestions for helping the students see themselves as part of the Church

Idea File #3: Meeting Individual Needs
Suggestions for addressing multiple learning styles and for adapting lessons for students with special needs

Idea File #4: Dealing with Popular Culture
Suggestions for incorporating the best (and eliminating the worst) of the messages students receive from society and the media

Idea File #5: Appreciating Diversity
Suggestions for incorporating multicultural experiences

Idea File #6: Connecting with Families
Suggestions for strengthening the classroom-home link

Idea File #7: Connecting with the Parish
Suggestions for integrating your class into the life of the faith community

Idea File #8: Overcoming Scheduling Limitations
Suggestions for dealing with busy schedules, time limitations, and housekeeping chores

Idea File #9: Fostering Catholic Morality
Suggestions for introducing and reinforcing Catholic moral teaching

Idea File #10: Assessing Progress
Suggestions for evaluating your own and the students' growth in faith, using a multitude of means

Idea Files materials are not tied to specific lesson plan pages. They're general in nature—the kinds of informative tips good catechists share with one another. The Idea Files are cross-referenced to other relevant parts of this Teaching Guide.

Each Idea File is designed to look like a bulletin board to which are attached notes, file cards, and memos. When you develop or hear of good ideas of your own, you might add them to these Idea Files pages, using removable sticky notes.

Establishing Group Atmosphere

Use or adapt any of these ideas to establish a positive and nurturing atmosphere in your class.

Get to Know the Students

Make sure each student feels welcomed, accepted, and safe. Learn the students' names, and call each student by name often. At the first class session, have the students introduce themselves and share favorite hobbies or activities. Throughout the year, allow the students to share events and information from their lives with family and friends, while respecting the need for privacy. Never force a student to share.

Begin Each Class by Gathering

It's not enough just to begin each religion class session with a prayer, or by taking roll. Students need help in making the transition from the rest of their day to the time they spend walking in faith together. Too often, prayer is used as a disciplinary measure, forcing the class into quiet. But gathering—the most important "first movement" of any religion class—must take into account who the students are and where they're coming from. Gathering welcomes the students and gives them the space to catch their breath. Gathering acknowledges the everyday experiences and concerns of the students, which are inseparable from their religious experience. Always take time for gathering activities before getting on with the spiritual, educational, and housekeeping tasks of the session.

For more Gathering suggestions, see The Importance of Gathering, *page T30.*

Help the Students Get to Know One Another

For the first few class sessions, have the students wear name tags. (This will help you get to know the students' names, too.) Have the students print their names on colorful tags. Provide art materials or magazine cutouts, and let each student create or choose a visual identifier for his or her name tag. You may wish to have the students choose partners and interview one another. After every student has been interviewed, let the students introduce their partners to the class, sharing one important thing he or she learned during the interview.

Make Your Room Their Room

To the extent that's practical, allow the students to shape the physical environment of the religion class. Take their suggestions as to the best seating arrangements. Let students design and decorate the prayer corner. If possible, set aside a bulletin board or an easel with chart paper for the students to decorate with the theme of the unit you're studying. Solicit the students' ideas and help when decorating the class space for seasons and feasts. If you share responsibility for classroom cleanup and maintenance with the students as well, they will feel a real sense of ownership.

Celebrate Special Days

Your religion class calendar should include all the important feasts and seasons of the Church year. Be sure to add your class's special occasions. You may wish to note birthdays, baptismal anniversaries, and name days (the feast days of the students' patron saints). Add parish and diocesan special days, too. Celebrate special days in a variety of ways, including sharing special snacks and creating decorations.

Set Group Goals

You and the students are on a mutual journey of faith, a shared pilgrimage. To build an atmosphere of community, work together to set class goals. Preview upcoming units or chapters with the students so they know what is ahead. Keep a class calendar with holidays and other special occasions clearly marked, so you can prepare and look forward together. Let the students know when you will be conducting formal assessments, and help them review the material in advance. You might want to chart the whole year as a road map, and have the students check off goals as you accomplish them.

E-Mail for: Walking by Faith

Subject: **Make Space for Prayer**
From: www.brownroa.com

Set aside a special place for prayer in your classroom. A prayer corner can be created by covering a small table with a cloth and placing a Bible on top. (A sturdy carton covered with patterned adhesive paper or a collage of magazine photos would also work well.) A crucifix and other simple religious images may be added according to custom and taste. (You might use figures from a folk-art nativity scene, for example.) The students can be encouraged to add their own decorative touches to the prayer corner each week by adding garden flowers or other natural objects and their own artwork. A CD or tape player with a stock of reflective music or favorite hymns helps add atmosphere. Large pillows or mats provide alternative seating. Please note that most local fire regulations prohibit using lighted candles in classrooms, especially with young students. Electric candles are a good alternative.

Share Joys and Concerns

As part of your gathering activities or as a regular part of classroom prayer, encourage the students to share their joys and concerns. Respect personal and family privacy, but let the students know that religion class is a safe place to share happy events—the birth or adoption of a sibling, a new pet, a team victory, an award—and concerns—a relative's illness, the death of a pet, a friend's moving away. Make time, too, to discuss the joys and concerns of your whole community, such as a parish festival or a natural disaster.

Arrange Seating for Sharing

Classroom arrangements can enhance or impede a positive group atmosphere. Arranging chairs or desks in a circle is one of the best ways to promote sharing. This is especially true if the students' regular classroom is arranged in more orderly rows. However, some students become easily distracted by sitting in a circle for the whole class period, so you may wish to save this arrangement for special parts of the religion class, such as discussion or prayer. As an alternative, arrange groups of chairs or desks in small clusters, or form two long curved rows of seats facing each other (the "banana split" formation). Although you may share classroom space, or be otherwise restricted in your ability to control seating, a certain amount of flexibility is always possible. If you do share space, be sure to return all chairs or desks to their regular formation at the end of class. You might arrange to rotate setup and cleanup chores with the class with whom you share space.

Building Faith Community

Use or adapt these strategies to help the students grow in their own spiritual and liturgical lives.

Choose Faith Partners

If your parish has both a Catholic school and a parish religion program, try to set up a Faith Partner program between the two. Students in the same grade in each teaching situation can be assigned as Faith Partners. Partners can write letters back and forth, exchange small treats or gifts, and get to know and support each other. This partnership might be maintained from year to year so the students could keep the same Faith Partners through their catechetical journey.

Ask Parishioners to Be Prayer Partners

Prayer is a good way to support students in the religious education program. Ask parishioners to volunteer as prayer partners for the students. Volunteers may draw names or choose from a list posted in the narthex of the church. As an alternative, have each volunteer choose a small wooden cross with a student's name on it. The cross may be kept in a pocket or purse as a continual reminder to include the student in the volunteer's prayers. Students should also include their parish prayer partners in their own prayers. Prayer partners might be invited to attend or to take a special part in liturgies and seasonal celebrations with the students. You may wish to post photographs of the students and their prayer partners in the parish hall.

Encourage Journaling

For students in Grades 1–6, the *Walking by Faith* program makes available a *Faith Journal*. The *Faith Journal* contains a variety of exercises and activities to help the students and their families explore the content of the religion class in a personal way. In addition to encouraging use of the *Faith Journal*, provide occasional journal experiences by posing questions for the students' private reflection. Remember that the journal experience is intended to be private. Students may share journal reflections if they choose, but should not be required to do so. Journal exercises should not be graded or counted toward homework points.

Get to Know the Saints

Use reference materials, lives of the saints, and the *Saints Walk with Us* feature in the student book to introduce the students to the "cloud of witnesses" that surrounds us on our journey of faith. Help the students identify (or choose) their patron saints. Learn about the patron saint of your parish and about any candidates for sainthood from your area of the country. Point out any statues or other artwork depicting saints in your parish church or school building. You might begin or end each class session by mentioning the saint or saints commemorated that day in the Church calendar.

Prepare for Mass

Spend some time each week helping the students prepare for Sunday Mass. Share the Scripture readings from the Lectionary, and discuss their meaning. This preparation time can also offer an opportunity to review the parts of the Mass and help the students practice the assembly's responses. You may occasionally follow up by asking the students to share their reactions to the previous Sunday's readings and homily.

Use Guided Meditation

Students find guided meditation a comfortable way to pray or reflect on the Scriptures. Guided meditation is not a gimmick or a form of hypnosis; it is a genuine spiritual discipline with a long history in the Church. Guided meditation helps students open themselves to the inspiration of the Holy Spirit and use their creative imagination in prayer. To use guided meditation, ask the students to sit comfortably. They may close their eyes to avoid distractions, or you can ask them to focus their attention on the cross or another religious image. Meditation can consist of storytelling, reflection questions, prayer, or a combination of all of these. Do not overuse this technique, but make use of it when you think it will be most effective for your students.

E-Mail for: Walking by Faith

Subject: Help Students Feel at Home with God's Word
From: www.brownroa.com

To familiarize students with the Scriptures, be sure they have access to the Bible. Ideally, each student will have his or her own copy of the Bible. The most familiar Catholic version, used in the Lectionary, is the *New American Bible*. (This is the version used for all Scripture citations in *Walking by Faith* Grades 3-6.) The *Catechism of the Catholic Church* cites the Catholic edition of the *New Revised Standard Version*. If it is not possible for each student to have a Bible, be sure there are sufficient copies available in class for the students to use.

Plan a Mass or Prayer Service

Work together with your students to plan a Mass or prayer service for the parish community sometime during the year. Have students choose a theme with appropriate readings, songs, and prayers. Encourage students to take on appropriate liturgical roles. Have the class make flyers to advertise the service and theme banners to hang in church. You may choose to work with other classes in the same grade level, or have all classes in the program participate.

For suggestions on incorporating the Walking by Faith *Music and Liturgy Resources into your class liturgies, see* Using Program Resources, *page T34.*

Pray All Ways

Help the students develop their own spirituality by varying your prayer celebrations. Introduce the students to the Church's rich treasury of prayer styles: formal and spontaneous, silent and sung, individual and communal. Make use of antiphonal prayer, in which the class is divided into groups to alternate verses or repeat refrains. Encourage the students to pray spontaneously in their own words and to compose prayers in various styles. Use collections of prayers from other times and places to expose the students to diversity in prayer.

Meeting Individual Needs

Use or adapt these general ideas to help you address the students' particular needs. Specific hints tied to the chapter content can be found on the lesson plan pages of this Teaching Guide.

Address a Variety of Learning Styles

All students differ in the ways they learn. Some students do well with words, mastering written or spoken language. Others deal in abstract concepts such as numbers. Still others learn best through visualization of content. Vary your teaching strategies to address different learning styles. Adapt the activities in the student book to meet the needs of your students. Remember that each of us is capable of learning in many different ways. By varying your strategies, you help the students enhance the range of their capabilities.

For more information on multiple learning styles, see Grade Five Overview, page T22.

Hope and Help for Learning Disorders

The term *learning disorders* refers to a complex of disabilities with a range of seriousness and a multitude of symptoms and causes. Learning disorders are difficult to diagnose, and students with undiagnosed or untreated learning disorders may experience low self-confidence, frustration, and anger. These students may be viewed, incorrectly, as disciplinary problems. Common learning disorders include difficulties with language and speech, writing, visual learning, memory, and thinking skills. A related complex of disabilities is known as attention deficit hyperactivity disorder (ADHD), which shows itself in excessive activity and inability to concentrate. In recent years, treatments have become available for many learning disorders, and support groups help students and their families deal successfully with these disabilities. If you have students with learning disorders in class, it is especially important to maintain contact with family members and to create situations in which students can grow in confidence. Other students in class should be enlisted as partners in this effort, and teasing must be firmly discouraged.

Establish Relationships with Family Members

Try to establish a relationship with the family members of students with special needs. Ask family members what strategies they use at home, and what they suggest you do in class, to help the student learn. Also ask what *not* to do for the student. Family members can often offer much input on how best to help the particular student. Be aware, too, that family members themselves may need help and direction. You may be as much of a resource for family members as they are for you.

Keep Everyone in the Mainstream

Students with disabilities—whether mental, physical, or emotional—need to be treated as much as possible like any other students. When you provide help to students with disabilities, try to do so without singling the students out. Allow students with disabilities as much independence as possible. Do not assume a student needs help; ask whether help is needed and, if so, what kind. The best thing you can do is to work with the class to make sure that all students are welcomed and appreciated for their particular gifts and strengths.

Use the Buddy System

To help students with individual needs, rely on the buddy system. Pair students so that those with physical, emotional, or mental disabilities, as well as those with learning disorders and those acquiring English, can get assistance from partners. You might also pair students with different learning styles, for example a visual learner and a student with strong verbal skills. Change partners occasionally, and allow both students in a partnership to assist each other, so that being a partner does not become burdensome.

Adapt for Students with Developmental Disabilities

Students with developmental disabilities may be assigned to special classes or, depending on the severity of the disability, may be mainstreamed into the regular class. In all cases, students with developmental disabilities should share some class activities, such as prayer and celebration, with other students. If you have students with developmental disabilities in class, you can make some adaptations to help them learn. Read aloud or use storytelling and role playing. Keep video presentations brief. Incorporate music and other rhythmic activities. Allow students with developmental disabilities to complete activities at their own pace. Provide items such as larger writing materials adapted to the students' needs.

E-Mail for: Walking by Faith

Subject: **Encourage Gifted Students**
From: www.brownroa.com

Sometimes being at the head of the class is a lonely place. Students who are gifted often absorb information so quickly they are left to watch the others catch up. Such students need additional challenges to hold their attention. If you notice students who seem to be ahead of the others, give them additional projects to work on. Let them supplement their lessons by drawing on the *Library Links* resources listed in your planning pages. Students could read the suggested books, access the multimedia, or contact the organizations for additional information. Gifted students may serve as tutors or project directors. However, be careful that extra work is seen as a challenge, and not perceived as either a reward or a punishment to the gifted student.

Communicate with Learners Acquiring English

If you have students in your class who are acquiring English, keep in mind that we all learn language in the same ways—by hearing it from other people and seeing it in print. To facilitate this learning, provide contextual clues when speaking—show pictures, use motion, and if possible, speak in the student's primary language. Don't be too concerned with making your English simple. Focus on the message you are communicating and you will automatically change your speech to make it easier to understand. Use dual-language flashcards to reinforce new vocabulary terms. Allow students to teach the class prayers and songs in their primary languages.

Be Flexible with Fidgets

Many students tend to fidget a lot during class. Fidgety students simply need to expend nervous energy. If they are distracting to other students, seat them on the outer edges of the group and let them fidget. If a student makes too much noise tapping a pencil on the desk, suggest that he or she tap it on something soft such as a jacket or sweater instead. Releasing that nervous energy helps students to concentrate on what you are teaching.

Dealing with Popular Culture

Use or adapt any of these strategies to make the students more aware of the world around them and help them deal with the positive and negative effects of popular culture.

Stay in Touch with the Real World

Discuss current events with the students. Include both positive and negative topics currently being discussed in newspapers and magazines or on TV, radio, or the Internet. Help the students see how these events affect their lives and the lives of others around the world. Explain the Church's position on particular issues. Ask the students what Jesus might think or do about the situations. Ask the students how they would respond. Have students write letters to the editor or send e-mail expressing their views. Include the needs of people around the world in your class prayers.

Tune In to Popular Music

Students receive many messages from the music they listen to. Some popular music carries disturbing messages about violence, sexuality, drug and alcohol use, racism, and attitudes toward women. Young students may react emotionally to melody and rhythm without recognizing inappropriate content in song lyrics, and may deny that the music they listen to reflects their personal values. But students need to be aware of the messages they're hearing. Listen to the music the students (and their older siblings) enjoy. When songs contain material counter to Christian values, point it out. But be sure to help the students listen for positive messages as well. No medium is completely negative, and helping students evaluate what they hear is better, in the long run, than bans and boycotts.

Address Social Pressures

Catholicism is often seen as a counter-culture to mainstream society. The students need to learn how to stand up for themselves and what they know is right. Talk with the students about the pressures they feel from others and from the media. These pressures might include how to dress, how to act, whom to be friends with, and how to have fun. Ask students to talk about the pressures that they feel and help them to open up by asking leading questions like, "Has anyone ever tried to tell you not to be friends with someone?" Don't be afraid to deal, in age-appropriate ways, with sensitive subjects such as drugs, alcohol, smoking, or sexual activity. Help the students see that they don't have to give in to negative pressure in order to fit in.

Watch TV Critically

Every year, the Human Family Institute—a foundation begun by Paulist Father Ellwood Kieser—awards Humanitas Prizes to the writers of television series episodes and TV movies that celebrate positive human values. One way to help the students sort through the "vast wasteland" of TV is to ask them to act as Humanitas scouts. When you or the students see a TV program that promotes the Christian values you are studying, talk about it in class. You might occasionally write a class letter to the producers or sponsors of positive shows, encouraging their efforts.

Evaluate Advertising

Young students are bombarded with advertising messages, primarily in the form of television commercials. Many of the programs students watch and the videos they see are thinly veiled commercials for toys and games. Some ads promote dubious values, or present stereotypical images. Help the students in your class evaluate the advertising messages they receive. Teach them to ask: (1) What is this ad trying to get me to buy or do? (2) What does the ad promise? (3) Is the ad's promise true? (4) Would buying or doing what this ad suggests reflect my Catholic faith? Reverse the process by having students create their own ads for positive Christian values.

Is Faith Fashionable?

Beginning at a very young age, students are pressured to be "in style." Students judge one another on appearances, looking for the popular name brands on shoes, jackets, and backpacks. Help the students see that what really matters is not how we look but who we are. Being in fashion is fine to a point, but it becomes wrong when fashion drives us to spend inappropriately, to judge others, to wear immodest or offensive styles, or to provoke violence, as in the wearing of gang colors.

E-Mail for: Walking by Faith

Subject: **Don't Get Caught in the Web**
From: www.brownroa.com

Computers are a real blessing in the classroom or library. Access to the Internet has revolutionized student research and interdisciplinary education. But online activities are full of pitfalls for the unwary. Young students should never spend time online without adult supervision, and efforts should be made to direct students to age-appropriate areas. Some positive computer connections for religion classes include exchanging e-mail with Catholic religion classes in other cities, states, or countries; accessing online versions of Catholic publications; keeping up with Church news such as the appointments of bishops and the canonization of saints; and making occasional use of Catholic CD-ROM resources or computer games.

Have Serious Fun with Comic Strips

Talking about comic strips can be a fun way to cover serious issues. Encourage the students to bring in comic strips that relate to topics you are covering in class. Discuss the characters' actions in the light of your Catholic values. Have the students act out alternative solutions or draw their own comic strips. You might also post comic strips in class for the students to read and enjoy.

Read All About It

When talking about the impact of popular media, we sometimes overlook the power of the printed word. Encourage the students to read. Obtain library copies of the books suggested in the *Library Links* section of the *Getting Ready* pages, and read them aloud or let the students read them during free time. Post a *Good Books* list and let the students add their recommendations. Encourage students to discuss books they've read that touch on religious themes.

Appreciating Diversity

Use or adapt these strategies to help the students develop their appreciation of the diversity of our Catholic culture and community.

Encourage Cultural Expression

The best evidence for the Church's cultural diversity is often right in your classroom. Encourage each student to find out about his or her cultural heritage and to share it with the rest of the class. Students may tell about or bring in examples of music, art, dance, food, or dress that are unique to their cultures. If any of your students and their families recently arrived in this country, ask the students to tell the class about their countries of origin.

Supplement Lessons with Diverse Religious Art

Christians from different parts of the world express religious images differently. Whenever possible, point out examples of religious art from different cultures. (Supplement those in the student book with examples from library books.) Ask the students to share examples of religious art reflecting their families' cultural roots. In addition to encouraging multicultural awareness and educating the students about religious imagery, sharing religious art that reflects all races and ethnicities reinforces the understanding that the Church is truly catholic.

Invite Families to Share Their Customs

Invite the families of all your students to join the class for a multicultural celebration. Have the students make and decorate a banner reading *We Are All God's Family* to hang in the classroom. Invite family members to bring in food, art, or other symbols of their cultures, or to dress in traditional clothing. If possible, ask families to bring pictures of their ancestors or their countries of origin. Encourage family members to tell stories about their cultural roots, share family history, or simply talk about their family's everyday activities. Be sure to check for food allergies before allowing the students to sample any foods in class.

Celebrate Saints' Days

There are saints from all over the world. Take advantage of feast days to learn more about particular saints and the cultures they come from. If possible, show the students how people of a saint's own country or culture depict that saint, rather than relying only on standard Western European iconography of saints. You might survey the students to find out their families' countries of origin, and learn more about the patron saints of these countries. What are some of the cultural symbols associated with saints, such as Patrick's shamrock and the kente-cloth robes of the African martyrs? How are saints' feast days celebrated in their native lands and cultures?

Plan Multicultural Seasonal Celebrations

Celebrate a multicultural holiday, such as a "Christmas Around the World." Work with teachers of other grade levels, and assign one country per grade or class. Each grade or class could learn one song or prayer from its assigned country and present it at a parish-wide celebration. At Easter time, have students find out more about Easter customs in other cultures. You might carry out simple activities such as decorating *pysanky* (Ukrainian-style Easter eggs) or making Russian Easter bread.

Deal with Socioeconomic Diversity

Don't ignore diversity in socioeconomic backgrounds, either among the students in your class or between your parish and others in the area. Students need to know from an early age that all people are equally loved by God and that all people have something to give to others. Too often, charitable activities or service projects give a false sense of "lucky us, helping those poor unfortunate others." Help the students see that what people have or don't have, materially, is not as important as how well they love and serve God and others.

E-Mail for: Walking by Faith

Subject: **Learn Other Languages**
From: www.brownroa.com

One important way to raise multicultural awareness is to have the students learn other languages. There are many prayers, phrases, and songs associated with religion class that might be translated into various languages. For example, the students could make a banner or mural with the words for *peace* in several languages. If students in your class are fluent in other languages, have them teach the class a simple prayer such as the Sign of the Cross in another language. Listen to recordings of popular hymns or Christmas carols in other languages. Don't forget to expose the students to simple terms in languages such as Latin, Greek, Hebrew, and Aramaic (the Church's "native languages") or American Sign Language.

Make a Quilt

A patchwork quilt, in which diverse fabric pieces are fashioned into a unified work of art, is a great symbol for the diversity of God's people. You might have the students create a class quilt. Ask each student to bring in a fabric square. (If possible, the fabric should have some family or personal significance.) Have the students decorate their squares with fabric paints or iron-on transfers. Make sure each student signs his or her square. Then join the pieces together into one design. (Let the students research quilt patterns, and enlist the aid of quilters in your parish community if necessary.) Display your quilt in the prayer corner throughout the year.

Partner with Another Congregation

Contact a church with a population different from your own. Possibilities include a Catholic parish with a different ethnic or racial balance, or another Christian denomination. You might arrange to partner with a congregation of another faith, such as a Jewish synagogue or a Muslim mosque in your area. Have the students write letters to students in the partner congregation, telling them about your parish and asking them about their faith community. If possible, visit each other's places of worship, or plan a celebration or service project both congregations could take part in.

Connecting with Families

Use or adapt any of these strategies to strengthen the connection between the religion classroom and the home.

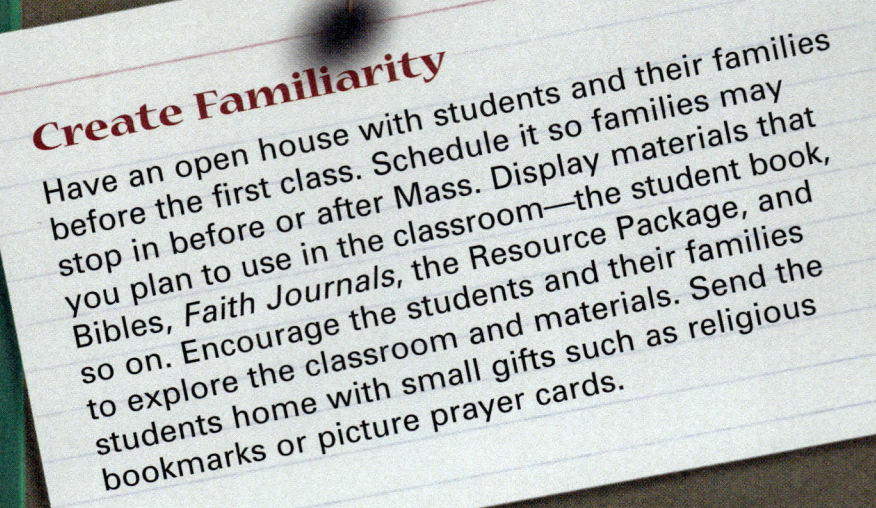

Create Familiarity

Have an open house with students and their families before the first class. Schedule it so families may stop in before or after Mass. Display materials that you plan to use in the classroom—the student book, Bibles, *Faith Journals*, the Resource Package, and so on. Encourage the students and their families to explore the classroom and materials. Send the students home with small gifts such as religious bookmarks or picture prayer cards.

Celebrate Family Life

Family life should be celebrated throughout the year, not just during holidays such as Thanksgiving or Christmas. To help promote the celebration of family life, select four or five dates for family gatherings. Include the Feast of All Souls (November 2) to recall family members who have died. You might also include a secular observance such as Arbor Day or Earth Day to celebrate God's gifts of creation. Have students make invitations for their families, and let them contribute to planning the celebration.

Keep in Touch

Begin the year by establishing an open line of communication with families. In the invitation you send to the students before the beginning of the school year, include a letter introducing yourself to the students' families. You may also want to send home a list of activities and materials needed for the class. Let families know you want their involvement. Ask family members to indicate areas of interest, committing to some level of participation. Make a point of visiting with families at coffee hours and other parish events. Periodically call family members to touch base with them. Send thank-you notes, progress reports, holiday greetings, and so on to strengthen the family connection.

For information on the Walking by Faith Family Letters, *see* Using Program Resources, *page T34.*

Send Home Familywork

Sending work home encourages family support. And there are many purposeful activities for families to do together. Consider making homework "familywork" on a regular basis, with the understanding that it serves the whole family, not just the student.

Encourage Family Prayer

As Catholics, we know prayer provides one of our strongest connections to God and to one another. Pray weekly prayers for families. Have the students think about the needs of their entire family, including those who live far away. Involve family members in the same activity by asking them at the beginning of the year to write a prayer for their students and for all students. Each week, choose a different prayer from the students' families to use as an end-of-day prayer.

Create a Family Photo Board

Students love to share pictures of their families, recalling vacations or fun activities that have been documented in photographs. Encourage your class to share pictures (with their families' permission) on a family photo board in your classroom. Change the pictures on a regular basis during the year. Establish themes for the board based on the Church calendar or the unit themes of the student book. Students will take great pride in showing off their families.

E-Mail for: Walking by Faith

Subject: **Capitalize on Your Connections**
From: www.brownroa.com

There are many activities that will support your curriculum off church grounds. Family members may have connections to places that may allow guided tours or provide further instruction. Plan field trips that encourage family involvement. Ask for volunteer drivers and chaperons. Families take great pride in sharing their occupations and vocations with students.

Plan Seasonal Family Nights

Invite families to join you for seasonal family nights. These events could be held at Thanksgiving, Christmas, Lent, and Easter. Begin the night with a prayer. Plan arts and crafts activities, such as holiday decorations, scenes with biblical characters, or even rosaries for families to make together. If possible, have family members make one craft to take home and another to give to a care center, hospital, hospice, or shelter.

Schedule a Family Retreat

Family members of students preparing for sacraments should be invited to come for a day of retreat to help prepare their children. Besides covering the basics of where to be and when, ask family members to share stories about when they celebrated the sacraments for the first time. For those students who aren't receiving sacraments, a retreat with family members could center on the theme of the student book. Plan activities and opportunities for much interaction and sharing.

Connecting with the Parish

Use or adapt any of these strategies to connect the students more directly with the parish community.

Get to Know Parish Ministers

Your parish staff is an important part of your class's journey of faith. Begin the year by scheduling a get-to-know-you celebration. Invite the pastor or administrator and other parish ministers to visit your class and introduce themselves. Schedule regular visits from parish ministers—to answer questions, or to join you for prayer and celebration—throughout the year.

Share the News

Use the weekly parish bulletin to acquaint the students with parish celebrations, activities, and personnel. Include in class prayer the names of parishioners who are sick or who have died. Send congratulatory messages from the class to newly baptized, confirmed, married, or ordained parishioners. Make use of your diocesan or regional Catholic newspaper as well. Read or post articles related to what you are studying. Take note of articles or photographs that refer to your parish. Encourage students to write letters to the editor to express opinions.

Celebrate the Eucharist

The Eucharist is the heart of the parish community. Make sure the students have ample opportunity to participate in the Mass. Even if the students attend special class Masses, make an attempt to provide a connection to the larger worshiping community. Invite parishioners (including the students' families) to join you for Mass. On occasion, have the class attend a regular daily Mass. Help the students prepare for Sunday Mass by going over the readings in class. Remind the students that we all have roles to play in the Eucharistic Celebration. Invite the students to become involved in liturgical ministries appropriate to their age and development.

Volunteer Time and Talents

As a class, give time to parish service ministries such as food banks, clothing drives, day care, or outreach to those who are homebound. Encourage the students to share their talents and abilities as their age and development allow. These efforts can also form a bridge to the larger community beyond the parish.

Learn Liturgical Music

Invite the parish music ministers to visit your class several times during the year. Help students become familiar with frequently used service music, such as settings of the acclamations and psalm responses. If your parish has a young people's choir or music group, encourage the students to join and participate.

Schedule a Parish History Project

Have the students work cooperatively to research the history of the parish. Research techniques might include interviewing parishioners, checking back issues of the diocesan newspaper, or exploring parish archives. The results of the research can be put together as a mural, book, photo album, or audiotape or videotape production. Share the presentation with the parish.

E-Mail for: Walking by Faith

Subject: **Tour the Parish Church**
From: www.brownroa.com

Don't assume that the students are familiar with the parish worship space. Arrange one or more visits to the church. You or a parish minister can point out the various ceremonial areas, architectural details, church art, vestments, and ritual objects, explaining their significance. Include information on the saint or mystery of faith for which your parish is named. You may wish to have the students work on a "map" of the church or create a written and illustrated or audiotape guide to the parish.

Participate in Sacramental Life

Arrange for your class to attend and participate in parish sacramental liturgies. If possible, attend celebrations of Baptism, Confirmation, Anointing of the Sick, and Matrimony as a class. Encourage student participation in both individual and communal celebrations of the Sacrament of Reconciliation. If a parishioner is to be ordained, try to arrange for your class to attend the ceremony. Before the class participates in or witnesses a sacramental celebration, review the rite and discuss prayers, symbols, and gestures the students will be experiencing.

Connect with Catholic Organizations

Your parish or diocese can supply information on Catholic organizations active in your area. Contact members of these organizations, who can provide assistance with class projects or information on involvement. Activities sponsored by the Catholic Youth Organization and Catholic Scouting are obvious choices for students, but don't ignore organizations that serve charitable, missionary, or social justice efforts.

Overcoming Scheduling Limitations

Especially in the parish school of religion, the scheduling of religion classes poses challenges. Use or adapt any of these strategies to help you make the most effective use of class time.

Share the Workload

Since your job is to teach, let the students themselves do the rest. Chores such as decorating the classroom, setting up and putting away chairs, setting up the prayer corner, and cleaning up can be delegated to the students according to their ages and abilities. When you need classroom assistants for special activities, consider inviting the students' family members, older students, or parishioners to pitch in.

Take Advantage of Opportunities

Religion class time is often the first to be sacrificed to other priorities, such as holiday celebrations and other extracurricular activities. If possible, take advantage of these occasions to build bridges between your class time together and the students' everyday lives. Obtain schedules of assemblies, special events, and holidays from the students' regular schools, and add these to your class calendar. Help the students make connections between religious values and such assembly topics as multiculturalism and drug-use prevention. Remind the students of the religious origins of holidays such as Christmas and Easter. Work together to create religious observances of secular holidays such as Thanksgiving and Memorial Day.

Streamline Housekeeping

Logistical tasks such as taking roll, collecting assignments, making announcements, and preparing paperwork to be taken home can eat up much of your class time. Allot the briefest possible time to accomplishing these tasks, and stick to your deadline. Sign-in sheets and check-off charts can be prepared in advance, as can homework folders and assignment sheets. It's important to provide a buffer space between any logistical tasks and the class time itself, so the students can make a graceful transition in and out of this special time together.

For more ideas on smooth transitions, see The Importance of Gathering, *page T30.*

Work with Other Teachers

Combine classes to cover special topics or celebrations that are common within the grade level or even across grade levels. Each teacher or catechist can cover part of the lesson. This lightens the workload for you, and makes an interesting change for the students.

Stay (Mostly) on Task

Use the Getting Ready pages before each chapter to help you allot time for classroom discussions and activities. Time spent in preparation can save you time later by allowing you to stay on task as much as possible. But remember to be flexible, too. Not all distractions are negative. Sometimes discussing the students' joys and concerns is more important than sticking to a rigid lesson plan.

E-Mail for: Walking by Faith

Subject: **Use Alternative Space**
From: www.brownroa.com

One difficulty in scheduling some religion class activities comes from the lack of available space. Shared classrooms can mean cramped quarters or limitations on rearranging seating or putting up decorations. Conducting a quiet prayer service in a crowded auditorium or parish hall shared by other classes can be very distracting. Ease your planning by exploring alternative class spaces well in advance. Are there classrooms or parish multi-purpose rooms you can use occasionally? Is it possible to celebrate prayer services or even conduct some class sessions in the church? Might the students' families or other parishioners host class sessions at home? If the weather permits, can you meet outdoors?

Organize Materials

Gathering the materials needed to carry out classroom activities can be a time-consuming headache. To streamline the process, be sure to check the *Materials* list in the planning chart on the Getting Ready pages for each chapter. Stockpile key materials such as art supplies in cardboard file boxes with handles or plastic storage bins for portability. Or let each student keep his or her own supply of art materials in a shoebox, lunch box, or plastic storage container.

Work in Groups

Instead of having each student answer a question or complete and share an activity, encourage the students to work cooperatively. Group discussion and cooperative activities are great timesavers, as long as you and the class are sufficiently prepared. Help the students form teams or working groups that stay together for a period of time (long enough to achieve a level of comfort and familiarity, but not so long as to become boring). Remember the importance of making sure that all students have the chance to participate as fully as possible.

For more suggestions on coping with time limitations, see Scheduling, pages T35–T37.

Give Sacramental Preparation Its Own Space

Preparation for the sacraments is not intended to substitute for catechesis, but in a busy religion program the temptation exists to save time by substituting. If students in your class are preparing to celebrate sacraments, work closely with families, parish staff, and other teachers and catechists to give this preparation its own special character. Ideally, sacramental preparation has its own schedule, with sessions meeting at other times than the regular religion program. If this is not possible, try team teaching sacramental preparation sessions with other parish ministers, involving families, or meeting somewhere other than your regular religion classroom.

IDEA FILES : T57

Fostering Catholic Morality

Use or adapt these strategies to enhance the material on moral formation provided in the student book.

Point Out Morality in Action

Help the students understand that morality involves how we live our lives every day. When you see the students making good moral choices, reflecting on the Church's moral teachings, and acting out of good conscience, make a point of mentioning it. Your acknowledgment may be public or private, depending on the situation. Encourage the students to be on the lookout for examples of everyday Christian morality in their own midst.

Review Decision-Making Steps

To help the students make good moral choices, frequently review with them the steps in decision making. (1) Think about the choice before you act. (2) Ask yourself "What is the right thing to do?" (3) Think about the results of your choice. (4) Ask yourself how Jesus would choose. (5) Compare your choice with the Great Commandment, the Ten Commandments, and the Beatitudes. (6) Talk about your choice with someone who can give you good advice. (7) Pray to the Holy Spirit for help.

Witness by Example

Students learn by example more easily than they learn from textbooks. So you yourself should be an example of how to live a Christian life. No one is perfect, but keep in mind that your actions and the way you treat others will be remembered longer than your words. Remember the respect with which Jesus, the greatest catechist, treated each of his listeners, and the ways in which he invited them to choose the path of God's kingdom. You are called to touch each student's life in the same way.

Encourage Moral Reflection

Remind the students of the importance of prayer and reflection in making moral decisions and of examining their consciences periodically. Include time for such reflection in your classroom prayer on a regular basis. Suggest that the students visualize themselves in a favorite place, talking with Jesus. What choice would he want them to make? Remind the students that they can perform this kind of meditation anytime they are faced with a moral choice.

Address Moral Questions

To clarify the Church's teaching on moral issues, invite your pastor or another knowledgeable parish minister to address the students. Invite the students to compose a list of questions in advance. The questions might be rooted in the material you are studying or may be prompted by events in the news (for example, students may be curious about the Church's view of such practices as cloning). Work with your guest speaker ahead of time to make sure he or she can respond to the students' questions in an age-appropriate and doctrinally sound manner.

E-Mail for: Walking by Faith

Subject: **Share Stories**
From: www.brownroa.com

```
Invite the students to share stories
they've read or TV programs or
movies they've seen that explore
moral questions. Bring up your own
examples, too. Discuss the following
questions: What choices did the
characters face? How did they come
to their decisions? What were the
results of their choices? Would you
have chosen differently? What do
you think Jesus would have told
the characters to help them choose?
```

Provide Role Models

When you find accounts of positive moral actions in the news media, share the information with the students. Together, find out more about real-life people who are acting on values consistent with the Church's teaching. Students' role models often come only from among entertainment and sports figures. Help them look to a wider range of witnesses.

Practice What You Preach

To help the students apply the moral principles they are learning in class, have them role-play various situations calling for moral choices. Suggest situations involving moral dilemmas (or have the students suggest them) and ask volunteers to act out the resolution. Evaluate the results together as a class.

Support Conscience Formation

In order to form their consciences properly, the students must be reminded frequently of the cornerstones of Christian morality. Take time to review the Great Commandment, the Golden Rule, the Ten Commandments, and the Beatitudes with the students on a regular basis. Point out the moral education contained in the Sunday Mass readings. Summarize, in age-appropriate language, moral statements made by the pope and the bishops.

Assessing Progress

Use or adapt any of these ideas to help you assess the students' progress in class and growth in faith.

Encourage Self-Assessment

Have the students write their own evaluations. At the end of the grading period, ask the students to think about what they have learned and what else they would like to know. If possible, talk with each student individually about his or her self-assessment. Remind the students of their successes, and discuss areas that need improvement. Help the students come to a realistic understanding of their strengths and weaknesses.

Make Portfolios

At the beginning of the year, have each student make his or her own portfolio in which to keep special assignments or activities completed throughout the year. Students can decorate their portfolios in class, or you can assign the project as homework and invite family involvement. Allow the students to choose the items they wish to place in their portfolios (prompts are provided under *Assessment Tip* in the *Resource Center* on your lesson plan pages). To use the portfolio as an assessment tool, periodically ask the students to share with you the contents of their portfolios. Discuss the significance of the choices to the students, and use the portfolio materials as the foundation of a mutual assessment process.

Provide Oral Reviews

Make use of opportunities for oral assessment. The *Share Your Faith* section of the unit review pages is intended to prompt oral review. Other oral review possibilities include asking the students to rephrase chapter lessons in their own words, encouraging discussion of key concepts, and having the students retell Scripture stories. The students' responses will help you measure their level of understanding.

Act Out the Lesson

In reviewing some lesson content, especially Scripture stories, material on the life of Jesus, and moral education, it may be appropriate to ask students to act out the lesson as a form of assessment. Have students think about what their characters might have felt or said. Encourage them to use simple props, masks, or costumes to get into character. Acting out a story or incident helps the students show creatively that they have understood the concepts covered in the text.

Play Games

Make up your own versions of popular games such as Pictionary® or Jeopardy®, with clues and answers related to concepts and vocabulary from the lesson. Divide the class into teams, or have partners compete together. Reward the winning team or partnership with a small treat, but stress that cooperation among team members or partners is more important than competition. Be sure to vary the composition of teams and partnerships often so all students have a chance to shine.

Let the Students Create Assessments

You might occasionally have the students create their own assessments. Students can work in teams to come up with assessment questions, fill-in-the-blank statements, or vocabulary quizzes. Have the teams test each other. Invite the students to suggest other ways of assessing understanding and progress.

E-Mail for: Walking by Faith

Subject: **Use Art for Assessment**
 From: www.brownroa.com

Have students draw pictures as a way of assessing their understanding of chapter content. Make it clear that these pictures will not be judged on artistic ability, but on the level of understanding they reflect. Artistic assessment exercises can include asking students to illustrate vocabulary terms, to visually retell a Bible story, or to draw themselves applying a particular moral value. Students might also create comic strips illustrating a lesson, or work together on a mural that will serve as a group assessment.

Evaluate Yourself

Don't forget to assess your own growth in faith throughout the year. Take time occasionally to reflect on the following questions: What were my goals for this chapter/unit? How well did I achieve my goals? What did I most enjoy sharing with the students? What did the students teach *me*? What areas of my catechetical ministry still need improvement?

For other opportunities for reflection and self-assessment, see Your Faith Journal *beginning on page J1.*

Invite Family Assessment

Once or twice a year, invite family members to assess the students' progress. You might compose a simple survey to send home with a family letter. Or ask each student to talk informally with his or her family about what he or she has learned, and ask family members to summarize for you the content of the conversation. Family assessment can also be scheduled as part of a mid-year or year-end open house.

Notes

Walking by Faith gives catechists and teachers opportunities to deepen their own spirituality and to grow in faith.

Your Faith Journal

This section of the Teaching Guide offers you a way to nourish your own spiritual development as you walk by faith with the students.

Your Faith Journal features one page of reflections for each chapter in the student book. Each page includes the *Catholics Believe* statement and its relevant citation from the *Catechism of the Catholic Church*, as well as the following:

- **Reflect**—questions and prompts for your own reflection on the chapter topic

- **Continue the Journey**—suggested activities for deepening your spiritual growth and understanding

- **Affirm**—a personal resolution to inspire and guide you

Writing rules are provided for you in this section, but you may wish to keep your written reflections in a separate journal or notebook to which you may add drawings, photographs, and other materials.

A note on the *We Reflect* page of each chapter's lesson plan pages reminds you to make use of *Your Faith Journal*. However, you may use these pages at any time before, during, or following your presentation of the chapter.

Reviewing completed *Your Faith Journal* pages at the end of each unit can be a helpful means of evaluating your progress as a catechist and your growth in faith.

Your Faith Journal — CHAPTER 1
Made for Each Other

God created humans to live in community.
Catechism of the Catholic Church, #1879

Reflect

What are the most important relationships in my life?

_____
_____
_____
_____

Why is being an active member of the Church important to my relationship with God?

_____
_____
_____
_____

How did God call me to be a part of the Church community?

_____
_____
_____
_____

How have I learned about God's love by being part of my parish?

_____
_____
_____

Continue the Journey

- Look through photographs of people you love. Think of the role each of these people has played in making you the person you are today. Thank God for their presence in your life.
- This week, make a point of telling those you care for how much they mean to you.
- Read *Ephesians* 4:1–16, and reflect on the author's vision of Church as Christ's Body.

Affirm

This week I will make an effort to greet someone whom I don't know.

Your Faith Journal — Chapter 2
The Family of Creation

All parts of creation are related. All creatures come from God and exist to give God glory.
Catechism of the Catholic Church, #344

Reflect

What are some signs of God's love that surround me every day?

_____
_____
_____

How do I treat the gifts of God's world as my "brothers" and "sisters"?

_____
_____
_____

What is my attitude toward people who are different from me?

_____
_____
_____

As a creature of God, how am I a sign of God's love to others?

_____
_____
_____

Continue the Journey

- Take a walk, watch a sunset. Drink in the beauty of God's world, and give praise and thanks for being a part of it.
- Read about the religious customs of another culture. How do the customs reflect the people's understanding of God?
- Read the Prayer of St. Francis at the end of the chapter. At the end, add some of your own lines of praise for the "brothers" and "sisters" you experience.
- Display and use some sacramentals at home, such as candles, holy water, or rosary beads.

Affirm

Today, in all my encounters, I will remember that I am made in God's own image.

Your Faith Journal — CHAPTER 3
Light of the World

God gives us grace, the free gift of God's own life, to bring all creation back into relationship with him.
Catechism of the Catholic Church, #1999

Reflect

With the presence of evil and suffering, how do I continue to believe in the goodness of the world that God created?

_____
_____
_____

Why is it important that I am free to choose or reject God's free gift of grace?

_____
_____
_____

In what ways have I recently experienced this gift?

_____
_____
_____

What are some places in my community that need the light of God's grace? How can I help that light shine?

_____
_____
_____

Continue the Journey

- Look for and affirm in others the ways they allow their "light" to shine. Send an encouraging note to someone, thanking the person for the good he or she does. By affirming others, you can be a channel of grace for them.

- Read *John 1:1–18*, and reflect on the imagery used to describe the meaning of Jesus for the world.

- Celebrate the Sacrament of Reconciliation. Focus on the ways God's grace has touched and healed you.

Affirm

Today I will remember and accept that God loves me not for what I do, but for who I am—God's unique gift to the world.

Your Faith Journal — CHAPTER 4
Mother of the Church

Mary, the mother of Jesus, continues to care for us as Mother of the Church.
Catechism of the Catholic Church, #969

Reflect

What role does Mary play in my life?

_____

_____

_____

_____

How does the story of Our Lady of Guadalupe enrich my appreciation of Mary's role in the Church today?

_____

_____

_____

_____

_____

Why is it important for my students to see how God is present to cultures other than their own?

_____

_____

_____

_____

Continue the Journey

- Pray a decade of the Rosary each day for five days. While praying, meditate on the Joyful, Sorrowful, or Glorious mysteries and the role Mary played in them.
- Place a picture or icon of Mary in a prominent place in your home. As you go about your daily life, think about Mary as a model of service.
- Research some of the ways in which other cultures honor Mary.
- Read and pray the Magnificat from Luke 1:46–55.

Affirm

I will try to say yes to God today as Mary said yes to becoming the mother of Jesus.

Your Faith Journal — CHAPTER 5
We Believe in God

Catholics believe in the mystery of the Holy Trinity: one God who is Father, Son, and Holy Spirit.
Catechism of the Catholic Church, #234

Reflect

How does Baptism make a difference in my life?

_____
_____
_____
_____

How does our belief that there is only one God affect my basic view of the world?

_____
_____
_____
_____

What does the mystery of the Trinity suggest to me about the nature of all relationships?

_____
_____
_____

Why is it important to know that there are truths about God we cannot fully understand?

_____
_____
_____

Continue the Journey

- Each time you pray the Sign of the Cross, consciously think about the Persons of the Trinity, and make an act of faith.
- Write a brief, personal creed, or statement of your beliefs, about God.
- At home, display the symbols of Baptism—water, oil, a candle—as reminders of your relationship with God.
- Look up your baptismal date, and mark it on your calendar to remind you to celebrate it in some way.

Affirm

Today I will remember that there is one God, and I will let no other person or thing become a "god" for me.

Your Faith Journal — Chapter 6
We Worship God

The Eucharist is the center of our life as Church.
Catechism of the Catholic Church, #752

Reflect

When do I find myself most often moved to pray?

_____
_____
_____

In what ways would I like to strengthen my prayer life?

_____
_____
_____

How does my experience of and participation in the Eucharist reflect its central place in my life?

_____
_____
_____

Why is it important for my students to understand the value of community worship?

_____
_____
_____

Continue the Journey

- Look through the Book of Psalms in the Bible. Pick a psalm that expresses your feelings, and pray it slowly and expressively.
- Set aside five minutes every day to be quiet and listen to your heart. Allow God to speak to you in the silence.
- Many parish bulletins publish the list of readings for the next Sunday. Read over and meditate on the passages at home before going to Mass.

Affirm

I will focus on deepening my relationship with God through prayer.

Your Faith Journal — CHAPTER 7
We Belong to God

The Church is a sign of God's new covenant with all people.
Catechism of the Catholic Church, #781

Reflect

How have I experienced God's faithfulness in my life?

_____
_____
_____

How well do I trust in God during difficult times? Why is trust an important part of a covenant?

_____
_____
_____

Which of the commandments do I find the most challenging?

_____
_____
_____

Why is it important for me to learn about the Jews, with whom we share common roots in faith?

_____
_____
_____

Continue the Journey

- Read *Exodus* 20—23. Note the many regulations, in addition to the Ten Commandments, that were part of the Sinai covenant between the Israelites and God.
- Make an effort to learn about the major Jewish holidays. Call a nearby synagogue, and ask for literature explaining these holy times.
- Read *Hebrews* 9:1–15 to understand how the author reinterprets the meaning of the Jewish covenant in light of the death and resurrection of Jesus.

Affirm

I will be faithful to God because of God's unconditional love for me.

Your Faith Journal — CHAPTER 8
Honoring Their Memory

Honoring the memory of the saints is a way to grow in faith.
Catechism of the Catholic Church, #957

Reflect

Who has shared the gift of faith with me in a significant way? What has that gift meant to me?

_____
_____
_____
_____

What is my idea of a saintly person? Who is such a person in today's world?

_____
_____
_____
_____

What would I do if I lived in a country where being a Christian could mean death?

_____
_____
_____
_____

What do I understand about the communion of saints?

_____
_____
_____
_____

Continue the Journey

- Using the *Catholic Encyclopedia* or *Butler's Lives of the Saints*, research the name of the saint that corresponds to your baptismal name or your Confirmation name. Find out some significant facts about that saint's life. Pray to him or her, asking for help in your daily life.

- Remember in prayer at Mass a loved one who has died. If you feel comfortable doing so, pray to that loved one, asking for intercession on your behalf.

- Write a note to someone who has helped you grow in faith. Thank that person for being a witness of faith to you.

Affirm

I remember how important others are in my faith journey, and I thank God for them.

Your Faith Journal — CHAPTER 9

Jesus Brings Good News

Jesus announced the coming of God's kingdom.
Catechism of the Catholic Church, #763

Reflect

What is the best news I have heard within the past week?

_____
_____
_____

How is Jesus' proclamation of the kingdom of God good news for me?

_____
_____
_____

How do I share the good news of the kingdom with those around me?

_____
_____
_____

The good news was accepted most readily in Jesus' time by those on the edge of society: the poor, the sick, the outcast. How can I stand with those who live on the edge?

_____
_____
_____

Continue the Journey

- Read Jesus' proclamation of the Beatitudes from *Matthew* 5. Think about how the "rules" of the kingdom seem to contradict what many people think is desirable and undesirable behavior.
- Volunteer to work with a social action ministry, such as the Society of St. Vincent de Paul or another group in your parish.
- Before or after Mass, discuss the Sunday readings with your family.
- Accepting the good news requires that we listen carefully. Make an extra effort this week to listen to others before formulating a response.

Affirm

Today I will be "good news" for all those I encounter.

Your Faith Journal — Chapter 10
New Life in Jesus

Jesus' love for us was so great that he sacrificed his life to save us.
Catechism of the Catholic Church, #609

Reflect

What are some signs of dying and rising that I see around me or that I experience personally?

_____
_____
_____
_____
_____

What are some areas of my life in which I need to let go of old ways in order to grow?

_____
_____
_____
_____
_____

How do I experience the Eucharist as a celebration of my own death and resurrection in Jesus?

_____
_____
_____
_____
_____

Continue the Journey

- To celebrate new life, plant some seeds and monitor their growth. Watch for other signs of new life around you every day.
- Read the story of the Passover festival in *Exodus 12*.
- Try fasting between meals or abstaining from meat one day a month, in addition to when it is required during Lent.

Affirm

Today I will let go of one thing that I fear in order to embrace the freedom of new life.

Your Faith Journal — CHAPTER 11
Jesus Works Through Us

We are members of the Body of Christ. We share our gifts and serve one another.
Catechism of the Catholic Church, #794

Reflect

What do I do about my need for love and care when I have been hurt or neglected?

_____
_____
_____

How do I help others in need without feeling superior to them or using power over them?

_____
_____
_____

What are my most important gifts for ministry?

_____
_____
_____

How do I allow others to use their gifts to serve me?

_____
_____
_____

Continue the Journey

- Read Paul's description of the function of gifts in the Body of Christ in 1 Corinthians 12:2–31.
- Make a list of what you consider to be gifts with which God has blessed you. Pray a prayer thanking God for each of them.
- A famous saying has it that "Christ has no hands but ours." The next time you help someone, think of it as Christ working through you.
- Be willing to listen and be present for someone without trying to "fix" the person's problem.

Affirm

Today I will "put on the mind of Christ" and act in his name.

Your Faith Journal — CHAPTER 12
A Time to Remember

We celebrate Advent to renew our hope for the second coming of Jesus at the end of time.
Catechism of the Catholic Church, #524

Reflect

What events in the lives of my parents or grandparents have had an impact on my family?

___

___

___

___

___

Why is it important to remember our ancestors in faith?

___

___

___

___

___

What does the hope of the second coming of Jesus mean to me?

___

___

___

___

___

Continue the Journey

- Explore the symbols of the Jesse tree in books and resources available through your parish or diocesan media center. Make a Jesse tree for your home or classroom.

- Go through your family photographs, and give thanks for the lives of your ancestors. Write a letter to a family member whom you seldom see yet appreciate and respect.

- Read *Isaiah 11* for a description of the messiah, a branch from the "root of Jesse."

Affirm

Each day I will try to live as if Jesus were coming again on that day.

Your Faith Journal — CHAPTER 13
The Church Works Together

We all help build the Body of Christ by using our special talents and abilities.
Catechism of the Catholic Church, #872

Reflect

In what ways do I share my time, talent, and treasure with my parish community?

_____
_____
_____
_____

What do I consider to be the mission of the Church?

_____
_____
_____
_____

What qualities do I admire in a Church leader? What is my attitude toward those in positions of authority in the Church?

_____
_____
_____
_____
_____
_____

Continue the Journey

- Find out if your parish has a mission statement. If one exists, ask for a copy. Reflect on how you personally serve your parish in light of its mission. If a mission statement does not exist, volunteer to organize a team of parishioners to help draft one.

- Begin your day with a morning offering prayer. Offer all that you do to God, and ask God to work through you during the day.

- Investigate the structure of the Church. Visit the Vatican web site on the Internet (http://www.vatican.va/). Contact the chancery of your diocese, and find out some basic facts about the diocese—number of parishes, number of members, and so on.

- Read about the life of Pope John XXIII and how he influenced the Church.

Affirm

Today I will use my unique gifts and talents in service to the Body of Christ.

Your Faith Journal — Chapter 14
One and Holy

The Church is unified because of the work of the Holy Spirit.
Catechism of the Catholic Church, #813

Reflect

How do I understand the Church to be one and holy?

_____
_____
_____
_____

How do I experience the Holy Spirit working in my life?

_____
_____
_____
_____

How is the Spirit calling me to holiness at this time in my life?

_____
_____
_____
_____

Why is being a member of the Catholic Church important to me?

_____
_____
_____
_____

Continue the Journey

- Read *Luke 4* to get a sense of the Holy Spirit's role in Jesus' life.
- Ask some of your friends and acquaintances what they think it means to be holy. See if any common features of holiness emerge.
- Many cities have churches of Catholic Rites other than the Latin Rite—such as the Maronite or the Byzantine Rite. If possible, attend a Catholic Mass in another Rite to see how the Eucharist is both universal and culturally conditioned.
- Look up the gifts of the Holy Spirit in the *Catechism of the Catholic Church* (#1831). Pray to the Holy Spirit, asking for the gifts you need.

Affirm

Today I will allow the Holy Spirit to fill my heart with love, the greatest gift.

Your Faith Journal — Chapter 15
Catholic and Apostolic

The whole Church is apostolic because it is founded on the apostles.
Catechism of the Catholic Church, #857

Reflect

Why is it important to me that the Church is catholic, or universal?

_____
_____
_____
_____
_____

How have I come to appreciate the fact that the Church was founded on the faith of the apostles?

_____
_____
_____
_____
_____

How can I contribute to the apostolic mission of the Church?

_____
_____
_____
_____
_____

Continue the Journey

- Talk to a good friend who belongs to a Christian Church of another denomination. Ask the person about how authority is exercised in that Church. How are decisions that affect the direction of the Church made? Share with the person your understanding of these ideas in the Catholic tradition.
- Consult the *Catholic Encyclopedia* for a list of the popes. Which ones were in office in your lifetime? Study the list. Reflect on some of the changes in the Church under various popes. What feelings does this evoke in you?
- Read *1 Corinthians* 1—2. Notice how Paul establishes his credentials as an apostle. Also note how he implores the Christians of Corinth to reconcile their differences. How is he exercising authority? Apostolicity?

Affirm

Today I thank God for the gift of faith that has been passed down to me. I will faithfully pass on this gift to others.

Your Faith Journal 📖 CHAPTER 16

The First Nativity Scene

The Son of God was born in a stable in Bethlehem.
Catechism of the Catholic Church, #525

Reflect

What are my fondest memories of nativity scenes from my childhood?

_____
_____
_____
_____
_____

What in the story of Jesus' birth is the most important element for my faith?

_____
_____
_____
_____
_____

How will I welcome Jesus this Christmas?

_____
_____
_____
_____
_____

Continue the Journey

- Compare the accounts of the nativity story in the Gospels of Matthew and Luke. What do they have in common? How do the details differ?
- Visit a local nativity scene. Take someone special with you.
- If possible, attend midnight Mass this year with your family. Imagine yourselves in the place of the shepherds, the first to visit the newborn Jesus.
- Read or tell the nativity story to your family on Christmas morning.

Affirm

This year I will continue to celebrate Jesus' birth from Christmas through the feast of the Epiphany.

YOUR FAITH JOURNAL : J17

Your Faith Journal — Chapter 17
Jesus' Law of Love

We are called to follow Jesus' law of love.
Catechism of the Catholic Church, #1970

Reflect

Who are the people in my life whom I find the most difficult to love? Why?

_____
_____
_____
_____

Who has been a good Samaritan to me when I most needed help?

_____
_____
_____

What has been the most difficult choice I have made recently? Did I make the most loving choice?

_____
_____
_____
_____

How does the Church help me be a more loving person on my journey of faith?

_____
_____
_____
_____

Continue the Journey

- Find out what your parish does to live Jesus' law of love.
- Choose a person whom you find difficult to love. Pray for him or her each day for a month.
- Take your family to a nearby care center or retirement home, and visit one or more of the residents.
- Invite someone who is not active in the Church to attend Mass with you this Sunday.

Affirm

Today I will try to love all those around me, especially those who do not love me.

Your Faith Journal 📖 CHAPTER 18

The Church Helps

The Holy Spirit, the word of God, and the teachings of the Church help us make good choices.
Catechism of the Catholic Church, #1785

Reflect

How can I become more conscious of the effect my choices have on others?

_____

_____

_____

Whom do I turn to when I need help making a difficult choice?

_____

_____

_____

How do the Holy Spirit and the Church help make moral decisions?

_____

_____

_____

How does my conscience help me make moral decisions?

_____

_____

_____

Continue the Journey

- Talk to someone you trust about a matter that is bothering you.
- Listen intently to those who share their struggles with you. Do not give advice or try to solve their problems. Just be there for them.
- Examine your conscience each night before you go to sleep. Seek God's forgiveness and healing in prayer.
- Ask forgiveness from someone whom you have offended.

Affirm

Today I will ask the Spirit for guidance in all my choices.

Your Faith Journal — Chapter 19
Faith, Hope, and Love

God gives us the virtues of faith, hope, and love to help us live as he wants us to live.
Catechism of the Catholic Church, #1813

Reflect

What concrete actions do I take to cultivate good habits?

_____
_____
_____
_____

How do I practice the virtues of faith, hope, and love in my daily activities?

_____
_____
_____
_____

How do the precepts of the Church relate to the virtues in my life?

_____
_____
_____

How do I encourage those for whom I am responsible in the positive practice of virtue?

_____
_____
_____
_____

Continue the Journey

- Read Paul's reflections on the three virtues of faith, hope, and love in 1 *Corinthians* 13.
- Read passages from William Bennett's *The Book of Virtues* or *The Moral Life*.
- Draw your own personal symbols of the virtues of faith, hope, and love, and hang them in a special place in your home.
- Make a point to affirm others, especially young people, when you see them practicing one of the virtues.

Affirm

Today I will notice others' virtuous deeds and commend them.

Your Faith Journal — Chapter 20
Strength Through Practice

Lent is a time of spiritual exercise.
Catechism of the Catholic Church, #1438

Reflect

How are solitude and quiet reflection important elements in my life with God?

_____
_____
_____
_____
_____

What are my priorities? Do some of my priorities need to change?

_____
_____
_____
_____
_____

This year, how will the days of Lent help me grow closer to God?

_____
_____
_____
_____
_____

Continue the Journey

- Find out the names of those being baptized at Easter in your parish. Pray for them during Lent.
- During this season of conversion, make a list of things in your life that you would like to change or do differently. Follow through with those changes.
- Use a Lenten devotional handbook. Resolve to spend at least five minutes each day in quiet prayer.
- Check your parish bulletin each week for Lenten activities. If possible, attend one or more of these.

Affirm

In this Season of Lent, I will allow God to mold and shape me according to his will.

Your Faith Journal — Chapter 21
We Become Part of the Church

The Sacraments of Initiation are the basis of every Christian life.
Catechism of the Catholic Church, #1212

Reflect

At this point in my life, what do Baptism and Confirmation mean to me?

_____
_____
_____
_____

What would I say to someone who asked me about becoming a member of the Catholic community?

_____
_____
_____
_____

How do I experience ongoing conversion, or change of heart, as a result of celebrating the Eucharist regularly?

_____
_____
_____
_____

How do I participate in welcoming new members into the Catholic community?

_____
_____
_____
_____

Continue the Journey

- Attend the Easter Vigil service this year, and join in welcoming the new Catholics.
- Read *Romans* 6:3–5 about the meaning of Baptism for Paul.
- Ask the coordinator of the catechumenate at your parish to give you names of candidates for initiation. Write each one a note of support, or have your class write letters to them.

Affirm

Today I will ask Christ to help me let go of sinful habits and embrace new life in him.

Your Faith Journal — CHAPTER 22

The Church Celebrates Healing

Jesus wants the Church to continue his work of healing in the Sacraments of Reconciliation and Anointing of the Sick.
Catechism of the Catholic Church, #1421

Reflect

What are some of the physical, psychological, or spiritual areas in my life in need of healing?

_____
_____
_____
_____

How does God work through other people to heal me?

_____
_____
_____

When was the last time I forgave someone? How did this also bring healing to me?

_____
_____
_____

What is the significance of the Sacrament of Reconciliation in my life?

_____
_____
_____
_____

Continue the Journey

- Take part in a communal Reconciliation service held in your parish.
- Attend a communal celebration of the Anointing of the Sick in either your own or another parish.
- Read about healing in the early Church in *James 5:14–16*.
- Pray for someone you know who is sick and in need of healing. If possible, visit someone who is ill.

Affirm

Today I will make an extra effort to forgive those who hurt me.

Your Faith Journal — Chapter 23
Sacraments of Service

Holy Orders and Matrimony are directed toward helping other people find God.
Catechism of the Catholic Church, #1534

Reflect

What is God calling me to in my life right now?

_____
_____
_____
_____
_____
_____

How can I serve God and others more fully in my chosen vocation?

_____
_____
_____
_____
_____
_____

How do I see my work as a way of ministering God's presence and love?

_____
_____
_____
_____
_____
_____

Continue the Journey

- If you are married, look through some of your wedding pictures. Recall what you felt that day and how you feel today about this vocation. Ask God to continue to strengthen you and your spouse.
- Talk with a young person about the meaning of vocation and the importance of choosing a life's work.
- Watch for opportunities at work to bring the light of the gospel to various situations.
- Take the opportunity to affirm and encourage a priest in his ministry. Pray for married couples who are having trouble in their relationships. Look for a retreat opportunity for yourself, or yourself and your spouse if you are married.

Affirm

Today I reaffirm my commitment to my vocation, and I pray for strength to live it out faithfully.

Your Faith Journal — CHAPTER 24
Hosanna!

Children and God's poor honored Jesus as he entered Jerusalem bearing witness to the coming of God's kingdom.
Catechism of the Catholic Church, #559

Reflect

When I shout the word *Hosanna*, from what would I like Jesus to save me?

_____
_____
_____
_____

As Holy Week begins, what are my feelings?

_____
_____
_____
_____

How can I personally welcome Jesus as king into my life?

_____
_____
_____
_____

What do the celebrations of Holy Week mean to me? How can I best celebrate these cornerstone events in the history of salvation?

_____
_____
_____
_____

Continue the Journey

- Take part in the celebration of the Easter Triduum at your parish.
- Watch one of the special Easter programs shown on television during this week. Or rent the video *Jesus of Nazareth*, and watch it with your family.
- Bring home blessed palms on Palm Sunday, and place them around a crucifix.
- Get outside this week, and notice any signs of new life in nature. Pray and thank God for the life that comes from death.

Affirm

This week I will let go of something in my life that I feel God is asking me to give up so I may experience new life.

Your Faith Journal — CHAPTER 25
Connected to the Past

The "family of God" is formed according to God's plan through the years of human history.
Catechism of the Catholic Church, #759

Reflect

What are some of the gifts I have inherited from my ancestors?

_____
_____
_____
_____

What are my earliest memories of the Church? How have they shaped and formed my faith?

_____
_____
_____
_____

Who are some of my favorite saints? What qualities in them do I admire?

_____
_____
_____
_____

Why is it important for me to know and understand some of the history of the Catholic Church?

_____
_____
_____
_____

Continue the Journey

- Research the lives of some members of your family who came before you. Learn about who they were and what they did.
- Discover the history of your parish.
- To enrich your appreciation of the Mass, research the early saints and martyrs mentioned in the Eucharistic Prayers.

Affirm

I remember and honor those who passed on the faith to me.

Your Faith Journal — Chapter 26
The Church Today

The kingdom of God in its fullness will come more quickly when we work with love to make the present better for everyone.
Catechism of the Catholic Church, #2046

Reflect

If I could solve one problem in the world today, which would I choose? Why?

_____

_____

_____

How do I envision the kingdom of God in its fullness?

_____

_____

_____

In what ways do I express solidarity with those who are poor and powerless?

_____

_____

_____

When I say the words "your kingdom come," what do I really mean?

_____

_____

_____

Continue the Journey

- Find out what your parish is doing to witness to the good news of Jesus, and join in. Give what you can to a Catholic organization that serves those who are poor and powerless.
- Ask your pastor or parish director of religious education for more information about the social teachings of the Church.
- Read *Matthew* 5 for Jesus' blueprint of the kingdom.
- When you pray before your evening meal, make a habit of praying for those who are hungry that night.

Affirm

Today I will do one thing to give witness to the kingdom of God, which is both present and yet to come in its fullness.

Your Faith Journal — CHAPTER 27
Hope for the Future

The Church will reach its full perfection when Jesus Christ comes in glory at the end of time.
Catechism of the Catholic Church, #1042

Reflect

What does John's image of the new heaven and the new earth mean to me?

_____
_____
_____
_____
_____

What signs of hope do I see?

_____
_____
_____
_____
_____
_____

How do I feel about death, specifically my own death?

_____
_____
_____
_____
_____
_____

Continue the Journey

- The *Book of Revelation* can be both hopeful and frightening. Read 21:1–7 for John's image of the second coming.
- To gain a better understanding of Revelation, read the introduction to the *Book of Revelation* in your Bible.
- Make a list of the things you would hope for if you had a vision such as John's in Revelation.
- Pray the Rosary using the Glorious Mysteries, and meditate on each mystery.

Affirm

Today I will not say the words, "I don't have time." Instead, I will give thanks to God for the gift of time and remember that I have all the time I need.

Your Faith Journal CHAPTER 28

Signs of New Life

The resurrection of Jesus from the dead is the central truth of our Church community.
Catechism of the Catholic Church, #638

Reflect

What are some of the signs of new life or transformation around me?

_____
_____
_____
_____
_____

How is Jesus' death and resurrection the central truth of my own faith?

_____
_____
_____
_____
_____

How can I be a sign of hope and new life to others?

_____
_____
_____
_____
_____

Continue the Journey

- In a prominent place in your home, display some symbols of new life.
- Welcome the neophytes (newly baptized) in your parish by attending the Easter Vigil and perhaps a reception for them afterward.
- Read and meditate on *Romans 6:3–9* and *8:11*, passages that pertain to Paul's Easter theology.
- Throughout your day, pray the prayer of the early Christians: "Jesus is Lord."

Affirm

Today I will shine with the joy of the risen Lord! Alleluia!

Notes